ASEAN LAW IN THE NEW REGIONAL ECONOMIC ORDER

The fast-growing last decade of strong economic growth of the Association of Southeast Asian Nations has played a critical role in Asia-Pacific regionalism and global trade. This book explores the concept of ASEAN law under the normative framework of the new regional economic order. It examines the roadmap of the new ASEAN Economic Community Blueprint 2025 by evaluating the impact of ASEAN trade agreements on domestic legislation on professional services, financial integration, investment disputes and digital trade. More importantly, it sheds light on the legal implications of ASEAN's agreements with China and India and the potential developments of megaregional trade agreements such as the CPTPP and the RCEP. Hence, the legal analysis and case studies in the book offer a fresh view of Asia-Pacific integration and bridge the gap between academia and practice.

PASHA L. HSIEH is an associate professor of law and Lee Kong Chian Fellow at Singapore Management University (SMU). He is also the co-chair of the Law in the Pacific Rim Region Interest Group of the American Society of International Law and an Executive Council member of the Society of International Economic Law. Prior to joining academia, he served as a legal affairs officer at the WTO Appellate Body Secretariat and as an associate at Shearman & Sterling LLP. He was awarded SMU's Lee Foundation Fellowship for Research Excellence in 2010 and received the Most Outstanding Legal Studies Teacher Award in 2015.

BRYAN MERCURIO is professor, Associate Dean (Research) and Vice Chancellor's Outstanding Fellow of the Faculty of Law at the Chinese University of Hong Kong. He is the author of one of the most widely used case books on WTO law (Hart Publishing, with S. Lester and A. Davies) and editor of the leading collection on bilateral and regional trade agreements (Cambridge University Press, with S. Lester and L. Bartels). Prior to relocating to Hong Kong in 2007, he taught as a tenured member of the faculty of law at the University of New South Wales and as a visiting scholar at universities in Australia and North America.

<u>ERRATA</u>

ASEAN Law in the New Regional Economic Order
Global Trends and Shifting Paradigms
Edited by Pasha L. Hsieh and Bryan Mercurio
ISBN 978-1-108-42499-8

On Page vi – The author's name for Chapter 14 should read **MAN YIP**.

On Page xiv (line 13) – YIP MAN should read **MAN YIP**.

On Page 271 – The author's name for Chapter 14 should read **MAN YIP**.

We would like to apologize to the author for this typographical error.

ASEAN LAW IN THE NEW REGIONAL ECONOMIC ORDER

Global Trends and Shifting Paradigms

PASHA L. HSIEH
Singapore Management University
BRYAN MERCURIO
Chinese University of Hong Kong

CAMBRIDGE
UNIVERSITY PRESS

CAMBRIDGE
UNIVERSITY PRESS

University Printing House, Cambridge CB2 8BS, United Kingdom

One Liberty Plaza, 20th Floor, New York, NY 10006, USA

477 Williamstown Road, Port Melbourne, VIC 3207, Australia

314–321, 3rd Floor, Plot 3, Splendor Forum, Jasola District Centre, New Delhi – 110025, India

79 Anson Road, #06–04/06, Singapore 079906

Cambridge University Press is part of the University of Cambridge.

It furthers the University's mission by disseminating knowledge in the pursuit of education, learning, and research at the highest international levels of excellence.

www.cambridge.org
Information on this title: www.cambridge.org/9781108424998
DOI: 10.1017/9781108563208

First published 2019

Printed and bound in Great Britain by Clays Ltd, Elcograf S.p.A.

A catalogue record for this publication is available from the British Library.

Library of Congress Cataloging-in-Publication Data
Names: Hsieh, Pasha L., editor author. | Mercurio, Bryan, editor author.
Title: ASEAN law in the new regional economic order : global trends and shifting paradigms / edited by Pasha L. Hsieh, Singapore Management University, Bryan Mercurio, Chinese University of Hong Kong.
Description: New York : Cambridge University Press, 2019. | Includes index.
Identifiers: LCCN 2018044263 | ISBN 9781108424998
Subjects: LCSH: ASEAN. | Law – Southeast Asia – International unification.
Classification: LCC KNE173 .A94 2019 | DDC 341.24/73–dc23
LC record available at https://lccn.loc.gov/2018044263

ISBN 978-1-108-42499-8 Hardback

CONTENTS

FIGURES

TABLES

NOTES ON CONTRIBUTORS

IRENE CALBOLI is a professor of law at Texas A&M University School of Law. She was a visiting professor and the deputy director of the Applied Research Centre for Intellectual Assets and the Law in Asia, Singapore Management University (SMU). Professor Calboli started her academic career at the University of Bologna, and has held visiting positions at King's College London, UC Berkeley, the University Complutense of Madrid, the Max Planck Institute for Innovation and Competition and National University of Singapore (NUS). Her scholarship focuses on the intersection between intellectual property and international trade. Her recent books include *Diversity in Intellectual Property: Identities, Interests and Intersections* (Cambridge University Press, 2015, with S. Ragavan) and *Research Handbook on Intellectual Property Exhaustion and Parallel Imports* and *Geographical Indications at the Crossroads of Trade, Development and Culture: Focus on Asia-Pacific* (Cambridge University Press, 2017, with W. L. Ng-Loy).

JULIEN CHAISSE is a professor of law at the Chinese University of Hong Kong (CUHK). Professor Chaisse is an award-winning specialist in international economic law with particular expertise in the regulation and economics of foreign investment. His research also covers other relevant fields, such as WTO law, international taxation and the law of natural resources. He has extensive experience as a practitioner and has been engaged as an expert, counsel and arbitrator in transnational dispute settlement. He is also regularly invited to provide legal advice and training courses on international economic law for international organizations, governments, law firms and private investors, including Ernst & Young, Maxwell Stamp, the United Nations ESCAP, the WTO, the ASEAN Secretariat, the European Commission, the Asian Development Bank and European and ASEAN member states. He is a member of the World Economic Forum's Network of Global Agenda Councils for the term 2016–18.

MICHELLE DY is legal counsel at AirAsia. She received her Juris Doctor degree, cum laude, from the University of the Philippines College of Law as the valedictorian of her 2011 class. She went on to obtain her LLM from New York University as a David Marshall scholar, and NUS, where she was awarded the Rajah and Tann Tax Prize. Michelle has worked as a legal consultant for the Securities and Exchange Commission, where she assisted in the formulation of policies geared toward deepening the Philippine capital market and promoting investor protection. She also provided technical assistance in the development of measures to prepare the Philippines for ASEAN capital market integration. She was a part-time lecturer at the Ateneo de Manila University and a research associate at the NUS Centre for Banking and Finance Law.

DEBORAH ELMS is the founder and executive director of the Asian Trade Centre (ATC) in Singapore. The ATC works with governments and companies to design better trade policies for the region. Dr. Elms is also Vice Chair of the Asia Business Trade Association (ABTA) and sits on the International Technical Advisory Committee of the Global Trade Professionals Alliance and is Chair of the Working Group on Trade Policy and Law. She is also a senior fellow in the Singapore Ministry of Trade and Industry's Trade Academy. Previously, she was head of the Temasek Foundation Centre for Trade & Negotiations and Senior Fellow of International Political Economy at the S. Rajaratnam School of International Studies at Nanyang Technological University. Her projects include the Trans-Pacific Partnership negotiations, the Regional Comprehensive Economic Partnership, the ASEAN Economic Community and global value chains. She has provided consulting on a range of trade issues to governments such as the European Union Delegation in Asia, the United Kingdom, the United States, Australia, New Zealand, Vietnam, including the United Arab Emirates, Sri Lanka, Cambodia, Taiwan and Singapore. She received a PhD in political science from the University of Washington, an MA in international relations from the University of Southern California and bachelor's degrees from Boston University. She publishes the Talking Trade Blog.

YOSHIFUMI FUKUNAGA is a Consulting Fellow at the Research Institute of Economy, Trade and Industry of Japan. With his expertise in international economic law and international political economy, he has published a number articles regarding the AEC as well as ASEAN+1 FTAs and the RCEP. He received an LLM from Harvard Law School and an MA in International Relations from the Fletcher School of Law and Diplomacy, Tuft University.

HENRY GAO is an associate professor of law at SMU and Dongfang Scholar Chair Professor at the Shanghai Institute of Foreign Trade. With law degrees from three continents, he started his career as the first Chinese lawyer at the WTO Secretariat. Before moving to Singapore in late 2007, he taught law at the University of Hong Kong, where he was also the deputy director of the East Asian International Economic Law and Policy Program. He has taught at the IELPO program in Barcelona and the Academy of International Trade Law in Macau, and was the academic coordinator to the first Asia-Pacific Regional Trade Policy Course sponsored by the WTO. He has advised many national governments as well as the WTO, the World Bank, the Asian Development Bank, APEC and ASEAN on trade issues. He sits on the Advisory Board of the WTO Chairs Program, which was established by the WTO Secretariat in 2009 to promote research and teaching on WTO issues in leading universities around the world.

PASHA L. HSIEH is an associate professor of law and Lee Kong Chian Fellow at SMU. He is also the co-chair of the Law in the Pacific Rim Region Interest Group of the American Society of International Law and an Executive Council member of the Society of International Economic Law. He holds Juris Doctor and LLM degrees from the University of Pennsylvania Law School, where he was a Senior Editor of the *University of Pennsylvania Law Review*. Prior to joining academia, he served as a legal affairs officer at the WTO Appellate Body Secretariat and as an associate at Shearman & Sterling LLP. His publications have appeared in the *Journal of International Economic Law*, the *Journal of World Trade*, the *Cornell International Law Journal* and peer-reviewed political science journals. His work has been cited by the Federal Supreme Court of Switzerland, the European Parliament and the OECD.

SUFIAN JUSOH is a Senior Fellow at the Institute of Malaysian and International Studies, National University of Malaysia and a consultant of the World Trade Institute, University of Bern, Switzerland. He is also a Distinguished Fellow at the Institute of Diplomacy and Foreign Relations, Ministry of Foreign Affairs, Malaysia. He is a barrister-at-law (England and Wales) of Lincoln's Inn, London. Jusoh holds an LLB from Cardiff Law School, an LLM (Merit), University College London and a Doctor in Law (summa Cum Laude/First Class) from the University of Bern. He is an investment law expert at the World Bank Group's Trade and Competitiveness team. He is also a consultant on investment policy and liberalization of services for ASEAN. Jusoh has advised some TPP members on negotiation issues.

JAE WOON LEE is an assistant professor at the CUHK Faculty of Law and specializes in aviation law and competition law. Having studied in Seoul (LLB at HUFS), Montreal (LLM at McGill) and Singapore (PhD at NUS), he has seven years of work experience in the airline industry. He has also acted as consultant to the Ministry of Foreign Affairs of the Republic of Korea on aviation law issues, and attended the International Civil Aviation Organization Legal Committee meetings and the Diplomatic Conference as a legal advisor to the Korean delegation. He has published many articles in international journals, and his monograph *Regional Liberalization in International Air Transport: Towards Northeast Asian Open Skies* was published in 2016.

HAN-WEI LIU joined the Department of Business Law and Taxation, Monash University as a Lecturer in 2018. He was an assistant professor at National Tsing Hua University in Taiwan. Dr. Liu works in the areas of law and technology, international economic law and international law. Prior to academia, he practiced with Baker & McKenzie and Russin & Vecchi. He earned his PhD, summa cum laude, from the Graduate Institute, Geneva where he was awarded a full scholarship by Kathryn Davis Foundation, and his master's degrees from Columbia and Oxford Universities on Taiwan Government Scholarship and British Chevening Scholarship, respectively. His publications appear in leading law journals, such as the *Journal of International Economic Law*, the *Journal of World Trade* and the *University of Pennsylvania Journal of International Law*. In 2013–15, he held visiting posts at Harvard Law School and Columbia Law School. His co-edited book, *Governing Science and Technology under the International Economic Order Regulatory Divergence and Convergence in the Age of Megaregionals* (with S. Peng and C. Lin), was published in 2017.

FEDERICO LUPO-PASINI is an associate professor at Durham Law School. He previously taught at Queen's University Belfast. His expertise focuses on international business law, law & economics, and financial regulation. He is particularly interested in international financial law and international economic law. He holds a master's degree in international law and economics from the World Trade Institute, and a PhD from NUS, where he researched in international financial regulation. Before moving to the United Kingdom, he worked for some years in southeast Asia and Australia, always on financial law and international economic integration. He started his career working as a trade policy expert, mostly in Vietnam and India. He lived for two years in Hanoi, where he worked for EU-Vietnam MUTRAP III, advising the Vietnamese government on WTO accession and ASEAN economic integration. Subsequently, he worked as a consultant for the World Bank, CUTS International, the ASEAN Secretariat and the ADB, and as a Research Fellow at the University of New South Wales (UNSW).

YIP MAN is an associate professor of law at SMU. Before joining academia, she worked as a disputes lawyer at WongPartnership LLP, practicing mainly in the area of international commercial arbitration. She researches in equity, contract, restitution and private international law. She has published in leading peer-reviewed journals, including *International and Comparative Law Quarterly*, *Cambridge Law Journal*, *Legal Studies* and *Lloyd's Maritime and Commercial Law Quarterly*. Her works have been cited by the Singapore Court of Appeal and the English High Court, as well as texts on various areas of private law. She has also acted as an expert witness on Singapore commercial law and private international law in an international commercial arbitration matter. In 2016, she was appointed the D. S. Lee Foundation Fellow in recognition of her research on issues of Asian business law.

BRYAN MERCURIO is professor, Associate Dean (Research) and Vice Chancellor's Outstanding Fellow of the Faculty of Law at the CUHK. Specializing in international economic law, he is a leading expert in the intersection between trade law and intellectual property rights. His work also frequently deals with free trade agreements, dispute settlement and, increasingly, international investment law. He is the author of one of the most widely used case books on WTO law (Hart Publishing, with S. Lester and A. Davies), and editor of the leading collection on bilateral and regional trade agreements (Cambridge University Press, with S. Lester and L. Bartels). Prior to relocating to Hong Kong in 2007, he taught as a tenured member of the faculty of law at UNSW and as visiting scholar at universities in Australia and North America. He has held visiting positions at a number of institutions in Asia, Europe and North America and is currently a Senior Fellow at the Melbourne Law School.

ELIZA MIK has worked in-house in a number of software companies, Internet start-ups and telecommunication providers in Australia, Poland, Malaysia, Australia and the United Arab Emirates. She advised on e-commerce, software licensing and patenting as well as technology procurement, PKI, data protection and provider liability. Throughout her professional career, Mik has maintained a keen interest in all developments (both legal and technical) pertaining to the Internet and its use as an enabler of commerce. Those interests resulted in the 2007 thesis "Contract Formation in Open Electronic Networks" at the University of Sydney. After joining SMU in 2010, Mik continued her research into the regulation of e-commerce, the interaction between contract law and technology and the use of the Internet as a platform for commerce. More recently, her sphere of interests has expanded to encompass the legal challenges inherent in the mainstream adoption of the Internet of Things. She teaches contract law, business law and the law of e-commerce.

LAVANYA N. is a research assistant at the ATC, and her academic interests include economic and business policy and planning. In addition, she is a recipient of the NUS Undergraduate Merit Scholarship. At ATC, she participated in projects related to trade in the ASEAN region, as well as in the planning and execution of The Digital Champion's Programme, which aims to enable MSMEs to capitalize on the digital trade platform.

MINH HUE NGUYEN is a trade policy analyst at the ATC. Nguyen is currently working on research projects on trade-related topics such as the TPP, the RCEP, the AEC and digital trade. She is also the Under-Secretary-General of the Asia Business Trade Association. She obtained her bachelor's degree in economics from Nanyang Technological University. She was among thirty-three scholars from ASEAN countries receiving the Singapore Ministry of Foreign Affairs scholarship in 2012. Prior to joining the ATC, Nguyen worked at Taylor & Francis Academic Publishing as a Journal Editorial Intern.

LUKE NOTTAGE is a professor of comparative and transnational business law at Sydney Law School, founding co-director of the

Australian Network for Japanese Law and associate director of the Centre for Asian and Pacific Law at the University of Sydney. He specializes in consumer product safety law, contract law, arbitration and corporate governance. He has published over a hundred refereed articles and book chapters. His eleven books include *ASEAN Product Liability and Consumer Product Safety Law* (2016, co-edited with S. Thanitcul), *Asia-Pacific Disaster Management* (2014, co-edited with S. Butt and H. Nasu), *Consumer Law and Policy in Australia and New Zealand* (2013, co-edited with J. Malbon) and *Product Safety and Liability Law in Japan* (2004). Nottage serves on the International Law Association's Committee for the International Protection of Consumers and has consulted on consumer law matters for law firms, ASEAN, the EC, OECD, UNCTAD, UNDP and the Japanese government.

JEANNIE MARIE PATERSON is a professor at Melbourne Law School who researches and teaches in the areas of contracts, consumer protection and consumer credit law. Her research centers on the effective protection of disadvantaged consumers, the impact of new technologies on consumer protection and the relationship between statute and the general law in consumer protection. Jeannie recently completed a Consultancy for the ASEAN-Australia Development Cooperation Program, "Supporting Research and Dialogue in Consumer Protection" (with C. Beaton-Wells, J. Malbon and L. Nottage). She is the convener of the Digital Citizens Network at Melbourne Law School.

NIMNUAL PIEWTHONGNGAM is a director of the DPU Praxis Center and a lecturer of Law at Dhurakij Pundit University. She holds a Doctor of Juridical Science degree in international trade law from Golden Gate University School of Law. Prior to joining Dhurakij Pundit University, she was appointed by the University of the Thai Chamber of Commerce as the executive director of the AEC Strategy Center. In this position, her main responsibility was to provide business and legal advice for businesses looking to enter the ASEAN market, especially in Cambodia, Laos, Vietnam and Myanmar. She worked at KPMG Thailand as a Tax and Legal Manager, where she advised clients on investing in ASEAN Countries focusing on the Myanmar Market. Her main focuses in her current position are advising Thai and foreign investors looking to invest in Myanmar and other ASEAN countries, and conducting various research projects related to ASEAN economic integration.

HENG WANG is an associate professor and the co-director of Herbert Smith Freehills CIBEL (China International Business and Economic Law) Centre, UNSW Faculty of Law and a University Visiting Professorial Fellow, Southwest University of Political Science and Law, China. He has published widely in journals including the *Journal of World Trade* and the *Cornell International Law Journal*. He has been a visiting professor at University of Ottawa, Case Western Reserve University, Yokohama National University and Xiamen University, and was a Max Weber Fellow at the European University Institute. He was an Executive Council member of the Society of International Economic Law and is a founding member of the Asian International Economic Law Network, a member of the Asian WTO Research Network, and an executive council member of all three Chinese societies of international economic law and WTO law. He is a recipient of top research awards and several major grants.

TRINH HAI YEN is the Vice Dean of the Diplomatic Academy of Vietnam (DAV) Faculty of International Law. She graduated with a BA from DAV Institute for International Relations, an MALD (Master of Arts in Law and Diplomacy) from the Fletcher School of Law and Diplomacy and a PhD in law from NUS. She has been a lecturer of international law at the DAV International Law Faculty since 2001, specializing in public international law, international investment law, international trade law and international human rights law. She has provided consultancy services for governmental and non-governmental organizations in Vietnam and published works on her areas of expertise, including investor-state arbitration, the ASEAN comprehensive investment agreement, and WTO law on dispute settlement. She is the author of a book titled *The Interpretation of Investment Treaties* (2014).

PREFACE

The Doha Round impasse has spurred the proliferation of trade and investment agreements, particularly in the Asia-Pacific region. The rise of populist nationalism has also posed new challenges to regional integration and the multilateral trading system. Against this backdrop, the fast-growing Association of Southeast Asian Nations has been attracting the attention of governments and enterprises.

In this collection, we seek to provide a valuable guide and legal analysis of the new ASEAN Economic Community Blueprint 2025 from regional and global perspectives. Our aim is to assess the theoretical concept of ASEAN law and the substantive impact of mega-regionals and bilateral agreements on commercial law and business operations.

This collection is a collaborative effort among legal experts who specialize in corporate law, international economic law and intellectual property law. Almost all contributors presented at the ASEAN Law Conference, which took place at Singapore Management University on December 7–8, 2017. The contributors have also incorporated the in-depth feedback provided by senior academics, legal counsels and officials from international organizations.

We thank SMU School of Law's Centre for Cross-Border Commercial Law in Asia (CEBCLA) for funding and organizing the conference. Professors Yeo Tiong Min and Goh Yihan (former and current Dean, respectively) and Tang Hang Wu, Academic Director of CEBCLA, as well as Mr Joe Ng at Cambridge University Press provided substantial support for the project. Detailed comments from Mr. Tan Tai Hiong of the ASEAN Secretariat, Mr. Marcus Bartley Johns of the World Bank, Professor Andrew Mitchell of Melbourne Law School and Gmeleen Tomboc of Sidley Austin LLP, tremendously benefited our discussion at the conference. SMU students Kent Chen Sixue, Terrance Goh, Belle The and Thong Ying Xuan also provided invaluable editing assistance.

Finally, we extend our gratitude to Professors Gary Chan, Christopher Chen, Weisteng Chen, Jean Ho, David Llewellyn and Yip Man for enriching the theme and structure of the book. With contributions from these distinguished colleagues, we hope to offer a fresh and holistic understanding of multifaceted ASEAN law in the new regional economic order.

ABBREVIATIONS

AANZFTA	ASEAN-Australia-New Zealand Free Trade Agreement
ABAC	ASEAN Business Advisory Council
ABIF	ASEAN Banking Integration Framework
ABMI	Asian Bond Market Initiative
ACFTA	ASEAN-China Free Trade Agreement
ACIA	ASEAN Comprehensive Investment Agreement
ACJEP	ASEAN-Japan Comprehensive Economic Partnership
ACMF	ASEAN Capital Markets Forum
ACPE	ASEAN Chartered Professional Engineer
ACPECC	ACPE Coordinating Committee
ADB	Asian Development Bank
ADR	Alternative Dispute Resolution
AEC	ASEAN Economic Community
AEC Blueprint 2015	ASEAN Economic Community Blueprint 2015
AEC Blueprint 2025	ASEAN Economic Community Blueprint 2025
AEM	ASEAN Economic Ministers
AFAS	ASEAN Framework Agreement on Services
AFIF	ASEAN Financial Integration Framework
AFTA	ASEAN Free Trade Area
AHKFTA	ASEAN-Hong Kong Free Trade Agreement
AHKIA	ASEAN-Hong Kong Investment Agreement
AHTN	ASEAN Harmonized Tariff Nomenclature
AIA	ASEAN Investment Area Agreement
AMS	ASEAN Member State
APEC	Asia-Pacific Economic Cooperation
AQRF	ASEAN Qualifications Reference Framework
ASAM	ASEAN Single Aviation Market
ASEAN	Association of Southeast Asian Nations
ATIGA	ASEAN Trade in Goods Agreement
ATISA	ASEAN Trade in Services Agreement
AWGIPC	ASEAN Working Group on Intellectual Property Cooperation
BIT	Bilateral investment treaty

CCS	Coordinating Committee on Services
CEPT	Common Effective Preferential Tariff Scheme
ChAFTA	China-Australia Free Trade Agreement
CJEU	Court of Justice of the European Union
CLMV	Cambodia, Lao PDR, Myanmar and Vietnam
CMDP	Capital Market Development Plan
CPTPP	Progressive Agreement for Trans-Pacific Partnership
CSFTA	China-Singapore FTA
CTC	Change in tariff classification
DSM	Dispute settlement mechanism
DSU	Dispute Settlement Understanding
EASA	European Aviation Safety Agency
EDSM	ASEAN Protocol on Enhanced Dispute Settlement Mechanism
EEA	European Economic Area
EHP	Early Harvest Program
EU	European Union
EUSFTA	EU-Singapore Free Trade Agreement
EVFTA	EU-Vietnam Free Trade Agreement
FDI	Foreign direct investment
FET	Fair and equitable trade
FTA	Free trade agreement
FTZ	Free trade zone
GATS	General Agreement on Trade in Services
GATT	General Agreement on Tariffs and Trade
GDP	Gross domestic product
GVC	Global value chain
HS	Harmonized System
IAI	Initiative for ASEAN Integration
ICSID	International Centre for Settlement of Investment Disputes
IGA	ASEAN Investment Guarantee Agreement
IIA	International investment agreement
IP	Intellectual property
ISDS	Investor-state dispute settlement
MAAS	Multilateral Agreement on Air Services
MAFLAFS	Multilateral Agreement for the Full Liberalization of Air Freight Services
MAFLPAS	Multilateral Agreement for the Full Liberalization of Passenger Air Services
MFN	Most-favored nation
MIC	Myanmar Investment Commission
MIL	Myanmar Investment Law

MIR	Myanmar Investment Regulations
MLEC	UNCITRAL Model Law on Electronic Commerce
MNP	Movement of Natural Persons
MOU	Memorandum of Understanding
MRA	Mutual Recognition Agreement
MSME	Micro, small and medium enterprise
NAFTA	North American Free Trade Agreement
NGO	Nongovernmental organization
NIEO	New International Economic Order
NREO	New regional economic order
NT	National Treatment
NTB	Nontariff barrier
NTM	Nontariff measure
OECD	Organisation for Economic Co-operation and Development
PTA	Preferential Trade Agreement
QAB	Qualified ASEAN Bank
RCEP	Regional Comprehensive Economic Partnership
RFPE	Registered Foreign Professional Engineer
RIATS	Roadmap for Integration of the Air Travel Sector
ROO	Rules of Origin
RVC	Regional Value Content
SAFTA	Singapore-Australia Free Trade Agreement
SEC	Securities and Exchange Commission
SEZ	Special economic zone
SICC	Singapore International Commercial Court
SIMC	Singapore International Mediation Centre
SMBD	Senior Management and Board of Directors
SME	Small and medium enterprise
TAC	Treaty of Amity and Cooperation in Southeast Asia
TFEU	Treaty on the Functioning of the European Union
TIG	ASEAN-China Agreement on Trade in Goods
TIS	ASEAN-China Agreement on Trade in Services
TPP	Trans-Pacific Partnership
TRIPs	Agreement on Trade-Related Aspects of Intellectual Property Rights
UN	United Nations
UNCITRAL	United Nations Commission on International Trade Law
UNCTAD	United Nations Conference on Trade and Development
USSFTA	United States-Singapore Free Trade Agreement
WCO	World Customs Organization
WEF	World Economic Forum
WTO	World Trade Organization

PART 1

ASEAN Agreements in the Global Context

1

ASEAN Law in the New Regional Economic Order: an Introductory Roadmap to the ASEAN Economic Community

PASHA L. HSIEH AND BRYAN MERCURIO

1.1 Introduction

The impasse of the WTO Doha Round has spurred the proliferation of trade and investment agreements, particularly in the Asia-Pacific region. The fast-growing ASEAN has been attracting the attention of governments and enterprises, increasing its importance to global value chains and the world economy. This book explores the theoretical concept of ASEAN law within the broadly defined discipline of international economic law. More specifically, it sheds light on the roadmap to the AEC Blueprint 2025 by evaluating the impact of regional agreements on the business and commercial aspects of laws.

The evolution of ASEAN is significant for global trade. First, with a strategic location and population of 640 million, ASEAN is a rising trade power. The ten-country bloc is Asia's third-largest economy, and is expected to ascend from the world's sixth to the fourth largest economy by 2030.[1] Owing to its geopolitical salience, ASEAN has become a priority trade partner for China, India, the EU and the United States. Second, the legalization of the AEC and ASEAN's external FTAs with major Asia-Pacific economies provides a valuable case study of South-South regionalism between developing nations.

Finally, ASEAN's FTA strategy plays a critical role in the development of mega-regional trade agreements. The United States' withdrawal from the TPP did not deter the remaining signatories from reviving the pact.

[1] ASEAN Economic Community Chartbook 2017 (2017), at 2; Victor Wong, *Compelling Case for Investing in Asean Region, The Straits Times*, Feb. 4, 2018, www.straitstimes.com/business/invest/compelling-case-for-investing-in-asean-region (last visited Jun. 29, 2018).

The eleven-party CPTPP was signed in March 2018.[2] It includes Brunei, Malaysia, Singapore and Vietnam. Another major initiative, the RCEP, is "an ASEAN-led process."[3] The sixteen-country RCEP will encompass the ten ASEAN Member States and incorporate the mechanisms of existing ASEAN agreements.[4]

ASEAN did not begin as an economic endeavor. In fact, the inception of ASEAN in 1967 was primarily driven by political considerations. Pursuant to the Bangkok Declaration, Indonesia, Malaysia, the Philippines, Singapore and Thailand established ASEAN as a loose security alliance against communist expansion.[5] The postcolonial mindset energized the "ASEAN Way," which rests upon noninterference and consensus-based principles.[6] The accession of Brunei in 1987 and the subsequent addition of four least-developed members, Cambodia, Laos, Myanmar and Vietnam (known as the CLMV countries), made today's ASEAN a ten-country bloc.[7] The development gap between earlier members and CLMV countries is often perceived to have created a two-tiered ASEAN, and gives rise to notable special and differential treatment provisions under ASEAN agreements.

ASEAN members signed the first economic agreement enabling preferential trading arrangements in 1977, but the objective was the promotion of economic cooperation rather than economic integration.[8] Preoccupied with cross-border commodity trade, the initiative was designed to ensure a commercially viable market for large-scale industrial products that selected Member States produced. This initiative failed to increase intra-ASEAN trade because Member States insisted upon lengthy exclusion lists and high tariff rates. Faced with global regionalism and the rise of China and India, ASEAN countries switched their focus to trade liberalization and formed the ASEAN Free Trade Area in 1992.[9]

[2] Comprehensive and Progressive Agreement for Trans-Pacific Partnership Ministerial Statement, Mar. 8, 2018.

[3] ASEAN Framework for Regional Comprehensive Economic Partnership (2011).

[4] Guiding Principles and Objectives for Negotiating the Regional Comprehensive Economic Partnership (2012).

[5] Rodolfo C. Severino, Southeast Asia in Search of an ASEAN Community: Insights from the Former ASEAN Secretary-General 1–11 (2006).

[6] ASEAN at 50: Achievements and Challenges in Regional Integration (2017), at 3–7.

[7] Walter Woon, The ASEAN Charter: A Commentary 10–12 (2016).

[8] Severino, *supra* note 5, at 214–25.

[9] *Id.*, at 222–5; Tham Siew Yean & Sanchita Basu Das, *Introduction: The ASEAN Economic Community and Conflicting Domestic Interests, in* Moving the AEC Beyond 2015: Managing Domestic Consensus for Community-Building 1, 3–4 (Tham Siew Yean & Sanchita Basu Das eds., 2016).

This initiative was not wholly successful, as insignificant margins of preferences and complicated administrative procedures necessary to meet the rules of origin led to the scheme's low utilization rate by businesses.[10]

In tandem with the development of the bloc was the beginning and evolution of the concept of unified ASEAN law, which consolidates separate ASEAN legal systems. A milestone of ASEAN is its transformation from an "association" to a "community," which represents a higher degree of legal integration.[11] Guided by the ASEAN Vision 2020, ASEAN leaders endorsed the plan for an ASEAN Community under the Bali Concord II in 2003.[12] The goal of the new institution is to establish three mutually reinforcing pillars, including the AEC, the ASEAN Security Community and the ASEAN Socio-Cultural Community.[13] The ASEAN Summit subsequently brought forward the deadline for the Community from 2020 to 2015.

As a critical constitutional moment, the adoption of the ASEAN Charter codified the bloc's established practice and conferred legal personality on ASEAN "as an inter-governmental" organization.[14] The ASEAN Charter thus alters the nature of the legal foundation for the institutional structure of ASEAN. In 2007, ASEAN states approved the AEC Blueprint 2015, which details the strategies for creating "a single market and production base."[15] Another historical step took place in December 2015 with the official launch of the much-anticipated AEC. To structure the roadmap for the post-2015 vision, ASEAN leaders adopted the new AEC Blueprint 2025, which targets the creation of "a deeply integrated and highly cohesive ASEAN economy."[16]

ASEAN law incorporates both internal and external dimensions that mutually accelerate economic integration. The internal dimension denotes multiple intra-ASEAN agreements, which underpin the AEC. The external dimension includes ASEAN+1 FTAs that ASEAN as

[10] See generally Bryan Mercurio, *Trade Liberalisation in Asia: Why Intra-Asian Free Trade Agreements Are Not Utilised By the Business Community*, 6 (1)Asian J. WTO & Int'l Health L. & Pol. 109, 110–36 (2011).

[11] Tang Siew Mun, *Is ASEAN Due for a Makeover*, 39 (2)Contemporary Southeast Asia 239, 243 (2017).

[12] Cha-am Hua Hin Declaration on the Roadmap for the ASEAN Community (2009–2015) (2009).

[13] *Id.*

[14] Charter of the Association of Southeast Asian Nations (2007) (ASEAN Charter), art. 3.

[15] ASEAN Economic Community Blueprint (2007), paras. 4–9.

[16] ASEAN Economic Community Blueprint 2025 (2015), paras. 3–7.

a group signed with its dialogue partners. From 2002 to 2017, ASEAN concluded FTAs with China, India, Japan, Korea, Hong Kong, Australia and New Zealand.[17] RCEP members also affirmed the pledge of the negotiating partners to integrate the legal mechanism consistently with coexisting ASEAN+1 FTAs.[18] These agreements have strengthened ASEAN centrality, a notion that the ASEAN Charter mandated to ensure the bloc's indispensable status in the region.[19]

After fifty years of ASEAN's progress, it has become urgent and necessary to have a comprehensive analysis of ASEAN law in national, regional and global contexts. Built on the latest AEC Blueprint 2025, this collection provides the most up-to-date examination of pressing legal issues that governments and investors face with respect to access to the ASEAN market. Each contributor closely considers these parameters and the operation of ASEAN law, reflecting its challenges to conventional theories of regional integration. This book therefore provides a rare opportunity to assess cutting-edge areas of ASEAN law not only from the conventional trade law angle, but also from commercial law and intellectual property perspectives.

In addition, this collection centers on the impact of the latest bilateral FTAs and mega-regionals on national legislation vis-à-vis commercial operations. Comparative case studies in selected countries and the implementation of recent bilateral agreements, including the China-Australia FTA and EU FTAs with Vietnam and Singapore, enrich the understanding of ASEAN law. The features highlighted in the chapters allow us to present fresh and holistic perspectives of Asia-Pacific regionalism and bridge the gap between theory and practice.

1.2 The Contextual Framework of the New Regional Economic Order

As the title of the book indicates, we situate ASEAN law in the context of the NREO and assess associated global trends and shifting paradigms.

17 ASEAN concluded the most recent ASEAN+1 FTA and investment agreement with Hong Kong in November 2017. For the history and framework of ASEAN's other external trade agreements, see David Chin Soon Siong, *ASEAN's Journey towards Free Trade*, *in* Economic Diplomacy: Essays and Reflections by Singapore's Negotiators 209, 217–42 (Chin Leng Lim & Margaret Liang eds., 2011).

18 Joint Leaders' Statement on the Negotiations for the Regional Comprehensive Economic Partnership (2017), para. 5.

19 ASEAN Charter, art. 2(2)(m); Woon, *supra* note 7, at 71–2; Amitav Acharya, *The Myth of ASEAN Centrality?*, 39 (2) Contemporary Southeast Asia 273, 274–8 (2017).

We propose the NREO as the normative framework to understand the contemporary dynamics of Asia-Pacific FTAs, which shape the evolution of ASEAN law.[20] The NREO represents the Global South's prodevelopment aspirations but is different from the movement of the NIEO. In the 1970s, the Group of 77 that included predominantly Asian and African states pushed for the United Nations to adopt the NIEO principles.[21] This group resorted to the UN Conference on Trade and Development to influence negotiations of the GATT, which Washington and Brussels had dominated.

In essence, the South requested a "just and equitable" economic order that demands absolute trade sovereignty and justified exceptions to cardinal trade norms such as the most-favored-nations principle.[22] To a certain extent, the South's agenda was advanced by prompting the GATT's incorporation of prodevelopment schemes, including special and differential treatment provisions and the Enabling Clause, which legalizes preferential market access for the South.[23] However, the NIEO quickly waned because of the divergent interests of the developing nations and, more decisively, the Thatcher-Reagan coalition's refusal to consider further demands.[24]

Since the Uruguay Round, the Washington Consensus – based on the North's concept of neoliberalism – became the dominant force for the trading system.[25] Under the single undertaking approach of the WTO, developing countries lacked bargaining power to confront the North. They were compelled to assume daunting obligations ranging from services to intellectual property under various agreements. Similar

[20] This normative framework can be explained by realist and dependency theories. Pasha L. Hsieh, *Reassessing the Trade – Development Nexus in International Economic Law: The Paradigm Shift in Asia-Pacific Regionalism*, 37 (3) Northwestern J. Int'l L. & Bus. 321, 337–41 (2017).

[21] GA Res. S-6/3201, Declaration on the Establishment of a New International Economic Order (May 1, 1974) (NIEO Declaration); The Early Days of the Group of 77, May 2014, https://unchronicle.un.org/article/early-days-group-77 (last visited Jun. 29, 2018).

[22] E.g., NIEO Declaration, *supra* note 21, Arts. 4 & 5; Antony Anghie, *Legal Aspects of the New International Economic Order*, 6 (1) Humanity 145, 147–9 (2015).

[23] Sonia Rolland, Development at the World Trade Organization 44–5 (2012); Tracey D. Epps & Michael J. Trebilcock, *Special and Differential Treatment in Agricultural Trade*, *in* Developing Countries in the WTO Legal System 323, 328–30 (Chantal Thomas & Joel P. Trachtman eds., 2009).

[24] James M. Cypher, The Process of Economic Development 238 (2014); Trade and Development Report (2014), at 67–8.

[25] John Williamson, *A Short History of the Washington Consensus*, *in* The Washington Consensus Reconsidered: Towards a New Global Governance 14, 16–17 (Narcís Serra & Joseph E. Stiglitz eds., 2008).

dynamics also prompted WTO-plus components to be included in FTAs between developed and developing nations. Much to the South's frustration, the NIEO movement failed to achieve its goals. Conceptually, the NIEO was preoccupied with North-South clashes in trade norms, whereas the current NREO focuses on new-generation South-South cooperation. In practice, the NREO has forged the collective power of developing countries through FTAs and reconstructed the neocolonial dependency of the South on the North.

The context of global regionalism is essential for understanding ASEAN law in the NREO. Global regionalism can be categorized into three major waves. The first wave occurred from the 1960s to the 1970s.[26] As ASEAN's initial preferential trade initiative illustrates, the prevailing import substituting policy that sought to increase the economies of scale by allocating regional industrial outputs largely collapsed in the developing world. The second wave took place in the 1980s and 1990s, when the United States and Europe galvanized the impetus for expediting regionalism.[27] Notable examples include NAFTA and the transformation from the European Single Market to the EU. The North-led bilateral agreements also resulted in the "domino effect" that invigorated South-based regionalism, such as the ASEAN Free Trade Area.[28]

The NREO emerged in what we call the "Third Regionalism," which refers to the third wave of global regionalism. The Third Regionalism has coincided with the Doha Round since the 2000s and gave rise to the AEC. The Third Regionalism encompasses distinctive characteristics. The five-fold growth of trade pacts in the past three decades, leading to 287 FTAs in 2018, evidences the unpresented speed of regionalism.[29] South-South FTAs (agreements between developing countries) now represent 75 percent of FTAs worldwide, whereas the number of North-South FTAs (agreements between developed and developing nations) dropped from

[26] Jagdish Bhagwati, *Regionalism versus Multilateralism*, 15 World Eco. 535, 538–39 (1992); World Trade Report 2011 (2011), at 52; Sungjoon Cho, *Breaking the Barrier between Regionalism and Multilateralism: A New Perspective on Trade Regionalism*, 42 Harv. Int'l L. J. 419, 426–57 (2001).

[27] Bhagwati, *supra* note 26, at 540–2; World Trade Report 2011, *supra* note 26, at 52–3.

[28] For the background, see Richard E. Baldwin, *Managing the Noodle Bowl: The Fragility of East Asian Regionalism*, Working Paper Series on Regional Economic Integration, No. 7 (2007), at 6–7; Amitav Acharya, *Foundations of Collection Action in Asia: Theory and Practice of Regional Cooperation*, ADBI Working Paper Series, No. 344 (2012), at 14.

[29] Regional Trade Agreements, www.wto.org/english/tratop_e/region_e/region_e.htm (last visited May 2, 2018); World Trade Report 2011, *supra* note 26, at 55.

60 to 25 percent.[30] These developments, along with the fact that more than half of the world's FTAs are in the Asia-Pacific, have led to paradigm shifts in world trade law.[31]

The deviation from the West-centric liberalization to multipolar trade governance has become a reality. The economic and geopolitical changes in the Third Regionalism have enabled the NREO to rejuvenate the South's efforts to alter the existing economic order. For instance, Asia's ascending power has contributed to the relative decline of US hegemony. The trade prong of President Obama's "pivot to Asia" strategy culminated in the TPP, which was perceived not only to strengthen ties with Asian allies but also to contain a rising China. Of course, the goodwill has been undone by soaring populist protectionism in the United States. Current President Trump's policies have eroded the intended strategic goals as well as damaged the cross-Atlantic alliance on which the previous NIEO was premised.

Furthermore, as illustrated by ASEAN Member States such as Indonesia and Vietnam, developing countries have switched their economic priorities from import substitution to export-driven orientation. This policy change resulted in more than 75 percent of Asian FTAs incorporating WTO-plus components.[32] To some extent, the increase of Asia's intraregional trade share to 57 percent has also lessoned regional economies' reliance on the developed markets.[33] The converging policies of Asian countries on ASEAN, including China's much ballyhooed "One Belt, One Road" initiative, Korea's New Southern Policy and Taiwan's New Southbound Policy, ought to strengthen the NREO in the Asia-Pacific.

The context of the NREO builds the theoretical foundation for ASEAN's development as an economic community. Its legal architecture in turn provides an alternative model for the Global South. It is true that political scientists often compare ASEAN with the European Union, but it is an oversimplification to characterize the AEC as an incomplete version of the EU. Some commentators similarly ignore different political backgrounds to argue for ASEAN to follow the European model. Despite its legalization process, the ASEAN Way continues to uphold its

[30] World Trade Report 2011, *supra* note 26, at 55–6; Asia-Pacific Trade and Investment Report 2016 (2016), at 90.

[31] Asia-Pacific Trade and Investment Report 2016, *supra* note 30, at 88.

[32] E.g., Richard Baldwin & Masahiro Kawai, *Multilateralizing Asian Regionalism*, ADBI Working Paper Series, No. 431 (2013), at 8–9.

[33] Asian Economic Integration 2017 (2017), at 16.

relevance in the bloc's operational structure. While ASEAN is an intergovernmental organization, the EU is a supernational institution. ASEAN's soft law approach based on horizontal integration makes it fundamentally different from the EU, which consolidates its members through a hard law, top-down approach. The EU's embedded problems with the euro crisis and border control contributed to the discontent that led to Brexit and populist nationalism in various European states. Hence, what the AEC envisions is intensifying its FTA-plus arrangements rather than pursuing the European version of a common market or customs union.

Two areas further exemplify the legal distinctions between ASEAN and the EU. First, EU treaties and regulations have "direct effect" to override national legislation, but the ASEAN Charter mandates that members "take all necessary measures" to implement ASEAN treaties.[34] National constitutions of ASEAN states are unlikely to be interpreted as granting regional agreements self-executing power.[35] Second, the treaty-making power provisions of the ASEAN Charter do not amount to the EU concept of competences conferred by Member States. For matters that fall with the EU's exclusive competences, the EU alone can negotiate and conclude international treaties that bind individual members. Nevertheless, ASEAN's power is severely restricted because it does not extend to the conclusion of agreements that would create obligations on individual states.[36] The legal obligation of ASEAN Member States is limited to the "endeavor to develop common positions and pursue joint actions."[37] A resultant political exercise is to convene the ASEAN Caucus meetings to converge stances before negotiating trade agreements. The practice of concluding external agreements by ten states collectively remains unchanged.

1.3 Consolidating the ASEAN Economic Community

As an integral part of the new ASEAN Community, the AEC marks a milestone in Asia-Pacific regionalism. The legalization of the AEC,

[34] ASEAN Charter, art. 5(2).

[35] See generally Diane A. Desierto, *ASEAN's Constitutionalization of International Law: Challenges to Evolution under the New ASEAN Charter*, 49 Colum. J. Transnat'l L. 268, 300–03 (2010–11).

[36] ASEAN Charter, art. 41(7); Rules of Procedure for Conclusion of International Agreements by ASEAN (2011), rule 1.

[37] ASEAN Charter, art. 41(4).

which connects ten diverse developing nations, exhibits the NREO by providing a new model for South-South cooperation. The AEC consolidates ASEAN agreements that govern trade in goods and services, investment and dispute settlement mechanisms.[38] The ATIGA integrates previous goods-related agreements that had been signed since the 1990s. The agreement aims to eliminate tariffs and nontariff measures and improve trade facilitation measures.

Based on its incremental modality, the AFAS enabled multiple rounds of negotiations that led to successive "packages" of services commitments. Having been negotiated as separate packages, the liberalization of air transport and financial services also forms an integral part of the AFAS. To facilitate the flow of intraregional professional mobility, ten states concluded the ASEAN Agreement on the Movement of Natural Persons and mutual recognition arrangements for selected professional services. In addition, the ACIA increases the bloc's competitiveness to attract FDI. Importantly, the ACIA consolidates former agreements to streamline the schedule of reservations and accord substantive benefits to investors. ASEAN has also developed multilayered schemes for the resolution of trade conflicts. While state-to-state disputes fall within the realm of the ASEAN Protocol for Enhanced Dispute Settlement Mechanism, the ACIA enables private investors to resort to investor-state arbitration.

Adopted in 2015, the AEC Blueprint 2025 succeeded its predecessor and is incorporated into the guiding document, "ASEAN 2025: Forging Ahead Together," which charts the roadmap of the ASEAN Community from 2016 to 2025.[39] To better understand the AEC, we now turn to a much-needed analysis of key differences between the AEC Blueprint 2015 and the AEC Blueprint 2025. In 2015, the implementation rate of original AEC goals was 79.5 percent.[40] On this basis, the AEC Blueprint 2025 pushes for further liberalization to realize the ASEAN Community Vision 2025. The new features of the Blueprint will similarly fortify the linkage between the ASEAN architecture with domestic business and commercial laws.

Five main characteristics are found in the AEC Blueprint 2025. The first characteristic, "A Highly Integrated and Cohesive Economy," comprises the most significant steps for the new phase.[41] The AEC

[38] For the timeline of the key agreements, see ASEAN at 50: A Historic Milestone for FDI and MNEs in ASEAN (2017), at 8–9.

[39] Kuala Lumpur Declaration on ASEAN 2025: Forging Ahead Together (2015).

[40] ASEAN at 50: Achievements and Challenges in Regional Integration, *supra* note 6, at 15.

[41] AEC Blueprint 2025, paras. 7–24.

Blueprint 2025 will create "a more unified market" by facilitating "the seamless movement of goods, services, investment, capital and skilled labour."[42] This language modifies the aspirations of the AEC Blueprint 2015 to form "a single market and production base."[43] The seamless movement provision suggests a step further than the previous Blueprint, which promoted the "free flow" of goods, services, investment and skilled labor and the "freer flow" of capital.[44]

Given that the bloc has achieved over 98 percent of the intra-ASEAN tariff elimination, ASEAN's tariff liberalization demonstrates clear progress for the AEC.[45] The key area for trade in goods is to strengthen the ATIGA and to manage proliferating nontariff measures that hinder the result of tariff liberalization. As for services trade, the target of the AEC Blueprint 2015 is to remove substantially all restrictions for remaining sectors was unmet. The AEC Blueprint 2025 will lower barriers to services trade and integrates currently fragmented commitments by enacting the ATISA. On the investment side, the ACIA will finalize the built-in agenda for decreasing or eliminating investment restrictions.

Tellingly, the AEC Blueprint 2025 substantially expands the coverage for financial integration. It seeks to bolster Qualified ASEAN Banks under the ASEAN Banking Integration Framework and facilitate capital market linkages for multi-jurisdictional equity and debt offerings. Moreover, the completion of national single windows for trade facilitation and regulatory reforms that enhance ASEAN's participation in global value chains illustrate the salient features of the new Blueprint.

The second characteristic of the new Blueprint, "A Competitive, Innovative and Dynamic ASEAN," is built on the previous Blueprint and reiterates regional cooperation of competition policy, consumer protection and intellectual property rights.[46] The new focus on sustainable economic development as the growth strategy reinforces ASEAN's collective commitments to the UN-led 2030 Agenda for Sustainable Development.[47] The third characteristic, "Enhanced Connectivity and Sectoral Cooperation," aims to implement the Master Plan on ASEAN

[42] *Id.*, para. 7.
[43] AEC Blueprint 2015, paras. 6 & 9.
[44] *Id.*, para. 9.
[45] ASEAN at 50: Achievements and Challenges in Regional Integration, *supra* note 6, at 15–18.
[46] AEC Blueprint 2025, paras. 25–44.
[47] Complementarities between the ASEAN Community Vision 2025 and the United Nations 2030 Agenda for Sustainable Development: A Framework for Action (2017), at 16–17.

Connectivity.[48] In particular, the ASEAN Single Aviation Market Implementation Framework will commence the review of aviation agreements and further liberalize air transport ancillary services. More developed than in the previous Blueprint, the AEC Blueprint 2025 pledges to promote e-commerce transactions by developing an ASEAN Agreement on Electronic Commerce. With the EU General Data Protection Regulation taking effect in 2018, the global community places additional importance on privacy in digital trade. The protection of personal data is also envisioned in the new Blueprint.

The fourth characteristic is "A Resilient, Inclusive, People-Oriented and People-Centred ASEAN."[49] The AEC Blueprint 2015 focused on the development of small and medium enterprises, whereas the AEC Blueprint 2025 extends the scope to cover micro enterprises.[50] Concrete steps are planned to increase the utilization of rules of origins under FTAs and the ASEAN self-certification scheme for exporters. Additionally, the new Initiative for ASEAN Integration Work Plan III will narrow the regional development gap by providing CLMV countries with additional capacity-building assistance.

The fifth characteristic, "A Global ASEAN," is to strengthen the principle of ASEAN centrality by orienting the bloc as the center of today's hub-and-spoke trade system.[51] The AEC Blueprint 2025 is far more ambitious than its predecessor. The latest ASEAN+1 FTA was concluded with Hong Kong in 2017. In addition to advancing the Doha Development Agenda, ASEAN's immediate priority is to accelerate RCEP negotiations and review and upgrade external FTAs. Finally, the success of the AEC hinges on an effective implementation mechanism. Departing from the conventional ASEAN Way, the AEC Blueprint 2025 mandates that the ASEAN Economic Community Council "enforce compliance of all measures."[52] The ASEAN Secretariat is also tasked with developing an enhanced monitoring framework.

[48] AEC Blueprint 2025, paras. 45–66.
[49] *Id.*, paras. 67–78.
[50] E.g., *id.*, paras. 68–9; AEC Blueprint 2015, para. 60.
[51] AEC Blueprint 2025, paras. 79–80.
[52] *Id.*, paras. 81–2.

1.4 The Approach and Outline of the Book

Based on the AEC Blueprint 2025, this book provides the most up-to-date and comprehensive analysis of ASEAN law in the new era of global regionalism, including recent developments that have taken place after the conclusion of the CPTPP. These developments have led to even more challenges. For instance, given the differences between the AEC Blueprint 2015 and the AEC Blueprint 2025, what are the prospects of ASEAN integration and implications for foreign investors? To what extent will the AEC and the new commitments within ASEAN's agreements with China and India influence the ongoing RCEP negotiations? How should multinational corporations and small and medium-sized enterprises effectively respond to the ASEAN architecture, particularly in diverse emerging markets such as the Philippines and Myanmar? Such questions have cast doubt on the conventional wisdom but have not been systematically addressed by the international and regional economic law literature.

In filling this gap and exploring pressing issues for academic and professional communities, this book is divided into four main themes: (a) ASEAN Agreements in the Global Context; (b) Services Trade and Financial Integration; (c) Investment Liberalization and Protection; and (d) Intellectual Property, Digital Trade and Consumer Protection. These themes collectively examine the concept of ASEAN law through the lens of the intersection of regional treaties and business and commercial laws. By focusing on the cutting-edge areas of ASEAN law, this collection distinguishes itself from the existing books that focus primarily on the rules of law or the regional public law framework.[53] Furthermore, various chapters provide insight into the legal regimes of ASEAN countries from comparative law perspectives. Using case studies, we take a holistic approach to understanding AESAN law at both national and regional levels. Built on the legal experts' findings, we have been able to identify actual gaps in the regional framework and suggest potential reforms based on best practices.

[53] E.g., Imelda Deinla, The Development of the Rule of Law in ASEAN (2017); Pieter Jan Kuijper et al., From Treaty-Making to Treaty-Breaking: Models for ASEAN External Trade Agreements (2015); Stefano Inama & Edmund W. Sim, The Foundation of the ASEAN Economic Community: An Institutional and Legal Profile (2015); Sanchita Basu Das et al. eds., The ASEAN Economic Community: A Work in Progress (2013).

1.4.1 ASEAN Agreements in the Global Context

Part 1 of the book discusses the "Global ASEAN" initiatives, since external context provides both the fundamental rationale and environment within which ASEAN law has operated.[54] The chapters center on systemic issues of ASEAN agreements' status vis-à-vis WTO obligations and RCEP negotiations. In particular, these chapters unveil the implementation of upgraded agreements that will shape mega-regionals and the Free Trade Area of the Asia-Pacific, which Asia-Pacific Economic Cooperation envisioned. Following this introductory chapter, Minh Hue Nguyen, Deborah Elms and Lavanya N in Chapter 2 assess the evolution and regional implications of the ATIGA, which governs ASEAN's trade in goods. They evaluate the status of ASEAN's tariff eliminations and rules of origin under the ATIGA and six ASEAN+1 FTAs. These current updates, as well as their observations of rising nontariff measures, benefit manufacturers and exporters.

Given the rise of China and its expanded trade ties with Southeast Asia, Heng Wang in Chapter 3 analyzes China's FTA strategy and its flexible approach to ASEAN. The ASEAN-China FTA is not only the first ASEAN+1 FTA, but also China's first FTA that has been upgraded. The new commitments under ASEAN's agreements with China and Hong Kong are expected to form the benchmark for RCEP negotiations. Of course, the enforcement of trade commitments entails a functional dispute settlement mechanism for resolving economic conflicts. In Chapter 4, Henry Gao analyzes systemic issues within dispute settlement mechanisms under ASEAN agreements and compares them with the system under the WTO Dispute Settlement Understanding. While ASEAN FTAs with China, Japan and Korea are largely consistent with the WTO and the ASEAN Protocol for Enhanced Dispute Settlement Mechanism, notable differences exist in panel procedures and alternative dispute resolution clauses. The RCEP's consolidation of these rules will empower developing countries and ensure ASEAN centrality in Asia-Pacific regionalism.

1.4.2 Services Trade and Financial Integration

After considering the global context surrounding and impacting ASEAN law, in Part 2 this collection turns to services trade and financial

[54] AEC Blueprint 2025, para. 79; ASEAN Economic Community 2025 Consolidated Strategic Action Plan (2015), at 47.

integration. These two intertwined areas are essential to both multilateral corporations and banks. Trade in services is the backbone of trade in goods and has been the critical driver for ASEAN's growth. The service sector now accounts for more than half of the bloc's Gross Domestic Product and FDI inflows.[55] Recognizing the prominence of services trade, ASEAN commenced negotiations under the AFAS in 1995. Ten packages of commitments covering main service sectors, along with separate packages for air transport and financial services, jointly form members' AFAS obligations.[56]

In Chapter 5, Bryan Mercurio provides a detailed overview of services commitments and reviews the structure and performance of the AFAS. Negotiating the ATISA, an integrated services agreement, is a top priority of the AEC Blueprint 2025. He argues for the ATISA to adopt trade-friendly principles, including most-favored nations and transparency. He also identifies the loophole in the flexibility scheme and how the CPTPP and the prospective Trade in Services Agreement may shape the ASEAN modality for scheduling services commitments. Markedly, among the four modes of trade in services, the movement of natural persons (Mode 4) directly enables professional mobility. In Chapter 6, Yoshifumi Fukunaga points out that ASEAN mutual recognition arrangements are distinct from those of the EU and the Trans-Tasman arrangement. In particular, the ASEAN scheme focuses on recognizing professional qualifications rather than facilitating the movement of professionals. By evaluating existing agreements that govern engineers, nurses and tourism professionals, this chapter offers the best practices for the AEC.

The following chapters consider cutting-edge areas of specific service sectors. The AEC Blueprint 2025 elaborates on the roadmap to financial integration.[57] Federico Lupo-Pasini in Chapter 7 explores the challenges to regulatory cooperation for the integration of ASEAN banks, which are not entitled to "single passport" rights like their EU counterparts. He explains the rationale for bilateral agreements that enable Qualified ASEAN Banks under the regional framework. By conceptualizing ASEAN's banking trilemma, he finds it difficult to simultaneously achieve the goals of financial sovereignty, financial stability and banking integration. Chapter 8 authored by Michelle Dy emphasizes a closely related issue of

[55] ASEAN Services Report 2017: The Evolving Landscape (2017), at 6, 16.

[56] *Id.*, at 25–9; Chairman's Statement of the Thirty Second ASEAN Summit, Apr. 28, 2018, para. 12.

[57] AEC Blueprint 2025, paras. 16–17; ASEAN at 50: Achievements and Challenges in Regional Integration, *supra* note 6, at 30–3.

financial inclusion, which energizes inclusive growth by allowing smaller-scale enterprises to raise financing in the capital market. In her chapter, she analyzes the impact of the Asian financial crisis and the ASEAN Capital Markets Forum Action Plan 2016–2020 on regulatory reforms. A comparison between the approaches adopted by the Philippine Securities and Exchange Commission and the Indonesian Financial Services Authority unveils different paths to capital market integration.

With international and ASEAN-based law firms expanding operations in the Asia-Pacific, Pasha L. Hsieh in Chapter 9 sheds light on the liberalization of transnational legal services. He examines the WTO concept of legal services and the business impact of legal provisions under the CPTPP, the Korea-US FTA and China's FTAs with Australia and Korea. Based on AFAS legal services commitments, he also deciphers new regulatory regimes in Singapore and Malaysia and law firms' corresponding structural changes. Moreover, as the world's only aviation market to possess as many aircraft on order as it has in its current operative fleet, ASEAN's budget carriers and national airlines such as Thai Airways and Garuda Indonesia substantially contribute to the flow of regional passengers.[58] To be better aware of the directions of the ASEAN Single Aviation Market, Jae Woon Lee in Chapter 10 explores current air transport and open skies agreements. This chapter also explains the commercial practice of joint venture airlines and ASEAN's remaining infrastructure and regulatory challenges.

1.4.3 *Investment Liberalization and Protection*

Due to its rapid growth and emerging markets, the ASEAN bloc has been an attractive investment magnet. One of the important economic rationales for forging an economic community is to ensure the bloc's competitiveness in attracting FDI. In the past two decades, ASEAN's FDI inflows have increased over six-fold, and the value of FDI now accounts for 21 percent of FDI stock in all developing nations.[59] Excluding intra-ASEAN trade, the top sources of investments come from the EU, Japan, the United States and China.[60] As FDI is a critical tool for development, the AEC Blueprint 2025 stresses improving the investment environment.

[58] Investing in ASEAN 2018–2019 (2018), at 88–9.

[59] ASEAN at 50: A Historic Milestone for FDI and MNEs in ASEAN, *supra* note 38, at xiii & 6–7.

[60] ASEAN Investment Report 2017: Foreign Direct Investment and Economic Zones in ASEAN (2017), at 4.

In the first chapter of Part 3, devoted to investment, Sufian Jusoh discusses the evolution of the ACIA as the central pillar that guides intra-ASEAN investment and examines the scope of national treatment and most-favored-nations provisions under the agreement. In addition, this chapter illustrates the ACIA's impact on domestic legislation by comparing investment law reforms in Laos and Myanmar. Notwithstanding different results, the two least-developed nations offer valuable lessons for ASEAN's investment policy and South-South FTAs. To complement the analysis of investment liberalization, Julien Chaisse in Chapter 12 emphasizes the investment protection that the ACIA accords to ASEAN investors. In particular, he explains key provisions on fair and equitable treatment, the prohibition of direct and indirect expropriation and the free transfer of funds. The role of the ATIGA and the AFAS in strengthening the investment environment is also examined in detail.

To enforce rights under investment agreements, ISDS is commonly included in bilateral investment treaties and FTAs, and entitles foreign investors to bring complaints against host governments before international panels.[61] However, such mechanism has attracted public criticism and has become the main source of global protectionism. ISDS is perceived as bypassing domestic courts' jurisdiction and as creating a "regulatory chill" that makes public policies vulnerable for multinational corporations' legal challenges. Reflecting these concerns, the CPTPP narrows the scope of ISDS under the original TPP by disallowing an investor to sue a host government on the basis of the investment agreement and by suspending the minimum standard of treatment pertinent to financial services.[62]

The EU's new policy to replace ISDS with an investment court system further complicates the debates.[63] The new system, which creates a permanent tribunal including an appellate mechanism for investor-state disputes, has been incorporated into EU agreements with Canada, Vietnam, Singapore and Japan.[64] Trinh Hai Yen in Chapter 13 observes

[61] See generally *Special Issue: International Investment Arbitration in Southeast Asia, in* 18 J. World Invest. & Trade 767, 767–1061 (Luke Nottage & Sakda Thanitcul eds., 2017).

[62] The Annex attached to the preamble to the CPTPP suspended certain Trans-Pacific Partnership provisions in Chapter 9 (Investment) and Chapter 11 (Financial Services); see also *CPTPP: The Five Countries that Won't Sue NZ, According to the Government*, Newshub, Mar. 9, 2018, www.newshub.co.nz/home/politics/2018/03/cptpp-the-five-countries-that-won-t-sue-nz-according-to-the-government.html (last visited Jun. 29, 2018).

[63] See generally State of the Union 2017: A Multilateral Investment Court (2017).

[64] The text of the EU-Singapore FTA was renegotiated following the 2017 judgment of the Court of Justice of the EU on the scope of the EU's competences in concluding trade

the fragmented nature of ISDS mechanisms by examining the legal designs under the ACIA and ASEAN's external investment treaties. She also focuses on the investment court system in the EU-Vietnam FTA and compares it with the WTO mechanism. Her findings suggest that the drawbacks of the EU initiative could result in an inflexibility of the court structure and confusing jurisdiction of the appeal tribunal.

In Chapter 14, Yip Man offers her insight into prodevelopment dispute resolution mechanisms for commercial and investment disputes.[65] Going beyond the ACIA, she addresses the practical need for small and medium-size investors to solve business disputes in a cost-efficient manner. She thus provides a comparative analysis of arbitration and mediation mechanisms in Indonesia, Vietnam and Singapore, including the innovative hybrid structure of the Singapore International Commercial Court. Similarly underscoring the development dimension, Nimnual Piewthongngam in Chapter 15 considers the role of CLMV countries in realizing the AEC's target as a single investment destination. Using the case study of Myanmar, she examines Aung San Suu Kyi's legal reforms in key areas covering investment law, telecommunications law and rules governing special economic zones. These first-hand observations offer an assessment of the actual correlation between the ASEAN framework and domestic legislation pertinent to investment.

1.4.4 Intellectual Property, Digital Trade and Consumer Protection

Part 4 of the book centers on the core elements that contribute to ASEAN's competitiveness, productivity and its participation in global value chains, as highlighted in the AEC Blueprint 2025. This part addresses regional and national frameworks on intellectual property rights, e-commerce and product safety standards. It also proposes best practices for realizing legal harmonization based on ASEAN's horizontal integration model. In Chapter 16, Irene Calboli investigates the relationship between intellectual property rights and the principle of free movement of goods in intra-ASEAN trade. In particular, she addresses

agreements. Released in Apr. 2018, the provisions on the international investment court are included in Chapter 3 (Dispute Settlement) of the EU-Singapore Investment Protection Agreement.

65 For a review of ASEAN's present dispute settlement barriers, see Locknie Hsu et al., Improving Connectivity between ASEAN's Legal Systems to Address Commercial Issues (2018), at 102–11.

domestic laws on trademark, copyright and patent exhaustion in ASEAN states such as Brunei, Cambodia and Malaysia and their impact on the regional flow of commercial goods. After finding the divergences among states and even in a single state's treatment of different types of intellectual property, this chapter provides NAFTA and EU experiences for the AEC's reference.

Significantly, with the escalating middle class and the prevalence of mobile phone use, ASEAN is now the world's fastest-growing Internet region.[66] By 2025, the population having Internet access in this region will triple to 600 million and e-commerce sales will soar to $88 billion.[67] The AEC Blueprint 2025 notes the indispensable roles of information and communications technology and e-commerce in accelerating trade and investment.[68] To assess the roadmap, Chapter 17 authored by Eliza Mik examines legal and regulatory challenges to facilitate e-commerce in ASEAN. More specifically, she offers insight into the impact of the UNCITRAL Model Law on Electronic Commerce on national legislation. Critical to commercial transactions, this chapter also investigates legal issues of electronic signatures, consumer protection and privacy rights.

In Chapter 18, Han-Wei Liu explores an intertwined topic on data localization, which has given rise to digital trade debates for the TPP and other FTAs. He considers various types of data storage requirements and data transfer restrictions, exemplified by the EU's General Data Protection Regulation. By deciphering recent personal data protection or privacy acts enacted in countries such as Indonesia and Singapore, he offers suggestions for ASEAN's enhanced connectivity. Furthermore, Luke Nottage and Jeannie Paterson in Chapter 19 evaluate ASEAN countries' consumer protection regimes in light of the AEC Blueprint 2025 and EU and East Asian jurisdictions. They find the harmonization of ASEAN consumer protection laws problematic. To substantiate their position, this chapter identifies the limited scope and enforcement weaknesses of ASEAN regulations on product safety and liability, as well as consumer protection laws.

Chapter 20 concludes the collection. ASEAN as a bloc for developing nations has transformed and progressed dramatically since its inception

[66] e-Conomy SEA Spotlight 2017: Unprecedented Growth for Southeast Asia's $50B Internet Economy (2017), at 3.

[67] *Id.*, at 5; Jonathan Camhi, *Southeast Asia's Set for Explosive e-Commerce Growth*, Bus. Insider, May 16, 2017, www.businessinsider.com/southeast-asias-set-for-explosive-e-commerce-growth-2017-5 (last visited Jun. 29, 2018).

[68] AEC Blueprint 2025, paras. 50–3.

in 1967. A sound legal architecture for implementing the AEC Blueprint 2025 is essential for consolidating the new economic community. Built on experts' findings of key issues at regional and national levels, we offer concise yet concrete legal and policy advice for ASEAN enterprises and governments. We hope these recommendations will contextualize ASEAN law in the new regional economic order and make ASEAN a unique model for the Global South.

2

The ASEAN Trade in Goods Agreement: Evolution and Regional Implications

MINH HUE NGUYEN, DEBORAH ELMS, LAVANYA N

2.1 Introduction

The ten countries in ASEAN celebrated fifty years with a grand party in November 2017. There was much to celebrate. By 2015, ASEAN – viewed collectively – would have been the sixth richest economy in the world and third in Asia (in terms of GDP share).[1] The GDP per capita across ASEAN increased more than 60 percent from $2,393 in 2007 to $4,034 in 2016.[2] This figure, of course, contains wide variations between Member States.

ASEAN members have also rapidly developed manufacturing sectors. Many Member States have built up extensive regional or even global value chains on the back of ASEAN integration efforts. The ten countries made strong commitments to achieve the AEC goal by the end of 2015. Progress can be seen in several areas such as zero or very low tariffs for goods moving between members.

However, after several decades of work, ASEAN remains far from its goal of achieving free trade with all ten members. The AEC has promised many things, and its primary goal is "free flow of goods, services, investment, skilled labour and freer flow of capital." Many obstacles are blocking the way. Most problems stem from the way ASEAN is structured and how the ten countries have chosen to implement common objectives at the domestic level. Four specific problems affect trade in goods: tariffs, rules of origin, nontariff measures and some other practical issues. Therefore, ASEAN has not gotten as close to its ambitious trade goals as might have been expected.

[1] Association of Southeast Asian Nations Economic Community Chartbook 2017 (2017), at 2.

[2] *Id.*, at 3.

This chapter will discuss ASEAN's journey toward achieving free trade in goods, their constant efforts and commitments and why the results remain below expectations. The first section will look at the two most important ASEAN agreements on trade in goods. The second section will assess the results of ASEAN's efforts and commitments by looking at the bloc's involvement in international and regional trade. The last section will then go into details on the reasons behind the slow progress of ASEAN toward its commitments for trade in goods.

2.2 ASEAN's Continual Forward Progress toward Free Trade in Goods

The ten ASEAN countries have consistently worked toward broader and deeper economic integration over the last five decades. The most noticeable benchmarks of this journey include: establishment of the AFTA, setting up of the AEC with a stronger focus on cross-border trade in goods, formation of the ATIGA, creation of the AEC Blueprint 2025 and ASEAN's participation in the RCEP. The sections below will describe these important benchmarks in further detail.

2.2.1 Starting with the AFTA

ASEAN achieved some modest levels of economic integration in the 1970s through preferential trading agreements and other cooperation measures. However, the ten-country bloc only started to grow substantially after the establishment of the AFTA in 1992.[3] The main mechanism to achieve the aforementioned goals was the CEPT.[4] This scheme required member nations to apply a tariff rate of between 0 and 5 percent on imported goods that originated within ASEAN while still allowing members the freedom to impose tariffs based on their own national schedules on goods originating outside the region.[5] Note that ASEAN has never tried to become a customs union with a common external tariff, like the European Union.

[3] Hall Hill & Jayant Menon, *ASEAN Economic Integration: Features, Fulfillments, Failures and the Future*, Asian Development Bank, No. 69, Dec. 2010, www.adb.org/sites/default/files/publication/28551/wp69-hill-menon-asean-economic-integration.pdf (last visited Aug. 26, 2017).

[4] *Id.*

[5] *Id.*

As more and more countries in the world adopted a strategy of economic integration at regional and international levels, ASEAN Member States saw a need for the region to work more closely toward more ambitious goals. In 2003, the ten countries declared the establishment of the AEC at the Ninth ASEAN Summit in 2003.[6] The AEC, though launched in 2003, was not implemented until 2015.[7]

The first pillar of the AEC was about establishing a single market and production base through the free flow of goods, services, investment, labor and capital among the ASEAN members. However, the movement toward a single goods market would not be successful just through the elimination of tariffs. Hence, the AFTA-CEPT was superseded by the ATIGA in 2010 – a more comprehensive agreement that aimed to address wider aspects concerning the movement of goods regionally.[8]

2.2.2 ATIGA: an Enhancement of AFTA-CEPT

ATIGA served as an enhancement to the AFTA-CEPT. The two agreements can be distinguished in four key ways. First, ATIGA provided for more comprehensive coverage in trade and goods with a stronger focus on other trade-related issues such as nontariff barriers, rules of origin, trade facilitation, customs, standards and sanitary and phytosanitary measures. Second, the agreement required all ten countries to have full tariff reduction schedules completed by 2015. Third, ATIGA put more effort into improving transparency. For example, Member States were obliged to inform all parties on the implementation of any new nontariff measures or the modification of existing measures. Last but not least, ATIGA provided new plans for trade facilitation in the region. The most significant initiatives included measures to remove nontariff barriers and the introduction of a self-certification system that allowed traders to declare that goods met the rules of origin of ATIGA without the need for a customs declaration form.

[6] A Blueprint for Growth ASEAN Economic Community 2015: Progress and Key Achievements (2015).

[7] *Id.*

[8] Chia Siowyue, *The ASEAN Economic Community: Progress, Challenges, and Prospects*, Asian Development Bank Institute, No. 440, Oct. 2013, http://www20.iadb.org/intal/catalogo/PE/2013/13156.pdf (last visited Aug. 26, 2017).

2.2.3 AEC Blueprint 2025 and the Regional Comprehensive Economic Partnership

As ASEAN approached the deadline for the AEC, members realized that they were struggling to meet the ambitious commitments. The target date was pushed back from January 1, 2015, to December 31, 2015. Even with this adjustment, much of the work remained unfinished. However, tariff elimination was largely completed, with 96 percent of tariff lines set at zero.[9]

ASEAN members then set up a new goal – the achievement of the ASEAN Blueprint 2025.[10] The first item on the agenda was the completion of all unfinished items from the original AEC. It fell to Lao PDR's chairmanship in 2016 to make this happen, as well as to decide which goals in the grand Blueprint should be prioritized. By the end of 2016, progress on unfinished items in the AEC had slowed to a crawl.

Instead, ASEAN Member States had largely shifted their focus to a more challenging economic target – the conclusion of negotiations in RCEP. ASEAN had already concluded six separate agreements with "Dialogue Partners" in the region – with China (2005), South Korea (2007), Japan (2008), India (2010), Australia and New Zealand (2010) and Hong Kong (2017). While each of these FTAs gave benefits to ASEAN member firms, they also complicated life for businesses, which had to take into account different rules in each of the five agreements. Officials realized that consolidating all five agreements into one could unleash new economic development for the region.

Hence, at the Leader's Meeting in late 2012, ASEAN began the process of negotiating a sixteen-party trade agreement in RCEP. Talks moved slowly at first, but began to pick up momentum soon after. By the end of 2017, officials had held twenty rounds of meetings. Ministers and Leaders announced substantial progress toward the conclusion of talks in time for ASEAN's fiftieth anniversary in Manila in November 2017.

The primary difficulties in reaching agreement in RCEP were two-fold. First, while each of the parties involved in the talks had existing agreements with ASEAN, not all of the members had existing agreements with one another. In particular, the Dialogue Partners did not have FTAs in common. Most notably, China had no agreement with India, nor with

9 Ministry of International Trade and Industry of Malaysia (MITI), *Table 1: Number of Tariff Lines at 0% in the ATIGA Tariff Schedule of 2016*, http://fta.miti.gov.my/miti-fta/resources/tb1.pdf (last visited Aug. 27, 2017).

10 ASEAN Economic Community Blueprint 2025 (2015).

Japan. Second, just because members had a previous commitment in place did not automatically mean that they were willing to replicate that pledge in a different setting with a larger group of countries. What a country might be able and willing to agree to in one environment is not automatically acceptable in a different situation. Therefore, even some of the ASEAN members were reluctant to open markets to all six Dialogue Partners at once.

While RCEP negotiations are underway, the ASEAN integration process has largely stalled, at least for trade matters. Most of the RCEP negotiators have been the same trade officials in charge of ASEAN trade. Once RCEP concludes, progress on the ASEAN Blueprint agenda is likely to resume. In fact, it is likely that ASEAN integration efforts will be enhanced from the experience of the RCEP negotiations. In the larger setting, ASEAN officials have had to caucus before every single round and have been forced to confront issues and resolve conflicts that have largely been papered over in the ASEAN setting – sometimes for years. The Dialogue Partners have frequently pressed ASEAN officials to come to a position on various issues, particularly over market access in goods, that the organization has never had to fully address. Many of the most sensitive goods sectors have had to be discussed and often even opened for liberalization in the RCEP context. Thus, when ASEAN returns to focus on the Blueprint, it should be prepared to go beyond what ASEAN members have achieved in the AEC.

2.3 ASEAN Free Trade Goals and the Reality

Throughout several decades of constant efforts to achieve improved economic development and integration, ASEAN has always prioritized liberalizing cross-border trade, broadening market access and facilitating SME involvement in global trade. As a result, the role of ASEAN has become more important in global trade over time. However, a closer look at the figures suggests that many of the more ambitious targets have not been met. The following section will examine why.

2.3.1 ASEAN's Involvement in Global Trade: Current State and Progress

One of the main reasons that ASEAN members have been diligently pursing freer trade for goods across the decades is to boost participation in global value chains (GVCs). Early on, strategic leaders in the region recognized the importance of embedding ASEAN companies into these wider manufacturing platforms as a key mechanism for achieving future economic growth. As individual economies, most ASEAN countries were too small to be attractive locations for multinational investment. Collectively, however, the region could offer a diverse and useful hub location for firms looking for new manufacturing sites. This would only work if ASEAN could open up trade in goods across the region in a way that matched the new needs of GVC companies.

GVCs have dramatically transformed the global economy over the past two decades. GVCs refer to the fragmentation of production processes, which allows exactly the right "slice" of production to be placed in exactly the right location. GVCs have been fostered through the liberalization and deregulation of trade, coupled with significant changes in technology and dramatic drops in the costs of transportation.[11] GVCs let developing countries, especially, enhance their involvement in global trade and diversify their exports. Without GVCs, developing countries are stuck requiring all the resources and expertise to manufacture all of the components of a product in order to enter a new line of business.[12] Prior to the emergence of GVCs, developing nations primarily exported raw materials while developed nations exported more complex products, and captured more of the value from the exchange. The expansion of GVCs now allows developing nations to integrate into different parts of the value chain.[13]

ASEAN countries are involved in GVCs through both backward participation, whereby they purchase foreign intermediate goods to manufacture exports, and forward participation, in which they sell inputs to foreign countries for their exports.[14] ASEAN nations, which are at different stages of development, have varying engagements in GVCs. Indonesia and Brunei have capitalized on their abundance of natural resources and still sell significant volumes of raw materials to other

[11] International Bank for Reconstruction and Development/The World Bank, *Measuring and Analyzing the GVCs on Economic Development*, www.wto.org/english/res_e/booksp_e/gvcs_report_2017.pdf (last visited Aug. 27, 2017).

[12] *Id.*

[13] *Id.*

[14] Javier Lopez-Gonzalez & Przemyslaw Kowalski, *Global Value Chain Participation in Southeast Asia – Trade and Related Policy Implications*, Oct. 2015, www.researchgate.net/profile/Javier_Lopez-Gonzalez/publication/291975538_Global_Value_Chain_Participation_in_Southeast_Asia_-_Trade_and_Related_Policy_Implications/links/56a88a5f08ae997e22bd6115/Global-Value-Chain-Participation-in-Southeast-Asia-Trade-and-Related-Policy-Implications.pdf?origin=publication_detail (last visited Aug. 27, 2017).

countries while Malaysia, Thailand, Philippines and Vietnam also manufacture a range of final goods. With 50 percent of the value added in exports originating from abroad, Singapore has the highest rates of backward participation among ASEAN nations.[15]

While ASEAN has consistently tried to achieve higher levels of integration in global and regional chains, trade figures show limited success. Despite years of movement toward better inter-ASEAN connectivity in goods in repeated commitments, intra-ASEAN's imports and exports have been moving slowly over the past sixteen years. Especially, intra-ASEAN trade has been sluggish over two decades in spite of the implementation of AFTA-CEPT, followed by ATIGA. Intra-ASEAN exports' contribution to GDP increased from 22.8 percent in 2000 to 24 percent in 2016. The increase in intra-ASEAN imports is even more insignificant, with a slight increase from 21.1 percent in 2000 to 22.1 percent in 2016.[16] This clearly shows some serious issues with ASEAN's ability to achieve its commitments and promises at the regional level. If these issues are not properly addressed, ASEAN's efforts to accelerate regional economic integration and trade liberalization will not bear fruit.

2.3.2 ASEAN SME Involvement in Global Trade

To achieve better involvement in GVCs, ASEAN has also had to engage its substantial SME sector. SMEs form the majority of enterprises in Southeast Asia and currently employ a large proportion of the domestic labor force. SMEs constitute more than 97 percent of enterprises and employ from 57 percent to 92 percent of the labor in ASEAN-7 countries.[17] Current trends in the global and regional economy increasingly highlight the opportunities that SMEs have for growth. These include several factors such as the increasing demand for customization, the rise of niche markets and the shortening of product life cycles.[18]

[15] *Id.*

[16] Data from ASEAN Statistics, *ASEAN Trade in Goods*, https://data.aseanstats.org/trade.php (last visited Aug. 27, 2017). Calculations were made by authors.

[17] ASEAN-7 refers to Brunei, Indonesia, Malaysia, Philippines, Singapore, Thailand and Vietnam. Asia-Pacific Economic Cooperation, *SMEs in the APEC Region*, Dec. 2013, APEC Policy Support Unit, Policy Brief No. 8, www.apec.org/-/media/Files/AboutUs/Infographics/20140519_infograph_sme_hires.jpg (last visited Aug. 30, 2017).

[18] Asian Development Bank Institute, *Integrating SMEs into Global Value Chains: Challenges and Policy Actions in Asia*, www.adb.org/sites/default/files/publication/175295/smes-global-value-chains.pdf (last visited Aug. 27, 2017).

SMEs are highly suited to meeting the demands that accompany these changes with more flexible production capabilities.

In general, there are many opportunities for SMEs in ASEAN to enhance their involvement in GVCs and leverage on them from both the input and output sides. Besides more opportunities for forward participation, SMEs can also supply inputs to larger domestic firms that export goods and services. Taking advantage of GVCs on the input side can also be highly beneficial for SMEs.[19] Export competitiveness has always been associated with effective and efficient sourcing of inputs.[20]

Despite the enormous potential that SMEs have as engines of growth for the ASEAN region, they only account for approximately a third of the total value added for exports in ASEAN.[21] In many ASEAN countries, SMEs contribute to less than 50% of GDP in 2013 (Brunei 22%, Malaysia 33%, Philippines 36%, Singapore 47%, Thailand 37% and Vietnam 40%).[22] SMEs export value shares range from 15% to 25% in Indonesia, Malaysia and Singapore, and 25% to 35% in Thailand and Vietnam.[23]

ASEAN has been paying more attention to SMEs over the past few years but little meaningful progress has been made. There are several challenges SMEs often encounter that prevent them from reaching their full potential. They are often constrained by the general lack of financial resources, technology, skilled labor, information on markets, networks and geographical isolation among others.[24] Issues at customs and the complexity of logistics in ASEAN at both the domestic and regional level can also be destructive to the growth of SMEs, especially when they are still struggling to equip themselves with suitable knowledge, skills and technologies. ASEAN will need to adopt more SME-friendly approaches that focus on enhancing SME competitiveness and facilitating SME involvement in global trade.

[19] *Id.*

[20] Asia-Pacific Economic Cooperation, *SMEs in the APEC Region*, Dec. 2013, APEC Policy Support Unit, Policy Brief No. 8, www.apec.org/-/media/Files/AboutUs/Infographics/20140519_infograph_sme_hires.jpg (last visited Aug. 30, 2017).

[21] Javier Lopex-Gonzalez & Kowalski Przemyslaw, *Global Value Chain Participation in Southeast Asia – Trade and Related Policy Implications*, Oct. 2015, www.researchgate.net/profile/Javier_Lopez-Gonzalez/publication/291975538_Global_Value_Chain_Participation_in_Southeast_Asia_-_Trade_and_Related_Policy_Implications/links/56a88a5f08ae997e22bd6115/Global-Value-Chain-Participation-in-Southeast-Asia-Trade-and-Related-Policy-Implications.pdf?origin=publication_detail (last visited Aug. 27, 2017).

[22] Asia-Pacific Economic Cooperation, *supra* note 20.

[23] *Id.*

[24] Asian Development Bank Institute, *supra* note 18.

2.3.3 The Complexity of ASEAN Market Opening

The creation of a common market for goods was supposed to include more than just tariff reductions. It was also intended to tackle various types of nontariff measures that prevented or slowed the movement of goods across ASEAN member borders. This included the harmonization of standards, recognition of testing and certifications, removal of barriers to investment and rules for fair competition. These other elements of the agenda have moved forward at a crawl.[25]

Countries trade more than just goods with one another, however. Starting in 1995, ASEAN also began discussions to open their markets for services to one another, with an initial opening at the end of 1997. Over time, the number of sectors covered by the agreement expanded as members gradually allowed greater competition within ASEAN in more service areas.[26] Barriers to investment also began to fall, starting with a limited agreement in 1998.

By 2007, most ASEAN countries had experienced strong economic growth. The per capita GDP had more than doubled for most.[27] The figures stood at $36,707 for Singapore, $32,443 for Brunei, $1,685 for Philippines and $1,859 for Indonesia. The newest members of ASEAN had much lower figures (Cambodia at $632 and Myanmar at $587, for example). Population sizes had also increased since the creation of AFTA, so the increase in per capita GDP for the original ASEAN6 countries was even more impressive than it first appeared. Indonesia now had 231 million people (up 47 million), Singapore had 5.16 million people and even Brunei had increased to 402,000.[28]

Most of the tariffs in ASEAN had fallen significantly. Yet, despite the decline in formal barriers to trade, intra-ASEAN trade levels remained quite low. In 2006, the total figure for exports was $193 billion, although Singapore alone accounted for almost 44 percent of the total.[29]

[25] The AFTA was replaced by the ATIGA on May 17, 2010. ATIGA consolidated various commitments on goods into one, more comprehensive legal instrument.

[26] The eighth package under the AFAS was signed in 2010. MRAs were signed to recognize qualifications between ASEAN members in surveying, architecture, nursing, engineering, dentistry and medical practitioners and accountancy starting in 2005.

[27] The World Bank Group, *GDP per capita (current US$)*, 2013, http://data.worldbank.org/indicator/NY.GDP.PCAP.CD (last visited Apr. 09, 2013).

[28] Population Statistics, *Growth of the Population per Country in a Historical Perspective, Including Their Administrative Divisions and Principal Town*, www.populstat.info/ (last visited Apr. 09, 2013).

[29] *See* WTO World Trade Developments 2006, Table I.22, Geneva: World Trade Organization.

By comparison, the WTO calculated global trade figures for the same year of nearly $11.8 trillion.[30] This meant that barely 1.6 percent of global trade was taking place between ASEAN countries.

The regional trade grouping had not met its original intention of being a single production base, nor was it attracting the levels of inward foreign investment that members thought possible. In 2007, it reached $69 billion.[31] In 2008, the intra-ASEAN FDI figure was $10.7 billion.[32] Both figures, again, were relatively small given the overall pool of global FDI.

2.4 Why Is ASEAN Still Far from Having Free Trade in Goods?

Thus, despite ample reasons for expecting free trade in goods, ASEAN has yet to really achieve this goal after years of effort. Tariffs are basically now set to zero across the region. This is a laudable accomplishment, but inter-ASEAN trade levels have barely budged, even with duty-free treatment of goods. Firms must therefore be facing additional market access barriers.

There are several reasons for why ASEAN's journey to achieve free trade has not been as successful as might be expected. The main difficulties stem from how ASEAN works as a group, how ASEAN countries reach mutual agreements and implement them and some practical issues of trade policies in ASEAN, including tariffs that still remain in place, difficult rules of origin, nontariff measures and some other practical issues.

2.4.1 Tariff Elimination

To help goods to move more easily and freely between ASEAN members, the ten countries agreed to eliminate tariffs – the most basic barrier to trade in goods. ASEAN started with CEPT in 1992, and upgraded their efforts under ATIGA in 2010.[33] By 2016, ASEAN had eliminated 96.01 percent of tariff lines. ASEAN-6[34] had removed up to 99.2 percent

[30] *Id.*

[31] ASEAN Secretariat, www.asean.org/communities/asean-economic-community/category/overview-14, (last visited Apr. 10, 2013).

[32] *Id.*

[33] MITI, *ASEAN Free Trade Area*, http://fta.miti.gov.my/index.php/pages/view/asean-afta?mid=50 (last visited Aug. 27, 2017).

[34] Brunei, Indonesia, Malaysia, Philippines, Singapore and Thailand.

of all tariffs while CMLV[35] had reached the number of 90.18 percent.[36] In other words, by 2016 under the AEC, the ASEAN-6 countries had duty free treatment for goods on all products except 0.8 percent of tariff lines for ASEAN companies.

After twenty-five years of constant efforts to eliminate tariffs for goods that move between ASEAN countries, the goal of having a free flow of goods remains one step away for all of ASEAN. While the ASEAN-6 have eliminated tariffs for more than 98 percent of their tariff lines, CMLV have reached only 89–92.5 percent. Part of the reason why the process has taken such a long time is because countries like CMLV have argued that they have needed longer phase-out periods so that their domestic sectors can adjust and adapt.

However, another important reason stems from the way ASEAN countries work together to reach an agreement. The method used by ASEAN members to cut tariffs and quantitative restrictions to one another, however, particularly under AFTA, was different from many other regional agreements. To simplify, for most FTAs elsewhere, the parties come together and cut tariffs to one another as a group. If Country A promises to lower barriers in canned tomatoes from 26 percent to 5 percent over a ten-year time frame, it extends this offer of tariff reductions to all the parties at the same time – every member gets the same tariff on canned tomatoes into Country A.[37]

However, ASEAN members have a number of particular challenges in creating a more common market. The members are an extremely diverse bunch in terms of per capita wealth, population and geographic size. Singapore's per capita GDP is significantly larger than the GDP of the rest (even of the original six members in 1992), even if its population size has always been much smaller. In 1992, when AFTA was negotiated, Brunei

[35] Cambodia, Laos, Myanmar and Vietnam.

[36] MITI, *Table 1: Number of Tariff Lines at 0% in the ATIGA Tariff Schedule of 2016*, http://fta.miti.gov.my/miti-fta/resources/tb1.pdf (last visited Aug. 27, 2017).

[37] Of course, only members get this benefit. Nonmembers of the group still must pay the 26 percent tariff. This is why many people refer to free trade agreements as preferential trade agreements, since they guarantee preferences or benefits to members that are not granted to nonmembers. To ensure that nonmember country firms do not have access to these tariff benefits, negotiators must also create ROO to ensure that only products "from" member countries qualify for the preferential rates on offer. It is only by examining both the tariff reductions and the rules of origin criteria that it is possible to determine how open or closed a particular market actually is to other members, as a country could lower tariffs but create such difficult ROO criteria that hardly any products actually qualify for use of the lower tariff rates.

and Singapore's per capita GDP was already over $15,000, while the Philippines was $819 and Indonesia was just $730.[38] Indonesia, however, dwarfs the rest in population and geographic size. In 1992, Indonesia's population was 184 million, while Singapore had 3.2 million people and tiny Brunei had only 269,000.[39] The extent of economic competitiveness varies quite a bit between them as well.

In part because of this diversity and also because the "glue" that holds ASEAN together is considerably less "sticky" than that in organizations like the European Union, ASEAN members have been much less eager to hand over sovereignty to the collective. They have been cautious about offering the same tariff liberalization, for example, to all parties simultaneously. Therefore, ASEAN trade opening for goods proceeded in a different manner.

During the period of negotiating CEPT, members split goods into four different categories. The first category (Inclusion List) had to be liberalized starting immediately.[40] Products in the second category (Temporary Sensitive List) could be protected from liberalization for an additional two to four years before being merged into the Inclusion List.[41] Items in the third category, the Sensitive List, could be protected for a longer period and were allowed higher tariffs in the interim.[42] Finally, a small list of goods could be placed on the General Exception list and excluded entirely from the FTA for reasons such as national security, public morals or the protection of human life and health.

[38] The World Bank Group, *GDP per Capita (current US$)*, 2013, http://data.worldbank.org/indicator/NY.GDP.PCAP.CD (last visited Apr. 9, 2013).

[39] Population Statistics, *supra* note 28.

[40] Products with tariffs of less than 20 percent had to be cut down to 0–5 percent faster than those with tariffs above 20 percent. When the four new members of ASEAN joined, they were given different deadlines to reduce tariffs to between 0 and 5 percent: Vietnam had until 2006, Laos and Myanmar had until 2008 and Cambodia until 2010. The ASEAN Secretariat notes that average tariffs on products on the original Inclusion Lists for the ASEAN 6 in 1993 was 12.76 percent. *See* Joint Media Statement of the Twentieth Meeting of the ASEAN Free Trade Area (AFTA) Council (Aug. 21, 2006).

[41] Products on the Temporary Sensitive List (TSL) were moved starting on Jan. 1, 1996, in five equal instalments, concluding on Jan. 1, 2000.

[42] Sensitive products were unprocessed agricultural products. They were eventually split into two categories. Most were moved to the Inclusion List starting between Jan. 1, 2001, and Jan. 1, 2003, with final tariffs of between 0 and 5 percent by 2010. Vietnam had to start the transition on Jan. 1, 2006, and complete the transition to 0 and 5 percent by Jan. 1, 2013. For Laos and Myanmar, the start date was 2008 with implementation by 2015. Cambodia had the same start date, but until 2017 for implementation of the sensitive list tariff reductions. The exception (Highly Sensitive List) was rice from Indonesia, Malaysia and the Philippines.

What makes ASEAN negotiations different, however, was that rather than cutting down tariffs on items like canned tomatoes to all ASEAN members simultaneously, ASEAN created a complex system of negotiating that looked closer to six bilateral deals than one regional agreement. This was because canned tomatoes were only opened under the agreement if and when more than one state agreed to open up canned tomatoes. If all countries placed canned tomatoes in the Inclusion List, then canned tomatoes would be subject to tariff reductions across the board in all ASEAN members. But, if Country B placed canned tomatoes in the Sensitive List instead, then Country A was not required to offer up tariff liberalization in canned tomatoes to Country B until such time as *both* Country A and Country B had placed canned tomatoes on the Inclusion List for liberalization. As a result, although AFTA was announced in 1992, tariff reductions to one another proceeded slowly.

2.4.2 A Side Trip through Tariff Liberalization

To liberalize trade in goods, officials use tariff schedules to determine product categories. Goods are arranged into different categories using a Harmonized System (HS) code.[43] HS codes can be thought of as a sorting system, with the greatest number of products bundled together at the two-digit level and more finely detailed information on products given as more digits are included. As an example, Preparations of Vegetables, Fruits, Nuts, etc. are found at the two-digit level in Chapter 20. Tomatoes prepared or preserved otherwise than by vinegar or by acetic acid is given the code 2002, at the four-digit level. Digging down further, the code 200210 gives greater detail on the product: Tomatoes, Whole or in Pieces (Prepared or Preserved; Excluding By Vinegar or Acetic Acid).

HS codes actually range from as few as two digits (where they aggregate into ninety-nine product categories) to as many as ten digits. In countries with eight or ten digits, canned tomatoes are likely given a separate tariff line from other types of whole or pieces of tomatoes (for example, those mixed with herbs). Because individual countries set the criteria for these lines themselves, there is no international standard that applies across all products at the eight- or ten-digit level (unlike the two-, four- and six-digit categories determined by the WCO).

[43] The World Customs Organization manages the system and revises it periodically.

Agreements that liberalize trade at broader levels can actually open up the market more than those that use domestic-level tariff headings. Take the example of tomatoes again. A country that agrees to drop tariffs to zero (i.e., duty free access for tomatoes) at the two-digit level for Chapter 20 will actually be dropping the tariff to zero on *all* Preparations of Vegetables, Fruits, Nuts, etc. This is likely to include a wide range of goods such as tomatoes, but also mushrooms, jams and jellies, nuts and fruit juices. But a country that agrees to open markets at the eight-digit level may only be opening the market for tomato paste.

When determining the level of market liberalization for any given agreement, it is therefore critically important to determine how tariff liberalization was conducted. Although it seems counterintuitive, if liberalization was done along tariff lines at the domestic heading level, then an agreement that included 98 percent of all lines may be quite comprehensive. This means that a country agreed to open up nearly all the market to their partner at the level of tomato paste or frozen orange juice. But if a country opened up 98 percent of the market on broader tariff lines, this may result in *less* market opening. This is because the country may have opted to keep the whole of Chapter 20, for example, closed or carved out the agreement as highly sensitive. No additional market access would be possible in any of the items in the chapter, including tomatoes, mushrooms, jams or fruit juices.

Chapter 20 may not seem particularly critical. However, given the relatively limited trade between some parties in FTAs, the bulk of trade between partners can often be localized to a very few tariff lines alone. If these items, like canned tomatoes, frozen orange juice or nonagricultural products like automobiles with engine sizes of 1000 ccs and below are excluded from market liberalization efforts, the final assessment of the impact of the FTA may be significantly less than it first appears.

Officials will often argue that their coverage should reach a certain target of, for example, 90 percent of trade in goods.[44] This generally means that 90 percent of tariff lines ought to be included with tariff reductions (and 10 percent of tariff lines can be excluded from cuts) at the end of the

[44] Countries are not supposed to sign an FTA with very poor coverage of goods because it would violate their commitments under the GATT/WTO. Under Art. 24 of the GATT, countries must include "substantially all trade" in their free trade agreements. This benchmark has not been defined by the members, but has been generally held to require something closer to 90 percent or more of lines for developed countries and slightly less for developing countries.

implementation period. Better agreements include commitments at or near 100 percent of lines.

In short, determining the potential for market access requires a careful analysis of the terms of any trade agreement. In the case of ASEAN, the complex mechanisms used to open markets to one another meant that the promises made in AFTA for trade in goods took until the full implementation of the agreement to bear fruit. It was not until the complete agreement was phased in and all tariff lines (except for the relatively modest number of items placed in the General Exception List)[45] were opened to one another that firms were finally able to take full advantage of market access across the partner countries.

2.4.3 *Rules of Origin*

Even once tariffs fell, firms continued to face new challenges in trading in ASEAN through sometimes complicated ROO. ROO are used to determine whether a good is considered as coming from a particular region or country. They are especially important in agreements like ASEAN, which offers companies the potential to pay no duties or tariffs at all on products, because Member States want to avoid giving this preference or benefit to non-ASEAN companies. These rules examine the origin of the materials used to produce a good or the transformation of the raw materials and components into a final or finished good.

Items that qualify as originating in ASEAN can take advantage of lower duties – now generally zero tariffs. Those that do not qualify have to pay higher tariffs at the border. Originating goods can be produced entirely with content from ASEAN, made from content that combines ASEAN with non-ASEAN content, or made from nonoriginating materials. The first category is not problematic – given that anything that has all-ASEAN content qualifies for ASEAN tariffs across the region. The latter two categories are more challenging. To determine whether a good made from at least partial nonoriginating materials can be considered as an originating good, different methods of rules of origin can be used.

[45] Mostly alcohol, tobacco and firearms products that are prohibited for moral or security reasons.

There are four main methods for determining rules of origin: Wholly Obtained,[46] CTC,[47] RVC[48] and Process Rules.[49] ASEAN uses all four for different types of goods. In addition, in ASEAN's various agreements with other trading partners, like ASEAN-China, ASEAN-South Korea, ASEAN-Japan, ASEAN-India and ASEAN-Australia-New Zealand, the qualifying ROOs can be different even for the exact same tariff lines and products. These differences can make life very complicated for companies.

The ATIGA provided for Wholly Obtained, RVC and CTC goods must have at least 40 percent of regional value content (or ASEAN value content). Second, all materials that are used to produce not wholly-obtained goods must go through a change in tariff heading (at the four-digit HS level).

The 40 percent of RVC requirement can be a challenge for some products or industries. Considering the fact that ASEAN is now the "manufacturing hub" of the world and that many countries are still struggling to move up the value chains from the lower end, a 40 percent RVC requirement can act as a barrier for many manufactured goods to move around freely and easily in ASEAN. For example, 40 percent can be too high for textile products when most of the high value cloth is often supplied from outside ASEAN such as China, Korea, Japan or the United States. This number can also be troublesome for the

[46] Under Wholly Obtained ROO, anything grown, harvested or dug up from the ground of a member state is considered originating. Nearly all fresh and frozen agricultural goods and most raw materials fit under these ROO.

[47] Under CTC or CTH, goods produced from nonoriginating materials have to go through a substantial transformation to be considered as originating goods. The tariff code of the final good has to be different from that of the materials used in the production. Whether the required changes are under tariff chapters, tariff headings or tariff subheading depends on rules specified in the tariff line of the trade agreement and on the goods.

[48] Under RVC, a certain percentage of the materials used to produce a good need to be originating from a certain region or country. The rest can be nonoriginating materials. The required percentages are different for different goods and different trade agreements.

[49] Under Process Rules, chemical goods qualify by being manufactured in a certain geographic space. This method recognizes originating chemical goods by looking at which chemical process occurs in which country or region to produce such a good. Some special goods might have their own rules of origin in some trade agreements such as textile and autos; Singapore Customs, *Handbook on Rules of Origin for Preferential Certificates of Origin*, May 2017, www.customs.gov.sg/~/media/cus/files/business/exporting%20goods/cert%20of%20origin/handbook%20on%20rules%20of%20origin%20for%20preferential%20certificates%20of%20origin%20ttsb%20apr%202016.pdf?la=en (last visited Aug. 27, 2017).

auto industry in ASEAN as a high percentage of auto parts are imported into ASEAN for the manufacturing process.

A calculation of RVC that is based on the customs value of traded goods can also be problematic for ASEAN companies. Several factors can add up to the risk borne by traders including exchange rate fluctuations, traceability and pricing of the materials and the need for disclosure of confidential business information such as suppliers' details. Each of these issues can make it problematic for firms to use RVC rules. Companies sometimes choose not to use the preferential tariff rates on offer simply because the ROO requirements are not worth the hassle of qualifying for the benefit of a lower duty.

In addition, rules of origin between ASEAN and other trading partners can be complicated. Under trade agreements between ASEAN and six major trading partners, both methods of RVC and CTC are used interchangeably. However, the use of RVC and CTC can be inconsistent across six trade deals. While the ASEAN-China FTA only allows RVC, ASEAN-India FTA requires *both* RVC and CTC criteria to be met (Table 2.1). The other three trade deals between ASEAN and Japan, Korea, Australia and New Zealand have the same rules of origin as ATIGA (Table 2.1). Only the AANZFTA had a plan to discuss the inclusion of a Process Rule after the trade deal came into force (Table 2.1).[50]

2.4.4 *Nontariff Measures in ASEAN*

As important as tariff barriers are to trade, another problem for firms are a set of issues lumped together under the heading of NTMs. NTMs are policy measures that are relevant to policy objectives of governments, such as food safety or environmental protection.[51] In some cases, these trade measures slip over and become barriers to trade when they become a tool for governments to intervene or control trade flows into or out of their countries. Even when some NTMs are created based on the legitimate concerns of policy makers, the impacts they have on trade can be disruptive and restrictive.[52]

Some governments make use of NTMs to protect domestic businesses from an influx of imports, especially when they have committed to eliminate or reduce the tariffs for these products. For example, the number of NTMs in ASEAN increased from 1,634 to 5,975 measures from 2000 to 2015, while

[50] Art. 18.4 in the full text of ASEAN Australia and New Zealand FTA.

[51] Lili Yang Ing, Santiago Fernandez de Cordoba & Olivier Cadot, *Non-Tariff Measures in ASEAN* (2016).

[52] *Id.*

Table 2.1 *The use of RVC, CTC and process rule in ASEAN FTAs*

	RVC	CTC	Process Rule
ATIGA	40%	Tariff Heading, four-digit level	Not mentioned
ASEAN-China FTA	40% and Product Specific Rules (PSR)	Not mentioned	Not mentioned
ASEAN-China FTA Upgrade	40% and PSR	Tariff Heading, four-digit level	Not mentioned
ASEAN-India FTA	35%	Tariff Subheading, six-digit level*	Not mentioned
ASEAN-Japan FTA	40%	Tariff Heading, four-digit level	Not mentioned
ASEAN-Korea FTA	40%	Tariff Heading, four-digit level	Not mentioned
ASEAN-Australia-New Zealand	40%	Tariff Heading, four-digit level	Being worked on by ROO Subcommittee
ASEAN-HKC FTA	40% and Product Specific Rules (PSR)	Tariff Chapter, two-digit level; Tariff Heading, four-digit level; Tariff Subheading, six-digit level	Not mentioned

* Only in the ASEAN-India FTA, both RVC and CTC are required. For others, only one criterion is required.
Source: Ministry of International Trade and Industry Malaysia (MITI).[53] Compiled by authors.

[53] MITI, Free Trade Agreements – Regional, https://fta.miti.gov.my/ (last visited Sep. 25, 2017).

during the same fifteen-year period the average tariff rates in the region dropped from 8.9 percent to 4.5 percent.[54]

Other governments stick to their own standards on various areas such as health and safety, hygiene and environment which may be stricter than international standards. This can cause obstacles for imported products to get into domestic markets. Some commonly used nontariff measures are technical barriers to trade, sanitary and phytosanitary measures, quantity control measures or export-related measures.

Even though ASEAN countries have reduced and eliminated tariffs substantially on intra-ASEAN goods over the past 15 years, intra-ASEAN trade increased only slightly (2.3 percent) from 23 percent in 2000 to 25.3 percent in 2014.[55] This modest increase could be linked to the sharp rise of NTMs in ASEAN within 15 years, an increase of 3.6 times.[56] Any trade plans that fail to understand and focus on NTMs might not yield the expected results.

Among ASEAN government agencies who often issue NTMs, Ministries of Health and Ministries of Agriculture (including forestry, plantation, fisheries) are the two agencies that have produced the highest number of NTMs. Each ministry accounts for more than 31 percent of the total number of NTMs in ASEAN.[57] This stems from the fact that most NTMs are based on health, food safety and hygiene concerns. The complexity and characteristics of NTMs differ across ten ASEAN countries because of differences in regulatory structures, economic concerns and trade focus.

One of the reasons why companies struggle to cope with NTMs in ASEAN is the lack of transparent, accurate and up-to-date information. When entering a new market, companies need to know and understand the existing domestic regulations that could affect their business strategy and their movement of goods. However, the lack of availability of crucial regulations and legal documents, particularly online and in one location, has remained one of the main obstacles to cross-border trade in ASEAN.

[54] *Id.*

[55] *Id.*

[56] *Id.*

[57] Lili Yang Ing, Cadot Olivier, Rizqy Anandhika & Urata Shujiro, *Non-Tariff Measures in ASEAN: A Simple Proposal*, in Non-Tariff Measures in ASEAN (2016).

2.5 Other Practical Issues That Affect Free Trade Movement in ASEAN

Trade in goods is not just about tariffs, rules of origin and standards. There are also a host of other practical issues that matter tremendously to firms trying to get goods across borders. Many of these issues have either not been taken up at all yet at the ASEAN level or have been insufficiently addressed to date. Three specific challenges are noted here – problems with logistics and customs procedures, the use of the ASEAN Harmonized Tariff Nomenclature and ASEAN Self-Certification schemes. Each issue highlights the types of real-world challenges that need to be tackled to allow ASEAN to deliver benefits that matter to firms moving goods in the region.

2.5.1 Logistics and Customs

Most ASEAN countries do not score well on international indexes that measure the efficiency and effectiveness of logistics and customs performance. The logistics performance indexes (LPI)[58] of most ASEAN countries in 2016 are relatively low in the ranking (Brunei 70, Cambodia 73, Indonesia 63, Laos 152, Malaysia 32, Myanmar 113, Philippines 71, Thailand 45 and Vietnam 64, out of 160 global countries).[59] This implies inefficient logistics systems across most of the region.

Even at the domestic level, the customs procedures in most ASEAN Member States are relatively burdensome for local companies. The WEF rating of customs procedure burden (from 1 = extremely inefficient to 7 = extremely efficient) shows that businesses in most ASEAN countries perceive their countries' customs procedures to be inefficient. The 2016 ratings are Cambodia – 3.1, Indonesia – 3.9, Malaysia – 5.2, Myanmar – 3.0, Philippines – 3.5, Thailand – 3.7 and Vietnam – 3.6, while the world average is 4.067.[60]

ASEAN has implemented several regional initiatives to improve logistics and customs performance to facilitate the cross-border movement of

[58] This index is based on the efficiency of customs clearance processes, quality of trade- and transport-related infrastructure, ease of arranging competitively priced shipments, quality of logistics services, ability to track and trace consignments and frequency with which shipments reach the consignee within the scheduled time.

[59] World Bank, Logistics Performance Index 2016 (LPI), https://lpi.worldbank.org/international/global (last visited Sep. 25, 2017).

[60] World Bank, Burden of Customs Procedure WEF 2016, https://data.worldbank.org/indicator/IQ.WEF.CUST.XQ (last visited Sep. 25, 2017).

goods intra-ASEAN. However, these initiatives have encountered some practical issues with implementation and slow progress.

2.5.2 ASEAN Harmonized Tariff Nomenclature or Tariff Code

To facilitate cross-border trade regionally and internationally, the WCO has developed the Harmonized System of Tariffs, a worldwide recognized product classification system. As described earlier, in the WCO system, universal codes have six digits that are the same for countries all over the world. However, the tariff codes at the domestic level often have eight to ten digits. Longer codes describe more specific products in the schedule. This means that even though the first six digits of the codes are the same for every country, the last two to four digits are different across countries. This difference and inconsistency has led to some challenges for companies selling the same product to many countries. Sometimes a company must use different tariff codes for the same products when exporting to different countries.

ASEAN has taken the initiative to address this issue by establishing an AHTN to have same tariff codes at eight-digit level across ASEAN countries. This AHTN aims to set up a common standard among ASEAN and to reduce the complexity of trading across borders for firms.

However, only after having to look up some products in the tariff schedules of ten ASEAN countries will one understand why this meaningful idea might not be delivering actual results on the ground. There are two main reasons for this. First, even though the first eight digits of the tariff codes are now meant to be consistent across ten countries, the difference in the last one or two digits (for countries who use nine-digit or ten-digit tariff codes) is still remarkable and troublesome for companies. Second, the AHTN has created product classifications (at eight-digit level) that are too broad and sometimes not comprehensive. This makes it extremely difficult for companies to figure out which tariff codes to use. In addition, this will also increase the chances that companies might not always argue successfully for the tariff codes they prefer at customs.

For example, to find the tariff code of a drinking straw in Thailand's tariff schedule (which uses eight-digit codes), one might end up finding no obvious matching tariff line at all.[61] A drinking straw could fall under

[61] Annex 2: Tariffs under the ASEAN Trade In Goods Agreement (ATIGA) in AHTN 2012 – Thailand, www.asean.org/wp-content/uploads/images/2012/Economic/AFTA

Table 2.2 *Kitchenware tariff code in Thailand tariff schedule*

AHTN 2012	Description
39.24	Tableware, kitchenware, other household articles and hygienic or toilet articles, of plastics.
3924.10.00	- Tableware and kitchenware
39924.90	- Other:
3924.90.10	- Bed pans, urinals (portable type) or chamber-pots
3924.90.90	- Other

Source: Annex 2: ATIGA in AHTN 2012 – Thailand[62]

kitchenware category (3924.10.00) or other household articles (3924.90.90) (Table 2.2). Many of the most innovative products get thrown into the "other" category every time. To get a trustworthy answer, a firm would have to ask either Thai customs officers directly or ask trade compliance companies, who might charge a substantial amount for providing this service.

2.5.3 ASEAN Self-Certification Scheme

The amount of paperwork traders must complete for their imports and exports could also be one of the main reasons they find the customs procedures burdensome. There are many certificate types that traders need to understand and know how to use. Each certificate only serves one particular purpose and goes with a customized form. For example, ASEAN-China FTA only uses Form E, ASEAN-Korea FTA recognizes Form AK, while AANZFTA only accepts Form AANZ.[63] This complicated paperwork requirement is both costly and time-consuming for companies

/annex/Annex%202%20(Tariff%20Schedules)%20-%20Thailand%20(AHTN%202012).pdf (last visited Aug. 27, 2017).

62 *Id.*

63 Singapore Customs, Application Procedures of Certificate of Origin and Export Permit Through TradeNet, Apr. 2015, www.customs.gov.sg/~/media/cus/files/business/exporting%20goods/cert%20of%20origin/handbook%20on%20the%20application%20procedures%20of%20certificate%20of%20origin%20and%20export%20permit%20via%20tradenet%20ttsb.pdf?la=en (last visited Aug. 31, 2017)

To address this issue, ASEAN has initiated a self-certification scheme, which aims to simplify the process of product certification by allowing certified exporters to declare and self-certify their exported products.[64] Under the self-certification system, exporters can avoid the burden of paperwork and administrative procedures of applying for certificates of origin. Instead of completing Form D and then submitting paperwork to customs officials to get the certificate of origin for products as required by the conventional system, certified exporters can now simply "self-declare" the country of origin on the commercial invoice of the products to make them eligible for favorable tariffs under ATIGA.[65] However, this scheme only applies to Form D, which means only for the use of ATIGA.

According to Singapore Customs, the potential savings of a fully implemented self-certification scheme could reach up to SG$1.08 million per year for around 850 exporters.[66] These cost and time savings could be extremely beneficial for exporters. As of 2017, Malaysia has appointed 184 certified exporters who are qualified for the self-certification system.[67] Even though this is an important step to advance trade facilitation in ASEAN, progress has been slow and adoption rates are still low. Firms have been reluctant to use self-certification schemes, in part because of a lack of knowledge about the system. But they are also often deterred because they worry about the potential for fines if anything goes wrong.

2.6 Conclusion

Over the past few decades, ASEAN has constantly made efforts to produce meaningful results for their trade agenda for goods. However, intra-ASEAN trade has remained stubbornly stuck at roughly 25 percent, largely due to several issues that still exist both at the domestic and regional level. Most of the problems are practical challenges that ASEAN officials have not yet tackled and that impede businesses from taking advantage of the opportunities presented by a ten-member

[64] MITI, Trade Facilitation in ASEAN, http://fta.miti.gov.my/index.php/pages/view/asean-afta?mid=50 (last visited Aug. 27, 2017)

[65] Singapore Customs, *ASEAN Pilots Self-Certification of Origin*, Singapore Customs Newsletter, Mar. 2011, www.customs.gov.sg/~/media/cus/files/insync/issue11/article_5.html (last visited Aug. 27, 2017).

[66] *Id.*

[67] MITI, *supra* note 64.

marketplace. While ASEAN leaders like to speak of ASEAN's rise as the sixth-largest global economy, a little more work resolving some of the key obstacles that prevent firms from joining regional value chains and unlocking the potential of greater trade would then make it possible to actually achieve the more ambitious goals announced over the past few decades in Southeast Asia.

3

Building toward the RCEP? Reflections on the ASEAN-China FTA

HENG WANG

3.1 Introduction

ASEAN is playing an increasingly important role in world economic governance, as evidenced by the RCEP negotiations between ASEAN and its FTA partners. The evolution of ASEAN law from the global perspective will cover a wide range of areas, including goods, services, intellectual property, investment and even social issues. The growing AEC will also exert current and prospective influence on the international economic legal order, including the increased attractiveness of the RCEP to other parties. Meanwhile, ASEAN may encounter legal challenges in its external interactions with Asia-Pacific economies, including China. Such interaction occurs at bilateral (i.e., China's FTAs with Singapore and ASEAN) and regional level (i.e., the RCEP). More broadly, it involves the complex interactions between the law of the WTO and FTAs. It is of immense significance to analyze the evolution of ASEAN law from a global perspective.

As highlighted in the AEC Blueprint 2025, ASEAN will continue to integrate the region into the global economy through trade pacts with partners, including the ACFTA. These trade pacts lay the foundation for ASEAN to "retain its centrality in global and regional engagements, where possible."[1] Among ASEAN's external FTAs, the ACFTA and the AHKFTA are of great significance. The ACFTA is one of the most important South-South FTAs for both parties, while AHKFTA is the first FTA to be signed by ASEAN over a period of around eight years.[2] The ACFTA is one of the earliest trade pacts concluded by China. It is also part of ASEAN's broader push toward concluding FTAs outside the

[1] Association of Southeast Asian Economic Community Blueprint 2025 (2015), para. 79.

[2] *ASEAN, HK to Sign Free Trade Agreement*, Xinhua, Sept. 10, 2017, www.chinadaily.com.cn/china/2017-09/10/content_31798251.htm (last visited Mar. 16, 2018).

multilateral WTO framework, in line with the proliferation of FTAs.[3] The AEC Blueprint 2025 emphasizes the importance of the ACFTA as well as the negotiations of the AHKFTAand the RCEP.[4] Notably, the ACFTA could affect the RCEP as ASEAN and China are among its parties. The AHKFTA and the AHKIA were signed in 2017[5] and represent the latest development of ASEAN in trade and investment.

This chapter will analyze the following questions: what is the approach of ACFTA? What are the implications of the ACFTA for the RCEP? What are the national implementation issues in ASEAN? The potential implications of the AHKFTA will be explored. Section 3.2 explores the approach of the ACFTA in comparison with other trade pacts of China, while other agreements of ASEAN will be discussed when needed. Section 3.3 analyzes the relevance of the ACFTA to the RCEP and its limits, followed by Section 3.4, which deals with the challenges in implementing the ACFTA. Section 3.5 concludes by summarizing the features of the ACFTA and looking into its future.

3.2 The Approach of the ACFTA

On the one hand, the ACFTA is comparable to China's other FTAs reflecting the country's pragmatic approach. These agreements are malleable, cooperation-oriented and WTO-based trade pacts. The malleability of FTA rules is partially attributable to the fact that trading partners' proposals are often adopted in China's FTAs. A writer observes that China prefers to work off the draft FTA provisions of its partners, such as Peru or Pakistan.[6] For instance, China has accepted comprehensive investment rules, which respond to partners' demands to a certain extent.[7] In the same vein, China largely adopted the ASEAN model as in the case of the Investment Agreement. The Framework Agreement on the ASEAN Investment Area served as a template for the negotiations of

[3] Nargiza Salidjanova et al., China's Economic Ties with ASEAN: A Country-by-Country Analysis, *in* U.S.-China Economic and Security Review Commission Staff Research Report 4 (2015).

[4] AEC Blueprint 2025, para. 79.

[5] *ASEAN, HK to Sign Free Trade Agreement, supra* note 2.

[6] Nargiza Salidjanova, *China's Trade Ambitions: Strategy and Objectives behind China's Pursuit of Free Trade Agreements, in* U.S.-China Economic and Security Review Commission Staff Research Report 22 (2015).

[7] Axel Berger, *Investment Rules in Chinese Preferential Trade and Investment Agreements: Is China Following the Global Trend towards Comprehensive Agreements?* (2013), www.die-gdi.de/uploads/media/DP_7.2013.pdf (last visited Mar. 16, 2018).

the Investment Agreement.[8] In the end, the Investment Agreement largely mirrors the ASEAN Comprehensive Investment Agreement, except for market access provisions.[9] Eventually, China followed the ASEAN format in several ACFTA agreements, including the TIG and DSM agreements, which adopts a similar template to the ASEAN Protocol on Enhanced Dispute Settlement Mechanism.[10]

In particular, the focus of ACFTA on cooperation is reflected in MOUs. Under the trade agreement, MOUs were signed to promote cooperation in areas such as standards, technical regulations and conformity assessment, as well as intellectual property. Reflecting functional cooperation proposed by China, MOUs were also concluded to facilitate cooperation in areas such as information and communications technology, as well as agriculture and transportation.[11] These economic activities are placed under the purview of the ACFTA Working Group on Economic and Technical Cooperation between ASEAN and China, and funding may be secured from the ASEAN-China Cooperation.[12] In the upgrading of the ACFTA, the parties will further explore economic cooperation in various areas, ranging from trade-related issues to SMEs and environment.[13] A similar arrangement can be found in some of China's FTAs.

The ACFTA resembles China's other trade agreements in terms of harvesting "low-hanging fruit" (such as tariff cuts) and building on the WTO norms. There are a very limited number of WTO-extra or WTO-plus obligations in China's FTAs, including the ACFTA. Preferring incremental development, China's FTAs do not focus on regulatory requirements. China's FTAs model on WTO norms. Even in the WTO-extra areas, WTO rules could be considered. For instance, the ACFTA[14] and some of China's FTAs, such as the China-New Zealand FTA,[15] incorporate exception clauses in investment rules that are modeled on Article XIV of the GATS.[16]

[8] Huiping Chen, *China-ASEAN FTA: An Investment Perspective, in* China-ASEAN Relations: Economic and Legal Dimensions 140 (John Wong et al. eds., 2006).

[9] Berger, *supra* note 7, at 23.

[10] Hidetaka Yoshimatsu, *Domestic Political Institutions, Diplomatic Style and Trade Agreements: A Comparative Study of China and Japan*, 15 New Political Economy 410, 410–11 (2010).

[11] *Id.*, at 411–12.

[12] ASEAN-China Free Trade Agreement (2002).

[13] China-ASEAN FTA Upgrading Protocol (2015), art. 7(II)(1).

[14] China-ASEAN Investment Agreement (2009), art. 16.

[15] China-New Zealand Free Trade Agreement (2008), art. 200(1).

[16] Bryan Mercurio, *Awakening the Sleeping Giant: Intellectual Property Rights in International Investment Agreements*, 15 J. Int'l Eco. L. 871, 905–6 (2012).

To sum up, the ACFTA and other trade pacts of China are not high-level ones. For instance, the ASEAN-China MOU on intellectual property[17] does not advance or alter the parties' positions in the international intellectual property regime except for its Article 3, which calls for greater protection of "genetic resources, traditional knowledge and folklore."[18] Like China's agreements with other countries, ACFTA does not provide national treatment regarding the pre-establishment of investment[19] that covers "admission," "establishment" and "acquisition" of investment. These agreements focus on investment protection rather than investment liberalization.

On the other hand, China adopts a more flexible approach toward ASEAN compared with its other FTA partners. The ACFTA adopts a more flexible approach than other FTAs of China. This flexibility is found in, among others, (1) the approach of ACFTA, (2) the special arrangement or rules for specific ASEAN countries and (3) other special treatment of the ACFTA. In general, the ACFTA adopts a step-by-step approach (first framework agreement and then specific agreements) rather than a single package in most of China's trade pacts. A number of ACFTA agreements were signed at different stages: the Framework Agreement,[20] the TIG,[21] the DSM agreement[22] and the TIS,[23] and the ASEAN-China Investment Agreement (Investment Agreement).[24]

The flexibility is also reflected in its progressive FTA approach. As an illustration, there are three protocols to amend the Framework Agreement[25] and two protocols to amend the TIG.[26] In services, the

17 Memorandum of Understanding between ASEAN and China on Cooperation in the Field of Intellectual Property (2009).

18 Peter K. Yu, The Incremental Development of the ASEAN–China Strategic Intellectual Property Partnership, http://ssrn.com/abstract=2657358, 6 (2015).

19 China-ASEAN Investment Agreement (2009), art. 4, 5.

20 China-ASEAN Framework Agreement (2002).

21 China-ASEAN Agreement on Trade in Goods (2004).

22 China-ASEAN Agreement on Dispute Settlement Mechanism (2004).

23 China-ASEAN Agreement on Trade in Services (2007).

24 China-ASEAN Investment Agreement (2009).

25 Protocol to Amend the Framework Agreement on Comprehensive Economic Co-Operation Between the Association of South East Asian Nations and the People's Republic of China (2003); Second Protocol to Amend the Framework Agreement on Comprehensive Economic Co-operation between the Association of Southeast Asian Nations and the People's Republic of China (2006); Third Protocol to Amend the Framework Agreement on Comprehensive Economic Co-Operation Between the Association of Southeast ASIAN Nations and the People's Republic of China (2012).

26 Protocol to Amend the Agreement on Trade in Goods of the Framework Agreement on Comprehensive Economic Co-operation between the Association of Southeast Asian Nations and the People's Republic of China (2006); Second Protocol to Amend the

parties agreed on the second package of commitments under the TIS in 2011. The flexibility is more evident in ACFTA than other FTAs of China regarding the frequency of FTA amendments and commitments.

China shows flexibility toward specific ASEAN countries in critical areas such as agriculture (e.g., EHP) and investment. Concerning agricultural trade liberalization, this flexibility is reflected in a number of aspects. The ACFTA provides for an EHP to cut tariffs on selected products, which is an integral part of the trade agreement.[27] It allows an eight-year early harvest period.[28] As an EHP, China signed a special agriculture deal with Thailand to open both countries' agricultural markets before the ACFTA came into force.[29] Being an essential element of the EHP, China has provided unilateral concessions to the ASEAN countries that feel they could not benefit much from the EHP.[30] The ACFTA emphasizes early harvest schemes that are not common in China's other trade agreements. As a distinct policy adopted by China, the offer of the EHP (eliminating tariffs on agricultural products before the normal track) was a critical decision for China, since agricultural liberalization was one of the most vital policy issues after its entry into the WTO.[31] The EHP under the ACFTA provided ASEAN countries with more generous terms than China would be required to under an arm's-length negotiation.[32] In contrast, it is observed that Chinese negotiators were less amenable to agricultural liberalization in talks with New Zealand than in the ASEAN negotiations, and the implementation of the ASEAN early harvest agreement has substantially increased exports of ASEAN countries' fruits and vegetables to China.[33]

The Investment Agreement also contains special provisions for several ASEAN member countries on major issues such as the scope of application

Agreement on Trade in Goods of the Framework Agreement on Comprehensive Economic Co-Operation between the Association of Southeast Asian Nations and the People's Republic of China (2010).

27 China-ASEAN Framework Agreement (2002), art. 6.1.

28 Nargiza Salidjanova, U.S.-China Economic and Security Review Commission Staff Research Report 16 (2015).

29 *China, Thailand Reach Trade Deal*, China Daily, Jun. 2003, www.china.org.cn/english/2003/Jun/66252.htm; China-Thailand, bilaterals.org, May 2012, www.bilaterals.org/?-China-Thailand (last visited Mar. 16, 2018).

30 Jiangyu Wang, *Association of Southeast Asian Nations–China Free Trade Agreement, in* Bilateral and Regional Trade Agreements: Case Studies 196 (Simon Lester & Mercurio Bryan eds., 2009).

31 Hidetaka Yoshimatsu, New Political Economy, 409, 414 (2010).

32 Yu, *supra* note 18, at 3.

33 Salidjanova, *supra* note 28.

and the denial of benefits. Concerning the coverage, the Investment Agreement only applies to investment that has been admitted in Thailand, and that has been specifically approved in writing for protection by the relevant authorities as per domestic law and policy.[34] Coming to the provision on the denial of benefits, Thailand could deny foreign investors the benefits of investment treaty protection when the investor is controlled by a person of a nonparty or the denying party.[35] Therefore, it is easier to meet the conditions for the denial of benefits in the case of Thailand. Under this special provision, there is no need to prove that the relevant juridical person lacks substantive business operations in another ACFTA party.[36] Moreover, the Philippines may deny foreign investors the benefits of the Agreement if the investment violates the so-called Anti-Dummy Law.[37] In this way, the domestic law of the Philippines is taken into account. Other special provisions for individual ASEAN members exist in the choice of the procedure in ISDS,[38] and the rate and payment of interest of compensation in the case of expropriation.[39]

Other special treatment in the ACFTA include the unique position of the ACFTA in China's FTAs (e.g., the utilization of the "enabling clause" of the WTO, the FTA upgrading, the higher level of national treatment in investment), and the treatment of newer ASEAN countries. The ACFTA is the only FTA for which China used the "enabling clause" of the WTO to ensure the WTO consistency of a lower-standard FTA with developing countries.[40] The ACFTA, which started with early harvest schemes in 2002 and was established in 2010, is the first and largest one that China has negotiated.[41] Notably, the ACFTA is also China's first FTA that has been updated.[42] In 2015, the Protocol to Amend the Framework Agreement on Comprehensive Economic Co-Operation and Certain Agreements thereunder between ASEAN and China (Upgrading Protocol) was signed.[43] For post-establishment national treatment in

[34] China-ASEAN Investment Agreement, art. 3.3.
[35] *Id.*, art. 15.2.
[36] *Id.*, art. 15.1(a).
[37] *Id.*, art. 15.3.
[38] *Id.*, art. 15.5.
[39] *Id.*, art. 8.3, footnote 6.
[40] Salidjanova, *supra* note 28, at 20–1.
[41] Chinese Ministry of Commerce Information Office, China and the ASEAN Concluded the Free Trade Area Upgrade Negotiations and Signed Upgrading Protocol (2015), http://fta.mofcom.gov.cn/article/chinadongmeng/dongmengnews/201511/29455_1.html.
[42] *Id.*
[43] China-ASEAN FTA Upgrading Protocol (2015).

investment, China has only granted Pakistan and ASEAN full national treatment, while other partners are treated as per "customary international law."[44] Moreover, flexibility is required for newer ASEAN members under the ACFTA. The Framework Agreement recognizes the need for flexibility,[45] and requires negotiations on trade in services and investments to consider special treatment and flexibility for the newer ASEAN members.[46] As another example, the TIG contains special and differential treatment and flexibility to newer ASEAN members.[47]

Within FTAs of ASEAN and its countries, China appears to take a more flexible approach than some ASEAN partners (such as Japan under the AJCEP).[48] This is reflected in the general arrangement of the ACFTA (i.e., the approach to establishing the FTA) and specific rules (e.g., the progressive tariff reduction). In the ACFTA, China is willing to accept ASEAN's formats of "framework agreement plus protocol plus annexes" and the step-by-step approach (from goods to services and then to investment) that was adopted in the AFTA, ASEAN-Korea FTA and AIA.[49] In contrast, the AJCEP adopts a single-undertaking approach, which covers goods, services, investment and economic cooperation in one pact.

From the perspective of the agreement(s) with specific ASEAN countries, China adopts a more accommodating approach toward ASEAN members than Japan. Differing from Japan, China signed a bilateral FTA with an ASEAN country (i.e., Singapore) only after signing the ACFTA. China was willing to sit down with all ten ASEAN members at the negotiation table from the outset.[50] The China-Singapore FTA was signed in 2008,[51] which was much later than the signing of the Framework Agreement, the TIG, the DSM and the TIS. In the AJCEP negotiations Japan took a "divide and conquer" approach: it signed FTAs

[44] Salidjanova, *supra* note 28, at 18.

[45] China-ASEAN Framework Agreement (2002), Recital 7 of the preamble.

[46] China-ASEAN Framework Agreement, art. 8.3.

[47] *See* e.g., China-ASEAN Agreement on Trade in Goods (2004), Annex 1, para. 6 (tariff reduction and/or elimination for tariff lines placed in the normal track), Annex 2, paragraph 3(iii) (reduction or elimination of the applied MFN tariff rates of tariff lines put in the sensitive track).

[48] It should be noted that these agreements also share similarities. For instance, ASEAN's trade pacts with China, Japan, Australia and New Zealand are not comprehensive ones compared to deep FTAs.

[49] Yoshimatsu, *supra* note 10, at 410.

[50] Salidjanova, *supra* note 28.

[51] China-Singapore Free Trade Agreement (2008).

with seven out of ten ASEAN countries before concluding the AJCEP to counteract the collective bargaining leverage of ASEAN.[52]

Such extra flexibility is also reflected in the specific rules. A progressive reduction of tariffs is a typical example. The ACFTA provides for a progressive reduction of tariffs over a number of years, which is flexible depending on different ASEAN countries. In the tariff reduction schedule of Brunei Darussalam under the ACFTA, ACFTA rates are set from 2010 to 2018.[53] For the Philippines, the rates are set from 2012 to 2018.[54] Such progressive tariff reduction arrangements are absent in the schedules of these two ASEAN countries under the AJCEP.[55]

3.3 From the ACFTA to the RCEP?

Besides bilateral FTAs such as the ACFTA, ASEAN attaches enormous importance to the RCEP. Through the RCEP, ASEAN will influence the shaping of the regional order and the nexus between multilateralism and regionalism. As an ASEAN-centric agreement, the RCEP primarily serves two ASEAN objectives: to propel closer intra-ASEAN integration and the deepening of the AEC, and to harmonize policies between ASEAN and its FTA partners.[56] As part of the strategic measures, ASEAN strives for (1) "a more strategic and coherent approach" toward external economic relations, (2) modern, comprehensive, and high-quality trade pacts that are more responsive to the needs of businesses and (3) strong support for the multilateral trading system and active participation in regional fora.[57] The RCEP will provide for a mega-FTA model that differs from the CPTPP, and may affect other FTA negotiations. Meanwhile, the RCEP is a complex matrix in itself, involving ASEAN and a number of other parties.

52 Salidjanova, *supra* note 28; Yoshimatsu, *supra* note 10 (by the end of 2008, Japan had concluded trade agreements with all ASEAN countries except for Laos, Cambodia and Myanmar).

53 Tariff Reduction Schedule of Brunei Darussalam under the ACFTA.

54 Tariff Reduction Schedule of the Philippines under the ACFTA.

55 Annex 1 – Schedule of the Philippines under the ASEAN-Japan Comprehensive Economic Partnership Agreement; Annex 1 – Schedule of Brunei under the ASEAN-Japan Comprehensive Economic Partnership Agreement.

56 Jeffrey J. Schott & Lu Zhiyao, *Asia-Pacific Regionalism after the TPP*, *in* US-China Cooperation in a Changing Global Economy 137 (Adam S. Posen & Ha Jiming eds., 2017).

57 AEC Blueprint 2025, para. 80.

3.3.1 *The Potential of the Contribution by the ACFTA to the RCEP*

The ACFTA could contribute to the development of the RCEP. The ACFTA and the AHKFTA, along with other ASEAN FTAs, lay a solid foundation for ASEAN to "retain its centrality in global and regional engagements, where possible."[58] From the Chinese perspective, the Upgrading Protocol will contribute to the RCEP negotiations and the development of the FTAAP.[59] China and ASEAN have similar positions in certain aspects. China and ASEAN support the multilateral trading system. The ACFTA largely follows WTO norms. The ASEAN FTA model also bears close similarities to China's "developing country" FTA pattern, highlighting regulatory cooperation rather than regulatory rights.[60] The ACFTA could further promote the consensus between China and the ASEAN countries. If so, the ACFTA could be a building block for the RCEP. It is advisable for China and ASEAN to cooperate to promote the RCEP negotiations.

In specific areas, the Upgrading Protocol envisages future work in the liberalization of trade in goods,[61] product-specific rules[62] and investment liberalization and protection.[63] Trade in goods and investment are the priority. This could reflect the vision of China and ASEAN for the future direction of economic integration. Both sides are likely to work together closely in these aspects of the RCEP negotiations. For trade in goods, China and ASEAN could cooperate on issues such as trade facilitation. In the most recent Chairman's Statement of ASEAN Summits, trade facilitation is emphasized by ASEAN as one of its eight priorities.[64] The ASEAN Trade Facilitation Framework is adopted as a priority deliverable.[65] China also supports trade facilitation,[66] which helps to

58 *Id.*, para. 79.

59 Chinese Ministry of Commerce Information Office, *supra* note 41.

60 Christopher M. Dent, *Free Trade Agreements in the Asia-Pacific a Decade On: Evaluating the Past, Looking to the Future*, 10 International Relations of the Asia-Pacific 201, 231 (2010).

61 China-ASEAN FTA Upgrading Protocol (2015), Ch. 5, para. 1.

62 *Id.*, Ch. 5, para. 2.

63 *Id.*, Ch. 5, para. 3.

64 Chairman's Statement of the Twenty-Eighth and Twenty-Ninth ASEAN Summits (2016), http://asean.org/storage/2016/08/Final-Chairmans-Statement-of-the-28th-and-29th-ASEAN-Summits-rev-fin.pdf.

65 *Id.*, at 8.

66 Zhong Nan, *Commerce Ministry Urges G20 Members to Back Trade Facilitation agreement*, Jul. 1, 2016, http://english.gov.cn/state_council/ministries/2016/07/01/content_281475383920672.htm (last visited Mar. 16, 2018).

promote the export of Chinese products. Concerning investment, the positions reflected in China's recent investment treaty practice are largely consistent with ASEAN practice.[67] For instance, China and ASEAN have a similar position in limiting the scope of the FET obligations.[68] The RCEP could, in turn, promote the future upgrade of the ACFTA. It is noteworthy that the ACFTA is a living or evolving agreement.[69] If properly managed, it could contribute to the negotiations and development of the RCEP.

3.3.2 The Limit of the Contribution by the ACFTA to the RCEP

The contribution of the ACFTA to the RCEP does face challenges and uncertainties. The scenario of the ACFTA is essentially different from that of the RCEP. First, the nature of the ACFTA and the RCEP is not the same. The ACFTA is a bilateral trade pact between China and ASEAN, although ASEAN consists of ten Member States. The flexibility of the ACFTA is due in large part to geopolitical considerations. China's initiation of the ACFTA was primarily driven to ease concerns of a "China threat" in Southeast Asia,[70] which may also involve concerns over China's WTO accession. It may help to explain why the ACFTA does not have an accession clause. It is arguably easier for China to be more flexible in the ACFTA given its limited coverage compared with the RCEP.

In contrast, the RCEP is a mega trade pact involving sixteen countries. Obviously, the RCEP differs from the ACFTA concerning the number of parties. For China, the RCEP will extend to new and major partners, i.e., Japan and India. Moreover, the progress of the RCEP cannot be solely decided by ASEAN and China, and other parties play an important role. ASEAN needs to coordinate with six partners in the RCEP negotiations. The RCEP talks proceed slowly due to the difficulties in engaging China, Japan and Korea to negotiate successfully with one another, and because

[67] Mark Feldman et al., The Role of Pacific Rim FTAs in the Harmonisation of International Investment Law: Towards a Free Trade Area of the Asia-Pacific 9 (2016).

[68] *Id.*, at 10.

[69] *Gao Hucheng Is Interviewed by the Xinhua News Agency on the Successful Signing of the China-ASEAN FTA Upgrading Protocol*, Xinhua News Agency, Dec. 2, 2015, http://english.mofcom.gov.cn/article/newsrelease/significantnews/201512/20151201199118.shtml (last visited Mar. 16, 2018).

[70] Yuzhu Wang & Tong Sarah Y, *China-ASEAN FTA Changes ASEAN's Perspective on China*, 2 E. Asian Policy 47, 47 (2010).

India has yet to participate in a trade pact of moderately high standards.[71] It is observed that India does not favor significant trade reform under the RCEP.[72] As another example, Australia and Japan may want high-level rules in the RCEP, which diverge from the position of other countries including India. In terms of existing agreements, the RCEP involves a complex net of trade and investment pacts. They include a number of ASEAN+1 FTAs, the FTAs among non-ASEAN parties and bilateral investment agreements.

Second, it remains unclear whether the ACFTA represents a coherent approach to regional economic integration. This is relevant to the RCEP as the ACFTA has value as a template for reference purposes. There are differences between the ACFTA and other ASEAN FTAs, which may complicate the RCEP negotiations. In some aspects, other ASEAN FTAs are more liberal than the ACFTA. For example, the ACFTA focuses on protection of investment rather than the protection and liberalization of investment in Japan's EPAs with single ASEAN members.[73] The ACFTA is a basic trade pact that does little beyond reducing tariffs and origin rules requirements for goods shipments.[74]

In certain aspects, the ACFTA is more trade-liberalized than other ASEAN trade pacts. As an example, China uses a different base of import tariff reduction compared with Japan in the trade agreements with ASEAN. It is similar to the approach in the ASEAN–Korea FTA. Both "the import value" and "the number of imported items" measures were adopted in the ACFTA and ASEAN–Korea FTA as the base for calculating the percentage of tariff cuts, while the value base alone was adopted in the AJCEP for Japan, permitting it to reduce the scope of market liberalization and exclude certain agricultural products.[75] The negative listing approach of the TIG (all tariff lines generally reduced and exceptions spelled out on an annexed list)[76] contrasts with the ASEAN-India and Japan-Singapore FTAs that adopt a positive listing approach whereby

[71] Meredith Kolsky Lewis, *The ASEAN–Australia–New Zealand FTA (AANZFTA), in* Bilateral and Regional Trade Agreements: Case Studies 131 (Simon Lester, et al. eds., 2015).

[72] Schott & Lu, *supra* note 56, at 137.

[73] Julien Chaisse, *The Shifting Tectonics of International Investment Law – Structure and Dynamics of Rules and Arbitration on Foreign Investment in the Asia-Pacific Region*, 47 Geo. Wash. Intl. L. Rev. 563, 615–16 (2015).

[74] Salidjanova, *supra* note 28, at 9.

[75] Yoshimatsu, *supra* note 10, at 406.

[76] A negative listing approach is adopted in the EHP to provide tariff cuts before the establishment of the ACFTA in 2010.

tariffs are reduced only for goods stipulated on a list by each party.[77] The negative listing approach covers all goods unless provided for in exceptions. Generally, it is more effective in tariff cuts than the positive listing approach.

In addition, the ACFTA is not comparable with other FTAs of China in issues such as regulatory requirements and new sectors. In this sense, it does not fit well with the aim of the RCEP to be a high-quality agreement.[78] Within China's FTAs, the ACFTA is a low-standard agreement compared with others such as China's trade pacts with New Zealand and Switzerland.[79] The ACFTA arguably focuses on market liberalization and contains fewer new regulatory obligations than China's recent FTAs with Korea and Australia. It is supported by the fact that China has only utilized the enabling clause once to ensure the WTO consistency of lower-standard FTAs with developing countries, which is the trade pact with ASEAN.[80] Concerning the future work program envisaged by the Upgrading Protocol, issues such as intellectual property and nontrade concerns are not the focus. China's agreements with Korea and Australia seek to promote regulatory improvements in certain, albeit limited, areas. The features of the China-Korea FTA are expanded coverage, highlighted focus on services and investment, increased nontrade concerns of competition and environment and enhanced good governance norms.[81] Non-trade concerns (e.g., environment) are starting to be addressed in the China-Korea FTA. The ChAFTA focuses not only on trade and investment facilitation through market liberalization, but also on carefully written good governance norms.[82] For new sectors, it appears that the ACFTA does not attach as much attention to them as the China-Korea FTA and the ChAFTA do. Going significantly beyond the ACFTA, China's recent agreements with Australia and Korea provide for preferential access to China's market in specific areas (e.g., information technology and retail services).[83]

[77] Wang, *supra* note 30, at 199.

[78] Joint Leaders' Statement on the Regional Comprehensive Economic Partnership (RCEP), Sep. 8, 2016, http://asean.org/storage/2016/09/56-RCEP_Joint-Leaders-Statement_8-September-2016.pdf (last visited Mar. 16, 2018).

[79] Salidjanova, *supra* note 28, at 22.

[80] *Id.*, at 21.

[81] Heng Wang, *The Features of China's Recent FTA and Their Implications: An Anatomy of the China–Korea FTA*, 11 Asian J. WTO & Intl. Health L. & Pol. 115, 115–54 (2016).

[82] Heng Wang, An Assessment of the ChAFTA and Its Implications: A Work-in-Progress Type FTA with Selective Innovations? 1–23 (2017).

[83] Salidjanova, *supra* note 28, at 9.

3.4 Challenges in FTA Implementation

A number of challenges exist in the implementation of the ACFTA and AHKFTA. This section will focus on the implementation of the ACFTA, since information on the newly concluded AHKFTA remains rather limited. Two points deserve attention at the beginning. One is that the implementation of the ACFTA varies from one ASEAN country to another due to a significant number of factors. These factors include the different development levels, individual ACFTA schedules and the bilateral trade surplus or deficit of ASEAN countries. As an example, different ASEAN countries may run trade surplus or deficits with China. ASEAN's goods trade with China has gone from surplus to an increased trade deficit in 2015,[84] although the causal link between trade deficit and ACFTA merits scrutiny.[85] The other is that some implementation challenges (e.g., the low FTA usage rate including its usage by SMEs[86]) are not unique to the ACFTA.

First, the ACFTA may negatively affect certain sectors of the importing country as the case with other trade pacts. A major challenge in the ACFTA implementation is the possible impact on industrial development (especially labor-intensive industries), since ASEAN-China trade (e.g., agricultural products) is considered more competitive rather than complementary in its character.[87] The ACFTA has caused concerns in certain sectors (such as steel, petrochemicals, cosmetics and herbal medicines) due to possible overwhelming competition from imports under the agreement.[88] It is observed that the implementation of the ACFTA does not bring significant economic benefits to improving the competitiveness of the Indonesian economy.[89]

Meanwhile, the implementation of the ACFTA is influenced by the dynamics and challenges of political and economic changes in the region,

[84] ASEAN Economic Community Chartbook (2016).

[85] Salidjanova, *supra* note 28, at 3–4.

[86] For instance, the TPP also presents challenges to SMEs, including the insufficiency of opportunities for SMEs, the complexity of rules, difficulties in interpretation and remained regulatory differences. *See* Heng Wang, *The Implications of the Trans-Pacific Partnership for SMEs: Opportunities and Challenges*, 6 KLRI J. L. & Legis. 45, 65–75 (2016).

[87] Ignatius Ismanto & Krishnamurti Indra, The Political-Economy of ASEAN-China FTA: An Indonesian Perspective, 22 (2014).

[88] Kevin Brown, *Biggest Regional Trade Deal Unveiled*, Financial Times, Jan. 2, 2010, www.ft.com/content/823707e4-f6f1-11de-9fb5-00144feab49a (last visited Jun. 28, 2018).

[89] Ismanto & Indra, *supra* note 87, at 26.

which could include internal factors in economic recovery.[90] For instance, one writer indicates that Indonesia is not very serious in addressing the opportunities and challenges of regional economic integration, and that the country faces internal constraints in the implementation of ACFTA.[91] In any case, adequate support to the sectors negatively affected by the ACFTA is crucial.

Second, the utilization rate of the ACFTA remains low. According to a WTO report, the ASEAN partners under the ACFTA had preference utilization rates of 12 percent, lower than Pakistan and New Zealand, which had utilization rates of between 20 and 30 percent of their exports to China.[92] There may be many reasons for the low usage rate of the ACFTA, such as different rules of origin (ROOs) that may lead to a noodle bowl effect as discussed below. Other reasons could include NTBs and the lack of information on the ACFTA. It is challenging to ensure that small businesses and farmers, who lack the expertise and funding to utilize the trade pacts, would benefit from the trade agreement. For instance, cooperation on regulation (e.g., food safety standards) will be desirable to reduce NTBs and help SMEs and small farmers to reap the FTA benefits.[93]

Third, the ACFTA consists of some out-of-date or "shallow" obligations, even after the FTA upgrading. A typical example is e-commerce. The Upgrading Protocol provides for cooperation in cross-border e-commerce.[94] It provides for information sharing and other cooperation without detailed obligations. The Upgrading Protocol has less detailed provisions compared with the counterpart of China's trade pacts with Korea and Australia that contain stand-alone chapters on e-commerce.[95] Therefore, one may argue that the ACFTA is not adequately prepared for e-commerce, since the rules may not be able to effectively deal with legal issues (e.g., intellectual property issues in e-commerce, electronic authentication, electronic signatures, paperless trading, online consumer protection and personal information

[90] For instance, the major challenge facing Indonesia in economic recovery is determined by internal factors such as political instability, rising terrorism, deteriorating infrastructure and stricter labor legislations. *Id.*, at 4, 26.

[91] *Id.*, at 26–7.

[92] Maria Donner Abreu, Preferential Rules of Origin in Regional Trade Agreements 29 (2013).

[93] For instance, there is concern about small farmers under the China-Thailand trade agreement, which involves food safety standards.

[94] China-ASEAN FTA Upgrading Protocol (2015), art. 7(III).

[95] China-Korea FTA (2015), Chapter 13; ChAFTA (2015), Ch. 12.

protection). As analyzed above, the ACFTA contains few WTO-plus or WTO-extra regulatory disciplines to address NTBs.

More broadly, the progress made by the Upgrading Protocol remains limited. The areas covered in the upgrading are product-specific rules, a *de minimis* rule, operational certification procedures, customs procedures and trade facilitation, the liberalization of services trade, investment promotion and facilitation, economic and technical cooperation and commitments to further strengthen trade and investment conditions.[96] Its focus seems to be origin rules, market opening and trade facilitation. However, it contains few new obligations in issues such as NTBs, nontrade concerns and investment liberalization.

Fourth, the relationship among the ACFTA, CSFTA and other trade or investment agreements (e.g., the RCEP) needs to be further clarified, and may lead to the noodle bowl effect. The lack of bilateral agreements between China and ASEAN countries (except for the CSFTA) exempts businesses from the job of checking both bilateral agreements and the ACFTA for FTA benefits. However, Singapore has concluded a bilateral FTA with China that is unique among the ASEAN countries. As a trade pact between an ASEAN Member State and its strategic trade partner, the CSFTA complements the ACFTA.[97] That said, for trade between Singapore and China, businesses and other stakeholders need to check both agreements and the RCEP, if it is concluded.

In the future, the AHKFTA is also highly relevant in this context. On the one hand, the ACFTA and AHKFTA may bring competition between Hong Kong and Singapore. The AHKFTA will effectively give Hong Kong access to the ACFTA, such as facilitating the staging of cargo and inventory in Hong Kong, enabling third-party invoicing from Hong Kong trading companies to buyers and sellers under the ACFTA.[98] As indicated by the Singaporean Minister for National Development, Lawrence Wong, "Singapore and Hong Kong are in healthy competition with each other ... But the competition is not a zero-sum game."[99] On the other hand, the ACFTA could benefit

[96] Ministry of Trade and Industry, A Guide to Understanding the ASEAN-China Free Trade Area Upgrade, www.mti.gov.sg/MTIInsights/SiteAssets/Pages/Guide-to-the-upgraded-ASEAN-China-Free-Trade-Area-(ACFTA)/ A%20Guide%20to%20Understanding%20the%20ACFTA%20Upgrade%20(final).pdf (last visited Mar. 28, 2018).

[97] AEC Blueprint 2025, para. 79.

[98] William Marshall, *Asean-HK FTA: What It Means for Hong Kong and Singapore*, The Straits Times, Sep. 20, 2017, www.straitstimes.com/opinion/asean-hk-fta-what-it-means-for-hk-and-spore (last visited Feb. 20, 2018).

[99] *Id.*

ASEAN countries including Singapore. For instance, it is reported that Philippines will tremendously benefit from the AHKFTA and AHKIA, as these two pacts will level up trade and investments relations through increased market access for Philippine businesses.[100] Meanwhile, it is interesting to see how the relationship of the AHKFTA and related AHKIA will be addressed, since the texts of these two agreements are not publicly available at the time of writing.

A number of questions remain open regarding the relationship among these agreements. How do we address the conflict, if any, among provisions of these agreements? How do we determine the forum to resolve disputes among the parties if they could not agree on it? The ACFTA does not prejudice the parties' right to resort to dispute settlement procedures of treaties to which they are parties.[101] In practice, it may depend on the choice of the complainant as its choice of forum will exclude other fora under the ACFTA.[102]

Taking Singapore as an example, the implementation of the ACFTA faces the noodle bowl effect arising from different FTA rules of origin. Regarding products that are not wholly produced or obtained in the ACFTA zone, the TIG used to only provide for the 40 percent value-added rule (the product needs to have 40 percent of its content originating from any ACFTA party).[103] This is the RVC rule. As pointed out by the Chinese Minister of Trade, the ACFTA ROOs are not flexible and origin determination is a complicated process.[104] The Upgrading Protocol brings a change to the rule in tariff heading (CTH) at the four-digit level of the Harmonized System: for goods classified in forty-six chapters of the Harmonized System that are not wholly produced or obtained in the ACFTA zone, they are originating goods if all nonoriginating materials used in the production of the goods have undergone a CTH at the four-digit level of the Harmonized System.[105] Either the RVC 40 percent rule or the CTH rule apply under the ACFTA. This resembles a number of ASEAN agreements (e.g., the ASEAN Trade in Goods Agreement, the AANZFTA, the AJCEP and the ASEAN-Korea FTA) but differs from the ASEAN-India FTA, which adopts RVC

[100] *ASEAN, HK to Sign Free Trade Agreement, supra* note 2.

[101] China-ASEAN Agreement on Dispute Settlement Mechanism (2004), art. 2.5.

[102] *Id.*, art. 2.6.

[103] China-ASEAN Agreement on Trade in Goods (2004), Annex 3, Rule 4(a)(i).

[104] *Minister of Commerce Interprets the China-ASEAN FTA Upgrading Protocol, supra* note 69.

[105] China-ASEAN FTA Upgrading Protocol (2015), Annex 1, art. 4.1(b).

35 percent and a change in tariff subheading (CTSH) for products that are not wholly produced or obtained in the FTA parties.[106] For products that are not wholly produced in the FTA parties, the China-Singapore FTA uses the RVC 40 percent rule,[107] and contains product-specific ROOs including a change in tariff classification[108] and process criterion for textile and textile products.[109] The Singapore-Australia FTA provides for the general rule of a specified threshold of local value content of either 30 or 50 percent, while each product has one corresponding specific ROO under the Japan-Singapore Economic Partnership Agreement, a significant portion of which requires 60 percent of local content.[110] The implementation of the ACFTA could face the noodle bowl effect arising from inconsistent ROOs under various agreements. Singaporean businesses may face different sets of ROOs (e.g., CTH and CTSH rules), and this will affect the usage of trade pacts.

Last but not least, other challenges exist. For instance, one challenge is how to implement the Upgrading Protocol and further upgrade the ACFTA. The Upgrading Protocol provides for few stringent regulatory disciplines, and the details of economic and technical cooperation have not been laid out. In the future, the ACFTA needs to address the challenge of deepening trade liberalization (including the further removal of NTBs) and cooperation while protecting regulatory autonomy.

3.5 Conclusion

The ACFTA is not a high-level and modern trade agreement compared with deep FTAs (e.g., the CETA and the TPP). On the one hand, the ACFTA does reflect a more flexible approach than other FTAs of China, but it is not a deep FTA. The flexible approach reflects a learning process, and both sides were exploring how to structure the FTAs at the same time as they were negotiating. The flexible approach is attributable to, *inter alia*, strategic considerations that should not be overlooked. The ACFTA carries political and economic implications and aims to promote the political and economic relationship between China and ASEAN. Moreover, the ACFTA differs from the US FTAs that attach greater

[106] Handbook on Rules of Origin for Preferential Certificates of Origin 25 (2017).
[107] China-Singapore FTA (2008), art. 13.2.
[108] *Id.*, at Annex 2, sec. B.1.
[109] *Id.*, at Annex 2, sec. B.2.
[110] Wang, *supra* note 30, at 201.

emphasis on deeper and binding commitments. It highlights narrow tariff considerations and regulatory cooperation, but does not contain stringent regulatory disciplines that require broader regulatory reform. On the other hand, the implementation of the ACFTA faces a number of challenges. As an example, its implementation depends on whether the ASEAN countries and the stakeholders deem the pact as a threat or an opportunity. If properly managed, the evolving ACFTA could contribute to the RCEP negotiations. However, it should be noted that the scenario of the ACFTA is markedly different from that of the RCEP.

The ACFTA will increasingly interact with other agreements. Among them, the RCEP and the AHKFTA are particularly relevant. During the ACFTA upgrade negotiations, both sides may want to wait for the conclusion of the RCEP. For the AHKFTA, it should promote the development of the economic relationship between China and ASEAN. Businesses could utilize either the ACFTA or the AHKFTA to tap the vast market of Mainland China. The AHKFTA will help firms to use Hong Kong as a gateway to conduct business with mainland China. Moreover, the AHKFTA may provide higher-level rules and liberalization than the ACFTA in key areas such as intellectual property and services trade.[111] It is possible that the RCEP, the AHKFTA and even the Mainland and Hong Kong Closer Economic Partnership Arrangement will be considered along with the ACFTA. Meanwhile, the AHKFTA may mean that there will be increased competition between Hong Kong and Singapore, but such competition is a healthy one.[112] To fully utilize these agreements, the understanding of them will be crucial. The challenges in FTA implementation should also be properly addressed. Therefore, the evolution of ASEAN law from the global perspective, including the development of the ACFTA and its interaction with other agreements, deserves close attention.

[111] Phila Siu, *"Hong Kong-Asean Free-Trade Deal to Be Signed by November": Philippine minister*, S. China Morning Post, Jul. 13, 2017, www.scmp.com/news/hong-kong/economy/article/2102420/hong-kong-asean-free-trade-deal-be-signed-november-philippine (last visited Feb. 20, 2018). The key elements of the FTA include tariff cuts, liberalization of trade and services and intellectual property cooperation.

[112] Charissa Yong, *Asean-Hong Kong Free Trade Agreement on Track to Be Inked This Year*, The Strait Times, Jun. 8, 2017, www.straitstimes.com/singapore/asean-hong-kong-free-trade-agreement-on-track-to-be-inked-this-year (last visited Feb. 20, 2018).

4

Dispute Settlement Provisions in ASEAN's External Economic Agreements with China, Japan and Korea

HENRY GAO

4.1 Introduction

Since its inception in 1967, ASEAN has helped to enhance not only the political cooperation of its member countries, but also the economic integration among them. In addition to promoting internal collaboration, another important task of ASEAN is to strengthen its ties with countries outside of the region. Over the years, ASEAN has signed many agreements with other countries. Among them, the agreements with its three big neighbors up north, i.e., China, Japan and Korea (CJK) are especially noteworthy due to ASEAN's troubled history with Japan and China. This started with the Japanese invasion during World War II, followed by the Chinese efforts to export revolution in the 1950s and 1960s by supporting communist parties and training soldiers for guerilla wars, as well as the Sino-Vietnamese War in 1979. With such unpleasant experiences, it was no surprise that ASEAN countries viewed the big powers from the north with suspicion. Indeed, one of the primary objectives for the founding of ASEAN in 1969 was to fend off the threat from other powers and "ensure their stability and security from external interference in any form or manifestation."[1] Given such historical background, the fact that ASEAN is willing to conclude agreements with the CJK countries provides strong testimony to ASEAN's commitment to regional integration.

[1] 1967 ASEAN Declaration, adopted by the Foreign Ministers at the First ASEAN Ministerial Meeting in Bangkok, Thailand on Aug. 8, 1967.

In recent years, the CJK countries have emerged as the largest trade partners of ASEAN countries. For example, since 2010, China has been the largest trade partner of ASEAN, while Japan and Korea are the third and fifth largest.[2] Taken together, their total trade accounts for more than 30 percent of ASEAN's external trade. With such strong and increasingly close economic ties, it is very important for ASEAN to maintain good relationships with the CJK countries. In this regard, international agreements provide the necessary platform for ASEAN to manage its trade relations with the CJK countries. Moreover, as the CJK countries are the biggest trade partners of ASEAN, ASEAN's trade agreements with them also provide good indications of how ASEAN manages its relationship with its trade partners.

Thus, this chapter will focus on ASEAN's trade agreements with the CJK countries. In particular, we will concentrate on the dispute settlement mechanisms in these agreements. Compared with the dispute settlement mechanisms within ASEAN's internal agreements, the dispute settlement mechanisms of ASEAN's external economic agreements provide a real litmus test for assessing the success of ASEAN in building a rule-based regime for two reasons. First, the external economic agreements provide a way to test the ability of ASEAN to respond to the pressures of larger, more powerful partners. The internal agreements are negotiated among ASEAN members, thus are less susceptible to power politics as the disparities among the members are relatively small. In contrast, the partners in ASEAN's external economic agreements are mostly big regional players or even global players, thus highly likely to apply strong pressures against ASEAN countries in the negotiations for the external agreements. Unless the ASEAN countries are able to stand together and resist such demands, the external economic agreements will be subject to heavy influences by the external partners. That is also why according to the AEC Blueprint 2025, one of the main areas of implementation of the Blueprint is "strengthening ASEAN's relationship with its external parties."[3] In that regard, studying the structure and design of the external economic agreements can tell us a lot about whether ASEAN countries can withstand external pressures.

[2] The 2010 data is available at *Table 20: Top Ten ASEAN Trade Partner Countries/Regions*, available at www.asean.org/images/2012/resources/external_trade/Table20_27.xls. The latest available data is for 2015, available at http://asean.org/storage/2016/06/table20_as-of-30-Aug-2016-2.pdf.

[3] ASEAN Economic Community Blueprint 2015, para. 1.

Second, as these agreements are negotiated by ASEAN as a whole, they are also quite different from the trade agreements negotiated by individual ASEAN members. Negotiating individual agreements is much easier as the particular ASEAN member can decide on its own. In comparison, when ASEAN countries negotiate agreements with external partners on a collective basis, they have to first negotiate among themselves in order to form a common position, then negotiate with the external parties to shape the agreements. On issues that are particularly difficult, they might have to go back and forth between external partners and ASEAN internal members before they can finalize their position. This is also confirmed in the AEC Blueprint 2015, which states that one of the strategic measures of ASEAN's global engagement is to "develop a more strategic and coherent approach towards external economic relations with a view to adopting a common position in regional and global economic fora."[4] Therefore, these external economic agreements also provide valuable insights on how well ASEAN can work as a whole and speak with a unified voice.

The rest of the chapter is organized as follows: in Section 4.2, the paper conducts a detailed critical analysis of the dispute settlement mechanisms in ASEAN's external economic agreements with the CJK countries by reviewing the main procedural rules of these mechanisms. Next, in Section 4.2.2 the paper discusses the difference among these agreements, and compares them with the WTO dispute settlement mechanisms. In Section 4.3, the paper concludes with thoughts on how these dispute settlement mechanisms might evolve in the future, especially in view of the ongoing negotiations for the RCEP.

4.2 Dispute Settlement Provisions in Economic Agreements

In general, the dispute settlement provisions in political agreements tend to be weak and informal, while those in trade agreements are usually much stronger and formal. In addition, while political agreements typically offer consultation or negotiation as the only means of dispute settlement, trade agreements offer the parties a variety of dispute settlement mechanisms, with the highly institutionalized WTO-style arbitration panel as the dominant model.

Japan included dispute settlement mechanisms as a chapter in its Comprehensive Economic Partnership Agreement with ASEAN, while China and Korea each includes in their respective FTA packages with

[4] *Id.*, para. 80.1.

ASEAN a separate agreement on DSMs. Their other economic agreements simply state that any dispute under these agreements shall be resolved through the procedures and mechanism as set out in the DSM agreement.[5] But there are some notable exceptions. For example, Article 8 of the 2009 MOU between ASEAN and China on Cooperation in the Field of Intellectual Property states that disputes shall be settled "amicably through mutual consultation or negotiation among All Participants through diplomatic channels, *without reference to any third party or international tribunal.*"[6] Similarly, Article 5.1.2 of the 2005 Framework Agreement on Comprehensive Economic Cooperation among ASEAN and Korea explicitly carved out trade in services and investment from the coverage of the DSM agreement. These provisions reflect the reluctance of the parties to enforce nontraditional trade issues such as services, investment and intellectual property rights.

4.2.1 *Typical Dispute Settlement Procedure*

In general, the dispute settlement procedures in the CJK countries' agreements are very similar to the one under the 2004 EDSM,[7] which in turn is modeled after the WTO DSU. This section discusses the main stages of dispute settlement in these dispute settlement mechanisms. It not only notes the common elements of these procedures, but also discusses their main differences with the WTO dispute settlement mechanism and the EDSM. These analyses provide key insights into the designs of these mechanisms and the rationales.

4.2.1.1 Consultations

Consultations in essence are bilateral negotiations. Because they are conducted directly between the disputing parties without the

[5] See e.g., art. 19 of the 2006 Protocol to Amend the Agreement on Trade in Goods of the Framework Agreement on Comprehensive Economic Cooperation between ASEAN and the People's Republic of China; art. 5.1 of the 2005 Framework Agreement on Comprehensive Economic Cooperation among the Governments of the Member Countries of ASEAN and the Republic of Korea; art. 19 of the 2006 Agreement on Trade in Goods under the Framework Agreement on Comprehensive Economic Cooperation among the Governments of the Member Countries of ASEAN and the Republic of Korea.

[6] Emphasis added by the author. 2009 Memorandum of Understanding between the Governments of the Member States of ASEAN and the Government of the People's Republic of China on Cooperation in the Field of Intellectual Property.

[7] 2004 ASEAN Protocol on Enhanced Dispute Settlement Mechanism.

involvement of third parties, it is usually easier to solve the disputes through consultations, and that is why they are included in both noneconomic and economic agreements. The difference between the two, however, is that the consultation provisions in the noneconomic agreements tend to be rather general and do not include detailed instructions, while the ones in the economic agreements are much more specific. They usually set out in detail the format, content and time limit for the consultation process. This is in marked contrast to the loose language in political agreements and reflects the legalistic nature of the economic agreements.

Similar to the WTO DSU, a party may file a request for consultations against a measure by another party that nullifies or impairs the benefits accruable to the complaining party under the covered agreements.[8] The request shall be submitted in writing to the responding party, and shall include the specific measures at issue, as well as the factual and legal basis, such as the provisions of the covered agreements allegedly breached.[9]

Interestingly, none of the three DSMs recognize nonviolation complaints, i.e., nullification or impairment caused by a measure that does not violate the WTO agreements.[10] The China DSM made this explicit by stating that "nonviolation disputes are not permitted under this Agreement."[11] The other two DSMs do not include such an explicit prohibition on nonviolation complaints. However, as they only recognize nullification or impairment caused by measures which are inconsistent with a party's obligation, or failure of a party to carry out its obligation,[12] we can infer that nonviolation complaints are implicitly excluded. In the view of the author, nonviolation complaints are mainly designed to deal with the problems of unforeseen developments caused by imperfect

[8] Article 4.1, 2004 Agreement on Dispute Settlement Mechanism of the Framework Agreement on Comprehensive Economic Co-Operation between the Association of Southeast Asian Nations and the People's Republic of China ("China"); art. 3.1, 2005 Agreement on Dispute Settlement Mechanism under the Framework Agreement on Comprehensive Economic Cooperation among the Governments of the Member Countries of ASEAN and the Republic of Korea ("Korea"); art. 62.1, 2008 Agreement on Comprehensive Economic Partnership among Member States of the Association of Southeast Asian Nations and Japan ("Japan").

[9] China, art. 4.2; Korea, art. 3.2; Japan, art. 62.2.

[10] See art. XXIII.b of General Agreement on Tariffs and Trade 1994; art. XXIII.3 of General Agreement on Trade in Services.

[11] China, Footnote 1 to art. 4.1.

[12] Korea, art. 3.1; Japan, art. 62.1.

treaty drafting. For a large international treaty like the GATT, it is impossible to have all the parties discuss whether such unforeseen developments should be allowed due to the high transaction cost. In contrast, for bilateral treaties like the CJK-ASEAN economic agreements, the transaction cost is much lower. Thus, it is much better for the parties to solve the problem through bilateral consultations in such cases rather than trying to force the case through the dispute settlement mechanism.

Upon receipt of the request for consultations, the respondent shall reply to the request within seven days and enter into consultations within thirty days.[13] The parties shall conduct the consultations with good faith and make every effort to reach a mutually satisfactory solution.

As consultation is conducted on a bilateral basis, the disputing parties might be reluctant to provide information for fear that such information might be used against them in later proceedings. To alleviate such concerns, the DSMs explicitly require the parties to provide sufficient information to enable a full examination of how the measure might affect the operation of the covered agreement. At the same time, to avoid the misuse of the information, the parties are also required to treat information provided by the other party as confidential. To enable frank discussions, the consultation process is also confidential and without prejudice to the rights of the parties under other proceedings. If consultations fail to settle the dispute within sixty days, the complainant may request the establishment of the panel.

In urgent cases, such as those concerning perishable goods, the time periods for starting and ending consultations are shortened to one-third of the original time periods, i.e., ten days and twenty days, respectively. This provision is of particular importance to ASEAN, which exports many fresh produce that are easily perishable.

While the economic agreements do not make this explicit, consultation seems to be the mandatory first step in the dispute settlement procedure. This conclusion is drawn from the provisions on the establishment of the arbitral tribunal, which can only be requested by the complaining party in any of the three scenarios: if the respondent fails to respond to the consultation request or to enter into consultations in time, or if the consultation fails to resolve the dispute after a certain period.[14]

[13] China, art. 4.3; Korea, art. 3.3; Japan, art. 62.3. Note that the deadline to reply to the request is ten days under the Japanese DSM.

[14] China, arts. 4.3 & 6.1; Korea, arts. 3.3 & 5.1; Japan, art. 64.1.

4.2.1.2 Establishment of Arbitral Tribunal/Panel

Upon the delivery of the request for the establishment of the panel, the panel shall be established automatically. As the arbitration panels are not standing bodies, they need to be composed on an ad hoc basis for each specific dispute. Normally, there are three members in the panel. Two of them are appointed by the complainant and respondent respectively, while the third – the chair – has to be agreed by the two parties. If any party fails to appoint its arbitrator within the time period provided for under the DSM, the arbitrator appointed by the other party shall be the sole arbitrator. As I will discuss in Section 4.2.3, this is an important change compared to the WTO DSU and solves the problem caused by blockage of the process through refusal by a party to appoint a panelist, especially by the respondent. If the parties cannot agree on the third arbitrator, they may request the Director-General of the WTO to appoint an arbitrator. If the Director-General is a national of one of the disputing parties, the Deputy Director-General or the officer next in seniority who is not a national of either party shall be requested to make the appointment. This provision is a good innovation as there is a real possibility of a national of the parties serving as WTO Director-General, such as Dr. Supachai Panitchpakdi, a Thai national who served as the WTO Director General in 2002–05.

To ensure the competence of the panel, the DSMs require panelists to "have expertise or experience in law, international trade, other matters covered by the covered agreements or the resolution of disputes arising under international trade agreements."[15] Given the dominance of the state in international trade affairs in most ASEAN and CJK countries, this requirement means that most panelists are probably government officials. Indeed, this seems to be consistent with the practice of these countries in the WTO, as they tend to nominate government officials to the indicative list for panelists. The problem with having government officials as panelists, however, is that they normally rule along the lines of their official national policy. To reduce this likelihood, the DSMs state that a panelist "shall be chosen strictly on the basis of objectivity, reliability, sound judgment and independence and shall conduct himself or herself on the same basis throughout the course of the arbitral panel proceedings."[16] Stricter rules apply to the Chair, who "shall not be a national of any party to the dispute and shall not have his or her

[15] China, art. 7.6; Korea, art. 6.6; Japan, art. 65.6.
[16] *Id.*

usual place of residence in the territory of, nor be employed by, any party to the dispute nor have dealt with the referred matter in any capacity."[17]

For the purpose of calculating the time periods under the DSM, the date of the establishment of the panel shall be the date on which the chair is appointed, or the thirtieth day after the receipt of the request for establishment of a panel in case of a sole-member panel.

4.2.1.3 Panel Proceedings

Once the panel has been composed, it shall fix the timetable for the panel proceedings.[18] To assist the panel, the DSMs also include annexes which set out the rules and procedures of the panel proceedings in detail. Of course, after consulting the parties, the panel may adopt additional rules and procedures for specific disputes.[19]

In general, the panel will hold two substantive meetings with the parties. Before each substantive meeting, the parties shall submit written submissions to the panel and the other disputing parties. The first round of submissions starts with the submission from the complainant, who usually uses this opportunity to substantiate its case by presenting the facts and making detailed legal arguments. This submission also helps the respondent to understand the factual and legal bases of the complaint, and to respond to them in its own submission. At the first substantive meeting, the complainant will present their arguments first, followed by the respondent. After the meeting, the parties shall submit another round of written submissions to rebut the arguments made by the other parties. These rebuttals will be presented at the second substantive meeting of the panel.

The submissions of the parties shall be kept confidential and made available only to the parties to the dispute and the panel, but there are two exceptions: first, a party is not precluded from disclosing its own position or the submission to the public; second, if a party submits a confidential version of a written submission, it shall provide a nonconfidential summary at the request of the other party to the dispute for disclosure to the public.

In addition to the written submissions and oral statements by the parties, the panel may also seek information from the parties by posing questions either in writing or orally.[20] Moreover, the panel may seek

[17] China, art. 7.6; Korea, art. 6.6; Japan, art. 65.2.
[18] China, art. 9.3; Japan, art. 68.7.
[19] China, art. 9.5; Korea, art. 10.1; Japan, art. 68.2.
[20] China, Rule 5, Rules and Procedures for the Arbitral Proceedings; Japan, art. 67.2.

additional information on the case from any person or institution.[21] In particular, the panel may seek advice on technical or scientific issues from experts.[22] Of course, such experts do not have the power to vote in respect of any decision to be made by the panel. In the interest of fairness, such information shall also be made available to the parties.

Given the language differences among the parties, the DSMs also explicitly require the panel proceedings and the documents submitted to the panel to be in English.[23]

After the substantive meetings, the panel shall meet to deliberate on the case and draft its report based on the written submissions and oral presentations of the parties, as well as additional information and expert advice it gathers from other sources. The deliberations shall be kept confidential,[24] and the report shall be drafted without the presence of the parties to the dispute.[25] As the function of the panel is to make an objective assessment of the dispute before it, including an examination of the facts of the case and the applicability of and conformity with the covered agreements, the panel report shall address both the factual and legal issues. In general, the report shall set out findings of facts and law together with reasons, including the applicability of particular provisions of the covered agreements to the current dispute as well as whether the parties have failed to carry out their obligations under the current agreements.[26]

During deliberation and drafting of the panel report, the members of the panel might disagree on certain issues. In such cases, the panel shall attempt to reach a decision by consensus or a majority vote if consensus could not be reached.[27] In the latter case, the panelist who is not in the majority may decide to write a dissenting opinion. However, even in such cases, the opinions of individual panelists shall be made on an anonymous basis.[28]

Following deliberations, the panel shall first issue an interim report or draft award setting out its findings and conclusions for review by the disputing parties.[29] The parties may comment on both the factual and

[21] China, Rule 8; Korea, art. 13.1; Japan, art. 67.3.
[22] China, Rule 8; Korea, art. 13.2; Japan, art. 67.3.
[23] China, art. 14; Korea, art. 16.
[24] China, art 9.4. Korea, Rule 21; Japan, art. 68.10.
[25] China, art 9.6. Korea, Rule 17; Japan, art. 69.1.
[26] Korea, art. 11.2.
[27] China, art. 8.5. Korea, Rule 20; Japan, art. 69.7.
[28] China, art. 9.6; Korea, Rule 17.
[29] China, art. 9.7; Korea, Rule 18; Japan, art. 69.2.

legal aspects of the report, and their comments shall be addressed by the panel in its final report.

The final report shall be released to the disputing parties within 120 days from the date of the establishment of the panel.[30] The time period may be shortened in case of urgency or extended if the panel has difficulty in issuing its report in time. The report shall be made available publicly within ten days of release to the disputing parties.[31]

To encourage the parties to seek a mutually satisfactory solution to the dispute, the panel may be suspended at any time before the issuance of the final report with the agreement of the parties.[32] If a solution is found, the panel proceedings may be terminated.[33] On the other hand, if the parties fail to reach a solution, the panel process may be resumed pursuant to the request of any party.[34]

4.2.1.4 Implementation, Compensation and Retaliation

If the panel finds against the respondent, the respondent is supposed to bring its measures into conformity with the panel report. However, the panel report might not specify how the panel recommendations shall be implemented. Instead, the parties are supposed to agree on the means to implement the recommendations.[35] Moreover, as it usually takes time for the respondent to change its measures through the domestic legislative process, the parties shall also agree on a reasonable period of time necessary for the respondent to implement the recommendations.[36] If the parties cannot reach agreement, they may refer the matter back to the original panel, which shall assess the consistency of the means proposed by the respondent.[37] If the parties disagree on whether or not the respondent has complied with the panel report, they may also refer the matter to the original panel for decision.[38]

If the respondent fails to comply with the panel's recommendations within a reasonable period of time, the complainant may request compensatory adjustment from the respondent in the form of tariff

[30] China, art. 9.8; Korea, art. 12.2; Japan, art. 69.6.
[31] China, art. 9.9. Korea, art. 12.3; Japan, art. 69.9.
[32] China, art. 11.1; Korea, art 8.1; Japan, art. 70.1.
[33] China, art. 11.2; Korea, art 8.2; Japan, art. 70.2.
[34] China, art. 11.1; Korea, art 8.1; Japan, art. 70.1.
[35] China, art. 12.2; Korea, art. 14.3.
[36] China, art. 12.2; Korea, art. 14.3.
[37] China, art. 12.2; Korea, art. 14.4.
[38] China, art. 12.3; Korea, art 14.5; Japan, art. 71.4.

reductions on other products.[39] If the parties cannot reach agreement on compensation, the parties may request the original panel to determine the proper level of retaliation.[40] As compensation and the suspension of concessions or benefits are temporary measures available in the absence of implementation,[41] they shall only continue until such time as implementation has taken place.[42]

4.2.1.5 Alternative Dispute Settlement Mechanisms

In addition to the normal dispute settlement process mentioned above, the three DSMs also include some alternative dispute settlement mechanisms. For example, all three DSMs include conciliation or mediation. In addition, the Korean and Japanese DSMs also include good offices. They shall only be undertaken if all the parties to the dispute agree to their use. They may be requested by any party, and they may start or terminate at any time. They may be pursued concurrently with the proceedings of the arbitral panel if the parties agree. These proceedings and the positions of the parties during such proceedings shall be confidential and without prejudice to the rights of the parties in any other proceedings.

The DSMs do not provide detailed rules on how good offices, conciliation or mediation should work. As these provisions are copied from Article 5 of the DSU, the parties might wish to refer to the explanations provided by the Director-General of the WTO, which state that good offices shall consist primarily of providing physical support and Secretariat assistance to the parties; conciliation shall consist of good offices plus the further involvement of the Director-General in promoting discussions and negotiations between the parties; while mediation shall consist of conciliation plus the possibility of the Director-General to propose solutions to the parties.[43]

4.2.2 Differences among the DSMs

As the Chinese and Korean DSMs take the form of stand-alone agreements, while the Japanese DSM is a chapter in its FTA, one might think

[39] China, art. 13.2; Korea, art 15.2; Japan, art. 71.3.
[40] China, art. 13.3; Korea, art 15.3; Japan, art. 71.3.
[41] China, art. 13.1; Korea, art 15.1; Japan, art. 72.1.
[42] China, art. 13.6; Korea, art 15.6.
[43] Art. 5 of the Dispute Settlement Understanding: Communication from the Director-General, WT/DSB/25, Jul. 17, 2001, Attachment B: Procedures for Requesting Action Pursuant to Article 5 of the DSU, footnote 15.

that the Japanese DSM is less detailed or legalistic than the other two. However, this is not the case as the provisions in the Japanese DSM are very similar to those in the other two.

At the same time, there are still some important differences among the three mechanisms. First, the Korean DSM is much more detailed than the Chinese and Japanese DSMs. For example, while the establishment of the panel does not need the approval of all parties under all three DSMs, only the Korean DSM explicitly states that the panel shall be established automatically upon delivery of the request to establish a panel, while the other two DSMs are silent on the issue.[44] Similarly, while both the Chinese and Korean DSM provide that a new panel shall be established if the original panel is unable to conduct its work, only the Korean DSM provides that the new panel shall apply the same time frame as the original panel.[45]

Second, the Korean DSM is more legalistic by providing more explicit guidelines on how to enforce certain obligations. For example, even if the respondent fails to implement the panel's recommendations, both the Chinese and Japanese DSMs require authorization from the panel before the complainant may retaliate.[46] In contrast, the Korean DSM states that the complainant may retaliate by simply providing a written notice of retaliation to the other parties.[47] While the same provision also allows the respondent to request a panel to rule on the legitimacy of the retaliation, the Korean rule provides a much stronger incentive for the respondent to implement the panel's recommendations as the burden of initiating the retaliation panel procedure is placed on the respondent rather than the complainant.

4.2.3 Comparison with the WTO Dispute Settlement Procedure

In these dispute settlement procedures, we can find many influences from the WTO DSU and the EDSM. For example, the provisions on the terms of reference of the arbitral panel are copied verbatim from the WTO. Similarly, the provisions on compensation and suspension of concessions also originated from the DSU. Given the maturity of the

[44] Korea, art. 5.3.
[45] Compare China, art. 7.7 and Korea art. 6.7.
[46] See China, art. 13.3; Japan, art. 72.2 & 71.4.
[47] Korea, art. 15.3.

WTO DSM, it is no wonder that it serves as a good model for the dispute settlement provisions in these agreements.

At the same time, some of the DSU provisions seem to have been blindly copied into these agreements with little consideration of their suitability. One example is the provisions on the interim report. The rationale for having such a step in the WTO DSM is probably to provide additional time for the parties to review the findings of the panel and decide whether or not to lodge an appeal. Without such a mechanism, the parties might not have sufficient time to digest the panel's findings and make an intelligent decision within the sixty-day period from the issuance of the final panel report and the submission of notice of appeal. As the CJK countries' economic agreements do not provide for the possibility of appeal, it is unclear what useful purpose such a mechanism would serve. Even worse, the provisions on the interim report could lead to two highly undesirable consequences.

First, it could result in the leakage of the interim report. While this frequently happens in the WTO,[48] it does not cause problems as the panelists are usually not nationals of the disputing parties.[49] In contrast, as the two nonchairing panelists in cases brought under the CJK countries' DSMs are appointed by the two disputing parties, they are very likely to be nationals of the parties, sometimes even officials of these parties. Leaking the report will subject them to political pressure at home through their national governments, and this could undermine the integrity of the panel.

Second, the parties could use the interim review to request a wholesale rewrite of the panel report. This has not happened in the WTO so far, because the DSU only allows the parties to request the panel to "review precise aspects" in the interim report.[50] In its report in the *Australian-Salmon* case, the WTO Panel ruled that this means that the parties cannot request the panel to make sweeping changes to the report.[51] Curiously, this language has not been copied into the CJK countries' agreements.

[48] Valerie Hughes, *The WTO Dispute Settlement System: A Success Story, in* Inter-Governmental Trade Dispute Settlement: Multilateral and Regional Approaches 115 (Julio Lacarte & Jaime Granados eds., 2004).

[49] This is prohibited by art. 8.3 of the DSU.

[50] Art. 15.2 of the DSU. See Hughes at 115.

[51] See Hughes, *supra* note 45, at 115. See Panel Report, Australia – Measures Affecting Importation of Salmon, WT/DS18/R and Corr.1, adopted November 6, 1998, as modified by Appellate Body Report WT/DS18/AB/R, DSR 1998: VIII, p. 3407, at para. 7.3.

While this might simply be the result of an oversight in drafting, it could well open up the floodgates of abuse by the parties to these agreements.

Another example is the provisions on suspension of benefits. As a form of self-help, this mechanism might not be useful for everyone. As explained by Valerie Hughes, if a developing country imposes high tariffs on imports from a noncomplying developed country, the level of trade affected might be too small to cause hardship to the developed country, while the developing country itself might suffer due to the higher tariffs.[52] Thus, such a measure has not been frequently used in the WTO. The same is true in the ASEAN-CJK context. The CJK countries are much bigger trade powers compared with most ASEAN member countries, even though Korea and China are both developing countries. Thus, if a CJK country fails to implement any panel decision, the winning ASEAN member countries might not be able to effectively retaliate, making it difficult to secure compliance. Furthermore, under the WTO, it is possible for the winning Member to suspend concessions in other sectors, especially services trade and TRIPS. Under the ASEAN-CJK agreements, however, retaliation is practically limited to goods trade as there are no substantial concessions on services and TRIPS. This further limits the utility of suspension of concessions. There are two possible ways to solve the problem: the first is the introduction of collective retaliation, which allows all ASEAN members to retaliate against their bigger neighbors from the north. The second is monetary compensation, whereby the winning party does not have to worry about any potential backfiring of retaliatory measures. However, as there are no precedents from the WTO, ASEAN might face substantial resistance from the CJK countries in introducing such innovative mechanisms in the agreements.

Of course, this does not mean that the drafters of the CJK countries' agreements simply copied the DSU without making any changes. To the contrary, a few provisions have been either deleted or modified by the CJK countries' agreements. The most conspicuous among them is the absence of a provision on an appellate mechanism in the CJK countries' agreements. This makes sense as the CJK countries' agreements are unlikely to generate a significant number of disputes to justify the establishment of a standing appellate tribunal.

[52] See Hughes, *supra* note 45, at 135. See also Julio Lacarte & Fernando Pierola, *Comparing the WTO and GATT Dispute Settlement Mechanisms: What Was Accomplished in the Uruguay Round?, in* Inter-Governmental Trade Dispute Settlement: Multilateral and Regional Approaches 60 (Lacarte & Granados eds., 2004).

Another change made by the CJK countries' agreements is the number of panelists. Under the DSU, each panel is usually composed of three panelists, but the number may be expanded to five.[53] In contrast, while the CJK countries' agreements also set the default panelist number at three, the panel could also include only one panelist. Such variations reflect the different procedures for the appointment of panelists: under the DSU, the panelists are proposed by the Secretariat and agreed by the disputing parties or appointed by the Director-General. Under the CJK countries' agreements, however, one panelist is named by each individual disputing party, with the third one to be agreed by the parties. Thus, under the CJK countries' agreements, the respondent could try to stall the process by refusing to name its own panelists. To prevent this, the CJK countries' agreements state that the panelist appointed by the complainant shall be the sole panelist if the respondent fails to appoint someone within the deadline. Such a problem would not arise under the DSU, where all panelists have to be agreed by the parties and the Director-General will appoint the three members if the parties fail to agree, making it impossible to have only one panelist.

The third change is of language, where the CJK countries' agreements explicitly state that English shall be the language used in the proceedings. This is an improvement over the DSU, where the requirement that the panel report shall be circulated only when it is available in all three official languages can lead to lengthy delays.[54] As there is no common language between the CJK countries and ASEAN members, the use of English – a common second language of all countries – can help make it easier to conduct the proceedings.

The last change concerns costs, where the CJK countries' agreements make the following arrangements: each party shall bear the costs of its appointed arbitrator; the costs of the Chair shall be born in equal parts by the parties to the dispute; other expenses of the panel proceedings shall be born in equal shares by the parties; and each party shall bear its own costs of participating in the dispute, including legal costs.[55]

With the exception of the last point, the cost arrangement under the CJK countries' agreements is completely different from that of the WTO, where costs of the panel and proceedings are borne by the WTO. Of course, this does not mean that the disputing parties do not have to

[53] Art. 5.8 of the DSU.

[54] Hughes, *supra* note 45, at 116.

[55] China, art. 15; Korea, art. 17; Japan, art. 73.

pay anything at all. As the WTO dispute settlement mechanism is funded by the general operating budget of the WTO, each WTO Member, including the disputing parties, also indirectly contributes to the operating expenses of the DSM through its payment of the membership fee. Nonetheless, as the payment is not directly associated with the dispute settlement activities, there is the potential for a free-rider problem. In practice, however, this has not been a major problem for the WTO, as most WTO cases are usually brought by or against the Members with bigger trade volumes. In the CJK countries' agreements, however, things are different. First of all, the members do not pay any membership fees. Furthermore, there is very little formal institutional structure handling the disputes. Thus, it makes sense to have the disputing parties contribute directly to the panel expenses.

4.3 Concluding Thoughts and Reflections

As we can see from our discussions above, the dispute settlement mechanisms in ASEAN's external economic agreements with the CJK countries are rather legalistic. This is quite different than the ones under its external political agreements, which usually prefer soft consultations over hard semi-judicial mechanisms.

In practice, however, the difference in the styles of dispute settlement mechanisms between the economic and noneconomic agreements might not matter much. After all, even though it is highly legalistic, the dispute settlement mechanisms in the CJK countries' economic agreements have never been used. In a way, this is not surprising, as dispute settlement mechanisms in most FTAs around the world have rarely been used. Instead, most countries prefer to use the WTO dispute settlement mechanism to handle their disputes with another WTO Member, even if both are members of an FTA with a well-designed dispute settlement mechanism. The main reason for such a preference is that the WTO dispute settlement mechanism has developed rich jurisprudence on trade issues, and is thus more predictable and reliable. Moreover, as the membership of the WTO is much bigger than any FTA, a ruling obtained through the WTO dispute settlement system can set a precedent for similar cases and deter other WTO members from adopting similar trade barriers. Thus, the difference in the dispute settlement mechanisms of the economic and noneconomic agreements might be of more theoretical rather than practical relevance.

Moreover, divergence in the approaches taken on economic and noneconomic agreements might not always be the case, especially as ASEAN countries seem to be moving toward a more legalistic approach even for internal noneconomic issues in recent years. The best example of this is the 2010 Protocol to the ASEAN Charter on Dispute Settlement Mechanisms (Hanoi Protocol), which provides for a rather formalized and legalistic approach even for noneconomic disputes.

According to one commentator, it is based on the EDSM, which in turn is based on the WTO DSU.[56] The author finds it hard to agree with this view. It is true that the Hanoi Protocol does indeed provide for consultations within a fixed timeframe, failing which the complainant may request the appointment of an arbitral tribunal.[57] However, the decision-making rule for the establishment of a tribunal/panel is very different under the two instruments. According to the Hanoi Protocol, an arbitral tribunal will only be established if the responding party explicitly agrees to the establishment of the tribunal.[58] In contrast, the Vientiane Protocol adopts the reverse/negative consensus rule as under the WTO DSU, which means that the panel shall be established unless the Senior Economic Officers Meeting decides by consensus not to establish a panel.[59]

Nonetheless, the Hanoi Protocol is still a big improvement over the rudimentary rules on dispute settlement under the TAC and the 2007 ASEAN Charter, as it explicitly provides for the possibility of arbitration by a court-like tribunal. Moreover, even though the establishment of the arbitral tribunal is subject to the consent of the responding party, no consent from the parties is required for the adoption of the arbitral award. Instead, once issued, the award of the arbitral tribunal shall be final and binding on the parties to the dispute,[60] and the parties are explicitly required to comply with the award.[61] In this respect, the Hanoi Protocol is even more legalistic than the Vientiane Protocol or the WTO DSU, as the panel reports under these two dispute settlement mechanisms still require the approval of the political bodies,[62] even though one

[56] See Walter Woon, *Dispute Settlement in ASEAN*, 1 (1) The Korean J. Int'l and Comp. L. 100, 100–01 (2013).

[57] *Id.*, at 101.

[58] Hanoi Protocol, art. 8.3–4.

[59] Vientiane Protocol, art. 5.1.

[60] Hanoi Protocol, art. 15.1.

[61] Hanoi Protocol, art. 15.1 & 16.1.

[62] See Vientiane Protocol, art. 9.

may argue that such approval is only a matter of formality because they follow the negative consensus rule.

As ASEAN is seeking to merge its economic agreements with the CJK countries under the RCEP,[63] the separate dispute settlement mechanisms under the individual agreements will need to be consolidated as well. Under the current agreements, each of the CJK countries has a separate dispute settlement mechanism with ASEAN on a bilateral basis. When one of the CJK countries has a dispute with the ASEAN countries, the other two CJK countries may not join the dispute settlement proceeding as co-complaints or third parties, but the other ASEAN countries may do so. In contrast, as the RCEP is a regional initiative, any of ASEAN's external partners will be able to join the dispute between an ASEAN country and another external partner. This will change the dynamics of the dispute settlement process and make individual ASEAN countries subject to more political pressures from external partners when they are involved in trade disputes.

To solve the problem, the author believes that ASEAN countries should use the opportunity of negotiating the RCEP to further strengthen the existing dispute settlement mechanism by making some structural changes. For example, ASEAN countries might consider changing the rule that each party nominates one panelist in a dispute, as this would politicize the dispute settlement process. Instead, the panelists shall be chosen from RCEP member countries that are not parties to the dispute. For this purpose, ASEAN countries might consider establishing an indicative list of panelists, or better still, setting up a permanent panel body, which shall be composed of one panelist nominated by each country in the RCEP. When a dispute arises, three panelists who are not nationals of the parties to the dispute shall be assigned to adjudicate the case on a random basis. This will ensure that panelists from ASEAN countries get more experience in dispute settlement, and will help to establish a rule-based system for the RCEP.

Also, under the current dispute settlement mechanisms, the costs of panel proceedings shall be split between the disputing parties. This might prevent smaller and poorer ASEAN countries from participating in dispute settlement proceedings as they do not have resources comparable to the non-ASEAN partners. ASEAN countries should propose changing it to the WTO model, i.e., a dispute settlement mechanism that is free for disputing parties and supported by the membership fees of member

[63] ASEAN Framework for Regional Comprehensive Economic Partnership (2012).

countries based on their respective trade volumes. This will help to alleviate the cost concerns for ASEAN members and make them more willing to participate in dispute settlement proceedings.

Of course, like any other dispute settlement mechanism, the success of the dispute settlement mechanisms in ASEAN's agreements with its external partners ultimately depends on the political will of ASEAN countries and their partner countries. However, other things being equal, a well-designed dispute settlement mechanism could help to depoliticize trade disputes and foster a culture of respect for the international rule of law among ASEAN and its partners. In the long term, the international rule of law provides the best way for ASEAN to achieve its aim of "maintain[ing] the centrality and proactive role of ASEAN as the primary driving force in its relations and cooperation with its external partners in a regional architecture that is open, transparent, and inclusive."[64]

[64] ASEAN Charter, art. 1 sec. 15.

PART 2

Services Trade and Financial Integration

5

Moving toward Liberalization: the ATISA and Beyond

BRYAN MERCURIO

5.1 Introduction

Statistically undercounted for decades, services play an important and growing role in the prosperity of both the domestic and world economy.[1] The growth of the services trade has, in large part, resulted from liberalization brought about by trade agreements. Without taking anything away from the difficulties in negotiating for the liberalization of trade in goods, trade in services is more complex for a host of reasons. Chief among these is that, in most cases, trade in services requires physical proximity and often interaction between the provider and consumer (cross-border trade – so-called Mode 1 – is the exception). The nature of this "behind the border" interface goes some way in explaining why nations restrict foreign providers' market access and give domestic providers preferences. The need to understand and to some extent untangle the web of regulations across areas which have traditionally been separate makes services negotiations even more complex and difficult. Yet another impediment is the diversity among the various service sectors and the multiplicity of market failures and regulatory frameworks to be taken into account in negotiations.

Services are incorporated into the multilateral system via the GATS, but incorporation into the WTO framework remains incomplete. Not only have issues such as subsidies, procurement and emergency safeguards been left for future negotiations, the agreement itself envisaged the progressive liberalization of initial market access and national

[1] The positive correlation between service sector share of GDP to per capita income is well-known. See e.g., Barry Eichengreen & Poonam Gupta, *The Two Waves of Service-Sector Growth*, Oxford Economic Papers (2011). For an example of a study demonstrating statistical undercounting, see Jane Drake-Brockman, *Access Through Presence: Australian Perspectives on Measuring Mode 3 Trade, in* Service Sector Reforms: Asia-Pacific Perspectives (Pierre Sauvé, Gloria Pasadilla & Mia Mikic eds., 2011).

treatment commitments. The "positive list" model of the GATS, whereby members select the sectors, subsectors and modes of supply which they are willing to liberalize combined with the negative listing of limitations to these commitments provides for a variable geometry of commitments between and among members. This approach also leaves gaps in coverage and a significant amount of protectionism. Thus, while the GATS provides a rich set of rules, the level of liberalization commitments is weak. With no meaningful advances to the GATS since its inception, services operate "with yesterday's rulebook [of] weak, incomplete, rules and the limited, regulatory precaution-laden, pre-internet, commitments of 1994."[2] Perhaps more discouraging, commitment offers made as part of the Doha Round of trade negotiations have been disappointingly shallow and unambitious.

Advancements in the level of commitments, architecture and WTO+ and WTO-X outcomes[3] have been achieved in bilateral and regional agreements.[4] In certain sectors, trade agreements have brought about increased market access opportunities for exporters and economic benefits for the liberalizing host country. But liberalization has not occurred across all sectors, and is somewhat disappointing overall. Sensitive sectors – including audio-visual, certain transport sectors and movement of persons – have seen few if any advances from the GATS. Likewise, in many FTAs (particularly South-South FTAs) liberalization commitments far too often "only marginally deepen," if at all, GATS commitments.[5] Even where significant

[2] Pierre Sauvé, *Towards a Plurilateral Trade in Services Agreement (TISA): Challenges and Prospects*, 5 (1) J. Int'l Commerce, Econ. and Pol. 1, 3 (2014).

[3] The term WTO+ refers to rules or market access commitments which go further than or qualitatively deepen existing rules or commitments. WTO-X refers to advances beyond those in the WTO. See Henrik Horn, Petros Mavroidis & Andre Sapir, *Beyond the WTO? An Anatomy of EU and US Preferential Trade Agreements*, Bruegel Blueprint Series Vol. VII (2009).

[4] Michael Gasiorek et al., *Qualitative Analysis of a Potential Free Trade Agreement between the European Union and India*, Centre for the Analysis of Regional Integration at Sussex (2007), http://trade.ec.europa.eu/doclib/docs/2007/june/Tradoc_135101.pdf (last visited Mar. 21, 2018) (noting India's 10 percent foreign equity ceiling in its Mode 3 Uruguay Round offer for certain key sectors, its 44.8 percent conditional offer in the Doha Round, and its applied rate of nearly a 70 percent ceiling in the sectors). See also Jeffrey Schott & Julia Muir, *Prospects for Services Trade Negotiations*, Peterson Institute for International Economics Working Paper, 12–17 (2012); Juan Marchetti & Martin Roy, *Service Liberalization in the WTO and in PTAs, in* Opening Markets for Trade in Services: Countries and Sectors in Bilateral and WTO Negotiations (Juan Marchetti & Martin Roy eds., 2008).

[5] Aaditya Mattoo & Pierre Sauvé, *The Preferential Liberalization of Services Trade*, NCCR Working Paper, No 2010/13, 57 (2010).

liberalization is achieved, there is the problem of "water," that is the gap level between the level of commitment and the applied regulatory norm. The prevalence of "water" led Roy, Marchetti and Lim to (somewhat bizarrely) conclude that FTAs "generally have provide [sic] for significant improvements over GATS commitments, *sometimes even leading to real liberalization of the market*" (emphasis added).[6]

There are now at least 122 trade agreements containing services, and the majority of new agreements include a comprehensive chapter. Most FTAs follow the negative list or positive list approach, with the former slightly outnumbering the latter and popular in the Americas and with developed countries (including select Asia-Pacific countries such as Australia, Japan, New Zealand and Singapore), and the latter popular with developing and most Asian countries (with the notable exception being the EU, which until recently favored the positive list approach). Under the negative list approach, parties liberalize all sectors and parts thereof except those identified in the "reservation lists," which preserve existing nonconforming measures (Annex 1) or make no/limited commitments to current or future measures, which can be maintained, modified or adopted (Annex 2) – the equivalent of an "unbound" in a positive list.

Although there is no reason why either approach should result in more or less liberalization than the other, there is solid evidence that the negative list approach results in substantially more liberalization than the positive list approach.[7] Of late, considerable architectural variation within and across FTAs has emerged, with experimentation in a growing number of agreements combining negative listing for investment or specific sectors while using a positive list for other sectors or modes of supply.[8]

[6] Martin Roy, Juan Marchetti & Hoe Lim, Services Liberalization in the New Generation of Preferential Trade Agreements (PTAs): How Much Further than the GATS?, WTO Staff Working Paper, ERSD-2006-07, 33 (Sep. 2006).

[7] See e.g., Martin Roy, Services Commitments in Preferential Trade Agreements: An Expanded Dataset, WTO Staff Working Paper, ERSD-11-18 (2011); Gary Hufbauer & Sherry Stephenson, *Services Trade: Past Liberalization and Future Challenges*, 10 (3) J. Int'l Econ. L. 605 (2007); Rudolf Adlung & Hamid Mamdouh, *How to Design Trade Agreements in Services: Top Down or Bottom-Up?*, WTO Staff Working Paper, ERSD-2013-08, 14–6 (2013).

[8] See generally Aaditya Mattoo & Pierre Sauvé, *Services, in* Preferential Trade Agreement Policies for Development: A Handbook 235–74 (Jean-Pierre Chauffour and Jean-Christophe Maur eds., 2011).

This chapter focuses on trade in services in ASEAN. For decades, trade in services has lagged due to government regulations, red tape and protectionism. The AFAS improved the situation, but the key in moving forward will be to incorporate new approaches/provisions as the Association transitions to the proposed ATISA. Following the objectives of the AEC Blueprint 2025 for a common market,[9] this chapter considers how the general rules can be improved to provide for greater transparency and good regulatory practices, increased liberalization and how to schedule commitments in a manner which reinforces the objectives of the AEC Blueprint 2025.

The chapter proceeds as follows: Section 5.2 reviews the structure and performance of the AFAS. While acknowledging that substantial progress has been made by AMS under the AFAS, the section also demonstrates that the Agreement has largely failed to provide meaningful liberalization or integration for ASEAN. Section 5.3 focuses on the proposed ATISA, which is currently under negotiation, and recommends the inclusion of several provisions which will help the AMS meet the goals of the AEC Blueprint. The recommendations focus on core principles such as most favored nation, transparency, liberalization targets and scheduling architecture rather than attempting to cover every potential negotiating topic.[10]

5.2 The ASEAN Framework Agreement on Services

The AMS have long recognized the importance of intra-ASEAN integration in the services sector, with the ASEAN Economic Ministers having signed the AFAS in 1995 in Bangkok, Thailand. Article 1 of the AFAS sets out the objectives:

- to enhance cooperation in services among Member States in order to improve the efficiency and competitiveness, diversify production capacity and supply and distribution of services of their service suppliers within and outside ASEAN;
- to eliminate substantially restrictions to trade in services among Member States; and

[9] Association of Southeast Asian Economic Community Blueprint 2025 (2015). See also, ASEAN Economic Community Blueprint (2007).

[10] For this reason, important issues such as rules of origin, government procurement and safeguards will not be discussed in this chapter.

- to liberalize trade in services by expanding the depth and scope of liberalization beyond those undertaken by Member States under the GATS with the aim of realizing a free trade area in services.

Despite these lofty goals, the AFAS merely set out a framework for liberalization between AMS through increased market access and national treatment. The ultimate success of the AFAS was always going to depend upon the will of the AMS to build upon the framework and continue liberalization efforts through actual commitments. The framework allowed for this to occur by covering all service sectors (later decisions ceded oversight of some sectors to other ministerial bodies/ mechanisms), and sought progressive liberalization "in a substantial number of sectors within a reasonable time-frame" by:

- eliminating substantially all existing discriminatory measures and market access limitations among Member States; and
- prohibiting new or more discriminatory measures and market access limitations.[11]

To date, successive rounds of negotiations (using progressively more stringent negotiating approaches to facilitate liberalization commitments) have culminated in nine packages of AFAS commitments.[12] These include a wide range of services sectors under the purview of the ASEAN Economic Ministers, such as business and professional services, construction, distribution, education, environmental services, healthcare, maritime transport, telecommunications and tourism. In addition to these AFAS packages, there have also been five packages of financial services commitments signed by ASEAN Finance Ministers and seven packages for air transport services signed by ASEAN Transport Ministers.

Consistent with the AEC Blueprint on Movement of Skilled Labor, ASEAN agreed to establish an MNP Agreement to facilitate movement of natural persons engaged in trade in goods, services and investments (signed in November 2012).[13] ASEAN has also established MRAs for selected professions: engineering, nursing services, architecture, land

[11] ASEAN Framework Agreement on Services, art. 3.

[12] The negotiations aim to achieve increasingly higher levels of commitment, which are set forth in service commitment packages annexed to the Framework Agreement.

[13] Operationalization of the Agreement on Movement of Natural Persons remains subject to ongoing discussion.

surveying, accountancy services, dental practitioners and medical practitioners.

The AEC Blueprint 2015 envisaged the removal of all restrictions to the trade in services by 2015, with priority sectors of air transport, healthcare, e-ASEAN and tourism and logistics having earlier timeframes of 2010 and 2013, respectively. Over the past decade, much work has been accomplished in successive negotiating rounds, notably in the expansion of the number of sectors to be liberalized and the deepening of liberalization commitments to include:

- no restrictions on service delivery via Mode 1 (cross-border trade) and Mode 2 (consumption abroad), except where there are bona fide regulatory reasons, such as public safety;
- gradual expansion of the foreign (i.e., ASEAN) equity participation permitted in each sector, to be no less than 70 percent by 2010 in the four priority sectors, and to be no less than 51 percent by 2010 and 70 percent by 2015 in all other sectors; and
- progressive removal of other limitations on market access via Mode 3 (commercial presence) by 2015.

The negotiators were also tasked with setting the parameters of liberalization and limitations on national treatment, liberalization of service delivery via Mode 4 (the movement of natural persons) and the liberalization of horizontal limitations on market access (i.e., limitations that apply across the range of services sectors), with commitments to be made in accordance with these parameters. While there were to be no *a priori* exclusions, the AEC Blueprint 2015 allowed for some flexibility in achieving these objectives, including via an ASEAN minus-X formula (where countries that are ready to liberalize can proceed first and be joined by others later) and a 15 percent margin of flexibility (from the eighth package).

On the positive side, the AFAS is the first FTA to experiment with formula-based market openings, most recently by adopting the liberalization packages and the ASEAN-X approach. ASEAN has also been innovative, such as through the use of variable geometry to market openings for certain members (e.g., Cambodia, Lao PDR, Myanmar and Vietnam). Overall, the AMS have shown themselves to be steady, if gradual, liberalizers while at the same time realistic in aims and willing to recognize the differing levels of development and capacity among members.

The aim of achieving the free flow of services by 2015 has not been met, and in the main, the performance of AFAS has not been particularly impressive or matched the expectations of traders. While the AFAS has achieved wider sectoral coverage than in the GATS, the rate of marginal preference is largely disappointing.[14] Likewise, the depth of commitments is on the whole rather meager. Furthermore, although ASEAN has attempted to improve transparency and predictability (such as by compiling and making available an inventory of barriers to trade in services to enhance transparency and identify limitations), these issues continue to hamper regional integration efforts and opportunities for traders.

That being said, it is important to realize that progress cannot simply be measured in terms of counting the number of sectors where commitments have been made and measuring the extent of the commitments[15] – such a count would give equal weight to each sector and mode of delivery, whereas some sectors and modes of delivery are more important than others in reality. For air and marine transport services, for example, Mode 1 is far more important than in the telecommunications sector, which relies on Mode 3. Mode 2, by contrast, is rarely if ever the most important.

Likewise, in every nation and economic partnership, some sectors and subsectors are far more important economically and politically than others. The comparative advantage of ASEAN is its linkages with the broader East Asian manufacturing and production networks as well as in the processing and export of primary products. Services that contribute to and advance productivity and efficiencies in these areas will be critical to continued success. For this reason, ASEAN priority sectors include air transport and logistics services. Other related key sectors would seem to include maritime and land transport, telecommunications, energy, insurance and finance. Even here, some subsectors (banking and insurance) are far more important than others (financial advisory services).

Most importantly, a simple count of commitments provides no indication of the effect on how actual policies, laws and regulations are applied. It is well known that there is significant "water" between commitments in services (and trade) and how policies, laws and regulations

[14] For comprehensive (if outdated) analysis, see Vo Tru Thanh & Paul Bartlett, Ten Years of ASEAN Framework Agreement on Services (AFAS): An Assessment, REPSF Project, No. 05/004 (2006).

[15] See Philippa Dee, *Does AFAS Have Bite? Comparing Commitments with Actual Practice*, 35 (C) J. Asian Econ. 1, 7–8 (2013).

are applied. Since commitments lag far behind practice, commitments extending beyond the GATS level may not result in economic gains. In this regard, Dee writes that "it remains an open question whether the services commitments under AFAS have been sufficiently bold to generate actual reform."[16] As a corollary, a simple count of commitments provides no signal of the work and reform still needed, whether at the domestic regulatory level or at the negotiating level, to resolve remaining difficulties and points of firm disagreement.

It is difficult to assess the actual result of liberalization commitments, and of actual practice versus commitments, due to the lack of sufficient information. In research conducted for the Economic Research Institute for ASEAN and East Asia, Dee gathered information reported by members and reached some conclusions on certain sectors. In some sectors, such as air transport and related sectors, commitments are minimal. Others, such as maritime transport, appear at first to be relatively liberalized, but several important restrictions remain upon closer inspection. These restrictions continue to hamper the integration of the regional network and deeper integration. Yet still in others, such as telecommunications, AMS remain cautious in their approach to liberalization, with substantial qualifications remaining even where a commitment has been made (especially in the key area of Mode 3). But here, the practice has gone beyond the commitments, which implies that the AFAS is not driving liberalization in the telecommunications sector and that there is scope for further commitments in the ATISA and subsequent negotiations.

Another important point to raise is that in more than a few cases, restrictions that do not exist in the AFAS schedules of commitments are being imposed. This seems most prevalent in the professional services, in particular accountancy, banking and insurance services. It also appears that unscheduled derogations from national treatment, in particular the discriminatory application of taxes and subsidies, have not been listed.[17] Such implementation lag, combined with non-AFAS related domestic regulations that further restrict market access, is harmful to the economy and unfriendly to business interests.

The picture of the AFAS is thus not altogether bright.[18] In fact, the World Bank's Services Trade Restrictiveness Index (STRI) database

[16] *Id.*, at 8.

[17] See in particular the medical and health services sector.

[18] See Thanh & Bartlett, *supra* note 14, at 39.

paints an unflattering picture of ASEAN's effective (i.e., applied) regulatory treatment of services.[19] Excluding Singapore, which operates a liberal regime and accounts for 51 percent of the region's services exports, ASEAN scores fairly poorly when measured against other regional groups overall, and particularly in important sectors such as banking, insurance, fixed-line and mobile telecommunications and retail distribution. In retail distribution, ASEAN ranked near the bottom, above only the Gulf Cooperation Council and the South Asia Free Trade Agreement. More worryingly, ASEAN scored at the bottom of all regional groupings in the maritime transport, accounting/auditing and legal sectors. The exception to these negative findings is the air transport (international) sector, where ASEAN is in the middle of the groupings. Just as worrying is the protection by modes, with the STRI showing little liberalization of Mode 2, with slightly better results for Modes 1 and 3. The above suggests that considerable scope exists for ASEAN members to offer deeper, competition-enhancing reforms in services markets in the ATISA (and FTAs with external partners).

5.3 Moving Forward: the ASEAN Trade in Services Agreement

Liberalization of trade in services and associated domestic reforms are fundamental to the realization of the AEC. The decision to establish the AEC has highlighted the need for AMS to remove restrictions affecting trade in services – including related foreign direct investment – and initiate related reforms. ASEAN's progress to date has been steady, but criticized for being too gradual and for not going far enough with liberalization targets and outcomes. There is also a feeling that intra-ASEAN liberalization has not received the same level of attention or ambition seen in some agreements negotiated by certain AMS with other nonparty countries. In addition, other issues have continued to plague progress, including opposition from domestic industry and sectors fearing displacement, weak regulatory oversight, confusion over necessary steps to liberalization, diversity of the member economies and demographics within the AMS.[20]

[19] It should be noted, however, that the STRI has been criticized for the limited number of subsectors it tracks and also for an inconsistent approach to data collection.

[20] Some of these issues are developed in Pierre Sauvé, Gloria Pasadilla & Mia Mikic eds., Service Sector Reforms: Asia-Pacific Perspectives (2011).

For these reasons, after two decades of AFAS, the ASEAN CCS committed to negotiating an enhanced and modern agreement, the ATISA. The ATISA offers ASEAN a once-in-a-generation opportunity to upgrade not only its trade in services agreement, but also the regulatory framework that operationalizes liberalization commitments. More specifically, owing to the nature of services, trade liberalization can be rendered valueless without a properly designed and functioning broader regulatory environment. In this regard, designing or maintaining a strong and well-functioning regulatory framework and environment can contribute to the aims of trade liberalization and indirectly to the aims of the AEC Blueprint for a common market. On the other hand, regulation which unnecessarily restricts competition – often the result of the regulator being closely tied or accountable to sectoral interests in the government or industry and in some cases of overlapping regulatory regimes – is a key impediment to economic growth. Impediments stemming from inappropriate regulation in the finance and several infrastructure-related service industries (telecommunications, energy, etc.) are well-known and thoroughly discussed in the literature.

This section will thus focus on strategies ASEAN could use to increase efficiency and combat unnecessarily restrictive effects on competition. The starting point of analysis will be that ambitious internal services commitments will lead to greater opportunities and economic growth. ASEAN has been consistent in this viewpoint, with such statements contained in official ASEAN documents. For instance, the ASEAN Vision 2020 (1997),[21] Bali Concord II (2003),[22] Bali Concord III (2011) and countless other documents envisage accelerated liberalization and integration of ASEAN and lay the initial groundwork for the attainment of these objectives.[23] The AEC Blueprint 2015 builds upon and encompasses the aims of these documents

[21] ASEAN Vision 2020 (1997).

[22] Declaration of Bali Concord II (2003). The Bali Concord II, in particular, declares that ASEAN "shall continue its efforts to ensure closer and mutually beneficial integration among its member states and among their peoples" and that it is "committed to deepening and broadening its internal economic integration and linkages with the world economy to realize an ASEAN Economic Community through a bold, pragmatic and unified strategy." Section B then sets out a goal of creating a "stable, prosperous and highly competitive ASEAN economic region in which there is a free flow of goods, services, investment and a freer flow of capital, equitable economic development and reduced poverty and socio-economic disparities in year 2020."

[23] These build upon the AFAS, which in itself reinforces the notion that trade liberalization and the ASEAN integration into a common market are at the core of its economic relations. See, in particular, the preamble.

and stresses the importance of liberalization of services and ultimate objective of the AEC:[24]

> Free flow of trade in services is one of the important elements in realizing ASEAN Economic Community, where there will be substantially no restriction to ASEAN services suppliers in providing services and in establishing companies across national borders within the region, subject to domestic regulations.

Statements made by high-placed officials consistently support the official documents. For example, Ong Keng Yong, Secretary-General of ASEAN, addressed the importance of services liberalization and integration for both internal and external benefits:[25]

> Trade in services cannot be isolated from trade in goods. The services sector is an indispensable part of our economies. Our growth in agriculture, manufacturing and natural resources production is dependent on the quality and spread of the related services. Indeed, without the services, we cannot grow. Without the services, our bargaining power is weakened. If we do not deal with the services sector, our economies will not be as attractive to the foreign investors. To put it very starkly, ASEAN's drive towards the AEC cannot be substantiated without a well-thought out policy of dealing with trade in services. Moreover, ASEAN cannot gain adequate leverage in its FTA negotiations with Dialogue Partners if we do not liberalize and accelerate ASEAN's trade in services.

Numerous other statements have recently been made, including that by the ASEAN Economic Ministers in 2014 which expressed determination and support for the "realization of the goals of ASEAN integration and commit[ment] towards advancing ASEAN's trade and investment facilitation and liberalization agenda so as to continue to bring prosperity and narrow the development gap in ASEAN."[26]

The objective of these documents and statements is clear – a deeply integrated economic community with free flow of trade and investment. These efforts have culminated in the AEC Blueprint 2025, which commends the AEC Blueprint 2015 for "advancing the services trade

[24] AEC Blueprint 2015.

[25] H. E. Ong Keng Yong, the Secretary-General of ASEAN, Towards a Free Flow of Services in ASEAN, Opening Speech (Jul. 5, 2005), www.asean.org/resources/2012-02-10-08-47-56/speeches-statements-of-the-former-secretaries-general-of-asean/item/towards-a-free-flow-of-services-in-asean-opening-speech-by-he-ong-keng-yong-the-secretary-general-of-asean (last visited Mar. 21, 2018).

[26] The Forty-Sixth ASEAN Economic Ministers' Meeting, Aug. 2014, Nay Pyi Taw, Myanmar, www.asean.org/images/Statement/2014/aug/JMS%20AEM%2046%20_Final.pdf (last visited Mar. 21, 2018).

liberalization agenda" but goes on to envisage a "deeply integrated and highly cohesive ASEAN economy," which will result in "more equitable and inclusive growth ... the principles of good governance, transparency, and responsive regulatory regimes."[27] The document also seeks to "reinforce ASEAN centrality in the emerging regional economic architecture by maintaining ASEAN's role as the center and facilitator of economic integration in the East Asian region [and] work towards a common position and enhance ASEAN's role and voice in global economic fora."[28]

The objective of the AEC is also clear – ASEAN seeks to "facilitate the seamless movement" of trade/investment and "create a unified market".[29] In order to meet this objective, the ATISA will need to "broaden and deepen services integration" in order to "facilitate industrial development, innovation, and efficiency [and] the maximization of potential contribution of the services sector to economic development and growth."[30] The AEC Blueprint 2025 also recognizes the importance of improving good governance, effective, efficient, coherent and responsive regulations and good regulatory practice in order to achieve its objectives.[31]

With these aims and objectives in mind, the remaining part of this section will set out issues and recommendations which should be borne in mind during the ATISA negotiations.

5.3.1 General Principles

Several general principles should be adopted to make the agreement more beneficial to AMS and more easily accessible and advantageous to traders.

5.3.1.1 Most Favored Nation

External partners that negotiate FTAs with ASEAN members tend to negotiate agreements with more ambition and which exceed the scope and depth of plurilateral negotiations with ASEAN. This is of course, rather curious, as one would expect a regional FTA among close partners to include a standard MFN clause. The AFAS does not contain a clause, but rather if one is to be read into the agreement it would be as a result of

[27] AEC Blueprint 2025, paras. 1, 6.
[28] *Id.*, para. 6.
[29] *Id.*, para. 7.
[30] *Id.*, para. 11.
[31] *Id.*, paras. 36–7.

Article XIV:1, which refers to and applies GATS where no specific provision has been written into the AFAS. If this is the case, the AFAS commitments in this regard are weak. This leaves only commitments made in an ASEAN FTA with a standard MFN clause, and not FTAs which AMS reach individually with external countries, subject to the provision. The fact that any commitment made in an ASEAN FTA automatically extends to all AMS – a built-in liberalization mechanism – ironically serves to discourage members from making deeper commitments in the plurilateral ASEAN-based negotiations.[32] Instead, AMS reserve their best offers for bilateral negotiations with third-party countries as such commitments are not then automatically extended to the other AMS.

The fact that AFAS+ commitments entered into by individual AMS with third countries do not flow back into ASEAN through an AFAS MFN clause is problematic for numerous reasons. One such reason is that negotiating partners have combated potential free riding by simply negotiating separate agreements with AMS prior to or in exclusion of negotiating with ASEAN (i.e., Japan and perhaps the European Union). In this regard, external partners can and are receiving preferences which exceed AFAS obligations in some sectors and subsectors. The completion and eventual coming into force of the CPTPP will exacerbate the problem (with Brunei Darussalam, Malaysia, Singapore and Vietnam as parties to the agreement). Moreover, as the larger service providers in the region enter the most FTAs, the commitments that would flow back to the other AMS would certainly benefit the community. In addition, the objective of the AEC is integration and a common market. While benefits may not flow equally to all members, the objective is to ensure ASEAN centrality and meaningful integration. These are at risk if members offer more preferable ATISA+ commitments to nonparty countries. For these reasons, the ATISA should enshrine the principle of MFN and ensure that any ATISA+ commitment made by one member to any external countries are automatically granted to all AMS.

It should be noted that a minority of FTAs include provisions which require a party to an agreement entering into a subsequent agreement and offering better terms/commitments to give consideration to a request by the other party or to enter into consultations regarding the possibility to extend the commitments to the original treaty partner – such a

[32] David Kleimann, *Beyond Market Access? The Anatomy of ASEAN's Preferential Trade Agreements*, 48 J. World Trade 629, 667 (2014).

provision exists in the ASEAN–Australia–New Zealand FTA (Chapter 8, Article 7). But given the objective of ASEAN integration, it is recommended that MFN clauses *automatically* apply and any ATISA+ commitment be granted to all ASEAN members.

5.3.1.2 Transparency

Services are heavily regulated and often subject to overlapping jurisdictional governance. Transparency disciplines in FTAs can lessen some of the confusion. Article 3 of the GATS sets out transparency obligations. Many FTAs also include an obligation to publish relevant measures and modifications as well as a requirement to notify partners of new measures potentially affecting trade in services. For the most part, these obligations are mere "best endeavors" rather than subject to dispute settlement.[33] Recent FTAs, most often with the United States as a negotiating partner, include requirements of a legally binding character.[34]

The AFAS contains no such disciplines on transparency other than the Article XIV:1 reference to GATS, which thus incorporates the GATS provisions into the AFAS. The lack of any substantial and direct provision in the AFAS undoubtedly played a role in one review concluding that "transparency in the AFAS can be viewed as relatively weak."[35] While some ASEAN members have agreed to certain transparency provisions in select FTAs, it is recommended that ASEAN follow the modern trend and impose legally binding transparency disciplines in the ATISA so as to demonstrate the seriousness of the ambition toward greater integration and a common market.

5.3.1.3 Market Access

In order to preserve the ambition of the AEC, it is imperative that the ATISA ensure genuine market access opportunities to traders. In short, the ATISA should offer greater market access opportunities than any existing trade agreement. For this reason, the ATISA should be an improvement on existing GATS commitments and Doha Round offers.[36]

[33] See e.g., Agreement Establishing the ASEAN-Australia-New Zealand Free Trade Area, Ch. 8, art. 11.

[34] See e.g., US–Colombia FTA, art. 11.8 and Ch. 19.

[35] Thanh & Bartlett, *supra* note 14, at 42.

[36] Several studies have shown that Doha Round offers remain significantly less ambitious than actual practice in many important sectors. See, e.g., Ingo Borchert, Batshur Gootiiz & Aaditya Mattoo, Restrictions on Services Trade and FDI in Developing Countries, World Bank, mimeo (2010).

Commitments should also not be allowed to be lower than in an FTA with any external country. Such standards should apply in all sectors and modes, including nondiscriminatory qualitative restrictions (which was an issue in some early agreements using a negative list approach).[37] Ideally, the ATISA will also commit members to scheduling market access and national treatment commitments to the prevailing regulatory norm, which would guarantee existing levels of access (so-called standstill).[38] In order not to discourage trial measures, the standstill clause could be made to be subject to exceptions to the extent that the members deem them necessary.

If the above recommendation is followed, the ATISA should be designed to automatically bind any subsequent liberalization (so-called ratchet). Again, the ratchet clause could be designed to take account of reservations for specified sectors, subsectors, or categories of measures.

The ATISA should be designed to automatically cover new services, which ensures a competitive environment as services develop and change over time. It is well understood, however, that the liberalization effect of such a design can and has been subject to significant reservations.[39]

5.3.1.4 Domestic Regulations, Convergence and Harmonization

Most FTAs do not seriously address the issues of domestic regulation, convergence and harmonization. If addressed at all, it is in a GATS Article VI-like manner focusing on procedural aspects of transparency and the prevention of measures that are unduly burdensome or a disguised restriction on trade. One exception is the European Union, which ensures through its internal rules that proportionality exists between regulatory means and objectives.[40]

37 See art. XVI of the GATS.

38 The use of a standstill clause is gaining momentum, and currently used in a number of agreements, including the EU–CARIFORUM and in all of Japan's recent bilateral agreements. For example, see CARIFORUM, Annex 4.VI(9).

39 See e.g., the US inclusion of an Annex in its FTAs that reserves its right "to adopt or maintain any measure that is not inconsistent with [its] obligations under Article XVI of the [GATS]."

40 This is foreseen in art. VI:4 of the GATS Agreement, which provides:

> With a view to ensuring that measures relating to qualification requirements and procedures, technical standards and licensing requirements do not constitute unnecessary barriers to trade in services, the Council for Trade in Services shall, through appropriate bodies it may establish, develop any necessary disciplines. Such disciplines shall aim to ensure that such requirements

This lack of convergence and harmonization is unfortunate, as regulations are diverse and have led to a problem of regulatory heterogeneity among trading partners. The diversity of regulations also creates additional problems, namely a lack of transparency and predictability for traders. The need for increased regulatory convergence and harmonization would seem even more appropriate to ASEAN as it progresses toward a common market. The AFAS does not specify any disciplines in domestic regulation.

Issues of licensing (requirements and procedures), qualifications, certification, standards, transparency and even special and differential treatment could be addressed in a more coordinated and progressive manner – again, with the aim of more complete integration of the ASEAN community. Drawing from the negotiating mandate in the Doha Round, and even incorporating by reference any future outcomes of the GATS Article VI:4 mandate, would be a starting point to approaching such issues. Yet it would be advantageous for ASEAN and its members to take a proactive approach to such issues so as to increase transparency and predictability, reduce costs and delays and improve efficiencies. This would, of course, include the expansion of breadth (e.g., to other sectors, such as tourism) and depth of MRAs in operation and those to be negotiated.

Moreover, by their very nature, most domestic regulations which are liberalized will be done on an (at least de facto) MFN basis. This will only add to the liberalization efforts. The reason is that for most countries it is simply neither feasible nor practical to maintain parallel regulatory regimes. For instance, when liberalizing a domestic regulation that limits the number of partners in a law firm to ten in an FTA, attempting to maintain it for non-FTA partners may result in undue compliance or enforcement costs.[41] This would also be the case for broader domestic regulations covering, among others, financial markets, consumer protection and the environment.[42]

are, inter alia: (a) based on objective and transparent criteria, such as competence and the ability to supply the service; (b) not more burdensome than necessary to ensure the quality of the service; (c) in the case of licensing procedures, not in themselves a restriction on the supply of the service.

[41] Pierre Sauvé & Anirudh Shingal, *Reflections on the Preferential Liberalization of Services Trade*, 45 J. World Trade 953, 959 (2011).

[42] *Id.*

5.3.2 *Specific Targets for Liberalization*

As mentioned, the AFAS includes specific liberalization targets. Continuing to do so in the ATISA is sensible, so long as it does not result in less ambitious commitments in the initial negotiations. The use of specific targets to liberalization can spur future negotiations and ultimately result in a richer set of commitments. But the targets themselves cannot be viewed as a panacea – they could very well lock in restrictions. For example, the 70 percent foreign equity limitation contained in the AFAS has not been free of implementation problems.

There are many different forms of specific targets for liberalization. For example, members should aim to schedule to the prevailing regulatory norm and allow for specific liberalization targets to progressively lower the restrictions. In this regard, the liberalization would not simply reduce "paper" restrictions, but would result in actual liberalization in furtherance of integration and the eventual common market. At the outset, the ATISA could also set out certain perimeters and a framework that establishes no *a priori* exclusion of sectors or modes of supply, the inclusion of regulatory disciplines, new rules and better offers than under previous negotiations and agreements.

Furthermore, the ATISA could build upon existing targets. For instance, members could commit to removing all market access and national treatment limitations on Mode 3, other than the 70 percent limit on foreign equity ownership. This perhaps seems more onerous than it is: where commitments have been made, a large number of AMS have already met this requirement in most sectors. In addition, while the framework set out to remove all but one limitation on national treatment per subsector in addition to the 15 percent margin of flexibility post-2015, it seems appropriate to establish a time period to remove the limitation and the flexibility. Targets could also be set for other existing exclusions (e.g., air transport services involving traffic rights).

Members should also consider setting out numerical benchmarks for future liberalization.[43] For instance, members could commit to removing *x* percentage of restrictions or to liberalize a minimum number of sectors within a set time period. Similarly, members should schedule further liberalizations in the Schedule in Commitment to ensure future liberalization through the use of so-called phase-in commitments. In this way, members commit to abolish existing restrictions or forgo the assumption

[43] In 2005, the GATS negotiators attempted to define numerical benchmarks, but without success. See WTO Document TN/S/M/16 (Oct. 28, 2005).

of new bindings by a specified period of time. Such phase-in commitments have been more popular in WTO accession commitment schedules than in FTAs; but the ATISA presents an opportunity for ASEAN to take the lead in this regard, which seems appropriate given the differing levels of development among ASEAN members.[44]

Moving to the focus for specific targets, it would seem appropriate to ensure particular attention is given to the priority sectors of tourism, healthcare, e-ASEAN, logistics and air transport. These sectors are important for growth in ASEAN, but it must also be stated that not all of them can be liberalized through trade policy alone. Cooperation from other regulatory agencies and departments would be necessary to achieve liberalization in quite a few of the sectors and subsectors. It is also recommended that key sectors with the highest levels of protection and with the most potential to produce economic gains be the focus of specific targets for liberalization. Such sectors would include distribution, energy, education, finance and even the thorny issue of cross-sectoral movement of persons.

Finally, members may wish to consider ways to deepen the liberalization packages in order to maximize returns. This would be done in combination with other negotiation-based deliverables such as a formula-based approach to market access and the removal of sector-specific or modal impediments (i.e., such as limitations on foreign equity or an economic needs test). Members may wish to consider ways to deepen the liberalization packages in order to maximize returns. One way to do so would be to utilize multi-sectoral clustering or the grouping of sectors with network properties. Examples of clustering would include sectors based around trade facilitation (transportation, distribution, customs brokerage, border management, etc.) and/or IT services, or both. Sectors with network properties would include waste disposal, water and energy and/or transportation-related services. The idea behind clustering and grouping is to simultaneously and holistically liberalize interdependent and interconnected and dependent sectors so as to increase efficiencies and economic gains. For some commentators, clustering represents a real opportunity to reshape the rules of the game in order to maximize efficiencies and gains.

44 Art. XX of GATS specifically allows the use of phase-in commitments.

5.3.3 *The 15 Percent Margin of Flexibility*

Announced in the "Joint Media Statement of the Forty-First ASEAN Economic Ministers Meeting" in August 2009, the 15 percent flexibility of the total modes of supply is not in line with the objective of an economic community:[45]

> The Ministers called for greater efforts to sustain the liberalization goals and looked forward to the recommendations of the Senior Officials on the parameters to liberalize the remaining limitations in trade in services in ASEAN by end of 2009. However, recognizing the need for flexibility, they endorsed the proposal for flexibility to be accorded to up to 15 percent of the total modes of supply in each package and to be used only as a last resort.

The reasons for adding this flexibility are not apparent from the statement and cannot be found on the ASEAN website or otherwise. The lack of explanation and transparency of the clause is cause for concern. Without full information, it is difficult to make a recommendation on whether the 15 percent margin of flexibility should be retained. However, the objectives of the AEC Blueprint 2025 and aims of the economic community suggest it should be eliminated.

If immediate elimination is impossible, it would seem practical and feasible to both disclose the justification for the flexibility and set a timeline in the ATISA for an orderly phase-out. In such circumstances, all members should be given a defined time period to phase out the flexibility and phase in the negotiated commitments. It may be that the members will differentiate between and among the membership, with some members being granted longer and staggered phase-out periods.

Moreover, as a legal matter, if the flexibility is not immediately eliminated the ATISA must anticipate and forestall any legal debate over the meaning of the clause. Thus, the text of the ATISA should fully explain the meaning of "up to 15 percent of the total modes of supply in each package" and, perhaps more importantly, of "to be used only as a last resort." In terms of the latter, at issue is deciding who is to determine whether this language equates to "necessary" or whether the flexibility was the "last resort." From a legal perspective, the vagueness of the flexibility is troubling and ripe for dispute. The ATISA must ensure clarity to prevent any dispute over the meaning of the flexibility, and ideally work toward its ultimate elimination.

[45] Joint Media Statement of the Forty-First ASEAN Economic Ministers' Meeting, Bangkok, Aug. 13–14, 2009, para. 24.

5.3.4 *Scheduling of Commitments*

Whatever one thinks of the merits of the positive list approach, it cannot be disputed that the trading world is moving beyond it to scheduling services commitments. Continuing to adhere to the positive list approach places ASEAN at a disadvantage vis-à-vis its trading partners and deepens a widening schism between ASEAN members. Countries that steadfastly maintain such an approach will be excluded from trade agreements being negotiated at this time. This includes not only ambitious bilateral and regional trade agreements, but also Geneva-based efforts such as the Trade in Services Agreement.[46] A negative list approach to scheduling should be utilized in the ATISA.

Some AMS, such as Singapore, are well versed and experienced in negotiating a negative list; others have begun the process through a "transparency list" approach (such as Brunei and the Philippines). Moreover, and perhaps most notably, Brunei, Malaysia and Vietnam have gained experience in the negative list approach in the Trans-Pacific Partnership, and its successor, the CPTPP. This willingness of a growing number of AMS to negotiate beyond a positive list approach could serve to isolate other members and could create disharmony within the economic community. Moreover, if some AMS are regularly scheduling using a negative list but others refusing to advance past a positive list, the impression of ASEAN as a unified trading bloc could be harmed, and its credibility as a trading group placed in doubt. Ultimately, ASEAN FTAs with external countries may be reduced to nothing more than a lowest common denominator agreement whereby members seeking actual liberalization and economic gains would negotiate separate bilateral agreements with the same external countries.

Moreover, a positive list approach to scheduling no longer seems in the wider interests of ASEAN. If a properly functioning economic community is the objective, then it is clear that ASEAN must take the necessary steps to do so. While a positive list approach is not theoretically less liberalizing than other approaches, in practice this is the case – almost without exception. Moreover, even a quick analysis of Singapore's

[46] It is noteworthy that one of the staunchest supporters of a positive list approach, China, agreed to use a negative list in its investment negotiations with the United States. This marks a departure from China's other 101 bilateral investment treaties. This decision, as well as the decision to grant national treatment in the "pre-establishment phase" of the investment, was reached at the US–China Strategic and Economic Dialogue in Jul. 2013. See further Len Bracken, *China Makes Market-Access Concession toward Investment Treaty with United States*, International Trade Daily, Jul. 12, 2013.

services commitments in various FTAs reveals that negotiating with a negative list approach yields more liberalization than does negotiating with a positive list approach.[47] The same is true when comparing the concessions of Singapore's partner countries.

The temptation to maintain a positive list approach is understandable – it is easier to be less ambitious and to entrench protections. One can, in theory, use the positive list approach to substantially liberalize services – but to do so requires immense political will to press ahead and resist the almost built-in expedients of the positive list approach. Moving into the unknown by adopting a negative list approach can be daunting, but proper preparation and careful planning can ensure a smooth transition.

There are also important qualitative differences between formats. Most notably, the negative list approach can have a positive effect on good governance.[48] The reason for this is clear, under a positive list approach the scheduling country does not have to supply information to trading partners relating to its current level and nature of discriminatory or access-limiting measures and regulations. Connected to this is the fact that the scheduling country can then make commitments which are below the prevailing norm/regulatory status quo.

This is to be contrasted to the negative list, which in Annex I requires the scheduling country to list reservations to liberalization in the form of the nonconforming measures. In this regard, not only is the negative list approach of Annex I more transparent, but it also only allows for reservations on *existing* nonconforming measures. In this regard, the negative list locks in the regulatory status quo and avoids the situation where commitments are below the prevailing regulatory framework (such treaties often contain a ratchet clause that automatically reduces reservations as the regulatory framework changes, thereby locking in future liberalization).[49] It has been suggested that such mechanisms lend credibility to a country and positively impact the flow of foreign direct investment, as investors are not only well-informed but are also assured against a reversal in policy.

[47] An exception is Singapore's FTA with Japan, which uses a positive list but is more liberalizing than Singapore's negative list agreement with Australia.

[48] See further Mattoo & Sauvé, *supra* note 8; Richard Baldwin, Simon Evenett & Patrick Low, *Beyond Tariffs: Multilateralizing Non-Tariff RTA Commitments, in* Multilateralizing Regionalism: Challenges for the Global Trade System (Richard Baldwin and Patrick Low eds., 2009); Sherry Stephenson, *Regional versus Multilateral Liberalization of Services*, 1 (2) World Trade Review 187 (2002).

[49] The standstill clause and ratchet mechanism now appear in South-South FTAs, such as in the agreements for Andean and CARICOM.

The requirement to list the nonconforming measures as a reservation is important, as it provides governments, traders and investors with useful and important information. Moreover, the requirement is also important, and beneficial, to the home country for a host of reasons – better interdepartmental and governmental communication, greater understanding of domestic impediments, easier to negotiate using a formula-based approach in the future, etc.[50] In addition, the generation of useful information can lead to dialogue between and among the various government departments and industries involved in the diverse range of service sectors and allow for a "regulatory audit" of measures, which will allow benchmarking against regional and international standards.

It should be noted that Annex II of the negative list is less transparent, as it allows a country to adopt, modify or maintain any nonconforming measure – the equivalent of the positive list "unbound." While some FTAs require the listing of existing nonconforming measures in Annex II, it is far from the norm. Moreover, several countries with a federal structure of government make use of Annex II to reserve all subnational laws and regulations, which can eliminate entire sectors (i.e., insurance, energy) from the scope of the liberalization commitments in the treaty.

Of course, the negative list approach has other hindrances in addition to Annex 2 being less transparent. The information gathering and coordinated approach to scheduling are administratively difficult and burdensome. Such burdens and difficulties may be, in the short term, beyond the capacity of some developing countries. The detrimental effects of such burdens could perhaps be outweighed by the benefits from improved governance and information garnered from the increased cooperation and a regulatory audit.

Moreover, there is a concern that by locking in to the regulatory status quo of an existing nonconforming measure in Annex 1, the scheduling country is thereafter prevented from introducing additional discriminatory or access-reducing measures. Given the amount of regulatory experimentation occurring in some developing countries, this is a valid concern.

A related concern is that the negative list approach also locks in liberalization and prevents the introduction of new measures even for

[50] See Mattoo & Pierre Sauvé, supra note 8; Pierre Sauvé & Simon Lacy, *A Handbook on Negotiating Preferential Service Agreements: Services Liberalization* (2013).

sectors that did not exist or were not regulated when the agreement was negotiated. While use of an Annex 2 list will go some way to assuaging concerns, there is of course negotiating pressure to limit the amount of reservations in that list.

In pushing toward an integrated ASEAN, members must recall that liberalization in services is unlike that of goods. For example, the long-term advantages that accrue to partner countries from preferential access in services are not necessarily reversed through the subsequent extension of benefits to other countries. This is because of the natural limit in the number of viable suppliers in certain sectors and because location-specific sunk costs play an important role in numerous sectors. Long-term advantages of preferential access include first mover status, better access to discretionary licenses, access in other regulated areas (particularly where no GATS commitments have been made), and familiarity with the supply chain network, with the customer base and with societal and business norms.

Likewise, Fink and Mattoo identified the importance of sequencing of liberalization in services due to the location-specific costs often necessary to establish and operate in most service sectors. This is especially the case with services, such as energy distribution, telecommunications and transportation, requiring large and expensive infrastructure or networks and where even temporary preferential access provides long-term market advantages and discourages market entrants.[51]

It should also be mentioned that other forms of scheduling exist. The least ambitious break from the positive list approach is the transparency list, used in conjunction with a positive list. With this approach, the parties agree to make public a nonbinding list, drafted in a format closely resembling that of an Annex 1 reservations document under a negative list approach, setting out all existing inconsistent measures. In addition to being nonbinding, the transparency list cannot be used against the scheduling country in dispute settlements or otherwise.[52]

In recent years, many hybrid forms of scheduling have emerged from bilateral and regional FTAs. These include variations from a positive list approach, requiring a negative list for national treatment while maintaining a positive list for market access, placing market access in an Annex II. Commitments can be subject to a positive list approach or

[51] Carsten Fink & Aaditya Mattoo, *Regional Agreements and Trade in Services: Policy Issues*, World Bank Policy Research Working Paper, No. 2852 (Jun. 2002).

[52] See e.g., Japan–Brunei Economic Partnership Agreement, art. 82.

maintaining a positive list approach for some sectors while adopting a negative list for other sectors. These are worth consideration, but it must be recognized that every hybrid introduces a level of complexity and potential confusion. For this reason, careful consideration and drafting must accompany any attempt to design or use a hybrid approach to scheduling commitments.

The architecture of the ATISA, together with the ambitions of member commitments, will determine whether the opportunity for reform is grasped or missed. Adopting a negative list approach will provide the AMS with the most appropriate tool to achieve the objectives of the AEC Blueprint 2025 and attain a meaningful AEC.

5.4 Conclusion

ASEAN has come a long way since 1992 in opening market access opportunities and working toward a more integrated community. Liberalized trade and a tighter economic community have contributed to the rising economic prosperity of AMS. The AEC Blueprint 2025 envisages even greater integration and economic community. The services sector could play a large role in contributing to future economic growth and ultimately in determining the success of the economic community. With the negotiation of the ATISA to replace the AFAS, ASEAN has a once-in-a-generation opportunity to provide a solid foundation for trade in services, growth and interconnectivity among AMS.

Negotiating the ATISA will not be a simple task. Services are inherently different from and more complicated to negotiate than goods. In many sectors, impediments to liberalization and integration are not trade barriers but rather well-entrenched domestic regulations. Further complicating negotiations is the fact that ASEAN consists of a diverse group of nations, all proud and culturally rich but at varied stages of economic development and with vastly different interests. To date, ASEAN has taken the less controversial but less ambitious route to trade in services and taken a GATS-style, positive list approach to scheduling commitments in its AFAS. This is understandable, as such a format is easier to negotiate than a negative list and requires less preparation and intergovernmental coherence. It also results in fewer commitments, meaning less liberalization, and restrained economic integration.

The trading world and several AMS have moved beyond a positive list approach to scheduling commitments. This has resulted not only in more liberalization, but also in increased transparency and predictability for traders. ASEAN should take the opportunity of the transition to the ATISA and embrace the objectives of the AEC Blueprint 2025. The ATISA should set ambitious targets for liberalization; and while ASEAN's makeup may necessitate variable geometry, such deviations from targets should be limited, clear and transparent. The ATISA should also contain an MFN clause guaranteeing that members receive the most favored treatment even if an individual member negotiates a separate FTA with another country or countries. Market access should be substantial, and the ATISA should ensure that commitments are not scheduled below the existing regulatory standard and status quo; in other words, members should not be allowed to have or maintain any gap between the applied regulations at the conclusion of the negotiations and what appears in the ATISA schedule. If exceptions and pullbacks to this principle are included in the agreement, they should be clear, transparent and limited. The ATISA should also include strongly worded clauses on transparency, as well as make a genuine attempt to strengthen regulatory coherence and MRAs in order to improve the efficiency of services and opportunities for traders.

The ATISA should move beyond the traditional positive list approach to scheduling commitments. The positive list approach is proven to deliver lower returns than other formats and will continue to do so absent extreme political will. A negative list approach to scheduling offers the AMS the best chance to achieve meaningful results. Regardless of scheduling format, the ATISA must ensure that information regarding reservations is available to governments and traders; transparency and predictability in itself can lead to greater efficiencies and economic growth.

The opportunity to redesign and craft the trade in services regime should not be treated lightly or squandered – trade in services has the potential to play a much larger and more sustained role in regional trade and growth. Its liberalization will not only benefit traders but also enhance economic growth among members and region-wide. It is understandable for AMS to be apprehensive as ASEAN transitions from the AFAS to the ATISA, but in order for the region to maintain and build upon its position as a trading bloc, it must be ambitious and not allow protectionist tendencies to override long-term opportunities. The risk of not showing leadership and ambition is that ASEAN as a trading group becomes the lowest common denominator, with the real market access opportunities coming from and being given to external partner countries. Such a situation can and should be avoided. The ATISA can and should be an ambitious twenty-first century agreement that accounts for the differing levels of economic development among the AMS and delivers economic growth and prosperity for the entire region.

6

Challenges of ASEAN MRAs on Professional Services

YOSHIFUMI FUKUNAGA*

6.1 Introduction

The primary objective of this chapter is to assess the implementation of MRAs on professional services of ASEAN to discuss challenges and ways forward. Other recent trends related to the movement of skilled labor are also briefly reviewed in the course of the discussion.

In 2007, the ASEAN leaders created their vision for a realization of the AEC.[1] The first pillar of the AEC Blueprint 2015, "a single market and production base," lists a variety of free-flow policies including free flow of skilled labor.[2] Several points on ASEAN's policies on the movement of labor should be noted. First, the AEC covers only skilled labor. A "migrant worker" (i.e., unskilled labor) issue, centering on the protection of rights, is considered a sociocultural community agenda.[3] Second, the AEC Blueprint 2015 limits its scope to allowing for "managed mobility or facilitated entry for the movement of natural persons."[4] Third, MRAs on professional services are understood as policy measures to achieve free flow of services rather than free flow of skilled labor.[5]

The idea to develop MRAs on professional services dates back to 1995, as mentioned in the AFAS.[6] It took ten years for ASEAN to come up with

* This chapter is built upon the background paper for the ASEAN Economic Community Scorecard Phase IV project of the Economic Research Institute for Association of Southeast Asian Nations and East Asia (ERIA). The author appreciates all the support from the ERIA and participants in the project.

1 ASEAN Economic Community Blueprint (2007).

2 *Id.*, para. 9.

3 ASEAN Declaration on the Protection and Promotion of the Rights of Migrant Workers (2007).

4 AEC Blueprint 2015, *supra* note 1, para. 33.

5 *Id.*, para. 21.

6 ASEAN Framework Agreement on Services (1995); as amended by the Protocol to Amend the ASEAN Framework Agreement on Services (2003), art. 5.

the first MRA on professional services, i.e., ASEAN MRA on Engineering Services,[7] signed in 2005. Since then, ASEAN has developed eight MRAs on eight professional services: engineers, nurses,[8] architects,[9] surveyors,[10] accountants,[11] medical practitioners,[12] dentists[13] and the tourism profession.[14]

These eight MRAs can be categorized into four groupings. The first category takes a three-step registration process in which a license or a certification originally recognized in a home country is recognized and registered at the ASEAN level before a license or a certificate is issued in a host country. ASEAN MRAs on engineers, architects and accountants fall into this category.[15] The second group of ASEAN MRAs, which covers nurses, medical practitioners and dental practitioners, does not establish a regional registration system.[16] Instead, a home country qualification can be recognized directly in a host country. The third pattern of ASEAN MRAs provides a single-step registration at the regional level (i.e., no country-level registration exists). The ASEAN MRA on Tourism Professionals falls into this category.[17] The last category is a framework agreement which provides only a framework for negotiating a future full-scale MRA. The surveyor profession remains at this framework agreement stage.[18]

ASEAN MRAs are quite different from those of the European Union and of Australia–New Zealand (Trans-Tasmanian arrangement).[19] In the European Union and Australia–New Zealand Closer Economic Relations Trade Agreement, there is "free movement of people." MRAs on

[7] ASEAN Mutual Recognition Arrangement on Engineering Services (2015).
[8] ASEAN Mutual Recognition Arrangement on Nursing Services (2005).
[9] ASEAN Mutual Recognition Arrangement on Architectural Services (2007).
[10] ASEAN Framework Arrangement for the Mutual Recognition of Surveying Qualifications (2007).
[11] ASEAN Mutual Recognition Arrangement Framework on Accountancy Services (2009); ASEAN Mutual Recognition Arrangement on Accountancy Services (2014).
[12] ASEAN Mutual Recognition Arrangement on Medical Practitioners (2009).
[13] ASEAN Mutual Recognition Arrangement on Dental Practitioners (2009).
[14] ASEAN Mutual Recognition Arrangement on Tourism Professionals (2012).
[15] ASEAN MRA on Engineering Services, art. 3; ASEAN MRA on Architectural Services, art. 3; ASEAN MRA on Accountancy Services, art. 4.
[16] ASEAN MRA on Nursing Services, art. 3; ASEAN MRA on Medical Practitioners, art. 3; ASEAN MRA on Dental Practitioners, art. 3.
[17] ASEAN MRA on Tourism Professionals, art. 3. See Section 6.4 of this paper for detail.
[18] ASEAN Framework Arrangement for the Mutual Recognition of Surveying Qualifications, *supra* note 10.
[19] ASEAN Handbook on Liberalization of Professional Services through Mutual Recognition in ASEAN: Engineering Services 19–23 (2015).

professional qualifications further facilitate such movement. ASEAN, in contrast, does not allow for the general movement of people; thus, the MRAs are also constrained by immigration regulations.

Several ASEAN initiatives are closely related to the MRAs. The first and most important is the ASEAN MNP Agreement signed in 2012.[20] ASEAN MRAs do not ensure the actual movement of professionals due to a lack of a clear link with immigration regulations. If implemented incorrectly, MRAs can hinder the actual movement of professionals (e.g., by setting many conditions). The MNP Agreement has a large potential to address such problems and facilitate the movement of skilled labor in the services sectors. The AQRF is another new initiative which potentially facilitates the implementation of ASEAN MRAs in the future, although not directly linked with the MRAs.

This chapter is structured as follows. Sections 6.2, 6.3 and 6.4 discuss and analyze the implementation of ASEAN MRAs on Engineering Services, Nursing Services and Tourism Professionals, respectively. In addition, these sections will look into the potential challenges faced by MRAs. Section 6.5 briefly reviews recent developments in two areas, namely the ASEAN MNP Agreement and the AQRF, and discusses the relevant measures provided in the new blueprint.[21] Section 6.6 articulates policy proposals for furthering ASEAN MRAs. Section 6.7 briefly discusses the implications of ASEAN MRAs for wider regional integration initiatives.

6.2 ASEAN MRA on Engineering Services

The ASEAN MRA on Engineering Services,[22] signed and entered into force on December 9, 2005,[23] is the first ASEAN MRA. The objectives of the MRA are to facilitate the mobility of engineering services professionals and to exchange information in order to promote the adoption of

[20] ASEAN Agreement on the Movement of Natural Persons (2012). The MNP Agreement does not cover any nonservices sector. Thus, large areas of manufacturing, which sits at the core of ASEAN single market and production base, are not covered at all in this new instrument.

[21] ASEAN, Kuala Lumpur Declaration on ASEAN 2025: Forging Ahead Together (2015); ASEAN Economic Community Blueprint 2025 (2015).

[22] ASEAN MRA on Engineering Services, *supra* note 7.

[23] ASEAN Legal Instruments, agreement.asean.org (last visited Jul. 30, 2017). The Agreement requires member states' individual notification of participation (art. 8.3). With the participation of Brunei Darussalam in January 2013, all member states have joined this initiative.

best practices.[24] The two objectives may conflict with each other; for example, when a best practice leads to stricter regulation.

The MRA sets up a three-step registration system: home country registration, ASEAN registration and host country registration. Professional engineers can apply to become an ACPE if they meet the qualifications (e.g., an engineering degree, a national registration and seven years of experience after graduation).[25] An ACPE shall then be eligible to apply and become an RFPE in the host country.[26] An RFPE, if approved, can practice the profession, but only in collaboration with local professionals.[27] In terms of institutional setups, regional and national institutions are involved. At the regional level, the ACPECC and its Secretariat are in charge of administering the MRA.[28] In each country, a monitoring committee and a Professional Regulatory Authority (PRA) are involved. The former takes the main responsibility in the national administration of the MRA in the home country (e.g., setting criteria and procedures to be an ACPE).[29] The latter's main role is the administration of RFPEs in the host country (e.g., approving ACPEs as RFPEs).[30]

The regional implementation has progressed smoothly: the ACPECC has been established, the Secretariat formed, the registration procedures for ACPEs established and the ACPECC website built.[31] As a result, ACPE registration is active with more than 2,000 ACPEs registered in total.[32] It is unknown whether or to what extent these regional activities have resulted in the adoption of best practices, which is the second objective of the MRA.[33]

The first element of national implementation of the MRA is whether a country has completed all the required actions to recognize the engineers certified in their respective jurisdiction as ACPEs. Such actions include submission of notification of participation,[34] establishment of a monitoring committee,[35] preparation and submission of Assessment

24 ASEAN MRA on Engineering Services, art. 1.
25 *Id.*, art. 3.1.
26 *Id.*, art. 3.3.1.
27 *Id.*, art. 3.3.2.
28 *Id.*, art. 4.3.5.
29 *Id.*, art. 4.1.
30 *Id.*, art. 4.2.
31 ACPE Coordinating Committee, http://acpecc.net/v2/ (last visited Aug. 12, 2017).
32 *Id.*
33 ASEAN MRA on Engineering Services, art. 1.2.
34 *Id.*, art. 8.3.
35 *Id.*, art. 4.2.

Statements[36] and screening and approval of domestic applicants by ACPE.[37] All the countries have completed these processes.[38] The second element of national implementation assessment is whether a country prepares its domestic regulation to accept ACPEs as RFPEs and implements such procedures.[39] The information is mixed on this point. According to a book published by the ASEAN Secretariat in 2015, Myanmar, the Philippines and Thailand have some rules for RFPE registration.[40] In addition, the ACPECC website shows that there are RFPE registrations taking place in Malaysia and Singapore.[41]

The ASEAN MRA on Engineering Services aims to facilitate the mobility of engineering services professionals as well as the exchange of information to promote the adoption of best practices on standards and qualifications.[42] However, since the signing of the Arrangement in 2005, only a small number of engineers have applied and registered as RFPEs in order to actually move across the ASEAN region.[43]

Although a lag in implementation is a contributing factor, it is by no means the sole factor for the low usage of RFPE registration. The larger problem is the fact that the MRA provides only limited benefits for engineers who wish to work overseas. There are other ways for engineers to work overseas than registering as ACPEs, and then as RFPEs. For example, Malaysia allows foreign engineers to work as professional engineers by applying for registration as Temporary Engineers,[44] regardless of whether such foreign engineers are ASEAN citizens or ACPEs. Similarly, some 30 percent of professional engineers registered in

36 Although the legal text of the ASEAN MRA on Engineering Services is not explicit in this point, the ACPECC website implies such a requirement by showing the status of the Assessment Statements by country. See ACPE Coordinating Committee, *supra* note 31.

37 ASEAN MRA on Engineering Services, art. 4.1.

38 ACPE Coordinating Committee, *supra* note 31.

39 ASEAN MRA on Engineering Services, art. 4.1.1.

40 Handbook on Liberalization of Professional Services through Mutual Recognition in ASEAN: Engineering Services, *supra* note 19, at 54, 68 and 75.

41 ACPE Coordination Committee website, *supra* note 31. There are seven RFPEs in total (one in Malaysia, two in the Philippines and four in Singapore). Unfortunately, the date of information is not provided. There is a contradicting statement in an academic paper in 2015 which claims that "there are no RFPEs actually registered in Singapore." See Hank Lim, Bernard Aw & Hoe Yeong Loke, *AEC Scorecard Phase IV: Furthering the Implementation of the AEC Blueprint Measures the Singapore Country Report*, ERIA Discussion Paper Series 2015–47 (2015), at 71.

42 ASEAN MRA on Engineering Services, art. 1.

43 See *supra* note 41.

44 Handbook on Liberalization of Professional Services through Mutual Recognition in ASEAN: Engineering Services, *supra* note 20, at 46.

Singapore are foreigners; none of them are registered as an RFPE.[45] Moreover, foreign engineers may work simply as consultants or corporate employees without violating domestic regulation by, for example, not signing legal documents.[46]

Fortunately, the financial cost of using the MRA is not prohibitive.[47] Some countries do not require any additional qualification for ACPEs to become RFPEs.[48] Yet, the current MRA does not ensure mobility because an RFPE must go through the immigration and work permit application processes separately.[49] The ASEAN MRA in principle does not give a right for independent practice.[50] Taking all these factors into consideration, the benefit of ASEAN MRAs as compared to alternative schemes may not be compatible with the cumbersome three-step registration.

6.3 ASEAN MRA on Nursing Services

The ASEAN MRA on Nursing Services, signed and entered into force on December 8, 2006,[51] is selected in this paper as an example of the three ASEAN MRAs on healthcare services. The objectives of the MRA are to facilitate the mobility of nursing services professionals within ASEAN, to enhance the exchange of information and expertise on standards and qualifications, to promote the adoption of best practices for professional nursing services, and to provide opportunities for capacity building and training of nurses.[52] Unlike the case of engineering services, this MRA does not aim at establishing a regional registration system of nurses (i.e., there is no "ASEAN Nurse" registration to be established).[53] Nurses registered in one ASEAN country may apply in another AMS to be

45 Lim, Aw & Loke, *supra* note 41, at 71.

46 Although not explicitly referring to engineers, a paper on the Indonesian implementation of AEC measures on services indicates such a situation in the context of architects and nurses. See Yose Rizal Damuri, *Services Sector Development in Indonesia and the Implementation of AEC Measures in Services*, CSIS Working Paper Series, WPECON-201603 (2016), at 16.

47 Taking the case of Thailand, the ACPE registration costs $100, while the RFPE registration fee is 4,000 Thai baht. See Sawowaruj Rattanakhamfu et al., *Thailand Country Study: ASEAN Economic Community Blueprint Mid-term Review Project*, ERIA Discussion Paper Series 2015-46 (2015), at 85.

48 Lim, Aw & Loke, *supra* note 41, at 68.

49 AFAS, art. 9.2.

50 MRA on Engineering Services, art. 2.9.

51 ASEAN Legal Instruments, *supra* note 23.

52 ASEAN MRA on Nursing Services, art. 1.

53 *Id.*, art. 3.

registered as a "Foreign Nurse" in the host country if they meet several conditions (e.g., a valid professional registration in the country of origin and a minimum three years of experience).[54] As such, the MRA on Nursing Services only takes a two-step approach.

As no regional registration system is to be developed, the regional actions designated in the MRA on Nursing Services are quite different from those stipulated in the MRA on Engineering Services. By June 2007, ASEAN established the ASEAN Joint Coordinating Committee on Nursing (AJCCN),[55] which has the mandate to facilitate the implementation of the MRA, among others.[56] The AJCCN has met more than twenty times since its inception, which has resulted in several milestone achievements.[57] In 2009, the AJCCN agreed on five domains of the ASEAN Nursing Common Core Competencies.[58] A dedicated website for AJCCN has been established, which compiles information about national regulations on nurses.[59]

As the MRA does not aim to establish a regional registration scheme, the national actions expected to be taken by each AMS differ from those for engineers (e.g., no monitoring committee is to be established). Thus, the major national implementation consists of regulatory reforms, including the establishment of procedures to recognize foreign nurses and the dissemination of such information to the public.[60]

Regulatory revisions are taking place in ASEAN to bring national regulatory schemes into conformity with the regional framework.[61] All the AMSs actually allow foreigners to provide nursing services in their territories in some way.[62] For example, Malaysia issues a temporary

[54] *Id.*, art. 3.1.

[55] ASEAN Joint Coordinating Committee on Nursing, AJCCN Achievements (2007–2015), www.asean.org/wp-content/uploads/2012/05/Summary-of-AJCCN-Achievement-2007-2015-Regional-and-National.pdf (last visited Aug. 11, 2017).

[56] ASEAN MRA on Nursing Services, art. 4.2.1.1.

[57] ASEAN Joint Coordinating Committee on Nursing (twenty-first meeting), *supra* note 55.

[58] Nursing Services (AJCCN), http://asean.org/asean-economic-community/sectoral-bodies-under-the-purview-of-aem/services/healthcare-services/nursing-services-ajccn/ (last visited Aug. 10, 2017).

[59] *Id.*

[60] National regulatory authorities involved in the implementation of the MRA were designated. See ASEAN MRA on Nursing Services, art. 2.6.

[61] ASEAN Joint Coordinating Committee on Nursing, *supra* note 55, 1–5. At least Brunei, Indonesia and Lao PDR revised their respective laws or regulations in 2014.

[62] ASEAN Joint Coordinating Committee on Nursing, *Temporary Licensing for Foreign Nurses*, www.asean.org/wp-content/uploads/images/2015/september/ajccn/AJCCN%20web-1%20Policy%20of%20Temporary%20Licensing%20for%20Foreign%20Nurses%2018th%20AJCCN.pdf (last visited Aug. 11, 2017), at 2–3.

practicing certificate to "a person who is registered as a nurse outside Malaysia" with the approval from the Nursing Board.[63] The Indonesia Nurses Act also allows foreign nurses to practice in Indonesia by proving their competences and acquiring a temporary STR (Certificate of Registration) and an SIPP (License for Practice of Nurses).[64] Typically, the period of such a temporary certificate is one year with the possibility of renewal.[65]

It is important to note, in the context of assessing the value of ASEAN MRAs, that those arrangements do not give preferential treatment to ASEAN citizens. For example, Section 18 of the Malaysian Nurses Act (Admission to the Register of person trained outside Malaysia) uses the word "any person . . . trained in any place outside Malaysia."[66] Section 10 of the Act (Temporary practicing certificate) does not distinguish ASEAN nurses vis-à-vis nurses registered in non-ASEAN countries.[67] Thus, the current framework does not give special attention to ASEAN, at least in the legal text.

Theoretically, there is a possibility that qualifications in other AMSs are considered favorable in the actual approval process of individual professionals. In most countries, a fundamental condition for foreign nurses to be registered in the host country is that their training in the country of origin is equivalent to that in the host country. The deeper understanding about nursing qualifications among the AMSs generated through AJCCN activities may facilitate such equivalent recognition or even convergence of such a training requirement.

Due to the lack of a regional registration system, there is no information about the usage of the ASEAN MRA on Nursing Services. Furthermore, as national regulations do not give privileges to ASEAN citizens, the impact of the ASEAN MRA on the actual movement of nurses across the ASEAN region is unknown.[68] Having said that, some studies show that there is movement of nurses in ASEAN, whether using the ASEAN MRA or otherwise. For example, 77 percent of non-Singaporean registered nurses are ASEAN citizens in Singapore,[69] and the share of ASEAN citizens is

[63] Malaysian Nurses Act 1950 (Act 14), sec. 10.

[64] Indonesian Nurses Act (Law Number 38 of 2014), arts. 24 & 25.

[65] ASEAN Joint Coordinating Committee on Nursing, *supra* note 62, 1–2.

[66] Malaysian Nurses Act 1950, *supra* note 63, sec. 18.

[67] *Id.*, sec. 10

[68] For example, while the Singapore Nursing Board publishes data on foreign nurses, it does not provide information about the origins of these foreign nurses. See Singapore Nursing Board, *Annual Report 2016* (2016), at 10.

[69] Lim, Aw & Loke, *supra* note 41, at 76.

increasing rapidly.[70] In contrast, there are officially no foreign nurses working in Indonesia as of 2016 despite the ASEAN MRA.[71] Just like engineers, many foreign nurses actually work in Indonesia as consultants.[72]

As one of the objectives of the ASEAN MRA on Nursing Service is to "promote adoption of best practices on professional nursing services,"[73] it is natural that some of these also aim to raise the standards required for professionals. These sometimes include changes that potentially reduce the movement of nurses across the region. In Indonesia, for example, all relevant regulations have been revised since the adoption of the ASEAN MRA.[74] However, the current regulations effectively limit foreign nurses in the provision of nursing services (only limited to specialists).[75] This is probably a result of concerns that Indonesian nurses will not be able to compete with an influx of foreign counterparts due to the relatively lower standards of nursing education in Indonesia. With the adoption of the Nursing Act in September 2014, together with other programs, Indonesia is aiming to raise the quality of Indonesian nurses.[76]

6.4 ASEAN MRA on Tourism Professionals

The ASEAN MRA on Tourism Professionals,[77] signed in 2012, is the eighth and newest MRA in ASEAN. The MRA entered into force in 2013.[78] All the Member States completed national procedures to join this endeavor by April 2016.[79]

"Tourism professions" cover as many as thirty-two job titles.[80] These job titles include both hotel services (front office, housekeeping, food production and food and beverage service) and travel services (travel agencies and tour operations).[81] For each type of service, there are four to

[70] *Id.*, 79.
[71] Damuri, *supra* note 46, at 16.
[72] *Id.*
[73] ASEAN MRA on Nursing Services, art. 1.3
[74] Damuri, supra note 46, at 16.
[75] *Id.*
[76] Indonesian Nursing Act, art. 3. Improvement of the quality of nurse and nursing service are the primary objectives of the Act.
[77] ASEAN MRA on Tourism Professionals.
[78] ASEAN Legal Instruments, *supra* note 23.
[79] *Id.* Art. IX (Final Provision) of the ASEAN MRA on Tourism Professionals requires a member state to establish a tourism professional certificate board (TPCB) and a national tourism professional board (NTPB) before the MRA becomes effective to that country.
[80] ASEAN MRA on Tourism Professionals, Appendix.
[81] *Id.*

seven different levels of services (e.g., from bellboy to front office manager for the front office), which add up to thirty-two in total.[82] It is important to note that "tour guide" was intentionally dropped from the scope.[83] Tour guide is a regulated profession in some countries to ensure tour guides' knowledge and understanding of their country's/region's history and culture. And so, the MRA covers only nonregulated professions. For instance, there is no regulation to become a bellboy or a waiter. Thus, the meaning of this MRA is quite different from all the other ASEAN MRAs that cover regulated professions.

The MRA on Tourism Professionals emphasizes common competency standards and a common curriculum.[84] Based on the ASEAN Common Competency Standards for Tourism Professionals,[85] ASEAN has established a Common ASEAN Tourism Curriculum.[86] Using the toolboxes for each job title, master trainers and master assessors are trained at the regional level, followed by national training for trainers and assessors. These regionally recognized trainers and assessors will train tourism professional candidates. After completing training, a professional is assessed and certified by a Tourism Professional Certification Board (national governmental body). Only then can the professional be recognized as a "Foreign Tourism Professional" in the ASEAN terminology. ASEAN has established the ASEAN Tourism Professional Registration System, which is a web-based facility to register foreign tourism professionals. The system also provides a matching function between jobseekers (Foreign Tourism Professionals) and potential employers. A legal instrument supporting the regional registration system was signed by tourism ministers in 2015.[87]

[82] *Id.*

[83] *Tour Guides Not Allowed to Work Freely in ASEAN*, VietNamNet Bridge, Oct. 22, 2014, http://english.vietnamnet.vn/fms/business/114732/tour-guides-not-allowed-to-work-freely-in-asean.html (last visited Feb. 26, 2018).

[84] ASEAN Mutual Recognition Arrangement on Tourism Professionals Handbook 13–26 (2013).

[85] *Id.*, at 13–18.

[86] *Id.*, at 19–26.

[87] Agreement on the Establishment of the Regional Secretariat for the Implementation of the ASEAN Mutual Recognition Arrangement on Tourism Professionals, signed in Jakarta, Indonesia (Dec. 30, 2015). The agreement is not effective yet as of the time of writing and is waiting for five Member States (Indonesia, Myanmar, the Philippines, Singapore and Vietnam) to complete their respective national procedures. See ASEAN Legal Instruments, *supra* note 23.

The ASEAN Secretariat's handbook lists various benefits for tourism professionals and the industry.[88] The first benefit is the facilitation of mobility of the tourism professionals based on tourism competency qualifications or certificates.[89] However, regional registration does not ensure job opportunities as the host country government has discretion in whether to recognize the eligibility to work in the country or not. On the other hand, regional recognition can help potential employers (e.g., hotels) to find professionals from other AMSs who meet certain standards by dramatically reducing information costs.

There are other benefits aside from the mobility of professionals: (1) enhancing conformity of competency-based training/education, (2) recognizing skills of tourism professionals, (3) improving the quality of tourism human resources and (4) enhancing the quality of tourism services.[90] The ASEAN MRA functions as a regional initiative to set and enhance quality standards in this unregulated profession.

6.5 Other Recent Developments

This section summarizes recent developments in ASEAN in the area of movement of skilled labor: the ASEAN MNP Agreement and the AQRF. Furthermore, ASEAN's vision for the second phase of the AEC building is discussed.

6.5.1 ASEAN MNP Agreement

The ASEAN Economic Ministers signed the ASEAN MNP Agreement in 2012,[91] a comprehensive Mode 4 services agreement. It specifies four types of movement of natural persons which can be potentially committed: (1) business visitors, (2) intracorporate transferees, (3) contractual service suppliers and (4) other categories as may be specified in the commitment schedules.[92] The Agreement covers all the

88 ASEAN Mutual Recognition Arrangement on Tourism Professionals Handbook, *supra* note 84, at 5.

89 *Id.*

90 *Id.*, at 4–5.

91 ASEAN MNP Agreement. The MNP Agreement does not cover any nonservices sector. Thus, large areas of manufacturing, which sits at the core of the ASEAN single market and production base, are not covered at all in this new instrument.

92 *Id.*, art. 2.1.

services sectors but does not cover nonservices sectors, despite the broader objective scope of the Agreement.[93] It also provides several clauses for procedural improvements, e.g., processing of applications and transparency.[94]

Most of the commitments focus on business visitors and intracorporate transferees.[95] All ASEAN countries have made commitments for intracorporate transferees and seven of them have made commitments for business visitors, except for Brunei Darussalam, Myanmar and Singapore.[96] Only a few countries (Cambodia, the Philippines and Vietnam) have made commitments for contractual services suppliers. The number of committed sectors varies across countries. Out of 154 services sectors, Brunei Darussalam and Cambodia have made commitments in as many as 153 sectors while Myanmar committed only in 59 sectors.[97] On average, AMSs have made liberalization commitments in 111 out of 154 sectors (i.e., 72.1 percent sectoral coverage), which is much broader than the sectoral coverages in the AFAS Eighth Package[98] (80.8 sectors on average, totaling 52.5 percent).[99] The depth of commitments (e.g., initial length of stay) differs among AMSs.[100]

6.5.2 ASEAN Qualifications Reference Framework

One of the challenges in facilitating the movement of natural persons, whether professionals or skilled labor, is the differences in national qualifications across countries. Such qualifications cover not only the licensing and certification aspects, but also broader qualifications such as basic education, technical and vocational training and higher education. ASEAN's new initiative, the AQRF, provides a possible solution to this

[93] *Id.*, Preamble, provides that it facilitates the movement of natural persons "engaged in the conduct of trade: in goods, trade in services, and investment" and hence does not limit the scope to trade in services.

[94] *Id.*, arts. 5 and 8.

[95] Yoshifumi Fukunaga & Hikari Ishido, *Values and Limitations of the ASEAN Agreement on the Movement of Natural Persons*, ERIA Discussion Paper Series, No. 2015–20 (2015).

[96] *Id.*, at 8–9.

[97] *Id.*

[98] Protocol to Implement the Eighth Package of Commitments under the ASEAN Framework Agreement on Services (2010). Until the ASEAN MNP Agreement came into force in 2016, member states made Mode 4 commitments in AFAS, which were superseded by the MNP Agreement. ASEAN MNP Agreement, art. 6.2.

[99] Fukunaga and Ishido, *supra* note 95, at 8–9.

[100] *Id.*, at 13.

situation.[101] The AQRF Governance and Structure, endorsed by three ministerial meetings in 2016, provides basic information about the AQRF.[102] The AQRF Committee, a regional governance body of AQRF, was established in February 2017.[103]

The AQRF is a regional common reference framework, which enables the comparison of national qualifications across the region. In the Indonesian education system, for example, there are diplomas called "S1" (a general high school diploma) and "D IV" (a vocational senior high school diploma). Are they equivalent to the "NC III," "NC IV" or "Diploma" of the Philippines?[104] The AQRF sets an eight-level regional qualification framework and links national qualifications to the regional ones.[105] The number of levels of national qualification frameworks differs among the Member States.[106]

One of the objectives of AQRF is to "support mobility," and as such the AQRF is recognized as complementing and supporting ASEAN MRAs.[107] As most ASEAN MRAs utilize national qualifications as the basis for regional recognition,[108] equivalence of national education and training is the key to the success of ASEAN MRAs. The AQRF thus helps facilitate the development of ASEAN MRAs. Furthermore, while the AQRF does not issue any regional certification, it certainly supports recognition of qualifications. As ASEAN MRAs cover only eight professional services, the AQRF has the potential to facilitate the movement of skilled labor outside the eight professions while waiting for the ninth MRA, which may take another decade.

The AQRF is considered voluntary in nature.[109] In the next step, ASEAN aims to establish referencing to the AQRF of at least two AMS by

[101] ASEAN Qualifications Reference Framework, http://asean.org/asean-economic-community/sectoral-bodies-under-the-purview-of-aem/services/asean-qualifications-reference-framework/ (last visited Aug. 5, 2017).

[102] ASEAN Qualifications Reference Framework: Governance and Structure, http://asean.org/storage/2017/03/ED-01-AQRF-Governance-and-Structure-document.pdf (last visited Aug. 12, 2017).

[103] ASEAN, Press Release of the First AQRF Committee Meeting, http://asean.org/asean-to-facilitate-regional-recognition-of-qualifications/ (last visited Aug. 5, 2017).

[104] Teresita R. Manzala, The ASEAN Qualifications Reference Framework (presentation uploaded on the website of Catholic Educational Association of the Philippines), http://ceap.org.ph/upload/download/20138/27222725873_1.pdf (last visited Aug. 5, 2017).

[105] ASEAN Qualifications Reference Framework, *supra* note 101.

[106] *Id.*

[107] *Id.*

[108] The ASEAN MRA on Tourism Professionals is the exception to this.

[109] ASEAN Qualifications Reference Framework, *supra* note 101.

2018.[110] In other words, no one can actually utilize the AQRF to compare national qualifications yet.

6.5.3 *ASEAN Economic Community 2025*

As the deadline of AEC 2015 approached, the ASEAN leaders adopted a new blueprint, the AEC Blueprint 2025, in November 2015.[111] The AEC Blueprint 2025 follows the basic structure of the previous blueprint, although the naming of pillars has changed. The first pillar in the AEC Blueprint 2015 was "a single market and production base" including the free flow of skilled labor. Now, the first pillar of the new blueprint is named as "a highly integrated and cohesive economy" that includes "facilitating movement of skilled labor and business visitors."[112]

Several points should be noted in this new blueprint. First, although the phrase "free flow" has disappeared, this does not, by itself, necessarily mean that ASEAN has lowered its ambitions. The AEC Blueprint 2015 stated its aim as "managed mobility or facilitated entry for the movement of natural persons"[113] and thus is better described as measures "towards a single market and production base."[114] Second, ASEAN MRAs on professional services, the AQRF and the ASEAN MNP Agreement are the main measures for achieving the "facilitating movement of skilled labor and business visitors."[115] Other measures listed in the AEC Blueprint 2015, such as facilitation of visa issuance,[116] are not explicitly mentioned. ASEAN documents are silent about the progress or achievement of these measures.[117] Third, the AEC Blueprint 2025 provides for four policy measures: (a) expand and deepen the commitments under the ASEAN MNP Agreement *where appropriate*; (b) reduce, if not standardize, the documentation requirements; (c) improve the existing ASEAN MRAs *if necessary*; and (d) *consider feasibility* of new MRAs.[118] As the wording indicates, ASEAN is cautious in committing to new measures in

[110] AQRF Governance and Structure, *supra* note 102, at 7.
[111] AEC Blueprint 2025.
[112] *Id.*, at 3 & 10.
[113] AEC Blueprint 2015, para. 33.
[114] Ponciano Intal, Jr. et al., ASEAN Rising: ASEAN and AEC Beyond 2015 120 (2014).
[115] AEC Blueprint 2025, para. 19.
[116] AEC Blueprint 2015, paras. 33–4.
[117] A Blueprint for Growth ASEAN Economic Community 2015: Progress and Key Achievements (2015). For the free flow of skilled labor agenda, ASEAN MRA on Engineering Services is recognized as the milestone achievement.
[118] AEC Blueprint 2025, paras. 20–21. Emphasis added by author.

the area of movement of skilled labor. Finally, several measures regarding the ASEAN MRA on Tourism Professionals, such as the expansion of covered job titles, are to be implemented by 2018.[119]

In sum, while ASEAN continues its efforts in the existing policy measures especially in terms of implementation, it faces challenges in advancing further toward a "free flow of skilled labor." The tourism profession, which covers mostly unregulated professionals, is a significant exception.

6.6 Policy Recommendations on ASEAN MRAs

This section provides policy recommendations on ASEAN MRAs based on the analyses in the earlier sections.

6.6.1 Increase the Benefits of ASEAN MRAs

One of the main problems hindering the actual usage of MRAs is the small benefits of ASEAN MRAs. A natural policy option, when taking the movement of professions as a serious policy objective, is to increase the benefits of ASEAN MRAs. In particular, alternative legal schemes should be taken as reference points in considering additional and real benefits. One possibility is to allow independent practice. Some countries are open to the possibility of independent practice in the case of architectural services. Another way to improve quality is to link ASEAN MRAs with visa or work permit processes. NAFTA provides an interesting model.[120] While NAFTA requires a visa in general, it provides a special facilitation measure for those who are recognized in NAFTA MRAs, that is, the nonimmigrant NAFTA visa.[121] A condition is that the applicant will work in a prearranged full-time or part-time job for an employer, and self-employment is not permitted. ASEAN may also consider systematic linkage between the ASEAN MRAs and the ASEAN MNP Agreement commitments. While these two measures are

[119] ASEAN Economic Community 2025 Consolidated Strategic Action Plan, Feb. 6, 2017, http://asean.org/aec-2025-consolidated-strategic-action-plan/, at 34 (last visited Feb. 26, 2018).

[120] See Handbook on Liberalization of Professional Services through Mutual Recognition in ASEAN: Engineering Services, *supra* note 19, at 87. A similar recommendation is included in this book.

[121] US Department of State, *Visas for Canadian and Mexican NAFTA Professional Workers*, https://travel.state.gov/content/visas/en/employment/nafta.html (last visited Aug. 12, 2017).

complementary to each other, there is no clear relationship between the two. For example, the MNP commitments in these sectors do not mention ASEAN MRAs and the commitment level is actually lower than the overall average liberalization level. The two instruments should be "synergized" with each other. Similarly, consistency between MRA and liberalization commitments in other modes of services, especially Mode 3 (commercial presence), should be well maintained to promote the actual movement of qualified professional services in the region.

6.6.2 *Identify Best Practices Regulations*

A most serious source of challenge in the movement of professionals is the variance in national regulations. Thus, in the long run, regulatory convergence should be considered at the ASEAN level. While all ASEAN MRAs aim to exchange information to adopt best practices,[122] such activities have not taken place. Best practices, which by nature are not binding, can provide a reference point to be used in comparing each country's regulation and, over time, can help national regulations converge across the region. Such a tool is established in the competition policy.[123] ASEAN should consider identifying the best practice regulations on regulated professions. In doing so, forming ASEAN-level professional associations can be a powerful tool.

6.6.3 *Involve All Stakeholders in a Policy Discussion*

Professional associations play critical roles in policy discussions on ASEAN MRAs. However, such discussions are dominated by professional associations and regulatory bodies (which often consist of members of the same professions), and can be easily captured by a protectionist mindset due to the fear of competition from foreigners. Service industries are increasingly understood as critical inputs to manufacturing in regional production networks. High quality and competitive price of construction are key factors for any factory. The users of professional services (e.g., manufacturing industries in the case of architects and engineers) should be duly involved in policy discussions.

[122] Tan Tai Hiong of the ASEAN Secretariat emphasized this aspect (best practice adoption) of the ASEAN MRAs, ASEAN Law Conference, Dec. 7, 2017 at Singapore Management University.

[123] ASEAN Regional Guidelines on Competition P*olicy* (2010).

6.6.4 *Expand the MRA to Cover Unregulated Professions*

An MRA is typically meant to give foreign professionals a local license or authorize the local practice of a profession. Yet, that is not the only benefit of MRA. It motivates member countries to review their qualification requirements, education and training programs. As a regional program, it encourages Member States to share their respective national regulatory (educational or other) practices. If a regional registration system is established (as they have been in the cases of engineers, architects and tourism professionals), it bridges the information gaps between potential employers and potential employees and thus enhances the mobility of skilled labor. These benefits, except for local licenses, can be pursued in unregulated professions as well. The ASEAN MRA on Tourism Professionals is a good example. It covers all tourism professionals except for tour guides, which are often regulated by law in host countries. It is not a typical MRA, as it has started building regional education and training programs for the professions to be implemented at the national level. An electronic regional registration system is expected to facilitate the job-matching process. Thus, one possible way forward for ASEAN is to expand MRA coverage to unregulated professions based on the experience of tourism professionals.

6.7 Implications for Asia-Pacific Integration

Several initiatives for wider regional integration are taking place in the Asia-Pacific region. First, while ASEAN has signed six FTAs with non-ASEAN economies: ASEAN-Australia-New Zealand FTA,[124] ASEAN-China FTA,[125] ASEAN-India FTA,[126] ASEAN-Japan FTA,[127] ASEAN-Korea

[124] Agreement Establishing the ASEAN-Australia-New Zealand Free Trade Area (2009). While the Agreement provides for a special chapter on the movement of natural persons (Ch. 9), the chapter on services (Ch. 10) does not set up MRAs.

[125] In terms of trade in services: Agreement on Trade in Services of the Framework Agreement on Comprehensive Economic Cooperation between the People's Republic of China and the Association of Southeast Asian Nations (2007). Only a general provision on recognition is included in the Agreement (art. 6).

[126] In terms of trade in services: Agreement on Trade in Services under the Framework Agreement on Comprehensive Economic Cooperation between the Association of Southeast Asian Nations and the Republic of India (2014). The Agreement encourages relevant bodies to prepare MRAs (art. 6.3).

[127] Agreement on Comprehensive Economic Partnership among Member States of the Association of Southeast Asian Nations and Japan (2008). The services chapter (Ch. 6, art. 50) is quite general and thus does not provide specific clauses on MRAs.

FTA[128] and a recently signed ASEAN-Hong Kong FTA,[129] none of them have set up an MRA on professional services. Second, ASEAN and six partners are in the process of negotiating the RCEP.[130] It is not known whether the negotiators are preparing a scheme for an MRA on professional services. Third, twelve countries in the Asia-Pacific region signed the TPP Agreement in 2016.[131] The TPP Agreement, which forms the basis of the CPTPP, pays special attention to the mobility of businesspersons with a special chapter on temporary entry for businesspersons.[132] The TPP Agreement also stipulates provisions on professional services (Annex 10-A).[133] A Professional Services Working Group is to be established to facilitate activities toward recognition of professional qualifications, licensing or registration.[134] While specific professions to be discussed in the Working Group are not stated in the Agreement, there is an indication that engineers and architects will be covered.[135]

ASEAN MRAs on professional services apparently go deeper as compared to these regional integration efforts. While ASEAN MRAs could provide rich insights to the future discussion of movement of professional services in a wider region, there should be much more effort made for ASEAN to show centrality.

[128] In terms of trade in services: Agreement on Trade in Services under the Framework Agreement on Comprehensive Economic Cooperation Among the Government of the Member Countries of the Association of Southeast Asian Nations and The Republic of Korea (2007). Article 6 of the Agreement provides a general clause on recognition.

[129] Free Trade Agreement between Hong Kong, China and the Association of Southeast Asian Nations (2017). While the agreement includes a clause on recognition of qualification requirements, qualification procedures, licensing and/or registration procedures for professional services, it does not set up any concrete mechanism to realize such recognition (Ch. 8, art. 6).

[130] Guiding Principles and Objectives for Negotiating the Regional Comprehensive Economic Partnership (2012). The participating non-ASEAN countries are China, Korea, Japan, Australia, India and New Zealand.

[131] Trans Pacific Partnership Agreement (2016).

[132] *Id.*, Ch. 12.

[133] *Id.*, Annex 10-1.

[134] *Id.*, at paras. 1–4 & 11.

[135] *Id.*, at paras. 5–7.

7

Banking Integration in ASEAN and the Challenges of Regulatory Cooperation

FEDERICO LUPO-PASINI

7.1 Introduction

An integrated market cannot exist without a thriving financial sector being able to channel capital where it is more needed and at competitive prices. Thus, when ASEAN leaders declared their goal to achieve a single ASEAN Economic Community by 2015, financial services were rightly seen as a key pillar of this regional economic architecture. This chapter will deal with probably the most important type of financial service in ASEAN: banking.

As of 2012, banks occupied the center stage in the ASEAN financial sector, accounting for around 80 percent of total financial assets.[1] However, compared with other regions of the world, the ASEAN banking sector was lagging behind. One of its main problems was the relatively low level of intra-ASEAN banking penetration, as the slice of the domestic market occupied by foreign banks was, and still is, mostly dominated by Asia-Pacific banks.[2] The lack of ASEAN "banking champions" among the elite groups of global banks was rightly seen as a barrier to the development of the regional banking market. More importantly, it was perceived as a potential obstacle for the evolution of ASEAN as a global player in financial rulemaking within the Financial Stability Board or the Basel Committee on Banking Supervision, the two main standard-setting organizations for the banking sector. Not surprisingly, the AEC Blueprint 2025 puts the creation of "indigenous ASEAN banks" as one of the key strategic measures to achieve an integrated and stable regional financial sector.[3] For

[1] Choong Lyol Lee & Shinji Takagi, *Assessing the Financial Landscape for the Association of Southeast Asian Nations Economic Community*, Asia and the Pacific Policy Studies 116, 120 (2014).

[2] Geert Almekinders, Satoshi Fukuda, Alex Mourmouras, Jianping Zhou & Yong Sarah Zhou, *ASEAN Financial Integration*, IMF Working Paper WP/15/34, 11 (2015).

[3] Association of Southeast Asian Nations Economic Community Blueprint 2025 (2015), sec. 17(i).

these reasons, the governors of the ASEAN Central Banks decided to enhance the efforts for the progressive regionalization of the banking market in 2015, with a vision of a single banking market by 2030 in which ASEAN banks could compete with the larger Australian, Chinese and European global banks.[4] How can ASEAN achieve this goal?

The history of European banking integration has taught very important lessons on the risks and challenges of creating a truly single banking market. The process of financial integration – and banking integration in particular – is a complex and multidimensional policy puzzle that needs to combine different areas including trade policy, investment protection, monetary policy and financial regulation.[5] Above all, it needs to combine different policy objectives that, very often, are difficult to reconcile. In the case of ASEAN, these challenges are augmented by the huge differences in the level of banking development and banking openness between countries. As I will demonstrate in this chapter, these differences impact profoundly on the political, economic and legal strategy of banking integration adopted by ASEAN, and can be rightly considered as the real economic underpinnings of ASEAN's unique model of banking integration. Unlike other experiences of regional banking integration, the ASEAN model entails very limited sacrifice of financial sovereignty, and it is based on a multispeed approach that favors preferential (often bilateral) cooperation rather than region-wide regulatory and policy convergence.

The chapter will be structured as follows: I will first discuss the challenges inherent to banking integration with regard to systemic risk and the fundamental role of policy cooperation in Section 7.2. I will then explain in Section 7.3 how economic and legal asymmetries among ASEAN countries require a discriminatory and preferential approach to regional banking integration. I will then introduce the question of supervisory cooperation in Section 7.4 and the financial trilemma in Section 7.5. The last part, Section 7.6, will discuss the ASEAN solution to the trilemma.

[4] ASEAN, Press Release, Joint Statement of the First ASEAN Finance Ministers' and Central Bank Governors' Meeting Kuala Lumpur, Malaysia, Mar. 21, 2015, Theme: Our People, Our Community, Our Vision, ASEAN Press Releases on Finance and Banking, www.asean.org/asean-economic-community/asean-finance-ministersmeeting-afmm/press-releases-statements/ (last visited Mar. 21, 2018).

[5] Bart De Meester, Liberalization in Banking Services: An International and European Perspective (2014).

7.2 Integration and Global Systemic Risk

The process of banking integration in ASEAN has a relatively short history that starts with the 2003 decision to progressively open ASEAN members' banking sectors to regional competition.[6] In the context of ASEAN law, this is currently dealt with under the AFAS, which includes eight packages of commitments on banking services.[7] As stated in the AEC Blueprint 2025, AFAS will probably be replaced in the future by the more ambitious ATIGA, which is nevertheless still largely under negotiation.[8] Like any agreement on trade liberalization, the AFAS sets out a platform whereby members commit to open their banking sectors to other ASEAN banking services providers by removing unnecessary regulatory and administrative requirements.[9] Banking liberalization alone through AFAS, however, was not sufficient to spur the growth of pan-ASEAN regional banks and increase banking integration in the region. Indeed, like the WTO General Agreement on Trade in Services, the AFAS does not deal with the real issues affecting banking integration: regulatory and supervisory policies.[10]

Prudential regulations and supervision are the bedrocks of banking policy. A good supervisory and regulatory framework can determine the direction of the entire financial and macroeconomic policy of a country.[11] Different bank capital requirements, for instance, can affect the level of liquidity in the market and the overall riskiness of the banking system. Concentration limits, another critical aspect of prudential policy, prevent banks from lending to or investing in certain sectors or assets classes beyond a certain point.[12] Supervisory rules and practices too are

[6] ASEAN, *Roadmap for Monetary and Financial Integration of ASEAN (RIA-Fin)*, ASEAN Finance Ministers Meeting in 2003.

[7] ASEAN Framework Agreements on Services (1995).

[8] AEC Blueprint 2025, sec. 17(i)(a).

[9] For a good overview, see Bryan Mercurio, *ASEAN Services Liberalization beyond 2015: Assessment and Recommendations*, Nathan Associates (Mar. 2016), www.nathaninc.com/sites/default/files/ASEAN%20Trade%20in%20Services%20Liberalization.pdf (last visited Mar. 16, 2018).

[10] Art. 2 of the GATS Annex on Financial Services explicitly excludes prudential regulation and other policies affecting consumer protection and financial stability from the scope of WTO law.

[11] Eddy Wymeersch, Klaus Hopt & Guido Ferrarini eds., Financial Regulation and Supervision: A Post-Crisis Analysis (2012); David Llewellyn, *Role and Scope of Regulation and Supervision, in* Handbook of Safeguarding Global Financial Stability: Political, Social, Cultural, and Economic Theories and Models (Gerard Caprio Jr. ed., 2013).

[12] John Armour, Dan Awrey, Paul Davies, Luca Enriques, Jeffrey Gordon, Colin Mayer & Jennifer Payne, Principles of Financial Regulation (2016), Chs. 3 and 26.

crucial to keep a financial system stable as they determine which credit institutions are licensed and allowed to participate in the financial system, and the penalties associated with the violation of banking laws and regulations. Not surprisingly, given the pivotal role banks play in shaping the economic trajectory of a country, both prudential regulation and bank supervision are historically kept as strictly national prerogatives with very little international harmonization.[13] Yet, asymmetries in national regulatory and policy requirements have a tremendous effect on the decision of a bank to operate abroad and, in turn, on the level of banking integration.

Like ASEAN, the European Union also considered financial integration as a key element for the completion of the European Single Market in the 1980s.[14] The experience of the European Union is particularly instructive of the various possible strategies to bypass regulatory discontinuities.[15] European authorities relied on three main mechanisms: mutual recognition of regulations, home country control and, later on, the Single Passport program. In the early days of the European banking market there was no single rulebook for banking. Indeed, Member States regulated and supervised their banks independently, with no substantial harmonization. The first strategy of European authorities, then, was to allow states to mutually recognize each other's regulatory banking frameworks in order to allow national banks licensed in one Member State to operate in another Member State without the need of the host country's regulatory approval. This was then complemented by home country control, whereby the home supervisor was competent for the supervision of domestic banks' branches abroad.

Both mutual recognition and home country control operationalize an extraterritorial application of domestic law into the partner country's territory, as they stretch the regulatory and supervisory powers of the home regulator to the countries where the multinational bank operates.[16] This strategy, however, soon proved not to be enough for the European Commission's ambition of a fully integrated market and, for this reason,

[13] Federico Lupo-Pasini, The Logic of Financial Nationalism: International Cooperation and the Role of International Law (2017); Federico Lupo-Pasini, *Financial Stability in International Law*, 18 Melbourne J. Int'l L. (2017).

[14] Larisa Dragomir, European Prudential Banking Regulation and Supervision: The Legal Dimension (2010).

[15] Ulrich Volz, *ASEAN Financial Integration in the Light of Recent European Experiences*, 30 Journal of Southeast Asian Economies 124 (2013); Douglas Elliot, *Lessons for Asia from Europe's History with Banking Integration*, ADBI Working Paper 462 (2014).

[16] Lupo-Pasini, *supra* note 13, at 72–5.

was replaced by the Single Passport program. This latter strategy, in particular, was instrumental in achieving quick regionalization of banking across the European Union, and it is still used for securities offerings. The Single Passport program indeed permits banks licensed in one of the EU Member States to access all other EU markets without the need of bilateral agreements. This means that once a bank obtains a license in an EU Member State, it can automatically operate in *all* other EU states without the need of regulatory approvals from the host authorities.[17]

Would this be a sensible approach to banking integration for ASEAN? Like the European Union, ASEAN's long-term objective is to have a dynamic banking market in which both wholesale and retail banks will be able to operate abroad with no additional regulatory and reporting requirements to those already applicable in their home jurisdictions. Keeping prudential requirements to the minimum necessary to guarantee safety indeed reduces those regulatory barriers that often hinder banks' expansions strategies. In this light, the AEC Blueprint 2025 clearly states the objective to "keep requirements for regulatory compliance to a minimum to reduce costs while remaining prudent."[18] Both mutual recognition and passporting are very effective integration strategies, as they bypass host countries' regulatory barriers and, therefore, protect primarily the interests of exporting nations and firms. Thus, a Single ASEAN Passport program would definitely incentivize ASEAN banks to penetrate foreign markets, thereby making integration much easier. In practice, an ASEAN bank licensed in Thailand would be able to operate automatically in Vietnam, Singapore, Philippines and Indonesia subject to the prudential requirements of the Thai banking authority. The host authorities in this case will not be able to refuse entry to the bank as long as it is lawfully licensed in one ASEAN country. Yet, since all those regulatory strategies entail a substantial reduction in the host country's regulatory and supervisory sovereignty, successful banking integration presumes a very high level of trust in the quality of partner members' regulatory and supervisory frameworks.[19]

[17] European Parliament, *Understanding Equivalence and the Single Passport in Financial Services: Third-Country Access to the Single Market*, European Parliament Think Tank, Feb. 9, 2017, www.europarl.europa.eu/thinktank/en/document.html?reference=EPRS_BRI(2017)599267 (last visited Feb. 24, 2018).

[18] AEC Blueprint 2025, sec. 17(i).

[19] Lupo-Pasini, *supra* note 13, at 82–4.

The concept of global systemic risk is key to understanding the rationales of supervisory banking cooperation.[20] To function efficiently, the financial sector relies on interconnectedness. Banks invest in each other in various forms: they buy similar types of financial assets and operate on the same infrastructures. These very tight connections, however, drastically increase the risk that a problem in one part of the financial system transmits instability to other areas through the various financial, infrastructure or psychological channels. In finance, this is called systemic risk.[21] Examples include panics, interbank contagion, fire sales or bank debt loops.[22] In a situation of financial integration, systemic risk stops being a simple national concern and, instead, becomes an international problem.[23] Indeed, because of their very nature, cross-border banks become the bridge through which systemic risk can be transferred from one financial system onto the other. Cross-border banks rely on a very centralized structure that connects the bank's different foreign operations, be they in the form of branches or subsidiaries. It is therefore very easy that a solvency or liquidity problem in the parent bank be transmitted to the various foreign branches or subsidiaries in a matter of hours.

The early days of European banking integration in the 1980s were plagued by international supervisory failures – among them, Banco Ambrosiano and Bank Credit and Commerce International – that showed how regulatory or supervisory loopholes in one country can become the Trojan horse through which instability is propagated across the regional or global banking network.[24] In an integrated global financial system, regulatory and supervisory coordination is therefore fundamental to achieving stability. As long as all members converge their prudential and supervisory standards, the automatic licensing at the core of Mutual Recognition or Single Passport will not constitute an insurmountable problem for the host authority, which can confidently

[20] See generally Federico Lupo-Pasini & Ross Buckley, *Global Systemic Risk and International Regulatory Coordination: Squaring Sovereignty and Financial Stability*, 30 Am. Univ. Int'l L. Rev. 665 (2015).

[21] Steven Schwarcz, *Systemic Risk*, 97 Georgetown L. J. 193, 204 (2008).

[22] Robert Kollmann & Frédéric Malherbe, *Financial Contagion*, *in* Handbook of Safeguarding Global Financial Stability: Political, Social, Cultural, and Economic Theories and Models (Gerard Caprio Jr ed., 2013).

[23] Lupo-Pasini & Buckley, *supra* note 20, at 46.

[24] See George Alexander Walker, International Banking Regulation: Law, Policy, and Practice 83–118 (2001).

rely on the soundness of the foreign bank. However, this requires the utmost level of regulatory and supervisory coordination.

7.3 Regional Disparities

In the context of ASEAN, policy coordination means having all ASEAN members agree on a prudential regulatory platform – a minimum level of regulatory harmonization – that guarantees a basic level of stability for all ASEAN banks; something similar to the minimum harmonization approach adopted by the European Union in the early days of European financial integration. Only by leveling up the supervisory and regulatory playing field to a common ASEAN standard will national supervisors feel comfortable in welcoming foreign ASEAN banks in their financial system. This, however, is a prohibitive goal in the medium-short term.

From a historical perspective, ASEAN's attempt to integrate financial markets with such huge structural, regulatory and economic differences has no precedent. When the European single market in financial services was created in the late 1980s and early 1990s, there was no major difference in the actual level of financial development of EU countries, even though certain markets had more depth and better oversight than others.[25] Moreover, EU national bank supervisors could benefit from substantial regional regulatory and supervisory convergence. Most EU supervisors were indeed members of the Basel Committee on Banking Supervision and applied largely similar supervisory standards, while their central banks had a long history of cooperation through the Bank for International Settlements.[26] European Union members therefore were put in the right conditions to trust each other's supervisory agencies and, in turn, their banks' licensing, prudential and supervisory regimes. Neither of these situations, however, applies to ASEAN, despite some central banks' cooperation on monetary policy under the Chiang Mai Initiative.[27]

[25] On this, see Rawi Abdelal, Capital Rules: The Construction of Global Finance 54–85 (2009).

[26] See Charles Goodhart, The Basel Committee on Banking Supervision: A History of the Early Years 1974–1997 (2011).

[27] Masahiro Kawai, *From the Chiang Mai Initiative to the Asian Monetary Fund*, ADBI Working Paper 527 (2015); Ramon Pacheco Pardo and Pradumna Rana, *Complementarity Between Regional and Global Financial Governance Institutions: The Case of ASEAN+3 and the Global Financial Safety Net*, 21 Global Governance 413 (2015).

The main obstacle to a single financial market in ASEAN is the differences in the level of financial development among members, especially between the ASEAN-5[28] and BCMLV countries.[29] ASEAN does not have the level of regulatory convergence that Europe had in the 1990s and 2000s. Not only are capital adequacy regulations applied very differently across the region, but the quality of supervision is remarkably dissimilar. Some countries can rely on vast pools of money and supervisory resources in the event of a banking crisis, but other countries do not offer the same guarantees. Moreover, the broader legal regimes applicable in the event of a bank insolvency are fundamentally different.[30] For these reasons, a Single Passport program for ASEAN would probably be too difficult to adopt, unless ASEAN members agree to a baseline framework with very low prudential requirements – an unpalatable option for all ASEAN-5 members.

Accommodating the different development needs of its members with the broader objective of integrating banking markets were therefore the main problems ASEAN finance ministers had to grapple with. The answer was found by giving members further flexibility to proceed with preferential liberalization in banking. This, essentially, means a model of selective banking integration based on three key pillars: MFN discrimination among ASEAN members, reciprocity of concessions between the two integrating members and the respect of national treatment.

7.4 Preferential Banking Integration: the Qualified ASEAN Bank Program

When ASEAN members decided to embank on the ambitious project of a more integrated ASEAN financial market, it became clear that the AFAS was not enough and a new template for financial integration was needed. This was achieved by a new initiative called the ASEAN Financial Integration Framework. Adopted in 2011 by the governors of the central banks, the AFIF provides some guidelines to the process of progressive regional financial integration.[31] AFIF's defining element is the approach to financial integration, which understands the different level of readiness of ASEAN members to financial integration and, for this reason,

[28] Original ASEAN founders: Indonesia, Malaysia, Philippines, Singapore and Thailand.

[29] Newer ASEAN members: Brunei, Cambodia, Lao PDR, Myanmar and Vietnam.

[30] Vivien Chen, Andrew Godwin & Ian Ramsay, *Cross-Border Cooperation in Bank Resolution: A Framework for Asia*, 1 S'pore J. Legal Studies 8, 8–13 (2016).

[31] ASEAN Financial Integration Framework, adopted by ASEAN Central Bank Governors and endorsed by the ASEAN Finance Ministers in 2011.

allows them to set their own milestones and timeline to integrate their financial markets. Key policy actions include the progressive removal of capital controls, financial market liberalizations, monetary cooperation, as well as capacity building to progressively reduce policy and regulatory asymmetries among members. AFIF's objectives to create a more integrated financial market are part of the broader financial regulatory architecture set out in the AEC Blueprint 2025. There, financial integration and financial stability were seen as two of the three main policy goals (the other being financial inclusion) underlying the process of regional convergence.[32]

Yet, given the AFIF's broad scope encompassing all financial services, and given the practical difficulties in enhancing banking integration, it became necessary to set out a more precise policy agenda for banking integration that would spell out the approach to supervisory and regulatory coordination among members.[33] This objective was achieved by the ABIF, a regulatory instrument that guides members in the process of progressive liberalization of the banking sector and in regulatory and supervisory coordination.[34] The ABIF was officially endorsed in March 2015 by the ten ASEAN central bank governors and became immediately operative. Although the text of the agreement is kept secret by the central banks, ASEAN acknowledges that the ABIF sets a few bedrock principles and provides guidelines with regard to the pace of liberalization of the banking sector, regulatory harmonization, supervisory convergence and systemic stability.[35] Like the AFIF, the ABIF also acknowledges the different stages of financial development of ASEAN members and their different readiness to open their market to foreign banks. In practice, this entails the utmost level of flexibility for ASEAN members with regard to the decision to integrate their banking sectors.

Thus, the strategy of banking integration adopted by ASEAN is based on the very opposite of the European Union's and rests on the principle of MFN discrimination. At the core of the ASEAN model lies the concept of QABs. The political rationale underlying the QABs is clearly set out in

[32] AEC Blueprint 2025, sec. 16.

[33] Asian Development Bank, *The Road to ASEAN Financial Integration: A Combined Study on Assessing the Financial Landscape and Formulating Milestones for Monetary and Financial Integration in ASEAN* (2013).

[34] ASEAN Banking Integration Framework, endorsed by the ASEAN central bank governors in Dec. 2014

[35] Maria Monica Wihardja, *Financial Integration Challenges beyond 2015*, ERIA Discussion Paper, ERIA-DP-2013–26 (2013).

the AEC Blueprint 2025, which sees bilateral integration as the best approach to reconcile ASEAN members' need for additional flexibility with regulatory convergence with the goal to spur local bank's regional expansion.[36] The legal basis of the QABs, on the other hand, is to be found in the Protocol to Implement the Sixth Package of Commitments on Financial Services (the Protocol) under the AFAS. Article 5 states:[37]

> For the purpose of deepening regional banking integration, in accordance with Article IV bis of the AFAS and guided by the principle of governance of ABIF ... two or more Member States may conduct negotiations and agree to liberalize their banking sector ... Any extension of preferential treatment in the banking sector to the remaining Member States on a MFN basis shall be voluntary on the part of the participating Member States.

The QABs system is, in its essence, a policy strategy that supports preferential integration in banking bilaterally or between a restrict group of members. Operationally, it does not rely on an established specific regulatory framework, but rather relies on the agreement reached by the two members that wish to integrate further, which decide autonomously the criteria required to grant QAB status.[38] In addition, the two members will decide the supervisory and resolution arrangements to which the banks will be subjected. The agreement is based on the principle of reciprocity. Once the two integrating members have agreed the regulatory and supervisory platform on which banking integration will operate among them, it will be up to the local banks to request QAB status from their home supervisory authority, which will be in charge of the screening and licensing. Once the license is given, the host authority will be obliged to grant market access to the foreign bank and treat it as a local bank. In addition, a Qualified ASEAN Bank should have operational flexibility in a host market, including the ability to carry out a range of banking activities and offer various products and services, as mutually agreed upon in bilateral negotiations. The ABIF simply provides a few criteria that must be respected, such as that the Bank must be headquartered in one of the ASEAN members.[39]

[36] AEC Blueprint 2025, sec. 17(1)(b).

[37] Protocol to Implement the Sixth Package of Commitments on Financial Services under the ASEAN Framework Agreement on Services, art. 5.

[38] Joint Statement of the First ASEAN Finance Ministers' and Central Bank Governors' Meeting (Mar. 21, 2015).

[39] *Id.*

The QAB program was welcomed by the ASEAN banking community as a useful step in the direction of progressive financial integration, and it is fully in line with ASEAN's long-standing approach of flexible preferential regional integration, the so-called ASEAN minus X formula.[40] This strategy allows ASEAN members to proceed autonomously in their integration agenda without having to wait for the other members. Given the huge disparities in prudential regulatory frameworks, banking, consumer protection and insolvency laws, as well as supervisory capacity, there is little doubt that asymmetric integration would work best in ASEAN. The ABIF requires each ASEAN member to have concluded at least one bilateral accord under the QAB framework before 2020. Since the adoption of the QAB platform, however, only a few members have signed bilateral agreements. In 2016, Bangko Sentral ng Pilipinas entered into an agreement with Bank Negara Malaysia and is expected to reach an agreement with two other supervisors.[41] The Malaysian Central Bank has already entered into bilateral agreements with the Indonesian and Philippine Central Bank,[42] while Thailand is about to enter into an agreement with Myanmar.[43] The QAP program is, however, not the only vehicle for banking integration as ASEAN banks can still choose to enter a foreign market through the normal route, simply by applying for a license. In fact, this seems to be still the preferred way for most ASEAN banks, which continue their strategy of expansion through representative offices or small branches to test the market before establishing a full subsidiary.[44]

[40] The formulation of this principle was first agreed in the AFAS 4 Package, and it broadly allowed ASEAN members that were willing to liberalize a certain service sector on a reciprocal basis to do so without having to extend the same concessions to other members.

[41] *ASEAN Banking Integration Framework Sets the Tone for ASEAN Economic Growth*, ASEAN Today, Jun. 7, 2017, www.aseantoday.com/2017/06/asean-banking-integration-framework-sets-the-tone-for-asean-economic-growth/ (last visited Feb. 24, 2018).

[42] Bank Negara Malaysia, *Regulatory Cooperation between Bank Negara Malaysia and Otoritas Jasa Keuangan on the Banking Sector*, Press Release, Aug. 1, 2016, www.bnm.gov.my/index.php?ch=en_press&pg=en_press&ac=4229&lang=en (last visited Feb. 24, 2018).

[43] Yukako Ono, *Myanmar Open Talks with Thailand on Reciprocal Banking Access*, Nikkei Asian Review, Nov. 29, 2016, https://asia.nikkei.com/Business/AC/Thailand-Myanmar-in-talks-to-give-banks-reciprocal-access (last visited Feb. 24, 2018).

[44] Yukako Ono, *Integration Is Slowly Taking Hold in ASEAN's Banking Sector*, Nikkei Asian Review, Nov. 21, 2016, http://asia.nikkei.com/Business/Companies/Integration-is-slowly-taking-hold-in-ASEAN-s-banking-sector?page=2 (last visited Feb. 24, 2018).

7.5 The ASEAN's Financial Trilemma

The Qualified ASEAN Banks program is a very useful and politically savvy strategy to promote banking integration in a region where sovereignty concerns and economic disparities would make it impossible to converge domestic financial policies. By allowing MFN discrimination, it permits a multilayered regional banking system in which integration will proceed at different paces. Yet, the QAB program does not deal with the actual mechanisms of supervisory and regulatory integration that make the bilateral banking integration among QAB states work. More specifically, it is unclear whether the QAB system operates as a home country model in which the supervision and prudential requirements are a matter for the home supervisory authority (as it was in the European Union), or as a host country-control model, in which the banks will be supervised and regulated differently in each country where they operate. Yet, the question of home-host coordination is probably the most crucial element for achieving successful and stable banking integration.[45]

Multinational banks operate through a complex corporate structure that relies on a parent bank and a network of affiliates.[46] Market access in banking is achieved through one of the two following modes: a branch or a subsidiary.[47] The difference between the two modes is fundamental from a regulatory and commercial perspective. A branch is nothing more than an office of the parent bank in a foreign territory. This means that the foreign branch does not have autonomous capital to finance its commercial operations abroad, but instead relies on the capital of the parent. Given that a branch is simply an operative arm of the parent bank in a foreign territory, it is generally supervised and regulated by the parent's authority, which is supposed to oversee the solvency of the branch abroad. In the event of a crisis for the banking group, the host authorities are in a very weak position because it will be very difficult for them to understand the true financial situation of the bank and intervene on time. History shows that the branches will be left with no funds as all the liquid assets will be repatriated in the home country to finance the debt of the parent bank.

[45] On home-host supervisory coordination, see Gerard Caprio Jr, Douglas Evanoff & George Kauffman eds., Cross Border Banking: Regulatory Challenges (2006).

[46] Dirk Schoenmaker, Governance of International Banking: The Financial Trilemma (2013).

[47] Eugenio Cerutti, Giovanni Dell'ariccia & Maria Martinez Peria, *How Banks Go Abroad: Branches or Subsidiaries?*, 31 J. Banking & Finance 1669 (2007).

Subsidiaries, on the contrary, are separate operations of the multinational bank. For instance, they can issue debt and raise capital autonomously and, in some cases, they are almost financially independent from their parent. A foreign subsidiary must be licensed and incorporated in the host territory as if it was a local bank. The host supervisor is, therefore, in charge of the prudential regulation and the supervision of the subsidiary, although it is expected that the parent bank will intervene in case of trouble with the subsidiary. For this reason, host authorities can supervise them much more easily than branches, subject them to local laws and regulatory standards and, if necessary, resolve them.

During both the normal supervisory stage and in the event of a crisis, the home and the host supervisors often fight to protect their own national interest, to the detriment of the broader stability of the multinational bank.[48] In the period before the actual declaration of insolvency of the bank, the home authority might have very few incentives to disclose the true state of the bank to the host supervisors. Since the home authority is the consolidated supervisor for the entire banking group (the entity with the "best view" of the true condition of the bank in its consolidated global structure), the host is therefore in a weak position as it can find out the true condition of the bank only when it is too late. Similarly, the host supervisor in charge of the subsidiary might refuse to disclose problems to the home authority.[49]

The worst scenario, however, occurs when the bank is in a situation of financial distress or actual insolvency. The European sovereign debt crisis and the global financial crisis have given various examples of supervisory conflicts in resolution, from the bankruptcy of Lehman Brothers, to the bailout of Fortis Bank, or the insolvency of the three major Icelandic banks. The tensions between the need to protect national interests and the obligation to guarantee the stability of the bank in its cross-border structure can come from multiple sources. In the context of a bailout, the home authority will suffer from a lot of political pressure to minimize the level of public intervention in the banking group, with the risk that only the domestic operations of the bank will be saved.[50] The literature reports

[48] Katia D'Ulster, *Cross Border Banking Supervision Incentive Conflicts in Supervisory Information Sharing between Home and Host Supervisors*, World Bank Policy Research Working Paper 5871 23–6 (2011); Eugenio Cerutti, Anna Ilyina, Yulia Makarova & Christian Schmieder, *Bankers without Borders? Implications of Ring-Fencing for European Cross-Border Banks*, IMF Working Paper, WP/10/247 (2010).

[49] Lupo-Pasini, *supra* note 13, at 78–84.

[50] See generally Schoenmaker, *supra* note 47.

various cases, the latest one being the collapse of Portugal's Banco Espirito Santo, in which the home authority has forced the parent bank to cut liquidity for its foreign subsidiaries or refused to support their operations. In a bail-in scenario, the home and the host supervisors could fight on the conversion of the bailinable debt. If not properly managed through private international law, the fight could easily end up in court.[51]

Given their importance in the context of the recent crises, the Financial Stability Board and the Bank for International Settlements have proposed various solutions to the problems of international coordination. First, supervisors and resolution authorities can now rely on regulatory standards to guide their intervention in the event of a crisis, most notably the FSB's *Key Attributes of Resolution Regimes for Financial Institutions*. If adopted and applied consistently by ASEAN members, these standards could reduce regulatory discontinuities and eliminate legal frictions between ASEAN supervisory authorities.[52] Second, home-host supervisory agreements are now complemented by the use of Supervisory Colleges and Crisis Management Groups. These two mechanisms group all the supervisory and resolution authorities in charge of a multinational bank under the same roof. Operationally, Colleges and Groups are established for each individual bank under the command of the consolidated supervisor, and require all national agencies (supervision, resolution and central banks) to meet once per year to monitor the solidity of the bank and discuss potential problems.

Yet, despite the efforts to converge supervisory resolution policies, it is extremely unclear whether the differing incentives of national authorities will be aligned in the event of a crisis.[53] The European crisis showed that, even with a long history of cooperation and a very similar regulatory framework, the political pressure for a national solution is sometimes too big to bear. Banks – and multinational banks, especially – are unique corporate entities with billions or even trillions of dollars of exposures. Understandably, domestic politics will often intervene directly or indirectly to push toward the protection of national interests, however perceived.[54] This inevitably turns into a zero-sum game in which the

[51] Lupo-Pasini and Buckley, *supra* note 20, at 57.

[52] On this, see Vivien Chen, Andrew Godwin & Ian Ramsay, *Cross-Border Cooperation in Bank Resolution: A Framework for Asia*, 1 S'pore J. Legal Studies 6–8 (2016).

[53] Thorsten Beck, *Regulatory Cooperation on Cross-Border Banking – Progress and Challenges after the Crisis*, National Institute Economic Review 235 (2016).

[54] Lupo-Pasini, *supra* note 13, at 90–118.

protection of one country's interests entails the sacrifice of another's, often putting the latter's financial stability at risk.

How, then, to address the challenges of cooperation in a situation of banking integration? Dirk Schoenmaker has conceptualized those difficulties in the so-called financial trilemma.[55] It is impossible to achieve full financial integration, financial stability and national control over banking policies at the same time. Only two of these three objectives can coexist. In the context of the ASEAN single banking market, the three options can be represented as follows.

The first option (Financial Sovereignty – Banking Integration in Figure 7.1) is to proceed to a model of banking integration based on branches, but in which supervision and resolution remain primarily national competences. In this model, the home authority will be in control of the bank in its consolidated structure, but with the possibility of each national supervisor to intervene in the event of a crisis. This is essentially the situation Europe was in before the crisis.[56] However, this model is prone to supervisory wars, as the higher the level of integration, the higher are the risks that coordination failures could destabilize the entire ASEAN financial system. For instance, if the bank conglomerate is systemically important in the host country, it is very likely that the home supervisor will refuse to bail it out or provide any sort of emergency support paid with its own taxpayers' money. In another possible scenario, the home and host authorities might engage in a ring-fencing war to protect local creditors, thus leading to a disorderly resolution.

The second option (Banking Integration – Financial Stability) is to proceed with a model of banking integration based on branches, but in which a supranational authority will be in charge of the regulation, supervision and resolution of the multinational bank. Essentially, this model of integration entails the loss of national sovereignty in favor of a supranational model of governance in which only one entity will be in charge of supervising regional banks. This option mimics the decision of Eurozone countries to create a European Banking Union in which only one supervisor – the Single Supervisory Mechanism – is in charge of Eurozone banks.[57] In the ASEAN

[55] Schoenmaker, *supra* note 47.

[56] Jean Pisani-Ferry & André Sapir, *Banking Crisis Management in the EU: An Early Assessment*, Economic Policy 341 (2010); Federico Lupo-Pasini, *Economic Stability and Economic Governance in the Euro Area: What the European Crisis Can Teach on the Limits of Economic Integration*, 16 J. Int'l Ec. L. 211, 211–56 (2013).

[57] Rosa Lastra, *Banking Union and Single Market: Conflict or Companionship?*, 36 Fordham Int'l L. J. 1190 (2013); Giuseppe Boccuzzi, The European Banking Union: Supervision and Resolution (2016).

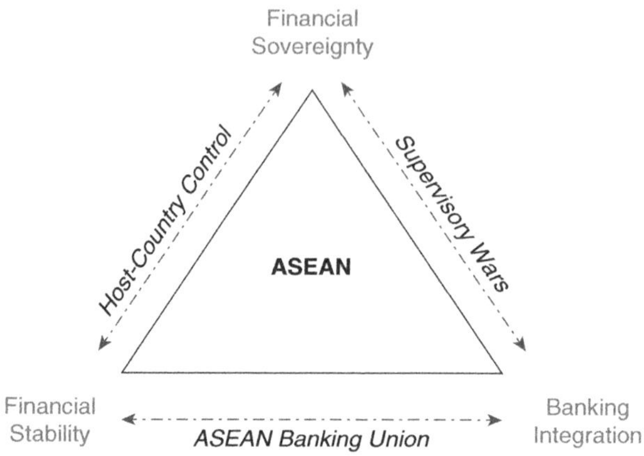

Figure 7.1 ASEAN's Banking Trilemma[59]

context, where integration is preferential, this model would envisage a "Single ASEAN Supervisor" in charge only of the supervision of ASEAN multinational banks, while national banks would remain under national control. This model has the advantage of eliminating supervisory wars, and therefore making banking integration much easier; banks, for instance, will have to deal with only one supervisor, and regulatory discontinuities will be eliminated. Nonetheless, this option requires the utmost level of political convergence among ASEAN nations, as sovereignty will be sacrificed and, very likely, some sort of fiscal solidarity be required.

The last option (Financial Stability – Financial Sovereignty) is to give up the dreams of a truly integrated ASEAN banking market and proceed with a purely national banking system in which financial policies remain fully national. In practice, this would entail a model of banking integration in which regional banks penetrate other ASEAN markets only through subsidiaries, and where regulation, supervision and resolution is still firmly in the hands of national authorities.[58] This model – also called "host country control" or "subsidiarization" – has the advantage of preserving national sovereignty and eliminating potential supervisory

[58] On host country control, see Avinash Persaud, *The Locus of Financial Regulation: Home versus Host*, 86 Int'l Aff. 637 (2010); Katharina Pistor, *Host's Dilemma: Rethinking EU Banking Regulation in Light of the Global Crisis*, ECGI Working Paper Series in Finance, No 286/2010 (2010).

[59] Author's interpretation based on Schoenmaker's Financial Trilemma, see *supra* note 47.

frictions, but at the expenses of banking integration as capital mobility will be highly reduced and regulatory frictions highly increased.

7.6 National Treatment and Host Country Control

The creation of supranational banking authorities is, at present, an impracticable option for ASEAN countries. With no experience in managing supervisory conflicts and very little regulatory convergence, giving up national sovereignty on such critical areas such as banking will be politically unwise and economically impracticable.[60] Moreover, as the European Banking Union shows, the need to establish a mechanism for fiscal solidarity among ASEAN members to finance the banking safety nets will inevitably create political tensions. On the other hand, it is likely that incentivizing banking penetration through branches will increase systemic risks.[61] If banking integration takes off and ASEAN banking conglomerates begin to emerge, ASEAN supervisors will eventually find themselves in the same situation European supervisors were in a few years ago. Before they even realize it, cracks in the banking system will emerge, and with them, the political pressure on national authorities to protect their own creditors and depositors. A new muddy banking crisis will unfold.

The most sensible option for ASEAN now is, undoubtedly, a model of banking integration based on host country control. The theoretical foundations of the ASEAN banking integration model were set in a 2013 ADB high-level report (ADB Report) on the path to closer financial integration in ASEAN.[62] In this document, the ADB proposes a three-dimensional approach to banking integration based on (1) equal access, (2) equal treatment and (3) equal environment. The ADB envisions a single market in which legal and regulatory requirements shall progressively converge so that banks will be not be treated unfavorably by the host regulators; essentially, a model based on national treatment rather than full non-discrimination. Yet, the report shies away from suggesting anything that would entail a loss of financial sovereignty or even home country control, not to mention the harmonization of regulatory requirements.

[60] On the politics-banking nexus, see Lupo-Pasini, *supra* note 56, at 211–56.

[61] The Warwick Commission on International Financial Reform, *Institutional Issues: The Locus of Regulation, Host or Home?*, Second Warwick Commission Report (2009).

[62] *The Road to ASEAN Financial Integration: A Combined Study on Assessing the Financial Landscape and Formulating Milestones for Monetary and Financial Integration in ASEAN* (2013).

The influence of the ADB Report was such that the QAB Program, a strategy devised in the Report, leaves central banks with the freedom to decide bilaterally how their home-host supervision and resolution can be structured. However, there is no legal obligation in the ABIF or the AFIF to adopt home country control or integrate through branches. On the contrary, given the ABIF's emphasis on equality of treatment and access, the regulatory pendulum seems to swing clearly in the direction of host country control. Hence, at present, given the difficulty of harmonizing laws and prudential requirements, ASEAN's approach is based on nondiscrimination. In practice, nondiscrimination means that foreign banks will be treated from a regulatory perspective as local banks. For instance, critical regulatory aspects such as capital adequacy requirements, liquidity ratios, concentration and exposure limits will be decided by the host authority. However, in order for a full nondiscriminatory approach to be applicable, it is necessary that the foreign banks enter the market only in the form of subsidiaries. Only by being locally incorporated can banks indeed have their own separate capital and assets.

Hence, what does host country control and subsidiarization mean for the future of the ASEAN banking market? In short, it means a choice for more sovereign control of the domestic financial system to the detriment of tighter and effective regional banking integration. A choice that would reduce the efficiency of cross-border banking conglomerates in allocating credit and slow down the process of regulatory and supervisory convergence. To understand why, it is necessary to look at the way global banks operate abroad.

The international finance literature has indeed predominantly advocated market penetration through branches as the best model for banking integration, as branches guarantee the highest level of capital mobility across the banking group.[63] This, in turn, reduces costs and increases profit margins for the global bank. From a financial perspective, the ideal corporate structure would indeed be one where funds are extremely mobile across the banking group in order to exploit interest rate differentials and market conditions; this would allow the company to raise money where it is cheaper and lend it where it is more profitable, all to the benefit of local consumers. Moreover, since branches are not locally incorporated, they do not require a lengthy and complex licensing procedure and, more generally, do not subject the bank to duplicative administrative and supervisory burdens.

[63] Cerutti et al., *supra* note 48.

However, in a subsidiary model, where the bank must be separately capitalized, funds must be raised in the host country, where interest rates could be higher. Moreover, moving assets across the banking group could be more difficult, thereby reducing the benefits of capital mobility. All this means that consumers of banking services will not be able to enjoy reduced costs of credit. From a purely regulatory perspective, one could argue that the sovereign control typical of a host country model will also reduce the incentives of countries to converge their regulatory and supervisory requirements, which is one of the ultimate long-term objectives of ASEAN. Because of the duplicative supervisory requirements, regional banks (especially smaller ones) might be hesitant to expand across borders. Having said that, a few countries have successfully embraced subsidiarization. For instance, both Mexico and New Zealand, two countries with open banking systems, require foreign banks to enter the market only through subsidiaries.[64] In the United States, the Federal Reserve issued a new regulation in 2014 whereby branches of foreign banks will be required to hold assets in the United States through a holding company; ultimately, a mild form of subsidiarization. Yet, their needs are very different from those of ASEAN, as the pressure to converge and level up domestic regulatory standards is much lower.

7.7 Concluding Remarks

To conclude, it is probably now too early to assess how regional integration will develop in ASEAN in ten or twenty years' time, and whether it will indeed lead to a pan-ASEAN banking market as envisaged by the AEC Blueprint 2025. This instrument tries to strike a very careful balance between the members' demands of policy space for development, the region's desire to bolster regional banking integration and the need to guarantee financial stability. Without committing too much to any of these objectives, and despite the breath of the AEC Blueprint 2025, it nonetheless provides sufficient guidance to ASEAN policymakers on the region's path toward an inclusive and safe regional banking market. However, it is safe to assume that the ASEAN model of integration will definitely not look like Europe's, at least from a regulatory perspective. As we said at the beginning of this chapter, banking integration requires regulators to make a painful choice between conflicting policy goals.

[64] Persaud, *supra* note 59.

While European regulators have always preferred regulatory models (be they Mutual Recognition or the Banking Union) that favor increased integration to the detriment of regulatory sovereignty, ASEAN regulators are clearly more conservative in their approach. Like in many other policy areas, what really defines ASEAN's attitude to integration is the emphasis on national control, even if this leads to slower integration and less effective regulatory convergence.

A different question is whether the ABIF will have any impact on future ASEAN Free Trade Agreements, such the RCEP. Given the early stages of negotiation of this agreement, which nonetheless comprises financial services, it is probably too difficult to divine whether the ASEAN approach will be used as a template. However, experience with other similar agreements suggests that the RCEP will have very little effect on actual banking integration. From a purely regulatory perspective, given the difficulty of the members to further open their financial sectors, and their distaste for regulatory convergence, it is difficult to see how the RCEP Trade in Services Chapter will be able to tackle extremely complex issues of regulatory and supervisory cooperation. Despite having the most sophisticated regulatory framework for Trade in Financial Services, even the most complex FTA negotiated so far – the Transpacific Partnership Agreement – felt short of addressing the most basic supervisory and regulatory issues that determine the actual level of regulatory convergence. It would be very surprising if future ASEAN FTAs go beyond that. From a policy perspective, regulatory convergence in financial services outside regional integration is actually determined mostly by unilateral regulatory changes rather international trade negotiations. Moreover, when cooperation takes place, the actual agreements on supervisory and regulatory cooperation, which are excluded from trade agreements by way of prudential carve-outs, are negotiated by central banks and financial supervisory authorities completely independently. Finally, from a purely business viewpoint, it is worth noticing that the Chinese, Korean and Australian banks with international ambitions have already established a commercial presence in key ASEAN markets.

8

The Shifting Sands of Capital Market Development and Integration in ASEAN: the Case of the Philippines and Indonesia

MICHELLE DY

8.1 Introduction

The plan to develop the capital markets of the members of ASEAN traces its origins to events which transpired long before the launch of the AEC project in 2003. In 1997, the ASEAN markets experienced a severe financial crisis which was partly blamed on the heavy dependence on banking institutions for access to finance. As a response, initiatives aimed at deepening the region's capital markets for it to become a viable financing alternative were adopted. This was subsequently superseded in 2003 by plans to streamline and harmonize capital market regulatory systems as part of the AEC's goal to have a freer flow of capital. This became an important milestone due to the overarching plan to have an ASEAN-wide financial integration between countries at different levels of development. This necessitated a careful planning of the proper sequencing of reforms, since opening up the members' markets to one another could lead to greater volatility and financial instability for the low-income members.[1]

In order to meaningfully participate in the financial integration initiative, the domestic markets of the members were expected to achieve "threshold conditions" first, such as "well-developed financial markets, high-quality institutions, good governance, sound macroeconomic policies, and trade integration."[2] Despite this realization, plans adopted to

[1] Geert Almekinders et al., *ASEAN Financial Integration*, 15 IMF Working Paper 1 (2015).

[2] *The Road to ASEAN Financial Integration: A Combined Study on Assessing the Financial Landscape and Formulating Milestones for Monetary and Financial Integration in ASEAN* (2013).

implement the AEC Blueprint 2015 were limited to region-wide measures, implying that members were to achieve these threshold conditions on their own. The new AEC Blueprint 2025 aims to resolve this problem by undergoing another paradigm shift to ensure that the financial sector is inclusive. Region-wide reforms are given less emphasis, and more attention is given to domestic reforms that aim to reduce the developmental gap among Member States.

With these regional developments as a background, it is now important to find out how ASEAN Member States have reacted as their reception and responses to the initiatives are crucial to the latter's success. Even if the AEC Blueprint 2015 failed to recommend a domestic sequencing of reforms, did the members seek to achieve the threshold conditions? Moreover, with the adoption of a new blueprint and a new paradigm, did the members also follow suit? To answer these questions, the country-level implementation of the capital market integration plan before and after the adoption of the AEC Blueprint 2025 shall be examined in two ASEAN Member States, Indonesia and the Philippines.

The rest of the chapter is divided as follows: Section 8.2 shall briefly trace the origins of capital market development and integration policy in ASEAN. Section 8.3 shall discuss the evolution and current status of Philippines' implementation of the capital market development agenda. Section 8.4 will then move to a discussion of Indonesia's implementation status and the evolution of its own capital market development program. Section 8.5 provides a comparative analysis of the two countries. Section 8.6 concludes.

8.2 The ASEAN Capital Market Integration Project

Even before talk of regional economic integration began, the development of the region's capital market had long been in the consciousness of the technocrats and civil servants working in this region. It all started in the 1980s as part of a series of reforms targeted toward financial liberalization. While the 1997 Asian financial crisis made countries rethink their financial liberalization plan, capital market development was left untouched and began to be promoted as a "spare tire" that would help alleviate the negative effects of bank credit crunches.[3] As part of this

[3] Alan Greenspan, *Do Efficient Financial Markets Mitigate Financial Crises?*, Remarks before the 1999 Financial Markets Conference of the Federal Reserve Bank of Atlanta, Georgia (1999).

heightened push toward the capital markets, the Asian Bond Market Initiative was launched. The program sought to develop a local currency bond market in Asia to solve the currency mismatch problem and render the region less vulnerable to the sudden reversal of capital flows. This initiative also reflected the regional concern that financial stability should be prioritized to prevent another financial crisis from happening.[4]

But before this initiative could fully take off, the AEC project was announced a year later in 2003.[5] Crucially, this also heralded a new era for capital market development in the region because instead of being merely treated as an alternative to bank financing, it was placed right at the center of the integration initiative as one of the ways to achieve AEC's goal of having a freer flow of capital.[6] It was also considered to have a very important role in facilitating cross-border trade and supporting the growth of the real economy, providing the initial connections between capital market development and economic growth. It was thought that since the development of alternative channels of financial intermediation such as the capital market enhances the overall efficiency of the financial system, it will also foster economic growth and development.[7]

However, the narrative of linking capital market development to economic growth and development cannot be explicitly seen in the 2015 Blueprint. The targeted measures to achieve free flow of capital failed to reflect themes of development and inclusive growth. These are instead found in the Implementation Plan issued by the ACMF, the taskforce set up by the ASEAN Finance Ministers in 2004 to manage the capital market development project, where specific mention was made of strengthening financial intermediation to support growth as one of the ultimate goals of the initiative.[8] Upon closer inspection of the measures, however, it can be gleaned that the said plan limited itself to the harmonization of the Member States' rules and regulations to facilitate cross-border access.[9] Strengthening the financial institutions of the Member States remained a domestic and fragmented affair.[10]

[4] Yung Chul Park & Charles Wyplosz, Monetary and Financial Integration in East Asia: The Relevance of European Experience (2008).

[5] Declaration of Association of Southeast Asian Nations Concord II (2003).

[6] ASEAN Economic Community Blueprint (2007), para. 31.

[7] Raymond Atje & Ira S Titiheruw, ASEAN Capital Market Integration: The Way Forward (2016).

[8] ASEAN Capital Markets Forum, The Implementation Plan (2009).

[9] 2003 Declaration of ASEAN Concord II, *supra* note 5.

[10] Michelle Dy, Capital Market Integration in the EU and ASEAN (2017).

This would remain as a key characteristic of the capital market development process in ASEAN.

This can be ascribed to ASEAN's propensity to use agreed-upon informal rules of engagement where legally binding instruments are avoided and nonbinding commitments in the form of soft law instruments are preferred.[11] Because of this, enforcement mechanisms are weak and have never been utilized.[12] Compliance is further weakened by the ASEAN minus X formula, a method of implementation unique to this region where flexibility is given to Member States to implement the initiatives only when they deem themselves ready.[13] This was rendered necessary due to the different levels of development by the Member States.

ACMF's harmonization project was not completed by its 2015 deadline. Despite this, the integration project is starting a new chapter with the adoption of the AEC Blueprint 2025. In this document, the link between capital market development and economic growth was strengthened and given more emphasis by putting financial inclusion as one of the three strategic pillars under the ASEAN financial integration agenda. By doing so, ASEAN gave itself a mandate to "broaden financial access to the underserved communities, tapping into their potential as a consumer base."[14]

The new ACMF Action Plan 2016–2020 also reflects the agenda to promote inclusiveness.[15] As will be seen later in the discussion of country-level measures to promote inclusion, regional financial inclusion is a bit different. Based on the proposed measures under the new ACMF Action Plan, a regional financial inclusive policy entails making it easy for issuers, investors and securities market professionals to access other markets within ASEAN and reducing the developmental gap among Member States to foster a more "meaningful participation" in the ACMF initiatives. To facilitate market access by issuers and investors in other jurisdictions, measures to harmonize rules and regulations and lower informational barriers on regional risk capital and credit information, especially for MSMEs, are being proposed.[16]

[11] Michelle Dy, *Coordination Games: The Challenge of Pursuing a Financial Integration Project in ASEAN*, 33 Chinese YB Int'l L. & Aff. 139 (2015).

[12] *Id.*

[13] Siow Yue Chia & Michael G. Plummer, ASEAN Economic Cooperation and Integration: Progress, Challenges and Future Directions (2015).

[14] ASEAN Economic Integration Brief (2017).

[15] ASEAN Capital Markets Forum, ACMF Action Plan 2016–2020 (2016).

[16] *Id.*

Also in the proposal are enabling the more sophisticated investors to participate in cross-border capital market activities and the promotion of increased mobility of capital market professionals within the region through the cross-recognition of educational qualifications.[17] A well-established investor protection regime in the region is also expected to encourage more ASEAN citizens to participate in the capital markets. Lastly and most importantly, capacity-building programs are now being prioritized so that the Member States which are lagging behind can implement the agreed-upon ACMF reforms.[18] This is in stark contrast to the old plan, where no similar initiatives can be found and members were left to devise their own capacity-building programs.[19] This, together with the ASEAN minus X formula, directly contributed to the minimal progress of the ACMF initiatives.

8.3 Philippine Capital Market Development: from Inclusive Growth to Structural Reform

Capital market development in the Philippines traces its roots long before ASEAN launched its own program as a reaction to the 1997 Asian financial crisis. After the dictatorship of Ferdinand Marcos ended and democratic institutions were reinstalled, the Philippine economy was in shambles. The capital market was underdeveloped and domestic savings were very low.[20] A project to revive the Philippine economy was launched in the early 1990s, and one of the measures proposed was to undertake reforms in the financial sector in order to stimulate investment-led growth from the private sector. Even before the link between capital market development and economic growth become popular globally, or at least within the ASEAN region, the Philippines already saw the importance of having deep and liquid capital markets as a contributor to economic growth.[21]

Due to the lack of technical capability and resources to undertake the needed reforms, the Philippine government tapped the technical assistance program of the Asian Development Bank (ADR) and sought its help in relation to measures needed to achieve its target objectives. After

[17] *Id.*
[18] *Id.*
[19] Dy, *supra* note 10.
[20] *Program Performance Audit Report on the Capital Market Development Program in the Philippines* (2003).
[21] *Id.*

being initially met with some resistance from industry groups, the first CMDP was launched in 1992.[22] Its primary goal was to develop the capital market as an alternative mode of financial intermediation to enhance allocative efficiency and foster economic growth. A developed capital market is also thought to form a virtuous cycle where better investment opportunities for domestic savers lead to an expansion of the economy, which then could lead to higher incomes, greater savings and increased investments.

In order to achieve this goal, measures formulated were targeted toward stimulating private sector activity, attracting portfolio investments from foreign sources and making the capital market in the Philippines a viable tool for the privatization of state-owned enterprises.[23] Two major reforms were undertaken: the first was the restructuring of the stock market by unifying the two stock exchanges operating in the country. Another was a push toward the devolution of some of the SEC's functions that were not directly related to capital market regulation, such as the jurisdiction to resolve intra-corporate disputes.[24] At the same time, the Capital Market Development Council was formed, consisting of representatives from the financial regulators and members of the industry. It was designed to be a public-private collaboration whose purpose is to recommend legislative and policy reforms aimed at promoting capital market development.

However, the said program did not have any impact as predicted according to the post-implementation assessment conducted by the ADB. It was found that the reforms undertaken were lopsided since it only focused on the stock market. The debt market was basically left alone because the Philippines already had a very active long-term commercial paper market. It was concluded that future capital market development programs should have a holistic approach and reforms should be system-wide to capture the spillover effects that changes in one sector could possibly cause in another.

Despite this, the initial CMDP produced some lasting results. For example, as a result of the amendments introduced in the Securities Regulation Code of the Philippines (SRC), it is now part of state policy for the SEC to promote the development of the capital market and the

[22] *Id.*
[23] *Id.*
[24] See Presidential Decree No. 902-A: Reorganization of the Securities and Exchange Commission with Additional Power and Placing the Said Agency under the Administrative Supervision of the Office of the President (1976).

democratization of wealth.[25] Since the link between capital market development and sustainable development received official recognition by the state, an evident policy shift was noticeable in measures targeted toward the former. One of this was the enhanced emphasis to equip the populace with tools to turn them into active contributors to the growth of the real economy instead of just being beneficiaries of government projects.

In contrast to the previous capital market development program, the first capital market development plan issued by the SEC in 2005 covering five years (2005 CMDP) contained measures that have a direct social impact on the Filipino population. One of these is the development of voluntary pension schemes aimed to encourage Overseas Filipino Workers (OFWs) to redirect some of their remittances to pension funds as a method of securing their financial independence in the future and ensuring that they have access to financial services.[26] In 2016, OFW cash remittances to the Philippines amounted to $26 million. It was estimated that even a 10 percent savings contribution from the remittances of these workers would significantly grow the pool of funds available for long-term investments via the Philippine capital market. A financial literacy drive measure was also proposed which aims to educate Filipino citizens on the benefits of savings and investments. The 2005 CMDP also advocated for the participation of the Philippines in the ASEAN regional integration measures and the convergence of its rules and regulations to global standards.[27]

By 2011, a state policy recognizing the importance of having a robust capital market to a development-oriented financial system had also been adopted in the national government's medium-term development plan (2011 MTDP).[28] From a top-down development model in the early 1990s, the 2011 MTDP fully embraced a bottom-up development process by recognizing that people living at the margins of society must be given an opportunity to take part in nation building and economic growth.[29]

The 2013 CMDP represented a paradigm shift with respect to the SEC's approach to capital market development by focusing on making Philippine financial markets regionally competitive and creating an

[25] Securities Regulation Code of the Philippines, sec. 2.

[26] Securities and Exchange Commission of the Philippines, Capital Market Development Plan (2005–2010) (2004).

[27] *Id.*

[28] NEDA, *Chapter 6: Towards a Resilient & Inclusive Financial Sector, in* Philippine Development Plan 2011–2016 181–204 (2011).

[29] *Id.*

"enabling regulatory environment for regional integration."[30] In contrast to the previous CMDP, it was more outward-looking and was written with ASEAN financial integration in mind. Focus was shifted to structural reforms from a previous emphasis on increased public participation in the capital market. The measures proposed were targeted at deepening capital market liquidity and stimulating a secondary market, such as the introduction of a repo market, the establishment of a market maker program, regulatory harmonization with other ASEAN jurisdictions, promulgation of new rules on securities lending, perpetual bonds and minimum public ownership requirement. Regulatory reforms were also planned to align market practices with regional standards such as introducing shelf registration and adopting regulations on exchange-traded funds and special purpose vehicles.[31] Providing capital market access to the public did not seem to be a major concern. Increased savings generation and resource mobilization were seen more as an effect of efforts to develop the capital market and no longer a primary focus, in contrast to the 2005 CMDP.[32]

Presently, the utilization of the capital market for financial intermediation still lags behind its traditional banking counterpart. As of the end of 2016, 81 percent of the total resources of the Philippine financial system came from banks and only 19 percent representing all other nonbank sources, such as the capital market and the insurance industry.[33] Talks are now ongoing to carry these structural measures into the new CMDP, but will now follow a sequential order of introducing reforms targeted toward capital market development.[34] This is rooted in the thesis that markets have a hierarchical order based on the degree of their complexity and the risks they create.[35] Based on this idea, the proposal is to develop the money market first and prioritize the development of the repo market, interest rate corridor and the overnight index swap before moving on to other financial market products – ending with

[30] Securities and Exchange Commission of the Philippines, CMDP Blueprint 2013–2017 (2010).

[31] *Id.*

[32] As stated in the 2013–2017 CMDP, one of its policy goals is to "achieve a macroeconomic environment that is more conducive to increased personal savings and long-term investment in promising corporate enterprises."

[33] Bangko Sentral ng Pilipinas, *Statistics* (2017), www.bsp.gov.ph/statistics/efs_fsa1.asp (last visited Mar. 16, 2018).

[34] Cem Karacadag, V. Sundararajan & Jennifer Elliott, *Managing Risks in Financial Market Development: The Role of Sequencing*, IMF Working Paper (2003).

[35] *Id.*

the equity markets, investment funds and derivatives at the top of the pyramid. As measures are gradually introduced in accordance with the hierarchical order, tools and institutions which are necessary to control both macroeconomic and financial risks will also be established including a robust corporate and government bond market, money market and foreign exchange markets.[36] One will also notice that the goals set for capital market development have become more specific. These include facilitation of post-trade transparency, enhancement of price discovery, reduction of friction costs, increase in domestic market liquidity, development of a robust yield curve, improvement of financial architecture and the diversification of the investor base.[37]

While the SEC's current priority is to develop a yield curve from government securities and develop a repo market as it relates to the curve, financial inclusion-related reforms as mandated by the 2025 Blueprint have been placed in the Central Bank of the Philippines' (BSP) charge.[38] Financial inclusion, as defined by the BSP, covers effective access to a wide range of financial services (including investments in the capital market), and includes increasing public confidence in the health and soundness of the Philippine financial system and educating the public on the different financial instruments and their rights as consumers.[39] An example of this is the regularly held investor education programs that teach the public about investing in the stock market and in mutual funds.[40] Other measures include introducing new financial products more attuned to the needs of retail investors and mid- and small-sized companies. One of these is the newly launched dollar-denominated securities to expand the investment options of investors with dollar holdings such as OFWs. Apart from the existing Small, Medium and Emerging (SM&E) board, the Philippine Stock Exchange is also exploring the possibility of opening a board for start-ups.[41]

36 *Id.*

37 Presentation of the Securities and Exchange Commission to the Capital Market Development Council Meeting (Apr. 10, 2017).

38 Interview with SEC official (May 17, 2017).

39 NEDA, *supra* note 28.

40 Iris Gonzales, *PSE, SSS Ink Deal to Boost Financial Literacy*, Philippine Star, May 23, 2016, www.philstar.com/business/2016/05/23/1585877/pse-sss-ink-deal-boost-financial-literacy (last visited Aug. 14, 2017); see also COL Financial Philippines, www.colfinancial.com/ape/Final2/home/investor_education.asp (last visited Aug. 14, 2017).

41 Keith Richard D. Mariano, *PSE Board for Start-Ups Proposed*, Businessworld Online, Jan. 23, 2017, www.bworldonline.com/content.php?section=Corporate&title=pse-board-for-start-ups-proposed&id=139426 (last visited Aug. 14, 2017).

Other structural reforms are also being pursued by the SEC, such as the recent amendment of the Implementing Rules and Regulations of the SRC allowing the shelf registration of securities. This would allow the Philippines to participate in regional note issuance programs.[42] Another is the agency's restructuring of its qualification requirements and licensing process for capital market professionals. Lastly, the SEC also adopted a new corporate governance code in January 2017, elevating the country's standards to be at par with regional and global best practices.

8.4 Indonesian Capital Market Development: from Resilience to Inclusive Growth

Just like the Philippines, Indonesia also implemented financial deregulation policies in the 1980s which led to a boom in its banking industry. By the time the 1997 Asian financial crisis hit Indonesia, the economy was highly dependent on bank financing and the nonperforming assets of the country's banks were staggering.[43] The economy suffered a severe contraction in growth, peaking at −13.7 percent in 1998.[44] Developments after the crisis were also similar as banks became highly risk averse and tightened their lending practices. Long-term financing became harder to come by.[45] To address this, financial sector reforms which aim to reduce the dependence on one financial sector alone (e.g., the banking sector), enhance the resilience of the financial sector and improve its risk-bearing capacity were seen as a crucial strategy.[46] To reduce dependence on banks, developing the capital markets to improve diversification of the financial sector and facilitating a more efficient facilitation of funds toward more productive investments were targeted.[47] Measures to achieve these included the strengthening of capital market supervision

[42] Securities and Exchange Commission of the Philippines, 2015 Implementing Rules and Regulations of the Securities Regulation Code (Republic Act 8799) (2015).

[43] Masaaki Komatsu, *Lessons from Financial Deregulation Policy, Financial Development and Crisis: Case of Indonesia, in* Financial Fragilities in Developing Countries 87–114 (Hiyasuki Mitsuo ed., 2007).

[44] Tulus T. H. Tambunan, *The Indonesian Experience with Two Big Economic Crises*, 1 Mod. Econ. 156, 156–67 (2010).

[45] Asian Development Bank, Proposed Loan for Subprogram 2 Republic of Indonesia: Capital Market Development Program Cluster (2009).

[46] *Id.*

[47] Capital Market Supervisory Agency – Ministry of Finance of the Republic of Indonesia, *Indonesian Capital Market Master Plan 2005–2009* (2005).

and legal certainty in capital market transactions, enhancing the roles and quality of market participants, expanding the alternatives of investment and financing in the capital market and developing a Syariah-based capital market.[48]

Also included in this suite of reforms was stimulating demand by expanding the domestic investor base. First, the Financial Services Authority of Indonesia, also known as OJK, started requiring stock exchange members to maintain a minimum number of domestic investors in their investor profile.[49] Second, financial education campaigns and financial literacy programs were launched targeting students in order to foster a culture of capital market investing early on. To ensure a successful financial literacy program, the government also proposed a partnership with Indonesian universities and held investment clinics nationwide on a regular basis. Third, the use of information technology was promoted in order to make access to information faster. Fourth, the quality of information disclosure was improved by aligning it with international standards and best practices. A proposal was also made to reduce the number of documents and information needed from businesses, especially for MSMEs, to raise money from the public without compromising the goals of investor protection. Fifth, the spread of capital market professionals around the Indonesian archipelago was encouraged to increase access to finance and guarantee institutions. Lastly, a more robust investor protection framework was established. This included improving investor quality through thorough Know Your Client procedures to assess the risk appetites and investment needs of Indonesian retail investors so that financial institutions can package and market their products accordingly. Confidence in the stock exchange was also enhanced through the establishment of the Securities Investor Protection Fund.

In all the capital market development programs adopted by Indonesia until 2014, there was a noticeable absence of any reference to the implementation of ACMF initiatives. At most, the 2005–2009 Capital Market Master Plan mandated the drafting of regulations in line with international standards and bilateral, regional and international agreements insofar as they refer to cross-border transactions, without mentioning specific agreements or standards.[50] This was also made with a caveat that this was to be done with the national interests of Indonesia in mind and the development

[48] *Id.*

[49] Ministry of Finance of the Republic of Indonesia, *The Capital Market and Non Bank Financial Industry Master Plan 2010–2014* (2010).

[50] *Id.*

of its capital markets. The document also insisted that the harmonization process should start with mutual recognition as a precondition.[51]

Despite the reforms introduced in the previously discussed documents, public access and utilization of the financial sector in the country remained low compared to its ASEAN neighbors. According to the World Bank, Singapore is the most financially inclusive country among the ASEAN-5 at 96 percent. Just behind are Malaysia and Thailand with 81 and 78 percent, respectively. Compared to these three countries, Indonesia is only 36 percent financially inclusive. Not far behind is the Philippines at a measly 31 percent.[52] With respect to the capital market, domestic investors now dominate the stock exchange, with 52 percent of the total ownership composition officially classified as domestic holdings compared to previous years.[53] While the number of domestic investors is slowly increasing, they still only constitute 1 percent of the total Indonesian population.[54] At least 30 percent of Indonesian households that borrow money still rely on the informal economy for their funding needs.[55]

The Indonesian Financial Services Sector Master Plan 2015–2019 (IFSSMP) marks the first time an inclusive capital market policy was explicitly expressed.[56] Concern for financial stability was retained but a new dimension was added: having financially inclusive policies was now deemed important in order to achieve financial stability. While the previous plans have always emphasized measures targeting increased utilization of the capital market to promote the diversification and financial stability of the financial sector, it was only in the IFSSMP that the capital market was seen to play an important role in ensuring that the Indonesian population, especially those in the low-income group, could have equitable and affordable access to finance to help them achieve financial independence.[57] It was also seen as a

[51] *Id.*

[52] Asli Demigurc-Kunt et al., The Global Findex Database 2014: Measuring Financial Inclusion around the World (2014).

[53] Indonesia Central Securities Depository, *Beyond Innovation: 2016 Annual Report* (2016); Anton Hermansyah, *Capital Market in Positive Trajectory This Year: OJK*, The Jakarta Post, Jun. 26, 2017, www.thejakartapost.com/news/2017/06/26/capital-market-in-positive-trajectory-this-year-ojk.html (last visited Aug. 11, 2017).

[54] *IDX eyes 200,000 more retail investors this year*, The Jakarta Post, Jan. 26, 2016, www.thejakartapost.com/news/2016/01/26/idx-eyes-200000-more-retail-investors-year.html (last visited Aug. 11, 2017).

[55] Indonesia Financial Services Authority, *Indonesian Financial Services Sector Master Plan 2015–2019* (2015).

[56] *Id.*

[57] *Id.*

key contributor to sustainable economic development in Indonesia and a provider of alternative sources for development financing.

To equip the general population with the right tools to knowledgeably access the capital market, there is now a heightened push to open access to financial services to all segments of the population. The National Strategy for Financial Literacy, a separate document issued by the OJK, enumerates measures to advance financial literacy in the country.[58] Under it, financial literacy programs were expanded to formal and informal streams. The informal stream targets housewives, fishermen and migrant workers (among others), while the formal stream is designed to be part of the curriculum of Indonesian schools. There are also plans to tap the public transportation network to access remote parts of the archipelago to deliver financial literacy programs.[59] Complimenting this is the creation of financial products specially tailored for lower-income groups called the "Laku Mikro." Since the banking and capital markets regulators are now housed under a single entity, bank products are also starting to be utilized to expand the investor base.[60]

Apart from these, there is also a push to make it easier for MSMEs to raise financing in the capital market through measures such as simplifying the requirements for making a public offering, creating an SM&E board in the Indonesian Stock Exchange and the granting of incentives to venture capital firms investing in start-ups operating in the priority economic sectors.[61] Currently, SM&Es can conduct an Initial Public Offering if they have a minimum of 100 billion Indonesian rupiah (IDR) in assets. There are plans to lower the threshold to 50 billion IDR.[62] The IFSSMP has also proposed more innovative ways of increasing the domestic investor base such as allowing the purchase of financial products using proceeds from a loan or a credit card and permitting mutual fund unit ownership transfers without undergoing the subscription and redemption requirement for limited cases.[63] Domestic investors will also be allowed to use electronic ID cards or Tax Amnesty

[58] Financial Services Authority of the Republic of Indonesia, *Indonesian National Strategy for Financial Literacy* (2013).

[59] Indonesia Financial Services Authority, *supra* note 55.

[60] *Id.*

[61] *Id.*

[62] *Global Business Guide – Indonesia, Indonesia's Capital Market: Growing beyond Expectations*, Global Business Guide (2017), www.gbgindonesia.com/en/finance/article/2017/indonesia_s_capital_market_growing_beyond_expectations_11764.php (last visited Aug. 11, 2017).

[63] Indonesia Financial Services Authority, *supra* note 55.

certificates to easily open investment accounts.[64] In relation to this, the Indonesian investors relying on the Tax Amnesty Law will also be allowed to invest their repatriated funds on selected capital market investment products.[65] These efforts might have already paid off. As of August 2017, Indonesia domestic market capitalization is valued at 6,319.55 trillion IDR, representing 9 percent growth from 2016.[66] Social media network technology is also being utilized in the country to create a "social network for stock traders" called the Stockbit. This platform enables members to copy the investment decisions of more experienced stock traders.[67]

The IFSSMP is also the first document containing specific initiatives on capital market development and integration based on the premise that the country should prepare itself for competition.[68] Two key measures are proposed: the first is the amendment of its regulations in order to facilitate cross-border offerings and efficiently resolve anticipated cross-border disputes as a result of increased activities across borders. Presently, the Indonesian Capital Markets Law 1995 requires foreign companies planning to do a public offering on the Indonesian Stock Exchange to have their prospectuses audited by an auditing commission recognized by OJK. This effectively bars cross-border offerings. The second entails institutional preparations such as the upgrading of capital market infrastructure, consolidation to fend off competition as well as the standardization of back office operations and online trading.[69]

[64] Global Business Guide – Indonesia, *supra* note 61.

[65] Financial Services Authority, *OJK Issues Regulation on Capital Market Investment Products to Support Tax Amnesty Program*, 2016, www.ojk.go.id/en/kanal/pasar-modal/berita-dan-kegiatan/siaran-pers/Documents/Pages/Press-Release-OJK-Issues-Regulation-on-Capital-Market-Investment-Products-to-Support-Tax-Amnesty-Program/SP-OJK-Terbitkan-POJK-Produk-Investasi-Pasar-Modal-ENGLISH.p, at 8–10 (last visited Aug. 11, 2017).

[66] Zubi Mahrofi, *OJK Hopes Capital Market More Mature, Ready to Face Competition*, Tempo. Co, Aug. 13, 2017, https://en.tempo.co/read/news/2017/08/13/056899506/OJK-Hopes-Capital-Market-More-Mature-Ready-to-Face-Competition (last visited Aug. 17, 2017).

[67] Nadine Freischlad, *Indonesia's Stockbit Simplifies Trading for Retail Investors*, Tech in Asia, Apr. 25, 2017, www.techinasia.com/trading-platform-stockbit-gets-funding-from-500-startups (last visited Aug. 11, 2017).

[68] Indonesia Financial Services Authority, *supra* note 55.

[69] *Id.*

8.5 One Region, Different Narratives

This chapter reveals that prior to the 2025 Blueprint, the objectives of capital market development at the regional level were not well aligned with similar state-level plans. While the former was concerned with the harmonization of rules and regulations within the region and the creation of cross-border markets, the two subject countries were more concerned with developing their own markets internally first. As a result, regional and state-level development programs lacked complementarity. This outcome was also exacerbated by the lack of capacity-building programs at the regional level to assist the low-income members who were lagging behind.

This chapter has also shown that the Philippines' and Indonesia's capital market development programs evolved differently even though they were both adopted as a result of the 1997 Asian financial crisis. As early as 2005, the Philippines already promoted the idea of achieving sustainable development through the capital market by encouraging public participation in it to achieve financial independence. However, a noticeable change took place in the 2013 CMDP. Structural reforms were prioritized over capital market access with the rationale that tools and institutions that are necessary to control both macroeconomic and financial risks are first needed before increasing access to the capital market. This did not necessarily mean that financial inclusion initiatives were completely abandoned – their implementation was instead transferred to the BSP. This resulted in a scaling back of initiatives to enhance capital market access and priority transferred to increasing access to basic financial services like loans and deposit accounts.

Even though the country's primary focus now is on the establishment of institutions and products that will promote financial deepening, it is still implementing measures to promote financial inclusion. However, these are limited in scope – most financially inclusive measures target domestic investors only. Compliance with ACMF initiatives is a different story, however. The Philippines is a signatory of all the ACMF MOUs, but the measures it has adopted pursuant to the regional integration project cannot be considered an implementation of them since they do not produce the outcomes stated in the MOU – for example, the adoption of the ASEAN disclosure standards. Instead, the measures adopted by the Philippines can be taken as preparatory steps toward regional harmonization of capital market rules. An example of this is the country's adoption of international standards on qualification requirements and best practices for the licensing process of its capital market professionals. While this does not implement the ACMF initiative of cross-recognition of qualifications on education and experience of market professionals, this brings the Philippines one step closer toward entering into mutual recognition agreements with other ASEAN members and enhancing the mobility of its capital market professionals to other countries in the region.

In defense of the SEC, the deviation away from increasing access to the capital market does not necessarily mean that it is completely abandoning it. Financial inclusion is not exactly an antithesis of capital market development. The Philippines just chose to deal with structural issues first, which will lay the necessary foundations for increased public participation in the country's capital markets. For example, the development of a yield curve from government securities will also stimulate the growth of the domestic corporate bond market. A robust corporate bond market means that more corporations will turn to the capital market to raise funds from the public instead of resorting to traditional bank financing. An increase in public participation in such a bond market could also stimulate the creation of innovative financial products catering to the different investment preferences of the public. These processes take time. Because of this, it is a reasonable assumption that the Philippines' implementation of its capital market development program is still aligned with the overall financial inclusion objectives of ASEAN.

Indonesia, on the other hand, has also been successful so far in operationalizing the 2025 Blueprint mandate to broaden financial access to the underserved communities. The country's financial access programs can be generally divided into two kinds: one that informs the general population of the existence of formal financial markets and how they can access them, and a second that is the creation of financial products that are tailored to retail investors' needs and financial capacities. Before the IFSSMP came along, the country centered its initiatives on making its financial sector stable and resilient. The reason for this was that it was one of the countries hardest hit by the 1997 crisis, suffering a 13.7 percent contraction in economic growth from 1997 to 1998 and the rupiah going from 2,500 to 10,000 per US dollar.[70] In contrast, Indonesia's GDP growth for the first quarter of 2017 was 5 percent. In May 2017, S&P upgraded the country's status to investment-grade.[71]

[70] Aarthi Sathya Swaminathan, *20 years after the Asian Financial Crisis, Indonesia Has Lessons Learned – and Warnings*, CNBC, Jul. 7, 2007, www.cnbc.com/2017/07/07/20-years-after-the-asian-financial-crisis-indonesia-has-lessons-learned–and-warnings.html (last visited Mar. 16, 2018).

[71] Hermansyah, *supra* note 53.

Despite this, improving access to the capital market has always been part of the country's capital market development program, although a financial inclusive policy only clearly surfaced in the IFSSMP. After the AEC was officially launched in 2015, Indonesia saw an intensification of initiatives to improve financial literacy and retail investor access to additional financial products in contrast to the Philippines. Indonesia's compliance with the ACMF initiatives, however, is similar to the Philippine experience. The measures named in the IFSSMP are merely preparatory steps toward regional harmonization of capital market rules. The current priority is to first make sure that the country's legal framework will be able to facilitate and support cross-border offerings.[72] Operationalizing this involves the amendment of its Capital Market Law and related regulations to better suit this purpose, the upgrading of capital market infrastructure and the standardization of back office operations.

With respect to harmonization of rules among ASEAN members and mutual recognition initiatives, OJK has expressed a preference for a bilateral approach over a multilateral one.[73] They also do not have a specific timeline for implementation of the ACMF MOUs – instead, they stated that they will do so "when the time is appropriate," i.e., when there are no significant impediments left to the MOUs' implementation.[74] Focus on financial inclusion and stability also indicates that they want to focus on strengthening the domestic market first before they open the doors more widely to foreign players. They have also expressed skepticism about the viability of the ASEAN capital market integration initiative in the absence of a strong inter-member cooperation on enforcement. Preference was also expressed for integration to happen organically – that is, driven by business decisions rather than governmental. They see the role of government as a mere facilitator rather than being an active player in the process.[75]

8.6 Concluding Thoughts

The adoption of the 2025 Blueprint brought a new milestone, as we are beginning to witness the two countries gradually internalizing the regional capital market integration initiative through the recalibration of their capital market development programs to complement existing ACMF

[72] Interview with OJK officials (Oct. 24, 2017).
[73] *Id.*
[74] *Id.*
[75] *Id.*

projects. We see this in the increasing concern shown by both countries with respect to competition from the other members due to increased integration.[76] We also find that the country-level reforms being adopted after the 2025 Blueprint are being aligned toward increasing public access to the financial markets. While there are slight variations in how the financial inclusion agenda is being woven into each jurisdiction's policy measures, the overarching direction in all of them is the same.

While the initiatives of the two countries and ASEAN with respect to promoting financial inclusion vary, and it is not yet clear whether such measures will enable cross-border transactions or enhance regional integration, it is still an important development because it shows that ASEAN is beginning to move in one direction, perhaps providing that much-needed momentum to speed up the implementation of the ACMF project. Moreover, measures implementing ACMF initiatives only form a part of the overall CMDP of the two countries; they are still in the process of working toward achieving the threshold conditions necessary to meaningfully participate in the regional capital market integration project.

The ACMF and ASEAN should take note of this development and adopt it to how capital market development programs in the region are designed. Instead of coming up with specific programs and products that all Member States are expected to implement at staggered periods, it might be better to give Member States the maximum flexibility to implement capital market development programs which are best suited for their respective markets.

While there seems to be a congruence between the concept of financial inclusion at the ASEAN level and the state level, the lack of legally binding instruments in the ACMF means that there is a fragmentation of the measures being implemented regionally and individually.

Since financial inclusion in the Philippines and Indonesia entails increasing retail investor access to financial services, this needs to be reflected in regional initiatives as well. For example, if the aim of the ACMF framework is to encourage the cross-border transfer of funds or encourage publicly listed companies to raise capital in other ASEAN jurisdictions, it is not enough that they create supply through the ASEAN Trading Link, Collective Investment Schemes or other schemes; demand must also be there.[77] Thus, the ACMF

[76] Mahrofi, *supra* note 66.

[77] As of Oct. 6, 2017, the ASEAN Trading Link officially ceased operations. See Andrea Tan, *Southeast Asian Stock Markets Quietly Kill Their Trading Link*, Bloomberg Markets, Oct. 13, 2017, www.bloomberg.com/news/articles/2017-10-13/southeast-asian-stock-markets-quietly-kill-their-trading-link (last visited Feb. 25, 2018).

must also make it easy for ASEAN citizens to easily access information on ASEAN public companies such as financial statements, annual reports and disclosure statements to encourage them to invest in nonresident companies. A way to do this is to have a single portal and repository where this information can be stored and easily accessed and retrieved by ASEAN citizens. Another proposal would be to harmonize Know Your Client procedures and have a central repository for this information so that investors do not have to go through the same burdensome process each time they want to open an investment account in another jurisdiction.

9

Transnational Legal Services in Asia: Legal Implications of the AEC and the CPTPP

PASHA L. HSIEH*

9.1 Introduction

Transnational legal services underpin today's multilateral business and investment. Liberalizing legal services is also pivotal to a high degree of economic integration that entails a free flow of professional services in diverse jurisdictions. From the inception of the WTO to the current Doha Round, international law firms and developed nations have been keen on placing legal services on trade agendas. With the economic power shifting to the Asia-Pacific, the total revenue of its legal services market has surpassed $83 billion and continued to grow at a rate of 3.9 percent.[1] Against this backdrop, this chapter examines trade in legal services in the fast-growing ASEAN.

As Asia's third largest economy and home to 640 million people, ASEAN is expected to ascend to the world's fourth largest economy by 2050.[2] The creation of the AEC and the goal of the AEC Blueprint 2025 to achieve "a highly integrated and cohesive ASEAN economy" make the study on transnational legal services critical to South-based regionalism in the new regional economic order.[3] By exemplifying the commitments and practice of ASEAN countries, I argue that governmental measures have often curtailed the liberalization of legal services under FTAs. To

* This chapter is the substantially revised and updated version of Pasha L. Hsieh, *Liberalizing Trade in Legal Services under Asia-Pacific FTAs: The ASEAN Case*, 18 (1) J. Int'l Eco. L. 153 (2015) and *ASEAN's Liberalization of Legal Services: The Singapore Case*, 8 (2) Asian J. WTO & Int'l Health L. & Pol. 475 (2013).

[1] *Legal Services in Asia-Pacific*, MarketLine (2017), https://store.marketline.com/report/ohme9405-legal-services-in-asia-pacific/#save-report (last visited Nov. 20, 2017).

[2] *ASEAN Matters for America/America Matters for ASEAN* (2017), at 3–5; Wee En Cheong, *Deepening Connectivity within ASEAN*, www.singaporesummit.sg/news_item.aspx?sid=47 (last visited Jun. 25, 2018).

[3] Association of Southeast Asian Nations Economic Community Blueprint 2025 (2015), para 3.

overcome such obstacles under the AEC Blueprint 2025, regional regulatory harmonization and national progressive measures are critical to the integration of the legal services market.

To substantiate my argument, Section 9.2 will provide the most updated examination of legal services negotiations under the WTO and Asia-Pacific FTAs. These pacts include FTAs of Australia, China and Korea, as well as the TPP, which was "reborn" as the new CPTPP in November 2017.[4] Section 9.3 will assess the concept of ASEAN law under the AEC framework and the weaknesses in ASEAN states' implementation of legal services commitments. Section 9.4 will explore Singapore's experiment to liberalize its regime on foreign law firms and lawyers vis-à-vis the country's commitments under ASEAN FTAs and bilateral agreements. It further sheds light on potential implications for Malaysia and other ASEAN states. Finally, Section 9.5 will provide the conclusion and recommendations that build ASEAN as an integrated legal services market.

9.2 Legal Services Negotiations in Global and Comparative Contexts

To expedite ASEAN's legal services integration, it is essential to understand the development of negotiations and key issues under the WTO and Asia-Pacific FTAs. To this end, I will first explain legal services commitments under the GATS and the initiative launched by the APEC. In comparison, I will also address the challenges to the implementation of the US-Korea FTA, the China-Australia FTA and the CPTPP, as well as their implications for ASEAN.

9.2.1 From the WTO to APEC

Under the WTO Services Sectoral Classification List, legal services constitute part of "professional services" and cover advisory and representation services related to legal proceedings.[5] In general, legal services exclude the administration of justice because it concerns "the exercise

[4] Trans-Pacific Partnership Ministerial Statement (2017), paras. 3–5.

[5] Services Sectoral Classification List, MTN.GNS/W/120, Jul. 10, 1991; Joint Statement on Legal Services, Communication from Australia, Canada, Chile, the European Communities, Japan, Korea, New Zealand, Singapore, Switzerland, the Separate Customs Territory of Taiwan, Penghu, Kinmen and Matsu and the United States, TN/S/W/34; S/CSC/W/46, Feb. 24, 2005, at 2–3.

of governmental authority" as defined by the GATS.[6] Forty-five members, including four ASEAN countries, made legal services commitments in the Uruguay Round.[7] Notwithstanding these WTO commitments, the hurdles to liberalization often arose from the lack of transparency, as well as nationality, residency and licensing and qualification requirements. These limitations have hindered the effectiveness of supplying legal services in four modes under the GATS, in particular Mode 3 (commercial presence) and Mode 4 (movement of natural persons).

Remarkably, the core of legal services liberalization reflects Australia's limited licensing proposal, which urges WTO members to devise a less burdensome regulatory approach to allow foreign law firms and lawyers to practice nonlocal law without the requirement to gain a right of audience in local courts.[8] Moreover, it encourages host states to allow international law firms to form partnerships or other forms of voluntary commercial association with other law firms. In 2006, Australia, the United States and other "Friends of Legal Services" countries also issued a collective request to further remove restrictions on legal services.[9] Forty-two WTO members, including five ASEAN states, submitted offers related to legal services.[10]

Notwithstanding the WTO efforts, the stalled Doha Round has rendered the negotiations ineffective. Legal services exporting countries thus shifted the focus to the twenty-one member APEC, which incorporates seven ASEAN states. APEC by its nature is a soft law-based forum, but its consensus of trade rules could transform to hard law obligations in the WTO and FTAs. Sponsored by six countries, APEC launched the Australia-proposed APEC Legal Services Initiative, which aims to enhance transparency of domestic regimes.[11] The inventory covers information on regulatory frameworks on Mode 4 (commonly known as "fly

[6] General Agreement on Trade in Services (1994), art. 1(3)(a) & (b).

[7] Annex III: Legal Services – Specific Commitments, *in* Legal Services: Background Note by the Secretariat, S/C/W/318 (2010), at 29–30.

[8] Negotiating Proposal for Legal Services Revision, Communication from Australia, S/CSS/W/67/Supp.1/Rev/1 (2001), at 2–5.

[9] Collective Request: Legal Services (2006), www.iatp.org/files/451_2_78786.pdf (last visited Nov. 21, 2017).

[10] WTO Services Negotiations – Derestricted Offers Relating to Legal Services (2010), www.americanbar.org/content/dam/aba/migrated/cpr/gats/derestricted.authcheckdam.pdf (last visited Nov. 21, 2017).

[11] APEC Legal Services Initiative, www.legalservices.apec.org/ (last visited Nov. 21, 2017); Completion Report for APEC legal Services Initiative, 2011/SOM1/GOS/006 (2011), at 2–3.

in, fly out" practice), full and limited licenses to practice law and rules on law firms' partnerships. Yet, as the initiative was a one-time project, the inventory information in the inventory has not been updated since 2010. APEC members' reported domestic rules were also incomplete due to APEC's voluntary approach.

9.2.2 *Bilateral FTAs and the CPTPP*

Multilateral initiatives at the WTO and the APEC have yet to achieve meaningful legal services liberalization. On the front of FTAs, the most "groundbreaking" agreement for liberalizing the legal market is the US-Korea FTA, which advances US law firms' interest to export legal services to Asia. The subsequent EU-Korea FTA incorporates comparable provisions. Both FTAs mandated three-phase liberalization under Korea's Foreign Legal Consultant Act.[12] Phase 1 allowed for the establishment of the representative offices of US and EU law firms, Phase 2 permitted these firms' cooperative agreements with Korean counterparts and eventually Phase 3 enabled joint ventures that permit the hiring of Korean-qualified lawyers.[13]

Nearly thirty foreign firms have entered Korea under the new scheme since EU and US FTAs took effect in 2011 and 2012, respectively.[14] In reality, the fee-sharing arrangement between foreign and Korean firms under Phase 2 had a marginal impact on the market. The final phase for EU and US firms that commenced in July 2016 and March 2017, respectively, was expected to bring paradigm changes.[15] However, the 2016 amendments to the FLCA significantly hindered the incentives for forming joint ventures.[16] The amendments not only impose a 49 percent equity cap on foreign firms in joint ventures, but also subject them to unlimited liability. The provisions that exclude joint venture firms from practicing certain areas, such as intellectual property, and that require

[12] E.g., Annex II-Korea-44–45, Korea-US FTA (2007). For the Korea-US Free Trade Agreement, deadlines for three stages of liberalization are set for 2012, 2014 and 2017, respectively.

[13] Marialuisa Taddia, *South Korean Legal Market, Life and Seoul*, The Law Society Gazette, Feb. 27, 2017, www.lawgazette.co.uk/practice/south-korean-legal-market-life-and-seoul/5059972.article (last visited Nov. 21, 2017).

[14] *Id.*

[15] *Id.*

[16] *Id.*; see Thomas M. Susman of the American Bar Association, Letter to the Ministry of Justice of the Republic of Korea, Apr. 11, 2016 (indicating the concerns about arts. 24 and 35 under the amended Foreign Legal Consultant Act).

Korean firms to be in operation for at least three years before joining the ventures have eroded the FTAs' liberalization mandate.

Following US and EU FTAs with Korea, the China-Australia FTA that came into force in 2015 is among the rare Asia-Pacific FTAs that incorporate legal services commitments.[17] Apart from the components that are akin to China's WTO commitments that permit foreign firms to operate representative offices for non-Chinese law practice, "innovative" FTA commitments relate to the Shanghai Pilot Free Trade Zone.[18] The FTA enables Australian law firms to form commercial associations with Chinese counterparts in the FTZ. Importantly, commercial associations are distinct from joint ventures, as both firms retain independent legal status, financial operation and liabilities. Furthermore, Australian firms that are established in the FTZ can contract with Chinese firms to exchange lawyers to act as legal counsels.

The China-Korea FTA includes similar provisions on Korean law firms in the FTZ.[19] The impact of FTZ-related legal services provisions remains to be seen. Yet, the Shanghai Municipal Bureau of Justice has previously granted the rights for commercial associations and mutual assignment of lawyers to foreign law firms regardless of FTA obligations.[20] Hence, in essence, the FTAs do not accord Australian and Korean law firms "extra" advantages.

In addition to the bilateral FTAs, the most noteworthy mega-regional agreement in the Asia-Pacific has been the twelve-party TPP, which includes provisions on "transnational legal services."[21] After US withdrawal from the TPP in January 2017, Japan and Australia have played a critical role in salvaging the deal. Certain countries, such as Vietnam, Canada and New Zealand (new Prime Minister Jacinda Ardern's center-left government), have voiced reluctance to keep the same commitments.[22] To strike a balance, eleven TPP countries reached a consensus "on the core elements of" the new CPTPP on the sidelines of the 2017 APEC meeting.[23] Signed in March 2018, the CPTPP, which incorporates

[17] FTA Text and Tariff Schedules, http://dfat.gov.au/trade/agreements/chafta/official-documents/Pages/official-documents.aspx (last visited Nov. 21, 2017).

[18] Annex III to Chapter 8, China-Australia FTA (2015), at 1060.

[19] Annex 8-A-2, China-Korea FTA (2015), at 80–62-64.

[20] For the two implementation measures, refer to http://en.pkulaw.cn/display.aspx?cgid=17693374&lib=law (last visited Nov. 21, 2017).

[21] Annex 10-A to Chapter 10, Trans-Pacific Partnership (2016) (TPP), art. 9.

[22] *Vietnam, Canada Holding up TPP*, Otago Daily Times, Nov. 10, 2017, www.odt.co.nz/news/national/vietnam-canada-holding-tpp (last visited Nov. 21, 2017).

[23] TPP Statement, *supra* note 4, para. 3 & Annex II – List of Suspended Provisions.

the agreed list of suspended provisions, will keep the TPP provisions largely intact. The CPTPP will be the mega-agreement that further liberalizes legal services in the Asia-Pacific. The TPP legal services provisions may also serve as the benchmark for the negotiations of the sixteen-country RCEP.

In my view, the TPP legal services provisions that will be incorporated into the CPTPP have certain salient features. Although the TPP reflects the concept of limited licensing in WTO negotiations, the provisions help clarify the "grey area" that countries neither currently prohibit nor specifically allow by law. First, the TPP permits foreign lawyers to participate in arbitration and mediation proceedings and to provide services on a fly in, fly out basis.[24] Often-raised obstacles for foreign lawyers, such as the minimum residency requirements, are further relaxed.[25] The TPP rules can thus facilitate foreign law firms to engage in commercial arbitration or ISDS claims that are expected to increase following the CPTTP's entry into force.[26]

Second, the TPP permits an international firm to choose the name it prefers (usually the firm name of its headquarters).[27] This technical issue can be of significance to legal service liberalization in ASEAN and the RCEP. For instance, the Philippine Constitution bestows the exclusive power to regulate "the admission to the practice of law" on the Supreme Court.[28] Since the Court's 1985 decision enjoined Baker & McKenzie from practicing law under its name due to its "alien law firm" status, its Manila office has practiced through a locally incorporated firm referred to as "Quisumbing Torres."[29]

9.3 The Legal Services Market in the AEC

The consolidation of the legal services market will fortify ASEAN's integration and its competitiveness to attract FDIs. In light of limited success in the WTO and FTAs, the ASEAN case may provide valuable lessons for South-based regionalism. Undoubtedly, ASEAN's legal systems are complex because they include common law, civil law, socialist law and Sharia law influenced by former colonial powers. Despite the

[24] Annex 10-A to TPP, Ch. 10, art. 10(b) & (e).
[25] *Id.*, art. 10(d).
[26] TPP, Ch. 9.
[27] *Id.*, art. 10(g).
[28] Const. of the Philippines (1987), art. VIII, sec. 5.5.
[29] Dacanay v. Baker & McKenzie, Adm. Case No. 2131 (1985).

legal diversity, the concept of ASEAN law has been in existence since the 1967 Bangkok Declaration gave birth to the bloc as a loose security alliance.

9.3.1 *Emerging ASEAN Law*

Distinct from the supranational European Union, ASEAN is "an intergovernmental organization" that has operated based on soft-law harmonization rather than the hard-law, top-down model.[30] From an economic perspective, ASEAN law encompasses internal and external dimensions. The creation of the AEC in 2015 culminated ASEAN's economic integration since the AFTA was forged in 1993.[31] The new AEC Blueprint 2025 will guide the direction of the AEC that comprises new-generation intra-ASEAN treaties. To remedy the AFTA's low utilization, the ASEAN Trade in Goods Agreement consolidated previous agreements on goods and reduced nontariff barriers.[32] As of 2017, the AFAS negotiations have led to the ratification of nine packages of services commitments.[33] The ASEAN Comprehensive Investment Agreement also streamlined the schedule of reservations and strengthened the ISDS mechanism.[34]

ASEAN's external FTAs also form an integral part of ASEAN law. Since 2002, ASEAN as a bloc has concluded six ASEAN+1 FTAs with seven Asia-Pacific countries.[35] The 2017 ASEAN-Hong Kong FTA and Investment Agreement constitutes the latest instruments under the ASEAN-plus framework. The AANZFTA is the most comprehensive, single-undertaking ASEAN+1 FTA. ASEAN FTAs with China, Korea and India have followed the incremental approach by enacting a framework agreement that facilitates the conclusion of sectoral agreements on trade in goods, trade

[30] Charter of the Association of Southeast Asian Nations (2007), art. 3.

[31] Masahiro Kawai & Kanda Naknoi, *ASEAN Economic Integration through Trade and Foreign Direct Investment: Long-Term Challenges*, ADBI Working Paper Series, No. 545 (2015), at 12–13.

[32] Stefano Inama & Edmund W. Sim, Rules of Origin in ASEAN: A Way Forward 4–27 (2015).

[33] The conclusion of the tenth and final package of commitments was postponed from 2015 to 2017. Chairman's Statement on the Twenty-Eighth and Twenty-Ninth ASEAN Summits, Sept. 6–7, 2016, at 10.

[34] ASEAN Comprehensive Investment Agreement: A Guidebook for Business & Investors (2013), at 9–11.

[35] *Free Trade Agreements with Dialogue Partners*, http://asean.org/asean-economic-community/free-trade-agreements-with-dialogue-partners/ (last visited Nov. 22, 2017); Joint Media Statement, The Signing of the ASEAN-Hong Kong, China Free Trade Agreement and ASEAN-Hong Kong, China Investment Agreement (2017).

services, investment and dispute settlement. AESAN+1 FTAs, the CPTPP, the RCEP and EU agreements with ASEAN states will collectively shape ASEAN law.[36]

Emerging ASEAN law buttresses the AEC integration and helps cultivate ASEAN law. Tellingly, selected firms have become well-known "ASEAN law firms," including Rajah & Tann of Singapore, Zaid Ibrahim & Co (ZICO) of Malaysia and DFDL of Laos.[37] These firms, which employ primarily ASEAN lawyers, have expanded their regional practice and gradually ascended to compete with international law firms in Southeast Asian transactions. Conferring preferential treatment on ASEAN lawyers and law firms in the region will strengthen their "home advantage" and facilitate cross-border investments in line with the AEC objectives. Hence, promoting transnational legal services in ASEAN is critical to the economic completeness of the bloc.

9.3.2 *Legal Services Commitments and Enforcement*

In the Uruguay Round, four ASEAN states entered into WTO commitments in legal services.[38] Cambodia, Malaysia, Thailand and Vietnam agreed to ease restrictions on advisory services relating to foreign law and international law.[39] Several ASEAN+1 FTAs also cover legal services commitments. These pacts include the ASEAN-Korea Trade in Services Agreement, the AANZFTA and the 2011 second package of commitments under the ASEAN-China Agreement on Trade in Services.

At the ASEAN level, legal services are not listed as priority sectors under the previous AEC Blueprint 2015, which aimed to enable "free flow of services."[40] The Blueprint's goal to "remove substantially all restrictions" on remaining services sectors by 2015 was not met.[41] Arguably for this reason, the AEC Blueprint 2025 altered the aspiration from "an

36 As of 2017, the European Union has concluded FTAs with Singapore and Vietnam and entered FTA negotiations with Indonesia and the Philippines. Overview of FTA and Other Trade Negotiations, www.consilium.europa.eu/media/31365/ongoing-trade-negotiations.pdf (last visited Nov. 22, 2017).

37 Rajah & Tann and Zaid Ibrahim & Co first developed the "ASEAN law firm" concept. Interview with a Malaysian lawyer (name withheld), Jul. 10, 2013.

38 Annex III: Legal Services – Specific Commitments, *in* Legal Services: Background Note by the Secretariat, *supra* note 7, at 29–30.

39 *Id.*

40 ASEAN Economic Community Blueprint (2007), paras. 6–10.

41 *Id.*, at 10.

ASEAN single market" to "a more united market" that will "broaden and deepen services integration."[42]

Although ASEAN states' legal services commitments have not met the expectations, ASEAN treaties have provided a framework for regional harmonization. Under the AFAS negotiations, the eighth package of commitments in 2010 first incorporated legal service commitments.[43] In comparison, the 2015 ninth package of commitments include certain characteristics. First, the number of ASEAN countries that made legal services commitments increased from five to seven.[44] For the first time, Singapore committed to more qualified international commercial arbitration services than conventional legal services. These developments left Myanmar and the Philippines the only countries that failed to commit to liberalizing legal services.[45]

Second, certain countries impose Mode 3 restrictions, evidenced by the requirement of Brunei, Cambodia and Vietnam for foreign firms to partner or associate with local firms and Laos' 49 percent foreign equity restriction.[46] While it is common to permit foreign firms to practice nonlocal law, Malaysia adopted a more restrictive stance by only allowing the supply of such legal services to offshore companies incorporated in the Federal Territory of Labuan. Lastly, ASEAN countries' Mode 4 commitments are independent from the ninth package of AFAS commitments. Instead, they are incorporated in the ASEAN MNP Agreement with the aim to facilitate intraregional "temporary entry and temporary stay."[47] Although Indonesia, Malaysia, Thailand and Vietnam made the Mode 4 commitments, they merely reflect the scope of practice permitted under Mode 3 commitments.[48] Moreover, Indonesia is the sole country that requires foreign lawyers to provide ten hours of "free skill and knowledge transfer" to local counterparts on a monthly basis.[49]

While ASEAN FTAs created a regulatory framework for harmonizing legal services rules, I contend that a gap between the regional agreements and the actual practice is evident. For instance, some ASEAN countries

[42] AEC Blueprint 2015, para. 6; AEC Blueprint 2025, paras. 3–6.

[43] Annexes to the Protocol to Implement the Eighth Package of Commitments under the ASEAN Framework Agreement on Services (2010).

[44] Annexes to the Protocol to Implement the Ninth Package of Commitments under the AFAS (2015).

[45] *Id.*

[46] *Id.*

[47] ASEAN Agreement on the Movement of Natural Persons (2012), art. 6.

[48] Annex I to the ASEAN Agreement on the Movement of Natural Persons (2012).

[49] *Id.*

simply "copied and pasted" their legal services commitments in these FTAs at different times without any significant improvement. Compared with treatment of their Australian or Chinese counterparts under ASEAN+1 FTAs, AFAS does not accord preferential treatment to ASEAN-based law firms and lawyers. This counteracts the AEC's objectives. Also, the WTO and FTA commitments can be misleading. Although the Philippines and Singapore made limited legal services commitments, they represent significantly different levels of liberalization. Both countries have highly regulated the legal profession, but Singapore has significantly liberalized the legal market in the past decade.

More importantly, the absence of Mode 4 commitment under the ASEAN MNP Agreement can pose challenges to international and regional law firms. A more recent case is Malaysia's proposed Legal Profession (Amendment) Act 2012, which made foreign lawyers' temporary advisory services related to non-Malaysian law illegal.[50] The rule may lead to the interpretation that even a Singapore-based general counsel could be barred from providing Singaporean legal advice to Malaysian subsidiaries. Although the Malaysian Bar Council later decided to amend the Act to permit foreign lawyers to temporarily practice up to sixty days each year, this incident illustrates the concerns.[51] It also highlights the rationale for the CPTPP to incorporate rules on the fly in, fly out practice.

9.4 The Legal Experiments of Singapore

Regional agreements and legal services commitments of respective countries serve as mechanisms to accelerate regional harmonization. Arguably, the ASEAN case demonstrates that countries' progressive, FTA-plus measures are more effective to accomplish legal services liberalization. Singapore, which has emerged as ASEAN's financial and legal hub, reinforces this contention. Home to more than 130 international law firms, the value of Singapore's legal services export has grown by 60 percent.[52] The 22 percent growth of cases filed before the Singapore

50 Legal Profession (Amendment) Act 2012, sec. 37(2A).

51 *Liberalisation of Legal Services*, www.malaysianbar.org.my/trade_in_legal_services_formerly_known_as_gats/liberalisation_of_legal_services.html (last visited Nov. 23, 2017).

52 Legal Services Regulatory Authority E-Services, www.mlaw.gov.sg/eservices/lsra/search-lawyer-or-law-firm/ (last visited Nov. 24, 2017); Speech by Minister for Law, K. Shanmugam, during the Committee of Supply Debate 2014, Mar. 5, 2014, www.mlaw.gov.sg/news/parliamentary-speeches-and-responses/speech-by-minister-during-cos-2014.html (last visited Jan. 29, 2018).

International Arbitration Centre evidences Singapore's status as a key commercial dispute resolution center.[53] The establishment of the Singapore International Commercial Court (SICC) in 2015 has further strengthened the country's regional competitiveness.

9.4.1 The Regulatory Framework for Foreign Law Firms

Singapore's liberalization of its legal services market and the impact of its FTAs provide important lessons for other ASEAN countries and the AEC. Under Singapore law, local firms are categorized as Singapore Law Practices. Foreign law firms operate under six schemes: Representative Offices, Foreign Law Practices, Formal Law Alliances (FLAs), Joint Law Ventures (JLVs), Qualifying Foreign Law Practices (QFLPs) and most recently Group Practices.[54] Although foreign firms have operated in Singapore since the 1980s, the Legal Profession Act (LPA) only governed local firms and left foreign counterparts out of the regulatory framework.[55]

The goal to boost its economic growth, keep talented lawyers in Singapore-based firms and promote the application of Singapore law in regional transactions galvanized the innovation of legal services rules in the 2000s.[56] The amendments to the LPA in 2000 for the first time required foreign law firms and lawyers to register and introduced the JLVs and FLAs.[57] In 2008, the QFLP scheme was introduced.[58] In 2015, the government set up the Legal Services Regulatory Authority to

[53] Yun Kriegler, *Singapore Sees Record-Breaking Numbers of Arbitration Cases*, Lawyer, Mar. 30, 2016, www.thelawyer.com/issues/online-march-2016/singapore-sees-record-breaking-numbers-of-arbitration-cases/ (last visited Jan. 29, 2018).

[54] Types of Licence or Registration, www.mlaw.gov.sg/content/minlaw/en/legal-industry/licensing-or-registration-of-law-practice-entities0/types-of-licence-or-registration.html (last visited Nov. 24, 2017).

[55] *Liberalisation of Singapore's Legal Sector: A Reflection*, 1 (2) AL-MIZAN 13, 14 (2013) (explaining that in 1981, to promote the Asian Dollar Market, Singapore "allowed foreign banks in Singapore to bring in solicitors . . . upon the Attorney-General's informal approval, to provide legal services for Asian dollar bonds . . . ").

[56] Report of the Committee to Develop the Singapore Legal Sector (2007), at 67 & 85; Second Reading Speech on Legal Profession (Amendment) Bill 2008 by Law Minister K. Shanmugam, Aug. 26, 2008, www.mlaw.gov.sg/news/parliamentary-speeches-and-responses/second-reading-speech-on-legal-profession-amendment-bill-2008-by-law-minister-k-shanmugam.html (last visited Jan. 28, 2018).

[57] Jeffrey Chan Wah Teck, *Liberalisation of the Singapore Legal Sector*, www.aseanlawassociation.org/10GAdocs/Singapore3.pdf (last visited Nov. 24, 2017), at 3–4.

[58] *Id.*, at 5–6.

consolidate supervisory and regulatory functions divided between agencies for Singapore and foreign law practices.[59]

The legislative changes to liberalize the legal sector have significantly influenced foreign law firms' structural operations and shaped Singapore's legal landscape. The practice of Freshfields illustrates the impact of evolving legal regimes. In 1980, Freshfields became the first foreign law firm in Singapore.[60] As an experiment to advance the professional standing and improve Singapore's status as a financial hub, the firm received an ad hoc license that permitted it to practice Singaporean law.

Because Freshfields' monopoly status as an international law firm with a strong litigation practice created tensions among local lawyers, the authorities requested that the firm phase out its Singapore law practice.[61] To accommodate its Singaporean lawyers, Freshfields helped establish a boutique litigation firm, Wong Yoong Tan & Molly Lim, in 1987.[62] Freshfields continued to operate as a foreign firm until it formed a JLV with Drew & Napier, a prominent local firm, in 2000. Given the Asian financial crisis and the shift of the firm's focus to China and Japan, Freshfields terminated the JLV and exited Singapore in 2007.[63] However, due to the booming ASEAN market, Freshfields relocated its Hong Kong-based partners and reopened its Singapore office in 2012.

Like Freshfields, almost 85 percent of Singapore-based foreign firms are Foreign Law Practices. Markedly, the incentive to practice Singapore law under FLAs, JLVs or QFLPs has not prompted most international firms to change their legal status. The reason is not the complexity of the application procedure, but rather the cost and need of having in-house Singapore law expertise. For instance, Nagashima Ohno & Tsunematsu serves primarily Japanese clients.[64] To meet the demand from an increasing number of Japanese small and medium-sized enterprises, it is important to cater to these companies' legal budgets by allowing them to retain flexibility in choosing Singapore law firm partners. Hence, being an FLA, JLV or QFLP would not advance the firm's business.

59 Trade Policy Review, Report by the Secretariat, Singapore, WT/TPR/S/343 (2016), at 68.
60 Interview with a UK lawyer (name withheld), Jun. 28, 2013.
61 *Id.*
62 *Id.* The firm was renamed as Wong Tan & Molly Lim LLC.
63 Suzi Ring, *Freshfields to Reopen in Singapore Five Years after 2007 Exit*, LegalWeek, Feb. 10, 2012, www.legalweek.com/legal-week/news/2145159/freshfields-reopen-singapore-2007-exit (last visited Jan. 28, 2018).
64 Interview with a Japanese lawyer (name withheld), Jun. 4, 2013.

9.4.2 *FTA-Plus Measures for Foreign Lawyers*

In addition to increasing the options for international law firms' operating models, Singapore's scheme has accorded FTA-plus treatment to foreign lawyers. Singapore has not made legal services comments under the WTO and AFAS frameworks. Nevertheless, the SAFTA and the USSFTA, which became effective in 2003 and 2004, have energized the change in Singapore's local profession. The USSFTA mandates that Singapore recognize Juris Doctor (JD) degrees conferred by Harvard, Columbia, Michigan and New York University law schools for admission to the Singapore bar.[65]

For the same purposes, the SAFTA and its 2016 amendments require recognition of Bachelor of Laws (LLB) and JD degrees obtained from ten Australian law schools.[66] Both FTAs apply to Singapore citizens and permanent residents who graduated from designated schools with a required standing. For foreign trade partners, the FTAs can be used to secure the export of legal education services. In 2015, Singapore authorities' removal of eight British law schools, which accommodated 30 percent of UK-educated Singaporean lawyers, evidences this issue.[67] The lack of an FTA thus made UK law schools vulnerable to Singapore's statutory changes.

Moreover, FTA-plus measures for foreign attorneys are exemplified by the legislative change to ease the requirement on ad hoc admission of Queen's Counsels (QCs) and the adoption of the Foreign Practitioner Examination (FPE). QCs are well-recognized barristers in common law countries. The 2012 LPA amendment, which abrogated the "sufficient difficulty and complexity" threshold for cases, accords the Singapore courts greater discretion to decide on the admission of QCs.[68] The Singapore High Court in *Re Caplan Jonathan Michael QC* stressed that the "special reason" criterion in the LPA would limit the admission of QCs to "exceptional" cases.[69] As of 2016, the SICC proceedings have also involved more than sixty foreign counsels, including QCs.[70]

[65] George Yeo's Letter to Robert Zoellick, May 6, 2003.

[66] Annex 4-III, Singapore-Australia FTA (2003) & Agreement to Amend the Singapore-Australia FTA (2006).

[67] Amelia Teng & Amir Hussain, *Shorter List of Approved UK Law Schools Welcomed*, The Straits Times, Feb. 26, 2015, www.straitstimes.com/singapore/courts-crime/shorter-list-of-approved-uk-law-schools-welcomed (last visited Jan. 28, 2018).

[68] Legal Profession (Amendment) Bill, 2012, Amendment of sec. 15:4(a).

[69] Re Caplan Jonathan Michael QC, (2013) SGHC 75, para. 75. One significant factor to consider is the availability of Singapore's QC equivalent, Senior Counsels or other attorneys to handle the case. *Id.*, paras. 66–70.

[70] Sundaresh Menon, Speech at the Global Pound Conference Series, Mar. 16, 2016, at 26.

Following the SAFTA and the USSFTA, the launch of the FPE further internationalized Singapore's legal landscape in line with the liberalization of foreign law firms. The FPE aims to draw foreign lawyers of high caliber to contribute to Singapore's commercial sector. The FPE is limited to foreign lawyers who have at least three years of relevant work experience and have worked, or will work, in Singapore-based firms.[71] Foreign lawyers who pass the FPE will be accorded a Foreign Practitioner Certificate, which qualifies them to practice "permitted areas" of Singapore law that covers primarily commercial law.[72] From 2012 to 2017, the Singapore Institute of Legal Education has held six FPE examinations.[73] As the number of foreign lawyers who passed the FPE remains very small, the impact of the scheme remains to be seen.[74]

9.4.3 *Implications of JLVs and QFLPs*

Singapore's experiments in the schemes of Joint Law Ventures and Qualifying Foreign Law Practices are instrumental for other ASEAN states and Asia-Pacific FTAs. The concept of a JLV is a new legal entity created jointly by a foreign firm and a local firm. Thus, it is distinct from a JLA, which merely facilitates an alliance between two freestanding firms without cross-ownership. A QFLP license would allow a foreign firm to practice permitted areas of Singapore law independent of a Singapore law firm partner. A QFLP can also form a Group Practice with another FLP.[75]

As for Mode 3 commitments under the AFAS, selected ASEAN states include partnership and association mechanisms for foreign law firms to work with local firms. The final phase of Korea's FTAs with the United States and the European Union similarly enabled the joint venture firms. Singapore's liberalization efforts have directly influenced Malaysia. To build the nation as an international Islamic financial center, Malaysia also introduced the International Partnership and Qualified Foreign Law Firm (QFLF) schemes, which are akin to Singapore's JLV and QFLP,

[71] Legal Profession (Foreign Practitioner Examinations) Rules 2011, rule 4(3).

[72] Fact Sheet 2, Legal Profession (Amendment) Bill: Foreign Practitioner Examination (2011), at 1.

[73] Final Report, Committee to Review the Regulatory Framework of the Singapore Legal Services Sector (2014), at 14, footnote 8; Guide to the 2018 Session of the Foreign Practitioner Examinations (2017), at 2.

[74] For instance, twelve candidates participated in the examination in 2016, but only seven passed it. Results of the 2015 (Postponed) Session of the Foreign Practitioner Examinations (2016).

[75] Types of Licence or Registration, *supra* note 54.

respectively.[76] Based on the Singapore case, I will analyze the potential problems for ASEAN states' reference.

As of 2017, only eight foreign firms formed JLVs in Singapore, and no firm has utilized the international partnership in Malaysia and the comparable scheme in Korea.[77] The common joint venture commitments under FTAs have proved to be unpopular. In Singapore, the JLV regime has undergone various stages of reforms since 2000. Singapore accorded preferential treatment to US and Australian law firms under the USSFTA and the SAFTA. The two FTAs eased requirements for establishing JLVs by reducing the number of resident foreign lawyers and the length of their relevant experiences.[78]

Nevertheless, a third of JLVs were dissolved from 2000 to 2005.[79] This "limited success" prompted the Singapore government to introduce an "enhanced JLV scheme" in 2008 to increase incentives for international firms to set up JLVs.[80] The 2008 scheme enabled the foreign firm of a JLV to share 49 percent of its constituent SLP's profits in the "permitted areas."[81] Despite the efforts, three of the "Big Four" firms, Drew & Napier, Wong Partnership and Allen & Gledhill, terminated their JLVs with Freshfields, Clifford Chance and Linklaters, respectively. The fundamental problem of JLVs lies in the management cultural differences in the JLV context, which ranges from partnership structures to standardized forms. Competing financial interests can also easily arise when the constituent FLP wishes to represent a foreign company that will compete with the Singapore firm's long-term local clients. These practical

[76] Lee Shih, *Malaysia's Liberalisation of Legal Services: One Year On*, Oct. 19, 2015, https://themalaysianlawyer.com/2015/10/19/liberalising-malaysia-one-year-on/ (last visited Jan. 28, 2018).

[77] Legal Services Regulatory Authority E-Services, *supra* note 52.

[78] For an overview of legal services under Singapore's FTAs with the United States and Australia, see Arfat Selvam, *Cross Border Legal Services in ASEAN under WTO*, www.aseanlawassociation.org/docs/w2_sing.pdf (last visited Nov. 27, 2017), at 76–78.

[79] Steven Chong, *Liberalisation of Legal Services Freeing the Legal Landscape: Is South-East Asia Ready?*, paper presented at the International Bar Association: Third Asia-Pacific Regional Forum Conference (2012), at 7.

[80] *Id.*, at 9; Yun Kriegler, *Singapore Flings: The Politics of Local Tie-ups Revealed*, Lawyer, Apr. 16, 2012, www.thelawyer.com/singapore-flings-the-politics-of-local-tie-ups-revealed/1012180.article (last visited Jan. 28, 2018).

[81] Allowing Singapore Law Practices More Flexibility to Grow and Enhance International Competitiveness, May 31, 2012, www.mlaw.gov.sg/news/press-releases/allowing-singapore-law-practices-more-flexibility-to-grow-and-enhance-international-competitiveness.html (last visited Jan. 28, 2018). In 2012, profit-sharing and holding of equity were increased to the 33 percent cap on the profits of the entire JLV in areas of cooperation. *Id.*

concerns should be of significance to FTA negotiators and legal services regulators.

Other than JLVs, Singapore's renewable, five-year QFLP license that permits the practice of commercial areas of Singapore law was introduced in 2008.[82] QFLP is also an FTA-plus measure, as it is not incorporated in any of Singapore's FTA commitments. As of 2017, there are nine QFLP firms in Singapore, and two Malaysia-based foreign law firms were granted similar three-year QFLF licenses.[83] Different from JLVs, QFLP licenses are awarded on a competitive basis. In Singapore, six and four leading US and UK-based international firms were accorded QFLP status in 2008 and 2013, respectively.[84] Except for Herbert Smith Freehills, all of the six firms in the "first batch" renewed their licenses in 2014. The QFLP firms have generated more than S$1.2 billion in revenue, with 80 percent coming from offshore transactions.[85]

Singapore's QFLP scheme provides an innovative regulatory example for foreign jurisdictions, including particularly the "closed" markets of Indonesia and the Philippines. Unique to other modes of foreign firms, QFLPs are required to commit to their growth in Singapore. The selection and renewal criteria include the value of its work, the number of the Singapore offices' resident lawyers, and whether the office can function as the firm's regional headquarters.[86] Compared with JLVs, eminent foreign firms are keen on pursuing QFLP licenses for reputational costs and cost efficiency. Potential clients will more likely retain international firms with QFLP licenses that would entitle them to practice Singapore commercial law.

[82] Legal Profession (International Services) Rules 2008, rules 3 & 11.

[83] Types of Licence or Registration, *supra* note 54. Trowers & Hamilton and Herbert Smith Freehills secured the Qualified Foreign Law Firm licenses in 2015 and 2017, respectively. Second foreign law firm to launch in Malaysia, Jan. 13, 2017, www.freemalaysiatoday.com/category/nation/2017/01/13/second-foreign-law-firm-to-launch-in-malaysia/ (last visited Jan. 28, 2018).

[84] Renewal of Qualifying Foreign Law Practice Licences Awarded in 2008, Feb. 28, 2014, www.mlaw.gov.sg/news/press-releases/renewal-of-qualifying-foreign-law-practice-licences-awarded-in-2.html (last visited Jan. 28, 2018).

[85] *Singapore Renews 5 QFLP Licences, HSF Opts Out*, Legal Business Online, Feb. 28, 2014, www.legalbusinessonline.com/news/singapore-renews-5-qflp-licences-hsf-opts-out/63776 (last visited Jan. 28, 2018).

[86] Renewal of Qualifying Foreign Law Practice Licences Awarded in 2008, *supra* note 84; Award of the Second Round of Qualifying Foreign Law Practice Licences, Feb. 19, 2013, www.mlaw.gov.sg/news/press-releases/award-of-second-round-qflp-licences.html (last visited Jan. 28, 2018).

Critical regulatory issues involving QFLPs should be highlighted. Effective monitoring is essential to ensure the goal of QFLPs to increase the hire of locally qualified lawyers. After receiving its QFLP status in 2013, Sidley Austin expanded its international finance team staffed by Singapore lawyers. Herbert Smith Freehills' decision not to renew the license was presumably because of its recruitment record and inability to generate expected revenues.[87] This underscores the challenge of maintaining QFLP status. In addition, ASEAN countries should be cautious as to the scope of permitted areas of law for QFLPs. An incremental approach to help QFLPs grow without jeopardizing local firms will need the authorities to limit QFLPs from bypassing the rule by creating an arrangement with local firms that are entitled to engage in local law practice, such as court proceedings.

9.5 Conclusion with Recommendations

Transnational legal services are of significance to the evolution of multifaceted ASEAN law and for the AEC to form a highly integrated services market. In tandem with the AEC structure, I have analyzed pertinent provisions and practices of various agreements, such as the CPTPP and bilateral FTAs that Australia, China and Korea concluded. I have argued that various forms of governmental measures have nullified the services commitments under FTAs, and that promoting regional regulatory harmonization and national progressive efforts are key to effective legal services liberalization. To buttress the argument, I have examined Singapore's FTA commitments and intertwined experiment in internationalizing the legal market, as well as the implications for ASEAN nations. I offer legal and policy recommendations below for ASEAN's legal services liberalization that may provide guidance for South-based regionalism.

First, regional transparency and harmonization of national rules are essential. Akin to the APEC initiative, ASEAN schemes should promote the transparency of domestic measures on the practice of law. In extending the ASEAN mutual recognition arrangement to legal services, a key step is for the AEC to harmonize recognition of law degrees and qualifications. An interim harmonization measure can be adopted on an

[87] Yun Kriegler, *Can Herbies Succeed in Singapore without the QFLP?*, Lawyer, Mar. 3, 2014, www.thelawyer.com/analysis/behind-the-law/can-herbies-succeed-in-singapore-without-the-qflp/3017033.article (last visited Jan. 28, 2018).

ASEAN-X basis. Second, with respect to Mode 3 practice, Indonesia and the Philippines should be persuaded to lift the ban on the commercial presence of foreign firms. As the Korea and Singapore experiments demonstrated, joint ventures are conventionally indicated in FTA commitments but are of minimum impact on liberalization in the market. Singapore and Malaysia have adopted QFLP schemes. Subject to required conditions, such schemes permit international law firms to practice permitted areas of local law and can provide guidance for ASEAN countries.

Finally, to effectuate the ASEAN MNP Agreement in legal services, Member States ought to clarify fly in, fly out practice. The Mode 4 commitments of four ASEAN parties to the CPTPP can be the benchmark. To fortify competitiveness of regional lawyers, creating an ASEAN law consultant mechanism can also enable ASEAN practitioners to provide foreign law services under more favorable conditions. Based on the lessons of Asia-Pacific FTAs, these measures will accelerate the liberalization of trade in legal services under the AEC Blueprint 2025.

10

ASEAN Air Transport Integration and Liberalization: A Slow but Practical Model

JAE WOON LEE[*]

10.1 Introduction

Air transport is a service enjoyed by virtually every country in the world. The airline industry is a major economic force in terms of its own operations and its impact on related industries. Indeed, aviation has played an integral role in the creation of the global economy and has been an integral component in the establishment of the AEC. Since ASEAN designated air transport (or air travel) as one of the twelve priority sectors for economic integration in November 2004,[1] significant integration and liberalization have taken place.

In a nutshell, the liberalization of air transport has fostered greater competition, resulting in lower fares for travelers, more people traveling, more choices in airlines and routes for passengers and improved levels of services (e.g., higher frequencies).[2] As to the impact on the broader economy, liberalization leads to increased air service levels and lower fares (which in turn boost the volume of traffic).[3] This can also bring about increased economic growth and employment.[4]

[*] Parts of this chapter are adapted from the author's monograph: Regional Liberalization in International Air Transport: Towards Northeast Asian Open Skies (2016) and updated to reflect recent developments.

[1] See Association of Southeast Asian Nations Framework Agreement for the Integration of Priority Sectors Vientiane, Lao PDR, Nov. 29, 2004, http://asean.org/?static_post=asean-framework-agreement-for-the-integration-of-priority-sectors-vientiane-29th-november-2004. Originally there were eleven priority sectors, namely: agri-based products, air travel, automotives, e-ASEAN, electronics, fisheries, healthcare, rubber-based products, textiles and apparels, tourism and wood-based products; logistics was added as a twelfth priority sector in 2006.

[2] Ian Kincaid & Michael Tretheway, *Chapter 19 Economic Impact of Aviation Liberalization*, *in* Liberalization in Aviation: Competition, Cooperation and Public Policy 345–49 (Peter Forsyth et al. eds., 2013).

[3] *Id.*, at 354.

[4] *The Economic Impact of Air Service Liberalization*, InterVISTAS-ga (2006).

The immediate impact of air transport liberalization is the emergence of new airlines as entry barriers for the industry are lowered or removed. Successful new entrants, including low-cost carriers (LCCs), have had a major effect on the ASEAN economy. Indeed, Southeast Asia is the most successful LCC market, where they command a market share of nearly 60 percent. This is remarkable compared to the market share of LCCs in other regions (40% in Western Europe, 32% in North America, 19% in the Middle East, 11% in Northeast Asia and 9% in Africa).[5]

The first phase of the ASAM was completed when the 2010 MAFLPAS was ratified by the tenth state, Indonesia, in April 2016 (discussed in Section 10.2). ASEAN is now looking at a greater level of integration as stated in the AEC Blueprint 2025:[6]

> Air transport: Strengthen the ASEAN Single Aviation Market (ASAM) for a more competitive and resilient ASEAN, through the following key measures:
>
> a. Advance safer and more secure skies in ASEAN;
> b. Enhance air traffic management efficiency and capacity through a seamless ASEAN sky; and
> c. Foster greater connectivity, including the conclusion of aviation agreements with Dialogue Partners.

The chapter will be structured as follows: In Section 10.2, I will first examine the development of the idea of the ASAM and the three key agreements of the ASAM and their implementing protocols. I will then address in Section 10.3 and Section 10.4 the common external relations strategy for the group and discuss collateral benefits arising from the ASAM. In Section 10.5 and Section 10.6 I will assess the success factors of ASEAN air transport integration and liberalization from a comparative perspective and analyze the remaining challenges to the ASAM. This chapter will end with Section 10.7 presenting the prospects of the aviation policy goals stated in the AEC Blueprint 2025.

10.2 The Three Agreements: Markets Access Liberalization

10.2.1 Overview

Understanding market access in international air transport requires that we first understand the concept of "Freedoms of the Air." In fact,

[5] Will Horton, Centre For Aviation (CAPA) Northeast Asia LCC Conference (2016) (unpublished manuscript).

[6] ASEAN Economic Community Blueprint 2025 (2015), para. 48.

Freedoms of the Air (the privileges that one state grants the carriers of other states to conduct activities in that state's sovereign airspace)[7] are frequently referred to in international air transport. The nine freedoms of the air are illustrated as below:[8]

First Freedom – For the aircraft of State A to overfly the territory of State B;
Second Freedom – For the aircraft of State A to make technical stops in the territory of State B;
Third Freedom – For the aircraft of State A to embark passengers and cargo in State A and disembark them in State B;
Fourth Freedom – For the aircraft of State A to embark passengers and cargo in State B and disembark them in State A;
Fifth Freedom – For the aircraft of State A, from a service originating in State A, to embark passengers and cargo in State B and disembark them in State C;
Sixth Freedom – For the aircraft of State A to embark passengers and cargo in State B, reroute them through State A, and disembark them in State C;
Seventh Freedom – For the aircraft of State A to embark and disembark passengers and cargo between State B and State C without a stop in State A;
Eighth Freedom – For the aircraft of State A, from a service originating in State A, to embark passengers and cargo in State B and disembark them in another point in State B;
Ninth Freedom – For the aircraft of State A, from a service originating in State B, to embark and disembark passengers and cargo between two points within State B.

After ASEAN designated air transport as one of the priority sectors for economic integration, the ASEAN transport ministers adopted the Action Plan for ASEAN Air Transport Integration and Liberalization 2005–2015 and the Roadmap for Integration of the Air Travel Sector.[9]

[7] Alan Khee-Jin Tan, *Liberalizing Aviation in the Asia-Pacific Region: The Impact of the EU Horizontal Mandate*, 31 Air & Sp. L. 432, 433 (2006).

[8] Jason R. Bonin, International Air Transport Liberalization in East Asia: A Regional Approach to Reform (unpublished PhD Thesis, National University of Singapore, 2013) at 81–5.

[9] ASEAN Economic Community Blueprint (2007).

Thus, negotiations on liberalizing air services have taken place in the larger context of ASEAN's economic integration.

The push toward ASEAN regional liberalization has been incorporated in several declarations adopted by the organization.[10] In 1995, ASEAN initiated discussions of "open skies" at a leaders' summit held in Bangkok, Thailand. Since then, the idea of ASEAN open skies has been reinforced by meetings of the ASEAN transport ministers and in various policy documents. The ASEAN Memorandum of Understanding (MOU) on Air Freight Services was signed in 2002, representing a first step toward the full liberalization of ASEAN air freight services.[11]

During their tenth meeting in 2004, the ASEAN transport ministers adopted the Action Plan for ASEAN Air Transport Integration and Liberalization 2005–2015 and the RIATS.[12] The Action Plan set the long-term goal of ASEAN regional liberalization as the "conclusion of an ASEAN Multilateral Agreement on Air Services by 2015 by significantly removing restrictions on market access so as to achieve a single air transport market."[13] Concurrently, the RIATS also specified the goals and target dates from 2005 to 2010.

This roadmap has been successfully incorporated into three formal legal agreements to be signed by ASEAN Member States.[14] The three agreements are the 2009 MAAS,[15] the 2009 MAFLAFS[16] and the 2010 MAFLPAS.[17] Although the Action Plan has not been implemented according to the suggested timetable, the fact that ASEAN used a concrete action plan to push ahead with regional

[10] Peter Forsyth, John King & Cherry Lyn Rodolfo, *Open Skies in ASEAN*, 12 J. Air Transport Management 143, 144 (2006).

[11] *Id.*

[12] *Action Plan for ASEAN Air Transport Integration and Liberalization Done at Phnom Penh, Cambodia*, *in* ASEAN Documents Series 2004 221–6 (2005).

[13] *Id.*, at 223.

[14] Alan Khee-Jin Tan, *Toward a Single Aviation Market in ASEAN: Regulatory Reform and Industry Challenges*, *in* 2013 Economic Research Institute for ASEAN and East Asia (ERIA) Discussion Paper 2013–22, 3, www.eria.org/publications/discussion_papers/toward-a-single-aviation-market-in-asean-regulatory-reform-and-industry-challenges.html (last visited Jun. 28, 2018).

[15] ASEAN Multilateral Agreement on Air Services Manila (2009).

[16] ASEAN Multilateral Agreement on the Full Liberalisation of Air Freight Services Manila (2009).

[17] ASEAN Multilateral Agreement on Full Liberalisation of Passenger Air Services Bandar Seri Begawan, Brunei Darussalam (2010).

liberalization was instrumental in achieving meaningful results. All three agreements and their protocols have been ratified by all ten of the ASEAN states.

10.2.2 The 2009 Multilateral Agreement on Air Services

The 2009 MAAS provided a step-by-step approach consisting of six implementing protocols that aim to ease market access liberalization in the region. Protocols 1 to 4[18] had a limited impact, mainly covering secondary cities in growth areas (subregions) straddling borders with neighboring states.[19] Protocol 5 allows unlimited Third and Fourth Freedoms between capital cities (A's carriers between A's capital and another capital, e.g., Singapore–Bangkok and vice versa by Singapore Airlines). Protocol 6 allows unlimited Fifth Freedom between capital cities (A's carriers from A's capital to C's capital via B's capital, e.g., Singapore–Kuala Lumpur–Hanoi routes, all by Singapore Airlines).

Starting with liberalization in the border area subregions (Protocols 1 to 4) was a sensible approach. However, since the designated points in the subregions covered by Protocols 1 to 4 are mostly secondary cities, the impact on air traffic volume has been negligible. Substantial air transport liberalization in ASEAN begins with Protocol 5 since this step addresses unlimited Third and Fourth Freedom traffic rights between ASEAN capital cities. Further, Protocol 6 provides unlimited Fifth Freedom traffic rights between ASEAN capital cities. In reality, however, Protocol 6 would not have much commercial impact since the ASEAN capital cities are not very far apart, and few airlines would seek to operate a Fifth Freedom capital city stop within ASEAN.[20]

[18] Protocol 1 – Unlimited Third and Fourth Freedom Traffic Rights Within ASEAN Sub-Region; Protocol 2 – Unlimited Fifth Freedom Traffic Rights Within ASEAN Sub-Region; Protocol 3 – Unlimited Third and Fourth Freedom Traffic Rights Between ASEAN Sub-Regions; and Protocol 4 – Unlimited Fifth Freedom Traffic Rights Between ASEAN Sub-Regions.

[19] Tan, *supra* note 14, at 4 (noting that "four such sub-regions have so far been identified [new sub-regions may be declared or existing ones expanded]: the Brunei, Indonesia, Malaysia and Philippines East ASEAN Growth Area [BIMP-EAGA]; the Sub-regional Cooperation in Air Transport among Cambodia, Lao PDR, Myanmar and Vietnam [CLMV]; the Indonesia, Malaysia, Singapore Growth Triangle [IMS-GT]; and the Indonesia, Malaysia, Thailand Growth Triangle [IMT-GT]").

[20] Alan Khee-Jin Tan, *The ASEAN Multilateral Agreement on Air Services: En Route to Open Skies?*, 16 J. Air Transport Management 289, 290 (2010).

10.2.3 The 2010 Multilateral Agreement for the Full Liberalization of Passenger Air Services

The MAFLPAS was designed to supplement the MAAS and to include the rest of the ASEAN cities. The MAFLPAS contains two protocols. Protocol 1 permits unlimited Third and Fourth Freedoms between all cities (A's carriers from A's capital to B's non-capital, A's non-capital to B's capital, and A's non-capital to B's non-capital, e.g., Philippine Airlines' Manila–Ho Chi Minh, Cebu–Jakarta and Cebu–Ho Chi Minh routes). Protocol 2 allows unlimited Fifth Freedom between all cities (except capital–capital–capital), e.g., Garuda Indonesia's Surabaya–Singapore–Bangkok, Jakarta–Kuala Lumpur–Ho Chi Minh, Jakarta–Chiang Mai–Hanoi and Jakarta–Kota Kinabalu–Cebu routes.

Indonesia joined the MAFLPAS as the last state on April 7, 2016 (compared with Singapore, the first state to join the MAFLPAS on March 25, 2011).[21] It is no surprise that bigger players are hesitant to join the trend of regional liberalization. Some examples are Indonesia in ASEAN, Egypt and Saudi Arabia among the Arab states, Brazil in Latin America, Fiji among the Pacific islands and Nigeria in Africa. In contrast, smaller countries with competitive airlines are the drivers of regional liberalization. Some examples include Singapore in ASEAN, UAE in the Arab region, Chile in Latin America and Ethiopia in Africa.[22] Clearly, they have more to gain than to lose in their respective regional liberalization groups.

10.2.4 The 2009 Multilateral Agreement for the Full Liberalization of Air Freight Services

The MAFLAFS, consisting of two protocols, deals with the liberalization of the cargo market. It aims to remove market access barriers for ASEAN carriers on the operation of air cargo transport. Protocol 1 provides unlimited Third, Fourth and Fifth Freedoms between designated points, e.g., Vietnam Airlines' Hanoi–Clark and Hanoi–Vientiane–Bangkok cargo routes. Protocol 2 allows unlimited Third, Fourth and Fifth Freedoms between all points with international airports, e.g., Vietnam Airlines' Ho Chi Minh–Singapore and Hanoi–Singapore–Manila cargo routes.

Generally, liberalizing air cargo services has been considerably less controversial than air passenger services. Governments tend not to care

[21] ASEAN Legal Instruments – Instruments of Ratification (2017).

[22] For the details, see Jae Woon Lee, Regional Liberalization in International Air Transport: Towards Northeast Asian Open Skies 62–92 (2016).

very much about how their exports arrive at destinations, as long as the cargo is transported efficiently and at a reasonable cost.[23] Indeed, nine out of ten ASEAN states ratified the MAFLAFS within two years of its adoption.[24] However, it took six years for Indonesia to join the MAFLAFS due to its national carrier's concerns that the extensive all-cargo operations of neighboring countries' carriers would affect its own cargo business.[25] As the biggest economy in ASEAN, it is understandable that Indonesia was slow to join the MAFLAFS.

10.3 The Common External Strategy

The ASAM has attempted to establish a common external relations strategy for the group. This is remarkable given that ASEAN does not have strong institutions with enforcement functions like the European Union. Moreover, ASEAN has yet to complete the integration of its internal market. In contrast, the European Union started to tackle external affairs after it had completed its internal market integration. The European Union marked the start of a common external aviation policy when the so-called open skies judgment was rendered on November 5, 2002 by the European Court of Justice,[26] while a single aviation market had already been established in 1993.[27] ASEAN's approach to a common external strategy has been different. Since the early stage of the ASAM, the Member States have been aware of the need to establish a common external strategy vis-à-vis third countries and regions.[28] At the request of the ASEAN Secretariat, the aviation expert group conducted a comprehensive study on the ASAM[29] and recommended that ASEAN adopt aviation Dialogue Partners including the

[23] Tan, *supra* note 14, at 28.

[24] ASEAN Legal Instruments – Instruments of Ratification (2017).

[25] Tan, *supra* note 14, at 28.

[26] *Developing the Agenda for the Community's External Aviation Policy*, EUR-Lex, Mar. 11, 2005, http://eur-lex.europa.eu/legal-content/EN/TXT/?uri=LEGISSUM:l24078 (last visited Jun. 28, 2018).

[27] Air Transport: Market Rules, European Parliament, Oct. 2017, www.europarl.europa.eu/atyourservice/en/displayFtu.html?ftuId=FTU_3.4.6.html (last visited Jun. 28, 2018).

[28] Alan Khee-Jin Tan, *Aviation Policy in the Philippines and the Impact of the Proposed Southeast Asian Single Aviation Market*, 34 Air and Space L. 285, 303 (2009).

[29] Ian Thomas et.al., *Developing ASEAN's Single Aviation Market and Regional Air Services Arrangements with Dialogue Partners, in* CAPA Consulting's 2008 report (Final Report, REPSF II Project No. 07/003) (2008).

three East Asian states of China, Japan and South Korea as an initial priority, followed by India and the European Union.[30]

10.3.1 China

ASEAN agreed with China to work toward an ASEAN-China Regional Air Services Agreement at the Sixth ASEAN-China Transport Ministers Meeting in 2007.[31] The result was the adoption of the 2007 ASEAN-China Aviation Cooperation Framework, which includes provisions for the gradual liberalization of cargo and passenger services.[32] It is worth noting that the ASEAN-China Free Trade Agreement was the explicit justification for the ASEAN-China Regional Air Services Agreement, which was subsequently adopted in 2010. The 2007 ASEAN-China Aviation Cooperation Framework states that the ASEAN-China Regional Air Services Agreement should be concluded by 2010 "to support the realization of the ASEAN-China Free Trade Agreement in 2010" and "to implement the agreement thereafter in line with the establishment of the ASEAN-China FTA."[33]

The ASEAN-China free trade area came into effect on January 1, 2010,[34] and, unsurprisingly, the Air Transport Agreement between ASEAN and China was adopted in November 2010.[35] The ASEAN-China Air Transport Agreement and its Protocol 1 provide for unlimited Third and Fourth Freedom access for airlines on both sides and effectively supersedes the capacity restrictions in the bilateral agreements between the individual ASEAN states and China (the bilateral agreements are still in place – only the

30 *Id.*

31 Gong Yu, *U.S. – E.U. Open Skies Deal and Its Implication for the Liberalization of International Air Transport Services: A Chinese Perspective*, 2 J. East Asia and Int'l L. 129, 153 (2009).

32 See ASEAN-China Aviation Cooperation Framework (2007), para. 6. "6. The substantive elements of this ASEAN-China Regional Air Services Arrangement would include, but not limited to, provisions for gradual liberalisation of cargo services as well as passenger services: (1) removal of restrictions to the number of points in the route schedule; (2) no limitations on third and fourth freedom traffic rights between ASEAN and China; (3) no limitations on fifth freedom traffic rights between ASEAN and China; (4) no limitations on frequency and capacity, as well as the type of aircraft; (5) charter operation as an element; and (6) multiple airline designation."

33 *Id.*

34 For a discussion of ASEAN-China FTA, See e.g., Sarah Y. Tong & Catherine Chong, *CHINA-ASEAN Free Trade Area in 2010: A Regional Perspective*, 2010 East Asia Institute (Background Brief No. 519) (2010).

35 For details, see Alan Khee-Jin Tan, *The 2010 ASEAN-China Air Transport Agreement: Placing the Cart before the Horse?*, 37 Air & Space L. 35 (2012).

capacity has changed).[36] The ASEAN-China Air Transport Agreement and its Protocol 1 have been ratified by China and all ten of the ASEAN states.[37]

The two sides concluded talks in 2013 for a new Protocol 2 on Fifth Freedom rights that would take the Air Transport Agreement beyond Third/Fourth Freedom liberalization. However, Protocol 2 offers only a finite list of secondary cities through which Fifth Freedom rights can be exercised. The Fifth Freedom routes that this would make possible are not commercially viable options. However, it is important to remember that Protocol 1 is one of the very few open skies agreements that China has signed. ASEAN carriers have unlimited penetration into all of China (with the exception of Hong Kong, Macao and Taiwan, points excluded in the ASEAN–China Agreement), which would not have been possible if the ten states had negotiated with China separately.

10.3.2 India

ASEAN has hoped to secure an open skies agreement with India from the very beginning. The ASEAN–India Aviation Cooperation Framework was adopted at the Fourteenth ASEAN Transport Ministers' Meeting in 2008, which hosted air services consultations by the ASEAN–India Working Group on Regional Air Services Arrangements.[38] Despite a promise to work toward concluding an Air Transport Agreement between ASEAN and India based on open skies principles covering both air freight and passenger services,[39] there has been no substantial progress thus far. Singapore is the most active in urging India to liberalize its aviation sector by concluding the ASEAN-India Air Transport Agreement.[40]

[36] See Air Transport Agreement between the Governments of the Member States of the Association of Southeast Asian Nations and the Government of the People's Republic of China (The ASEAN-China Air Transport Agreement), ASEAN-China art. 23; see also Tan, *supra* note 14, at 22.

[37] ASEAN Transport Instruments and Status of Ratification (as of May 2018), http://asean.org/storage/2017/05/Ratification-status-Transport-Agreement-as-of-May2018_AT-00000002.pdf (last visited Jul. 19, 2018).

[38] 2016–2020 Plan of Action to Implement the ASEAN-India Partnership for Peace, Progress and Shared Prosperity, at 2.4.4 (2004).

[39] Plan of Action to Implement the ASEAN-India Partnership for Peace, Progress and Shared Prosperity (2010–2015).

[40] Nirmala Ganapathy, *India Should Engage More with ASEAN, Increase Aviation and Maritime Links: Vivian Balakrishnan*, The Straits Times, Nov. 1, 2017, www.straitstimes.com/asia/south-asia/india-should-engage-more-with-asean-increase-aviation-and-maritime-links-with (last visited Jun. 29, 2018).

10.3.3 *Japan*

The ASEAN–Japan Working Group on Regional Air Service Arrangement was established in 2014. Since then, the two parties have been meeting annually. On a bilateral level, Japan has signed open skies agreements allowing the Third and Fourth Freedoms for passenger and cargo services with eight ASEAN states.[41] The key issue is the Fifth Freedom, and specifically Fifth Freedom operation via the Tokyo airports of Haneda and Narita. Japan has already opened all cities except Tokyo to Fifth Freedom operation in its bilateral air services agreements with six ASEAN states: Vietnam, Malaysia, Myanmar, Singapore, Indonesia and Brunei. From Japan's perspective, opening Tokyo to unlimited Fifth Freedom could have undesirable results, such as multiple Singapore Airlines flights per day departing from Singapore and arriving in major US cities (Los Angeles, New York and Chicago, for example) via Tokyo. Allowing unlimited and likely profitable Fifth Freedom routes (e.g., Singapore–Tokyo–Los Angeles) is not an easy policy decision for Japan. Thus, it is expected that the ASEAN-Japan Regional Air Service Arrangement will be concluded in the near future while excluding Tokyo from the Fifth Freedom.

10.3.4 *South Korea*

ASEAN is actively looking to establish a new collective agreement with South Korea. Just as with Japan, the Fifth Freedom is the biggest obstacle here. In fact, South Korea is more sensitive than Japan in terms of the Fifth Freedom. While Korea has signed open skies agreements permitting the Third and Fourth Freedoms with six ASEAN members (Vietnam, Malaysia, Myanmar, Thailand, Cambodia and Laos), none of these air services agreements contain the unlimited Fifth Freedom. Although ASEAN is calling for the convening of the ASEAN–Korea Working Group on Air Services Arrangements,[42] it is unlikely that they will reach a meaningful agreement in the near future.

[41] Namely, Thailand, Vietnam, Malaysia, Myanmar, Singapore, Indonesia, Brunei and the Philippines.

[42] ASEAN, Twenty Third ASEAN Transport Ministers Meeting Oct. 12, 2017, Singapore – Joint Ministerial Statement, Oct. 12, 2017, http://asean.org/storage/2017/10/23rd-ATM-Final-JMS.pdf.

10.3.5 The European Union

The European Union and ASEAN agreed to commence negotiations on a comprehensive air transport agreement between the two regions in 2014. A prime motivation of this initiative was to neutralize the formidable Middle Eastern carriers that capture a significant amount of traffic in the EU–ASEAN market.[43] At the same time, the two parties are negotiating not only market access issues but also various topics including fair competition.[44] Reflecting these ambitious goals, the initiative has been named the ASEAN-EU Comprehensive Air Transport Agreement. Since both the European Union and ASEAN are willing to adopt the agreement, it is expected to be concluded soon. This will be the first ever region-to-region aviation agreement. It will be interesting to watch not only the substantive changes this agreement brings to these two regions, but also its impact on other parts of the world.

10.4 Collateral Benefits: Formation of Joint Venture Airlines

Market access liberalization is the most noticeable fruit of ASEAN's aviation integration. To a lesser extent, the common external strategy has also been making progress. In addition, the emergence of joint venture airlines in ASEAN is a collateral but significant benefit of ASEAN's aviation integration. Indeed, this collateral benefit complements ASEAN's lack of "ownership and control" liberalization.

Along with market access liberalization, the relaxation of ownership and control requirements is the other significant legal hurdle for air transport liberalization. The ownership and control restriction is the traditional requirement that an airline must be substantially owned and effectively controlled by nationals of the state that designates it for international air transport and under whose flag the airline is

[43] Alan Khee-Jin Tan, *The Proposed E.U. – ASEAN Comprehensive Air Transport Agreement: What Might It Contain and Can It Work?*, 43 Transport Policy 76 (2015); *Aviation: EU-ASEAN Aviation Summit Proposes "Open Skies" Agreement*, Feb. 12, 2014, http://asean.org/aviation-eu-asean-aviation-summit-proposes-open-skies-agreement/ (last visited Jun. 28, 2018).

[44] *EU, ASEAN Second Round of Negotiations for a Region-to-Region "Free Skies" Agreement*, UNIEROPA J. (2007), http://unieropajournal.com/eu-asean-hold-second-round-of-negotiations-for-a-region-to-region-free-skies-agreement/ (last visited Jun. 29, 2018).

operated.[45] In other words, foreign ownership in an airline designated by a particular state is restricted, typically to less than 50 percent ownership.

The EU broke with this tradition by introducing the concept of the "community carrier" for the first time. As a general principle, Article 52 of the Treaty of Rome (1957) (which is now Article 49 of the TFEU)[46] provides for the right of establishment and prohibits restrictions on the freedom of establishment for nationals of a member state in the territory of another member state. The aviation-specific EU Regulation 2407/92 (1992) stipulates that EU Member States shall grant an air carrier an operating license if the air carrier meets safety and finance requirements and is majority-owned and effectively controlled by EU Member States and/or their nationals. Thus, ownership and control of air carriers in EU Member States no longer necessarily means *national ownership and control*, but instead have been redefined as *EU ownership and control*.[47] These liberalization and integration efforts make it possible for EU carriers to have subsidiaries in other EU Member States. For instance, Lufthansa's subsidiaries include SWISS (based in Zurich but wholly owned by Lufthansa), Austrian Airlines (based in Vienna but wholly owned by Lufthansa) and Air Dolomiti (an Italian regional airline but wholly owned by Lufthansa).

In ASEAN, the wholly owned subsidiary strategy is not legally allowed. None of ASEAN's regional air transport agreements deal with the right of establishment for ASEAN investors. Admittedly, MAAS and MAFLPAS provide for a so-called "ASEAN community carrier," which is similar to the EU community carrier. However, the contracting state can reject the application of an ASEAN community carrier, even if the airline is substantially owned and effectively controlled by ASEAN interests. This means that there is no guarantee that an ASEAN community carrier will be able to access all countries in ASEAN, and this uncertainty is a manifest disadvantage for any investor planning to establish an ASEAN community carrier.[48]

[45] Isabelle Lelieur, Law and Policy of Substantial Ownership and Effective Control of Airlines: Prospects for Change 1 (2003).

[46] Treaty establishing the European Economic Community; See the explanation of "freedom of establishment" available at *The European Single Market*, European Commission, http://ec.europa.eu/internal_market/top_layer/living_working/services-establishment/index_en.htm (last visited Jun. 29, 2018).

[47] Peter P. C. Haanappel, The Law and Policy of Air Space and Outer Space: A Comparative Approach 136 (2009).

[48] Alan Khee-Jin Tan, *Toward a Single Aviation Market in ASEAN: Regulatory Reform and Industry Challenges*, compiled in Economic Research Institute for ASEAN and East Asia (ERIA) Discussion Paper Series 20 (2013).

However, joint venture airlines formed by two different ASEAN nationalities are commonplace in ASEAN. These joint venture airlines typically use the 51/49 model (that is, majority ownership by the local interest and minority ownership by the foreign parent airline). Table 10.1 summarizes the ownership and control structure of joint venture airlines, mostly LCCs, in ASEAN.

AirAsia pioneered the joint venture model in the region. In the case of AirAsia's subsidiaries in other ASEAN states, the local owners hold a majority share, while the parent airline group only has a minority stake. Certainly, this adheres to the traditional 51/49 practice.[50] However, it is less clear whether the requirement of "effective control"

Table 10.1: *The ownership and control structure of ASEAN LCC joint ventures*[49]

Country/ Territory	Joint Venture Airline	Local Shareholder/s	Foreign Shareholder/s
Indonesia	Indonesia AirAsia	Pin Harris – 20% and Sendjaja Windjaja – 31%	AAIL (wholly owned subsidiary of AirAsia Berhad) – 49%
Indonesia	Indonesia AirAsia X	PT Kirana Anugerah Perkasa (PTKAP) – 51%	AirAsia X Berhad – 49%
Malaysia	Malindo Air	National Aerospace and Defence Industries – 51%	Lion Air – 49%
Philippines	Philippines AirAsia	F&S Holdings – 16%; TNR Holdings – 16%; Alfredo Yao – 13% and Michael Romero – 16%	AAIL (wholly owned subsidiary of AirAsia Berhad) – 40%
Singapore	Jetstar Asia	Westbrook Investments Pte. Ltd. – 51%	Qantas Airways – 49%

[49] Adapted and updated from Lee, *supra* note 22, at 72–3.

[50] Under the laws of the Philippines, however, at least 60 percent of its capital must be held by Filipino citizens.

Table 10.1: (*cont.*)

Country/ Territory	Joint Venture Airline	Local Shareholder/s	Foreign Shareholder/s
Thailand	Thai AirAsia X	Tassapon Bijleveld – 41% and Julpas Kruesopon – 10%	AirAsia Berhad – 49%
Thailand	NokScoot	Nok Mangkang Co. Ltd. (wholly owned subsidiary of Nok Airlines) – 49% and Pueannammitr Co. Ltd. – 2%	Scoot Pte. Ltd. – 49%
Thailand	Thai Lion Air	Thai investors (undisclosed) – 51%	Lion Air – 49%
Thailand	Thai AirAsia	Asia Aviation – 55%	AAIL (wholly owned subsidiary of AirAsia Berhad) – 45%
Thailand	Thai Vietjet Air	Kan Air (Somphong Sooksanguan) – 51%	Vietjet – 49%
Vietnam	Jetstar Pacific	Vietnam Airlines – 69% and Saigontourist Travel Services – 1%	Qantas Airways – 30%;

applies since the managing expertise and strategic decisions may come from the parent foreign airline (the minority owner).[51] Typically, the local majority shareholders have no experience with aviation.

These joint ventures were only possible because ASEAN integration and liberalization were underway. In essence, ASEAN governments have relaxed the effective control test for other ASEAN companies who invest in LCC joint ventures in the region.[52] It is doubtful that the same joint ventures would have been approved if a totally foreign carrier (e.g., a US carrier) had proposed the subsidiaries to the local governments.

[51] Tan, *supra* note 14, at 18.

[52] See Jae Woon Lee & Michelle Dy, *Mitigating "Effective Control" Restriction on Joint Venture Airlines in Asia: Philippine AirAsia Case*, 40 Air & Space L. 231 (2015).

10.5 Success Factors

This section will discuss the success factors of ASEAN air transport integration and liberalization. In brief, ten ASEAN states, ASEAN as an institution and airlines in ASEAN have properly fulfilled their roles. There are three factors that other regional groups can learn from the ASEAN model.

10.5.1 All States Are Better Off

States typically liberalize their aviation markets when it is to the benefit of their national carriers, including the traditional flag carriers and the newer LCCs. Conversely, states generally do not open their markets when their carriers are not interested in liberalization. For policymakers, the interests of national carriers are often considered part of the national interest.[53] States are becoming less defensive about national airlines in general, and the benefits of air transport liberalization for consumers and the economy as a whole are widely acknowledged. Even so, its benefits for national airlines are still the real drivers of liberalization.

In other words, the success of national airlines (not necessarily state-owned companies but companies owned and operated by the state's nationals) is the key to convincing self-interested governments that open skies agreements make their airlines better off. If national airlines are not willing to enjoy the fruits of liberalization, there must be a clear benefit to the economy as a whole, and thus for the national interest. Not only airlines from Singapore (a traditional aviation power in the region) but also airlines from Vietnam, Indonesia, the Philippines and Malaysia (such as Lion Air, VietJet, Cebu Pacific and AirAsia) have enjoyed remarkable growth because of ASEAN's liberalization. This has also had a positive impact on countries like Thailand, Laos, Cambodia and Myanmar, which rely on the tourism industry. In short, each ASEAN state has benefited from ASEAN's liberalization.

10.5.2 Gradual Approach

ASEAN's approach has been gradual and patient. Indeed, ASEAN's aviation integration started with modest goals (Protocols 1 to 4 of the MAAS), and pursued more ambitious goals at a later stage. That was a realistic approach

[53] See Peter Forsyth, Liberalization in Aviation: Competition, Cooperation and Public Policy 403 (2013).

given that ASEAN has no central government or supranational institutions (unlike the European Union), and that it consists of ten states (more Member States than is ideal for close negotiations). Given a system in which reluctant states could hold up the entire project, a gradual approach was inevitable. Although progress was slow, ASEAN deserves credit for the good results.

10.5.3 Role of Airlines

Although the liberalization of market access has evidently facilitated the growth of LCCs, LCCs themselves also promote policy reform and liberalization.[54] In 2006, when the idea of an ASEAN regional liberalization was gaining support, the rapid development of LCCs in ASEAN put pressure on regulators to give access to more international routes and accelerated its liberalization process.[55] When ASEAN Member States adopted the MAAS in 2009, emerging LCCs served as one of the main drivers for this development.[56] The significant air traffic growth by LCCs and the success of LCCs (particularly AirAsia) prompted the ASEAN states to push for greater regional liberalization.[57]

10.6 Remaining Challenges

10.6.1 Insufficient Infrastructure

As growth in air traffic surpasses the available runways, parking and passenger processing capacity at terminals, airport slot shortage is becoming an issue in many airports around the world. Because of a combination of infrastructure constraints and political decisions, airports in Bangkok, Jakarta and Manila do not get capacity until long after they need it.[58] Jakarta's Soekarno-Hatta airport is heavily congested, with its current terminals operating well above its capacity of 22 million

54 See Xiaowen Fu, Tae Hoon Oum & Anming Zhang, *Air Transport Liberalization and Its Impacts on Airline Competition and Air Passenger Traffic*, 49 (4) Transportation J. 24, 35 (2010).

55 See Forsyth, King & Rodolfo, *supra* note 10, at 150.

56 See Forsyth, *supra* note 53, at 35.

57 *Id.*

58 Danny Lee, *As Singapore's Changi Airport Soars, Is HK$141 Billion Upgrade too Little too Late for Hong Kong?*, South China Morning Post, Nov. 3, 2017, www.scmp.com/news/hong-kong/economy/article/2118143/singapores-changi-airport-soars-hk141-billion-upgrade-case.

passengers (it served about 60 million passengers in 2014[59]), and its two runways are fully utilized during peak hours. Airlines seeking to add flights at the Soekarno-Hatta airport have to operate in very unpopular periods, such as before 6:00 a.m.[60] Thus, Indonesia's ratification of Protocols 5 and 6 of the 2009 MAAS does not effectively change anything since few new flights can be launched from Jakarta.

Similarly, the Philippines' ratification of Protocols 5 and 6 of the 2009 MASS is linked with the country's aviation policy of restricting access to Manila's congested Ninoy Aquino International Airport while fully opening Clark Airport, which is located about 80 km from downtown Manila.[61] The insufficiency of infrastructure affects the ability of air carriers to exercise market access rights granted to states under ASEAN's aviation liberalization.

10.6.2 Lack of Shared Vision

Now that the Third, Fourth and Fifth Freedoms of the air have been granted in ASEAN, the logical step is opening up the Seventh Freedom (the Sixth Freedom is simply a combination of the Third and Fourth Freedoms, so it does not require an international agreement). However, the Seventh Freedom – an airline's right to carry traffic between one foreign country and another without service to its home country – is typically viewed as a serious threat to local air carriers.[62] Most ASEAN states would not move toward relaxing the Seventh Freedom without a tangible benefit for their national carriers or people.

In relation to the ASEAN–China Air Transport Agreement, Professor Alan Tan draws attention to the fact that an individual ASEAN airline

[59] Emirsyah Satar (former CEO of Garuda Indonesia), *The Next Biggest Growth Opportunities for Indonesia's Airline Market*, Address to the Seventh Annual Aviation Outlook Asia Conference (Oct. 29, 2014) (unpublished).

[60] *Jakarta Halim Airport Re-opening Frees Soekarno-Hatta Slots for Citilink, Garuda, AirAsia, Lion Air*, CAPA, Jan. 12, 2014, http://centreforaviation.com/analysis/jakarta-halim-airport-re-opening-frees-soekarno-hatta-slots-for-citilink-garuda-airasia-lion-air-147479 (last visited Jun. 28, 2018); For instance, Mandala Airlines started flights at 4:30 a.m. in Jakarta because the carrier cannot get any airport slots later in the day. See Kyunghee Park & Jasmine Wang, *Jakarta 4:30 A.M. Flights Show Budget Carriers Outgrow Airports*, Bloomberg, Feb. 4, 2013, www.bloomberg.com/news/2013-02-03/jakarta-4-30-a-m-flights-show-budget-carriers-outgrow-airports.html (last visited Jun. 28, 2018).

[61] See Alan Khee-Jin Tan, *Aviation Policy in the Philippines and the Impact of the Proposed Southeast Asian Single Aviation Market*, 34 Air & Space L. 285 (2009).

[62] Alan Khee-Jin Tan, *Prospects for a Single Aviation Market in Southeast Asia*, 34 Ann. Air & Sp. L. 253, 271 (2009).

can only connect from its home territory to China, while Chinese carriers can effectively connect any point in China with any point in each of the ASEAN states.[63] For this reason, he argues, "ASEAN governments must start allowing each other the seventh freedom of the air if they are to carry traffic between any point in ASEAN and China" and adds that allowing the Seventh Freedom is "the only strategic way to match the Chinese airlines' ability to do the same thing."[64] However, the Seventh Freedom – which would allow, for example, a Thai carrier to station aircraft in Singapore and operate a route to Indonesia – continues to be resisted by most ASEAN states and their airlines.[65]

10.6.3 Incomplete National Commitments

Although all ten states have ratified the three agreements, some Member States have included significant reservations to the agreements when they have implemented them through domestic legislation and policies. Indonesian Presidential Regulation No. 12/2016 states that only five Indonesian airports are part of the agreement: Soekarno-Hatta International Airport (Jakarta), Kualanamu International Airport (North Sumatra), Juanda International Airport (East Java), Ngurah Rai International Airport (Bali) and Sultan Hasanuddin International Airport (South Sulawesi). Although these are all major airports in Indonesia, the Presidential Regulation is a significant departure from the original commitment to open all cities. For political reasons, Laos has not yet freed up Vientiane and Luang Prabang for Thai carriers. Furthermore, the Philippines is limiting access to Manila's Ninoy Aquino airport due to capacity and overcrowding concerns.[66]

10.7 Concluding Remarks

Overall, the ASEAN Single Aviation Market model should be praised for its steady progress and be regarded as a good and realistic example of

63 See Alan Khee-Jin Tan, *New Heights for ASEAN-China Community Diplomacy in Aviation*, East Asia Forum, Jun. 23, 2017, www.eastasiaforum.org/2017/06/23/new-heights-for-asean-china-commercial-diplomacy-in-aviation/#more-73763 (last visited Jun. 28, 2018).

64 *Id.*

65 *Id.*

66 James Jordan, *ASEAN Liberalization: Open Skies Achieves Full Ratification*, Holman Fenwick Willan LLP, May 2016, www.hfw.com/ASEAN-liberalisation-open-skies-achieves-full-ratification-May-2016 (last visited Jun. 28, 2018).

what the regional approach can achieve. ASEAN successfully completed the basic integration of the aviation market by providing the Third, Fourth and Fifth Freedoms of the air for both passenger and cargo services. According to the aviation policy goals stated in the AEC Blueprint 2025, ASEAN is now focusing on three pillars: aviation safety, air traffic management and connectivity.

Aviation safety has always been a primary concern of international aviation. The legal framework for aviation safety regulation is more collaborative and less controversial than any other topic in aviation law.[67] The problem ASEAN is facing is that the level of aviation safety in its ten Member States varies considerably.[68] According to a universal safety oversight audit program conducted by the International Civil Aviation Organization, the effective implementation scores of four ASEAN states are lower than the global level.[69] To develop ASEAN's civil aviation market, it is necessary to bridge this gap. How to achieve that goal is debatable. One idea is to forge a common aviation safety regulator in ASEAN that would be similar to the European Aviation Safety Agency (EASA) in the European Union. The EASA, founded in 2002, pursues technical harmonization in air transport to ensure the highest common level of safety. However, an ASEAN aviation regulator seems a long way off, and many ASEAN stakeholders still believe that aviation safety should be left to national regulators.[70]

Enhancing air transport efficiency and capacity is another goal. In the AEC Blueprint 2025, ASEAN uses the term "seamless ASEAN sky." ASEAN obviously adapted this concept from the European Union's Single European Sky (SES). The SES is an initiative to reform the architecture of European air traffic management in order to meet future capacity and safety needs at a European rather than a local level, thereby increasing the overall efficiency of the European air transport system.[71] The creation of a seamless ASEAN sky by way of the integrated

[67] Brian F. Havel & Gabriel S. Sanchez, The Principles and Practices of International Aviation Law 173 (2014).

[68] See ICAO, *Annual Safety Report Asia Pacific Region 2017*, (2017), www.icao.int/APAC/RASG/Documents/annual%20safety%20Report%202017.pdf (last visited Jun. 28, 2018).

[69] *Id.*

[70] Khettiya Jittapong & Kanupriya Kapoor, *ASEAN Air Safety Regulator May Still Be Decades Away*, Reuters, Dec. 16, 2015, www.reuters.com/article/us-airlines-asean-regulation/asean-air-safety-regulator-may-still-be-decades-away-idUSKBN0TZ0MB20151216 (last visited Jan. 30, 2018).

[71] See *Frequently Asked Questions (FAQ) on EUROCONTROL*, EUROCONTROL, www.eurocontrol.int/faq/corporate (last visited Jan. 30, 2018).

management of airspace will be beneficial to ASEAN aviation. Compared to an ASEAN aviation safety regulator, establishing a common air traffic system in ASEAN is a more realistic way to enhance the safety and efficiency of air traffic.

Lastly, ASEAN set the goal of fostering greater connectivity by concluding aviation agreements with Dialogue Partners. As the Seventh Freedom would be very difficult to achieve, ASEAN will focus on external relations. In doing so, ASEAN should bear in mind the challenges of its Dialogue Partners. When its Dialogue Partners negotiate with ASEAN, there is no guarantee that the ten ASEAN Member States (and particularly the states in which the Dialogue Partners are interested) will ratify the agreement in question. For instance, one Dialogue Partner might want Indonesia in an agreement it signs with ASEAN. But that agreement might be only ratified by a few like-minded states in ASEAN, not by Indonesia. In that case, the Dialogue Partner would lose the advantage of signing an agreement with ASEAN. This is not the case when non-EU states negotiate with the European Union, because the European Union has a supranational mechanism in place. In other words, the failure to strengthen internal coordination within ASEAN's ten states could weaken its ability to negotiate matters related to common external relations. In sum, ASEAN will make slow but steady progress in the years to come as it has for the last decade. It will be interesting to see how and to what extent ASEAN can achieve its goals by 2025.

PART 3

Investment Liberalization and Protection

11

Investment Liberalization in ASEAN: Moving from Myths to Reality

SUFIAN JUSOH

11.1 Introduction

ASEAN is an important player in the regional and global value chain where a final product is made from various components sourced from different locations. ASEAN economies serve as part of a global chain of products and services where the ASEAN Agreements and the AEC serve to integrate the value chain between ASEAN Member States and the world. In fact, ASEAN economies are forming part of the regional value chain (RVC), which is contributed to by the expansion of operations by multinational companies, the increasing capacity of local firms in producing inputs used in the various stages of value chains in ASEAN and regional integration in ASEAN through the establishment of the AEC in 2015.

Thus, it is important to analyze the ASEAN Comprehensive Investment Agreement[1] from the perspective of linking the economy of ASEAN countries through the GVC and the RVC. The GVC and RVC, which will have to be linked to both trade in goods and trade in services, are governed in the ATIGA[2] and the AFAS[3] respectively. This will make the three agreements a set of interrelated – rather than stand-alone –

[1] The Association of Southeast Asian Nations Comprehensive Investment Agreement was signed in 2009 and entered into force 2012. For a review of the Regional and Global Value Chain and ASEAN, see Ayako Yamaguchi, *Global Value Chains in ASEAN*, Institute for International Monetary Affairs Newsletter, No. 1 (2018), Jan. 4, 2018, at 1–15.

[2] The ASEAN Trade in Goods Agreement was signed in 2009 and entered into force in 2010. ATIGA replaced the earlier Agreement on the Common Effective Preferential Tariff of the ASEAN Free Trade Area 1992. The main objective of ATIGA is to establish an integrated market and production base with a free flow of goods by 2015, one of the goals of the formation of the AEC.

[3] The ASEAN Framework Agreement on Trade in Services 1995, is designed to allow for the free flow services and the freer flow of skilled labor respectively.

agreements that promote the free flow of trade in goods and services and free flow of capital within ASEAN.

ASEAN countries, including newer countries such as the Lao Peoples' Democratic Republic (Lao PDR) and Myanmar, will be able to utilize the three ASEAN agreements in order to diversify their economies through trade and investment. To achieve the objective of diversifying the economy and increasing FDI, Lao PDR and Myanmar will need to further liberalize their economies. New investment policies in both Lao PDR and Myanmar may be benchmarked against the liberalization pillar of the ACIA.

This chapter undertakes the task by examining the investment laws and policies in Myanmar and Lao PDR, two newer ASEAN members. Myanmar enacted the Myanmar Investment Law in October 2016[4] and has issued the Myanmar Investment Rules 2017,[5] whereas Lao PDR has enacted the Law of Investment Promotion 2016.[6] The new Myanmar Investment Law adopts all four pillars of ASEAN, including the pillar of liberalization. Nevertheless, the biggest challenge for the new law is how the new government treats investment liberalization through the updating of the negative list, and whether the new negative list will be more liberalizing and reflective of the commitments undertaken in the ACIA. The issue for Lao PDR is whether the new law will be able to address the rationalization of the negative list, which is under the control of two ministries, namely the Ministry of Planning and Investment and the Ministry of Industry and Commerce.

In Section 11.2, the chapter will briefly discuss the formation of the AEC, from the Bali Concord II to the ASEAN Charter. Section 11.3 will then discuss the main provisions of the ACIA, with special focus on the liberalization pillar, in particular the liberalization of investment sectors. This is followed by discussion on the standards of NT, MFN and SMBD.

Sections 11.4 and 11.5 of the chapter will then discuss recent investment policy reform processes in Lao PDR and Myanmar, mainly from the perspective of liberalization as stated in the ACIA. In conclusion, the chapter then makes several recommendations on how to further improve the liberalization reform processes in Lao PDR and Myanmar.

[4] The Pyidaungsu Hluttaw Law No. 40/2016, The 2nd Waning of Thadingyut, 1378 ME (Oct. 18, 2016).

[5] Ministry of Planning and Finance Notification No. 35 / 2017, The 3rd Waxing of Tagu, 1378 ME (Mar. 30, 2017).

[6] No. 14/NA Vientiane Capital (Nov. 17, 2016).

11.2 The ASEAN Economic Community

ASEAN took the first step toward regional integration with the signing of the Bali Concord II, which was endorsed at the Ninth ASEAN Summit in October 2003.[7] The Bali Concord II consists of three pillars, namely the ASEAN Security Community (now the ASEAN Political-Security Community), the ASEAN Economic Community and the ASEAN Socio-Cultural Community. The Bali Concord II is followed by the Bali Concord III "ASEAN Community in a Global Community of Nations."[8] The Bali Concord III covers all the main pillars of ASEAN, namely Political-Security Cooperation, Economic Cooperation and Socio-cultural Cooperation.

The transformation of ASEAN from a loose organization into a legal entity is enhanced by the signing of the ASEAN Charter on November 20, 2007.[9] Under the ASEAN Charter, ASEAN aims to create a single market and production base which is stable, prosperous, highly competitive and economically integrated with effective facilitation of trade and investment in which there is free flow of goods, services and investment; facilitated movement of business persons, professionals, talents and labor; and freer flow of capital.

To expedite the formation of the AEC, ASEAN leaders agreed to the AEC Blueprint 2015 at the Thirteenth ASEAN Summit held in Singapore in 2007. The AEC Blueprint consists of four key pillars, namely a single market and production base, a highly competitive economic region, a region of equitable economic development and a region fully integrated into the global economy.[10] The AEC Blueprint 2015 is succeeded by the AEC Blueprint 2025, which maps out ASEAN's ten-year strategic plan in the three areas of political-security, economic and socio-cultural pillars to further deepen and consolidate regional integration.[11]

Among other aspects, ASEAN looks to further increase investment liberalization, increase market access and reduce barriers to investment. Reducing barriers to market access is very important to ASEAN in view of the latest statistics showing that FDI into ASEAN has reduced by 20 percent in 2016 to US$ 96.7 billion, which is in line with the global

[7] Declaration of ASEAN Concord II (Oct. 7, 2003).

[8] Bali Declaration on ASEAN Community in a Global Community of Nations (Nov. 17, 2011).

[9] The ASEAN Charter, Nov. 20, 2007, entered into force on Dec. 14, 2008.

[10] ASEAN Economic Community Blueprint (2007).

[11] ASEAN Economic Community Blueprint 2025 (2015).

trend of reduced FDI flows.[12] ASEAN has outlined strategic measures to enhance investment flows into ASEAN, mainly on the issue of liberalization. To increase investments, ASEAN plans to provide effective implementation of the modality on the elimination or improvement of investment restrictions and impediments, and to identify appropriate approaches or mechanisms for the phasing out and/or reduction of the ACIA Reservation Lists. At the same time, ASEAN will continue to undertake and, where necessary, enhance the Coordinating Committee on Investment Peer Review Mechanism, which is mainly conducted in conjunction with the OECD.[13]

Nevertheless, a few challenges remain for the AEC.[14] There is still an economic and development gap between ASEAN Member States, especially between the ASEAN-6 and the newer ASEAN countries. In terms of FDI, there is a big gap between the FDI received by Singapore compared to the remaining ASEAN nations: Thailand, Malaysia and Indonesia (which are economically the most important countries after Singapore); the Philippines, Vietnam, Cambodia, Lao PDR and Myanmar (where most investments are resource-seeking given the wealth of mineral and water resources and a pool of relatively cheap labor). The third challenge lies in behind-the-border issues, which relate to legacy issues such as domestic regulations prior to the formation of ASEAN and ASEAN Community. These impose various obstacles to the full liberalization of investment in ASEAN.

11.3 The ACIA and Investment Liberalization

The ACIA was signed by the ASEAN Economic Ministers in 2009. It replaced and consolidated two earlier agreements, namely the IGA and the AIA. The ACIA is designed to enhance the flow of cross-border investment and promote the freer flow of capital by turning ASEAN into a more competitive economy and an attractive destination for FDI whilst increasing intra-ASEAN investment in both goods and services.[15]

[12] UNCTAD Global Investment Trends Monitor, *Foreign Direct Investments and Economic Zones in ASEAN, Special Edition*, No. 27, Nov. 16, 2017, at 1.

[13] AEC Blueprint 2015, para. 65.

[14] *OECD Southeast Asia Investment Policy Perspectives* (2014).

[15] For a serious discussion on the ASEAN Comprehensive Investment Agreement, see Julien Chaisse & Sufian Jusoh, The ASEAN Comprehensive Investment Agreement: The Regionalisation of Laws and Policy on Foreign Investment (2016).

Beyond the mere consolidation of earlier regional pacts, the ACIA is an enhanced agreement that encompasses four pillars: liberalization, facilitation, protection and promotion. The approach taken in the ACIA is to provide the best standard or approach in every pillar. What this means is that although ASEAN countries are encouraged to liberalize within the agreed sectors, they are also required to provide protections to ASEAN Investors investing within their territories. Such protections meet the standards under international best practices, such as fair and equitable treatment, full protection and security, free transfer of funds and direct and indirect expropriation only under certain conditions and compensation.

Investment liberalization in the ACIA responds to the needs of businesses looking to expand across national frontiers. Intra-ASEAN liberalization facilitates the efficient deployment of capital within ASEAN. The ACIA offers a platform for ASEAN nations to liberalize investment by lowering entry and postentry barriers faced by investors. Its provisions provide for more liberalization compared to its predecessor agreements. The ACIA provides for the progressive liberalization of investment regimes, and ASEAN members have committed to lift restrictions progressively in the ten sectors covered under the ACIA.

The approach on liberalization of investments in the ACIA is to remedy shortcomings in the both the IGA and the AIA. The benefits of the ACIA are extended to ASEAN Investors and foreign-owned ASEAN-based investors.

The IGA, being the first investment agreement between ASEAN nations, did not provide for any investment liberalization. Rather, the IGA was more of a BIT type, which only deals with the protection of investments and investors normally addressed by a BIT. The liberalization approach in the AIA was more complicated with the existence of the Temporary Exclusion List and the Sensitive List of Investments for ASEAN Investors and foreign investors.

Hence, the ACIA has to take a different step and approach to ensure economic sustainability in the region by encouraging ASEAN and non-ASEAN investments in the region. The ACIA provides for the progressive liberalization of investment regimes. This covers five sectors, namely, manufacturing and services incidental to manufacturing, agriculture and services incidental to agriculture, fishery and services incidental to fishery, forestry and services incidental to forestry and mining and quarrying and services incidental to mining and quarrying.[16] In terms of

[16] ACIA, art. 9.4.

liberalization, the ACIA covers both FDI and Portfolio investment (compared with the AIA, which refers to FDI only).

The concept of progressive liberalization allows ASEAN countries, especially the newer ASEAN members, to liberalize their investment sectors based on their economic development and national policy objectives. The principle of "progressive liberalization" follows the mechanism in use within the WTO, especially in relation to the liberalization of the services sector under the GATS, where its approach was also adopted by ASEAN in the AFAS. The GATS recognizes the need of developing countries to liberalize their economy and trade over time.[17] The principle also includes the concept that the government should not backtrack on liberalization or reintroduce restrictions that have been removed once the liberalization of sectors occurs.

Nevertheless, the ACIA allows each ASEAN state to provide reservations to the liberalization under the Schedules.[18] Under Article 10, an ASEAN member may, for a period of twelve months after the submission of a schedule, adopt measures or modify its reservations for prospective applications to investors and their investments in the liberalized sectors. This is provided so that such measures or modification shall not adversely affect any existing investors and investment.[19] After the twelve-month period any Member State may, however, reach an agreement with any other Member State to adopt, modify or withdraw any measure provided that such action may not adversely affect any existing investors or investments.[20] The ASEAN member that imposes the new measures must also not force investors, by reason of their nationality, to sell or otherwise dispose of an investment existing at the time of the measures, unless such requirement has been specified in the approval.[21]

[17] Art. XIX of the GATS calls for achieving progressively higher liberalization and promoting the interests of all participants on a mutually advantageous basis and to securing an overall balance of rights and obligations. The mandate further states that negotiations shall take due regard for national policy objectives and the level of development of individual members, both overall and in individual sectors. It also states that there shall be appropriate flexibility for individual developing countries for opening fewer sectors, liberalizing fewer types of market transactions, progressively extending market access in line with their development situation and flexibility of attaching market access conditions to foreign service suppliers.

[18] ACIA, art. 9.

[19] ACIA, art. 10.

[20] *Id.*

[21] *Id.*

Apart from the sectoral liberalization, the ACIA also subscribes to the principle of nondiscrimination, which provides for NT[22] and MFN[23] treatment to investors and covered investments within the ambit of the ACIA. In general, this means that ASEAN Investors and their investments are not to be discriminated against in any of the ASEAN economies where they invest or where their investments are in. NT extends to admission, establishment, acquisition, expansion, management, conduct, operation or other disposition of covered investments in an ASEAN nation. The MFN treatment to ASEAN Investors and their covered investments covers both the pre-establishment and postestablishment stages of an investment. The MFN provision is subject to an exception, either to "(a) any sub-regional arrangements between and among Member States; alternatively, (b) any existing agreement notified by Member States to the AIA Council pursuant to Article 8(3) of the AIA Agreement."[24]

At the same time, the ACIA allows investors to select senior management personnel irrespective of their nationality, allowing investors to seek the best talents in the field and to be able to work with people whom they can trust.[25] The ACIA also ensures that ASEAN countries do not impose performance requirements that may put investors and their investment at a disadvantage over local investors or other third-country investors.[26]

Nevertheless, there are a few remaining challenges in the implementation of liberalization of investments in ASEAN. First, many ASEAN nations are not able to fully liberalize investments in the relevant sectors, mainly due to legacy and constitutional issues. In a few ASEAN states, some sectors remain reserved for domestic investors, by law or constitution, requiring legislative processes to take place. Secondly, many ASEAN countries, especially the newer ASEAN members, still do not have a deep understanding of the main provisions of the ACIA. For example, some of the ASEAN countries are not able to design effective investment negative lists to attract FDI and to reduce regulatory burden for FDIs and domestic investments. Finally, the ACIA has to be read together with the other ASEAN Agreements, mainly the AFAS. For instance, the provisions on commercial presence under the AFAS have to be read together with the

22 ACIA, art. 5.
23 ACIA, art. 6.
24 *Id.*
25 ACIA, art. 8.
26 ACIA, art. 7.

protection pillar of the ACIA. One cannot read the AFAS provisions on commercial presence in isolation from the protection pillar of the ACIA.

11.4 The Law on Investment Promotion 2016 of Lao PDR

11.4.1 FDI of Lao PDR

Lao PDR is located within the Greater Mekong Region, bordering China, Cambodia, Myanmar, Thailand and Vietnam. Lao PDR is a member of the United Nations, the WTO and ASEAN. Lao PDR is a landlocked lower middle-income economy, with a total population of around 6.758 million people, a total GDP of $15.81 billion at 2016 exchange rates, GDP growth of 6.7 percent in 2017.[27] Under the Seventh National Socio-Economic Development Plan 2011–2015, Lao PDR expects a continuous annual growth rate of 8 percent per annum, which requires a total investment of $15 billion in total. The Asian Development Bank predicts that the Lao PDR GDP will grow at a rate of 6.8 percent in 2016 and 7.0 percent for 2017 and 2018 – the third highest in ASEAN, after Cambodia and Myanmar.[28]

To promote Lao PDR as an investment destination and to provide minimum protection to foreign investors and their investments, Lao PDR has signed twenty-six international investment agreements. These includes countries such as Australia, Burma, Cambodia, China, Cuba, Denmark, France, Germany, India, Indonesia, Japan, Kuwait, Malaysia, Mongolia, Netherlands, North Korea, Pakistan, Philippines, Russia, South Korea, Singapore, Sweden, Switzerland, Thailand, the United Kingdom and Vietnam. At the same time, Lao PDR is also a member of ASEAN free trade agreements that possess investment chapters, namely the ASEAN-Australia-New Zealand FTA, the ASEAN-Korea FTA, the ASEAN-Japan FTA and the ASEAN-China FTA.

Lao FDR has seen an increase in FDI into the country, both in terms of FDI flows and FDI stock. In 2016, Lao PDR received a total of $890 million, compared to $1.19 billion in 2015.[29] The increase in FDI

[27] See *Lao PDR*, The World Bank Open Data, https://data.worldbank.org/country/lao-pdr (last visited Mar. 22, 2018).

[28] *The Asian Development Outlook (2017) Update: Sustaining Development Through Public-Private Partnership*, Asian Development Bank, www.adb.org/ado2017-update (last visited Nov. 6, 2017).

[29] *Lao People's Democratic Republic Fact Sheet*, World Investment Report 2017, http://unctad.org/sections/dite_dir/docs/wir2017/wir17_fs_la_en.pdf (last visited Nov. 6, 2017).

inflows has also led to an increase in FDI stock in the same period, which sees an FDI stock of $5.639 billion at the end of 2016. However, this figure is significantly lower than its peers – Cambodia has an FDI stock of $16 billion, while Myanmar has an FDI stock of $22.66 billion in the same period.[30]

Most of the economic growth is linked with the use of the country's natural resources.[31] About 80 percent of FDI in Lao PDR is made up of natural resource-seeking investments, mainly in the mining and quarrying (primarily copper) sectors and the generation of hydropower from rivers in the country. Most of the FDI come from China, Vietnam, Korea, France and Japan. At the same time, some investors are looking at Lao PDR as an efficiency-seeking investment location, mainly to diversify their production base in Thailand and to enter the Mekong Region, including China.[32]

In the latest data available at the time of writing, in 2015 Lao PDR had approved twenty-seven projects valued at $1.267 billion from either wholly foreign-owned or joint venture companies. Differentiating by sectors, most of the investments are still in the mining sector, with nine projects amounting to $183 million, while the electricity generation sector has two projects amounting to $568 billion and the agricultural sector has three projects amounting to $466 million.[33] This shows that Lao PDR is still relying on natural resources such as water, mining and agriculture for investments. In agriculture, most investments deal with cash crops such as coffee and tea, but Lao PDR also needs to start looking at other areas of agriculture such as rice and other important food products. Lao PDR needs to ensure that the investments are properly implemented according to plan. There have been cases where approved investments were improperly implemented due to the lack of monitoring, evaluation and enforcement capacities of the relevant authorities in Lao PDR.

[30] *Id.*

[31] *Investment Law Reform: A Handbook for Development Practitioners*, The World Bank (2010). There are generally four typologies of investments, namely, natural resource seeking, market seeking, efficiency seeking and strategic asset seeking.

[32] *Laos Investment Climate Statement 2015*, United States Department of State (2015).

[33] *Approved Foreign and Domestic Investment Projects by Sector*, Investlaos, www.investlaos.gov.la/images/Statistics/rpt_Invest_Summary_Sector1A_2015.pdf (last visited Nov. 6, 2017).

11.4.2 Laos' Legal Reforms

The Law on Investment Promotion 2016 (LIP 2016) revises the Law on Investment Promotion 2009 (LIP 2009) and its relevant decrees, including the Decree on the Implementation on the Investment Promotion Law and Annexes. Namely, these are the Decree on Promoted Activities and the List of Investment Promoted Zones and on Concession Activities. The LIP 2016 adopted a wide range of amendments to the LIP 2009, with more than 80 percent of the provisions of the law being amended or new.

The first overall impression that emerges from reviewing the LIP 2009 is that it seems to reflect a policy that hesitates between a centrally planned economy, decentralization and a market economy, or that it is ambiguous toward private investment. In some aspects, the legislation is quite liberal. For instance, it includes few explicit restrictions as to the sectors which investors can invest in; in other aspects, it includes a number of provisions that allow government authorities to interfere with investment projects or exercise very ample discretion.

In reforming the national investment policy, Lao PDR takes into account the best practices and the four pillars contained in the ACIA. The adoption of the ACIA's four pillars is discussed among the policymakers at the inception stage of the investment policy reform process. The OECD, as part of the ASEAN investment policy peer review process, recognizes that the LIP 2016 was amended to align it with international good practices, the ACIA and WTO Commitments.[34] This shows that Lao PDR considers the standards set out in the ACIA's four pillars to be an important benchmark for the country to emulate in reforming the country's investment laws and policies.

The LIP 2016 partly meets the progressive liberalization provisions in the ACIA. The LIP 2016 allows investors to invest in all investment sectors and areas in Lao PDR, apart from the sectors prohibited by law, such as those areas considered detrimental to national security, the natural environment, public health and national culture.[35] At the same time, the LIP 2016 provides for the creation of a List of Controlled Businesses[36] and Concession Businesses,[37] which calls for the screening

[34] *OECD Investment Policy Reviews: Lao PDR*, Jul. 2017, at 33. This report contains peer-reviewed information and recommendations. However, the OECD does not intervene in the lawmaking process in the ASEAN Member State concerned.

[35] Law on Investment Promotion of Lao PDR, art. 4.

[36] LIP, art. 34.

[37] LIP, art. 41.

of any investments included in the list. The list reflects the need for investors to undergo a screening process at the entry phase prior to registration of the enterprise. A potentially long list of Controlled Businesses and Concession Businesses subject to screening goes against international best practices, which encourage reduced screening of investments at the entry stage.

The LIP 2016 also lists promoted sectors, namely agriculture, industry, handicraft and services.[38] For example, in certain agricultural sectors and animal breeding, foreign investors are allowed to have 100 percent ownership.[39] In addition, businesses located within Special Economic Zones, such as the Savan-Seno Special Economic Zone, are allowed to have 100 percent foreign ownership.[40]

In addition, it is also important to read the LIP 2016 together with the Law on Enterprise 2005[41] and the relevant decrees, including the Restricted, Conditional and Prohibited Lists; the Laws on the Special Economic Zones, including the Prime Minister's Decree on Special Economic Zone 2010; the Prime Minister's Decree 148/PM of 2003 on the Savan-Seno Special Economic Zone; and the Prime Minister's Decree 177 of 2003 on the Management Regulations and Incentive Policies Regarding the Savan-Seno Special Economic Zone. The array of different laws dealing with investments may confuse investors at times. It would therefore be good if Lao PDR could consolidate all these laws in the future.

The negative list under the Law on Enterprise 2005 cannot be equated with the Schedule of Reservations or the negative list in the ACIA and other IIAs. This is because the Schedule of Reservations or the negative list in the ACIA or the IIA basically consists of exclusions to certain types of commitments, such as the NT and the SMBD obligations of the liberalized sectors in the IIA. For example, the Schedule of Reservations under the ACIA only relates to the five sectors initially liberalized under the ACIA. In the Schedule of Reservations however, Lao PDR focuses on mining, quarrying, manufacturing, agriculture and fisheries. In the later amendments to the Schedule of Reservations dated August 27, 2012, Lao

[38] LIP, art. 49.

[39] Interview with Dr. Sithong Phiphakhavong, Deputy Director General of the Department of Livestock and Fisheries of the Ministry of Agriculture and Forestry, Lao PDR, and Mr. Khamtanh Thadavong, Deputy Director General of the Department of Agriculture of the Ministry of Agriculture and Forestry (Sep. 2015).

[40] See for example, Prime Minister Decree 177 of 2003, art. 9.

[41] Law on Enterprise 2005 (No. 11/NA) (Promulgated by Decree No. 29/PO of Dec. 9, 2005).

PDR further liberalized the manufacturing sector by removing restrictions on foreigners investing in, among other areas, production, processing and preserving of meat and meat products (cattle, pigs, sheep, horse); fish processing and storing; fruit and vegetable processing; and the manufacturing of nonalcoholic beverages, soft drinks and pure drinking water.[42]

The negative list under the Law on Enterprise 2005 is wider than the Schedule of Reservations. The MOIC issued three different types of lists under the Enterprise Law, namely Restrictions to FDI in the areas only reserved for Lao people (Reserved List);[43] the conditional business category for Foreign Investors (Conditional List);[44] and the list of prohibited sectors (Prohibited List).[45]

The three lists are generally market access documents, which limit access to either domestic investors only or to foreign investors after having met certain conditions. The Reserved List allows access to the sectors in question, subject to the issuance of the Enterprise Registration Certificate(s) and necessary operational licenses from the relevant ministry. The Conditional List states the minimum capitalization requirements for foreigners in each sector. The prohibited list generally closes off the listed sectors to private investors.

Compared to the Schedule of Reservations under the ACIA, the Restricted and the Conditional Lists includes service sectors such as production, transmission and distribution of electricity in specific segments; urban and land passenger and cargo transport services; as well as radio and television broadcasting, print media and recording activities.

However, as the Restricted and Conditional Lists are subject to domestic law, it is the prerogative of Lao PDR to include or exclude sectors from the two lists. In the same way as Lao PDR can include sectors in the Restricted and Conditional Lists, Lao PDR can also further liberalize sectors including those that are identified as promoted sectors, such as agriculture, manufacturing (including food processing and downstream activities of agriculture products), mining and mining equipment manufacturing, creative, innovation and information technology, leisure and tourism, education services and health services through the domestic law. In preparing the domestic lists, Lao PDR has to ensure, however, that the

[42] Lao PDR, Schedule of ACIA, Supplement 1, LA/RL5/Rev.1 (Aug. 27, 2012).

[43] Notification on Reserved Business Category List for Lao People No. 1328 (Jul. 13, 2015).

[44] Notification on Conditional Business Category List for Foreign Investors (Conditional List) No. 1327 (Jul. 13, 2015).

[45] Notification on Prohibited Business Category List No. 1592 (Aug. 26, 2015).

lists are justified against the national policy objective, and are based on objective and necessary measurements.

In actual fact, the minimum capital requirement which foreign investors have to maintain but is otherwise inapplicable to domestic investors is already a form of discrimination. This goes against the national treatment obligation or the concept of nondiscrimination mentioned in the LIP. Additionally, the lack of precise drafting in the law provides a ground for uncertainty for the actual implementation of the law.

On the SMBD front, the LIP 2016 allows investors to administer and manage investment businesses[46] and to hire labor,[47] and for foreign investors, foreign experts and their families to reside within the territory of Lao PDR according to the terms of investment and employment contact, respectively.[48] However, these provisions are silent as to whether investors are free to select the senior management and board of directors as envisaged in the ACIA, and thus it can be safe to assume that there are no restrictions on the selection of senior management personnel and the board of directors.

In addition, the LIP 2016 does not offer clear-cut provisions on the NT and MFN standards. Despite providing that "investors have equal rights to invest and to have their benefits protected under the laws and regulations of the Lao PDR and international treaties to which Lao PDR is a party of,"[49] LIP 2016 does not provide any clear provision on how the NT and MFN obligations will operate among and between foreign and domestic investors. Although it is safe to assume that ASEAN Investors and other investors coming from countries where Lao PDR has an IIA with will receive NT and MFN, the same treatments will not, however, apply to investors coming from outside of ASEAN or countries which Lao PDR does not have any IIA with.

11.5 The Myanmar Investment Law 2016

11.5.1 FDI of Myanmar

The Republic of the Union of Myanmar lies in a very strategic location, between China to the northeast, India and Bangladesh to the west and northwest, Thailand to the east and Lao PDR on the northeast. This

[46] LIP, art. 65.
[47] LIP, art. 66.
[48] LIP, art. 67.
[49] LIP, art. 60.

makes Myanmar an important economic destination as it is situated in one of the most economically dynamic and important regions in Southeast Asia. Myanmar has a population of about 52.8 million people.[50] Myanmar became a British colony in 1885 and was ruled directly from India, which also influenced the government and civil service system, laws and policies, as well as the court system in the country. Internationally, Myanmar is a member of the United Nations, the WTO and ASEAN.

After more than fifty years in economic isolation, the economy of Myanmar has largely stagnated since 1997 due to poor macroeconomic management, large public sector debt, economic sanctions and a sharp decline in foreign investment.[51] The subsequent opening up of Myanmar's economy to trade and investment in 2010 marked a new beginning for private sector development. In 2012, GDP in current US dollars was estimated at $56 billion, making its per capita income of $876 ($1,405 in purchasing power parity terms) one of the lowest in Asia.[52] This has grown to $67.43 billion in 2016, making a per capita income of $1,275, and puts Myanmar in the lower middle-income country category.[53]

Agriculture dominates Myanmar's economic structure, as expected from the country's very low per capita income, accounting for 29 percent of GDP but over 52 percent of employment and 20 percent of exports.[54] On the other hand, manufacturing contributes to 20 percent of GDP, with garments and wood product as the major exports.[55]

Prior to the closing of the country and after its opening to external investment Myanmar had been and continues to be an important trade and investment destination, either from the perspective of natural resource-seeking investment, with its vast untapped natural resources

[50] See *Myanmar*, The World Bank Open Data, https://data.worldbank.org/country/myanmar (last visited Mar. 22, 2018).

[51] *Myanmar Unlocking the Potential*, Asian Development Bank (2014).

[52] *Myanmar: Second Review under the Staff-Monitored Program – Staff Report and Press Release*, IMF Country Report, No. 14/91 (2014), www.imf.org/external/pubs/ft/scr/2014/cr1491.pdf (last visited Mar. 22, 2018).

[53] *World Bank List of Economies*, https://datahelpdesk.worldbank.org/knowledgebase/articles/906519-world-bank-country-and-lending-groups (last visited Nov. 6, 2017); *Myanmar*, The World Bank Open Data, https://data.worldbank.org/country/myanmar (last visited Nov. 6, 2017).

[54] *Myanmar, 2017–2021 Building the Foundations for Inclusive Growth*, ADB Country Partnership Strategy, Mar. 2017, at 2.

[55] *Id.*

and minerals, oil and gas reserves and fertile land for agriculture; or market-seeking investment, with its large and growingly sophisticated consumers; or efficiency-seeking investment, with its plan to become an export hub; and even strategic asset-seeking investment such as those seeking banking and financial services licenses.

The ASEAN Business Outlook Survey 2014 by the American Chambers of Commerce finds that Myanmar is one of the most attractive countries for new business expansion in ASEAN, apart from Indonesia, Vietnam and Thailand.[56] Myanmar has been receiving a steady flow of FDI into the country. Myanmar's FDI inflows improved from $584 million in 2013 to $2.19 billion in 2016. The FDI stock in Myanmar improved from $16.7 billion in 2013 to $22.66 billion at the end of 2016.[57]

Although the FDI inflow into Myanmar is still small compared to the overall FDI inflow into ASEAN as a whole, Myanmar is catching up fast with its peers in the region, especially when compared to the FDI inflow into Cambodia and Lao PDR.

According to figures released by the Directorate of Investment and Company Administration (DICA) of the Ministry of Finance and Planning of Myanmar, a great majority of investments in the country are still in the natural resources sector, led by the oil and gas industry (154 approved projects, worth $22 billion or 30.09 percent of approved FDI), followed by power (14 approved projects, worth $20.7 billion or 27.81 percent of approved FDI) and manufacturing (811 approved projects, worth $9.2 billion or 12.3 percent of approved projects).[58]

11.5.2 Myanmar's Investment Policy Reform

To ensure that Myanmar continues to attract quality investments, including those with responsible business conduct, Myanmar has started to diversify its sources of investment from countries in ASEAN, Europe, Japan, Korea and the United States.[59] Most importantly, based on the

[56] *ASEAN Business Outlook Survey 2014*, www.uschamber.com/sites/default/files/legacy/international/files/ASEAN%20Survey%202014.pdf (last visited May 18, 2015).

[57] *Country Factsheet: Myanmar*, World Investment Report 2017, http://unctad.org/sections/dite_dir/docs/wir2017/wir17_fs_mm_en.pdf (last visited Nov. 6, 2017).

[58] Foreign Investment of Permitted Enterprises as of Sep. 30, 2017, Directorate of Investment and Company Administration, Myanmar, www.dica.gov.mm/sites/dica.gov.mm/files/document-files/fdi_sector_2.pdf (last visited Nov. 6, 2017).

[59] *Id.*

present author's assessment, Myanmar is sending signals around the world that investors and investments are welcome in Myanmar, that Myanmar investment laws and policies are based on internationally acceptable standards of treatment, liberalization, protection and dispute prevention and dispute settlement procedures.

There are several steps that Myanmar took in order to gain the trust of investors. One of these is to review investment laws and policies with the assistance of the World Bank and funded by the United Kingdom, Australia and Japan. Another encompasses investment promotion activities, mostly sponsored by host countries such as the United Kingdom, Japan, South Korea and the United States. The third type of activity is direct engagement at the government-to-government level in entering into IIAs, including FTAs with investment chapters.

In reviewing its investment policies, Myanmar adopts internationally acceptable standards based on the OECD peer review process of the Policy Framework for Investments. Three principles apply throughout the Framework: policy coherence, transparency in policy formulation and implementation and regular evaluation on the impacts of existing and proposed policies.[60]

Myanmar, following the recommendations of the OECD Investment Policy Review, brought in the World Bank Trade and Competitiveness team to assist them in adopting internationally acceptable standards in investment policy. Myanmar agreed to prepare a new investment law covering both domestic and foreign investment that is clear, succinct and adopts the best international practice principles, including principles that are already applicable to most foreign investment in Myanmar through the IIAs that Myanmar has concluded. One has to note that the OECD only provides a peer review mechanism and is not involved in the design of Myanmar's investment policies or laws.

The new Myanmar Investment Law was passed by parliament in October 2016.[61] The MIL came into force with the adoption of the Myanmar Investment Regulations 2017.[62] The MIR and MIL cover both domestic and foreign direct investment (not portfolio investments) and apply to both existing and new investments. The MIL adopts recommendations and proposals made by the World Bank, IFC and other

[60] OECD, *supra* note 34.

[61] The Pyidaungsu Hluttaw Law No. 40/2016, The 2nd Waning of Thadingyut, 1378 ME (Oct. 18, 2016).

[62] The Government of the Republic of the Union of Myanmar, Ministry of Planning and Finance Notification No. 35 / 2017, The 3rd Waxing of Tagu, 1378 ME (Mar. 30, 2017).

partners and involves close consultation with the private sector and civil society in Myanmar. Further, the MIL is benchmarked against internationally accepted standards for investment legal frameworks as contained in the ACIA as well as in IIAs.

The adoption of the standards set out in the ACIA is based on the understanding by Myanmar officials that the ACIA is an important document to be benchmarked with. The officials were of the view that the four pillars of the ACIA coupled with the concept of progressive liberalization reflect Myanmar's needs to adopt internationally acceptable standards of international investment policy framework, while at the same time being able to promote investment liberalization at the country's own pace.

The MIL adopts the best international standards in terms of investor protection, investment entry and investment incentives. In terms of investor protection, the new law goes beyond what is included in the Foreign Investment Law 2012[63] and the Citizen Investment Law 2013.[64] The new law adopts best practice standards for the treatment of investors, including a strong guarantee of currency (profit/capital) transfer, which normally only applies to foreign or nonresident investors. The new law adopts the criteria of residency and not nationality to define who is a foreign investor; a Myanmar citizen who is nonresident and invests in Myanmar (i.e., an expatriate) would then benefit from that provision as a foreign citizen investor would.

The MIL offers strong protection against the risk of both direct and indirect expropriation. The MIL also offers a strong guarantee of nondiscrimination. The strongest standard internationally is one that incorporates the NT and MFN principles. The NT and MFN language in the MIL is based on the corresponding provision in the ACIA. In relation to NT, Section 47(a) of the MIL states that "the Government shall accord to foreign investors and their direct investments, treatment no less favorable than it accords to Myanmar citizen investors in respect of the expansion, management, operation, and the sale or other disposition of direct investments according to this Law except any way stipulated in Laws, rules and notifications."[65]

The MFN provision is in Section 47(b) of the MIL, and it states that "the Government shall accord, in like circumstances, to foreign investors and

[63] The Pyidaungsu Hluttaw Foreign Investment Law, Pyidaungsu Hluttaw Law No. 21/2012, The 3rd Waning of Thadingyut, 1374 ME (Nov. 2, 2012).

[64] The Pyidaungsu Hluttaw Law No. 18, The 7th Waning of Waso, 1375 ME (Jul. 29, 2013).

[65] MIL, sec. 47(a).

their direct investments from one country, treatment no less favorable than that it accords to investors of any other country and their direct investments in respect of establishment, acquisition, expansion, management, operation, and the sale or other disposition of direct investments."[66]

Under the MIL, "all investment is allowed without restriction in Myanmar except as specified in the Negative List."[67] In addressing investment entry, the new law clearly defines who can invest and where one can invest, as well as the types of restrictions that may exist for foreign investment either at the horizontal or sectoral level.

The MIL addresses issues related to market access by providing for a promoted sector list and a restricted sector list (otherwise known as the negative list). The MIR lists out prohibited sectors for investments in Myanmar.[68] The MIR also explains the process of issuing and identification of promoted sectors and restricted sectors.[69] The Government of Myanmar has issued a notification of promoted sectors, which will determine investment activities to receive tax incentives through profit tax holidays.[70] Restricted sectors are normally addressed through a periodic notification, which has been the case for Myanmar since 2014.

There is an indication that the list can be amended "from time to time" by the Myanmar Investment Commission and in consultation with government bodies and the private sector.[71] In the author's view, a better solution would have been to (a) set a fixed periodicity for the review of the negative list, and (b) adopt the principle that "changes to the negative list are only possible in the direction of liberalization."

An updated investment restriction list will be issued which includes a list of activities reserved for the Union (or the government), investments not allowed to be carried out by foreigner investors, investment business allowed only in the form of joint ventures with Myanmar firms or citizens and investment businesses to be carried out with the approval of the relevant ministries. Any business activity not mentioned on the list is considered open to wholly owned foreign investors.

To be able to invest in Myanmar, investors would require a permit if they invest in certain sectors that require it as noted under Section 36 of

[66] MIL, sec. 47(b).
[67] OECD, *supra* note 34.
[68] MIR, Rule 12.
[69] MIR, Rules 17–23.
[70] Myanmar Investment Commission Notification No. 13 /2017, The 5th Waxing of Tagu, 1378 ME (Apr. 1, 2017), Classification of Promoted Sector.
[71] MIL, secs. 44, 45.

the MIL, or to seek an endorsement if they wish to acquire land or fiscal incentives in sectors not requiring an MIC permit. The MIR explains the requirements and the approval process for the issuance of permits and endorsements. These include categories of investments considered to be strategic (based on location, sectors and threshold of investments). The MIR also clarifies the power of the state and regional governments to issue endorsements for land rights and incentives for investments below $5 million as of August 2017, this amounted to roughly K 6 billion.[72]

As in the case of Lao PDR, Myanmar's negative list under the MIL caters for the domestic investment policy environment and this, to a certain extent, has been reflected in the Single Reservation List under the ACIA. The Myanmar Single Reservation List under the ACIA focuses on national treatment restrictions in the manufacturing of alcoholic drinks, cigarettes, pulp and papers, pharmaceutical drugs and services related to the manufacturing of pharmaceutical drugs, petroleum refining and services incidental to fisheries.[73] In the revised Schedule of Reservations, Myanmar further liberalized foreign investment in the distilling, blending, rectifying, bottling and marketing of all kinds of spirits, beverages and nonbeverages (ISIC 1551); manufacturing of malt and malt liquors, beer and other brewery products (ISIC 1553); manufacturing of soft beverages, aerated and nonaerated products (ISIC 1554); and the manufacturing of cigarettes (ISIC 1600).[74]

The Myanmar Investment Commission has issued the latest negative list through Notification No. 15/2017.[75] The List of Restricted Activities follows the method prescribed in the Myanmar Investment Law and the Myanmar Investment Rules. The list includes nine sectors allowed to be carried out only by the States, twelve sectors allowed to be carried out only by Myanmar nationals (closed to foreigners), and twenty-two sectors to be carried out in the joint venture format between Myanmar nationals and foreigners. The list adopts sectors under the ISIC/ CPC, and it is much narrower compared to the previous negative lists. However, the list also contains 128 subsectors requiring permits or licenses from line ministries.[76] Arguably, these subsectors should not

[72] MIR, Ch. VII.

[73] MM/RL1/Rev.1. AIA 16–06 Suppl. Notes and Revised RL (MM) (2013).

[74] Myanmar Schedule of ACIA Supplement 1, MM/RL1/Rev.1.

[75] Myanmar Investment Commission Notification No. 15 /2017, The 14th Waxing of Tagu, 1378 ME (Apr. 10, 2017), List of Restricted Investment Activities.

[76] *Id.*

be in the negative list as they do not concern investment liberalization and market access. In addition, one needs to investigate whether these permits or licenses are necessary and do not constitute de facto barriers to market access.

The new negative list addresses an earlier concern that the negative list contained too many sectors subject to restrictions. Due to rapid changes to the National Negative List, Myanmar may have to amend the Schedule of Reservations under the ACIA in order to make both lists compatible and consistent with each other.

Many sectors are subject to foreign investment ceiling (in effect a forced joint venture). Many projects will have to obtain MIC permits even when applying for a piece of land. A "permit" seems to correspond to the approval that was given by MIC upon successfully being screened under the previous law. The fact that some investments will not require any permit and that others will only necessitate an "endorsement" is *a priori* progress over the universal screening that was required under the previous law, provided that the endorsement process is indeed lighter, less burdensome than the screening and approval process.

In dealing with employment issues and in line with SMBD provisions in the ACIA, the MIL allows investors to appoint qualified persons of any nationality as senior managers, technical and operational experts, provided that the investors shall arrange capacity building programs to train Myanmar citizens to take over these jobs in the future. In addition, investors are required to appoint Myanmar citizens for jobs which do not require special skills. To ensure that workers are protected, investors are also required to enter into employment contracts with their workers, in which they will be granted all entitlements and rights.

Myanmar is undertaking steps to implement the provisions of the MIL, which includes making sure that the provisions of the MIL are properly enforced. To ensure that enforcement is in place, Myanmar is forming an investor aftercare committee and an investor grievance mechanism to address investors' concerns and to see to it that government agencies work hand in hand with investors.

11.6 Conclusion and Recommendations

The reforms of the investment policy in the Lao PDR and Myanmar are based on the desire of both ASEAN countries to increase the level of investments – domestic and foreign – in their respective countries. As the ACIA is an IIA between ASEAN members, both countries decided to adopt the main principles in the ACIA, including the liberalization pillar, when designing the national investment policy reform. In fact, many stakeholders, such as the OECD and the World Bank, promoted the use of the ACIA as a benchmark for the investment policy reforms in Lao PDR and Myanmar. By adopting the ACIA as the benchmark, the two ASEAN economies are also indirectly adopting the principle of progressive liberalization of investment sectors and other treatment of investors, including NT and MFN obligations.

The approach taken by Myanmar and Lao PDR sets an important precedent for ASEAN and for South-South FTAs. Myanmar and Lao PDR being the newer ASEAN members brought the principles and the pillars of the ACIA into their national investment policy and law, paving the way for ASEAN countries to adopt not just the principles and pillars of ACIA, but also potentially other ASEAN documents and agreements. In the case of Myanmar, the MIL adopted, albeit with some modifications, the terms of NT, MFN, expropriation and transfer of funds.

The adoption of the ACIA's principles and pillars by Lao PDR and Myanmar also shows that developing countries may negotiate and set their own standards that meet the development expectations and the needs of the South. The principle of progressive liberalization and the innovation of the Single Reservation List are two examples of the main ACIA provisions that take into account the needs and the development expectations of the least developed and developing countries. These two principles provide comfort for countries like Lao PDR and Myanmar to adopt South-South treaties like the ACIA into the national legal system without a fear of overcommitting to international standards that may hamper domestic development policies and objectives.

However, while the reform process undertaken by the two ASEAN states has led to the adoption of the LIP 2016 and the MIL 2016, it has also brought in different results. This is shown in Table 11.1 below.

First, Lao PDR's LIP 2016 does not directly address investment liberalization. The lack of a clear definition of the negative list combined with the List of Controlled Business and Concession Business risks making the regime too restrictive. As of now, the negative list falls under the purview of the Law on Enterprise, and these two laws are governed by two different ministries, the Ministry of Planning and Investment and the Ministry of Industry and Commerce, respectively. This is different from Myanmar, where investment liberalization is governed by the MIC, whose secretariat is DICA, under the Ministry of Planning and Finance.

Table 11.1: *Comparisons of liberalization in the Lao PDR and Myanmar*

Areas of liberalization	Provision in the Lao PDR Law of Investment Promotion	Provision in Myanmar Investment Law
• Reduce negative list • Promoted Sector List	• LIP 2016 does not address liberalization or negative list as it is addressed in the Enterprise Law 2005 • LIP 2016 addresses promoted sectors	• MIC has the power to issue notifications prescribing promoted, restricted or prohibited sectors
• National Treatment and Most Favored Nation treatment	• No clear NT provision apart from provision of nondiscrimination	• Adopts the ACIA treaty language for both MFN and NT

In the case of Myanmar, it should start looking at reducing the number of sectors in the negative list. This will allow Myanmar to become more attractive to foreign and domestic investors. It is recommended for Lao PDR to have a single national negative list that includes both general businesses and concession businesses. The list should be short, with sectors only included based on sound public policy reasons. Language used for general-controlled and specific-controlled businesses could be replaced by "restricted/prohibited businesses," which is in line with terms used internationally. Moreover, the provision on investor conditions will likely discourage and prevent innovations as many innovative businesses are start-ups, which may not have experience and success stories. The Investment Law and negative list should provide clear guidance to domestic and foreign investors as to whether they can invest or not, whether their participation is limited in any way, whether there is any special approval process and whether there are any differences between domestic and foreign investment, etc.

Second, the Lao PDR's LIP 2016 does not directly address the provisions of NT and MFN. Instead, Lao PDR prefers the NT and MFN treatment to be addressed by the IIAs. This also means that only investors from those countries having an IIA with Lao PDR will benefit from these nondiscrimination treatments. On the other hand, Myanmar takes a different approach, where it adopts treaty language for the national treatment and most favored nation obligations from the ACIA. This means that Myanmar does not treat investors differently, irrespective of their origin and whether or not they come from a country that Myanmar has an IIA with. Myanmar is seen as more liberalizing and more welcoming for foreign and domestic investors. It is good international practice to liberalize market access for foreign investors as far as possible so that foreign investors can enter the domestic market on the same footing as national investors.

This chapter shows that despite having undertaken the investment policy process at almost the same time, Lao PDR and Myanmar have achieved different results. The LIP 2016 has partially met the standards and best practices contained in the ACIA, whilst the MIL adopts many best practices in the ACIA, especially by adopting the principle of progressive liberalization and negative list investment liberalization. Thus, in undertaking the reform of investment law and policy, it is important for Lao PDR to ensure full compliance with the four pillars and best practices contained in the ACIA. Hence, the chapter recommends that in reforming its investment law, Lao PDR should, among other measures, enhance the level of liberalization by improving the law's provisions as well as NT and MFN treatment.

12

The ACIA: Much More Than a BIT of Protection for Foreign Investors?

JULIEN CHAISSE

12.1 Introduction

One very important document in the establishment of the AEC is the ACIA.[1] This chapter reviews the performance of the ACIA from the standpoint of the laws and policies that specify the regionalization of investments in the Asia-Pacific Region.[2]

ASEAN established the ASEAN Economic Community through the AEC Blueprint 2025 in 2015.[3] The ACIA, within its confines, portrays ASEAN as a stand-alone investment front, with a view to encouraging the free flow of capital as well as fostering competitive trade and investment throughout the region, thereby playing a prominent role in the "Global ASEAN."[4] Therefore, this chapter analytically examines the investment laws and proceedings in order to unveil its weaknesses and strengths, and how it affects the ASEAN Community.

First, this chapter starts with a critique of ASEAN as a unanimous trade community, followed by a review of the establishment of the ACIA, its major functions in the control of the ASEAN free flow of investment agenda and how it controls and guarantees investment security.[5] To assess trade and investments, particularly the role of the ACIA in enhancing investments through trade under the ATIGA[6] and

[1] Association of Southeast Asian Countries Comprehensive Investment Agreement (2007).

[2] *Id.*

[3] ASEAN Economic Community Blueprint 2025 (2015).

[4] For ASEAN's partners, ASEAN 2025 means a stronger, more visible and united ASEAN, with a greater role and voice in global economic fora and increased contribution to global economic governance. This is the concept of "Global ASEAN" that was endorsed in the AEC Blueprint, paras. 79 & 80.

[5] This chapter draws on Julien Chaisse & Sufian Jusoh, The ASEAN Comprehensive Investment Agreement – The Regionalization of Laws and Policy on Foreign Investment (2016). The book provides a full discussion of the many issues outlined here.

[6] ASEAN Trade in Goods Agreement (2010).

the AFAS,[7] this chapter will discuss the correlations between the ACIA and the investment decision-making process. In concluding, the chapter will deliberate on issues affecting countries bordering on some ASEAN Member States, which should be addressed to complete the ACIA's implementation.

12.2 Investment in Southeast Asia: the Value of ASEAN

One of the greatest landmarks in Southeast Asia was the formation of ASEAN in 1967 by its five original Member States (Indonesia, the Philippines, Singapore, Malaysia and Thailand). In the years that followed, Cambodia, Brunei, Laos PDR, Myanmar and Vietnam joined the bloc, making ASEAN a ten-member organization.[8]

One achievement of ASEAN is its current GDP, which is valued at $2.7 trillion as of 2017.[9] It began in 1997 with the ASEAN vision 2020, at which time the ASEAN GDP was $694 billion[10] with a 5 percent compound annual growth rate.[11] The GDP projections of the ASEAN economy were $1 trillion and $2 trillion in 2005 and 2020, respectively.[12] Remarkably, in 2006, albeit a year later than projected, ASEAN reached the $1 trillion mark.[13] More interestingly, ASEAN exceeded all expectations by crossing the $2 trillion benchmark in 2011, which was nine years earlier than projected.[14] Consequently, ASEAN's combined GDP is now instead projected to reach $4 trillion in 2020.[15]

In terms of market size, ASEAN sits between China and India, both of which are simultaneously ASEAN's competitors and collaborators. The bloc is one of the world's largest markets, with a standing population of about 630 million (higher than North America or the European Union).[16] Remarkably, 60 percent of this population is less than twenty-five years old.

[7] ASEAN Framework Agreement on Services (2010).

[8] Timor Leste is now an observer country and waiting for full membership of ASEAN.

[9] PricewaterhouseCoopers, Global Economy Watch: Economic integration: the key to unlocking ASEAN's export potential?, Oct. 2017, at 1.

[10] Ministry of Trade and Industry (Malaysia), Forecast: ASEAN GDP, Share in Global GDP and GDP/Capita (2013), www.miti.gov.my/miti/resources/fileupload/ASEAN_GDP%20Forecast.pdf (last visited Apr. 24, 2018).

[11] *Id.*

[12] *Id.*

[13] *Id.*

[14] *Id.*

[15] IMF's Database on World Economic Outlook, Oct. 2017.

[16] *Id.*

In spite of the global economic and financial crisis in many parts of the world, the entire ASEAN community remains a chosen and highly competitive ground for FDI, and it continues to receive FDI as well as contribute to other economies in the form of outward FDI. The attraction of investors to the region is fostered by ready-made resources, as well as export-oriented, market-seeking and efficiency-seeking outlooks. The growth of FDI, as perceived and envisioned by the ASEAN Member States, is also somewhat driven by the launch of the AEC in 2015 and the envisioned AEC 2025.

However, the entire AEC (investment sector included) is confronted by two major challenges.[17] First, among the ASEAN Member States, Singapore tends to receive the highest FDI as compared to the others. Other important FDI destinations include Thailand, Malaysia and Indonesia. Most of these countries' investments are highly resource seeking, with access to a wealth of minerals and water resources and relatively cheap labor. Second, with the exception of Myanmar, Indonesia and Malaysia, intra-ASEAN trade and investments are comparably lower than with external partners. Notably, in 2015, ASEAN countries received more FDI from non-ASEAN partners than from within the bloc.[18]

Studies suggest that an increase in intra-ASEAN trade is directly proportional to an increase in intra-ASEAN stock and investment flow. Economically speaking, trade and investment are interdependent, particularly in the era of global value chains. For instance, to obtain an end product, various components (raw materials) have to be sourced from various locations. Therefore, an investor would choose to maximize returns in one or more of these locations in order to create a product or part of a product. For the cycle of commerce to be complete, the investor will have to trade the finished product by exporting all or some part of the component or the finished product. In that regard, the investor will also have to be fully involved in the trade, i.e., by importing components and/or exporting finished products in part or in whole.

It is generally believed that investment only entails trading in the main sector (goods or tangible products), but this should no longer hold true. Trade in goods and trade in services are becoming inseparable, especially as cross-border trade increases, making investment in services via

[17] Organisation for Economic Co-operation and Development, Southeast Asia Investment Policy Perspectives, at 11–2 (2014), www.oecd.org/daf/inv/investment-policy/Southeast-Asia-Investment-Policy-Perspectives-2014.pdf (last visited Mar. 26, 2018).

[18] ASEAN, *Foreign Direct Investment Net Inflows, Intra- and Extra-ASEAN* (2016), http://asean.org/storage/2015/09/Table-25_oct2016.pdf (last visited Mar. 26, 2018).

commercial presence more paramount. Thus, investment in commercial presence has become an important aspect of FDI, providing the link between the flow of trade in goods and trade in services.

FDI involves the flow between trade in goods and trade in services; thus, FDI acts as a substitute as well as a complement to trade, especially as efficiency-seeking and strategic asset companies are looking for optimum productive locale from where they can finish and export their products.[19] Conversely, services sector investments lead to an increased level of service supply, which in turn leads to exports between parties. One can conclusively say that the choice of ASEAN as an investment destination is a function of the intense growth in trade in both goods and services.

As shown by Chaisrisawatsuk et al., one very remarkable thing in the ASEAN and OECD countries is the self-augmenting relationship between trade (dual) and FDI, where trade induces FDI and vice versa.[20] Another study demonstrates the fact that the Asian countries, including ASEAN, that received the highest FDI flows are the ones with the highest output in terms of exportation,[21] bringing us to the conclusion that FDI is beneficial to trade. For instance, the Australian Trade and Investment Commission states that "inbound foreign direct investment into Australia over past decades, for example in the mining and food manufacturing industries has been a key driver of growth for Australia's exports, as well as growth of the domestic economy."[22]

12.3 The ASEAN Comprehensive Investment Agreement

ASEAN has deployed various investment structures throughout the ASEAN territories to serve as economic tools portraying the bloc as a dominant, single investment center in the Asia-Pacific region.[23]

[19] OECD, *supra* note 17, at 27.

[20] Santi Chaisrisawatsuk & Wisit Chaisrisawatsuk, *Imports, Exports and Foreign Direct Investment Interactions and Their Effects, in* Towards coherent policy frameworks: understanding trade and investment linkages – A study by the Asia-Pacific Research and Training Network on Trade 97 (Nagesh Kumar et. al. eds., 2007).

[21] Fredrik Sjoholm, *Foreign Direct Investments in Southeast Asia*, Research Institute of Stockholm Working Paper, 1 (2013).

[22] Christina Goodman, *Overseas Investment of Australian Companies, Trade and Investment Note*, Austrade Economics 4 (2015).

[23] This section and some of the subsequent paragraphs draw from the monograph by Julien Chaisse & Sufian Jusoh, ASEAN Comprehensive Investment Agreement: The Regionalisation of Laws and Policy on Foreign Investment (2016).

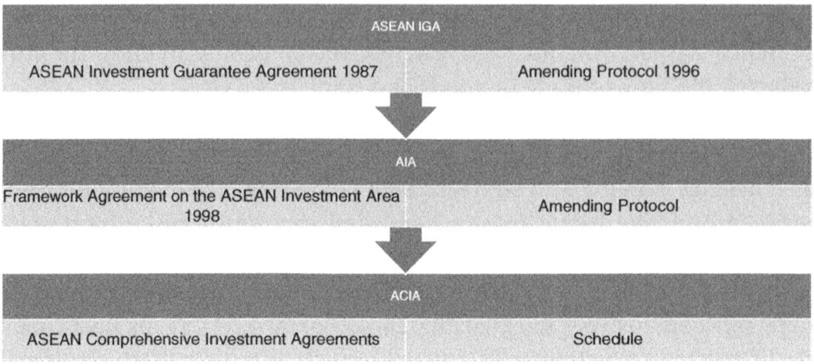

Figure 12.1 Development timeline of the ASEAN Comprehensive Investment Agreements

Through dialogue, ASEAN and its Member States have entered into different PTAs and BITs,[24] with the common goal of positioning ASEAN as an appealing destination for various investment types (natural resource-seeking, market-seeking, efficiency-seeking or strategic asset-seeking).[25]

On February 26, 2009, the ASEAN economic ministers signed the ACIA, bridging the IGA and the AIA. The ACIA, as an enhanced regional pact, is designed to embrace four pillars: liberalization; expedition; security; and advancement, and also entails new features to facilitate and encourage the inflow of FDI.

During the Cebu Declaration of the Twelfth ASEAN Summit in 2007 to transmute ASEAN into a free flow investment destination, the ACIA was designed to supplement two other imperative legitimate systems in the AEC, specifically the ATIGA and the AFAS. For the ATIGA, it was signed in 2009, but its operation had only begun in 2010, while the AFAS had come into play in 1995. These two systems are intended to permit the free stream of merchandise and ventures and a more liberated stream of skilled workers individually. Notably, from the developmental perspective, ASEAN is seen as an international group operating as one. Thus,

[24] As stated by Simon Lester & Bryan Mercurio, many of the so-called FTAs favour certain countries in trade relations and are discriminatory rather than "free trade." The term "PTAs" encompasses many different kinds of bilateral and regional trade agreements and it underscores their common denominator, which is to establish preferences for the signatories over others in trade relations. See Simon Lester & Bryan Mercurio, *Bilateral and Regional Trade Agreements: Commentary and Analysis* 4 (2009).

[25] Sufian Jusoh, ASEAN Investment Agreements: A Tool of Economic Diplomacy in Meeting the Objectives of ASEAN Economic Community Blueprint (2014).

since its inception, ASEAN has worked to redefine and promote its flexibility within its original key concept (i.e., the free flow of investment within the AEC).

12.3.1 Investment Flow and Liberalization in ASEAN

During the Asian financial crisis of 1997–98, the ASEAN states that were most affected by the crisis negotiated for the ASEAN IGA and the AIA agreements as a form of a "liberalization of trade" agreement. However, this was later still deemed not progressive enough to handle the post-financial crisis recovery efforts of the affected ASEAN states. Crucially, this was because of the Sensitive Investment List as well as the Temporary Exclusion List for both ASEAN and foreign investors that are contained in the AIA agreement. As a remedy, the ACIA agreement came into play to ensure that ASEAN would become an investment center by encouraging ASEAN states to lower the entry and postentry barriers faced by investors over time so as to attract more investors from within and outside the AEC.

Economic development and sustainability in the region are both the core vision and responsibility of the ACIA. Consequently, it has to employ various measures and approaches in encouraging both ASEAN and non-ASEAN investments in the region. The so-called liberalization of trade approach of the ACIA is a need-response pattern of assisting businesses looking to expand across the border of their origin countries. Hence, there is a need to lower the entry and postentry barriers faced by investors.

ACIA provisions are rather unique and more concessional in design compared to its preceding agreements, where ASEAN states have committed to progressively lift restrictions in the ten sectors covered by Article 9.4 of the ACIA. This is in line with the developmental blueprint of the AEC. This concept of progressive liberalization allows for the ASEAN states, especially the newer Member States, to apply the concept to their investment sectors within the boundaries of their national and economic development policy objectives.[26]

[26] The principle of progressive liberalization follows the mechanism in use within the World Trade Organization, especially in relation to the liberalization of the services sector under the GATS, the approach that was adopted by ASEAN in the AFAS. On the notion of progressive liberalization, *see* Julien Chaisse & Debashis Chakraborty, *Deconstructing Services and Investment Negotiations – A Case Study of India at WTO GATS and Investment Fora*, 14 *J. World Investment & Trade* 44, 44–78 (2013). The General Agreement on Trade in Services recognizes the need for the developing countries to liberalize their economy and trade over time. Article XIX of the GATS calls for achieving progressively higher liberalization and promoting the interests of all participants on

Against the backdrop of economic development and AEC's trade expansion vision, individual AEC governments are not allowed to backtrack on liberalization or reintroduce the previously removed restrictions. The ACIA, in a proposal to further liberalize other sectors subject to the collective agreement by all Member States, covers five main liberalized sectors: manufacturing, fisheries, agriculture, forestry mining and quarrying and all the related services.[27] The expanded scope of the ACIA allows it to not only cover FDI but also portfolio-investments, which is one of the ways it differs from the AIA, which only covers FDI. Article 10 of the ACIA provides for a concise procedure for adjustment of commitments or reservations and includes a provision for compensatory adjustments to ensure that there is a balance of benefits for ASEAN investors and foreign-owned ASEAN-based investors. This accounts for the flexibility of the ACIA. The ACIA is designed to be unbiased in principle, giving room for the rules of NT and MFN to apply to investors and investments covered within the scope of the ACIA. This means that, in general, ASEAN investors and their investments are to be treated equally, irrespective of the ASEAN states from which they originate. Simultaneously, this principle gives investors the freedom to choose SMBD and select the best talents from various fields irrespective of nationality. It also restricts Member States from imposing performance requirements, which may provide local investors an advantage over foreign investors and their investments.

According to Article 10 of the ACIA, an ASEAN state can modify its reservations for prospective investors and their investments for up to a period of twelve months after the initial submission of a schedule, provided that the modifications shall not affect any existing investors and their investments. However, a stringent maintenance of the restrictive measures outlined in the ACIA limitations list can limit the benefits of MFN, NT and SMBD.

a mutually advantageous basis and for securing an overall balance of rights and obligations.

[27] In terms of liberalization, the ACIA enshrines provisions that accommodate the expansion of scope of this Agreement to cover other sectors in the future, such as art. 3(3)(f) "services incidental to manufacturing, agriculture, fishery, forestry, mining and quarrying; and (g) any other sectors, as may be agreed upon by all Member States."

12.3.2 *Facilitation and Transparency*

It is extremely important for businesses to be abreast of information in relation to territorial governmental measures, particularly on businesses and investment-related issues such as restrictions or liberalization or licensing requirements as it affects their interests. In this regard, the ACIA particularly makes provision for transparency. In explicitly spelling out such information, for instance on the removal of barriers to investments,[28] the ACIA ensures that it is simple enough for the public to be aware of the laws, mandates, prescriptions and administrative declarations that affect their interests.[29] This will also enable them to "participate in their development" and request a review of their application under domestic law.[30] However, the UNCTAD suggests a broader view in terms of transparency (i.e., the availability of information for investors and participants to make informed decisions and meet obligations and commitments) as it relates to the protection and promotion of international investments. Thus, it is important that participants possess an "information-seeking" attitude as part of the investment process.[31]

From a political and business point of view, transparency as purported by the ACIA is interlinked with politics with respect to business risks; at the peak of transparency, political and legal risks to business are reduced to the bare minimum. Transparency decreases dangers and vulnerabilities, advances tolerant venture, lessens opportunities for bribery and corruption, reveals shrouded investment hindrances and adheres to a meaningful boundary among certifiable and less real policy objectives. This helps investors to manage "thin" principles, neutralizes "conflicting prerequisites" circumstances between home country or host country, adds to the level playing field among firms and encourages manageable improvement.[32] The ACIA requires each ASEAN state to make available to the ASEAN Investment Council any investment laws, regulations and administrative guides that serve as measures or any form of agreement at the international level that relates to investors and their investments, so as to ensure that businesses benefit from the ACIA. This obligation, being in line with Article 21 of the ACIA, requires that each ASEAN state

[28] Asia Pacific Economic Cooperation Leaders' Statement to Implement APEC Transparency Standards (2002).

[29] *Id.*

[30] *Id.*

[31] United Nations Conference on Trade and Development, *Transparency* 3 (2004).

[32] OECD, Public Sector Transparency and the International Investor (2003).

makes this information available via an enquiry point in response to the request or inquiries of potential investors or the other Member States.

Despite the requirements of this obligation, Member States maintain a few exceptions to this "flexibility" concept as a necessity, in order to conceal confidential information pertaining to the state and its business investments. This is supported by Article 21(2), which clearly negates the disclosure of any confidential information. Under this Article, an ASEAN state is not required to disclose any confidential information pertaining to particular investments and/or investors if the disclosure will interfere with law enforcement or otherwise be contrary to the public interest, or may undermine the legal commercial interests of certain public or private juridicial persons.

12.3.3 Investment Protection

Among all of the investment agreements made by ASEAN, the ACIA has better and clearer provisions that ensure better coverage in terms of business protection. A number of minimum guarantees are provided as a key to the long-term growth and operation of businesses and commercial activities in the ASEAN territories. These guarantees ensure that investments and investors are treated equally in a fair and nondiscriminatory manner. The ACIA provides instruments of protection such as FET, prohibition of expropriation without adequate compensation, free transfer of funds and full investment security while adopting international best practices in protecting investors.

In a concession, each ASEAN state has agreed to extend FET to the investments covered in their respective territories.[33] The treaties provided by Article 11 of the ACIA, which is similar in context to that of case law, provides a practical meaning of the ACIA FET clause. Essentially, this implies that: (1) the host ASEAN state will be bound by the rule of law in exercising its power and that such an exercise will not be arbitrary; (2) the host ASEAN state will have to ensure access to judicial or administrative tribunals or procedures for a review of such measures; and (3) ASEAN investors who are parties to the proceedings must be given the right to legal representation as well as the opportunity to appeal any adverse outcome.

As implied by the provisions of Article 11 of the ACIA, providing full security for covered investments entails protection of the physical

[33] ACIA, art. 11.

properties of the investment from attacks in the event that there is a territorial crisis, insurgency or chaotic public protests occurring within the boundaries of the host ASEAN state. The investment treaties often include various forms of full "protection and security" provisions, but they have little or no impact on the application of the standard.[34]

As specified by the ACIA, ASEAN states are required to guard against inappropriate and unlawful direct and indirect expropriation without adequate compensation of the involved parties (investors). However, not all government actions interfering with foreign investors are seen as indirect expropriation; this is because each ASEAN state reserves the right to regulate investment activities within its territory.

Annex 2, section 3 of the ACIA specifies that an indirect expropriation action or series of actions must be reviewed using a case-by-case, fact-based request that takes the following factors into consideration: (1) whether the action creates an antagonistic impact on the economic value of an investment; (2) whether the activity breaks the government's written commitments to the investor (by contract, permit or other legal documentation); and (3) whether the government's actions, including its goal, is unbalanced with the public purpose. Additionally, the measures enforced by the ASEAN states must be based on fair treatment in design and must be applicable in terms of protecting legitimate public welfare goals (for example, public health, security and the environment).

It is paramount for an investor to consider as part of the host state's commitment its permit to transfer funds into and out of it (host state). On the other hand, it is also important for the host state to have regulatory parameters to check the inflow/outflow of capital, as well as sometimes streamline the transfer of funds. Earlier commitments posed no restrictions on the transfer of funds, even when some circumstantial crises such as balance of payments are sufficient cause to control inflow/outflow of capital.

The GATS provisions restrict sectoral controls on the flow of capital where a member state has spelt out specific commitments in its national commitment schedule, regardless of which the IMF's rules restrict the control of funds transfer in relation to current transactions. However,

[34] The Parkerings v. Lithuania Award found that it is generally accepted that the variation of language between the formulation "protection" and "full protection and security" does not make a significant difference in the level of protection a host state is to provide. *See* Parkerings-Compagniet AS v. Republic of Lithuania, ICSID Case No. ARB/05/8, Award, Sep. 11, 2007, para. 354.

these rules do not apply to capital transactions. That said, funds transfer disputes rarely involve resort to the measure of investor-state arbitration.

More recent agreements have involved an issue whereby the host state has legitimate reasons to restrict funds transfer through specific treaty provisions, though with specific exemptions to the exchange of assets commitment. Article 13 of the ACIA specifies the freedom of every ASEAN investor in conducting transfers without delay in relation to its investments into and out of its location within the ASEAN states' territories. This specification includes the following forms of transfers: contribution to capital; profits, capital gains, dividends, royalties, license fees or any other fees, interest or other forms of income emanating from the investment; proceeds from the total or partial sale or liquidation of its investments; payments under a contract, including a loan agreement; payments of compensation in cases of strife or lawful expropriation; payments from settlement of a dispute; and earnings or other remuneration of personnel who are employed and allowed to work in relation to the investment in that territory. This is driven by the fact that capital and asset management freedom is paramount to the successful operation of any business.

Furthermore, it would be considered restrictive to require a specific hard currency of exchange or transfers (e.g., EUR or USD). Therefore, the ACIA specifies that such transfers can be made in "freely usable currency" as determined by the investors. The term "freely usable currency" basically implies that the moneycan be used to make payments for global transactions, and that is broadly traded on the main exchange markets.

Despite the specifications in Article 13, there are quite a number of exceptions to the provisions stated therein, especially where an ASEAN state may legitimately forestall or postpone funds transferred under the context of an equitable, nondiscriminatory, and good-faith application of its laws and regulations, with respect to indebtedness or the insurance of the privileges of creditors; trading securities, prospects, options or derivatives; criminal or correctional offenses and the recuperation of the proceeds of crime; financial reporting or record keeping of transfers at the request of law enforcement or financial regulatory authority; in compliance with court orders or judicial proceedings; tax assessment; social security, retirement or necessary saving plans; severance for employees; and customs forced by the Central Bank or other relevant authorities of that ASEAN ember state.

In its protection extension, the ACIA assures non-ASEAN investors of adequate protection, on the condition that the non-ASEAN investors set up a legal entity in one of the ASEAN states. The initially established entity becomes an ASEAN investor by establishing another legal entity in its target destination in another ASEAN state. Substantially, the initial entity must own and control the latter entity (i.e., have power to name a dominant part of its directors or to legitimately coordinate its activities), and the former entity must perform substantive business operations in the ASEAN state where it was built up.

In cases where the value of an investment is impaired or invalidated by the host country's activities or inactions or failure to settle on choices, dispute settlement may be resorted to in response. The ACIA furnishes concerned investors with direct access to dispute settlement procedures such as domestic court action, conciliation, mediation or international arbitration.

The ACIA provides an ISDS mechanism that only applies to post-ACIA investment disputes, i.e., after March 29, 2012. It should be noted that it is not an ACIA procedure for investors to resort to domestic court action before requesting consultation or filing for arbitration. Rather, investors are free to exercise any preferred method of dispute settlement. However, in the event that they have any dispute, they may refer it to a local court within the host country.

Investors reserve the right to initiate or continue local court proceedings. Notwithstanding, in the event that arbitration is the favored dispute resolution strategy, the investor is required to postpone any local court procedures in writing.

The ACIA recognizes the fact that, with an ever-increasing number of firms, entrepreneurs and professionals flocking into the ASEAN market, there can be disagreements between individual investors and their respective host states. It therefore contains a detailed chapter on the provisions for dispute settlement. This is due to the commitments of the ASEAN states to guarantee protection so as to ensure smooth operation, expansion and diversification activities for businesses across regional borders.

12.3.4 Investment Decision-Making Process

Different studies demonstrate that international investment agreements, such as the ACIA, do not by and large contribute to expanded investment streams between the parties to the agreement.[35] This is especially so for

[35] Here, a few relatively recent examples should suffice to demonstrate this fact. E.g. UNCTAD's World Investment Report (2003) at 89 held that "BITs play a minor role in influencing global FDI flows . . . The policy framework is at best enabling, having by itself little or no effect on FDI flows . . . As a rule, IIAs tend to make the regulatory framework

agreements involving small and medium enterprises, which may not have sufficient resources to orchestrate enough information to upgrade their comprehension of the content of the agreement, which would then be a reason for the lack of in depth knowledge of the investment agreement.

The second factor stems from the perspective of the international investment agreement. As a matter of fact, it is thought to have a complex effect on businesses as well as investors. Using PTAs and similar agreements as a reference point, one should note that these agreements may not have standard terms and provisions. Also, there can be diverse sets of provisions over a similar subject which will increase the cost of doing business. For example, an increase in the complexity of trading arrangements and expenses for commercial trading organizations in comprehension and consenting to the administrative necessities of every agreement. Hence, organizations and investors would favor some type of harmonization among the PTAs and international investment agreements.

However, in the face of improvements in liberalization and market access, investors are likely to utilize PTAs as well as international investment agreements. This is consistent with certain studies which have concluded that PTAs and BITs are less important in an investor's preference list and have little or no impact on investment decisions, except on the ground that such PTAs or BITs provide for investment liberalization. Market access is one important factor that greatly influences FDI flow. Direct access to the investment market/destination or using the investment destination as an access route to the intended investment destination or to another market greatly contributes to the signing of an investment treaty; it also contributes to increases in FDI flow.

In their study on foreign investment protection and liberalization,[36] Berger, Busse, Nunnenkamp and Roy confirmed the importance of liberal admission rules such as NT provisions in the establishment

more transparent, stable, predictable and secure – that is, they allow the economic determinants to assert themselves. And when IIAs reduce obstacles to FDI and the economic determinants are right, they can lead to more FDI. But it is difficult to identify the specific impact of the policy framework on FDI flows, given the interaction and relative importance of individual determinants." Andrew Paul Newcombe & Luis Paradell, Law and Practice of International Investment Treaties (2009).

[36] Axel Berger, Matthias Busse, Peter Nunnenkamp & Martin Roy, *Do Trade and Investment Agreements Lead to more FDI? Accounting for Key Provisions inside the Black Box*, 10 Int'l Eco. & Eco. Policy 247, 247 (2013).

phase in promoting bilateral FDI flow.[37] Therefore, creating free market access as well as establishing provisions on nondiscrimination[38] and fair treatment of investors in terms of international investment agreements are very important in attracting investors to specific destinations.[39] Similarly, certain studies have shown that commerce is greatly enhanced by international treaties, given that countries create easier access to the market by establishing low barriers to business with other countries, allowing firms to benefit while also enabling easy export back to the home country.[40]

Subsequently, the ASEAN-Australia-New Zealand Free Trade Area treaty and the like have great potential in reducing the cost of production in the host countries. This is because it allows/creates access to cheaper input materials, especially in respect of efficiency-seeking investments. Certainly, a most favorable assessment of the investment climate is a product of economic reforms and trade liberalization.[41]

12.3.5 Relation with the ATIGA and the AFAS

FDI information is comprised of both interests in the primary areas and the commercial presence in trade in services.

The ATIGA and the AFAS, in combination with the ACIA agreement, provide a deeper platform where it becomes comparatively cheaper for multinational corporations to secure their inputs from local sources

[37] *Id*, at 268.

[38] See Tim Büthe & Helen V. Milner, *The Politics of Foreign Direct Investment into Developing Countries: Increasing FDI through International Trade Agreements?*, 52 Am. J. Pol. Science 741, 741 (2008); Tim Büthe & Helen V. Milner, *Foreign Direct Investment and Institutional Diversity in Trade Agreements: Credibility, Commitment, and Economic Flows in the Developing World, 1971–2007*, 66 World Politics 88, 88 (2014).

[39] Tom Kenyon & Yotam Margalit, *Does Joining International Treaties Attract Foreign Investment? Experimental Firm-Level Evidence*, Columbia University Working Paper (2014).

[40] See Matthias Busse, Jens Königer & Peter Nunnenkamp, *FDI Promotion through Bilateral Investment Treaties: More than a Bit*, 146 Rev. World Economics 147 (2010); Peter Egger & Michael Pfaffermay, *The Impact of Bilateral Investment Treaties on Foreign Direct Investment*, 32 J. Comp. Eco. 788 (2004); Eric Neumayer & Laura Spess, *Do Bilateral Investment Treaties Increase Foreign Direct Investment to Developing Countries?*, 33 World Development 1567 (2005); Jeswald Salacuse & Nicholas P. Sullivan, *Do BITs Really Work? An Evaluation of Bilateral Investment Treaties and Their Grand Bargain*, 46 Harvard Intl. L. J. 67 (2005); and Jennifer Tobin & Susan Rose-Ackerman, *When BITs Have Some Bite: The Political Economic Environment for Bilateral Investment Treaties?*, 6 Rev. Intl. Org. 1 (2011).

[41] Kenyon & Margalit, *supra* note 40.

within the host country, while they simultaneously enjoy protection against political risks in the event of direct and indirect investment and property seizure, denial of justice, unfair treatment and other government misconduct. These economies act as a component of the worldwide chain of product and services, while the ASEAN agreements and the AEC serve to integrate the value chain between the ASEAN Member States and the global community.

One of the mutual benefits of the investor-host agreement is that the said multinational corporation, in expanding their operations, increases the production capacity of local firms (within the host country) in terms of supply of input used in all stages of the ASEAN value chain and regional integration as well, through the establishment of the AEC in 2015.[42] As a result, the ASEAN states have become part of the RVC. The major sectors featured as part of the RVC include automobile, electrical and electronics and agribusiness. Additionally, it is reported that ASEAN's value contributions to the region's aggregate exports are high and have expanded, from 65 percent in 1995 to 69 percent in 2011.[43] This improvement shows that foreign and local companies have not only channeled their input sourcing from the region, but have also increased it in creating components or finished products in their associated value chains. Not only does this make ASEAN an appealing investment destination to investors in the existing RVC, it also creates a new set of RVC within the ASEAN.

One of the major steps taken by the AEC in support of the free trade area agenda is the adoption of the ATIGA, which is designed to build up a coordinated market and production base with a free stream of products by 2015. The ATIGA contains a few components to guarantee acknowledgment of the free stream of products within the ASEAN, including tariff liberalization, evacuation of nontariff barriers, rules of inception, business facilitation, customs, guidelines and conformance, sanitary and phytosanitary measures. To encourage transparency and consistency, Annex 2 of the ATIGA gives the full Tariff Reduction Schedule of every ASEAN state and it explains the duty rates to be applied to every item/product for every year up to 2015. The ATIGA liberalizes market product flows through the disposal of both intraprovincial duties and nontariff barriers, which should expand the productivity and intensity of ASEAN's manufacturing sector in the global market.

42 *FDI Development and Regional Value Chain, ASEAN Economic Report 2013–2014* (2014).
43 *Id.*, at xix.

The AFAS came into force in 1995. It aims to foster collaboration among the ASEAN states in terms of trade in services, thereby enhancing the proficiency and intensity of the ASEAN services industry; to expand production limits, supplies and the distribution of services; and to wipe out significant barriers as well as liberalize trade in services by extending the profundity and extent of liberalization beyond those embraced under the GATS of the WTO. The AFAS coined the trade-in-services definition in Article I.2 of GATS. Trade-in-services under AFAS adopts a four-fold definition as specified in GATS. This definition depends on the location of the supplier and the consumer at the time of the exchange. In accordance with Article I:2 of GATS, trade-in-services entails services provided from the domain of one member into the region of some other member (Mode 1 – Cross-border exchange); in the region of one member to the services purchaser of some other member (Mode 2 – Consumption abroad); by a service provider of one member, through commercial presence, in the region of some other member (Mode 3 – Commercial presence); and by an administration provider of one member, through the presence of a temporary worker of member in the region of some other member (Mode 4 – Presence of natural persons).

12.3.6 Issues and Challenges Ahead

Other than being an important document aimed at making ASEAN a most attractive investment destination, the ACIA has several aspects that are yet to be implemented. One important fact is that there are no stand-alone comprehensive investment policies with region-wide coverage; the available policies are only geared toward individual Member States, with investment laws varying from one ASEAN state to another.

Another paramount measure that needs to be embarked upon by ASEAN is to project a more positive image of the ACIA as a tool of trade designed to attract investors and investments into the ASEAN region through social strategies. The unique and favorable nature of the ACIA that differentiates it from other agreements lies in its inception as a regional agreement, where the involved parties arrive at a certain point of agreement to liberalize investment sectors while at the same time shouldering the role of protection for both investors and their investments in all sectors. The critical need for promoting the ACIA is due to the speculation that international investments may have a major impact on investment decision-making processes.[44] Generally, investors do not always consider the presence of international investment agreements, including investment chapters in the PTA or the existence of investor protections including the ISDS mechanism, at the point of making the investment decision.

Again, ASEAN as a conglomerate needs to project and promote itself as a single entity and an investment-ready destination, instead of individual ASEAN states promoting themselves as separate destinations. Similarly, the ASEAN states need to begin a full implementation of the AEC Blueprint 2025. As projected by the ASEAN leaders in the document, it is envisioned that by 2025 ASEAN will be exceedingly coordinated and durable; competitive, innovative and dynamic; with upgraded connectivity and sectoral collaboration; and a stronger, comprehensive and people-oriented, people-focused community incorporated into the worldwide economy.

The entire ASEAN community and its pioneers unanimously uphold a common agenda of attaining the status of an exceptionally coordinated and strong regional economy, characterized by high economic development with a view to expanding trade, investment and employment creation; enhancing the region's ability to react to global challenges and mega trends; propelling a single market plan through enhanced commitments in trade-in-goods and through effective resolution of nontariff barriers; accomplishing further integration in trade-in-services; and ensuring a more consistent flow of investment, skilled labor, businesspeople and capital.

As part of the AEC Blueprint 2025, the AEC will create a competitive, innovative and dynamic community that encourages durable product development. Moreover, the AEC will project an improved regional framework with upgraded connectivity and sectoral cooperation. This will include key sectoral policies crucial to the viable operationalization of the economic community; a versatile, comprehensive people-oriented and people-centered community that fosters fair development and comprehensive growth; a community with improved micro, small and medium enterprise development strategies and cooperation to reduce the development

[44] See how some investors have structured or restructured their investments to size the benefits of investment treaties and/or arbitration Julien Chaisse, *The Issue of Treaty Shopping in International law of Foreign Investment – Structuring (and Restructuring) of Investments to Gain Access to Investment Agreements*, 11 Hastings Busi. L. J. 225 (2015).

gap; and a community with greater financial/economic opportunities, which embraces poverty eradication.

The ASEAN pioneers additionally envisage that in 2025 the AEC will conduct its external economic relations in a more precise and reasonable manner and be a central and major facilitator of regional economic relations in East Asia.

In its post-2015 vision, ASEAN states will keep on working on the strategic review of the ACIA embedded agenda, including the treatment of permanent residents and prohibition of performance requirements. Another area of importance to ASEAN is the ACIA amendment procedure, which provides the instrument for amending the ASEAN states' reservation lists. This review will be with particular regard to their continuous liberalization efforts as well as the efforts of ASEAN to showcase the region as a single investment destination; and to additionally enhance their individual investment regimes through continuous investment promotion and facilitation projects. Considering the fact that ASEAN states are true contenders for FDI and that most Member States have their individual investment policies that specify some form of performance requirements, the ACIA agenda review will pose many challenges.

12.4 Conclusion

There is an agreement, reflected in the ACIA, that cross-border trade has a positive role to play in each of the ten ASEAN states and that speculators ought to be urged to keep up and extend their ventures all through the district. Similarly, it is trusted that more speculators will emerge in the coming years. This is the foundation of the ACIA, and it goes a long way toward clarifying why the ASEAN states hold in esteem the development and improvement profits that can flow from expanded economic cooperation and the way it offers possibly huge favorable circumstances for organizations working together across the district. The ACIA liberalization initiative completely accommodates and encourages investment in three categories of investment sectors that cover conceivably profitable sectors such as manufacturing, agriculture, fishery, forestry, mining and related services.

With respect to liberalized sectors, the ACIA, as part of its commitments, requires ASEAN states to treat new investments and investors in line with the standards of the NT and MFN clause. Restrictions on the nationality of senior management and boards of directors are additionally lessened under the ACIA. For instance, through the ACIA, ASEAN states will be expanding their receptiveness to cross-border exploration, manufacturing and servicing in the oil and gas industry. There will likewise be fewer obstacles for cross-border supply chains; for instance, in the textile sector, where input materials are being collected in one ASEAN Member State and handled in another, an article of clothing can be created in a third ASEAN Member State.

The ACIA features quite a number of advantages over previous agreements and investment instruments, such as a guarantee of fair and nondiscriminatory government regulations, more extensive scope within ASEAN and clearer substantive protection guarantees. This is particularly true for the ACIA's far-reaching and regulatory utilization of NT and MFN treatment principles over how host governments regulate investors and investments. For instance, the ACIA's nondiscriminatory provisions cover both ASEAN and non-ASEAN investors. Another good example of clarity is that of its criteria for legal expropriation, and its commitment to FET as well to full protection and security.

In the event of sudden regulatory changes, the ACIA reacts to the worries of foreign businesses by addressing such changes in a proficient, straightforward and legitimately binding manner. Previously, investors had to rely on the diplomatic protection of their home country government; therefore, the ASEAN states collectively committed to a rule-based dispute settlement system by specifying the investor-state dispute settlement provisions that allow individual investors to pursue complaints for alleged breaches of agreements and to safeguard their property rights without requesting the help of their governments.

The ACIA offers various alternative dispute settlement procedures (incorporate intervention, placation and international arbitration); of these, arbitration is the most preferred and most relevant to major disputes and subsequently is the subject of the greater part of the ACIA standards. Investor-state arbitration under the ACIA offers the following extra advantages: judges are autonomous from the host state and not subject to political pressures; improved consistency may come from the current ascent in case law and arbitral awards; in particular, perhaps, arbitral awards involve restricting decisions that can be implemented universally.

Pursuant to the AEC Blueprint 2025, ASEAN will continue to enhance its efforts in fostering economic expansion by using efficient, productive, rational and responsive controls and good administrative practice to improve the investment environment. ASEAN will likewise guarantee that the ACIA will contribute toward the further reconciliation of ASEAN into the worldwide economy by embracing a more rational approach with the perspective of attaining a full position in local and global economic fora.

13

Fragmented Approaches to Investor-State Dispute Settlement Mechanisms in Intra-ASEAN And Extra-ASEAN Investment Treaties

TRINH HAI YEN*

13.1 Introduction

In the effort to establish the AEC, ASEAN has set the goal of improving its regional legal framework on foreign investments to enhance "its competitiveness in attracting foreign direct investment (FDI) as well as intra-ASEAN investment," which is believed to have the effect of promoting and ensuring dynamic development of ASEAN economies.[1] To enhance regional integration, the Blueprint states that ASEAN Member States will realize "a more comprehensive investment agreement which should be forward looking, with improved features, provisions and obligations by considering international best practices that would increase the investor confidence in ASEAN." This has led to the conclusion of the ACIA.

Chapter 11 focuses on the investment liberalization provisions of the ACIA and Chapter 12 provides an overview of salient features of the ACIA, including a brief introduction to its dispute settlement mechanisms. This chapter provides a critical analysis of the ISDS mechanism from a comparative perspective. It examines one of the objectives in the ACIA, which is to strengthen investor-state dispute settlement mechanisms to "provide *enhanced protection* to all investors and their investments to be covered under the comprehensive agreement."[2] ASEAN

* The opinions expressed in this chapter are those of the author, and do not reflect in any way those of the institutions with which she is affiliated.

[1] A Blueprint for Growth ASEAN Economic Community 2015: Progress and Key Achievements (2015).

[2] *Id.*, para. 27 (emphasis added).

Member States, therefore, have endorsed a favorable approach to a system granting greater procedural rights to investors.

The AEC Blueprint 2025 focuses on implementing the ACIA to further enhance the attractiveness of ASEAN "as an investment destination globally through the establishment of an open, transparent and predictable investment regime."[3] It emphasizes the promotion aspects of the ACIA, as well as scheduling to eliminate or improve investment restrictions and impediments and to find ways of phasing out or reducing the ACIA Reservation Lists. Consequently, the ACIA dispute settlement mechanisms are not likely to be modified or affected by initiatives like that of the European Union on the investment court system. In addition, this Blueprint states clearly that the Association is determined to work toward further integrating the AEC into the global economy through developing a more strategic and coherent approach toward external economic relations with a view to adopting a common position in regional and global economic fora as one of the strategic measures.[4]

Within several years of the adoption of the AEC Blueprint in 2007, ASEAN concluded the ACIA and four other regional investment treaties with external partners China, South Korea, Australia, New Zealand and India.[5] This intensive and robust treaty-making aims not only to realize the plan of ASEAN's attractiveness as an investment destination but is also commensurate with ASEAN's legalization approach, starting with the ASEAN Charter, which officially announces the existence of ASEAN as an international organization with legal personality.[6]

The following sections will first examine the investor-state dispute settlement mechanisms in all existing ASEAN investment treaties that have been concluded since the adoption of the AEC Blueprint 2015 in 2007. Despite the absence of a common investment treaty template, the

[3] Association of Southeast Asian Nations Economic Community Blueprint 2025 (2015), paras. 14–15.

[4] AEC Blueprint 2025, para. 80(i).

[5] *See* Agreement on Investment of the Framework Agreement on Comprehensive Economic Cooperation Between the Association of Southeast Asian Nations and the People's Republic of China (2009); Agreement on Investment under the Framework Agreement on Comprehensive Economic Cooperation Among the Governments of the Member Countries of the Association of Southeast Asian Nations and the Republic of Korea (2009) (ASEAN-South Korea Investment Agreement); Agreement Establishing the ASEAN-Australia-New Zealand Free Trade Area (2009); Agreement on Investment under the Framework Agreement on Comprehensive Economic Cooperation Between the Association of Southeast Asian Nations and the Republic of India (2004) (ASEAN-India Investment Agreement).

[6] *See* Charter of the Association of Southeast Asian Nations (2007), art. 3.

parallel negotiations of these treaties have resulted in marked similarity in their substantive and structural design, including provisions on ISDS. Therefore, normative integration into a common regional ISDS framework appears to be possible.

Yet, close scrutiny of the details of ISDS provisions suggests a fragmented approach in the ASEAN investment treaties reflecting the nature of an international investment regime customized between specific parties. The chapter will discuss the responses of ASEAN Member States to the European Union's initiative for an international investment court to replace traditional international arbitration in the European Union's FTAs with Singapore and Vietnam, which reveals the potential of further fragmentation in ASEAN's position on ISDS. This chapter will then reassess the ISDS in the ACIA in light of the AEC's goal of strengthening ISDS to provide enhanced protection to investors and their investments covered under the ACIA. It will demonstrate the possible dormant status of the ACIA's ISDS and recommend a course of action to avoid this.

13.2 Fragmented Approach to Investor-State Dispute Settlement in ASEAN's Investment Treaties

Replacing the single provision on investor-state disputes in the IGA[7] with a sophisticated, full-fledged section addressing concerns over the conduct of present arbitration cases, the ACIA is a major development from its predecessor agreement in this respect. In addition to this intra-ASEAN investment treaty, the other abovementioned ASEAN investment treaties with external partners were all signed in 2009, with the exception of the ASEAN-India Investment Agreement, which was concluded five years later. Despite the absence of a common investment treaty template, the parallel negotiations of these treaties and ASEAN's coordinated position have resulted in marked similarity in their substantive and structural design, including provisions on ISDS. Nonetheless, since they are specifically negotiated by groups of states, though their diversity is defined by the change of only one or two partners, the ISDS mechanisms are fragmented not only in the form of separate treaties but also in their features and formats.

Prima facie, ASEAN investment treaties share the main traditional characteristics of ISDS mechanisms. First, they provide for two-stage ISDS: prearbitration and arbitration. Investors are obliged to explore

[7] *See* ASEAN Agreement for the Promotion and Protection of Investments (1987).

amicable means of resolving their disputes with the host states within 180 days of the receipt of the request for consultations.[8] Second, the treaties offer investors the right to choose various arbitration rules or for a, including, notably, the Convention on the Settlement of Investment Disputes between States and National of other States (ICSID), ICSID Additional Facility Rules, the arbitration rules of UNCITRAL, the Regional Centre for Arbitration at Kuala Lumpur or any other regional center for arbitration in ASEAN.[9] Third, they include a waiver of diplomatic protection by the home state of investors.[10] Fourth, except for the ASEAN-China Investment Agreement, they emphasize that arbitral awards are final and binding upon disputing parties, which is generally also provided in applicable arbitration rules.[11] This basic structure of ISDS makes arbitration an available international forum for foreign investors to settlement disputes on an equal footing with sovereign host states. It does, however, leave various procedural questions unanswered.

State experience in investor-state arbitration leads to progressive developments of ISDS in ASEAN investment treaties. Based on international best practices,[12] they add important procedural improvements to enhance predictability and clarity as well as to preserve state control over this international adjudicative system. They all provide that foreign investors may submit their disputes to international arbitration within three years of their becoming aware of a treaty breach.[13] Second, dual nationals possessing the nationality of the host state may not initiate arbitration against that state.[14] Except for the ASEAN-South Korea Investment Agreement, all other ASEAN investment treaties require

[8] *See* ASEAN Comprehensive Investment Agreement (ACIA), art. 31; AANZFTA art. 19; ASEAN-India Investment Agreement, art. 20(5), (6); ASEAN-South Korea Investment Agreement, art. 18(4); ASEAN-China Investment Agreement, art. 14(3).

[9] *See* ACIA, art. 33(1); AANZFTA, art. 21(1); ASEAN-India Investment Agreement, art. 20 (7); ASEAN-South Korea Investment Agreement, art. 18(5); ASEAN-China Investment Agreement, art. 14(4).

[10] *See* ACIA, art. 34(3); AANZFTA, art. 22(3); ASEAN-India Investment Agreement, art. 20 (29); ASEAN-South Korea Investment Agreement, art. 18(13); ASEAN-China Investment Agreement, art. 14(8).

[11] *See* ACIA, art. 41; AANZFTA, art. 28(4); ASEAN-India Investment Agreement, art. 20 (23); ASEAN-South Korea Investment Agreement, art. 18(14).

[12] AEC Blueprint 2025, *supra* note 4, para. 26.

[13] *See* ACIA, art. 34(1)(a); AANZFTA, art. 22(1)(a); ASEAN-India Investment Agreement, art. 20(8)(a); ASEAN-South Korea Investment Agreement, art. 18(7)(a); ASEAN-China Investment Agreement, art. 14(6)(a).

[14] *See* ACIA, art. 29(2); AANZFTA, art. 18(2); ASEAN-India Investment Agreement, art. 20 (19), (20); ASEAN-South Korea Investment Agreement, art. 18(2); ASEAN-China Investment Agreement, art. 14(2)(b).

express written waiver of the right to initiate or continue parallel proceedings before the courts or administrative tribunals of the host state, which seems unnecessary with the presence of a clear fork-in-the-road clause making final the choice of listed adjudicative procedures by an investor.[15] The adoption or enforcement of a taxation measure is governed by a distinct procedure allowing more control by the state parties concerned over the process of dispute settlement.[16] These treaties also address the right to seek interim measures of protection to preserve the disputing investor's rights and interests.[17]

Notwithstanding the possible convergence into a common regional ISDS framework based on strikingly similar provisions, the divergences in the ASEAN investment treaties reverse this trend. They share some new features but differ in other aspects. The investment agreements between ASEAN and South Korea, China and India have single-provision ISDS that are less detailed than those of the other two ASEAN investment treaties, the ACIA and the AANZFTA. More importantly, in terms of substantive content, the ACIA, AANZFTA and the ASEAN-India Investment Agreement contain further modifications to any arbitration rules or fora chosen by investors on some important issues. First, arbitrators must have "expertise or experience in public international law, international trade or international investment rules, and be independent of, and not be affiliated with or take instructions from the disputing Party, the non-disputing Party, or disputing investor." Frivolous claims manifestly without legal merits can be addressed early in the arbitral proceedings. Transparency clauses are introduced to encourage respondent states to make arbitral decisions and awards public. State parties to these three agreements may intervene in the interpretation of treaty terms by way of joint interpretation. Finally, they require the enforcement of arbitral awards in the territory of the contracting states.

The added characteristics have significant implications for both the host state and foreign investors. Arbitration becomes more controllable

[15] *See* ACIA, art. 33(1), 34(1)(c); AANZFTA, art. 21(1), 22(1)(c); ASEAN-India Investment Agreement, art. 20(7), 20(8)(b)(iii); ASEAN-South Korea Investment Agreement, art. 18 (6); ASEAN-China Investment Agreement, art. 14(6)(b)(iii).

[16] *See* ACIA, art. 36(6)–(9); AANZFTA, art. 25(6), (7); ASEAN-India Investment Agreement, art. 20(19), (20); ASEAN-South Korea Investment Agreement, art. 18(8)–(11); ASEAN-China Investment Agreement, arts. 14(9), (10).

[17] *See* ACIA, art. 34(2); AANZFTA, art. 22(2); ASEAN-India Investment Agreement, art. 20 (19), (20); ASEAN-South Korea Investment Agreement, art. 18(12); ASEAN-China Investment Agreement, art. 14(7).

Table 13.1: *Fragmented features of investor-state dispute settlement mechanisms in ASEAN investment treaties*

Fragmented features	ACIA	AANZFTA	ASEAN-India Investment Agreement	ASEAN-South Korea Investment Agreement	ASEAN-China Investment Agreement
Qualification of arbitrators	Art. 35	Art. 23	Art. 20(10–11)	N/A	N/A
Preventing frivolous claims	Art. 36 (2–3)	Art. 25(2–3)	Art. 20(12–16)	N/A	N/A
Transparency	Art. 39	Art. 26	Art. 20(17–18)	N/A	N/A
States' joint interpretation	Art. 40 (2–3)	Art. 27(2–3)	Art. 20(19–20)	N/A	N/A
Enforcement of arbitral awards	Art. 41(9)	Art. 28(7)	Art. 20(27)	N/A	N/A

for states because of the explicit right to intervene with state joint interpretation, specified qualification of arbitrators and screening of claims manifestly without merit. However, the population in the host state might not be content with hortatory transparency clauses, which are supposed to inform them of internationally challenged governmental measures. Investors can be reassured of the enforcement of arbitral awards in case they prevail in their disputes, especially when they are resolved under arbitration rules without intrinsic enforcement mechanisms.

At the tip of the iceberg, therefore, normative integration into a common regional ISDS framework appears to be possible. However, close scrutiny of details in ISDS provisions suggests fragmentation in the ASEAN investment treaties reflecting the nature of an international investment regime customized between specific parties. Investors cannot adopt the pick-and-choose strategy because the MFN standard granting them no less favorable treatment than that of investors from other states is not applicable to investor-state dispute settlement procedures,[18] subject to further negotiation[19] or is absent[20] in ASEAN investment treaties. These entangled offers to arbitration send mixed signals to the competitiveness of ISDS in the intra-ASEAN investment regime and make it difficult to anticipate how ASEAN investors or foreign investors can find it more legally beneficial in ASEAN host states.

13.3 The EU Initiative for an International Investment Court: the Potential Converging Point for an ASEAN Common Position on ISDS

Virtually all investment treaties provide for international arbitration, which has been frequently used to settle disputes between foreign investors and states. The settlement of over 800 disputes by treaty-based arbitration[21] has raised concerns about inconsistent and unintended interpretations of states' treaty obligations.[22] This situation is arguably

[18] ACIA (2009), n. 4, art. 6; ASEAN-China Investment Agreement art. 5(4).

[19] ASEAN-South Korea Investment Agreement, arts. 4, 27.

[20] *See* ASEAN-India Investment Agreement; AANZFTA, Ch. 11.

[21] *Special Update on Investor-State Dispute Settlement: Facts and Figures*, IIA Issue Note, No. 3, UNCTAD/DIAE/PCB/2017/7 (2017).

[22] *See* e.g., Muthucumaraswamy Sornarajah, *A Coming Crisis: Expansionary Trends in Investment Treaty Arbitration, in* Appeals Mechanism in International Investment Disputes 51–73 (Karl P. Sauvant & Michael Chiswick-Patterson eds., 2008); Muthucumaraswamy Sornarajah, *The Retreat of Neo Liberalism in Investment Treaty*

rooted in the ambiguous and general wording of investment treaty provisions,[23] the ad hoc nature of investor-state arbitration,[24] the lack of appeal bodies,[25] alleged proinvestor interests of the arbitrators or arbitration system[26] and interpretation methods used by arbitrators.[27]

Debates over perceived deficiencies of ad hoc international arbitration center more on how to modify it rather than on how to find a better alternative to it. The idea of an investment court to replace traditional, long-established investor-state arbitration mechanisms in IIAs was rarely discussed. The European Union has recently proposed the use of an international investment court for investor-state disputes and successfully persuaded Vietnam and Canada to replace arbitration with that model in their Free Trade Agreements.[28] The rationale for such a sea change replacing the long-recognized and utilized arbitration method is to solve its problems such as ad hoc nature, conflicts of interest and arbitrators' lack of full impartiality.[29] The ad hoc nature of arbitrators' appointment allegedly interferes in their ability to act independently and to properly balance investment protection against the right to regulate or provide financial incentives to multiply ISDS cases.[30] The underlying

Arbitration, *in* The Future of Investment Arbitration 291 (Catherine A. Rogers and Roger P. Alford eds., 2009).

[23] *See* e.g., Charles H. Brower II, *Structure, Legitimacy, and NAFTA's Investment Chapter*, 36 Vand. J. Transnat'l 37, 59–63 (2003); Ian Laird & Rebecca Askew, *Finality Versus Consistency: Does Investor-State Arbitration Need an Appellate System?*, 7 J. App. Prac. & Process 285, 286 (2005).

[24] *See* e.g., August Reinisch, *The Issues Raised by Parallel Proceedings and Possible Solutions*, *in* The Backlash against Investment Arbitration: Perceptions and Reality 115 (Michael Waibel et al., eds., 2010).

[25] *See* e.g., David Gantz, *An Appellate Mechanism for Review of Arbitral Decisions in Investor-State Disputes: Prospects and Challenges*, 39 Vand. J. Transnat'l 39, 39–76 (2006).

[26] *See* e.g., Vicki Been & Joel C. Beauvais, *The Global Fifth Amendment? NAFTA's Investment Protections and the Misguided Quest for an International "Regulatory Takings" Doctrine*, 78 N.Y.U. L. Rev. 30, 35–7 (2003); Olivia Chung, *The Lopsided International Investment Law Regime and Its Effect on the Future of Investor-State Arbitration*, 47 Va. J. Int'l L. 953, 956–7 (2007); Gus Van Harten, *Perceived Bias in Investment Treaty Arbitration*, *in* Michael Waibel et al., eds., The Backlash against Investment Arbitration: Perceptions and Reality 433 (2010).

[27] *See generally* Trinh Hai Yen, *The Interpretation of Investment Treaties* (2014).

[28] European Union-Vietnam Free Trade Agreement (2016) (agreed text); and Comprehensive Economic and Trade Agreement (2016); EU-Singapore Free Trade Agreement.

[29] *Investment in TTIP and beyond – the Path for Reform*, European Commission Concept Paper, May 5, 2015, at 6. http://trade.ec.europa.eu/doclib/docs/2015/may/tradoc_153408.PDF (last visited Mar. 21, 2018).

[30] *Id.*, at 6, 7.

reasons for replacing the current arbitration mechanism with the investment court system, therefore, are to ensure the impartiality and independence of adjudicators and to prevent the risk of unforeseen interpretation of investment treaties, thereby promoting consistency and predictability in investment treaty jurisprudence.[31] Ultimately, it aims to safeguard "the right to regulate of host states and to achieve legitimate policy objectives, such as public health, safety, environment, public morals and the promotion and protection of cultural diversity."[32]

Amidst sustained enthusiasm in redrafting ISDS across ASEAN's investment treaties, the European Union's revolutionary initiative of an alternative means resembling the two-tier adjudicative system of the WTO has been a litmus test for fragmentation in ASEAN's investment regime. Two ASEAN members, Singapore and Vietnam, have reached agreement on foreign investment with the European Union.[33] The ISDS in these agreements differentiates with those of ASEAN investment treaties in some important issues such as emphasis on mediation, more stringent requirements on transparency, incorporation of a code of conduct for arbitrators, the roster of tribunal members, specified qualifications and fixed remuneration for members of tribunal.

The most radical change in the EU ISDS proposal is an international investment court. The European Union and Vietnam have included an investment tribunal system in their agreed draft EU-Vietnam Free Trade Agreement (EVFTA) of January 2016. Although no terms such as courts or judges are mentioned in the treaty text, the provisions follow closely the EU's proposal on an investment court system without substantial modifications. In contrast to the EVFTA's smooth switch from arbitration to investment court, the EU-Singapore Free Trade Agreement (EUSFTA) resists the change and focuses on improving arbitration choice instead.

The European Union is targeting more FTAs with ASEAN Member States, or ideally with ASEAN as a whole, replacing all existing European Union Member States' investment treaties in the exercise of its competence for the protection of investments conferred in 2009.[34] The opposite negotiation outcomes in the EVFTA and the EUSFTA suggest further

[31] *See* Sornarajah, *supra* note 22, at 7–8.

[32] *See* Sornarajah, *supra* note 22, at 2.

[33] Free Trade Agreement between the European Union and the Republic of Singapore (2015); EVFTA, *supra* note 28.

[34] *See* Treaty on the Functioning of the European Union art. 3, 2012 OJ C326/47 (consolidated version).

fragmentation in ASEAN ISDS, because it would be difficult to form a common ASEAN response to the EU position. Investors in ASEAN investment areas, therefore, are likely to face diverse distinct offers of dispute settlement means. It will be a challenge to ASEAN's determination in developing "a more strategic and coherent approach towards external economic relations with a view to adopting a common position in regional and global economic fora."[35] The Court of Justice of the European Union makes the prospect for the ASEAN plan more complicated and unpredictable when opining that treaties with ISDS are subject to the consent of individual EU Member States to be bound.[36]

13.3.1 Singapore's Response: a Switch from Modified Arbitration to the Investment Court System

An ASEAN host state might want to weigh reforming the arbitration mechanism against an alternative option, a new quasi-judicial investment court. This was Singapore's initial approach in the EUSFTA in response to the EU proposal. To prevent inconsistencies and unintended arbitral interpretations of the EUSFTA, states parties may issue subsequent interpretations through the EUSFTA Trade Committee, which are binding upon arbitral tribunals established under that Agreement.[37] Moreover, these tribunals are expressly obligated to interpret the EUSFTA in accordance with the Vienna Convention on the Law of Treaties.[38] A code of conduct of arbitrators is added to ensure their impartiality and independence.[39] This Agreement also requires publication of documents exchanged or used in arbitral proceedings and public hearings.

One might find a corrective appeal mechanism which was absent in the previously released EUSFTA text as a crucial tool to avoid inconsistent jurisprudence, although it envisages further consideration by the treaty committee of this option.[40] It is, however, not integrated into the current investor-state arbitration system in all investment treaties including this Agreement. This option was already explored in the Working Paper of the ICSID Secretariat,

[35] AEC Blueprint 2025, para. 80(i).
[36] CJEU, Opt. 2/15, para. 292 (May 16, 2017).
[37] EUSFTA, art. 9.19(3).
[38] EUSFTA, art. 9.19(2).
[39] EUSFTA, Annex 9-F.
[40] EUSFTA art. 9.30(1)(c).

Suggested Changes to the ICSID Rules and Regulations,[41] and in the US Model BIT of 2004 and the Dominican Republic-Central American-United States Free Trade Agreement.[42] The ICSID Secretariat then considered that such appeal system was premature due to technical and policy issues.[43] Some commentators also found the option unappealing.[44]

A salient feature of this ISDS compared to ASEAN investment treaties and the EVFTA is the mediation mechanism. Detailed rules are developed to encourage "comprehensive and expeditious procedure with the assistance of a mediator."[45] This can serve as a competitive advantage and promise a new trend in the development of ASEAN ISDS.

The recently released text of the EU-Singapore Investment Protection Agreement (negotiated texts as of April 2018) revealed a switch from resistance to approval of the EU investment court system, which will be discussed in detail below in the EVFTA text.

[41] *See Possible Improvements of the Framework for ICSID Arbitration, Discussion Paper*, Oct. 22, 2004, https://icsid.worldbank.org/en/Documents/resources/Possible%20Improvements%20of%20the%20Framework%20of%20ICSID%20Arbitration.pdf (last visited Mar. 19, 2018).

[42] Appendix D of the 2004 US Model Treaty provides that "within three years after the date of entry into force of this Treaty, the Parties shall consider whether to establish a bilateral appellate body or similar mechanism to review awards rendered under art. 34 in arbitrations commenced after they establish the appellate body or similar mechanism." *See also* Annex 10-F of the Dominican Republic-Central American-United States Free Trade Agreement, Aug. 5, 2004 (DR-CAFTA).

[43] *Suggested Changes to the ICSID Rules and Regulations*, Working Paper of the ICSID Secretariat, May 12, 2005, para. 4, https://icsid.worldbank.org/en/Documents/resources/Suggested%20Changes%20to%20the%20ICSID%20Rules%20and%20Regulations.pdf (last visited Mar. 19, 2018).

[44] E.g., Barton Legum, *Options to Establish an Appellate Mechanism for Investment Disputes, in* Appeals Mechanism in International Investment Disputes 231-40 (Karl P. Sauvant & Michael Chiswick-Patterson eds., 2008); Jan Paulsson, *Avoiding Unintended Consequence, in* Appeals Mechanism in International Investment Disputes 241–65 (Karl P. Sauvant & Michael Chiswick-Patterson eds., 2008); Asif H. Qureshi & Shandana Gulzar Khan, *Implications of an Appellate Body for Investment Disputes from a Developing Country Point of View, in* Appeals Mechanism in International Investment Disputes 267–78 (Karl P. Sauvant & Michael Chiswick-Patterson eds., 2008); Muthucumaraswamy Sornarajah, *Toward Normlessness: the Ravage and Retreat of Neo-Liberalism in International Investment Law, in* The Yearbook on International Investment Law and Policy 2009/2010 641 (Karl P. Sauvant ed., 2010).

[45] EUSFTA, Annex 9-E.

13.3.2 Vietnam's Response: Investment Court System in the EVFTA and Its Challenges

The investment court system in the EVFTA is a radical departure from modified arbitration in the EUSFTA in terms of a two-tier structure, tenured members and appeal mechanism. These new features aim to realize the expectations of its investors of a more superior choice for investor-state disputes to ensure consistent and intended application of their treaties, notably through a permanent appellate mechanism.

From the investors' perspective, the investment court system is not a completely different regime from the international arbitration offered in other ASEAN investment treaties since it retains the most important value – an international dispute settlement mechanism consisting of independent adjudicators where the foreign investor may seek enforcement of its rights conferred under investment treaties. The EVFTA does not leave the foreign investor with solely domestic remedies by continuing the phenomenal offer in international investment law of an international adjudicative mechanism for private actors to bring claims against sovereign states.

Vietnam's acceptance of the EU initiative might result from considerations of its attractiveness in the view of both the host state and the foreign investor. Nonetheless, there is the question of an inconsistent approach across its investment treaties. Moreover, the system can present challenges to its implementation and proliferation. It is modeled after the WTO dispute settlement mechanism with modifications, though it can also be compared with courts in the EU system.[46] The following comparative analyses with the WTO system reveal some drawbacks of the EVFTA model.

13.3.2.1 Inflexibility of the Tribunal Structure

The EVFTA Tribunal, or the Tribunal of First Instance as it is called in the EU proposal, consists of nine members appointed by the Trade Committee, three of whom are nationals of a Member State of the European Union, three are nationals of Vietnam and three are nationals of third countries.[47] Its function is similar to that of an arbitral tribunal in the traditional arbitration mechanism. A structural switch from an ad hoc disputing party-appointed arbitral tribunal to a permanent

[46] *See generally* Steffen Hindelang, In Pursuit of an International Investment Court: Recently Negotiated Investment Chapters in EU Comprehensive Free Trade Agreements in Comparative Perspective (2017).

[47] EVFTA, art. 12(2), § 3 (Resolution of Investment Disputes).

contracting-party appointed court is intended to reduce the risk of contradictory interpretations and adjudicators' conflict of interests by being involved in multiple cases. Nonetheless, semipermanency in the Tribunal structure should be weighed against flexibility and disputing party autonomy in selection of the Tribunal members to make this institution attractive to both investor claimants and negotiating partners who still favor arbitral systems in the majority of IIAs. There are three main reasons for making the Tribunal more flexible and party-autonomy based.

First, inflexibility, which is reflected in the composition of the EU first instance tribunal in two aspects, is not necessary. Appointments of Tribunal members must be made by the appointing authority, the Trade Committee, which is composed of representatives of contracting parties[48] rather than disputing parties. Moreover, the number of Tribunal members is temporarily fixed and subject to consensual procedure to be changed. Although in the future the Trade Committee may decide to increase or to decrease this number by multiples of three,[49] the division of three members[50] to hear a dispute brought before an EVFTA tribunal is currently confined to this list.

Conversely, the WTO Understanding on Rules and Procedures Governing the Settlement of Disputes (DSU) allows disputing parties to determine the members of panels which serve as the WTO first instance institution of dispute settlement. Party autonomy and flexibility in the composition of WTO panels are highly respected, reflected in ad hoc composition for each individual dispute, the number of panelists[51] and the selection of nationals or non-nationals of disputing parties[52] from the indicative nomination lists of the Secretariat or not.[53] Since the WTO

[48] EVFTA, art. X.1(2), Ch. XX, provides that "the Parties hereby establish a Trade Committee comprising representatives of the Union and Viet Nam."

[49] EVFTA, art. 12(3), § 3.

[50] EVFTA art. 12(4) provides that "the Tribunal shall hear cases in divisions consisting of three Members, of whom one shall be a national of a Member State of the European Union, one a national of Vietnam and one a national of a third country. The division shall be chaired by the Member who is a national of a third country."

[51] According to art. 8.5 of the DSU, WTO panels are generally composed of three persons, although the disputing parties can agree to a panel composed of five panelists.

[52] DSU art. 8.3 provides that "citizens of Members whose governments are parties to the dispute or third parties . . . shall not serve on a panel concerned with that dispute, *unless the parties to the dispute agree otherwise*" (emphasis added) (footnote omitted).

[53] DSU art. 8.6 provides that "the Secretariat shall propose nominations for the panel to the parties to the dispute. The parties to the dispute shall not oppose nominations except for compelling reasons." However, "compelling reasons" are not defined and subject to the discretion of disputing parties.

rules and practice[54] prioritize party agreement on panel composition, they show less concern over the impartiality and independence of panelists. While the EVFTA requires members of the Tribunal and of the Appeal Tribunal not to be affiliated with any government,[55] the WTO accepts panelists as "governmental and/or non-governmental individuals, including persons who have served on or presented a case to a panel, served as a representative of a member or of a contracting party to GATT 1947 or as a representative to the Council or Committee of any covered agreement or its predecessor agreement, or in the Secretariat."[56] The DSU does not address the challenge of panelist independence. The only guidance in the selection of panel members is that it should ensure "their independence, a sufficiently diverse background and a wide spectrum of experience."[57]

In the context of investor-state disputes, party autonomy contributes to creating more trust in the dispute settlement process. Increasing IIA contracting parties' control is more justified in the composition of the Appeal Tribunal, the authority of which is to promote the correct and consistent application of international investment rules rather than to directly solve specific disputes. Therefore, it is understandable that treaty-contracting parties should appoint of the Appeal Tribunal's members.

Second, in addition to the disadvantage of inflexibility and removal of investors' autonomy in selecting members of the first instance tribunal, there is a financial disincentive in the European Union's proposed design as compared with ad hoc arbitration and the WTO structure. The financing scheme of dispute settlement institutions is a notable method shared by both the EU investment court system and the WTO with a view to preventing conflict of interests. While the disputing parties bear the costs of arbitration, including the fees and expenses of arbitrators, the expenses of members of investment courts and WTO panels or Appellate Body are covered jointly by all the contracting parties. However, while the WTO first instance institution does not impose pre-proceeding fees, the EU investment courts generate financial sunk costs because of a monthly retainer fee to ensure that their members shall be available at all times and on short notice, and shall stay abreast of dispute settlement activities

[54] Peter Van Den Bossche, The Law and Policy of the World Trade Organization: Text, Cases and Materials 236 (2005).

[55] EVFTA, art. 14, § 3.

[56] DSU, art. 8.1.

[57] DSU, art. 8.2.

under the IIA in question.[58] Some governments, especially in developing countries, might not be willing to accept and incur this retainer fee. An ad hoc first instance mechanism would relieve this regular financial burden, not to mention its attractive features of flexibility and disputing parties' determination of its members. If the criteria for selecting members of the tribunal render its composition more party autonomy-based and subject to less stringent generalized objective requirements, the tribunal's composition and function will accommodate more various needs of disputing parties.

Finally, there is a concern over the lack of qualified candidates who are nationals of contracting parties to serve as members of tribunals in the investment court system. For example, in the case of the EVFTA, no Vietnamese nationals have been involved in investment treaty arbitration. If the selection of the first instance tribunal depends solely on the autonomy of disputing parties with general qualifications and is not required to be allocated by nationality, the search for potential candidates to serve in tribunals will be less demanding. Modifications in the structure of the Tribunal of First Instance in the EU proposal are, therefore, desirable. Flexible selection criteria and ad hoc establishment of the first instance tribunal to prioritize party autonomy and a broader pool of potential adjudicators should relieve the concerns over excessive state control and prostate system, as well as reduce the financial burden of a monthly retainer fee.

13.3.2.2 Confusing Jurisdiction of the Appeal Tribunal

Unlike the rejection of an appeal facility in the EUSFTA, the EVFTA establishes appellate tribunals.[59] The Appeal Tribunal in the EVFTA, as well as in the EU proposal on an investment court system, is entrusted with the most important goal of the system, that is, to ensure consistency and predictability of the investment treaty concerned. The design of this institution, however, creates some challenges to its efficiency and sustainability.

First, the jurisdiction of the tribunal is so comprehensive that it can essentially be a retrial of a case. The grounds for appeal are: (a) that the Tribunal has erred in the interpretation or application of the applicable law; (b) that the Tribunal has manifestly erred in the appreciation of the facts, including the appreciation of relevant domestic law; or (c) those

[58] *See* e.g., EVFTA art. 12, paras. 13–14, art. 13, § 3.

[59] EVFTA, arts. 27(7), 28.

provided for in Article 52 of the ICSID Convention, insofar as they are not covered by (a) and (b).[60] It encompasses the ICSID Convention bases for award annulment, which are confined to protecting the technical integrity of arbitration proceedings[61] and the WTO Appellate Body substantive review of legal issues in the panel report.[62] The mandate of the WTO appeal institution is limited to issues of law addressed in the panel report with a clarification through its practice that whether a panel has made an objective assessment of the facts can be a legal question within the scope of appellate review.[63]

The EU Appeal Tribunal is given an additional and uncommon power of appellate review in both international and domestic courts. It can assess the appreciation of the facts of the first instance tribunal. While making the scope of its review very comprehensive, this provision underrates the contribution of the first instance procedure to the resolution of investor-state disputes. The settlement of specific disputes with detailed examination of facts and law is mainly entrusted to first instance institutions. The function of factual review is further challenged by the time limit for the appeal procedure. The EVFTA requires that, as a general rule, appeal proceedings shall not exceed 180 days from the date a party to the dispute formally notifies its decision to appeal to the date the Appeal Tribunal issues its decision, and in no case should the proceedings exceed 270 days.[64] An EU Appeal Tribunal will have to carry out a thorough re-examination of every aspect of a dispute to ensure not only consistency and correctness of legal interpretations, but also of the factual conclusions of the first instance tribunal. It is not clear why this institution should be given such a broad mandate if its main mission is to prevent conflicting legal determinations of the first instance tribunal and

[60] EVFTA, art. 28(1) § 3.

[61] Art. 52 of the ICSID Convention lists the following annulment grounds: the Tribunal was not properly constituted; the Tribunal has manifestly exceeded its powers; there was corruption on the part of a member of the Tribunal; there has been a serious departure from a fundamental rule of procedure; or the award has failed to state the reasons on which it is based.

[62] DSU art. 17(6) provides that "an appeal shall be limited to issues of law covered in the panel report and legal interpretations developed by the panel."

[63] Appellate Body Report, *EC Measures Concerning Meat and Meat Products (Hormones)*, WTO Doc. WT/DS26/AB/R, WT/DS48/AB/R (adopted Feb. 13, 1998), para. 132. *See also* Appellate Body Report, *Korea – Taxes on Alcoholic Beverages*, WTO Doc. WT/DS75/AB/R, WT/DS84/AB/R (adopted Feb. 17, 1999), para. 162. *See also* Peter van den Bossche, The Law and Policy of the World Trade Organization: Text, Cases and Materials 236 (2005).

[64] EVFTA, art. 28(5) § 3.

promote predictability and consistency in the application of the treaty concerned.

Second, having the competence of reviewing awards issued by the first instance tribunal, the Appeal Tribunal is supposed to have an apparent higher authority from its composition and more strictly controlled integrity than the first instance tribunal. This is not reflected in the EVFTA and the EU proposal because both two-tier tribunals are governed by almost identical rules of composition and ethics. Their members are selected when they meet the requirements of expertise in public international law and of the qualifications required in their respective countries for appointment to judicial offices, or are jurists of recognized competence.[65] The only difference in the wording is a qualifier, "the highest" in the phrase "highest judicial offices" regarding the qualification of a member of the Appeal Tribunal.[66] There is no difference applied to the phrase "jurists of recognised competence." Both are required to be unaffiliated with any government.[67] One could reasonably draw a conclusion that members of the first instance tribunal and Appeal Tribunal are subject to the same selection criteria. Besides, they are both employed on a semi-permanent basis, having to be "available at all times and on short notice, and shall stay abreast of dispute settlement activities"[68] under the investment treaty concerned. They are appointed for a four-year term, renewable once[69] and paid a monthly retainer fee.[70]

Therefore, the proposed higher retainer fee for members of the Appeal Tribunal cannot be justified from selection criteria.[71] The design of appeal tribunals in the EU proposal follows closely the WTO rules on its Appellate Body. It would be a better structure in terms of crediting higher inherent authority to investment appeal tribunals if this proposal also adopts the WTO model of an ad hoc first instance panel, which makes selection criteria both more flexible and less demanding than those of the appeal institution and necessitates no monthly retainer fee. Removing the power of reviewing questions of fact of appeal tribunals,

[65] EVFTA, arts. 12(4), 13(7) § 3.

[66] EVFTA, art. 13(7) § 3.

[67] EVFTA, art. 14 § 3.

[68] EVFTA, arts. 12(13), 13(13) § 3.

[69] EVFTA, art. 12(5), 13(5) § 3.

[70] EVFTA, arts. 12(14), 13(14) § 3.

[71] The EU suggests a monthly retainer fee for members of the Appeal Tribunal of €7,000 per month in art. 10(12), and for members of the Tribunal of First Instance of €2,000 per month in art. 9(12) of its proposal for Investment Protection and Resolution of Investment Disputes.

therefore, should enhance its efficiency in terms of the proceeding's time limit and at the same time fulfill its fundamental function of ensuring predictability and consistency in legal determinations of the investment court system.

A general observation reveals that the WTO prioritizes sustainability, flexibility and state autonomy. The EU proposal appears to prioritize legitimization by creating public authority for and state control over dispute settlement institutions. It actually reaffirms state superiority in the relationship with private parties, foreign investors at the international level. For any legal framework to be sustained and develop, however, efficiency and flexibility should be given priority over formality and legitimization. This also applies to reforms in the international investment regime, including those of dispute settlement mechanisms.

13.4 Conclusion

Whichever model – modified arbitration or an international investment court – prevails in the ASEAN regional ISDS framework will be determined by its attractiveness in comparison with traditional arbitration. The purpose of strengthening the ISDS provisions clearly stated in the AEC Blueprint suggests that ASEAN Member States want to send positive signals on a credible investor-state dispute settlement mechanism. The ACIA contains two less appealing aspects for foreign investors compared to other investment treaties. Its ISDS contains prostate features which are absent in the ASEAN-China and ASEAN-South Korea Investment Agreements as discussed in Section 13.2. The ACIA clarifies frequently invoked substantive protection standards to contain the most restrictive state obligations. For example, its fair and equitable treatment provision is limited to a single meaning, an obligation "not to deny justice in any legal or administrative proceedings in accordance with the principle of due process,"[72] while in other investment treaties it is open for interpretation of equivalent customary international law or contains a list of various obligations.

Recent conclusions of investment treaties have further put their regional concerted plans on ISDS to a test. Negotiations with the European Union have initially resulted in distinct ISDS in separate treaties with two individual ASEAN Member States. Recently, Singapore joined Vietnam in accepting an introduction of the two-tier court system in their treaties

[72] *See* ACIA, art. 11(2)(a).

with the European Union. A permanent investment court with broad competence is expected to be a "systemic shift" to solve problems of investor-state arbitration.[73] Although it has unclear prospects in the ASEAN investment area, not only because it will be difficult to form a common position of ASEAN countries regarding this issue, EU Member States will have to reach agreement among themselves on treaties containing ISDS clauses after the Court of Justice of the European Union found that ISDS was a shared competence with EU Member States and that FTAs with the European Union will require ratification from its Member States.[74] Finally, with diverse offers of ISDS for foreign investors, the existing fragmentation of ISDS frameworks in ASEAN investment treaties is challenging the objective of enhancing competitiveness in attracting foreign as well as intra-ASEAN investment.

[73] *See* Steffen Hindelang, In Pursuit of an International Investment Court: Recently Negotiated Investment Chapters in EU Comprehensive Free Trade Agreements in Comparative Perspective 204 (2017).

[74] CJEU, Opt. 2/15, para. 292 (May 16, 2017).

14

Pro-Development Dispute Resolution Mechanisms and Norms for Investment and Commercial Disputes in ASEAN

MAN*

14.1 Introduction

The establishment of the AEC in December 2015 marked an important milestone in the acceleration of regional economic integration. In the next ten years, according to the AEC Blueprint 2025, an area of focus for ASEAN is the development and promotion of MSMEs. Transnational transactions within and with ASEAN will therefore continue to rise, which will undoubtedly lead to a concomitant increase in the volume as well as the complexity of disputes.

This chapter explores the strategic development of innovative approaches to facilitate the resolution of investor-state and commercial disputes in ASEAN. It argues that the creation of new dispute settlement mechanisms will enhance the economic development of ASEAN states, drive the growth of small and medium enterprises and ultimately achieve the wider objective of more equitable and inclusive economic growth in the region.

The first part of the chapter, Section 14.2, provides an overview of the existing dispute settlement landscape, identifying the weaknesses and gaps. Owing to space constraints, the survey focuses on the dispute settlement mechanisms provided in the ASEAN Comprehensive Investment Agreement (ACIA) and within the domestic legal systems of Indonesia, Vietnam and Singapore.

* The author would like to thank Bryan Mercurio, Pasha L. Hsieh, Jean Ho, Federico Lupo-Pasini, Han-Wei Liu, Nadja Alexander and Dorcas Quek Anderson for their insightful comments. All errors and views are the authors' own. The author also gratefully acknowledges the excellent research assistance provided by Melissa Ng.

In light of the weaknesses of the existing dispute settlement mechanisms discussed in Section 14.2, the chapter then explores in Section 14.3 strategic approaches for the development and improvement of dispute settlement mechanisms and norms for both investor-state as well as commercial disputes.

14.2 The ACIA and Domestic Dispute Mechanisms

Although ASEAN is represented as a single economic entity, one must not overlook the socioeconomic, political and legal diversity within ASEAN which, in part, accounts for the differences in the legal infrastructures of ASEAN States. And dispute settlement is a critical, if not central, part of the legal infrastructure of ASEAN. Ultimately, commercial actors need to be confident that the legal rights and obligations they have contracted for will be enforced, and in an efficient manner. The need for such assurances in the case of MSMEs is even more acute, as they neither have the bargaining power to reach advantageous settlements with counterparties nor the finances to sustain protracted dispute resolution processes.

Owing to space constraints, my survey on existing dispute settlement mechanisms focuses on recent developments: the ACIA dispute settlement mechanism and the case studies of Indonesia, Vietnam and Singapore.[1] The treatment of the ACIA shall be focused on the evaluation of the strengths and weaknesses of its dispute settlement regime.[2] Indonesia, Vietnam and Singapore are selected for study because of the diversity in legal history and systems.[3] Singapore, in particular, is chosen for closer scrutiny in view of its recent efforts at introducing a variety of innovative initiatives in dispute resolution.

The establishment of the ACIA and an overview of how the ACIA controls investment flows in ASEAN and guarantees investment protection have been dealt with in great detail in Chapters 11 and 12. An important form of investment protection under the ACIA, as highlighted in Chapter 11, is the ACIA's dispute settlement regime. This chapter examines that regime in greater depth. The ACIA was undoubtedly a significant step in ASEAN's

1 This chapter does not focus on mechanisms found in bilateral treaties.

2 For a detailed discussion of ACIA, *see* Trinh Hai Yen, *Fragmented Approaches to Investor-State Dispute Settlement Mechanism in Intra-ASEAN and Extra-ASEAN Investment Treaties, infra* Chapter 20.

3 For an overview, *see* Michael Pryles ed., Dispute Resolution in Asia (2002), Chs. 6 (Indonesia), 10 (Singapore) and 13 (Vietnam).

development of comprehensive investor-state dispute settlement (ISDS) mechanisms for disputes involving a Member State of ASEAN and an investor of another Member State. Four features of the ACIA framework are of note. First, the ACIA does not preclude an investor from pursuing administrative or court processes in the host state.[4] Second, the investor and the host state may at any time during the process commence conciliation.[5] Third, the ACIA prescribes a consultation-binding adjudication dispute settlement process.[6] Finally, in turning to binding adjudicative processes, the investor may choose between domestic court proceedings or arbitration of various forms, including arbitration under the ICSID Convention and the ICSID Rules of Procedure for Arbitration Proceedings, ICSID Additional Facility Rules, UNCITRAL Arbitration rules, arbitration at regional arbitration centers or, where the parties have agreed, any other form of institutional arbitration.[7]

The core strength of the ACIA ISDS framework lies in the promotion of arbitration,[8] which is effective in leveling the playing field for the investor against the host state.[9] In particular, it enables small to medium-sized investors (which could include MSME) – who have no power to appeal to their home states for help[10] – to have direct recourse to dispute settlement processes. Neutrality and impartiality are further undergirded under the ACIA by the requirement that the third arbitrator on the arbitral panel, who is the presiding arbitrator, shall be a national of a "non-Member State."[11]

Nevertheless, the ACIA mechanism may be criticized for promoting complicated processes in light of its tiered, multipronged approach.[12]

4 ACIA, art. 29(4).

5 ACIA, art. 30.

6 ACIA, arts. 31 and 32.

7 ACIA, art. 33.

8 John Frangos, *Investor-State Arbitration in the ASEAN Economic Community*, 22 Asia Pacific Regional Forum News (Jan. 2015), www.tilleke.com/sites/default/files/2015_Jan_Investor-State_Arbitration_AEC.pdf (last visited Mar. 19, 2018).

9 *See* concerns outlined in A. Giardina, *The International Centre for Settlement of Investment Disputes between States and National of Other States, in* Essays on International Commercial Arbitration 214 (Peter Šarčević ed., 1989).

10 *See* Pearlie Koh, *Enhancing Economic Co-operation: A Regional Arbitration Centre for ASEAN*, 49 Int'l & Comp. L. Q. 390, 396 (2000).

11 ACIA, art. 35(1)(b).

12 H. E. Mr. Krit Kraichitti, *Dispute Settlement Mechanisms for ASEAN Community: Experiences, Challenges and Way Forward*, Workshop on Trade and Investment ASEAN Law Association Twelfth General Assembly, Feb. 25–28, 2015, www.aseanlawassociation.org/12GAdocs/workshop5-thailand.pdf (last visited Mar. 19, 2018), at 10.

One commentator notes the presence of two inconsistent provisions in the ACIA concerning the path to arbitration.[13] Generally, investment treaties prescribe either a fork-in-the-road provision or a waiver provision in relation to investors' election of dispute settlement mechanisms. It is observed that Article 33(1) of the ACIA is a fork-in-the-road provision as it allows the investor to choose between the different kinds of adjudicative processes; but Article 34(1)(c) of the ACIA clearly represents a waiver provision by stating the choice of arbitration would consequently require the waiver of the right to dispute resolution in domestic courts.[14] One way to resolve the apparent inconsistency is to interpret Article 34(1)(c) as being triggered only upon an election for arbitration under Article 33(1)(b)–(f).[15] Its function is to reinforce and clarify what the choice of arbitration means: that is, no recourse to court proceedings. In other words, if the investor chooses litigation in domestic courts, Article 34(1)(c) is not brought into play.

Further, an inherent limitation of the ACIA ISDS mechanism is that it can only be invoked in respect of industries covered under the ACIA,[16] whose scope may be further circumscribed by reservations made by the Member States.[17] Finally, there may be concern that the ACIA mechanism has yet to be tested, although this concern would abate over time with utilization. Overall, the ACIA is a laudable development by raising ASEAN's dispute settlement standards to be on par with, or at least close to, international standards. More broadly, the ACIA functions as a gateway toward more innovative dispute resolution mechanisms, as its structure is sufficiently flexible to capture a variety of mechanisms that may be developed both at the domestic as well as regional levels. The section below considers the domestic dispute mechanisms under the existing laws of three ASEAN countries: Indonesia, Vietnam and Singapore.

14.2.1 Indonesia

The Indonesian legal system is based upon Dutch civil law, although many new laws incorporate common law principles. Culturally, the philosophy underpinning Indonesian society – Pancasila – seeks

[13] Trinh Hai Yen, The Interpretation of Investment Treaties 246 (2014).

[14] *Id., see* footnote 1181.

[15] I thank Jean Ho for her helpful comments on how the apparent inconsistency between art. 33(1) and art. 34(1)(c) may be resolved.

[16] *See* ACIA, art. 3(3). *See also* Frangos, *supra* note 8.

[17] *See* ACIA, art. 9.

consensus and discourages contention.[18] Litigation in Indonesian courts is thus rarely resorted to for the resolution of commercial disputes. Other reasons for avoiding litigation in the Indonesian courts include: protracted court proceedings, uncertainty and unpredictability of outcomes, language barriers[19] and costs.[20] Litigation in foreign courts is not a viable alternative if there is a need to enforce the foreign judgment in Indonesia, as Indonesia is currently not a party to any treaty for the recognition and enforcement of foreign judgments.

14.2.1.1 The Rise of Arbitration

Arbitration is increasingly the preferred mechanism for the resolution of commercial disputes.[21] Although arbitration has been recognized and used since the mid-nineteenth century, it was not until 1999 that Indonesia had comprehensive arbitration legislation[22] – the Law Concerning Arbitration and Alternative Dispute Resolution, Law No. 30 of 1999 (the Arbitration Law).[23] Notably, Indonesia has been a contracting state of the New York Convention on Recognition and Enforcement of Foreign Arbitral Awards (the New York Convention) since 1981.[24] The most commonly used local arbitral institution in Indonesia is Badan Arbitrase Nasional Indonesia (BANI).[25] BANI maintains its own panel of arbitrators comprising both local and international arbitrators. There are also other arbitral institutions that have been set up for dispute settlement in specific industries.[26]

[18] Karen Mills, *National Report for Indonesia, in* ICCA International Handbook on Commercial Arbitration (Jan Paulsson and Lise Bosman eds., 2016).

[19] Proceedings must be conducted in Indonesian. In PT Bangun Karya Pretama Lestari v. Nine AM, the Indonesian Supreme Court upheld the ruling by the High Court of West Jakarta that contracts not written in the Indonesian language are unenforceable under Indonesian law. *See further: Commentary: Indonesian High Court Upholds Ruling that Contracts be Written in Indonesian*, Jones Day, Dec. 2015, www.jonesday.com/files/Publication/202d219d-d9e4-4656-b25d-3071c32a870d/Presentation/PublicationAttachment/e5a54e8d-9240–4111-a178-374d0be20912/Indonesia_High_Court_Upholds.pdf (last visited Mar. 19, 2018).

[20] Pheo M. Hutabarat, *Indonesia, in* The Dispute Resolution Review 374, 377, 389 (Richard Clark ed., 2013).

[21] Mills, *supra* note 19, at 3.

[22] *Id.*, at 1.

[23] This legislation is not based on the UNCITRAL Model Law.

[24] Indonesia has not entered into any other treaty for the enforcement and recognition of awards.

[25] *See* BANI Arbitration Center, www.baniarbitration.org/ (last visited Mar. 19, 2018).

[26] For example, the Capital Market Arbitration Board that was set up in 2002 to handle civil disputes arising out of the capital market through out-of-court mechanisms.

A weakness in the current Indonesian law on arbitration is that "public policy" is not a clearly defined or recognized legal concept and courts have "considerable discretion" in its application. The Arbitration Law uses the phrase "public order" instead of public policy, which is the more internationally established terminology. Moreover, notwithstanding proposals for a definition of public order, none was ultimately included in the legislation.[27] Article 66 of the Arbitration Law states that international arbitration awards[28] "may only be enforced in Indonesia if they do not violate public order." On a plain reading, at least, public order is conceptually distinct from public policy.

14.2.1.2 Court-Annexed Mediation

Consistent with the Indonesian ideology of amicable dispute settlement, mediation of various forms has long been practiced in Indonesia.[29] Under Article 45 of the Arbitration and ADR Law, the arbitral tribunal is required to first attempt to encourage the parties to settle their disputes amicably before the commencement of the arbitral hearing. There are various organizations in Indonesia that provide alternative dispute resolution services and/or training.[30] To date, Indonesia has not adopted the UNCITRAL Model Law on International Commercial Conciliation.

The latest development concerns the push for court-annexed mediation. In February 2016, the Indonesian Supreme Court promulgated Regulation No. 1 of 2016 on Mediation Procedures in Courts (the Mediation Regulation), which obliges disputing parties to attempt mediation of their civil disputes before pursuing litigation in the courts. Most remarkably, the Mediation Regulation introduces a "good faith" provision, requiring parties and their lawyers to undertake the process of mediation in good faith – including to attend and actively participate in the process. In June 2016, the Chief Justice of the Supreme Court issued Decree No. 108/KMA/SK/VI/2016 regarding the Organization of Mediation Procedures in Court (the Mediation Decree) to set out in detail the process of mediation, rules on the

[27] Mills, *supra* note 19, at 49.

[28] According to art. 1(9) of the Arbitration Law, an "international arbitration award" is an award delivered by an arbitration institution or arbitrator(s) outside of Indonesia or an award deemed to be such under Indonesian law.

[29] *See* Mas Achmad Santosa, *Development of Alternative Dispute Resolution (ADR) in Indonesia*, ASEAN Law Association, Dec. 1, 2003, www.aseanlawassociation.org/docs/w4_indo.pdf (last visited Mar. 19, 2018).

[30] Examples: Pusat Mediasi Nasional, BANI Arbitration Centre and the Indonesian Academy of Independent Mediators and Arbitrators.

education and certification of mediators and mediators' code of conduct.[31] However, court-annexed mediation has not been effective in helping parties reach settlements.[32] It is observed that court-annexed mediation is still generally being regarded as a "tick-box" exercise.[33]

14.2.1.3 ISDS Mechanisms

Turning now to consider ISDS mechanisms, Indonesia ratified the ICSID Convention in 1968. Indonesia has also signed many BITs. It has been observed that almost half of the publicly available BITs provide for similar dispute settlement mechanisms: tiered dispute settlement involving parties' first attempt to amicably resolve their dispute through consultation/negotiation, failing which the dispute may be submitted for resolution by arbitration or conciliation under the ICSID Convention.[34] Further, Article 32 (Chapter XV) of Investment Law No. 25 of 2007 sets out various options for settlement of disputes arising between the Indonesian government and an investor: amicable settlement, arbitration under Indonesian law, alternative dispute resolution under Indonesian law, international arbitration or litigation in Indonesian courts.

Significantly, in March 2014, the Indonesian government announced that it intended to let its existing BITs expire without renewal.[35] The intention, it is said, is to allow Indonesia to develop a new model BIT with better terms for the country.[36] This provides an opportunity to rethink the ISDS framework, in particular, the balance between protection of investors and protection of the host states.[37]

[31] *See Mediation Court Procedures and Regulations in Indonesia*, Indonesia-Investments, Sep. 26, 2016, www.indonesia-investments.com/business/business-columns/mediation-court-procedures-and-regulations-in-indonesia/item7221 (last visited Mar. 19, 2018).

[32] Benny Riyanto, *Remodelling and Repositioning of Court's Mediation in Indonesia*, Diponegoro L. Rev. 28, 31 (2016).

[33] Herbert Smith Freehills, *ADR in Asia Pacific: Spotlight on Indonesia*, ADR in Asia Pacific Guide Issue 3, Feb. 2017, www.herbertsmithfreehills.com/latest-thinking/adr-in-asia-pacific-spotlight-on-indonesia (last visited Mar. 19, 2018).

[34] *See generally* Loretta Malintoppi & Charis Tan, Investment Protection in Southeast Asia: A Country-By-Country Guide on Arbitration Laws and Bilateral Investment Treaties 136–8 (2016).

[35] Indonesia and Argentina mutually agreed to terminate their BIT.

[36] Michael Ewing-Chow & Junianto J. Losari, *Indonesia Is Letting Its Bilateral Treaties Lapse so as to Negotiate Better Ones*, Financial Times, Apr. 16, 2014, www.ft.com/content/20c6c518-c16c-11e3-97b2-00144feabdc0 (last visited Mar. 19, 2018).

[37] Investors may still benefit from the provisions of regional treaties (such as the ACIA) and Free Trade Agreements to which Indonesia is a party. *See* Alvin Yeo & Smitha Menon,

14.2.2 Vietnam

Vietnam, whilst remaining a socialist society, has transformed into a more market-oriented economy since the introduction of the *doi moi* reforms in 1986. It joined the World Trade Organization in 2007 to accelerate its integration into the global trade and investment system. To date, Vietnam has signed many bilateral investment treaties and eleven free trade agreements.[38] The Vietnamese legal system, civil law in nature, has developed significantly for the purpose of creating a favorable environment to grow its foreign direct investment sector.[39] Vietnam is also a contracting state of the New York Convention[40] since September 12, 1995.

14.2.2.1 Litigation and Foreign Arbitration

Gaps and limitations, nevertheless, remain in the Vietnamese legal infrastructure for dispute settlement. In principle, a foreign investor may pursue the resolution of its disputes with the state or a Vietnamese party through litigation in the Vietnamese courts, domestic arbitration or arbitration overseas. Litigation in Vietnamese courts is considered as a last resort by businesses.[41] The establishment of the Vietnamese Economic Court – which deals with a variety of commercial disputes – in 1994 has not given businesses significantly greater confidence in the Vietnamese judiciary. Notwithstanding the increasing use of the Economic Court, there is a general sense of mistrust by both businesses and lawyers arising from a number of causes, including inefficiency, ineffective enforcement of judgments,[42] incompetence, a lack of transparency in the process and perceived partiality towards state-owned enterprises.[43]

Indonesia – Arbitrating with Foreign Parties: A Closer Look at Indonesia's Approach to Investor-State Dispute Settlement, 3 *Asian Dispute Review* 124, 128–9 (2016).

[38] *See Free Trade Agreements*, Asia Regional Integration Center, https://aric.adb.org/fta-country (last visited Mar. 19, 2018).

[39] *See generally* Hop Dang, *Legal Issues in Vietnam's FDI Law: Protections Under Domestic Law, Bilateral Investment Treaties and Sovereign Guarantees*, *in* Foreign Investment and Dispute Resolution Law and Practice in Asia 223 (Vivienne Bath & Luke Nottage eds., 2011).

[40] Note, however, that Vietnam has made three reservations.

[41] Pip Nicholson & Minh Duong, *Legitimacy and the Vietnamese Economic Court*, *in* New Courts in Asia 31, 46–7 (Andrew Harding & Penelope Nicholson eds., 2010).

[42] This issue arises from the institutional separation of enforcement of judgment from the courts. Under the Vietnamese system, the Ministry of Justice is responsible for the enforcement of judgments. *See* P. Nicholson & Minh Duong, *Legitimacy and the Vietnamese Economic Court*, *in* New Courts in Asia 37–8 (Andrew Harding & Penelope Nicholson eds., 2010).

[43] *Id.*, at 46–7.

Foreign investors' preference is for arbitration abroad.[44] Overseas arbitration is more advantageous when compared with domestic arbitration, given the inadequate processes and underdeveloped laws of the latter.[45] However, it is more difficult to enforce a foreign arbitral award in Vietnam.[46] Procedurally, an application to a Vietnamese court is required for the enforcement of a foreign arbitral award. A domestic arbitral award, in contrast, is directly enforceable.[47] Moreover, it is generally perceived that Vietnamese courts are disinclined against enforcing foreign arbitral awards.[48]

Further, Vietnamese law does not recognize the concept of international public policy. The New York Convention provides that an arbitral award may be refused recognition/enforcement if it "would be contrary to the public policy of that country." However, the implementing Vietnamese legislation of the New York Convention, the 1995 Ordinance on Recognition and Enforcement of Foreign Arbitral Awards, chose the wording of "the fundamental principles of Vietnamese laws."[49] The same wording was retained in the Civil Procedure Code, which replaced the 1995 Ordinance. The new Civil Procedure Code, dated November 15, 2015, continues to keep the "fundamental principles of Vietnamese laws" provision, notwithstanding a proposal to adopt and follow the New York Convention provision strictly.[50] It has been said that the breach of Vietnamese law in itself may constitute contravention of the fundamental principles of Vietnamese laws.[51] Currently, there is no official guidance issued by the authorities on the proper interpretation of this ground.[52]

[44] Dang, *supra* note 39, at 234.

[45] *Id.*, at 235.

[46] *Id.*

[47] *See* Law on Commercial Arbitration (No: 54/2010/QH12), art. 66.

[48] Tyco Services Singapore Pte Ltd v Leighton Contracts (VN) Judgment No. 02/pTDS dated Jan. 21, 2003 (Court of Appeal of the Supreme People's Court of Vietnam), is frequently cited as an example of judicial unfriendliness toward the recognition and enforcement of foreign arbitral awards. *See also* commentary in Hew R. Dundas, Dzungsrt & Associates LLC, *National Report for Vietnam (2015)*, *in* ICCA International Handbook on Commercial Arbitration 1–46 (Jan Paulsson & Lise Bosman eds., 2015).

[49] Art. 16.2(b).

[50] Nguyen Manh Dzung & Nguyen Thi Thu Trang (Dzungsrt & Associates LLC), *Countries report on the public policy exception in New York Convention – Vietnam* (Mar. 15, 2016).

[51] Richard Garnett & Kien Cuong Nguyen, *Enforcement of Arbitration Awards in Vietnam*, 2 Asian Int'l Arbit. J. 1, 142–5 (2006).

[52] There has been guidance issued by the Research of Institution of Judicial Science of the Supreme People's Court, but it is only available in Vietnamese. *See* Nguyen Manh Dzung & Nguyen Thi Thu Trang, *supra* note 40. Arguably, one may draw some guidance from the Supreme People's Court's Resolution 01/2014/NQ-HDTP dated Mar. 20, 2014 on the

Finally, in respect of investor-state disputes, Vietnam has yet to become a signatory to the ICSID Convention. This means that investors bringing a claim against the Vietnamese government have no recourse to ICSID arbitration.

Yet, it should not be missed that Vietnam has made some recent progress in improving its dispute settlement infrastructure. It is to these efforts that we now turn.

14.2.2.2 The EVFTA and Legal Reforms

Vietnam and the European Union signed the EVFTA on May 29, 2015,[53] which is expected to come into force in 2018. A detailed treatment of the EVFTA – critically examining its strengths and weaknesses – is found in Chapter 13. This part of the discussion will consider the EVFTA from the perspective of legal innovation and shall be more brief, in view of the analysis offered by Chapter 13. Investment disputes arising under the EVFTA will be settled by an independent two-tier investment tribunal system incorporating an appeal mechanism. Further, the EVFTA, to ensure greater transparency, directly addresses issues such as third-party funding[54] and ethics,[55] and incorporates the UNCITRAL Rules on Transparency in treaty-based investor-state arbitration.[56] This new dispute settlement mechanism will challenge and thus grow the competence of Vietnamese agencies in participating in investment disputes.

On the commercial arbitration front, Vietnam's promulgation of Law No. 54 on Commercial Arbitration (LCA) evinces its commitment to promote arbitration and adopt a more open attitude. The LCA widens the scope of arbitral disputes beyond disputes arising from commercial activities. The LCA also relaxes qualifications of arbitrators to include in special cases individuals with specialised expertise and practical experience, as well as abolishing the requirement of Vietnamese nationality. The possibility of having foreign arbitrators may make arbitration in Vietnam more attractive to foreign investors.[57] The introduction of

interpretation and application of "contrary to the fundamental principles of Vietnamese law," a ground for the setting aside of Vietnamese arbitral awards. But such a solution results in a fragmented approach toward the interpretation of the New York Convention.

53 For a detailed analysis on the EVFTA ISDS mechanism, *see* Trinh, *supra* note 2.

54 *Id.*, art. 11.

55 *Id.*, art. 14.

56 *Id.*, art. 20.

57 Dinesh Raj Shiwakoti, *A Review of Vietnam's Law No 54 on Commercial Arbitration*, 2 Asian Dispute Review 1, 61 (2014).

foreign arbitrators[58] is also likely to invigorate Vietnamese arbitration practice.

Finally, on February 24, 2017, the Vietnamese Government issued Decree No. 22/2017/ND-CP (Decree No. 22), the first piece of Vietnamese law on commercial mediation.[59] The legislation came into effect on April 15, 2017, and is inspired by the UNCITRAL Model Law on International Commercial Conciliation. Two interesting aspects of the legislation are worth highlighting. First, it encourages foreign mediation centers to establish branch or representative offices in Vietnam, and these offices may establish their own panel of mediators, provided that the mediators meet the prescribed qualifications. Secondly, the legislation addresses the issue of enforceability of mediated agreements by providing a mechanism to convert the agreements into court judgments. Mediation has certainly garnered interest and attention from the Vietnamese legislator.[60]

14.2.3 Singapore

Singapore, a common law jurisdiction, has always been committed to maintaining an open economy.[61] The year 2014 saw the conclusion of the EUSFTA, the first free trade agreement concluded between the European Union and an ASEAN country, and which is on track to be ratified in 2019. An in-depth discussion of the EUSFTA – and its comparison with the EVFTA – is found in Chapter 13. This chapter turns to consider more recent innovative approaches by Singapore to address the needs of modern dispute settlement. Notably, in recent years, Singapore has taken on a leadership position in offering dispute resolution services, especially where resolution of commercial disputes is concerned.[62] More recently, Singapore, in tandem with the rise of ASEAN and the

[58] *See* list of foreign arbitrators listed on the Vietnam International Arbitration Centre panel, http://eng.viac.vn/foreign-arbitrators-p3.html-trang-2? (last visited Mar. 23, 2018).

[59] *See generally* Nguyen Manh Dzung & Dang Vu Minh Ha, *Enforcement of Mediated Settlement Agreements in Vietnam: A Step Forward the International Trend?*, Kluwer Arbitration Blog, Jul. 2, 2017, http://kluwerarbitrationblog.com/2017/07/02/deposition-japan-u-s-based-international-arbitration/ (last visited Mar. 23, 2018).

[60] *See also* EVFTA, Ch. 8, sec. 3, art. 5.

[61] *See generally* Malintoppi & Tan, *supra* note 33, Ch. 9 (Singapore).

[62] *See* Jane Croft, *Singapore Is Becoming a World Leader in Arbitration*, Financial Times, Jun. 3, 2016, www.ft.com/content/704c5458-e79a-11e5-a09b-1f8b0d268c39?siteedition=intl (last visited Mar. 23, 2018).

development of Asia more broadly, has launched various initiatives to attract disputes business.[63] Three recent developments form the focus of this part of the discussion.

14.2.3.1 Bespoke Investment Arbitration Rules

The Singapore International Arbitration Centre (SIAC) has enjoyed continued success in attracting private disputes, recording its highest number of new cases in 2017 – 452 new cases filed in that year from parties coming from 58 countries.[64] Leveraging on the SIAC's reputation, Singapore is turning towards attracting investor-state disputes. The SIAC included a provision under rule 3.1(d) of its 2013 edition of the SIAC Rules[65] that disputes arising out of a noncontractual instrument, citing investment treaties as an example, may be referred to SIAC arbitration. This provision is retained in the 2016 SIAC Rules. This initial step was then followed by the release of a set of bespoke rules for investment arbitration – the SIAC Investment Arbitration Rules 2017 (IA Rules), which came into effect on January 1, 2017. The IA rules are a hybrid of traditional investment arbitration and commercial arbitration, and their application is not constrained by objective criteria such as the existence of a qualifying "investor" or "investment" that applies under the ICSID Convention.[66] The IA Rules also explicitly provide for circumstances under which third parties may make submissions to the SIAC Court[67] and directly address the issue of third-party funding.[68]

The IA Rules would be favored by parties who adhere to strict timelines in the dispute resolution process, but it is unclear if efficiency of processes by itself would persuade ASEAN nations to adopt the IA Rules.

[63] Sanum Investments Ltd v Government of the Lao People's Democratic Republic (2016) 5 SLR 536 was the first case brought under a bilateral investment treaty before the Singapore court.

[64] This is a 32 percent increase from the number of cases filed in 2016. *See SIAC Announces New Records for 2017*, SIAC, Mar. 7, 2018, www.siac.org.sg/images/stories/press_release/2018/[Press%20Release]%20SIAC%20Announces%20New%20Records%20for%202017.pdf (last visited Mar. 23, 2018).

[65] Both the 2013 and 2016 editions are available in languages other than English.

[66] *See* ICSID Convention, art. 25.

[67] IA Rules, art. 29.

[68] IA Rules, art. 24(i). The tribunal has the power to order the disclosure of third-party funding arrangements, the identity of the third-party funder and such other details related thereto, as well as take into account such arrangements in ordering costs (art. 33.1).

14.2.3.2 Innovative Litigation Framework

Moreover, the Singapore International Commercial Court was launched into operation on January 5, 2015. This specialist court, created as a new division in the Singapore High Court, hears international and commercial disputes.[69] The terms "international" and "commercial" are widely defined under the SICC rules – notably, disputes can be considered international and/or commercial if the parties have agreed that they are of such nature.[70] There are two main ways in which the SICC takes jurisdiction, where (1) the parties have submitted a written jurisdiction agreement to the SICC; and (2) proceedings have been transferred from the Singapore High Court to the SICC.[71]

The SICC litigation framework has a strong arbitral practice influence. For instance, the SICC may, on a party's application, order that rules of evidence other than those found under Singapore law be applicable to the case.[72] Foreign law may be determined on the basis of submissions in SICC proceedings instead of proof for cases involving foreign law elements.[73] Parties may also apply for a confidentiality order in respect of the proceedings or the outcome. Further, alongside experienced Singapore judges,[74] the SICC also boasts a panel of eminent international jurists. At the time of writing, fifteen international judges – drawn from civil and common law jurisdictions – have been appointed.[75] To enhance the portability of Singapore judgments (including SICC judgments) abroad, Singapore has signed and ratified the Hague Convention on Choice of Court Agreements.[76]

Relevantly, the SICC may also hear investor-state disputes, provided the state has submitted to the jurisdiction of the SICC under a written jurisdiction agreement.[77] However, notwithstanding its capabilities and

[69] *See* a detailed commentary in Man Yip, *The resolution of disputes before the Singapore International Commercial Court*, 65 Int'l & Comp. L. Q. 439 (2016).

[70] Order 110 rule 2(a)(iv) and (b), Singapore Rules of Court.

[71] To date, the cases heard by the SICC are cases transferred from the Singapore High Court.

[72] *See* O 110 r 23 of the Rules of Court (Amendment No 6) Rules 2014.

[73] *See* O 110 r 25 of the Rules of Court (Amendment No 6) Rules 2014.

[74] *See Judges*, SICC, www.sicc.gov.sg/Judges.aspx?id=30 (last visited Mar. 23, 2018).

[75] *See further Four New Judges Appointed to the Singapore International Commercial Court*, Channel News Asia, Jan. 3, 2018, www.channelnewsasia.com/news/singapore/four-new-judges-appointed-to-singapore-international-commercial-9828592 (last visited Mar. 23, 2018).

[76] The implementing legislation under Singapore law is the Choice of Court Agreements Act 2016.

[77] Mediation Act, sec. 12.

arbitral-like procedures, the SICC's main caseload will likely be commercial disputes. Notwithstanding its branding and less parochial set up, the SICC remains a domestic court. States may be unwilling to submit their disputes for resolution in a foreign national court. As for commercial disputes, whether the SICC will be an attractive regional dispute settlement option would depend on the enforceability of its judgments in ASEAN Member States, which would in turn depend on the laws of the other members and the existence of enforcement treaties.

14.2.3.3 Comprehensive Mediation Framework

Finally, the Singapore International Mediation Centre[78] was recently set up to promote mediation in the region, including ASEAN states such as Brunei, Cambodia, Laos, Myanmar, Philippines and Indonesia. Furthermore, a new piece of legislation, the Mediation Act 2017 (Mediation Act),[79] has been passed by the Singapore Parliament to introduce a more comprehensive framework for commercial mediation.

Most notably, the Mediation Act enhances the enforceability of mediated settlement agreements – which could only be enforced as contracts in common law – by allowing these agreements, if all parties to the agreements so consent, to be recorded as a court order and enforced as such.[80] Where enforcement is sought abroad, however, the enforceability of the Singapore court order would depend on private international law rules and existing treaty arrangements between the states on enforcement and recognition of foreign judgments. Importantly, the Mediation Act only applies where the mediation is wholly or partly conducted in Singapore or where the mediation agreement provides for Singapore law or the Mediation Act to apply.[81] Obviously, the Mediation Act and the services of the SIMC would be most readily availed of by Singapore businesspeople, as well as appeal to commercial parties who desire a neutral venue and/or a neutral law for the mediation of their disputes.

Mediation is, however, not reserved only for the settlement of private disputes. Yet, the triggering criteria of the Mediation Act, given the

[78] *See* Singapore International Mediation Centre, http://simc.com.sg (last visited Mar. 23, 2018). It works in partnership with the Singapore International Mediation Institute: www.simi.org.sg (last visited Mar. 23, 2018).

[79] For a commentary, *see* Dorcas Quek Anderson, *A Coming of Age for Mediation in Singapore?: Mediation Act 2016* 29 Sing. Acad. L. J. 275 (2017).

[80] Mediation Act, sec. 12.

[81] *Id.*, sec. 6.

Singapore bias, might restrict its adoption in investor-state disputes where neither party is Singaporean. The comfort level of conducting the mediation in Singapore, whether wholly or partly, or for Singapore law to apply to the mediation agreement would undoubtedly vary across the ASEAN Member States. Foreign investors are generally unable to bargain on an equal footing with the host states. A similar strand of concern would also arise in relation to the use of the SIMC's services. In particular, its panel of mediators comprises experts from mainly developed and non-ASEAN countries.[82] Some ASEAN Member States may consider their interests as not being adequately understood by these experts given their legal-cultural backgrounds. That said, the SIMC may increase its regional influence by setting up branch/representative centers in ASEAN countries, to the extent that this is possible under local laws.

14.3 The Way Forward

Based on the above analysis of the dispute settlement landscape of Indonesia, Vietnam and Singapore, three reflections emerge. First, for a variety of reasons, litigation in national courts is not the preferred mode of dispute settlement. Save in the case of Singapore, efforts are generally not dedicated to improving litigation as a viable mechanism, even in the case of commercial disputes.

Secondly, following from the first reflection, governmental inclination is to promote arbitration and mediation as dispute settlement mechanisms for both investor-state and commercial disputes. In the case of Indonesia and Vietnam, arbitration laws are not fully aligned with international standards. Specifically, Vietnamese laws on arbitration do not sufficiently support the "jurisdiction neutral" feature of arbitration. As for mediation, different approaches have developed in the three jurisdictions. Diversity, a facet of flexibility, is desirable, but some thought should be given to harmonizing practices and norms at the broader level so as to enhance mediation's potential as an effective and reliable means of dispute resolution within ASEAN.

Finally, in view of the developments taking place in Indonesia, Vietnam and Singapore, it may be said that there is an emerging trend of reforming ISDS models.[83] Such a trend is beneficial and to be

[82] *See Mediators*, SIMC, http://simc.com.sg/mediators/ (last visited Sep. 27, 2017).

[83] Of course, the motivations for the reforms may differ, and in the case of Vietnam, it was initiated by the European Union. Nevertheless, the effect is the same: changes are or will be taking place.

encouraged. The question is, how can ASEAN garner the momentum and facilitate reforms at the regional level so as to promote harmonization to counter fragmentation in approaches?

Building on the analysis in Section 14.2, I take a forward-looking perspective and consider how ASEAN can work toward developing more pro-development dispute settlement mechanisms and processes. In charting the way forward, ASEAN should be mindful of the emerging global and regional trends in dispute settlement. ASEAN should encourage the adoption of key international norms and practices in dispute settlement. While national innovations are desirable and encouraging, they are not always successful or comprehensive. Furthermore, ASEAN should start thinking about regional harmonization and leadership in dispute settlement, such as the establishment of a regional dispute settlement center. I propose additional initiatives that ASEAN should focus on in the next five years to accelerate the achievement of its aims.

14.3.1 Notable Trends

There are four notable trends in the global and regional dispute settlement scene. There is increasing interest in using mediation for ISDS – either in tandem with arbitration or replacing it.[84] Regionally, ADR accords with the generally more conciliatory approach of ASEAN Member States toward conflict management. In particular, mediation is being actively developed for the resolution of commercial disputes, as attested to by recent developments in Indonesia, Vietnam and Singapore discussed in Section 14.2. Mediation would facilitate the growth of MSMEs given that it is generally less costly than arbitration and, if successful, it allows both parties to emerge as winners without irreparably damaging their business relationship.

Secondly, arbitration is of increasing importance in the settlement of commercial disputes[85] and investor-state disputes in ASEAN. ASEAN Member States are becoming more exposed to and educated about this

[84] Esme Shirlow, *The Rising Interest in the Mediation of Investment Treaty Disputes, and Scope for Increasing Interaction between Mediation and Arbitration*, Kluwer Arbitration Blog, Sep. 29, 2016, http://kluwerarbitrationblog.com/2016/09/29/the-rising-interest-in-the-mediation-of-investment-treaty-disputes-and-scope-for-increasing-interaction-between-mediation-and-arbitration/ (last visited Mar. 23, 2018).

[85] *See* Marquise Clarke, *Successfully Resolving Commercial Disputes: An Overview of Arbitration in ASEAN*, ASEAN Briefing, Jun. 28, 2016, www.aseanbriefing.com/news/2016/06/28/asean-arbitration.html (last visited Mar. 23, 2018).

dispute settlement mechanism, either through the entry into bilateral/multilateral treaties or homegrown culture. Indeed, even the SICC, a Singaporean initiative, adopts an arbitral-like litigation framework to increase its appeal to potential users. Taking into account the trend of favoring the use of mediation, the norm for ASEAN should move towards a tiered dispute settlement framework that combines mediation-arbitration and actively encourage parties to insert tiered dispute resolution clauses into their contracts.

Thirdly, there is a prominent global trend of reforming current ISDS frameworks for investor-state disputes,[86] as a result of criticisms directed at the existing mechanisms.[87] For example, the UNCTAD is reviewing ISDS norms and proposing reforms along five paths:[88] promoting ADR; remodeling; limiting investor access to ISDS; introducing appeal mechanisms; and creating a standing international investment court. Notably, individual countries including Indonesia, the United States and India are unilaterally initiating review and reform of their BITs or international investment agreement models along the UNCTAD's paths of reform.[89]

Fourthly, various countries are currently creating specialist courts to better compete for judicial business.[90] Within ASEAN, Singapore is the first Member State to seriously undertake innovative court reform. Singapore's case study provides an occasion to consider if more efforts should be made to improve litigation as a viable option for settlement of commercial disputes. The costs of using arbitration, notwithstanding its

[86] Yeo & Menon, *supra* note 37, at 124.

[87] *See World Investment Report 2015: Reforming International Investment Governance*, Table IV.5 at 147, http://unctad.org/en/PublicationsLibrary/wir2015_en.pdf (last visited Sep. 27, 2017).

[88] *See Reform of Investor-State Dispute Settlement: In Search of a Roadmap*, UNCTAD IIA Issues Note, No. 2 (Jun. 2013), http://unctad.org/en/PublicationsLibrary/webdiaepcb2013d4_en.pdf (last visited Mar. 23, 2018).

[89] *See* summary in *Taking Stock of IIA Reform*, UNCTAD IIA Issues Note, No 1 (Mar. 2016), http://unctad.org/en/PublicationsLibrary/webdiaepcb2016d3_en.pdf (last visited Mar. 23, 2018), at 5–8.

[90] For example, the United Kingdom has launched the Financial List, a specialist court, to deal with financial disputes. Elsewhere in Europe, France, Netherlands, Belgium and Germany have taken steps to establish their respective versions of international commercial courts, hoping to take judicial business from London in the post-Brexit world. To serve the disputes needs of the Belt and Road initiative, China has also announced plans to set up three international commercial courts in Beijing (headquarters), Xian and Shenzhen to provide litigation, arbitration and mediation services. *See* further Andrew Godwin, *International Commercial Courts*, Chinese Busi. L. J., Dec. 13, 2017, www.vantageasia.com/international-commercial-courts/ (last visited Mar. 23, 2018).

many advantages, may make it an unattractive option in smaller disputes. Transparency of arbitral proceedings may also be a concern for some parties.[91] The question is whether commercial parties should be afforded a wider spread of feasible dispute settlement options. There is a more pertinent point: the concept of a specialist court, in the form of a regional initiative, can be a future development for ASEAN. Rethinking dispute settlement mechanisms need not only take the direction of dejudicializing the process. There is every merit to innovating within a judicial framework as it would enable the development of commercial law and regional expertise – which may be much needed in some jurisdictions where the law is uncertain. This point will be discussed further below.

14.3.2 International Standards

Adopting international standards for dispute settlement is a crucial step in ASEAN's path towards an improved framework. This must be undertaken at two levels: regional and national. The ACIA represents a regional effort in aligning dispute settlement norms with international standards.

Nationally, ASEAN Member States should be more proactive in considering becoming a signatory to existing dispute settlement and related international instruments. Reyes has suggested the adoption of six Hague Conventions to better harmonize civil procedures and commercial laws in ASEAN as well as reflect international standards.[92] Of the six, three are closely related to dispute settlement: the 1965 Convention Service Abroad of Judicial and Extrajudicial Documents in Civil or Commercial Matters; the 1970 Convention on the taking of Evidence Abroad in Civil or Commercial Matters; and the 2005 Convention on Choice of Court Agreements.[93] In respect of international instruments that have already been ratified by the ASEAN Member States, there

[91] Sundaresh Menon, *Adjudicator, Advocate or Something in between?: Coming to Terms with the Role of the Party-Appointed Arbitrator*, 34 J. Int'l Arbi. 347 (2017).

[92] Antonio Reyes, *ASEAN and The Hague Conventions*, 22 Asia Pacific L. Rev. 26 (2014).

[93] These international instruments are given by way of example and do not exhaust the number of instruments that ASEAN Member States should consider signing. In the field of mediation, for instance, two instruments are of note: United Nations Convention International Settlement Agreements and UNCITRAL Model Law on International Commercial Conciliation. *See* further: Nadja Alexander, *A Convention on the Enforcement of iMSAs … AND a New Model Law*, Kluwer Mediation Blog, Mar. 16, 2018, http://mediationblog.kluwerarbitration.com/2018/03/16/convention-enforcement-imsas-new-model-law/?utm_source=feedburner&utm_medium=feed&utm_campaign=Feed%3A+KluwerMediationFull+%28Kluwer+Mediation+-+Latest+Entries%29&print=pdf (last visited Mar. 23, 2018).

should be greater efforts to promote consistent application. For instance, public policy as a ground for refusal to enforce a foreign arbitral award under the New York Convention should be given more consistent treatment across the ASEAN states. Further, several ASEAN nations do not presently have any clear laws or are not parties to treaties for the recognition and enforcement of foreign judgments, rendering litigation in a neutral forum a non-option.

Alignment of practices at the national level is crucial and could be strategically propelled by regional efforts to promote and educate on international standards, if regional harmonization cannot be readily achieved in the short to medium term. Further, regional standardization could be expedited if certain Member States with similar legal systems (for example, Singapore, Malaysia, Brunei and Myanmar) join forces to adopt certain sets of international standards to create pressure on or provide reference for other members to follow suit.

14.3.3 Regional Dispute Settlement Systems

There was a recent proposal to set up an ASEAN arbitration center by the ABAC. The ABAC suggests that the ASEAN arbitration center "could assist in governing arbitration matters and to standardize arbitration classification within the region."[94] At the time of writing, such a center has yet to be established. Some may question if this move is necessary given the existence of established international arbitration centers. However, international arbitration centers have their limitations, especially for the achievement of regional harmonization.[95]

Relevantly, the establishment of an ASEAN dispute settlement center provides an opportunity for ASEAN Member States to design a mechanism that is suited for the needs of the region. Indeed, such a center could incorporate the desirable features of the existing mechanisms whilst avoiding their shortcomings, thereby reducing the amount of work that is required.[96] Such a region-based center would also be better able to develop ASEAN jurisprudence and thus facilitate the harmonization of commercial laws and practices. Importantly, an ASEAN-based institution,

[94] *Malaysia 2015: Business for the People*, ASEAN Business Advisory Council Report to ASEAN Leaders, www.aseanbac.com.my/_content/events/pdf/ASEANBAC_Report_to_ASEAN_Leaders_April_2015.pdf (last visited Mar. 23, 2018).

[95] *See* Koh, *supra* note 10, at 400–2.

[96] *See* discussion of desirable features, *id.*, at 405–08.

whether an arbitration center, a specialist court,[97] a mediation center or a dispute resolution center incorporating all three mechanisms, would have the added benefit of developing ASEAN expertise, "composed of members who are appointed specifically because of their 'insider expertise,' who are attuned to ASEAN legal traditions and policies."[98] The ASEAN expertise and jurisprudence can in turn inform and modify international best practices and norms in dispute settlement, enabling the international dispute settlement landscape to become culturally more balanced.

14.3.4 Other Developments

ASEAN should further focus on two initiatives in the next five years. First, online dispute resolution is a feasible development and one that would greatly reduce costs for MSMEs in the resolution of commercial disputes. Online dispute resolution is most suited for the conduct of mediation and simple litigation/arbitration. The online mechanism also avoids the inconvenience of travel where the dispute involves parties based in different jurisdictions. In tandem with the development of online dispute resolution is the acceleration of technology acceptance and accessibility across the ASEAN Member States. This project could be initially promoted at the national level and led by international mediation or ADR centers. Pilot programs could then run at a regional level.

Second, there should be greater judicial collaboration and interaction in the region. This could be launched on two levels. Formal collaboration in terms of mutual assistance in legal matters, such as interpretation of foreign laws, recognition and enforcement of foreign judgments,[99] interim measures, etc. Moreover, there could be interaction through judicial education, training and research. For example, the Singapore Judicial College has an international training arm. It also runs an empirical judicial research programme to promote innovation in judicial studies, practices and policies, which also has the effect of enabling the

[97] There has been suggestion for establishing an ASEAN court: *see* Perfecto V. Fernandez, *Law and Culture in ASEAN: Towards New Structures for Economic-Cultural Development*, *in* ASEAN Identity, Development and Culture 328 (Ram P. Anand & Purificacion C. Quisumbing eds., 1981).

[98] Koh, *supra* note 10, at 402–3.

[99] *See* a significant step taken toward establishing a regional instrument for the recognition and enforcement of foreign judgments in Asia led by Singapore: Adeline Chong (project lead and editor), *Recognition and Enforcement of Foreign Judgments in Asia*, ABLI Legal Convergence Series, 2017, http://abli.asia/LinkClick.aspx?fileticket=I0rTeJ0yljw%3d&portalid=0 (last visited Mar. 23, 2018).

international community to have a better understanding of Singapore's legal system. Collaboration and interaction on these two levels will undoubtedly enable the building of trust between the judiciaries of the different countries and progressively facilitate harmonization of practices in court-based dispute settlement.

14.4 Conclusion

The success of ASEAN economic integration is in part dependent upon the availability of reliable and efficient dispute settlement mechanisms to handle the disputes that will arise in the ten rapidly developing economies. Further, developing user-friendly dispute settlement mechanisms that can be readily utilized by MSMES – placed in different circumstances from big-time commercial entities – will be a major project going forward. The successful promotion of MSMES will undoubtedly facilitate "more equitable and inclusive economic growth in ASEAN."[100]

The survey of the dispute settlement landscapes of Indonesia, Vietnam and Singapore as well as regional instruments such as the ACIA reveals that much work remains to be done. This chapter suggests that while individual innovation/improvement in each ASEAN Member State is crucial, concerted efforts to harmonize approaches and norms at the regional level must be pursued vigorously to develop ASEAN methods and jurisprudence that will enhance the level of trust and cooperation across the ten Member States.

[100] *See also ASEAN 2030: Towards a Borderless Economic Community* (2014), http://scnavigator.avnet.com/wp-content/uploads/2015/04/ASEAN2030.pdf (last visited Mar. 23, 2018).

15

The AEC and Regulatory Reforms in CLMV Countries with a Special Focus on Myanmar

NIMNUAL PIEWTHONGNGAM

15.1 Introduction

The ultimate goal of ASEAN is to create an ASEAN-integrated market. To advance this goal, all requirements for the establishment of the AEC must be met. ASEAN recognizes, however, the challenging developmental gap between the original members of ASEAN, namely Singapore, Malaysia, Indonesia, Philippines, Thailand and Brunei Darussalam (ASEAN-6), and its newer, less developed members, Cambodia, Lao PDR, Myanmar and Vietnam. The IAI was implemented through the IAI Work Plans. The IAI Work Plans I (2002–08)[1] and II (2009–15)[2] constituted an integral part of the AEC Blueprint 2015[3] to provide technical assistance to the CLMV countries to help narrow their developmental gap. This assistance increases the capacity of the CLMV countries to keep pace with the implementation of regional commitments toward deeper economic integration.

Section 15.2 of this chapter introduces the status and progress of commitment implementation under the AEC Blueprint 2015 of the CLMV countries. Undoubtedly, increasing foreign direct investment (FDI) flow in the CLMV countries will enhance those countries' development, which, in turn, will narrow the economic gap among ASEAN members. Section 15.3 of this chapter discusses the role the CLMV countries play in drawing FDI into ASEAN, which further helps ASEAN become a single investment destination. Section 15.4 focuses on Myanmar as a prime example of FDI influx. As a case study, Myanmar demonstrates how regulatory reforms and the implementation of commitments to ASEAN have led to development and growth. The chapter

1 Initiative for ASEAN Integration Work Plan I (2002).
2 Initiative for ASEAN Integration Work Plan II (2009).
3 Association of Southeast Asian Nations Economic Community Blueprint (2008).

concludes by surveying how legal reforms and Myanmar's implementation will help ASEAN become the primary investment destination, as the AEC Blueprint 2025 projects.[4] Finally, Section 15.5 emphasizes challenges regarding regulatory reforms that Myanmar has been facing and provides recommendations in order to help Myanmar cope with the regulatory reforms and implementation of commitments under the AEC.

15.2 The CLMV Countries and Their Overall Implementations of the AEC: Progress and Challenges

The implementation of the commitments of the AEC had already begun by the time the CLMV countries joined ASEAN. For this reason, the CLMV countries received a special timeframe, a so-called grace period, to comply with the commitments of the AEC. Additionally, the ASEAN-6 recognized the extent to which the newer members' development differed from their own. In turn, this developmental gap affected the CLMV countries' abilities to implement the complex ASEAN commitments and agreements. In response, ASEAN launched the IAI Work Plans to (1) assist the CLMV countries in contributing to the AEC's long-term goals; (2) help the CLMV countries enhance their capacity to implement all commitments; and (3) narrow the developmental gap between the ASEAN-6 and the CLMV countries. With support from the ASEAN-6 and other dialogue partners, the CLMV countries made significant progress in implementing the commitments of the AEC Blueprint 2015 and continue implementing their obligations under the AEC Blueprint 2025. According to the IAI Work Plan III,[5] ASEAN affirmed that the capacity building, technical assistance and infrastructure development provided in the IAI Work Plans I and II have contributed to such impressive progress. Moreover, ASEAN realized that despite the impressive progress made in prominent development gaps among ASEAN members, the CLMV countries still require assistance from the ASEAN-6 to continue implementing their commitments to the AEC Blueprint 2025. For this reason, ASEAN still lends support to the CLMV countries by including the IAI Work Plan III as an integral part of the AEC Blueprint 2025.

Trade facilitation is one of five strategic areas on which Work Plan III focuses. The other four areas Work Plan III addresses include (1) food and agriculture; (2) micro, small and medium enterprises; (3) education;

[4] ASEAN Economic Community Blueprint 2025 (2015).

[5] Initiative for ASEAN Integration Work Plan III (2016).

and (4) health and well-being.[6] In implementing the CLMV countries' AEC commitments, trade facilitation measures were set to simplify and harmonize trade procedure under international standards. Trade facilitation issues in the CLMV countries remain challenging for those states. Persisting major trade facilitation issues in the CLMV countries include: (1) nontariff barriers (NTBs); (2) complex documentary compliance for importing and exporting; (3) inefficiencies within the custom clearance process; and (4) time and cost associated with the current trade facilitation.[7] Therefore, the trade facilitation actions set under Work Plan III attempted to assist the CLMV countries in (1) lowering the incidence of trade distorting NTBs; (2) reducing the time and cost of customs and border procedures; (3) harmonizing or mutual recognition of products, conformance and technical standards; and (4) improving market access through stronger participation in the WTO.[8]

Moreover, the regulatory agencies of the CLMV countries lack standardized adoptions and conformance assessments, which results in weakened implementation of existing ASEAN agreements. Work Plan III's trade facilitation measures and actions also aim to reduce regulatory barriers that impede trade. Numerous NTMs exist in the CLMV countries and other ASEAN members and have yet to be eliminated. For example, in 2016, Cho Cho Thein and Zin Zin Naing studied existing NTMs in Myanmar and discovered that there were thirty-six regulations observed as NTM-related regulations.[9] The study revealed that, similar to most ASEAN Member States, technical barriers to trade measures, sanitary and phytosanitary measures and export-related measures played a significant role in the incidence of NTMs. As NTMs continue to impede intra-ASEAN trade, the actions and programs under Work Plan III are designed to help ASEAN states, especially the CLMV countries, confront NTMs and other trade facilitation challenges. Through the implementation of Work Plan III, for example, the ASEAN nations will witness a reduction in the incidence of trade-distorting NTMs through well-coordinated reform and standard regulatory practices.

[6] *Id.*, at 7.

[7] Nimnual Piewthongngam & Prasert Vijitnopparat, *Trade Facilitation: Cost of Non-Cooperation to Consumers in the ASEAN Economic Community* (2014), www.asiafoundation.org/resources/pdfs/TradeFacilitationCostofNonCooperationtoConsumersintheASEANEEconomicCommunity.pdf (last visited Nov. 6, 2017), at 25–8.

[8] IAI Work Plan III, *supra* note 5, at 16.

[9] Cho Cho Thein & Zin Zin Naing, *Report on Non-Tariff Measures in Myanmar* (2016), www.asiafoundation.org/resources/pdfs/TradeFacilitationCostofNonCooperationtoConsumersintheASEANEconomicCommunity.pdf (last visited Nov. 6, 2017), at 105–6.

There are common issues most ASEAN Member States will continue to face, particularly involving the delay in implementing commitments under the ASEAN agreements. While the delay is due to many factors, all have been hampered by the slowness of each respective government's decision-making in liberalizing trade in goods, investment, services and the capital market, as well as the strategic movement of skilled labor in ASEAN contexts. Legal and regulation reform is indeed a sluggish process. Further compounding the problem is the age-old habit of implementing agreements with flexibility rather than standardization. In becoming ASEAN's way of dealing with the implementation of commitments, there remains no punishment for slow action or inaction. Thus, apart from a tariff elimination commitment on trade in goods, the progress of implementation of other commitments is underwhelming. Additionally, the deadline for establishing the ASEAN Economic Community by 2015 has since passed, but there is still negligible progress on implementation in other areas of commitments, particularly the commitment on the elimination of nontariff barriers.

Any Member State can address an issue arising from the implementation of ASEAN's agreements against another ASEAN member by using the ASEAN Dispute Settlement Mechanism, but at the time of writing, the well-written dispute settlement mechanism of ASEAN has never been used. In 2015, ASEAN announced various accomplishments toward realizing the AEC Blueprint 2015; concurrently, however, many obligations remained unimplemented. Consequently, ASEAN set forth the ASEAN Blueprint 2025 new targets, frameworks and action plans to fulfill the outstanding obligations. While ASEAN has made a marginal impact due to slow implementation, many ASEAN Member States have individually entered into bilateral and multilateral free trade agreements with other countries. For example, Vietnam signed a free trade agreement with the European Union, the EVFTA,[10] on May 29, 2015. The EVFTA is expected to be ratified by 2018 and will subsequently come into effect in 2019. This bilateral agreement is projected to create massive trade opportunities for Vietnam that will yield a tremendous impact on the Vietnamese economy.

In addition, many major countries in other parts of the world have been forming trade relationships regionally and beyond. For instance, Brazil, Russia, India and China have formed a forum called BRICs to

[10] Free Trade Agreement Between the European Union and the Socialist Republic of Vietnam (2015).

enhance collaborations among parties in many sectors including economics, trade and investment. Will this phenomenon, coupled with the slow implementation of commitments under the AEC, dilute the attractiveness of ASEAN economic integration? ASEAN cannot afford the diversion of FDI and intra-ASEAN investments to other regions. Accordingly, all ASEAN states must accelerate their implementation of the commitments under the AEC Blueprint 2025 to continue attracting ASEAN and foreign investors alike. If any ASEAN country shows a reluctance to do so, a challenge during the implementation process would surface.

While ASEAN economies are implementing schedules of commitments under various agreements of the AEC scheme, they must also focus on improving their policies and legal structures to attract both foreign investment into ASEAN and intra-ASEAN investment so as to turn ASEAN into a world-class investment destination. More importantly, the newer members – the CLMV – will play critical roles in drawing inflows of FDI into ASEAN. To improve their capacity to attract both foreign and ASEAN investments, the CLMV countries should put their best efforts toward enhancing their business and investment climates. Moreover, the CLMV countries should also focus on nurturing their ability to follow the implementation progress of the ASEAN-6. This will enable the CLMV countries to realize the commitments laid down in the ASEAN Blueprint 2025 and further close the gap between the original members and the newer members. In addition, ASEAN should focus on attracting ASEAN investors to increase intra-ASEAN investment on a global level. ASEAN Member States should implement the commitments of the ACIA,[11] without any further delay, to liberalize, facilitate, promote and protect cross-border investment among ASEAN economies. This will help to enhance the competitiveness of the investment environment in ASEAN.

15.3 The CLMV's Duty to Fulfill ASEAN's Goal As a Single Investment Destination

Based on the ASEAN Statistics Database in 2016, the GDP growth of the CLMV countries from the years 2011–16 was higher than in ASEAN-6 during the same period.[12] In 2016, the GDP growth of the CLMV countries

[11] ASEAN Comprehensive Investment Agreement (2007).

[12] ASEAN Statistics Database, www.aseanstats.org (last visited Nov. 6, 2017).

was at 6.9 percent while that of the ASEAN-6 was at 4.3 percent; overall ASEAN GDP growth was at 4.7 percent during the same year. Further, the GDP growth of the CLMV countries during the first half of 2017 indicates higher rates, and it is expected that this pattern will continue. Undoubtedly, FDI contributes to the CLMV countries' development by contributing to infrastructure upgrading, people development and job creation. Vietnam is a prime example of how FDI may bring transformative and positive change. Attracting foreign investment has been an important component of the growth strategies of most ASEAN Member States. To draw FDI inflows into the ASEAN region, ASEAN should encourage the CLMV countries to become like an ASEAN "magnetic field," drawing in investments throughout the region.

The CLMV countries offer many important advantages to foreign investors, including but not limited to (1) vast low-cost labor pool; (2) rich natural resources and raw materials; and (3) emerging markets and special benefits from the ASEAN Economic Community. However, investors remain concerned about the uncertainty of the implementation of rules and regulations, especially in emerging countries. Hence, regulatory reform is essential to the CLMV countries. Cambodia, Lao PDR and Vietnam have done well in their legal reforms, helping them to increase their FDI inflows. Vietnam serves as an example of success to its peers. The total legal makeover of Vietnam has created dramatic changes and impressive improvements to Vietnam's FDI that reportedly grew by 28 percent in 2015. According to a statistical report from Trading Economics, Vietnam's FDI reportedly increased by $2.7 billion in the third quarter of 2017.[13]

Vietnam has indeed closely followed the ASEAN-6 in its economic and development growth. According to the World Bank's *Doing Business Report 2017*,[14] Singapore, Malaysia and Thailand ranked in the top third of all 190 countries surveyed. Singapore was ranked second, whereas Myanmar ranked 177th, which is in the bottom twenty of all countries surveyed. For the CLMV countries, Vietnam was ranked 82nd, whereas the rest of the group ranked in the bottom half of the full set of countries surveyed. For the "Starting a Business" indicator shown in the same report, only Singapore, Brunei Darussalam and Thailand made it into the top 100 of 190 countries, while the other seven ASEAN countries

[13] *Vietnam's Foreign Direct Investment*, https://tradingeconomics.com/vietnam/foreign-direct-investment (last visited Nov. 5, 2017).

[14] The World Bank, *Doing Business 2017: Equal Opportunity for All* (2017), www.doingbusiness.org/reports/global-reports/doing-business-2017 (last visited Nov. 6, 2017).

were ranked outside the top 100 of all countries sampled. The "Ease of Doing Business" and "Starting a Business" rankings[15] serve as a valuable indicator for ASEAN countries, particularly the CLMV countries, to realize that their system of setting up and running limited liability companies (LLC) and businesses does not facilitate an enterprise-friendly business and investment environment. Furthermore, the amount of time spent and number of procedural steps for setting up an LLC in most ASEAN Member States except Singapore are too complex and lengthy. For example, setting up an LLC in Cambodia involves nine procedural steps and ninety-nine days to set up the company. Thus, improving the business registration process and procedures will make the CLMV countries more attractive for FDI. Myanmar has shown promising gains in its ranking since undergoing legal and economic reforms in 2011. According to the "Starting a Business" ranking of the *Doing Business Report 2017*, Myanmar has made a vast leap from 170th to 146th place in the rankings.

Among the CLMV countries, Vietnam's investment regimes are more liberal than its peers. It is worth examining how Vietnam has turned itself into one of the most attractive ASEAN countries, drawing huge amounts of FDI. To magnetize foreign investments, Vietnam not only gives special privileges to foreign investors but has also improved and simplified business setup and investment processes with clear and transparent rules and regulations. Intal recognizes that Vietnam has been much more successful in attracting FDI than most of the other ASEAN members by providing greater protection to its investors and eliminating unfair treatment of foreign investors with regard to their rights to establish businesses and investments in Vietnam.[16] Furthermore, Vietnam has also improved its regulatory regime, including institutional and procedural changes, that governs FDI.

Cambodia and Lao PDR have also undergone processes of regulatory reforms that have contributed to the improvement and development of both countries' economies. The next part examines the investment regulatory reform process of Myanmar, which is presently one of the more interesting countries for international investors.

[15] *Id.*

[16] Ponciano S. Intal Jr., *AEC Blueprint Implementation Performance and Challenges: Investment Liberalization* (2015), www.eria.org/ERIA-DP-2015–32.pdf (last visited Nov. 6, 2017), at 19.

15.4 Myanmar's Regulatory Reform

The OECD refers to Myanmar as one of Asia's leading economies in the early 1960s, with a per capita income of more than three times than that of Indonesia and twice that of Thailand.[17] The OECD recalls that Myanmar's first departure from self-imposed isolation in 1988 coincided with political turmoil, which led to increasingly stringent sanctions in major markets, particularly the United States, Canada, Australia and the European Union, while other countries imposed certain restrictions, such as Japan, which cut off most of its aid to Myanmar.[18] Subsequently, investments from most OECD countries were quickly withdrawn from Myanmar.

After President Thein Sein took over with a new government in 2011, Myanmar swung its doors wide open to the world for the first time in nearly six decades and began its first steps toward reform. After its period of isolation, Myanmar urgently needed to develop to catch up with the other ASEAN Member States and the rest of the world. Opening up the country to foreign investments and building a robust investment climate for FDI was indeed essential to Myanmar's development. To date, Myanmar continues to work on legal, regulatory and economic reforms to attract foreign investment. Indeed, many laws and regulations have been modified and enacted in this vein. Melissa Crouch points out that legal reforms often occur at moments of political conflict, crisis and change, and this is also the case for Myanmar.[19] She also adds that legal reforms may be undertaken in various forms to update, amend or replace existing laws, to introduce a new policy or to set a strategic direction in a particular area of reform.[20]

On November 8, 2015, Myanmar marked a turning point when Aung San Suu Kyi's National League for Democracy won approximately 80 percent of all contested seats. It was considered to be a landslide victory in the general election. Myanmar has undergone dramatic changes in the last five years, including modernizing its legal and regulatory framework. The influx of FDI, led by China, Singapore and Thailand, and later Hong Kong and the United Kingdom, has brought remarkable improvements

[17] Organisation for Economic Cooperation and Development (OECD), *OECD Investment Policy Reviews: Myanmar 2014* (2014), www.oecd.org/daf/inv/investment-policy/Myanmar-IPR-2014.pdf (last visited Nov. 6, 2017), at 23–4.

[18] *Id.*

[19] Melissa Crouch, Legislating Reform? Law and Conflict in Myanmar: War, Politics, Religion 221 (2016).

[20] *Id.*

to the country's development.[21] Myanmar's FDI figure has seen high growth rates. According to statistics from the Directorate of Investment and Company Administration, the top investment sectors in 2016–17 were (1) oil and gas; (2) power; (3) transport; and (4) communication and manufacturing.[22]

What exactly does Myanmar have to offer to foreign investors? The enormous potential business and investment opportunities in Myanmar derive from its strategic location, namely in that it shares the longest border area with another ASEAN member, Thailand. Myanmar also borders India and China, two of the world's largest economies and free trade agreement partners with ASEAN. Foreign investors in the manufacturing sector foresee significant opportunities for manufacturing goods in Myanmar and being able to export to its neighboring countries. In addition, Myanmar also shares a border with Lao PDR and Bangladesh. Myanmar has abundant natural resources, including oil and gas, valuable gemstones, gold and top-quality jade as well as other minerals and elements of high commercial value, such as uranium. Notably, Myanmar also offers low-cost labor with its large population of nearly fifty-five million. With a large and growing population, Myanmar serves as one of the newest emerging economies with a huge potential market.

There is no question of why Myanmar is highly rated as an investment destination in ASEAN and is listed as one of the most attractive commercial opportunities in the world. Myanmar's peers – Cambodia, Lao PRD and Vietnam – have also updated and reformed their laws and regulations relating to foreign investment. Though Myanmar has made remarkable improvements in its development, The country must, however, expedite the process of legal and economic reforms and considerably improve its attractiveness for foreign investment. While Myanmar offers rich investment opportunities and now boasts a stabilized government, foreign investors remain skeptical of its legal reforms, and the guarantee of protection of foreign investments. These main concerns are critical to the investment environment in Myanmar.

The legislative framework of Myanmar was laid down by the British government during the Colonial Era from 1826 to 1947. Most of its laws

[21] Directorate of Investment and Company Administration, *Foreign Investment of Permitted Enterprises (as of Jun. 30, 2017)*, www.dica.gov.mm/sites/dica.gov.mm/files/document-files/fdi_country_1.pdf (last visited Nov. 6, 2017).

[22] Directorate of Investment and Company Administration, *FDI by Sector*, www.dica.gov.mm/en/topic/foreign-investment-sector (last visited Nov. 6, 2017).

were based on British legislation dating back to the eighteenth century. In addition, Myanmar's legal system was also derived from the Colonial model during the time when Britain ruled the country. While enacting many necessary new laws, Myanmar is hindered by many other laws that remain outdated and inadequate. Crouch recalls that by 1890 the Indian Codes generally applied to all of Myanmar as a province of British India.[23] She also observed that main bodies of many major areas of laws, such as criminal, contract and property law, were copied wholesale from India, and many, such as the Penal Code, remain largely unaltered and are in force today.

Additionally, one of the most important laws in the country, the Myanmar Companies Act[24] (formally Burma Companies Act) promulgated in 1914 is a verbatim copy of the Indian Companies Act of 1913. This particular legislation was brought into Myanmar during the colonial period. The Myanmar Companies Act of 1914 has been the legal foundation for incorporating legal entities in Myanmar for more than a hundred years. Nothing in the Act has undergone changes except the registration and other government fees. However, in 2015, the Myanmar government desired to modernize the Myanmar Companies Act of 1914 and align it with international standards to provide flexibility in foreign investment. Hence, a new Myanmar Companies Law was drafted in 2015 and proposed to be approved by the parliament.

Myanmar faces the challenges of transforming itself into a law-abiding and regulation-based country capable of attracting and maintaining business and investment, as well as of meeting international standards. No one can deny that foreign investments will greatly impact the development of Myanmar and the quality of life of its people through infrastructure improvement, transfer of technical know-how and the development of human resources. Myanmar requires complete legal reform, however, to create an appealing business and investment environment to attract FDI inflows. To do so, Myanmar must modernize its many outdated laws, which is no small feat as noted later on. For instance, Myanmar will have to enact intellectual property laws to protect the intellectual property rights of its citizens and foreign investors.

To pursue legislative reforms, a parliamentary Committee on the Rule of Law, Peace and Stability chaired by Aung San Suu Kyi was established

[23] Melissa Crouch, *The Layers of Legal Development in Myanmar* (2014), https://papers.ssrn.com/sol3/papers.cfm?abstract_id=2510404 (last visited Nov. 6, 2017).

[24] Myanmar Companies Act of 1914 (formerly known as Burma Companies Act 1914).

in August 2012. The Committee on the Rule of Law, Peace and Stability was formed to review existing legislation and make recommendations on amending or revoking laws. In addition, the Attorney General's Office is responsible for reviewing newly drafted laws to ensure compliance with Myanmar's international commitments. Furthermore, the Pyidaungsu Hluttaw[25] Legal Affairs and Special Cases Assessment Commission (ASCA Commission) was formed in November 2011 to assess and review all existing legislation and propose recommendations to the Myanmar Union Parliament on abolishments, revisions and new enactments. This ASCA Commission was previously comprised of thirty-five well-experienced and qualified members, thirty-one of whom were ordinary citizens and four of whom were members of Parliament.

On March 1, 2016, the ASCA Commission's mandate was renewed by the new government, which designated twenty-three new members and appointed Thura U Shwe Mann, the former speaker of the Pyithu Hluttaw, as chairman of this Commission. A total of 239 new laws have been enacted since 2011, and 85 of them required secondary legislation to be promulgated. Without the by-laws, those new registrations could not be entered into forced. However, at least 45 of the 85 new laws are still awaiting their by-laws.[26] Take, for example, the Competition Law,[27] which was enacted on February 24, 2015, and came into effect on February 24, 2017. Pursuant to Article 56(a), the implementation rules and regulations of the Competition Law of 2015 should already have been issued. However, to date, the rules and regulations that should serve as implementing tools to provide clarifications including procedures and directions of the Competition Law of 2015 remain unpublished.

Overall, new legislation as well as draft laws appear to favor FDI. Myanmar has liberated many sectors to foreign investment, including retail and wholesale businesses which were previously strictly off-limits for foreign investment. Foreign investment restrictions on retail and wholesale business sectors are indeed common in many ASEAN countries like Thailand, and in Asian countries like Korea and Japan. As such, many international retailers have set their eyes on Myanmar since it opened up in 2012. While many countries and companies seek to invest in this brand-new emerging market, investors face many challenges – not

[25] Pyidaungsu Hluttaw is Myanmar's Union Parliament.
[26] Thomas Kean & Nyan Hlaing Lynn, *supra* note 26.
[27] The Competition Law (Pyidaungsu Hluttaw Law No. 9/2015).

only underdeveloped infrastructure, but also regulations that have yet to meet international standards.

Legal reform in Myanmar has caused sharp concern for foreign investors. Many investors are skeptical about the transparency of laws and the uncertainty of their implementation by the authorities. In addition, bureaucracy continues to keep investors at bay from a land filled with golden opportunities. Therefore, bureaucratic reform is essential to the country's development and should be done concurrently with legal reform.

Since 2011, Myanmar has undergone many amendments and enactments of laws. While much has to be done before Myanmar's laws are fully aligned with international good practices, Myanmar has done more than it could ever have expected. The following key registration updates and upgrades show how reforming legal instruments significantly improves the investment opportunities and the investment climate in the country.

15.4.1 The New Myanmar Investment Law and Its Key Implications

Since Myanmar opened its doors to the world and welcomed foreign investment, the country's previous and current governments have made impressive developments in legal reform. More than 200 registrations have been enacted and amended. Along the way, however, problems arose from the rush to draft new laws and to revise old laws. From a practical point of view, too many laws were put into the reform process during a short period of time. Some of the laws are likely to be revised again because vague language was used that created unclear provisions and allowed for uncertain interpretation. In addition, the sheer volume of newly revised and newly enacted laws has meant that lawyers have difficulty interpreting new versions of the laws and regulations and appropriately advising their clients. Many new laws introduced new procedures with no precedents to follow. Furthermore, guidelines came much later after the main laws were enacted. A perfect example is the reform of the Myanmar Foreign Investment Law of 1998 (MFIL of 1988)[28] that was later replaced by the Foreign Investment Law of 2012 (FIL of 2012),[29] which in turn was superseded by the Myanmar Investment Law of 2016 (MIL of 2016).[30]

[28] The Union of Myanmar Foreign Investment Law (The State Law and Order Restoration Council No. 10/88).

[29] Foreign Investment Law (The Pyidaungsu Hluttaw Law No. 21/2012).

[30] Myanmar Investment Law (The Pyidaungsu Hluttaw Law No. 40/2016).

The FIL of 2012 opened up many sectors for foreign investment, ranging from investment in infrastructure to finance and banking to communication. In addition, the 2012 version launched new procedures and required additional documents for the Myanmar Investment Commission Permit (MIC Permit). It took several months before related rules and regulations were published and came into effect. During this period of vacuum, no investment proposals were submitted to the MIC due to a lack of clear procedures and regulations. On October 18, 2016, the FIL of 2012 was revoked when President Htin Kyaw signed the Myanmar Investment Law of 2016 as the newest law that combined the Myanmar Foreign Investment Law of 2012 and the Myanmar Citizens Investment Law of 2013[31] into the MIL of 2016 as a single code that governs all investment activities covering both domestic and foreign investors. The most important law for foreign investment has been revised on three occasions. Moreover, there were major changes in the versions, including investment incentives and application and approval processes. This part of the chapter will investigate key issues that arise from the latest reform of investment of Myanmar.

The Myanmar Investment Law of 2016 was followed by its specific implementing rules, the Myanmar Investment Rules,[32] in March 2017. Though the implementing rules under the Myanmar Foreign Investment Law were being observed by the MIC, there was a vacuum-like situation where foreign investment was stagnant while investors awaited the implementing rules of the new MIL of 2016. All prepared investment applications were temporarily interrupted because foreign investors were waiting for new rules and regulations for the MIL. Even after the implementing regulations were announced, there was a delay while foreigners and their legal advisors studied how to provide advice on investment plans and applications as investors sought to maximize the investment incentives available to them. The MIL of 2016 stated that only promoted areas would be eligible under the new scheme. Therefore, some investment projects that had qualified for MIC permits under the FIL of 2012 may not qualify under the new regime. In the event that the investment projects did qualify, they may have received fewer privileges or incentives than those available under the previous version of 2012.

Apart from this issue, the MIL of 2016 not only merged two important investment laws together, but also introduced the new concept of

[31] Myanmar Citizen Investment Law (The Pyidaungsu Hluttaw Law No. 18/2013).

[32] Ministry of Planning and Finance Notification 35/2017, *Myanmar Investment Rules.*

dividing the investment areas into three zones and granting different investment incentives to the promoted areas in each of the three zones based on the development of the areas. The new zoning scheme caused a substantial problem for investors who had already prepared business and investment plans or even applications for acquiring MIC Permits under the previous investment law. These investors needed to prepare new applications and undergo the new application process set forth under the MIL of 2016. Moreover, investors likely had to reevaluate their investment plans in view of the change in investment incentives. This circumstance arose under Section 75 of the MIL of 2016, which indicated that income tax exemptions would be granted based on MIC Zones.[33]

Based on general practice, investors prefer and plan to invest in major economic and commercial cities, namely Mandalay and Yangon. Only some townships in both cities are located in Zone 2, and most of the townships are in Zone 3, which offers fewer income tax incentives. For the sake of Myanmar's citizens, it is essential to spread wealth and economic development opportunities throughout the country, rather than centering those opportunities in a few select regions such as Yangon or Mandalay.

Pursuant to Notification 10/2017 "Designation of Development Zone" dated February 22, 2017,[34] there are three designated MIC Zones to which investors may apply for income tax exemptions based on the zone in which they plan to invest. For Zone 1 (regions that are the least developed), promoted businesses will be eligible for a corporate income tax exemption of up to seven years. For Zone 2 (regions that are moderately developed), promoted businesses will be eligible for a corporate income tax exemption of up to five years. Most areas in Mandalay and Yangon are defined as regions that are adequately developed and, as such, receive the least income tax exemption of up to three years for promoted businesses to be located in those areas. Moreover, unlike the earlier versions of the FIL of 2012, the tax incentives will not be granted automatically. Investors must submit tax incentive applications to the MIC, and only promoted business sectors are qualified. Consequently, there is no guaranty for the income tax exemptions, and the exemption decisions are left entirely up to the MIC.

[33] The Pyidaungsu Hluttaw Law, *supra* note 33, sec. 75.

[34] Myanmar Investment Commission Notification 10/2017, *Designation of Development Zone*.

Indeed, investment promotion zoning is a means to improve the quality of life of Myanmar's people in underdeveloped areas. However, this could cause impediments to foreign investments due to the lack of basic infrastructure, particularly power supply and good road networks in most of the areas in Zone 1 and Zone 2. In addition to the lack of good infrastructure, foreign and local investors have raised many safety and security concerns about doing business in those remote areas. There are many local ethnic groups in those remote but promoted areas, some of which do not fully support the government. There are also armed rebellions in some of those remote rural areas. On top of that, foreign investors may have difficulties finding skilled labor and professionals to work in Zone 1 and Zone 2. The Myanmar Government should take this into serious consideration.

Though there are many positive upgrades in the new MIL of 2016, the zoning concept does not seem to encourage foreign and local investors to invest in Myanmar due to the challenges they must face in the lesser-developed Zones 1 and 2 in order to receive maximum incentives and privileges. Until sufficient infrastructure, stability of investment environment and real security in those areas are improved, investors will likely opt for fewer benefits and set up businesses and investments in more readily attractive areas such as Zone 3.

15.4.2 Opening up Banking, Monetary and Financial Sectors

Myanmar's exchange rate was previously a critical issue, not only for foreign investment, but also for the country's businesses and people because the official rate was extremely low compared to the informal exchange rate. There were considerable foreign exchange restrictions, which discouraged foreign investors in Myanmar. To solve this issue, the Foreign Exchange Management Law[35] was enacted in August 2012 (amended in 2015), and implementing regulation was issued in August 2014. Since the enactment of the Myanmar Exchange Management Law of 2012, the value of the Myanmar Kyat (MMK) is determined by a daily dollar auction at the Central Bank of Myanmar. However, since Myanmar started using the managed floating system during the time of writing, the MMK exchange rate against USD has been weak and subject to frequent fluctuation.

[35] Foreign Exchange Management Law (The Pyihtaungsu Hluttaw Law No. 12/2012).

The Central Bank of Myanmar (CBM) was established in 1948 to oversee all matters related to the banking sector. The CBM was functioning under the Ministry of Finance and Revenue until the new Central Bank of Myanmar Law was enacted in 2013. Pursuant to the Central Bank of Myanmar Law of 2013,[36] the CBM is now an autonomous institution. However, the CBM is nominally still under the Ministry of Finance and Revenue. In 2014, Myanmar liberalized its banking sector, granting banking licenses to nine foreign banks from Australia, China, Japan, Malaysia, Singapore and Thailand. There were four licenses awarded to banks from Vietnam, India, Taiwan and South Korea, with a total number of thirteen foreign banks in Myanmar.

On January 28, 2016, the newly elected government passed the Financial Institutions Law[37] to provide a framework and guidelines for all types of banks including commercial, state-owned and foreign banks. In addition, the new law also provides rules for nonbank financial institutions as well. This new law replaced the Financial Institutions Law of 1990, which failed to provide detailed and comprehensive rules and guidelines for governing local financial institutions. In contrast, the new law incorporated international standards on compliance including anti-money laundering provisions. Myanmar's liberalization of the banking and finance sectors is ahead of its schedule of commitment under ACIA. In plain words, the new laws related to banking and finance have not only brought in tremendous investments from foreign investors but also brought Myanmar's citizens more access to financial services. Myanmar got its first automatic teller machine in 2012, and citizens now can use various debit card and credit card services. As of November 6, 2017, Myanmar has twenty-four locally owned private banks, thirteen foreign banks and forty-nine representative offices of foreign banks and finance companies.[38]

15.4.3 Telecommunication Law: the Leaping Frog

Before the end of the military government in 2011, the telecommunication sector was very undeveloped. Landline telephone and mobile services were insufficient. Furthermore, internet access was only available to a limited number of subscribers and the service was very slow.

[36] Central Bank of Myanmar Law (The Pyihtaungsu Hluttaw Law No. 16/2013).

[37] Financial Institutions Law (The Pyidaungsu Hluttaw Law No. 20/2016).

[38] Central Bank of Myanmar, www.cbm.gov.mm (last visited Nov. 6, 2017).

Reportedly, there were limited numbers of SIM cards for mobile phones and one SIM card cost as much as $6,000 in 2009. In response, telecommunication reform took root in 2013 when the government enacted the Telecommunication Law of 2013[39] as a basic framework for companies operating in the telecommunications sector. The new law repealed the Telegraph Act 1885 and the Wireless Telegraph Act that previously governed the Information and Communication Technology sector in Myanmar. The Telecommunication Law of 2013 opened up the mobile telecommunication sector to both local and foreign operators. The Myanmar government awarded two telecom licenses to two fully foreign-owned operators, namely, Telenor of Norway and Ooredoo of Qatar, in 2013. After opening up the telecommunication sector to two foreign operators, Myanmar went from having almost nothing for communicating – not even sufficient land line phone service – into a country that has a very high number of mobile phone subscribers and yields extremely high growth in telecom-related businesses such as mobile headsets and accessories. The newest telecom operator, Telecom International Myanmar Company Limited (TIMC), launched its MyTel brand in June 2018. The TIMC is a consortium of Viettel from Vietnam, Star High Public Company Limited, which is a subsidiary of the military-owned conglomerate Myanmar Economic Corporation, and a group of eleven local companies, Myanmar National Telecom Holding Public Limited.

A report in 2015 by the telecom equipment supplier Ericsson suggested that 6 percent of the world's new mobile subscribers came from Myanmar, making it the fourth-fastest growing mobile market in the world.[40] Now, data-enabled SIM cards cost around $1.50 each. This is an affordable price for Myanmar's population and has made voice and data services vastly accessible. In January 2017, Digital Asia reported a rapid growth in Myanmar's online population, where at least 33 million of 54 million people living there have active mobile subscriptions.[41] Additionally, the smartphone usage rate was reported to be at 80 percent at the time of the study.

[39] Telecommunications Law (The Pyihtaungsu Hluttaw Law No. 31/2013).

[40] Jyrki Härkki, *Telecommunication Sector in Myanmar*, Digital in Asia, Jan. 9, 2017, https://digitalinasia.com/2017/01/09/myanmar-33-million-mobile-users-smartphone-usage-80/ (last visited Feb. 19, 2018).

[41] *Myanmar 33 Million Mobile Users, Smartphone Usage 80%*, Digital in Asia, Jan. 9, 2017, https://digitalinasia.com/2017/01/09/myanmar-33-million-mobile-users-smartphone-usage-80/ (last visited Feb. 19, 2018).

With the rapid improvement of the telecom sector, Myanmar has now opened itself to the world. Internet services, SMS services and even money transfer services have been introduced to consumers. The leaping upgrade also supports e-commerce businesses, which are now starting to become an important communication tool. The new Telecommunications Law of 2013 is part of the telecommunication reform and serves as a perfect example of how foreign investment can contribute to the development of Myanmar as well as improve the quality of life of its people. Because of the telecommunication law reform, more than 30 million people in Myanmar can now connect with others in the country and around the world.

15.4.4 Special Economic Zones: Easing the Tensions

Another example of legal reform boosting Myanmar's attractiveness as an investment destination is the introduction of the Special Economic Zone Law of 2011 and Dawei Special Economic Zone Law of 2011, which was subsequently replaced by the Myanmar Special Economic Zone Law[42] in the year 2014 (MSEZL of 2014). Currently, there are three Special Economic Zones in Myanmar, namely Thilawa, Kyaukphyu and Dawei. However, only the Thilawa SEZ has started operating. This law allows foreigners to invest in SEZs with certain investment incentives, such as an income tax exemption for the first seven years starting from the date of commencement of commercial operations of the investment business in the Free Zone, and income tax exemption for the first five years starting form the first date of commencement of commercial operations of the investment business in the Promotion Zone, etc. Most importantly, under the MSEZL of 2014, foreign investors may have the right to lease land in the long-term or make productive use of land for fifty years, with twenty-five-year renewal periods.

The MSEZL of 2014 not only offers good investment opportunities and eases difficulties, but also provides decent privileges for foreign investors. For instance, the Thilawa Special Economic Zone provides not only investment incentives but also robust infrastructure and the long-term land lease option. In general, foreigners in Myanmar can lease land and other immovable properties such as housing, apartments, office space and condominiums for only one year at a time. Foreign investors can lease government properties for a longer period if they apply for an

[42] Myanmar Special Economic Zone Law (The State Peace Development Council Law No. 8/2011).

MIC Permit to obtain a fifty-year long-term lease, with the possibility of renewal for twenty years. For this reason, the SEZ scheme offers an alternative option for foreign investors to obtain long-term land lease rights and makes nongovernment properties accessible. The SEZ scheme from the Myanmar Government has undoubtedly enhanced foreign investments. The government will need to continue promoting and expanding the SEZ scheme at least to the other two SEZs that remain underdeveloped still.

15.4.5 Reforming Myanmar Companies Act

The new Myanmar Company Law (MCL of 2017)[43] was enacted on December 6, 2017 and came into force on August 1, 2018. The new law replaced the Myanmar Companies Act of 1914 and the Special Companies Act of 1950 as well as all notifications, rules, orders and subordinate instruments made under both laws. This is a pivotal piece of legislation that reforms how companies are regulated, and it describes and provides guidance on the rights of foreign and local joint venture companies. Furthermore, the MCL of 2017 is expected to serve as a tool to encourage more foreign investments. The new important improvements are abolishment of the "Permit to Trade" – a form of business license in the Myanmar Companies Act of 1914, which requires a foreign company to obtain prior registration of a company. In addition, a company will no longer be required to state its intended objectives in the Memorandum of Association and in the Articles of Association as Section 5(A)(iii) of the MCL of 2017 states clearly that a company is entitled to full legal capacity to carry on any business and activity. Pursuant to Section 60(B) of the MCL of 2017, a share will not have a nominal or par value. Furthermore, this new law allows a company to hold shares of different classes. Moreover, the MCL of 2017 introduces the new legal definition of a foreign company by allowing companies registered in Myanmar to have up to 35 percent of their shares owned by foreign shareholders without being deemed as foreign companies. This will allow foreign investors to participate in business activities that were previously restricted solely to Myanmar companies. Together with the inception of the MCL of 2017, a new electronic registry system, the Myanmar Companies Online (MyCo), was also introduced. The new electronic company registration system is expected to simplify the

[43] Draft Myanmar Company Law (2017), www.dica.gov.mm (last visited Nov. 6, 2017).

registration process. However, all existing companies as well as overseas corporations registered in Myanmar prior to August 1, 2018 are required to re-register by January 31, 2019. Although there is no fee for re-registration, this requirement creates a burden for existing entities. In addition, if an entity fails to re-register on MyCo within the prescribed period, the Registrar may take action to strike its name from the register and publish notice thereof in the Gazette. Upon publication in the Gazette of such notice, the company will be dissolved. Moreover, such an entity will not be allowed to carry on any business in Myanmar. However, prior to its name being struck off the register, the Registrar may restore such an entity and may determine any fee payable for such restoration.

15.4.6 *Priority Laws to Be Reformed*

In September 2016, the Myanmar Legal Affairs Commission issued a letter setting out a list of forty-eight laws including a new Trademark Law, Copyright Law and Foreign Employment Law as priority laws that will be enacted in the near future. This announcement signals the emphasis on ongoing legal reform in Myanmar. Investors and legal practitioners can only hope that the new proposed laws will provide clear and transparent provisions that will further create a good business and investment environment. Investors are still hoping for more investment protection and guarantees from the Myanmar government.

15.5 Conclusion

As previously discussed, numerous changes are afoot in the laws and regulations of Myanmar. A significant number of laws have been amended, revoked and redrafted during the regulatory reform period. Crouch argues, however, that the law after the 2008 Constitution is not to be considered a "big bang." She has evaluated the legal reform as a slow and complex process that builds on successive, and at times contradictory, layers of development.[44] Those newly updated and modernized laws aim to support a good and liberal environment for investment. However, these new changes have certainly resulted in some difficulties and uncertainties for investors as well as legal practitioners. Lawyers have had to study the many new laws and regulations enacted from 2011 until

[44] Crouch, *supra* note 23.

the present in order to provide accurate advice and give legal support to investors based on the new legislation. Additionally, since the laws previously used are outdated, law schools and law professors are then required to update their curriculums and law programs to keep abreast with the new legislation. Laws and regulations which law students study today may be outdated tomorrow. In fact, more than 200 laws have been enacted and more will come into effect. This means that law lecturers and all stakeholders need to study these new laws from the beginning. Meganathan observes that Myanmar's legal system, once admired throughout the region, languished under military rule. She added that the government shuttered the most prestigious faculty of law at Yangon University in response to the uprising led by students in 1988. Profoundly, even after the government allowed the law school to reopen, no lawyers were trained there until 2014.

This matter must be seriously taken into account. Myanmar must lay a solid foundation for its legal professionals to be well trained and to become experts in their own Myanmar laws. Unfortunately, at the present time, the country does not have enough qualified local lawyers to support the influx of foreign investments. Due to this lack of local lawyers who possess a good foundation in corporate law as well as experience in international businesses and investments, there are now more than fifty international law firms set up under Myanmar's jurisdiction, where most of these foreign law firms are led by foreign lawyers. This chapter encourages the Myanmar government, its legal profession organizations and its universities to develop Myanmar's legal professions along with legal reforms to help create sustainability of legislative and administrative reforms.

The FDI influx in the last five years has positively impacted both the Myanmar economy and its people. There is impressive progress in its economic and legal reforms. However, one can argue there are numerous other actions that must be taken and laws to be reformed. In fairness, we must recognize the fact that this country, which had been isolated for six decades, has improved dramatically. Myanmar exceeded expectations when, as a newly open country, it turned into one of the fastest growing economies in Asia in such a short period of time. It is clear that the government prioritizes legal reforms and focuses heavily on attracting FDI. However, the government should also provide transparency and open communication with foreigner investors. At the very least, foreign investors should know what laws will be changed. In the past, the new proposed laws were drafted in secret and the names of the laws that were to be amended or revoked were not released. This situation improved when the government asked for opinions from the public and investors during the drafting of the new Myanmar Companies Law and the MIL of 2016. There is no question that regulatory reform is the right track toward creating a better investment climate. While focusing on drawing in FDI, it is essential to balance the interests of both foreign investors and Myanmar's citizens to ensure sustainable development.

The ADB acknowledged that Myanmar has undergone extensive reforms since 2011, which can lead to long-term success in economic and human development. However, the ADB views that if Myanmar maintains harmony of both economic and human development and a vision for growth that is based on an integrated, well-planned and coordinated design, the country is slated to become one of Asia's leading economies, as it was once before.[45]

Myanmar has made impressive changes in opening up to foreign investment and reducing restrictions on trade and investment. However, Myanmar must continue working and tracking its commitments in the ASEAN context to reap the benefits of being a Member State of ASEAN. To boost overall growth, the ADB urges Myanmar to increase economic integration both regionally and globally. Moreover, Myanmar should continue improvement of its business and investment environment in order to transform itself into one of the region's most attractive destinations for FDI.[46]

The manufacturing sector in Myanmar is developing at a high rate of growth. Investors foresee that Myanmar will be a production hub with special privileges from ASEAN's free trade in goods. Goods manufactured in Myanmar and certified as ASEAN products can be circulated with as low as 0 percent tariff within an ASEAN territory that has more than 600 million people. Moreover, ASEAN has six free trade agreements with six major countries (ASEAN+6), namely India, China (including Hong Kong), Japan, South Korea, Australia and New Zealand. Also, through the Regional Comprehensive Economic Partnership, ASEAN seeks to achieve a modern, comprehensive, high-quality and mutually beneficial economic partnership agreement among the dialogue negotiation partners. The total population within ASEAN+6 is nearly half of the world's population. Furthermore, Myanmar has been awarded special benefits under the Generalized System of Preferences from the European

[45] Asian Development Bank, *Myanmar: Unlocking the potential* 174 (2014).
[46] *Id.*

Union and other developed countries, making up for the benefits revoked as part of the economic sanctions against the country in the 1990s. This preferential treatment will help make Myanmar even more attractive as an investment hub, elevating it to one of the top choices for investors. Myanmar has everything working in its favor, now it is up to Myanmar to use the rule of law and make full use of its strengths during this critical period of growth.

The gap among ASEAN-6 and the CLMV countries has been narrowing gradually, slowly but steadily. The improvement of the CLMV countries' development and their investment environment will bring ASEAN closer to its dream/goal of being a single investment destination. Developed ASEAN Member States should share their experience in legal reform with Myanmar. Furthermore, the ASEAN countries should also provide support while Myanmar works to modernize its legal education and assist Myanmar as it seeks to create stable change while undergoing legal reform. Myanmar should not just wait for support from ASEAN or any countries. It is in a position to learn from the legal makeovers of Cambodia, Lao PDR and particularly Vietnam, which has used legal reform as a major tool to completely transform the country into one of the more attractive investment destinations not only in ASEAN, but in all of Asia. The learning process and steps of legal reform in the CLMV will mean nothing if Myanmar does not put well-thought action plans in place and take serious actions in legal, economic and human development. Moreover, Myanmar should urgently consider making an implementation plan to implement commitments under the AEC Blueprint 2025 while undertaking economic and legal reforms. In so doing, Myanmar will soon walk side by side, not behind, with other ASEAN members toward the ASEAN Economic Community in 2025.

PART 4

Intellectual Property, Digital Trade and Consumer Protection

16

Free Movement of Goods and Intellectual Property Exhaustion in ASEAN: a Road Block in the ASEAN Way?

IRENE CALBOLI

16.1 Introduction

In this chapter, I analyze the relationship between IP rights and the principle of free movement of goods in the context of cross-border trade among the countries that are members of ASEAN. Building upon my previous research on this topic with respect to the EU and other free trade areas such as NAFTA, I analyze the application of the principle of IP exhaustion – according to which the owners of IP rights are no longer entitled to control the distribution of their products after the first lawful sale in the market – and the impact of the existing national variations in the application of this principle among ASEAN members on the free movement of goods within ASEAN. In particular, I assess the type of domestic positions adopted today by ASEAN Member States on trademarks, patents and copyright exhaustion and whether these domestic positions permit the importation of genuine goods from other ASEAN members.

The chapter proceeds as follows. In Section 16.2, I offer a brief primer on ASEAN, ASEAN's principles of consensus and noninterference of national policies (the ASEAN Way) and the lack of substantive harmonization of IP rules to date, including the principle of IP exhaustion. In this section, I also explain the relationship between the principle of IP exhaustion and the free movement of goods with respect to cross-border trade and the alternative systems that are followed today by national jurisdictions – notably in regard to national, international and regional exhaustion. In Section 16.3, I survey the approaches adopted by individual ASEAN countries regarding trademark, patent and copyright exhaustion and note the inconsistency of these approaches, which either combine a variety of domestic approaches favoring national or international exhaustion, or simply do not address the issue of IP exhaustion. In Section 16.4, I criticize this inconsistency and take the view that ASEAN members should adopt consistent national rules in order to effectively promote free movement of goods within ASEAN.

Certainly, considering the more pressing issues and the generalized lack of enforcement of IP rights across ASEAN, the harmonization of domestic regulations on IP exhaustion may not be a priority for ASEAN states at this time. Yet, economic integration is set to intensify, and differences in domestic exhaustion regimes will become increasingly scrutinized as potential barriers to legitimate trade within ASEAN. Thus, I suggest that ASEAN countries could follow one of two options in this respect. In particular, ASEAN states could agree on a common solution of regional exhaustion, even though that solution is not advisable as it would impose an ASEAN-centric trade policy, which may run against the national interests of ASEAN states and be contrary to the ASEAN Way. Instead, it would be advisable that ASEAN members consistently adopt a domestic policy in favor of IP exhaustion with respect to all IP rights. This would allow ASEAN states to decide their respective trade-related agendas with non-ASEAN countries and may create less friction with the ASEAN Way.

Due to the limited scope of this chapter, my analysis is limited to the trade in physical goods (sold both through traditional channels in the brick-and-mortar environment and online) and does not extend to the (increasingly relevant) issue of free movement of digital goods. Similarly, I only incidentally elaborate on the impact of contracts (primarily licensing agreements), particularly the instances where contracts are used to limit the resale of products in foreign markets. These agreements are recognized as valid in some (but not all) jurisdictions in ASEAN. In the same context, I do not address the competition-related aspects of these contracts, which could be found to represent anticompetitive practices. Finally, my analysis does not include a detailed review of the level of development nor data related to the domestic economies and industries in each ASEAN state. This data may be relevant to justify different national policies on exhaustion at this time, yet again only the adoption of consistent rules on this issue can promote and guarantee long-term effective functioning of an ASEAN internal market.

16.2 A Brief Primer on ASEAN, the ASEAN Way and the Relationship between Intellectual Property Exhaustion and Free Movement of Goods

ASEAN was established in 1967[1] with the aim of integrating the ASEAN members into a regional economic organization. ASEAN countries adopt fundamental principles of consensus and noninterference with national policies.[2] This approach is different from the approach adopted, for example, by European Union members, and is defined as the ASEAN Way. In addition, ASEAN did not create institutions in charge of developing, administering and ruling on issues related to ASEAN-focused policies, such as the European Parliament, European Commission, and CJEU (formerly the European Court of Justice, ECJ). In 2003, the ASEAN states resolved to establish an ASEAN Community, and in 2007 they adopted the ASEAN Charter.[3] One of the pillars of the ASEAN Community was the creation of the AEC, launched in 2015.[4] The AEC aims to integrate ASEAN members' markets into a single market that comprises the free movement of goods, services, investment, capital and skilled labor.[5] The foundation of the ASEAN market can be traced to the Declaration on the ASEAN Economic Community Blueprint.[6] In 1992, ASEAN countries also signed an Agreement on the Common Effective Preferential Tariff Scheme for the AFTA[7] in order to foster regional economic integration and eliminate tariff and nontariff barriers.[8]

1 The Association of Southeast Asian Nations Declaration (Bangkok Declaration), Bangkok (1967).

2 Treaty of Amity and Cooperation in Southeast Asia, 2012 O.J. (L 154) 6 (1976).

3 Declaration of ASEAN Concord II (Bali Concord II) (2003); Charter of the Association of Southeast Asian Nations (2007).

4 Cebu Declaration on the Acceleration of the Establishment of an ASEAN Community by 2015 (2007): ASEAN members committed to accelerate the establishment of the ASEAN Economic Community in the Cebu Declaration on the Acceleration of the Establishment of an ASEAN Community by 2015. The ASEAN Community consists of the three pillars of the ASEAN Security Community, the ASEAN Economic Community and the ASEAN Socio-Cultural Community. These form the Roadmap for an ASEAN Community 2009–2015.

5 AEC Blueprint 2015, para. 9. For a detailed analysis of the creation of the AEC, see Stefano Inama & Edmund W. Sim, An Institutional and Legal Profile (2015).

6 AEC Blueprint 2015, *supra* note 5, para. 11, 13 & 14.

7 Agreement on the Common Effective Preferential Tariff Scheme for the ASEAN Free Trade Area (1992) (CEPT-AFTA).

8 ASEAN Trade in Goods Agreement (2009), art. 8(d) (stipulating that the protection and enforcement of IPRs may constitute a general exception to the prohibition to nontariff barriers within ASEAN; the ATIGA replaced the earlier CEPT-AFTA scheme signed in 1992).

As part of the process of ASEAN integration, in 1995 the ASEAN countries adopted the ASEAN Framework Agreement on Intellectual Property Cooperation[9] (Framework Agreement) aiming at establishing cooperation in several IP-related areas, including copyright and related rights, patents, trademarks, industrial designs, geographical indications, trade secret and layout designs of integrated circuits.[10] To date, however, this cooperation has focused primarily on administrative matters such as interoperability between and assistance with domestic procedures adopted for patent and trademark searches, and the creation of regional databases. Various intra-ASEAN IP-related initiatives[11] have been adopted, including the Hanoi Plan of Action,[12] the ASEAN Intellectual Property Rights Action Plan 2004–2010[13] as part of the Vientiane Action Programme 2004–2010,[14] the Work Plan for ASEAN Cooperation on Copyright,[15] the ASEAN Intellectual Property Rights Action Plan 2011–2015[16] and the ASEAN Intellectual Property Rights Action Plan 2016–2025.[17] Also, ASEAN addresses external cooperation with non-ASEAN countries and international organizations. The AWGIPC was established in 1996 pursuant to the IP Framework Agreement. The AWGIPC serves as a "consultative group" and comprises the IP offices of the ten ASEAN Member States.[18]

However, no harmonized substantive rules on IP rights have been adopted by ASEAN members. Nonetheless, IP laws across ASEAN are largely harmonized, as ASEAN countries are part of the WTO and have aligned their national laws with the principles set by TRIPS.[19] Still, TRIPS

[9] ASEAN Framework Agreement on Intellectual Property Cooperation (1995).

[10] *Id.*, art. 3(1).

[11] For an introduction of ASEAN IP initiatives, see Elizabeth Siew-Kuan Ng, *ASEAN IP Harmonization: Striking the Delicate Balance*, 25 Pace Int'l L. Rev. 129, 137–60 (2013).

[12] ASEAN, Hanoi Plan of Action, adopted at the Sixth ASEAN summit in 1998 in Vietnam (1997).

[13] Intellectual Property Rights Action Plan 2004–2010 (IPR Action Plan 2004–2010).

[14] Vientiane Action Programme 2004–2010 (2004).

[15] Work Plan for ASEAN Cooperation on Copyright (2006).

[16] ASEAN IPR Action Plan 2011–2015.

[17] ASEAN IPR Action Plan 2016–2025.

[18] ASEAN Working Group on Intellectual Property Cooperation 367–89.

[19] *See* Agreement on Trade-Related Aspects of Intellectual Property Rights, Apr. 15, 1994, Marrakesh Agreement Establishing the World Trade Organization, Annex 1C, Legal Instruments – Result of the Uruguay Rounds Vol. 31, 33 I.L.M. 83 (1994). With the exception of Myanmar, all ASEAN members are members to the Paris Convention for the Protection of Industrial Property and to the Berne Convention for the Protection of Literary and Artistic Works, the two most relevant international agreements harmonizing national IP laws pre-TRIPS, which also considerably harmonized substantive laws on IP

only provides for common minimal standards, and ASEAN members could consider adopting common standards and harmonizing national laws beyond the levels set forth by the TRIPS standards, similarly to what has been done, for example, by the Member States of the European Union with respect to several IP norms across the EU.[20]

To turn to the specific topic of this chapter, ASEAN nations have neither adopted a common policy with respect to IP exhaustion nor discussed the domestic regulation of this principle in the context of the ASEAN internal market or in order to guarantee the free movement of goods within ASEAN.[21] Hence, there is an inherent tension between the enforcement of national IP rights, the principle of IP exhaustion and the principle of free movement of goods in relation to cross-border trade.[22] More precisely, as elaborated below in this paragraph, the adoption of one approach on exhaustion versus another (notably international versus national versus regional exhaustion) directly translates to permitting, or not permitting, importation/exportation of genuine goods across national borders by third parties. Not surprisingly, the tension between the principle of exhaustion and free movement of goods becomes more acute when it relates to the application of this principle within free trade areas or customs unions, as the objective of these regional organizations is precisely to promote the free movement of goods within the territory of the organizations.[23] As I have elaborated at length in my previous scholarship, it was precisely the need to create an internal market where goods could freely flow that brought the European Union to adopt a common approach on the issue of IP exhaustion as a matter of EU law.[24]

Generally, the principle of IP exhaustion is based on the premise that IP rights should not be used to control the distribution of a product, or

across all members. *See* Paris Convention for the Protection of Industrial Property, Mar. 20, 1883, as revised Jul. 14, 1967, 21 U.S.T. 1583, 828 U.N.T.S. 305; The Berne Convention for the Protection of Literary and Artistic Works, Sep. 9 1886, as revised Jul. 24, 1971, and as amended Sep. 28, 1979, 102 Stat. 2853, 1161 U.N.T.S. 3.

20 *See* Herman Cohen Jehoram, *Harmonising Intellectual Property Law within the European Community*, 23 Int'l Rev. Intell. Prop. & Competition 622 (1992).

21 *See infra* Section 16.3.

22 *See e.g.*, the various contributions in Irene Calboli & Edward Lee eds., Research Handbook on Intellectual Property Exhaustion and Parallel Imports (2016).

23 *See e.g.*, Irene Calboli, *Market Integration and (the Limits of) the First Sale Rule in North American and European Trademark Law*, 51 Santa Clara L. Rev. 1241 (2011).

24 *See e.g.*, Irene Calboli, *Reviewing the (Shrinking) Principle of Trademark Exhaustion in the European Union (Ten Years Later)*, 16 Marq. Intell. Prop. L. Rev. 257 (2012).

a batch of products, after their first release into the market. With respect to international trade, the key inquiry is whether IP rights of genuine products are exhausted upon distribution in the national or foreign markets. To date, there is no international agreement on these issues, and Article 6 of TRIPS explicitly emphasizes that TRIPS does not address the issue of IP exhaustion.[25] Left to their discretion, countries tend to adopt the national policy that best promotes national interests by balancing the interests of (1) IP owners who desire control of cross-border trade of their products and the ability to set prices; (2) third-party importers importing/exporting the goods that they lawfully purchased (generally in lower-cost markets to be exported to higher-cost markets); and (3) governments favoring either the protection of national markets and allowing price discrimination within these markets, or having an open market and international competition.

Notably, national jurisdictions generally adopt one of three approaches: international, national or regional exhaustion. Under the principle of *international* exhaustion, the rights of IP owners to control the further distribution of a good, or a batch of goods, exhaust after the first sale of the goods regardless of the country where this first sale has occurred.[26] Unauthorized imports in the jurisdictions following this principle are considered to be lawful. In contrast, under the principle of *national* exhaustion, the rights of IP owners are exhausted after the first sale of a good, or a batch of goods, only if this first sale has occurred in the national territory. In turn, unauthorized imports can be stopped at the border or legitimately seized after importation on the basis of infringement, even though these goods are genuine goods.[27] Finally, under the principle of *regional* exhaustion, the rights of IP owners are exhausted after the first sale of a good, or a batch of goods, only if the sale has occurred in one of the member countries of a regional organization that follows this principle as a common rule for all members. Under this system, the imports of products originating from third countries remain unlawful and can be stopped as infringement. To date, this approach is the common policy adopted by EU Member States, which reflects the concern between balancing free movement of goods and protecting regional IP rights and trade interests.[28]

[25] TRIPS, *supra* note 19, art. 6.

[26] See e.g., Calboli, *Market Integration, supra* note 23, at 1252–6.

[27] *Id.*

[28] *Id.*

Ultimately, countries remain free to select their respective policies on IP exhaustion based on a variety of national interests, including the size of their markets and the level of development. Hence, free movement of goods in a free trade area or regional organization can be secured only by limiting, among other trade-related barriers, the enforcement of national IP rights toward genuine goods.[29] To this end, all members of a free trade area or regional organization should thus consistently apply a system of exhaustion – regional or international – that can assure that goods can freely move within that area or organization.

16.3 Current National Positions on Intellectual Property Exhaustion in ASEAN Member States

16.3.1 National Rules on Trademark Exhaustion

As I mentioned in Section 16.2, ASEAN nations have not engaged in any substantive harmonization of national trademark laws to date, including the principle of trademark exhaustion. In the absence of any fixed provisions or guidelines, ASEAN members remain free to decide what system of trademark exhaustion they prefer to adopt domestically based on their respective national interests (or experience) on the issue. In particular, based on a survey of the current trademark laws, the exhaustion rules followed by ASEAN countries can be divided into three separate groups: Singapore, Vietnam, Malaysia, the Philippines and Thailand follow a system of international exhaustion through legislative provisions or case law; Cambodia and Lao PDR follow a system of national exhaustion based on legislative provisions that, however, have not yet been applied by the courts; and Indonesia, Brunei and Myanmar do not have a specific rule on exhaustion (or in the case of Myanmar no trademark law is enacted in the country at this time).

Notably, in Singapore, the Trade Marks Act[30] excludes trademark infringement for products that have been distributed in the market "whether in Singapore or outside Singapore" with the "express or implied consent (conditional or otherwise)" of the trademark owners in Article 29(1).[31] To avoid strategic assignment of trademarks, imports are also permitted if the Singapore trademark and the foreign mark are owned by

[29] *Id.*

[30] Singapore Trade Marks Act (Chapter 332, 2005 Revised Edition) (Singapore).

[31] *Id.*, § 29(1).

related entities, and courts have ruled that the owner of the Singapore trademark would be deemed to have implicitly consented to the first sale of products abroad.[32] The exception to this rule applies when "the condition of the goods has been changed or impaired after they have been put on the market" or "the use of the registered trade mark in relation to those goods has caused dilution in an unfair manner of the distinctive character of the registered trade mark."[33] In Singapore, courts have applied these provisions in several instances and consistently admitted the import of genuine products into Singapore.[34] Similarly, in Vietnam, Article 125(2)(b) of the Intellectual Property Law[35] provides statutory support for the principle of international trademark exhaustion.[36] Notably, the provision does not address the issue of products of different quality, but states that the following does not constitute infringement: "circulating, importing, exploiting utilities of products having been lawfully put on the market, including overseas markets, except for products put on the overseas markets not by the mark owners or their licensees."[37]

In Malaysia, the Trade Marks Act uses a more convoluted language, which provides a statutory exception against infringement for the imports of genuine goods.[38] In particular, Section 40(1)(d) provides that it does not constitute infringement to use a mark (protected in Malaysia) with respect to products "connected in the course of trade" with the trademark owners as long as the trademark "has not subsequently removed or obliterated it."[39] Moreover, the judiciary in Malaysia has explicitly embraced the application of the principle of international trademark exhaustion in the *Panadol* case.[40] In this case, the court held that the parallel import of goods sharing a common origin should be allowed.[41] Still, this case is the only

[32] Revlon Inc. v. Cripps & Lee Ltd. [1980] Fleet Street Reports 85 (C.A.).

[33] Singapore Trade Marks Act, at § 29; See Ng-Loy Wee Loon, Intellectual Property Law of Singapore, 401–2 (2014).

[34] See Ng-Loy, *supra* note 24, at 400.

[35] Law on Intellectual Property (No. 50/2005/QH11) (2005) (Vietnam). This law was amended in 2009 by Law No. 36/2009/QH12, amending and supplementing a Number of Articles of the Law on Intellectual Property, Jun. 19, 2009 (Vietnam). However, the trademark exhaustion provision, art. 125, remained unchanged.

[36] *Id.*, art. 125(2)(b).

[37] *Id.*

[38] Trademark Act (Act 175 of 1976, as last amended by Act A1138 of 2002), Jun. 21, 1976 (Malaysia).

[39] *Id.*, § 40(1)(d).

[40] Winthrop Products Inc. & Anor v. Sun Ocean (M) Sdn Bhd & Anor [1988] 2 M.L.J. 317.

[41] *Id.*

case dealing with the issue of trademark exhaustion in Malaysia to date, and the court did not address the parallel importation of goods of different origins or with materially different qualities.[42]

Differently, in the Philippines, the Intellectual Property Code does not explicitly include a provision on exhaustion.[43] According to Article 166, importation of an article into the Philippines, which copies or simulates a mark registered in the Philippines, is an infringement.[44] Since parallel imports involve genuine products – while the provision refers to counterfeits or infringing products – it is supported that the principle of international exhaustion applies to the importation of genuine goods. In addition, neither the Intellectual Property Code of the Philippines nor the Philippine courts have addressed issues relating to goods of materially different qualities for different markets thus far. Similarly, Thailand also has no express legislation regarding the exhaustion of trademark rights.[45] Nevertheless, the Thai Central Intellectual Property and International Trade Court[46] and the Thai Supreme Court have embraced international trademark exhaustion in their decisions.[47] In particular, in a 1999 decision, the Thai Central Intellectual Property and International Trade Court allowed the parallel import of genuine goods bearing the same mark from Singapore to Thailand, stating that trademark rights are internationally exhausted because trademark owners have already fairly received rewards from the first sale of the goods. This decision was affirmed by the Supreme People's Court of Thailand in 2000.[48]

On the other hand, Cambodia and Lao PDR have both adopted a system of national trademark exhaustion. In particular, Article 11(c)

[42] Lazaros G. Grigoriadis, Trade Marks and Free Trade: A Global Analysis 483 (2014).

[43] Intellectual Property Code of the Philippines (Republic Act No. 8293) (1997) (Philippines) *as amended by* Implementing Rules and Regulations of the Republic Act No. 9502 of 2008, Jul. 4, 2008 (Philippines) *as amended by* Republic Act No. 10372, Feb. 28, 2013 (Philippines).

[44] *Id.*, art. 166.

[45] Trademark Act, B.E. 2543, sec. 44 (1991) (consolidated as of 2000) *as amended* up to Trademark Act B. E (No. 3) B.E. 2559 (2016) (Thailand). See Vichai Ariyanuntaka, *Exhaustion and Parallel Imports in Thailand, in* Parallel Imports in Asia 98–100 (Christopher Heath ed., 2004).

[46] Thailand Central Intellectual Property and International Trade Court Decision No. 16/ 2542 (1999).

[47] Thailand Supreme Court Decision No. 2817/2543 (2000).

[48] Thailand Supreme Court Decision affirmed *Decision No. 16/2542* (1999) in decision No.2817/2543 (2000).

of the Cambodian Law[49] provides that "the rights conferred by registration of a mark shall not extend to acts in respect of articles which have been put on the market in the Kingdom of Cambodia by the registered owner or with his consent."[50] Similarly, Lao PDR's Law on Intellectual Property states[51] in Article 57(3)(1) that "no individual or organization . . . [other] than the trademark owner" is entitled to undertake any activity or act as described in paragraph 1 of the Law of Lao PDR without the authorization of the trademark owner, "except as otherwise provided in this Law"[52] and "any such acts without authorization shall be considered to be an act of infringement."[53] Based on the language of these provisions, parallel imports seem to be forbidden in Lao PDR.

Finally, Indonesia and Brunei Darussalam do not seem to have adopted, to date, any relevant statutory provision on trademark exhaustion and no judicial decision on the issue can be found so far in either country. In the case of Indonesia, this position is further reinforced by the absence of any specific provision in the new law on trademarks adopted in 2016.[54] On one hand, it appears that Indonesia admits imports from other ASEAN members, and in general from foreign jurisdictions. On the other hand, however, based on the current provision of Article 94 on injunctions, the opposite could also be supported, that the trademark owner or its licensee could prohibit the importation of genuine goods as trademark infringement.[55] Similarly, in Brunei, the statutory language does not specifically make provisions for trademark exhaustion and parallel imports.[56] However, based on the language of Section 82(5) of the Trade Marks Act, it seems that imports are allowed for goods bearing the trademark which has been put in any country "other than Brunei Darussalam by or with the approval of the proprietor" of the registered trademark.[57]

Myanmar also has not adopted any provision on trademark exhaustion to date, as it does not currently have a law on

[49] Law Concerning Marks, Trade Names and Acts of Unfair Competition of the Kingdom of Cambodia (2002) (Cambodia).

[50] Grigoriadis, *supra* note 42, at 488.

[51] Lao People's Democratic Republic Intellectual Property Laws (Law No. 01/NA of Dec. 20, 2011) (Lao PDR).

[52] *Id.*, art. 57(3)(1).

[53] *Id.*

[54] Law on Trade Marks and Geographical Indications (Law No. 20 of 2016) (Indonesia).

[55] *Id.*, art. 94.

[56] Trade Marks Act (Ch. 98, 2000 Rev. Ed.) (Brunei).

[57] *Id.*, § 82(5).

trademarks. However, a draft trademark law has been approved by the Myanmar Attorney General's Office and has been under review in the Parliament of Myanmar since 2014. As reported by the International Trademark Association, Article 41 of the Myanmar Draft Trademark Law adopts the principle of international exhaustion, while Article 42 "prevents the importation of goods which have been altered after their initial sale."[58]

16.3.2 National Rules on Patent Exhaustion

Similar to trademarks, the ASEAN cooperation regarding patent rights has so far not led to substantive harmonization, including with regard to the principle of exhaustion, even though it seems that the majority of countries prefer a system of international exhaustion either explicitly or implicitly. In particular, the analysis of current patent laws shows that the exhaustion rules followed by ASEAN members can be divided as follows: countries that adopt a system of international exhaustion through legislative provisions or case law, namely Cambodia, Malaysia, Vietnam and Singapore; countries that adopt a system of national exhaustion based on legislative provisions, such as Indonesia and the Philippines; and countries that do not have a specific rule on exhaustion, namely Brunei, Lao PDR and Thailand (or in the case of Myanmar, no patent law is enacted in the country at this time). Yet, a fourth subgroup can be identified, as Singapore, Indonesia and the Philippines treat pharmaceutical products differently for the purpose of patent exhaustion. Notably, Singapore follows a de facto system of national exhaustion if the resale is prohibited by contract, while Indonesia and the Philippines adopt international exhaustion.

In particular, in Cambodia, Article 44 of the Law on the Patents, Utility Model Certificates and Industrial Designs[59] states that patent rights do not extend to acts related to "articles which have been put on the market in the Kingdom of Cambodia or outside the Kingdom of Cambodia by the owner of the patent or with his consent."[60] To date, no case has been decided with respect to parallel imports into Cambodia. Similarly, the Patents Act of Malaysia[61] provides, in Section 58A, that it is not an

[58] International Trademark Association, Comments by the International Trademark Association on the Myanmar Draft Trademark Law, §§ 41, 42, www.inta.org/advocacy/documents/january82013comments.pdf (last visited Jan. 28, 2017).

[59] Law on Patents, Utility Models and Industrial Designs (2003) (Cambodia).

[60] *Id.*, art. 44.

[61] Patents Act 1983, *as amended* by the Patents (Amendment) Act 2006 (Malaysia).

infringement "to import, offer for sale, sell or use" any of the following: "any patented product" or "any product obtained directly by means of the patented process or to which the patented process has been applied, which is produced by, or with the consent, conditional or otherwise, of the owner of the patent or his licensee."[62] The provision additionally clarifies that "patent" "includes a patent granted in any country outside Malaysia in respect of the same or essentially the same invention as that for which a patent is granted under this Act."[63] This provision was first introduced into the Malaysian Patents Act by the Patents (Amendment) Act of 2000, which was prompted by concerns regarding the AIDS/HIV pandemic in the late 1990s and the related need to access affordable medicines.[64] Similarly, in Vietnam, the Intellectual Property Law[65] permits the circulation, importation and exploitation of utilities of products that have been lawfully put on the market, including overseas markets in Article 125(2)(b), except for products put on overseas markets without the mark owners' or their licensees' consent.[66] No judicial decision in this area has been adopted so far in Vietnam.

Singapore also follows international exhaustion in patent law.[67] Section 66(2)(g) of the Patents Act states, in particular, that it is not an infringement of a patent to import into Singapore a patented product or a product obtained by means of a patented process or to which a patented process has been applied, if the product "was produced by or with the consent (conditional or otherwise) of the patent proprietor" or any of his licensees.[68] For this purpose, a "patent" is defined to include a patent granted in any country outside Singapore in respect to the same or substantially the same invention for which the patent is granted. Singapore also applies the concept of "deemed consent," according to which any condition restricting the resale of the product outside the territory of manufacturing or first sale shall be disregarded for the purpose of determining if the product was produced with consent. The same applies to the conditions imposed in licensing agreements.[69] However, Singapore follows a stricter approach

[62] *Id.*, § 58A.
[63] *Id.*
[64] See John Chong, *Exhaustion and Parallel Imports in Malaysia*, *in* Parallel Imports in Asia 133–5 (Christopher Heath ed., 2004).
[65] Law on Intellectual Property (No. 50/2005/QH11) (2005) (Vietnam).
[66] *Id.*, art. 125(2)(b).
[67] Patents Act (Ch. 221, 2005 Rev. Ed.) (Singapore).
[68] *Id.*, § 66(2)(g).
[69] *Id.*, § 51(1)(c).

regarding pharmaceuticals. First, imports of patented pharmaceuticals are not allowed if the products have not been previously sold or distributed in Singapore by the patent owner or with her consent (this principle is referred as "first mover advantage"). Second, imports can still be blocked when the pharmaceuticals have been imported as a result of a breach in the contract between the patent owner and her licensees, including outside Singapore.[70]

Indonesia and the Philippines are the two ASEAN states that follow an explicit system of national exhaustion with a specific exception for the imports regarding pharmaceutical products. Specifically, the 2016 Patent Law of Indonesia[71] grants patent owners the exclusive right to prohibit that other parties, *inter alia*, "import" patented products or products derived from the patented products.[72] Third parties may still import these products for the purpose of "research, experiment, or analysis" when the use would not prejudice the interest of patent holders and is noncommercial.[73] More generally, Article 167 provides that the general prohibition against imports does not apply to imports of patented pharmaceuticals that were lawfully marketed outside Indonesia.[74] This exception is based directly on the need to "to ensure a reasonable price and satisfy the justice of a pharmaceutical product is necessary for human health."[75] Similarly, the Philippine Intellectual Property Code[76] includes the right of "selling or importing" the patented product or products obtained directly or indirectly from a patented process as part of the exclusive rights that are granted to the patentee in Section 71.[77] Moreover, Section 72(1) states that patent owners cannot prevent third parties, without authorization, from "using a patented product which has been put on the market in the Philippines by the owner of the product, or with his express consent."[78] Hence, this principle does not apply in the case of pharmaceuticals. In particular, Section 72(1) clarifies that, regarding "drugs and medicines," "the limitation on

70 *Id.*, § 66(3).

71 Law of the Republic of Indonesia No. 13 of Jul. 28, 2016, on Patents (Indonesia).

72 *Id.*, art. 19(1)–(2) and art. 160.

73 *Id.*, art. 19(3).

74 *Id.*, art. 167.

75 *Id.*, Explanation to art. 167.

76 Intellectual Property Code of the Philippines (Republic Act No. 8293) (1997), *as amended by* the Republic Act No. 10372 (2013) (Philippines).

77 *Id.*, § 72.

78 *Id.*, § 72.1.

patent rights shall apply after a drug or medicine has been introduced in the Philippines or anywhere else in the world by the patent owner, or by any party authorized to use the invention." Moreover, the provision continues, "the right to import the drugs and medicines contemplated in this section shall be available to any government agency or any private third party."[79]

Last, Brunei,[80] Lao PDR[81] and Thailand[82] belong to the category of countries without specific rules on patent exhaustion. In these countries, whether the parallel importation of genuine products that were sold overseas with the proprietors' consent constituted infringement may depend on the contents of the contracts signed between the proprietors and the relevant parties concerned. These countries generally strive to ensure access to affordable pharmaceutical products for their citizens. Thus, it could be speculated that courts in these countries may rule in favor of international patent exhaustion should a case be brought over the nature – lawful or unlawful – of parallelly imported pharmaceutical products. Finally, Myanmar does not have an applicable patent law, even though the Burma Patents and Designs (Emergency Provisions) Act 1946 came into force in 1993.[83] In 2015, the government of Myanmar published a New Draft Patent Law, which is still pending approval. The new law includes procedural and substantive provisions. However, it remains unclear how the principle of patent exhaustion would be addressed in the new law.

16.3.3 National Rules on Copyright Exhaustion

Regarding copyright, ASEAN nations again follow diverse positions on exhaustion. To date, ASEAN members' positions can be divided into the following groups: Singapore, which follows a system of international exhaustion through explicit legislative provisions, and countries that follow national exhaustion based on legislative provisions or interpretation thereof, such as Cambodia, Lao PDR, Vietnam and Malaysia; countries that do not have a specific rule on exhaustion but could be could be seen as

[79] *Id.*

[80] Constitution of Brunei Darussalam, Order made under art. 83(3), Patents Order (2011) (Brunei).

[81] Lao People's Democratic Republic Intellectual Property Laws (Law No. 01/NA of Dec. 20, 2011) (Lao PDR).

[82] Patent Act B.E. 2522 (1979), *as amended by* the Patent Act (No. 2) B.E. 2535 (1992) and the Patent Act (No. 3) B.E. 2542 (1999) (Thailand).

[83] Patents and Designs (Emergency Provisions) Act of 1946.

supporting national exhaustion, namely the Philippines and Myanmar (which still apply the colonial copyright law); and countries without a clear policy altogether, namely Brunei, Indonesia and Thailand.

Initially, Singapore's treatment of copyright exhaustion was also unclear. In particular, Sections 32 and 104 of the Copyright Act[84] state that copyright infringement occurs with the "importation for the purpose of sale or hire and other commercial activity" of an article for which "the importer knows or ought reasonably to know that the making of the article was carried out without the *consent* of the owner of the copyright."[85] In this respect, it was initially unclear whether the consent referred to in the provisions was that of the copyright owner in Singapore or, instead, the copyright owner in the country where the products were first marketed (in the instances of separate ownership). The Copyright Act was amended in 1994 in order to clarify the meaning of the provisions. Notably, specific language was added to clarify that "the reference to the owner of the copyright" indicates "the person entitled to the copyright in respect of its application to the making of an article of that description in the country where the article was made" even if the same person did not own the copyright in Singapore.[86] In other words, the language of the statute was amended to clarify that Singapore supports international copyright exhaustion. The 1994 Amendment Act also clarified that the existence of copyright owners' consent is determined without regard to any "condition as to the sale, distribution or other dealings in the article after its making."[87]

In contrast, in Cambodia, the Law on Copyrights and Related Rights provides for a system of national exhaustion.[88] Notably, Article 21 states that "the author has exclusive right to act by him/herself or authorize someone to the following," which include "(d) public distribution by sale, rental of the original or a copy of the work that has not already been subject to a sale or transfer of ownership authorized by the owner of copyright" and "(e) importation into the country, the reproduction copies of his/her works."[89] Similarly,

[84] Copyright Act (Ch. 63, 2006 Rev Ed) (Singapore).

[85] *Id.*, §§ 32, 104. See Public Prosecutor v. Teo Ai Nee [1993] 3 S.L.R.(R.) 755 (finding that, under Section 25(2), the consent relevant to assess whether the copyright owner had consented to the distribution of the products was the consent of the copyright owner in Singapore; the same applied to the interpretation of consent with respect to the manufacturing of the products).

[86] Copyright Act (Ch. 63, 2006 Rev Ed) § 25(3).

[87] *Id.*, § 25(4).

[88] Law on Copyrights and Related Rights of 2003 (Cambodia).

[89] *Id.*, art. 21.

Article 98 of the IP Laws of Lao PDR[90] states that the author or copyright owner "shall have the exclusive right to carry out or authorize the importation or exportation of the original or any copy of the work."[91] Moreover, Article 98 provides that the author or copyright owner of literary and artistic works shall have the exclusive right of "reproducing such work in any manner or form including distribution of copies of such works."[92] Even though both countries' national laws do not specify whether the provisions refer to sales or transfer that occurred nationally or abroad, it seems that the national laws refer to the first national distribution since the importation of unauthorized articles is prohibited. The same applies in Vietnam, where the Law on Intellectual Property[93] provides that the authors shall have exclusive rights to "distribute or import original works or copies thereof."[94] The principle of national exhaustion is further confirmed under Article 28, which specifies that the acts of "exporting, importing or distributing copies of works without permission of copyright holders" constitute copyright infringement.[95]

In Malaysia, the leading interpretation also favors national exhaustion. Section 36(2) of the Copyright Act provides that the "copyright is infringed by any person who, without the consent or licence of the owner of the copyright, imports an article into Malaysia for the purpose of ... (b) distributing the article ... (c) by way of trade, exhibiting the article in public, where he knows or ought reasonably to know that the making of the article was carried out without the consent or licence of the owner of the copyright."[96] Moreover, Section 13(1)(e) grants copyright owners the exclusive right to the "distribution of copies to the public by sale or other transfer of ownership."[97] The Copyright Amendment Act of 2000 additionally clarified that "the exclusive right to control the distribution of copies refers only to the act of putting into circulation copies not previously put into circulation in Malaysia and not to any subsequent

90 Lao People's Democratic Republic Intellectual Property Laws (Law No. 01/NA) (2011) (Lao PDR).

91 *Id.*, art. 98.

92 *Id.*

93 Law on Intellectual Property (No. 50/2005/QH11) (2005) (Vietnam).

94 *Id.*, art. 20.

95 *Id.*, art. 28.

96 Copyright Act 1987 Act 332 § 36(2) (Malaysia).

97 *Id.*, § 13(1)(e).

distribution of those copies or any subsequent importation of those copies into Malaysia."[98]

A similar conclusion applies in the Philippines. In particular, the Intellectual Property Code does not include "importation" as part of the exclusive rights granted to copyright owners. Yet, Article 177(3) provides that copyright owners can control "the first public distribution of the original and each copy of the work by sale or other forms of transfer of ownership."[99] Once again, the provision does not differentiate between products that have been first distributed in foreign countries and those that have been distributed in the Philippines. This could suggest that the distribution rights would be exhausted after the first distribution anywhere. However, Article 190 of the Code offers a detailed list of the exceptions under the heading "importation for personal purposes," which seems to indicate that commercial importation is not to be permitted.[100]

In Myanmar, the 1914 Copyright Law of Burma is still the official national law.[101] This legislation is modeled after the 1911 Copyright Act of the United Kingdom, and refers to the 1911 Act in its Annexes.[102] Under Section 6, the copyright owner has the power to control the importation of copyrighted articles into Burma, which implies a system of national copyright exhaustion.[103] The Act also refers to Section 2(2) of the 1911 Copyright Act, according to which any person who distributes, for the purposes of trade or to such an extent to prejudicially affect the owner of the copyright, or imports for sale or hire, any work which to her knowledge infringed copyright, may commit an act of copyright infringement.[104] Hence, a similar position seems to be adopted in the 2015 draft of a new copyright law that is currently under review in Myanmar. In particular, it seems that national exhaustion will continue to apply, even though the English summary of the draft indicates that the law would be modified so as to guarantee that "international

[98] *Id.*, § 13(1)(a). See also Class One Video Distributors Sdn Bhd & Anor v. Chanan Singh a/l Sher Singh & Anor, [1997] 5 M.L.J. 209.

[99] Intellectual Property Code of the Philippines (Act No. 8293) (1997), § 177.3 (Philippines).

[100] *Id.*, art. 190.

[101] Copyright Act of 1914 (Myanmar).

[102] Copyright Act of 1911 (UK); Copyright Act of 1911 (Myanmar).

[103] Copyright Law of Burma of 1914, § 6.

[104] Copyright Act of 1911, § 2(2).

exhaustion applies to works imported by a natural person for personal purposes."[105]

Finally, Indonesia's law remains ambiguous. Under the revised Copyright Law of 2014,[106] there is no mention of a specific right of importation for authors or copyright owners. Nonetheless, Article 9(1)(e) explicitly states that the author or owner of a copyright has the right to distribute the work or a copy of it.[107] However, this principle is limited by Article 11, which provides that the economic rights to perform the work or the distribution of copies as referred to in Article 9(1)(e) do not apply to the works or the copies that have been sold or have transferred ownership. Still, the provision does not clarify if the right of distribution is exhausted by the first sale or transfer in Indonesia or in a foreign country. To date, no judicial decision seems to have been issued on this point. Similarly, in Thailand, under the Copyright Act,[108] there is no specific right to import or distribute the copyrighted work or copy of it, even though Section 15 mentions the right of "communication to the public," which could potentially include the right of distribution.[109]

Moreover, even though Section 31 states that "whoever knows or should have known that a work is made by infringing the copyright of another person" and imports such works into the country is deemed to infringe copyright under Section 31(4),[110] this provision could be referring to counterfeit products and not to genuine imports. This position seems to be corroborated by the new Section 32(1),[111] which, based on the unofficial translation of the Act, reads "[the s]ale of an original or copy of a copyright work by a person legally acquiring ownership of the original or the copy of such copyright work shall not be deemed a copyright infringement."[112] Last, in Brunei, the language of the Emergency (Copyright) Order grants copyright owners the exclusive

[105] See Draft Myanmar Copyright Law Published in Kyemon Newspaper (The Mirror), Jul. 9, 2015, www.eifl.net/sites/default/files/resources/kyemon_mirror_9july2015_key_points.pdf (last visited Dec. 12, 2017).

[106] Law of the Republic of Indonesia (No. 28 of Sep. 16, 2014) (Indonesia).

[107] *Id.*, art. 9(1)(e).

[108] Copyright Act B.E. 2537 (1994) (Thailand).

[109] *Id.*, § 15.

[110] *Id.*, § 31.

[111] Copyright Act (No. 2) B. E. 2558 (2015) (Thailand).

[112] See the unofficial translation of the amendments to the Copyright Act of 1994 in Thailand, http://web.krisdika.go.th/data/outsitedata/outsite21/file/COPYRIGHTACT_(NO.2),_B.E._2558_(2015).pdf (last visited Dec. 12, 2017).

rights "to issue copies of the work to the public" in Article 18(1)(b).[113] Article 20 further clarifies that "(1) the issue to the public of copies of a work is an act restricted by the copyright" and that "(2) references . . . to the issue to the public of copies of a work are to the act of putting into circulation copies not previously put into circulation, whether in Brunei Darussalam or elsewhere."[114]

However, the provision clarifies that this does not apply to the following "(a) any subsequent distribution, sale, hire or loan of those copies; or (b) any subsequent importation of those copies."[115] By reading the language of the provisions, one may argue that parallel imports fall within the exception to the application of Article 18 as per the wording of Article 20(2)(a) and (b). The ultimate position on whether Brunei adopts a system of international or national copyright exhaustion remains a matter for the judiciary or the legislative authority to clarify. To date, no case has been decided in Brunei.

16.4 Free Movement of Goods and the Necessity of Consistency: International Exhaustion as the Way Forward for ASEAN?

In summary, the above survey indicates that divergences still apply regarding, trademark, patent and copyright exhaustion in different ASEAN countries. Divergences also characterize domestic policies on exhaustion with respect to specific rights – i.e., differences in the treatment of trademark, patent and copyright exhaustion – with the same ASEAN nations. For example, Cambodia, Lao PDR, Malaysia and others apply different policies on exhaustions based on the type of right at issue. These differences are relevant as commercial goods are often protected under more than one type of IP rights, and thus different policies on IP exhaustion at the domestic level may result in IP owners leveraging one type of rights in order to block the import of genuine goods into the national market.[116] The table

[113] Constitution of Brunei Darussalam, Order under § 83(3), Emergency (Copyright) Order (1999) (Brunei).

[114] *Id.*, art. 20(1).

[115] *Id.*

[116] See Irene Calboli & Mary LaFrance, *The Case for a Legislative Amendment Against "Accessory Copyright" for Gray Market Products: What Can the U.S. Learn from Singapore and Australia?*, Sing. J. Legal Stud. 253 (2013); Irene Calboli, *Corporate*

below highlights again the current national policies on IP exhaustion of ASEAN countries:

Country	Trademark Exhaustion	Patent Exhaustion	Copyright Exhaustion
Brunei	Unspecified	Unspecified	Unspecified
Cambodia	National	International	National
Indonesia	Unspecified	National (except pharmaceutical)	Unspecified
Lao PDR	National	Unspecified	National
Malaysia	International	International	National
Myanmar	Law not yet in force	Law not yet in force	Law not yet in force
Philippines	International	National (except pharmaceutical)	National
Singapore	International	International (except pharmaceutical)	International
Thailand	International	Unspecified	Unspecified
Vietnam	International	International	National

Certainly, there can be several (and possibly very legitimate) reasons at the basis of these national divergences, and these could be based on the current status of development and the domestic trade policies of individual ASEAN nations, including free trade agreements with non-ASEAN countries. As mentioned in Section 16.2, the issue of regulating IP exhaustion remains one of the most delicate across many sovereign states, as it entails regulating the enforcement of national IP rights, and in turn may affect national trade policies.[117] Thus, it is common for the members of free trade agreements and free trade areas to not address this issue unless these members intend to promote free movement of goods within the free trade areas.[118]

In particular, not all members of a free trade area or regional organization may desire to achieve a full-scale market integration. Instead,

Strategies, First Sale Rule, and Copyright Misuse: Waiting for Answers from Kirtsaeng v. Wiley and Omega v. Costco (II), 11 Nw. J. Tech. & Intell. Prop. 221 (2013).

[117] See discussion in Section 16.2.

[118] North American Free Trade Agreement, art. 1704 (1993); Trans-Pacific Partnership Agreement, art. 18.11 (2015); Regional Comprehensive Economic Partnership, art. 1.5 (2015).

countries may desire to achieve a lower level of market integration based on national interests, and based on their respective level of economic development as well as market size and type of domestic industries. Notably, some countries may have a priority interest in protecting their domestic markets from foreign imports, and thus may prefer a system of national exhaustion, while other countries may have a priority interest in allowing a larger number of foreign products into their markets, and thus may opt for a system of international exhaustion. Moreover, countries with strong patent- and technology-driven industries but less strong trademark-intensive industries may opt for national patent exhaustion and international trademark exhaustion. In contrast, countries with trademark- or copyright-intensive industries but without a strong technology-driven industry may opt for national trademark and copyright exhaustion and international patent exhaustion.

For example, in the mid-1990s the members of NAFTA decided to join in a free trade area not to create an internal market, but for other reasons.[119] Notably, the United States and Canada joined NAFTA primarily to produce at lower costs in Mexico (and import back or sell internationally products manufactured at lower costs), while Mexico joined primarily as it sees it as a source of foreign direct investment from the United States and Canada.[120] Thus, like TRIPS members, NAFTA members harmonized several intellectual property standards, but did not harmonize their national rules on exhaustion.[121] It is a fortuitous coincidence that NAFTA members consistently practice international trademark[122] and copyright exhaustion (with some exceptions in Canada for books) that permit parallel imports within their respective territories.[123] Yet, NAFTA members still differ on their domestic treatment of patent exhaustion, as Mexico practices national

[119] NAFTA, *supra* note 118, art. 1701(1).

[120] See Calboli, *Market Integration, supra* note 23, at 1256.

[121] See Kenneth W. Abbott & Gregory W. Bowman, *Economic Integration in the Americas: A Work in Progress*, 14 Nw. J. Int'l L. & Bus. 493, 493–6 (1994) (discussing the 1990 initiation of NAFTA negotiations between the United States and Mexico); Richard Bernal, *Regional Trade Arrangements in the Western Hemisphere*, 8 Am. U. J. Int'l L. & Pol'y 683, 697 (1993) (discussing the proposal of NAFTA in the 1990s).

[122] NAFTA, *supra* note 118, art. 102 ("The objectives of this Agreement … are to … eliminate barriers to trade in, and facilitate the cross-border movement of, goods and services between the territories of the Parties … promote conditions of fair competition in the free trade area.") *Id.*

[123] Pierre-Emmanuel Moyse, *Canadian Colonial Copyright: The Colony Strikes Back, in* An Emerging Intellectual Property Paradigm, Perspectives from Canada 107 (Ysolde Gendreau ed., 2008).

patent exhaustion while the United States and Canada follow international patent exhaustion.[124] The NAFTA model – i.e., the choice of silence on the issue of IP exhaustion as part of the agreement, like in TRIPS – has been the basis for other free trade agreements between different countries worldwide, in which some countries seek cheaper production costs while others seek foreign direct investments and market access.

Hence, effective free trade in free trade areas or regional organizations that would like (or state that they would like) to create an internal market can be secured only by limiting, among other trade-related barriers, the domestic enforcement of IP rights when this enforcement can represent a barrier to legitimate trade. This includes the application of a system of national exhaustion of IP rights, as this principle necessarily translates to legally preventing the import of genuine products from other countries (including those that are members of the same area or organization), and thus blocks the free movement of goods. As a result, members of a free trade area or regional organization that desire to effectively build an internal market need to decide whether they intend to enforce the legal conditions necessary so that all goods, including goods covered by existing IP rights, can freely move across their territory. In particular, these conditions need to include the adoption of one of two possible approaches on IP exhaustion: either a system of regional or international exhaustion, applied consistently (1) by all country members of the free trade area or regional organization, or (2) for all types of IP rights to prevent IP owners leveraging restrictive provisions on one type of rights when multiple rights can be used to protect a product (or different parts of it).

In this context, the process of market integration of the European Union (which today extends to the EEA) can be taken as a useful example. EU/EEA members decided to harmonize their national policies on exhaustion, and adopted similar standards to remove any disguised barriers to effective intra-EU/EEA trade.[125] Only

[124] Impression Products, Inc. v. Lexmark International, Inc., 581 U.S. 1523 (2017); Eli Lilly & Co. v. Novopharm Ltd., [1998] 2 S.C.R. 129 (Can.).

[125] Article 34 of the Consolidated Version of the Treaty on the Functioning of the European Union (2010), as amended following the entering into force of the Treaty of Lisbon on December 1, 2009. The TFEU states that "quantitative restriction on imports and all measures having equivalent effect shall be prohibited between Member States." This principle supersedes the general principle in art. 36, according to which European Union members can prohibit or restrict "imports, exports or goods in transit" based upon "the protection of industrial and commercial property." Moreover, the prohibition under art.

very serious concerns relating to health, security or public policy in member countries could be invoked to supersede this principle.[126] Several leading cases by the ECJ (and later the CJEU) assisted in settling uncertainties, and the CJEU prioritized the free movement of goods versus the exercise of IP rights in most instances.[127] Nevertheless this full-force integration of markets does not extend beyond the territory of the EU/EEA, as EU/EEA members decided to adopt regional exhaustion, and genuine products coming from outside the EU/EEA can be legally stopped at the will of trademark owners as trademark infringement.[128]

To date, ASEAN countries adopt a halfway solution between EU/EEA and NAFTA members. Notably, ASEAN nations have already taken important steps toward creating an internal market through the AFTA and the AEC Blueprint 2015. The latter specifically states that the "free flow of goods is one of the principal means by which the aims of a single market and production base can be achieved."[129] Still, the level of economic integration achieved, and perhaps the level that is possible at this time, has not yet reached the same level that can be seen in the EU/EEA markets. Instead, even though the AFTA has reduced intra-ASEAN tariffs on most products, tariffs still exist on products (especially the most relevant products for national economies, such as rice or sugar)

36 "shall not . . . constitute a means of arbitrary discrimination or a disguised restriction on trade between Member States." *Id.*

126 See discussion in Section 16.2.

127 Apostolos G. Chronopoulos & Spyros M. Maniatis, *Trademark Exhaustion and Its Interface with EU Competition Law, in* Research Handbook on Intellectual Property Exhaustion and Parallel Imports 367 (Irene Calboli & Edward Lee eds., 2016); Guido Westkamp, *Exhaustion and the Internet as a Distribution Channel: the Relationship between Intellectual Property and European Law in Search of Clarification, in* Research Handbook on Intellectual Property Exhaustion and Parallel Imports 367 (Irene Calboli & Edward Lee eds., 2016).

128 See e.g., Carl Steele, *"Fortress Europe" for Trademark Owners*, Trademark World 14 (1998) (summarizing the relevance of the ECJ's decision in *Silhouette* in creating a closed trading block among member countries).

129 In 2007, a Protocol to provide special consideration for rice and sugar was signed in Makati City, Philippines. Protocol to Provide Special Consideration for Rice and Sugar, ASEAN, Aug. 23, 2007; In 2010, following the signing and entry into force of the ATIGA, a revision to the protocol was adopted that provides "the need to amend the Protocol to take into account the entry into force of the ASEAN Trade in Goods Agreement." See Protocol to Amend the Protocol to Provide Special Consideration for Rice and Sugar, ASEAN (2010), http://investasean.asean.org/files/upload/00%20Protocol%20Amendment%20Protocol%20Rice%20and%20Sugar%20(2010)(1).pdf (last visited Jan. 28, 2017).

coming from other ASEAN states.[130] Accordingly, it may not necessarily be a reflection of ASEAN countries' desire to effectively integrate their markets in the long term that domestic laws on IP exhaustion still diverge. For comparison, EU/EEA countries diverged on the issue for several decades after the launch of the EEC in 1957, and harmonized their laws on IP exhaustion only in the 1990s.[131]

Even though not in the immediate future, ASEAN states will need to decide whether they would like to proceed with full market integration as announced in the AEC Blueprint 2015 and as part of the AEC. Should they decide to proceed in this direction, ASEAN members would need to decide what IP exhaustion approach they would like to adopt, either as individual ASEAN members or as AEC as a whole.

As mentioned earlier, ASEAN countries have two options to achieve a fully operating internal market where goods can freely move, including goods protected by IP rights. They could opt for an EU-EEA-type system of regional exhaustion, for which all ASEAN states would need to change their national laws and decide to allow intra-ASEAN free movement but not allow parallel imports from outside ASEAN. Or they could opt for a system where each ASEAN nation would follow a principle of international exhaustion for all domestic IP rights. In the latter case, most ASEAN members would still be required to shift or clarify their domestic policies in favor of a generalized principle of international exhaustion. Hence, each ASEAN member would also be able to continue a nationally independent trade policy and admit as legal imports goods coming also from countries outside ASEAN. As I mentioned in the Introduction, the latter solution seems to be the solution more in line (for the time being) with the principle of noninterference (or perhaps "less interference") and the ASEAN-Way, as ASEAN nations would not be required to grant other ASEAN states preferential treatment over third-party foreign countries and could continue independent trade-related policies with these countries while still creating the legal conditions for goods to freely move across ASEAN.

[130] ASEAN Free Trade Area (AFTA Council), http://asean.org/asean-economic-community/asean-free-trade-area-afta-council/; see also *ASEAN Free Trade Area (AFTA): An Update* (2014), http://asean.org/?static_post=asean-free-trade-area-afta-an-update (last visited Jan. 28, 2017).

[131] See Irene Calboli, *Trademark Exhaustion and Free Movement of Goods: A Comparative Analysis of the EU/EEA, NAFTA, and ASEAN*, in Research Handbook on Intellectual Property Exhaustion and Parallel Imports 367 (Irene Calboli & Edward Lee eds., 2016).

In summary, even though there may be legitimate reasons, including nationally-driven trade policies, for ASEAN states to retain the current inconsistent status quo regarding the regulation of IP exhaustion at the domestic level, the exercise of domestic IP laws should not entail the creation of barriers to the free movement of legitimate genuine goods within ASEAN in the long term. Simply put, this amounts to a disguised barrier to legitimate trade within ASEAN and stands against the principle of free movement of goods that has been adopted as one of the defining principles of ASEAN and the AEC. Accordingly, ASEAN countries should consistently adopt rules that would not permit the domestic enforcement of IP rights to interfere with the free movement of goods across ASEAN so long as the goods at issue are genuine. The rules do not need to be put in place immediately, but they need to be put it in place at a certain time, or else the ASEAN and the AEC would not enjoy a fully functioning internal market.

16.5 Conclusion

Different countries adopt different solutions regarding the principle of IP exhaustion based on a variety of conditions, including the size of national markets, level of development as well as historical and geopolitical factors. National solutions may later evolve and change, again depending on changes in these conditions and based on national interests. Free trade areas and regional organizations are also created based on a variety of (often diverse) national interests of the participants. When one of the objectives of these areas or organizations is the creation of a regional internal market, consistent national rules on IP exhaustion are necessary, even when this may imply changes in national policies. At a certain point in time, ASEAN states may need to decide on a common strategy that would guarantee free movement of goods within ASEAN. This would include the regulation of domestic policies on IP exhaustion. As ASEAN countries may prefer to continue following the ASEAN Way and avoid interference in other members' national policies, then ASEAN countries could opt for domestic solutions of international exhaustion for all IP rights. These solutions would both facilitate the free movement of goods within ASEAN and leave ASEAN members free to decide their domestic trade policies with other countries.

17

Legal and Regulatory Challenges to Facilitating e-Commerce in ASEAN

ELIZA MIK

17.1 Introduction

E-commerce is commonly portrayed as a contributor to economic growth and an integrating force for ASEAN. The facilitation of e-commerce is thus largely associated with the harmonization of laws and regulations in this area.[1] Unsurprisingly, ASEAN is the first developing region to prepare a unified e-commerce legal framework.[2] To date, harmonization efforts have centered on electronic transactions laws, the assumption being that the latter will create legal certainty for the recognition of electronic contracts.[3] Such efforts may, however, be insufficient. As e-commerce often involves high-volume and low-value cross-border transactions, its facilitation may require more prosaic endeavors, such as coordinating customs procedures, tax rates and invoicing standards.[4]

Moreover, the provision of a *legal* framework for e-commerce cannot, by itself, guarantee its success. The viability of e-commerce depends on the existence of a robust telecommunication infrastructure, user-friendly online payment systems and efficient distribution networks.[5] The creation of a conducive legal framework for cross-border e-commerce constitutes part

[1] e-ASEAN Framework Agreement (2000), art. 5; Association of Southeast Asian Nations Economic Community Blueprint 2025 (2015); ASEAN ICT Masterplan 2015.

[2] Reference Framework for Electronic Commerce Legal Infrastructure (2001) (Reference Framework).

[3] *See* United Nations Conference Trade and Development, *Review of e-Commerce Legislation Harmonization in the Association of Southeast Asian Nations* (2013) (UNCTAD Review), at 8.

[4] The ASEAN Single Window initiative expedites cargo clearance and promotes regional integration by enabling the electronic exchange of border documents, *see* http://asw.asean.org.

[5] *Maximizing the Development Gains from e-Commerce and the Digital Economy* (2017) TD/B/EDE/1/2.

of a larger picture, comprising multiple regional initiatives addressing a wide spectrum of issues. This chapter is confined to a discussion of the high-level challenges inherent in the regulatory and legislative initiatives aimed at promoting e-commerce in ASEAN.

17.1.1 Scope of Discussion: the Blueprints

To delineate the scope of the discussion, the AEC Blueprint 2015, adopted in 2008, is compared with the AEC Blueprint 2025, adopted in 2015. The AEC Blueprint 2015 aimed at implementing the AEC by 2015[6] and declared the need to establish a legal infrastructure for electronic commerce. The planned actions included:[7]

(1) the preparation of domestic legislation on e-commerce,
(2) the development, implementation and harmonization of the legal infrastructure for electronic contracting and dispute resolution and
(3) the mutual recognition of digital signatures.

The AEC Blueprint 2015 also mentioned the need to develop consumer protection measures.[8] It envisaged that between 2008 and 2009, member countries would enact their e-commerce laws, implement harmonized principles for electronic contracting and for online dispute resolution as well as adopt a regional framework for the mutual recognition of digital signatures.[9] Between 2010 and 2011, member countries were to update and/or amend relevant legislation in line with regional best practices in e-commerce, as well as adopt guidelines on other cyberlaw issues.[10] Between 2014 and 2015, a harmonized legal infrastructure for e-commerce was to be established. The AEC Blueprint 2015 focused on the transactional aspects of e-commerce and on the mutual recognition of digital signatures. Consumer and privacy protections were addressed only marginally. According to the 2013 UNCTAD report, the aims of the AEC Blueprint 2015 have been largely achieved, especially concerning the enactment of legal instruments focused on electronic contracting.[11]

6 ASEAN Economic Community Blueprint 2015 (AEC Blueprint 2015), at 2.
7 *Id.*, para. 59.
8 *Id.*, para. 42.
9 *Id.*, at 53.
10 *Id.*
11 UNCTAD, *Review of e-Commerce Legislation Harmonization in the Association of Southeast Asian Nations*, at 5.

The current AEC Blueprint 2025 emphasizes financial integration and the development of retail payment systems.[12] Moreover, it acknowledges that e-commerce requires innovative ways of protecting and *promoting* consumer interests. This in turn requires comprehensive national and regional consumer protection systems enforced through effective legislation, redress mechanisms and public awareness.[13] Unsurprisingly, the establishment of an ASEAN consumer protection framework constitutes a key strategic measure. The AEC Blueprint 2025 emphasizes the need to develop interoperable, mutually recognized, secure and user-friendly e-identification and authorization (electronic signature) schemes.[14] In comparison to its predecessor, it is more consumer-centered, recognizing that the promotion of e-commerce necessitates more than a broad declaration that contracts can be formed electronically.

17.1.2 Roadmap and Caveats

As ASEAN does not have a legal superstructure permitting an EU-style, top-down approach to create a unified regime for e-commerce, its facilitation largely depends on the adoption of common reference frameworks that can serve as legal "templates" guiding the enactment of domestic laws and regulations in the respective jurisdictions. The choice of an adequate reference framework, accompanied by its consistent implementation and enforcement, is therefore crucial. With this in mind, this chapter critically reviews existing initiatives aimed at facilitating e-commerce, with particular focus on the selection of appropriate models to guide regulatory and legislative efforts. It commences with a clarification of the term "e-commerce" and "e-commerce laws." Following the recommendations made in the Blueprints, it examines (1) the promotion of the MLEC[15] as a template guiding the enactment of e-commerce legislation; (2) the claim that e-commerce requires the use of electronic and/or digital signatures – a claim that logically precedes issues of mutual recognition; and (3) the challenges of creating innovative privacy and consumer protection regimes. This chapter addresses initiatives concerning substantive law. Before proceeding, it is pertinent to differentiate between:

[12] AEC Blueprint 2025, at 7–8.

[13] *Id.*, at 10–11.

[14] *Id.*, at 24.

[15] UNCITRAL Model Law on Electronic Commerce with Guide to Enactment (1996) with additional art. 5 *bis* as adopted in 1998.

- commercial dealings and dealings with public authorities, i.e., between e-commerce and an area popularly referred to as e-Government. This chapter addresses only *commercial* interactions. Many provisions in e-commerce instruments, such as the production of originals, the retention of records or the creation of electronic identities may, of course, be relevant for both areas.
- e-commerce and ICT infrastructure, i.e., between commercial interactions *enabled by* the Internet and the infrastructure *comprising* the Internet. The latter is a precondition of e-commerce but is usually regulated in different legal areas, such as telecommunications law. Legal instruments addressing the investment in and promotion of ICT infrastructure do not, theoretically, fall in the category of e-commerce.

17.1.3 Defining "e-Commerce"

The OECD defines e-commerce as "the sale or purchase of goods or services, conducted over computer networks by methods specifically designed for the purpose of receiving or placing orders."[16] Similarly, the AEC Blueprint 2015 regards e-commerce as the "online trade in goods."[17] Both definitions emphasize the *transactional* aspects of e-commerce and bring it within the scope of contract law, a system of rules governing commercial exchanges that underpins most modern market economies. The logical conclusion is that the legal area most relevant to e-commerce is contract law. Interestingly, the principles of contract law are formulated in broad terms and are, in most circumstances, sufficiently flexible to accommodate online transactions. It is thus questionable whether discrete laws facilitating e-commerce are indispensable – at least with regards to its transactional aspects. Initiatives aimed at facilitating e-commerce should therefore inquire whether the *contract laws* in the relevant jurisdictions require any amendment to enable online transaction. Three points arise:

17.1.3.1 Two Discrete Regimes?

The creation of a bespoke legal regime for e-commerce accompanied by a broad definition of the term may render it difficult to ensure a *separate* coexistence of traditional and e-commerce-specific rules.

16 *OECD Guide to Measuring the Information Society* (2011).

17 AEC Blueprint 2015, para. 59.

The dangers of a broad definition are illustrated by the Lao Law on Electronic Transactions, which describes e-commerce as "the purchase, sale and other exchange of goods or services between individuals, legal entities or organizations *using electronic means*."[18] This leaves open to interpretation whether a transaction concluded over the phone constitutes e-commerce. While phones constitute "electronic means," it is unlikely that the regulatory intent was to introduce special rules governing transactions concluded over the phone. Arguably, e-commerce is "just commerce" and such divisions are unwarranted. All regulatory initiatives should therefore be (or should *have been*) preceded by: (a) a precise delineation of the regulatory target (what is e-commerce? what are "electronic means?"); (b) an examination whether existing rules require supplementation; and (c) a debate whether the presence of two potentially overlapping regimes promotes legal certainty.

17.1.3.2 The Neglected Areas

While it is easy to proclaim the primacy of agreement in business-to-business (B2B) transactions, the same cannot be said about business-to-consumer (B2C) transactions, particularly in the online context. Unsurprisingly, recent ASEAN e-commerce initiatives emphasize the need for adequate privacy and consumer protection regimes.[19] While every ASEAN jurisdiction has laws governing commercial exchanges (i.e., contracts), only few jurisdictions have comprehensive laws in the areas of privacy and consumer protection.[20] It is therefore puzzling why, to date, ASEAN initiatives have focused on the *transactional* aspects of e-commerce, prioritizing the creation of legal instruments in an area that already has sufficient laws and is, historically, resistant to harmonization[21] – that of contract law. Meanwhile, areas with insufficient or no laws – those of consumer protection and privacy – have been neglected.

18 Lao Law on Electronic Transactions, No 20/NA, Dec. 7, 2012, art. 3 (emphasis mine).

19 AEC Blueprint 2025, p 24; e-ASEAN Framework Agreement, art. 5.

20 *Policy Digest 3: Consumer Protection Laws and Regulations for Online Purchasing, in* ASEAN Consumer Protection Digests and Case Studies: A Policy Guide (Volume I), 30–2 (2014).

21 Michael Joachim Bonell, *The CISG, European Contract Law and the Development of a World Contract Law*, 56 Am. J. Comp. L. 1 (2008).

17.1.3.3 The "Law" of e-Commerce?

The terms "e-commerce law(s)" or "e-commerce legislation" constitute potential sources of confusion. It is also debatable whether the very concept of e-commerce law is warranted. While it could be argued that e-commerce law is, at its core, confined to contract law, it must be acknowledged that the term is often used more broadly, in reference to legal areas that are unrelated to the transactional aspects of e-commerce, such as domain names, intermediary liability or unsolicited commercial communications.[22] Contrary to what is implied by various ASEAN initiatives, however, one can hardly imagine that a single instrument could address all legal issues *surrounding* online transactions. It seems more correct to speak of a "legal infrastructure" or "framework" for e-commerce because these terms expressly recognize the broad spectrum of challenges that must be addressed. Despite declarations concerning the need for legal *frameworks* for e-commerce, ASEAN initiatives have centered on the enactment of electronic transaction legislation.[23] The realization that such instruments *by themselves* can do little to facilitate e-commerce seems of relatively recent origin.

17.2 The UNCTRAL Instruments – the Transactional Aspects of e-Commerce

Two UNCITRAL instruments, the MLEC and, more recently, the Convention on Electronic Contracting,[24] are promoted as legal templates for jurisdictions with little or no e-commerce regulations. Focusing on contract law, these instruments prohibit any discrimination of contracts originating in electronic form and any disparity of treatment between electronic communications and paper documents.[25] These prohibitions are regarded as "enabling" e-commerce by removing doubts about the enforceability of contracts formed online. To date, multiple ASEAN jurisdictions have enacted domestic legislation based on either the MLEC or the Convention. For example, Malaysia has copied the

[22] The Directive 2000/31/EC of 8 Jun. 2000 on certain legal aspects of information society services, in particular electronic commerce, in the Internal Market, O.J. 2000 No. L 178, Jul. 17, 2000 (e-Commerce Directive), which combines multiple legal areas under the umbrella term "e-commerce."

[23] UNCTAD Review, at 5–10.

[24] Convention on the Use of Electronic Communications in International Contracting, Nov. 23, 2005, U.N. Doc. A/60/21.

[25] UNCITRAL Model Law on Electronic Commerce, art. 8, Explanatory Note, para. 129.

provisions of the MLEC almost verbatim.[26] Singapore has adopted the modified wording of the Convention and added sections concerning electronic signatures, certification authorities and intermediary liability.[27] The Philippines substantially follow the MLEC but supplement their Electronic Commerce Act with provisions governing specific aspects of online contracting, such as carriage of goods and transportation documents.[28] Indonesia's legislation addresses multiple issues related to the digital economy, such as domain names and dispute resolution.[29] The provisions addressing electronic transacting seem to follow the MLEC but, upon closer examination, reveal an idiosyncratic mixture of legal and technological misunderstandings.[30]

Lao models the relevant sections of its e-commerce instrument on the MLEC,[31] but also includes provisions on electronic signatures, dispute resolution and intermediary liability.[32] A similar approach is adopted in Myanmar,[33] Thailand,[34] Brunei Darussalam[35] and Vietnam,[36] all of which follow (to a greater or lesser extent) the wording of the MLEC and add provisions governing other aspects of online transacting.

It is worth observing that (a) the adoption of the MLEC in individual ASEAN jurisdictions is by no means uniform and that the individual "electronic transactions acts" often address legal issues that are unrelated to the transactional aspects of e-commerce; and (b) to date, only Singapore and the Philippines have acceded to the Convention. More importantly: the choice of the MLEC as the baseline for e-commerce legislation appears questionable.

[26] Malaysia, Electronic Commerce Act 2006.

[27] Singapore, Electronic Commerce Act 2010, secs. 18, 22 and 26.

[28] Republic Act No. 8792 of Philippines Electronic Commerce Act of 2000, for example sec. 16 (2) addresses electronic transactions made through banking networks, sec. 25 regulates actions relating to contracts of carriage of goods and sec. 26 deals with transportation documents.

[29] Law of The Republic of Indonesia Number 11 of 2008 Concerning Electronic Information and Transactions, arts. 23–6.

[30] *See* arts. 17–22, particularly arts. 21 and 22 seem to conflate problems of message integrity and problems of automation.

[31] Law on Electronic Transactions, No 20/NA, Dec. 7, 2012, arts. 8–12.

[32] Law on Electronic Transactions, No 20/NA, Dec. 7, 2012, arts. 40–5.

[33] The Electronic Transactions Law (The State Peace and Development Council Law No. 5/2004), arts. 21–9.

[34] Electronic Transactions Act B.E. 2544 (2001).

[35] Electronic Transactions Act 2008, arts. 11–5.

[36] Law on E-Transactions 51/2001/QH10 of 25/12/2001 of the 10 Legislature, Session No. 10.

17.2.1 An Outdated Model?

The MLEC may be outdated and simply inadequate, creating a situation where the laws modeled after its provisions may be unable to accommodate – not to mention facilitate – e-commerce transactions. The MLEC dates back to 1996, a time when e-commerce was in its infancy. The instrument itself constitutes an adaptation of UNCITRAL's prior work relating to Electronic Data Interchange (EDI),[37] which refers to the automated exchange of structured data on the basis of *prior agreement* between sophisticated commercial entities communicating over closed, proprietary networks.[38] Principles deriving from such relationships can hardly serve as a template for legal instruments facilitating transactions in open, public networks between businesses and consumers, who have no prior dealings with each other. To aggravate matters, the drafters of the MLEC possessed a limited understanding of the technologies involved.[39] Many provisions prove, upon closer scrutiny, better suited to email, telex or static PDF files than to interactive websites or apps – not to mention such modern but prevalent online phenomena as transactions in information or the "sharing economy." Given that the MLEC (and hence the Convention) relies on an outdated understanding of e-commerce and given that online commercial practices have continued to evolve beyond EDI and email, ASEAN's promotion of these instruments seems unfortunate.

17.2.2 Legal Obstacles to Electronic Contracting?

The MLEC governs all electronic communications pertaining to the formation or performance of a contract.[40] Contracts have, however, never been regulated because of the manner they are formed. Contract law is generally indifferent to how intention is communicated. The UNICTRAL instruments imply, however, that many legal requirements prescribe the use of traditional paper documentation and thus

[37] MLEC Guide to Enactment, at 1.

[38] The Electronic Messaging Services Task Force, *The Commercial Use of Electronic Data Interchange – A Report and Model Trading Partner Agreement*, 45 Bus. L. 1645 (1990).

[39] Amelia Boss, *The Evolution of Commercial Law Norms: Lessons to Be Learned from Electronic Commerce*, 34 Brooklyn J. Int'l L. 673, 687 (2009).

[40] *See* Sieg Eiselen, *The Interaction between the Electronic Communications Convention and the United Nations Convention on the International Sale of Goods, in* The United Nations Convention on the Use of Electronic Communications in International Contracts (Amelia H. Boss & Wolfgang Killian, eds., 2008), at 333–52

impede the adoption of e-commerce.[41] Interestingly, such "legal requirements" are nonexistent in contract law. Formalities, such as writing or signatures, are often required by statute[42] or by the contracting parties themselves. From the perspective of contract law – and the MLEC and the Convention purport to facilitate electronic *contracting* – the electronic form does not pose an obstacle to valid on-line transactions because contractual intention can be manifested in any manner,[43] including tweets or websites. Although some statutes or regulatory instruments may not be amenable to broad interpretations to accommodate dematerialized communications, and hence require amendment or even replacement, it is necessary to distinguish between the need to update legislation from the need to update contract law. It is also necessary to differentiate between questions of substantive law and questions of evidence. Writing and signatures are, in most jurisdictions, not prerequisites of enforceability. They may, however, significantly facilitate proof of a transaction.

17.2.3 A Substantive Interference?

As virtually all mass-market consumer transactions are devoid of any formalities, it is doubtful whether e-commerce transactions require a "removal of obstacles." If the UNCITRAL instruments confined themselves to confirming the enforceability of online contracts, they could be regarded as an attempt to alleviate any remaining concerns in this area. Unfortunately, both instruments go further and introduce *substantive* provisions regarding online contracting. Consequently, they create a discrete regime for e-commerce transactions that may differ from and interfere with the principles of contract law governing traditional transactions. For example, MLEC Article 10 determines when and where electronic communications are deemed to have been dispatched or received, thereby directly affecting the determination of the time of contract formation. Its wording is, however, not only technically inconsistent (due to UNCITRAL's misunderstanding of the Internet infrastructure) but also more suitable to email than to web-based transactions, which dominate e-commerce. MLEC Article 14 contains complex provisions governing acknowledgments of receipt that requires multiple exchanges of messages before a contract is deemed concluded.

41 MLEC Explanatory Note, para. 50.

42 *See e.g.*, Civil Law Act (Cap. 43) (Rev. ed. 1985) (Sing.).

43 Skeptical readers are invited to recall the last time they signed a document when making a purchase on amazon.com.

This mechanism introduces legal uncertainty as to contractual communications, such as offers or acceptances, that have been received but remain unacknowledged. ASEAN jurisdictions that have adopted those provisions[44] will, inevitably, face difficulties in establishing the precise moment of contract formation.

Traditionally, the legal principles governing the time of formation are formulated in broad terms that are amenable to case-specific interpretations. The MLEC, however, imposes an inflexible regime that cannot accommodate constant technological change. For example, in Singapore, which is a common law jurisdiction, a contract is concluded when acceptance is *communicated* to the offeror or when the parties *reach* agreement.[45] In Thailand, which is a civil law jurisdiction, "a contract between persons at a distance comes into existence at the time when the notice of acceptance *reaches* the offeror."[46] The terms "communicate" and "reach" allow for many, technology-specific interpretations. The MLEC provisions, however, associate the formation of a contract with, depending on the circumstances, electronic messages entering (a) "an information system outside of the control of the originator," (b) a "designated information system" or electronic messages being retrieved by the addressee. Given the broad definition of "information system" and the problems surrounding the concept of "designation," the said provisions are difficult to apply in practice as they replace a broad, flexible principle with one that is rigid and technically incorrect.[47] The preparatory works reveal that UNCITRAL did not examine whether the substantive provisions introduced by the MLEC were compatible with existing principles or whether such principles could accommodate electronic transactions without legislative assistance. In sum, the introduction of substantive provisions in the MLEC creates a parallel, incompatible and possibly redundant regime for online contracts.

[44] *See e.g.*, Malaysia, Electronic Commerce Act 2006, art. 24; Philippines sec. 20; Indonesia art. 20; Thailand Electronic Transactions Act B.E. 2544 (2001) sec. 19.

[45] *See generally*, Andrew Phang & Boon Leong ed., The Law of Contract in Singapore (2012), Ch. 3.

[46] Thai Civil and Commercial Code, sec. 361.

[47] *See* Eliza Mik, *Certainty at Last? A "New" Framework for Electronic Contracting in Singapore*, 8 J. Int'l Comm. L. & Tech. 160 (2013).

17.3 Creating Trust: Digital and Electronic Signatures

ASEAN initiatives emphasize the need to enact laws regulating (and promoting the adoption of) electronic and digital signatures. Purportedly, the success of e-commerce hinges on the widespread adoption and cross-border recognition of electronic and/or digital signatures. The latter are commonly promoted as a method of confirming the identity (i.e., authenticating) of the other party and as a functional equivalent of traditional signatures. Unnecessary confusion, however, derives from an inconsistent use of terminology. "Electronic" signatures relate to any electronic representations of a name, such as those found on the bottom of emails, whereas "digital" signatures have a narrow technical definition and rely on asymmetric cryptosystems.[48] ASEAN initiatives refer to both terms interchangeably, creating a situation where regulatory proposals and existing legal instruments[49] require meticulous analysis to establish the underlying intent. To illustrate: the AEC Blueprint 2025 directs ASEAN members to establish "inter-operable, mutually recognized, secure, reliable and user-friendly e-identification and authorization (electronic signature) schemes."[50] Such schemes are, however, difficult to envisage in relation to *electronic* signatures, which are only words on the screen and cannot be evaluated in terms of reliability or security. It is also difficult to imagine how names could be mutually recognized or interoperable.

Arguably, the AEC Blueprint 2025 tried to remain technologically neutral while, at the same time, assuming that only digital signatures can facilitate e-commerce. Only the latter raise issues of mutual recognition in the context of cross-border transactions (see below). This conclusion can also be reached in light of other ASEAN proposals.[51] To date, many ASEAN jurisdictions have enacted legislation addressing digital and electronic signatures, either as stand-alone instruments[52] or as part of their electronic transaction legislation.[53] The focus on signatures seems, however, misguided.

[48] Bruce Schneier, Applied Cryptography 34 (1996).

[49] *See e.g.*, the Vietnamese Law on E-Transactions (51/2005/QH11); Indonesian Law Concerning Electronic Information and Transactions, arts. 11–16.

[50] AEC Blueprint 2025, at 24.

[51] *See e.g.*, Reference Framework, paras. 14 and 15.

[52] *See e.g.*, Malaysia, Digital Signature Act 1997.

[53] *See e.g.*, Singapore Electronic Transactions Act (2010).

17.3.1 Some Common Misunderstandings

ASEAN initiatives assume that e-commerce requires the ability to authenticate the other party. It is overlooked, however, that in traditional transactions parties rarely have an assurance that the other party is who he claims to be. The ability to authenticate is thus not an inherent characteristic of traditional transactions that must be preserved or recreated online. It is always the parties themselves who decide how much risk they are willing to assume. How the parties authenticate each other largely depends on the subject matter and value of the transaction. Authentication seems more important in cross-border transactions, particularly in case of delayed payment or when there is a risk of latent defects in the contractual subject matter. This does not mean, however, that the law should prescribe a specific authentication technology.[54] Moreover, the assumption that traditional signatures are indispensable for authentication is incorrect. Signatures are generally not a method of authentication because they need not be legible or even biometrically related to the signatory. People are not identified by their signatures, but by their government-issued identification cards or passports. Lastly, signatures are rarely a prerequisite of enforceability because contract law, as indicated, contains virtually no formal requirements.

17.3.2 Problems of Authentication and the Mutual Recognition of Signatures

ASEAN initiatives incorrectly assume that digital (or electronic) signatures are technically capable of authenticating the other contracting party. An explanation is necessary. Digital signatures rely on the mathematical correspondence between the private and the public key in asymmetric cryptosystems. For digital signatures to work, the public key must be accessible to everyone, the private key – exclusively to its authorized user. Multiple problems arise.

17.3.2.1 Establishing a Legal and Technical Infrastructure

A trusted third party must guarantee that a given key pair belongs to a specific person. Consequently, digital signatures require a Certification Authority (CA), which manages the issuance of Digital Certificates

[54] This was the case with Directive 2000/46/EC on the taking up, pursuit of and prudential supervision of the business of electronic money institutions, which was repealed after eight years as it stifled the development of e-money in the European Union.

(DCs).[55] A DC contains information about the person it was issued to (subscriber) and the public key. When issuing a DC, the CA must confirm the subscriber's identity.[56] If a CA does not correctly authenticate the potential subscriber, the digital signature is worthless because the subscriber can obtain the DC under a fictional name. It is, however, difficult to ensure that CAs in different jurisdictions are equally diligent in this process, particularly in the absence of common standards and procedures. At present, each ASEAN jurisdiction has a different legal regime governing the establishment of CAs and the manner they issue DCs.[57] For example, in Lao or Myanmar CAs are registered entities,[58] while in Singapore[59] their operation is largely unregulated. This raises problems when it comes to the mutual recognition of digital signatures and cross-certification of CAs. For example, the Vietnamese Law on Electronic Transactions states that the government recognizes the validity of foreign e-signatures if they are equally reliable as those issued in accordance with Vietnamese laws.[60] Consequently, parties from different ASEAN jurisdictions would have to ensure that their digital signatures comply with their local laws and with the laws of the jurisdiction of their counterparty.

Even if both parties adopted the highest common technological denominator, there would be no guarantee that their digital signatures will be recognized in the counterparty's jurisdiction. The administrative and technical overhead accompanying cross-border transactions involving digital signatures issued in accordance with different procedures seems impossible to bear – for both consumers and online businesses. The difficulties of cross-border certification, and hence the mutual recognition of digital signatures, are, however, generally underestimated. It is overlooked that such mutual recognition requires an intricate regulatory

[55] Neil Ferguson & Bruce Schneier, Practical Cryptography 29 (2003).

[56] Dorothy Anderson, *What Trust is in These Times? Examining the Foundation of On-line Trust*, 54 Emory L. J. 1441 (2005).

[57] *C.f. see e.g.*, Singapore, which does not prescribe a licensing regime for CAs with Laos, which requires that CAs be authorized and registered with the relevant ministry, *see* Lao Law on Electronic Transactions, No. 20/NA, Dec. 7, 2012, 26–9; *see also* Reference Framework, paras. 28–31, 54–7.

[58] Lao 28, Myanmar The Electronic Transactions Law.
(The State Peace and Development Council Law No. 5/2004) at 12–8.

[59] Singapore Electronic Transactions Act 2010.

[60] Vietnam, Law on E-Transactions 51/2001/QH10 of 25/12/2001 of the 10 Legislature, Session No. 10; art. 27.

framework encompassing cooperating CAs and a comprehensive regional agreement addressing the technical standards governing CAs.

17.3.2.2 The "Private Key" Problem

Digital signatures only guarantee that a message was "signed" with a specific private key. They cannot ensure that the key was used by the subscriber. The problem lies in securing the private key. Given the frequency of network and device compromises, there is a high risk of private keys being used by unauthorized persons. Consequently, any legal framework accompanying digital signatures must allocate liability for compromised private keys.[61] For the subscriber, the problem lies in safeguarding the private key and avoiding liability for its unauthorized use. For the party relying on a digital signature, the problem is that even a detailed examination of a DC (i.e., confirmation that the public key corresponds to the private key used in creating the digital signature) cannot reveal who used the private key.

For example, the Vietnamese Law on Electronic Transactions obliges the subscriber, among others, to "have means to avoid the unauthorized use" of his private key and to ensure the integrity of the information of a DC.[62] The first requirement is nearly impossible to achieve from a technical standpoint, as it requires the subscriber to store the private key off-line, use sophisticated biometric access controls and have in-depth expertise of network security. The fulfillment of the second obligation largely depends on the reliability and responsiveness of the CA. The latter controls the DC and introduces updates to its contents, such as suspensions or revocations. The same instrument obliges the party relying on the "e-signature" to "verify its reliability" as well as the validity of the DC.[63] Again, the relying party is practically unable to verify either – unless he is to examine the technology underlying the specific digital signature and the manner it was deployed, as well as the manner CAs issue DCs. Relying parties always face the risk of subscribers claiming that their private key was used without authorization. The presence of

[61] Jane Kaufman Winn, *The Hedgehog and the Fox: Distinguishing Public and Private Sector Approaches to Managing Risk for Internet Transactions*, 51 Admin. L. Rev. 955 (1999); *see also* Digital Signature Act 1997 (Malaysia) and ETA Singapore 2010, neither of which addresses liability allocation comprehensively.

[62] Vietnam Law on E-Transactions, art. 25; *c.f.* sec. 43 of the Malaysian Digital Signature Act 1997, which provides that "the subscriber named in the certificate assumes a duty to exercise reasonable care to retain control of the private key and prevent its disclosure to any person not authorized to create the subscriber's digital signature."

[63] Vietnam Law on E-Transactions, art. 26.

a CA changes nothing in this regard because the CA cannot control the security of the private key. It can only confirm that the DC (and the key pair) was issued in accordance with the relevant regulations and that it contains accurate information concerning the subscriber.[64] In practice, the use of digital signatures requires technological sophistication, specifically with regards to the ability to safeguard the PINs or passwords protecting the private keys.[65] Such sophistication cannot, however, be expected in jurisdictions where consumers lack basic experience with credit cards and online payments.

17.3.2.3 Lessons from Other Jurisdictions

ASEAN's continued promotion of digital signature laws is surprising given that, to date, such laws have proven unsuccessful. The first digital signature law, the Utah Digital Signature Act, was repealed in 2007.[66] Similarly, the EU Digital Signatures Directive,[67] which promoted digital signatures in a commercial context, has been replaced with a Regulation of a narrower scope that focuses on the cross-recognition and interoperability of national electronic identification schemes, predominantly in the context of public services.[68] The European Commission found that private parties had not been using digital signatures in e-commerce transactions and that simpler electronic signature applications had become available.[69] There is no single example of digital signatures contributing to the success of e-commerce.[70] Even in those ASEAN jurisdictions that have market economies, modern internet infrastructures and digital signature laws (Malaysia and Singapore), their use is virtually nonexistent.

[64] This is exemplified by secs. 34 and 36 of the Malaysian Digital Signature Act 1997.

[65] An effective digital signature scheme would require that each use of the private key relied on biometric access controls.

[66] Utah Code. Ann. §§ 46-3-101 (1999); the bill repealing the Utah Digital Signature Act was signed into law in 2006. S.B. 20, 2006 Leg., Gen. Sess. (Utah 2006).

[67] Directive 1999/93/EC on a Community framework for electronic signatures O.J. 2000, No. L013, Jan. 19, 2000.

[68] Regulation No 910/2014 on electronic identification and trust services for electronic transactions in the internal market and repealing Directive 1999/93/EC.

[69] *See* Report on the Operation of Directive 1999/93/EC on a Community Framework for Electronic Signatures, 5.2, COM (2006) 120 final.

[70] Aside from being part of the https protocol, which creates secure connections between web servers and clients.

In practice, problems of authentication and liability allocation are solved in a less technology-intensive manner. Most e-commerce vendors, such as Amazon or Lazada, require the establishment of an account, which involves the consumer agreeing to standard terms and, quite often, the provision of payment information. The terms usually state that customers must protect their account information (e.g., password) and are liable for any activity originating therefrom. Individual purchases usually involve authentication mechanisms by the consumer's bank, which issued the credit card.[71] The liability for unauthorized transactions is apportioned by contract and partially absorbed by the financial institutions providing the payment infrastructure. Digital signatures are not an indispensable component of a legal framework facilitating e-commerce. Their use may be confined to government-sanctioned authentication schemes enabling online interactions with public authorities, such as the electronic filing of tax returns.

It is thus unfortunate that many legal instruments designed to enable e-commerce are dominated by provisions governing the establishment of certification authorities.[72] ASEAN jurisdictions should de-emphasize the importance of digital signatures laws. The focus should instead be placed on the development of secure online payment mechanisms. In mass-market consumer transactions, identity seems less important than the ability to pay. The accompanying risks are usually spread among the financial intermediaries enabling the transaction.[73] The facilitation of e-commerce requires the introduction of regulations obliging banks and credit card companies to absorb the cost of unauthorized online transactions – not the use of digital signatures.

17.4 Other Areas

The facilitation of e-commerce is increasingly associated with the establishment of consumer and privacy protection regimes.[74] In many ASEAN jurisdictions, these areas are, however, underdeveloped. Some general

[71] An example of such scheme is Verified by Visa.

[72] *See e.g.*, the Myanmar Electronic Transactions Law (The State Peace and Development Council Law No. 5/2004) secs. 12–18.

[73] *See e.g.*, in the United States, the Federal Reserve Board promulgated Regulation E (12 C.F.R. Part 205) to implement the EFTA pursuant to authority granted under 15 U.S.C. § 1693b. 15 U.S.C. § 1601 (1982); in the European Union the Payment Services Directive 2 (2015/2366) governs unauthorized credit card transactions, including mobile and internet payments.

[74] AEC Blueprint 2025, at 13.

observations pertaining to both privacy and consumer protection are necessary. Optimally, all ASEAN jurisdictions should adhere to similar principles: uniform frameworks in the areas of privacy and consumer protection would alleviate many concerns that consumers have in relation to cross-border transactions. The selection of an adequate reference model becomes all the more pertinent. Moreover, both consumer and privacy protections require a careful balancing exercise: the interests of online consumers must be weighed against the interests of online businesses, especially SMEs, which may be unable to bear a heavy burden of regulatory compliance. The facilitation of e-commerce is, after all, associated not only with empowering consumers but also with empowering online vendors.

17.4.1 Consumer Protection

Although ASEAN has undertaken some consumer protection initiatives,[75] many ASEAN jurisdictions have only rudimentary laws in this area.[76] The problem does not lie in the lack of e-commerce-specific instruments, but in the lack of basic consumer protections in general, such as those concerning product safety or the prohibition of unfair commercial practices. For example, while Singapore and Malaysia have relatively comprehensive protective regimes,[77] Laos, Cambodia and Myanmar are only beginning to address basic consumer issues.[78] In many jurisdictions, the introduction of consumer protections in e-commerce must be preceded by the creation of fundamental protections in traditional transactions. Although ASEAN provides few guidelines in this area, there are multiple international models that provide points of reference.[79] This discussion addresses only consumer

[75] *See* e.g., ASEAN Strategic Action Plan for Consumer Protection (ASCAP) was developed to elaborate on the consumer protection measures under the AEC Blueprint 2025.

[76] *Policy Digest 3: Consumer Protection Laws and Regulations for Online Purchasing, in* ASEAN Consumer Protection Digests and Case Studies: A Policy Guide (Volume I) 30–2 (2014); *see also*: D. K. Round & S. Zeljka, *Globalisation and Consumer Protection in East Asia: Is It a Zero-Sum Game?*, 12 Asian-Pacific Economic Literature 39 (2003).

[77] Singapore, Consumer Protection (Fair Trading) Act 2004; Malaysia, Consumer Protection Act (CPA) 1999.

[78] *See* country reports in ASEAN Australia Development Cooperation Program Phase II (AADCP II), *Roadmapping Capacity Building in Consumer Protection in ASEAN* (2011).

[79] *See e.g.*, OECD Guidelines on Consumer Protection in the Context of Electronic Commerce (2000); United Nations Guidelines for Consumer Protection (2016) UNCTAD/DITC/CPLP/MISC/2016/1.

protection in e-commerce, recognizing the idiosyncrasies of new transacting environment. Arguably, there is a greater need for protection in e-commerce than in traditional transactions because online fraud and deception assume novel forms. Additional problems concern the information density and cognitive challenges inherent in the online environment. To date, only Malaysia boasts regulations specifically tailored to online transactions.[80]

17.4.1.1 Providing Information

Consumer protection is usually associated with the provision of information, the assumption being that informed consumers can protect their interests and make better decisions. Regulatory efforts must, however, acknowledge that instruments based exclusively on the provision of information have had limited success[81] and that effective consumer protection must, more generally, enable consumers to make choices and protect them from misleading or deceptive practices. Consequently, e-commerce-specific instruments should ensure that information is provided in a manner allowing for the special characteristics of the online environment.[82] This has been recognized by the US Federal Trade Commission, which addressed the difficulties of making effective online disclosures and emphasized the challenges of hypertext and information density.[83] The problem is particularly pertinent in ASEAN, where consumers access the Internet predominantly via their mobile phones, i.e., through smaller screens. The FTC explained that, among others, a disclosure is effective only if presented in a manner that makes it "clear and conspicuous." It also acknowledged that many consumers might find it difficult to "discover" information if the latter is viewable only upon the activation of hyperlinks or requires additional scrolling. Arguably, consumer protection instruments must also allow for the fact that many ASEAN consumers are particularly vulnerable due to their limited familiarity with the Internet[84] and novel forms of misconduct, such as phishing or spamming.[85] ASEAN initiatives should thus

[80] Malaysia, Consumer Protection Act 1999, Consumer Protection (Electronic Trade Transactions) Regulations 2012.

[81] Stephen Bainbridge, *Mandatory Disclosure: A Behavioral Analysis*, 68 Univ. Cin. L. Rev. 1023 (2000).

[82] United Nations Guidelines for Consumer Protection (2016), at 15, 20.

[83] Federal Trade Commission, *Dot.com Disclosures: How to Make Effective Disclosures in Digital Advertising* (2013).

[84] United Nations Guidelines for Consumer Protection (2016), at 7.

[85] Patrick Quirk and John A. Rothchild, *Consumer Protection and the Internet*, *in* Handbook of Research on International Consumer Law 333, 335 (Geraint Howells et al. ed., 2011).

acknowledge that the mere provision of information may be insufficient. More proactive educational efforts may be necessary.

In selecting a regulatory model for ASEAN initiatives for e-commerce-specific consumer protection, a useful legal framework can be found in the European Union. It combines information requirements with certain substantive rights on the side of online consumers and, most importantly, contains provisions capable of accommodating technological change. For example, EU consumers must be provided with detailed information about the product or service and be able to easily contact the trader.[86] Online traders must explain the technical steps required to conclude the contract, provide technical means for identifying and correcting input errors and immediate acknowledgments of the receipt of online orders.[87] These protections seem particularly important for less experienced consumers. The terms governing a particular transaction must be accessible, capable of storage and reproduction[88] and written in understandable language.[89] EU consumers are also protected from unfair standard contract terms[90] as well as false and misleading advertising.[91] In addition, they have the right to withdraw from online contracts without penalty and without providing any reason.[92]

The EU model can be regarded as the high benchmark of consumer protection that, given its high cost of compliance, may be difficult to follow in less developed ASEAN jurisdictions. The right of withdrawal alone would encounter significant obstacles as it involves cross-border returns of goods. While it is unrealistic to copy the EU model, some of its aspects should be borne in mind – particularly with regards to the requirements to explain the transacting sequence or to provide error-correcting screens. Another EU instrument, the Directive on Unfair Commercial Practices (UCPD), seeks to enable consumers to make meaningful choices.[93] To this end, it prohibits certain practices without any qualifications. For example,

[86] Directive 2011/83/EU of Oct. 25, 2011 on consumer rights, O.J. 2011, No. L 304/64, Nov. 22, 2011, arts. 5, 6, 7, 8.

[87] E-Commerce Directive, arts. 5, 10 and 11.

[88] *Id.*, art. 10.

[89] Directive 93/13/EEC of Apr. 5, 1993 on unfair terms in consumer contracts, O.J. 1993 No. L 95/29, Apr. 21, 1993; art. 5.

[90] *Id.*, art. 3.

[91] Directive 2006/114/EC of Dec. 16, 2006 concerning misleading and comparative advertising, O.J. 2006 No. L 376/21, Dec. 27, 2006; art. 5.

[92] Directive 2011/83/EU of Oct. 25, 2011 on consumer rights.

[93] Directive 2005/29/EC of May 11, 2005 concerning unfair business-to-consumer commercial practices in the internal market, O.J. 2005, No. L149/22, Jun. 11, 2005 (UCPD).

Article 5 contains a general prohibition of unfair commercial practices, practices that are contrary to the requirements of professional diligence and materially distort or are likely to materially distort the economic behavior of the average consumer.[94] A material distortion occurs when a practice impairs the consumer's ability to make an informed decision, "causing the consumer to take a transactional decision that he would not have taken otherwise."[95] The generality of Article 5 aims to ensure that the directive is "future proof." The UCPD also prohibits the provision of false information or correct information presented in a manner that deceives or is likely to deceive.[96] The said directive curbs abusive marketing and sales practices associated with profiling and personalization techniques.

17.4.1.2 Addressing Disputes and Complaints

A discrete set of challenges concerns the cross-border character of e-commerce. The latter should not facilitate fraud (given the ease of establishing a website as compared to a physical outlet) or otherwise enable vendors to avoid liability due to the fact that consumers from different jurisdictions are less likely to sue. At a minimum, online vendors must obey the laws of the jurisdictions where they offer their goods and services. It is also paramount to guarantee that consumers can seek redress in their home jurisdiction and rely on effective dispute resolution mechanisms. Apart from ensuring that consumers cannot be contractually bound to arbitrate or to sue in remote forums, as is the case in the United States,[97] it becomes necessary to create cheap and efficient complaints-handling mechanisms and/or online dispute resolution frameworks.[98] Many difficulties of cross-border enforcement could, arguably, be alleviated by the introduction of online dispute resolution mechanisms, which provide an accessible and low-cost method of obtaining redress.[99] ASEAN could benefit from instruments and proposals in other jurisdictions.[100] In addition to establishing active consumer

[94] UCPD, arts. 5, 8, 9.

[95] UCPD, art. 2 (e).

[96] UCPD, art. 6 and 7.

[97] *See* the Federal Arbitration Act 9 U.S.C. § 2; AT&T Mobility LLC v. Concepcion 131 S. Ct. 1740 (2011).

[98] United Nations Guidelines for Consumer Protection (2016), at 9.

[99] Amy J. Schmitz, *Building Trust in eCommerce through Online Dispute resolution*, *in* Research Handbook on Electronic Commerce Law (John A. Rothchild ed., 2016).

[100] *See e.g.*, Directive 2013/11/EU on Alternative Dispute Resolution for Consumer Disputes, 2013 OJ (L 165) 63; or the UNCITRAL Technical Notes on Online Dispute Resolution (2017).

protection agencies and promoting cooperation between them, ASEAN members should join the International Consumer Protection and Enforcement Network (ICPEN),[101] which is a platform for sharing consumer protection issues, including best practices and legislative reforms. Notably, ICPEN encompasses an online initiative, econsumer.gov, aimed at educating consumers about scams and online abuses.[102] To date, only Vietnam and the Philippines have joined this organization. As the creation of consumer protection regimes remains low on the agenda,[103] "interim" consumer protections could be achieved by means of educational efforts.

17.4.2 Privacy

Space constraints prevent a comparative review of ASEAN privacy initiatives. The present section addresses only those aspects of privacy that are directly relevant to e-commerce. To date, ASEAN has not proposed a single, uniform regime that could be used as a template by those jurisdictions that lack regulations in this area. There are also no international privacy agreements in Asia, which could impose obligations concerning the contents of privacy laws.[104] Consequently, the privacy frameworks (if any) in the respective ASEAN jurisdictions have been influenced by various instruments, such as the OECD Privacy Guidelines and the European Union Data Protection Directive. They vary in scope, strength of enforcement and general recognition of the need to protect consumers online. At present, Cambodia, Myanmar, Brunei and Laos have virtually no legal instruments in this area.[105] Only the Philippines has a comprehensive privacy law that covers both the public and private sectors,[106] while Malaysia and Singapore have narrowly formulated laws covering most of their private sector.[107] Vietnam and Indonesia have

[101] *See* International Consumer Protection and Enforcement Network, www.icpen.org (last visited Mar. 16, 2018).

[102] *See* International Consumer Protection and Enforcement Network, *Staying Safe Online*, www.icpen.org/staying-safe-online (last visited Mar. 16, 2018).

[103] *See* ASEAN, *Strategic Action Plan for Consumer Protection (ASAPCP) 2016–2025: Meeting the Challenges of a People-Centered ASEAN beyond 2015*, which sets the timeline for modernizing consumer protection legislation for 2020–25, Appendix.

[104] Graham Greenleaf, Asian Data Privacy Laws 478 (2014).

[105] *See generally*, *id.*

[106] The Philippines Data Privacy Act 2012.

[107] Malaysia, Personal Data Protection Act 2010; Singapore, Personal Data Protection Act 2010.

sectoral laws governing only their e-commerce and consumer sectors.[108] Thailand's limited privacy protections apply only to the public sector.

17.4.2.1 Privacy Risks in e-Commerce

The need for e-commerce-specific privacy protections must be seen against a broader background. The digital economy predominantly relies on advertising and abounds in what are best described as barter transactions involving the exchange of personal information for the right to access to online resources.[109] Many e-commerce businesses are built exclusively around the collection and commercial utilization of the information generated by consumers during their online activities. The ability to process personal information by means of new technologies, such as predictive analytics, gives online businesses unprecedented transactional advantages, including the ability to manipulate consumer behavior. An example is personalization, the user-specific display of online content, where personal information is used to determine the maximum price that can be charged.[110] Modern privacy regulations must acknowledge the commercial value of personal information as well as the risks arising from its collection, processing and subsequent utilization. The principles relevant in the e-commerce context concern restrictions on the manner online businesses are allowed to collect, process and utilize personal information, including the extent to which they are permitted to share such information with third parties, including entities located in foreign jurisdictions. All privacy instruments are characterized by a tension between the interests of the businesses that collect and utilize personal information for such purposes as direct marketing or profiling and the interests of online consumers (or data subjects) whose personal information may be used to their disadvantage.

Logically, it is more beneficial for e-commerce businesses (but less beneficial for consumers) to face fewer (if any) limitations on what

[108] Vietnam, Law on E-Transactions of 2005, Law on Information Technology 2006 (No. 67/2006/QH11); Indonesia, Regulation of the Government of the Republic of Indonesia Number 82 of 2012 Concerning Electronic System and Transaction Operation, unofficial government English translation, implementing the Information and Electronic Transactions Law (No. 11 of 2008).

[109] J. Whittington & Ch. J. Hoofnagle, *Unpacking Privacy's Price*, 90 NC. L. Rev. 1328, 1331 (2012).

[110] Tal Z. Zarsky, *"Mine your own Business!" Making the Case for the Implications of the Data Mining of Personal Information in the Forum of Public Opinion*, 2 Yale J. L. & Tech. 55, 19–22 (2002–2003).

information they are permitted to collect, how they are obliged to collect it and how they allowed to utilize it. Examples are the obligations to inform data subjects of the purpose of collection and the need to adhere to such purpose in the subsequent utilization of the personal information. The more specific the stated purpose and the more restrictions on using the information for secondary purposes, the better for the data subject. The strength of privacy protections in e-commerce can be measured by the difficulty of obtaining consent to the collection and utilization of personal information, by the level of disclosure concerning the primary purpose of collection and the degree of leniency granted to businesses in utilizing the information for secondary purposes.

17.4.2.2 Consent and Notice (Disclosure)

Most privacy regulations permit the collection, processing and use of personal information on condition that online consumers are informed about and consent to such practices.[111] A popular manifestation of this approach takes the form of privacy policies, which are placed in the lower sections of most websites. Instruments relying on notice assume that given the opportunity to inform themselves, consumers will give their consent with the full realization of its implications. Such an assumption is incorrect. Privacy protections based on notice and consent have proven generally ineffective.[112] Moreover, as consent need not be informed or express, it can be implied from almost any behavior, such as the continued use of a website. For example, the Singapore Personal Data Protection Act 2012 (PDPA) permits consent to be deemed.[113] Instruments that do not require explicit consent or do not prescribe the manner of its expression[114] produce the same outcome. The resulting ease of obtaining consent renders many privacy protections ineffective, if not illusory. When creating e-commerce-specific privacy protections, it is thus necessary to appreciate the limited effectiveness of instruments based on notice and consent.

[111] *See e.g.*, Singapore, PDPA 2012 sec. 13; Philippines, Data Privacy Act 2012, sec. 12; PDPA (Malaysia), sec. 6; Vietnam, Law on E-Transactions of 2005, art. 46.

[112] Fred H. Cate, *The Failure of Fair Information Practice Principles, in* Consumer Protection in the Age of the Information Economy 341, 342 (Jane Kaufman Winn ed., 2006).

[113] *See* PDPA, sec. 15.

[114] *See e.g.*, the Vietnam Law on E-Transactions of 2005, art. 46(2) and the Philippines Data Privacy Act sec. 12.

It is also necessary to acknowledge the significant differences between the EU, the US and the OECD approaches. The OECD and United States prioritize the demands of the modern marketplace. For example, the OECD Guidelines,[115] which served as a template for privacy instruments in multiple Asian jurisdictions[116] and also underlie the APEC Privacy Framework,[117] seem to limit the collection and uses of personal information but allow any such limitations to be overridden by notional notice and consent requirements. Interestingly, the recently updated OECD Privacy Framework recognizes the risks inherent in personalization techniques,[118] and the fact that consumers find it increasingly difficult to make informed choices related to their personal information. Nonetheless, it largely retains the principle that if online consumers are notified of the fact and purpose of collecting their personal information, online businesses can engage in the said activities without further restrictions.[119] Similarly, the US approach "substitutes" substantive limitations on the collection and processing of personal information with notice and consent requirements.[120]

Despite different regulatory techniques, most ASEAN instruments permit the collection, processing and commercial utilization of personal information for virtually any purpose (including profiling) on condition that customers receive certain information and provide their implied consent. It could be argued that this approach relies on a universally accepted model. It must, however, be acknowledged that the technological developments in the area of automated data processing and the accompanying ability to use the personal information to the disadvantage of consumers require a re-evaluation of all approaches that implicitly facilitate such processing. Protections relying on consent and disclosure might have been sufficient in an era where less personal information was

[115] OECD Guidelines on the Protection of Privacy and Trans-border Flows of Personal Data, OECD Doc. (C 58 Final) (1980).

[116] *See e.g.*, Australian Privacy Act of 1988; New Zealand Privacy Act of 1993.

[117] APEC Privacy Framework (2005).

[118] OECD Privacy Framework (2013), arts. 20, 66, 82, 83.

[119] OECD Privacy Framework (2013), basic principles of national application 7, 8, 9, 10; *see also* the Singapore Personal Data Protection Commission, *Public Consultation for Approaches to Managing Personal Data in the Digital Economy* (Jul. 2017), which seeks to limit the instances where consent and notice are required in order to accommodate recent technological advances.

[120] The United States has no single comprehensive system of privacy protection and relies on an inconsistent patchwork of federal and state laws, as well as self-regulatory measures.

being collected and where its subsequent utilization was limited. Online businesses should permit their consumers, to the extent possible, to conduct their activities anonymously or minimize the amount of information collected.[121]

17.4.2.3 Protections from Automated Processing

In selecting a model for privacy protection, it is worth considering the recently adopted EU General Data Protection Regulation (GDPR).[122] The Regulation specifically recognizes that the automated processing of personal information may result in profiling and economic discrimination.[123] While it does not expressly prohibit profiling, numerous provisions significantly limit its negative effects. For example, consumers have the right to object to their personal information being processed for purposes of personalized marketing.[124] The GDPR requires that consumers receive specific information about the purposes of processing and the presence and consequences of any profiling techniques. It also significantly restricts the processing of personal information for purposes other than those for which such information was originally collected.[125] Moreover, consumers have the right not to be subject to a decision based solely on automated processing, which significantly affects them. An example of such automated decision is the discovery or prediction of a person's preferences, interests or geographical location.[126] Profiling is only allowed where expressly authorized by law, for example, for fraud and tax-evasion prevention, or on the basis of express consent.[127] The latter requires a clear affirmative act establishing a freely given, specific, informed and unambiguous indication of agreement to the processing of personal information.[128] Consent is not freely given if, among others, the consumer has no genuine choice or is unable to refuse or withdraw consent without detriment.[129]

[121] Greenleaf, *supra* note 106, at 486.

[122] Regulation 2016/679 on the protection of natural persons with regard to the processing of personal data and on the free movement of such data, and repealing Directive 95/46/EC (General Data Protection Regulation).

[123] GDPR, art. 4(4).

[124] GDPR, art. 21.

[125] GDPR, arts. 5 and 6.

[126] GDPR, art. 22, recital 71.

[127] GDPR, art. 22.

[128] GDPR, art. 4(11) definition of consent.

[129] GDPR, recital 42, art. 7.

In sum, the GDPR not only imposes tedious disclosure requirements, but also enhances the act of consent, making it more difficult to override the substantive protections contained therein. In evaluating this approach, ASEAN legislators face the challenge of balancing the right of online consumers with the interests of online businesses – a challenge rendered even more difficult by the fact that less sophisticated online consumers may be unaware of their right to privacy and ignorant of the risks of automated data processing. Although it is tempting to disclaim the GDPR as setting too high a standard in privacy protection, it must be acknowledged that such a standard might be necessitated by the very fact that consumers in less technologically advanced ASEAN jurisdictions may require more protection – persons unfamiliar with data mining and profiling techniques can hardly be expected to understand the relevant notices and provide their consent with a rudimentary appreciation of the implications of having their personal information processed and shared.

17.4.2.4 Restrictions on Exports of Personal Information

It is logical to assume that there should be restrictions on exports of personal information to jurisdictions lacking adequate privacy protections. Modern privacy instruments should thus specify the conditions in which such exports are permitted, e.g., whitelisting the countries to which such information can be exported, providing contractual protections directly enforceable by the data subjects or imposing liability on data processors for the acts of entities the personal information was exported to. Unfortunately, it is frequently implied that the modern, global economy requires uninhibited cross-border data flows leading to a situation where restrictions on personal data exports are often regarded with reluctance. The fact that unlimited data flows between jurisdictions with differing protections might weaken or even annihilate protections given to consumers in their local jurisdiction is often overlooked.[130] Interestingly, the adoption of more consumer-oriented export restrictions may be negatively affected by the e-Commerce Chapter in the TPP,[131] which regards such restrictions as trade barriers or discriminatory measures. Parties to the TPP must allow the cross-border transfer of personal information to another jurisdiction for the conduct of an investor or service supplier's business, even if the latter lacks adequate protections.[132] As a result, jurisdictions with instruments favoring online

130 *See* Greenleaf, *supra* note 106, at 500–1.

131 Trans-Pacific Partnership Agreement, Ch. 14, Electronic Commerce.

132 *Id.*, Ch. 14, art. 14.11.

consumers would be unable to protect their privacy by conditioning cross-border transfers of personal information on compliance with their privacy regimes.[133] The TPP approach would, effectively, force ASEAN to adopt a regime least favorable to online consumers. The creation of a harmonized legal privacy framework thus seems even more important: if the protections accorded to online consumers are similar throughout ASEAN, the imposition of export restrictions seems largely unnecessary.

17.5 Conclusion

Virtually all ASEAN e-commerce initiatives emphasize the scarcity of available resources. Going forward, it is necessary to ensure that such resources are used efficiently. To date, many initiatives can be regarded as misplaced or simply unnecessary. Instead of removing nonexistent barriers to e-commerce in contract law or promoting the use of digital signatures, governments and legislatures should focus on creating adequate consumer protection regimes and instruments safeguarding the online privacy of their citizens. An indiscriminate adherence to UNCITRAL instruments must be replaced with the recognition that the most successful jurisdictions in e-commerce do not rely on the MLEC. Many instruments in the area of e-commerce were premature and relied on untested assumptions as to their very necessity. ASEAN jurisdictions lagging behind in the development of e-commerce laws may thus enjoy an unexpected advantage as their initiatives can be guided by mistakes made in other, purportedly more advanced jurisdictions. While it seems too late to reverse or repeal instruments based on the MLEC, it seems recommendable to examine the extent the UNICTRAL instruments have actually facilitated the adoption of e-commerce. It is also necessary to distinguish between the transactional aspects of e-commerce, which are generally governed by contract law, and such adjacent areas as consumer and privacy protection. Regulatory efforts must shift to the latter and focus on making the online environment safer for less technology-savvy consumers.

[133] Although Chapter 14 permits exceptions to this principle, the exception seems difficult to use as it forces the relevant government to prove that it has a "legitimate public policy objective" and that such measure does not constitute a disguised trade restriction or discriminatory measure, *see generally*: Burcu Kilic & Tamir Israel, *The Highlights of the Trans-Pacific Partnership e-Commerce Chapter* (2015), www.citizen.org/sites/default/files/tpp-ecommerce-chapter-analysis.pdf (last visited Feb. 26, 2018).

Although ASEAN initiatives emphasize the need to adopt "international standards," it must be observed that such standards may not exist. It is also difficult to select a single ASEAN jurisdiction to serve as a model for other members. It is, however, possible to cooperate in order to establish which of the existing solutions adopted by individual ASEAN jurisdictions had a positive effect on the adoption of e-commerce. The fact that an ASEAN member has enacted laws in the relevant area does not imply, of course, that such laws are immutable and incapable of improvement. ASEAN members must maintain an open mind and learn from one another. It is also recommended to adopt a global view of the e-commerce environment and contemplate legislative and regulatory solutions from outside of ASEAN. Moving forward, all ASEAN jurisdictions (both those that have privacy legislation and those that have shortcomings in this area) must re-evaluate their existing or planned instruments in light of technological progress and with a full appreciation of the risk inherent in automated data processing. E-commerce will only flourish if consumers can trust that their personal information is not used against them. ASEAN initiatives should also refrain from formulating e-commerce instruments in rigid or technology-specific terms, and aim to create laws and regulations that are capable of broad interpretations to accommodate the technological progress. Of equal importance is the acknowledgement that while the provision of information (be it in the context of consumer or privacy protection) is important, the special characteristics of the online environment must be allowed for in prescribing how such information is to be presented.

Additional developments can be expected once the RCEP is finalized.[134] Unfortunately, the RCEP negotiations are held in secret and the text of the e-commerce chapter is not publicly available. The limited resources indicate that the chapter will address, among others, paperless trading, electronic authentication, online consumer protection, the nondiscriminatory treatment of digital products, customs duties on electronic transmissions and the online protection of personal information.[135] The TPP Chapter on e-Commerce provides only

[134] The Twentieth Regional Comprehensive Economic Partnership Trade Negotiating Committee (TNC) meeting was held Oct. 17–28, 2017 in Songdo, Incheon, Korea. At present, it is expected that the RCEP will only be finalized in 2018.

[135] Regional Comprehensive Economic Partnership Negotiations, Discussion Paper on Electronic Commerce, May 2017, http://dfat.gov.au/trade/agreements/rcep/Pages/rcep-discussion-paper-on-electronic-commerce-may-2017.aspx (last visited Mar. 16, 2018).

rudimentary guidance in the area of e-commerce, as its provisions are drafted in a broad manner and can be regarded as instructions as to *what* has to be done but not *how* it has to be done. There is, however, no mention of more specific principles or a recommended regulatory model. Moreover, most of the provisions of the Chapter deal with areas that can be regarded as adjacent to e-commerce, such as customs duties, the nondiscriminatory treatment of digital products or the promotion of competition in Internet access.[136] In sum, while ASEAN members must diligently observe any further developments with regards to the RCEP and the TPPA, these instruments seem unlikely to provide detailed guidance for the creation of e-commerce-specific instruments.

[136] *See* Trans-Pacific Partnership Agreement, Ch. 14, arts. 14. 3, 14.4 and 14.10.

18

Data Localization and Digital Trade Barriers: ASEAN in Megaregionalism

HAN-WEI LIU

18.1 Introduction

While unfettered data flows serve as the backbone of the open Internet and enable various new applications over the cloud, an increasing number of countries are recently putting up barriers against cross-border information flows. Although governments often justify such intervention by way of privacy, cybersecurity or national security, such movement – dubbed as "data localization" – has worried cyberlaw scholars and industry stakeholders and engendered heated debates among the trade community.[1] The WTO, created before the dot-com bubble, offers limited answers but a set of anti-protectionism proxies (e.g., nondiscrimination, necessity) to address this issue. The stagnated multilateral negotiations thus led countries to focus on bilateral and regional efforts to manage such emerging challenges.[2]

This chapter provides an overview of the challenges and opportunities facing ASEAN amid this worrying trend. The digital population in ASEAN is on the rise. As of 2016, the world's Internet users

[1] This chapter follows the definition offered by Laura DeNadis, who loosely describes data localization as covering any measures that require "content intermediaries store customer data within the country in which the customer resides," "when or how data is able to 'cross borders,'" "taxes on data exports" and "requirements for consumer consent, and rules about storing duplicate or backup data locally." We take this liberal view for a practical reason: these measures, whatever their forms, can implicate the ability of transborder data mobility and digital trade and should be considered in this context. Also, we use the terms "data protection" and "privacy" interchangeably, though they can have different meanings, depending upon the jurisdictions. *See* Laura DeNardis, *Five Destabilizing Trends in Internet Governance*, 12 I/S: J. L. & Pol'y for Info. Soc'y 113, 128 (2015).

[2] Joshua P. Melzer, A New Digital Trade Agenda 9 (2015), http://e15initiative.org/wp-content/uploads/2015/07/E15-Digital-Economy-Meltzer-Overview-FINAL.pdf (last visited Dec. 16, 2017).

amounted to more than 3.4 billion; most of them are located in Asia-Pacific.[3] Southeast Asia alone accounts for over 339 million of the digital population and has around 306 million active social media users, and these numbers are set to increase.[4] Data localization may have broader ramifications for the lives of a huge digital population, business operations and government functions in ASEAN. Normatively, there are two interlocking implications. First, regionally, ASEAN members' approaches to controlling data transfer, either individually or collectively, have a direct bearing on the full realization of the potentials envisaged by the AEC Blueprint 2025.[5] Also, their regulatory approach may have implications for the shaping of the international economic order. Many ASEAN members have been actively participating in recent megaregionalism, notably, the TPP and the RCEP. Presumably, given the formidable power of these combined markets, these initiatives may spill over into other fora and serve as a template on digital trade governance. The developments of new laws or policies on data flows both within and outside ASEAN would be a dynamic, mutually reinforcing process that deserves consideration.

The aim of this chapter is threefold: to provide the key background, to underscore the need for action and to explore the role of ASEAN in the way forward. To this end, in Section 18.2, I first address the rationales, forms and, more crucially, the ramifications of data localization measures from the perspective of international trade. Section 18.3 then considers digital trade barriers to information flows in the context of ASEAN. By stocktaking the way each ASEAN state approaches cross-border data flows, I underscore the implications of such balkanized cyberspace for ASEAN integration. Such implications lead to new developments amid megaregionalism, which may shed light on the way in which ASEAN address data localization measures in the future. Section 18.4 concludes.

[3] *See Internet Users in the World*, Internet Live Stats, www.internetlivestats.com/internet-users/#byregion (last visited Dec. 29, 2017).

[4] Simon Kemp, *The Full Guide to Southeast Asia's Digital Landscape*, TechinAsia, Feb. 8, 2017, www.techinasia.com/talk/full-guide-southeast-asia-digital-landscape-2017 (last visited Dec. 29, 2017).

[5] *See infra* 50 and accompanying text.

18.2 Global Spread of Data Localization: an Emerging Challenge for Digital Trade

The earliest efforts to control data flows date back to the 1970s.[6] Such efforts gained new momentum after Edward Snowden's leaks, which intensified debates on the limits of intelligence operations[7] and set off the alarm for privacy and data protection. Governments around the globe have been called upon to take what measures they see fit to rebuild trust in the online environent. Rightly or wrongly, one way to achieve this is to prohibit data from "travelling through the territory or infrastructure of 'untrustworthy' nations."[8] Today, over a dozen governments in developed and developing worlds – including some ASEAN members – have or are contemplating relevant policies.[9] These measures vary in terms of objectives, scope and enforcement, which may be roughly grouped into three types, as detailed below.[10]

18.2.1 Rationales and Typology of Data Localization

18.2.1.1 Type I: Forced Local Data Storage

Governments in this camp take the strictest stance by requiring data to be stored in facilities physically located within a geographic border. Given its implications for the RCEP and thus ASEAN members, China's measures are of particular significance here. Long before the passage of its Cybersecurity Law,[11] China has addressed cross-border data flow in a relatively piecemeal fashion with several laws on overarching issues (e.g., Law on Guarding State Secrets, which generally prohibits data from

[6] Christopher Kuner, Transborder Data Flows and Data Protection Law 26–7 (2013); Allan Gotlieb et al., *The Transborder Transfer of Information by Communications and Computer Systems: Issues and Approached to Guiding Principles*, 68 Am. J. Int'l L. 227, 246 (1974).

[7] Scott Shane, *Ex-Contractor Is Charged in Leaks on N.S.A. Surveillance*, N.Y. Times, Jun. 21, 2013, www.nytimes.com/2013/06/22/us/snowden-espionage-act.html?mcubz=1 (last visited Dec. 29, 2017).

[8] Jonah Force Hill, *The Growth of Data Localization Post-Snowden: Analysis and Recommendations for U.S. Policymakers and Industry Leaders*, Lawfare Research Paper Series 3 (2014), https://lawfare.s3-us-west-2.amazonaws.com/staging/Lawfare-Research-Paper-Series-Vol2No3.pdf (last visited Dec. 29, 2017).

[9] *See generally* Anupam Chander & Uyên P. Lê, *Data Nationalism*, 64 Emory L. J 677 (2015).

[10] *See* Shin-Yi Peng & Han-Wei Liu, *The Legality of Data Residency Requirements: How Can the Trans-Pacific Partnership Help?*, 51 J. World Trade 183, 190 (2017).

[11] Cybersecurity Law of the People's Republic of China (promulgated by the Standing Committee of the National People's Congress, Nov. 7, 2016, effective Jun. 1, 2017).

leaving China if it is deemed to comprise "state secrets")[12] and numerous sector-specific regulations on transborder data transfer.[13] A more full-fledged framework on data transfer can be found in, among others, Article 37 of the Cybersecurity Law, which requires "personal information" and "other important data" collected or generated in mainland China by "critical information infrastructure operators" (CII operators) to be stored within the country's borders.[14] The terms "other information" and "CII operators" are given a rather broad scope. The former refers to "all kinds of information that, recorded electronically or through other means and taken alone or together with other information, is sufficient to identify a natural person's identity."[15] The latter would, per the draft "Critical Information Infrastructure Security Protection Regulations," cover any business operating in public communication and information services, finance, public services, energy, water resources, transportation, electronic communications and others. Worse, such local data storage mandates may arguably have no exemption for data about foreigners and overseas companies.[16]

18.2.1.2 Type II: Sector-Specific Data Storage Requirements

Countries in this camp subject cross-border data flows to certain requirements, narrowing down the scope of local data storage to selected sectors. For instance, in Australia, the Privacy Act 1988 and its implementation regulations – Australian Privacy Principles (APP) and APP Guidelines – generally requires an entity to take "reasonable steps to ensure that the overseas recipient does not breach the APPs" before disclosing personal information; such entity should also be accountable for "any acts or practices of the overseas recipients" in relation to violation of the APPs.[17] Additionally, under the My Health Records Act 2012, firms managing health-related data are required to either outsource to

[12] The Law of the People's Republic of China on Guarding State Secrets (promulgated by the Standing Committee of the National People's Congress, Sept. 5, 1998, as amended on Apr. 29, 2010).

[13] *See e.g.*, Notice to Urge Banking Financial Institutions to Protect Personal Information (promulgated by the People's Bank of China, Jan. 20, 2011).

[14] Cybersecurity Law, *supra* note 11, art. 37.

[15] *Id.*, art. 76.

[16] Graham Greenleaf & Scott Livingston, *China's New Cybersecurity Law – Also a Data Privacy Law?*, 144 Privacy Laws & Bus. Int'l Rep. 1-7 (2017).

[17] Off. of the Australian Info. Comm'r, *Australian Privacy Principles Guidelines: Privacy Act 1988*, Ch 8, at 3, www.oaic.gov.au/agencies-and-organisations/app-guidelines/ (last visited Dec. 29, 2017).

companies physically located in Australia or maintain local data centers. A similar approach can be found in two Canadian provinces.[18]

18.2.1.3 Type III: Restrictions on Data Transfers

Strictly, countries that follow this model do not "localize" data for they do not mandate local data storage. Nevertheless, as illustrated in the case of the European Union, such an approach could prohibit data from crossing the border.[19] In the European Union, cross-border data flows have long been regulated under the 1995 Data Protection Directive 95/47/EC.[20] This directive prohibits personal data from being exported outside the European Economic Area unless third countries maintain "an adequate level of protection," as determined by the European Commission.[21] Only thirteen countries are deemed as offering such a level of protection.[22] In 2001, the Commission approved the EU-US Safe Harbor Framework, allowing qualified US firms to transfer data. Absent such equivalency findings, data export is only allowed by way of statutory derogations (e.g., consent of data subject) or where "adequate safeguards" are in place.[23] In practice, such derogations can be read so strictly that it inhibits data flows; thus, alternative mechanisms like binding corporate rules (BCRs) and model contracts are recommended for massive and repeated data transfers.[24]

[18] Peng & Liu, *supra* note 10, at 188.

[19] *See generally* W. Kuan Hon, Data Localization Laws and Policy: The EU Data Protection International Transfers Restriction Through a Cloud Computing Lens (2017). Note, however, that local data storage requirements can still be found, from time to time, within certain European Union Member States. To abolish the barriers to intra-EU data flows while ensuring competent authorities' access to data, the Commission proposed the "Regulation on Free Flow of Non-Personal Data." *See* Eur. Comm'n., Press Release, *State of the Union 2017: A Framework for the Free Flow of Non-Personal Data in the EU*, http://europa.eu/rapid/press-release_IP-17-3190_en.htm (last visited Dec. 20, 2017).

[20] Directive 95/46/EC of the European Parliament and the Council of Oct. 24, 1995 on the Protection of Individuals with Regard to the Processing of Personal Data and on the Free Movement of Such Data.

[21] *Id.*, arts. 2(a) and 25.

[22] Recognized countries include Andorra, Argentina, Canada, Faeroe Islands, Guernsey, Israel, Isle of Man, Jersey, New Zealand, Switzerland and Uruguay. *See Commission Decision on the Adequacy of the Protection of Personal Data in Third Countries*, http://ec.europa.eu/justice/data-protection/international-transfers/adequacy/index_en.htm (last visited Dec. 23, 2017).

[23] Data Protection Directive, *supra* note 20, art. 26(1).

[24] *See e.g.*, Phil Lee, *Why You Shouldn't Rely on Consent for (Most) Data Transfer*, Fieldfisher, http://privacylawblog.fieldfisher.com/2016/why-you-shouldn-t-rely-on-consent-for-most-data-transfers/ (last visited Dec. 29, 2017); Working Party, *Working*

Recent years have witnessed a major sea change: the Safe Harbor scheme was invalidated and replaced by the Privacy Shield,[25] and as of May 2018, the Data Protection Directive will be repealed by the GDPR.[26] Although the GDPR tightens up control over information flows,[27] the basic framework does not dramatically deviate from its predecessor: data flows outside the EEA region are generally prohibited unless otherwise permitted.

In short, under the EU approach, which serves as a template for various jurisdictions, including for some ASEAN countries, there are no explicit onshore data storage requirements. The extent to which such a model impacts trade depends on the red tape surrounding the permitted transferring machines in practice.[28]

18.2.2 Reflections: Data Protection or Data Protectionism?

Government intervention in cyberspace often justifies itself on one or more of the following grounds: privacy and cybersecurity, foreign surveillance, law enforcement and economic mercantilism.[29] Whatever the concern, the costs of these policies are significant for the digital economy; many of them, moreover, may not be sustained upon a closer examination.

Much of regulatory interference citing cybersecurity and privacy is grounded on the premise that data transferred and stored overseas is less secure. This claim is somewhat exaggerated, though. Cybersecurity is, technically, "a function of how a product is made, used, and maintained, not by whom or where it is made."[30] Therefore, "physical access to a server or other device containing data is neither a necessary, nor

Document on a Common Interpretation of Article 26 (1) of Directive 95/46/EC October 1995, at 6-9, 2093/05/EN, WP 114 (Nov. 25, 2005).

25 Case C-362/14, Schrems v. Data Prot. Comm'r, 2015 E.C.R.

26 Regulation (EU) 2016/679 of the European Parliament and of the Council of Apr. 27, 2016 on the Protection of Natural Persons with Regard to the Processing of Personal Data and on the Free Movement of Such Data, and Repealing Directive 95/46/EC.

27 The GDPR has, for instance, taken into account the *Schrems* judgment by raising the bar to require "essential equivalency" in assessing a third country's data protection scheme. *Id.*, rec. 104.

28 One of the GDPR's purposes was, according to the European Commission, to cut the red tape, while protecting personal data. *See e.g., Fact Sheet: Data Protection Day 2015: Concluding the EU Data Protection Reform Essential for the Digital Single Market*, Jan. 28, 2015, http://europa.eu/rapid/press-release_MEMO-15-3802_en.htm (last visited Dec. 26, 2017).

29 *See generally* Chander & Lê, *supra* note 9, at 714–39.

30 Statement, Digital Europe, US Information Technology Industry Council and Japan Electronics and Information Technology Industries Association, Global Information and Communications Technology Industry Statement: Recommended Government

a sufficient, condition for access to information in an intelligible form."[31] The actual issue facing policymakers is not so much about geographic location, but how logical access to data can be secured, i.e., data located physically in Germany but not managed securely, as a commentator nicely point out, "may turn out to be accessible from anywhere on the planet."[32] The same argument goes to foreign surveillance. It is not a secret that foreign intelligence agencies rely on a range of techniques like malware to hack into systems; thus, a government's strategies to keep data "inside a heavily secured and monitored ironclad firewall do not necessarily mean that it cannot be accessed by those on the other side of the earth."[33] By forcing firms to use local servers rather than those managed by their global counterparts, which are driven by fierce market competition to take more rigorous security measures to attract customers, data localization rules increase, rather than decrease, the risk of surveillance activities.[34] Worse, legally speaking, local data storage can even facilitate the operation of foreign surveillance as their overseas activities are subject to less oversight.[35]

Yet, this does not mean that the physical location of data plays no role here. In fact, it turns on two government functions: counterintelligence and law enforcement. On the former, local data storage can give domestic intelligence agencies greater regulatory hook for their operations, which may arguably serve as additional leverage for them to negotiate with their foreign counterparts such as the NSA in information sharing.[36] This is questionable, though, as it has much less, if anything, to do with cybersecurity or privacy protection as such but simply serves as a negotiating tactic. For law enforcement, by contrast, it appears to make sense because keeping data at home can make it easier to gather evidence and prosecute crimes. But again, this claim can be largely undercut by a less intrusive alternative, i.e., Mutual Legal Assistance Treaties (MLAT). Although MLATs are often criticized for their cumbersome process, it requires

Approaches to Cybersecurity (Jun. 2012),www.itic.org/dotAsset/69ec38f0-e17b-44df-9ac3-6fa9052c743c.pdf (last visited Dec. 29, 2017).

31 Christopher Millard, *Forced Localization of Cloud Services: Is Privacy the Real Driver?*, 2 IEEE Cloud Computing 10, 12 (2015).

32 *Id.*, at 12.

33 Chander & Lê, *supra* note 9, at 715–16.

34 *Id.*, at 717; *see also* Patrick Ryan et al., *When the Cloud Goes Local: The Global Problem with Data*, 46 Computer 54, 57 (2013).

35 Chander & Lê, *supra* note 9, at 715.

36 Hill, *supra* note 8, at 25.

regulatory reforms to cut red tape head on.[37] If governments can effectively have lawful access to data across jurisdictions, it is not necessary to resort to those more trade-restrictive data localization measures, which can break the Internet and impede digital trade.[38]

Domestic economic development is yet another open secret. Many governments see data localization as a convenient way to tap into the wealthy cyberspace.[39] Keeping data – the new currency in this digital economy – at home may, in the eyes of some, help local economies by spurring technology transfers and inward investment, thus creating more jobs in domestic markets.[40] Such a claim is questionable, though, from both macro and microeconomic perspectives. At the macro level, studies have well documented the loss of total social welfare: China's data localization measures, for instance, would reduce its domestic investment by 1.8 percent and exports by 1.7 percent, and result in welfare costs of up to $63 billion.[41] Similar negative effects can be found in other economies.[42] Similarly, at the micro level, local data storage would burden startups and entrepreneurs by reducing the supply of available server space in the global market and making it more expensive.[43] Studies show that local firms would be required to pay from 30 percent to 60 percent more for their computing needs than if there is no local data storage mandate.[44] Such financial burdens can deter, rather than encourage, inward investment and startups. On balance, the costs of

37 *Id.*, at 37.

38 *See also* Peter Swire & Justin D. Hemmings, *Mutual Legal Assistance in An Era of Globalized Communications: The Analogy to the Visa Waiver Program*, 71 N.Y.U. Ann. Surv. Am. L. 687, 711 (2017).

39 In Europe, for instance, Deutsche Telekom has been a powerful advocate for localization initiatives in order to reduce the US firms' hegemony in the ICT market. Similar initiatives like the Europe Cloud have also attracted attention. *See e.g.*, W. Kuan Hon et al., *Policy, Legal and Regulatory Implications of a Europe-Only Cloud*, 24 Int'l J. L. & Info. Tech. 251 (2016).

40 Neha Mishra, *Data Localization Laws in a Digital World: Data Protection or Data Protectionism?*, The Public Sphere 137, 145 (2016).

41 Matthias Bauer et al., *The Costs of Data Localisation: Friendly Fire on Economy Recovery*, Eur. Ctr. For Int'l Political Econ., Occasional Paper No. 3, 2014, www.ecipe.org/app/uploads/2014/12/OCC32014__1.pdf (last visited Dec. 30, 2017).

42 *See id.*

43 Cody Ankeny, *The Costs of Data Localization*, TechWonk Blog, www.itic.org/news-events/techwonk-blog/the-costs-of-data-localization (last visited Dec. 30, 2017).

44 Leviathan Security Group, *Quantifying the Cost of Forced Localization* (2015), www.leviathansecurity.com/blog/quantifying-the-cost-of-forced-localization (last visited Dec. 30, 2017).

prohibiting data export can outweigh the benefits as contemplated in the first place.

Admittedly, economic efficiency is a yardstick used to assess data localization. It can be naïve to label any regulatory initiatives restricting data flows as "protectionism" by overlooking the fact that they may also serve to protect human rights, ethical considerations, freedom of speech and other social values. To distinguish "data protection" from "data protectionism" can be problematic: it rests upon how those antiprotectionisms are read and applied to these measures on a case-by-case basis. From a systemic perspective, therefore, a more appropriate question facing the trade community is perhaps how to design the default rule on international data flows by reconciling regulatory diversities and various cultural, economic, social and political underpinnings. In recent years, the ramifications of data localization have triggered trans-governmental cooperation to moderate this trend through trade negotiations. ASEAN members have played a role in these endeavors, as discussed in Section 18.3.

18.3 Challenges and Opportunities for ASEAN in the Balkanized Cyberspace

As in other countries, certain ASEAN countries also restrict free information flows. In what follows, we examine the ramifications of such measures and new developments that aim to mitigate the unwanted consequences.

18.3.1 Taking Stock: Data Localization and a Disconnected ASEAN

ASEAN leaders in the AEC Blueprint 2015 set their goal of economic integration as the free movement of goods, services, investment and skilled labor and freer flow of capital among Member States by 2015.[45] The blueprint is committed to creating, specifically, "a single market and production base," "a highly competitive economic region," "a region of equitable economic development" and "a region full integrated into the global economy."[46] The desire to bring together ten states that vary considerably in economic, social and political underpinnings led

[45] Association of Southeast Asian Nations Economic Community Blueprint (2007).
[46] *Id.*

ASEAN leaders to adopt the Masterplan on ASEAN Connectivity (MPAC).[47] This strategic document has two broader, interrelated functions. Internally, enhancing connectivity along three dimensions – physical, institutional and interpersonal – would reduce the transaction costs, time and travels and bridge the development divide between the "core" and the "periphery."[48] The intraregional connectivity, in turn, serves as a pathway to other areas and helps ASEAN to maintain its centrality in the evolving dynamics. The physical infrastructure is the building block because part of this region – especially in less-developed members – is still suffering from structural weakness.

Central to the physical layer is the Internet, which, along with the ICT infrastructure, is "fundamental to supporting trade, facilitating investments, and enlarging markets through its ability to facilitate information exchange, to connect people, to support delivery of services, and to reduce the cost of business and trade-related transactions."[49] Because of the e-ASEAN Framework Agreement, the role of ICT has been underscored in several initiatives, including the ASEAN ICT Masterplan 2015 (AIM 2015), the MPAC and their respective follow-up initiatives, e.g., AIM 2020, MPAC 2025 and the AEC Blueprint 2025. As compared with its earlier vision, the ACE Blueprint 2025 places greater emphasis on the need for digital technology and identifies ICT and electronic commerce as a key driver for trade, investment and the development of SMEs in the region.[50] For years, a series of initiatives like the ASEAN Broadband Corridor worked toward "enhanced connectivity" as enshrined in the AEC Blueprint 2025 by creating the physical network.[51] However, these efforts on physical networks would be less fruitful without institutional underpinnings. This is particularly so because of the ramifications of ASEAN members' diversified approaches to cross-border data flows, as illustrated below.

18.3.1.1 Type I: Indonesia and Vietnam

Citing the need for data security and promotion of a domestic ICT industry, Indonesia has passed and considered several initiatives to

[47] Masterplan on ASEAN Connectivity, www.asean.org/storage/images/ASEAN_RTK_2014/4_Master_Plan_on_ASEAN_Connectivity.pdf (last visited Dec. 30, 2017).

[48] *Id.*; Sanchita Basu Das, *Understanding the MPAC, in* Enhancing ASEAN's Connectivity (Sanchita Basu Das ed., 2013).

[49] MPAC, *supra* note 47, at 15.

[50] ASEAN Economic Community Blueprint 2025 (2015), at paras. 2, 24, 45.

[51] *See generally* Arne Jeroschewski et al., *Connecting Southeast Asia Through Broadband, in* Enhancing ASEAN's Connectivity, *supra* note 48, at 72–90.

keep data at home. The Electronic Information and Transactions Law No. 11 of 2008 (EIT Law) laid down the basic framework on data protection. EIT Law was amended and supplemented several laws and regulations, including the Regulation No. 82 of 2012 Concerning Electronic Systems and Transactions Operation (Regulation 82) and the Regulation No. 20 of 2016 on Personal Data Protection in Electronic Systems (Data Protection Regulation).

Of great concern is Regulation 82 and the Data Protection Regulation. Regulation 82 requires the "electronic system operator for the public services" to place "data center and disaster recovery center in Indonesia territory for the purpose of law enforcement, protection, and enforcement of national sovereignty to the data of its citizens."[52] Although Regulation 82 did not explicitly define the scope of "electronic system operator for the public services," some referred to the draft on the regulation concerning the registration procedure for electronic system providers and read this term as loose enough to apply to "almost all websites and online applications such as newspapers or information and social platforms."[53]

The Data Protection Regulation issued by the Ministry of Communication and Informatics (MOCI) in 2016 can be problematic, too.[54] Electronic system operators are required by this regulation to have onshore data centers and data recovery centers if they engage in "public services." As the term "public service" remains undefined, as in Regulation 82, it can be problematic in practice.[55]

Like China, Vietnam has a long history of keeping certain data outside of the country's borders.[56] Recently, Vietnam revealed strong interests in

[52] Regulation Concerning Electronic System and Transaction Operation, Law No. 82 of 2012, art. 17(2) (Indonesia), www.flevin.com/id/lgso/translations/JICA%20Mirror/english/4902_PP_82_2012_e.html (last visited Dec. 30, 2017).

[53] Chander & Lê, *supra* note 9, at 698.

[54] *See ITI Forced Localization Strategy in Indonesia*, Info. Tech. Indus. Council, www.itic.org/public-policy/ITIForcedLocalizationStrategyBriefs.pdf (last visited Dec. 30, 2017).

[55] Mark C. Innis, *Indonesia: New Regulations on Personal Data Protection*, Baker McKenzie, www.bakermckenzie.com/en/insight/publications/2016/12/new-implementing-regulation-personal-data/ (last visited Nov. 1, 2018). As of this writing, it is reported that the Indonesian government is currently working on a draft amendment to Regulation 82 to clarify the requirements for those multinational enterprises with global data center arrangements with their offshore group entities. In this regard, *see* Mark C. Innis, *General Data Localization Requirements in Indonesia*, Baker & McKenzie, https://www.bakermckenzie.com/en/insight/publications/2018/07/general-data-localization-requirements (last visited Nov. 1, 2018).

[56] Graham Greenleaf, Asian Data Privacy Laws: Trade and Human Rights Perspectives 365 (2014).

data localization. In 2013, Vietnam passed the Decree on Information Technology Services (Decree No. 72). This decree not only follows tradition by prohibiting online speech and content to the detriment of "national security, social order and safety" but introduces restrictions requiring firms to physically locate at least one server within the country to operate most Internet-based services.[57] More recently, the National Assembly of Vietnam passed the new Law on Cybersecurity in June 2018, which will come into effect in January 2019. The Law on Cybersecurity will impose local data storage requirements for certain categories of information including "personal information," "data about users' relationship" and "all other data generated by users in Vietnam," though many of these terms are left undefined at the moment.[58]

18.3.1.2 Type III: Malaysia and Singapore

In 2010, Malaysia enacted the Personal Data Protection Act (PDPA) – the first of its kind in force in ASEAN.[59] In contrast with the approach by Indonesia and Vietnam in terms of cross-border transfer, the Malaysian PDPA is somewhat similar to the EU model. Data users are generally required by the PDPA not to "transfer any personal data of a data subject to a place outside Malaysia unless to such place as specified by the minister, upon the recommendation of the commissioner, by notification published in the Gazette."[60] Such a whitelist was not released until 2017, when Malaysia's Personal Data Protection Commissioner issued the Public Consultation Paper (PCP) No. 1/2017 entitled Personal Data Protection (Transfer of Personal Data to Places outside Malaysia) Order. This list contains proposed jurisdictions, including the EEA and countries recognized by the European Union under the Data Protection Directive, Dubai International Finance Centre, as well as major Asia-

[57] Yee Chung Seck & Thanh Son Dang, *Vietnam National Assembly Passes the Law on Cybersecurity*, https://globalcompliancenews.com/vietnam-law-cybersecurity-20180702/ Baker & McKenzie (last visited Nov. 1, 2018). For the full Vietnamese text of this law, *see Toàn văn Luật An ninh mạng trình Quốc hội thông qua*, thư viện pháp lauat, https://thuvienphapluat.vn/van-ban/Cong-nghe-thong-tin/Luat-an-ninh-mang-2018-351416.aspx (last visited Nov. 1, 2018).

[58] US-ASEAN Business Council & Info. Tech. Indus. Council (joint letter to Vietnamese Minister Son, Ministry of Info. & Communications) (Jan. 6, 2015), http://cloud.chambermaster.com/userfiles/UserFiles/chambers/9078/File/ICT/2015/VietnamOTTCircular-USABC-ITILetterFINAL.pdf (last visited Dec. 30, 2017).

[59] *See* Greenleaf, *supra* note 56, at 318–35.

[60] Personal Data Protection Act 2010 § 129 (Act No. 709) (Malaysia).

Pacific economies, e.g., Australia, China, Hong Kong, Japan, the Philippines, Singapore, South Korea, Taiwan and the United States.[61]

Additionally, the PDPA sets out certain exemptions to enable data flows in cases where, say, "the data subject has given his consent," "the transfer is necessary for the performance of a contract between the data subject and the data user," "the transfer is necessary for the conclusion or performance of a contract between the data user and a third party" that is either "entered into at the request of the data subject" or "in the interest of the data subject"; the data user has "taken all reasonable precautions and exercised all due diligence" to ensure that the personal data will not be processed in the recipient country in a way that would contravene the PDPA; or for the public interests as determined by the regulator.[62]

Singapore's Personal Data Protection Act 2012 takes a similar form to its Malaysian counterpart in terms of cross-border data flows.[63] The Singaporean PDPA prohibits offshore transfers unless the organization ensures that they will follow PDPA obligations related to exported personal data while it remains under its control, and the overseas recipient is bound by legally enforceable obligations to provide a standard of protection "comparable to" those set by the PDPA.[64] However, besides a general exemption granted by the regulator on a case-by-case basis,[65] the Personal Data Protection Regulation 2014 offers exceptions similar to those found in Malaysia's PDPA and the European Union's GDPR to enable data exports (e.g., data subject's consent, necessity for the performance of the contract and BCRs).[66]

18.3.1.3 The Rest in ASEAN: Even Weaker to Nonexistent

The remaining ASEAN states are far less rigorous in controlling data transfers. In the Philippines, the Data Privacy Act of 2012 permits export of personal information without specific prerequisites, though organizations engaged in the transfer of data "shall be responsible for any personal data under its control or custody, including information that has been outsourced or transferred to a personal information processor or a third

[61] Public Consultation Paper (PCP) No. 1/2017 entitled Personal Data Protection, www.pdp.gov.my/images/pdf_folder/PUBLIC_CONSULTATION_PAPER_1-2017_.pdf (last visited Dec. 30, 2017).

[62] Mala. PDPA, *supra* note 60.

[63] For an appraisal, *see e.g.*, Warren B. Chik, *The Singapore Personal Data Protection Act and an Assessment of Future Trends in Data Privacy*, 29 Computer L. & Sec. Rev. 554 (2013).

[64] Personal Data Protection Act 2012 § 26 (1) (2012 S.S. 26) (Singapore).

[65] *Id.*, § 26 (2).

[66] Personal Data Protection Regulation 2014 §§ 9-10 (Singapore).

party for processing, whether domestically or internationally, subject to cross-border arrangement and co-operation."[67] International transfer of "sensitive information," e.g., race, color, age, health or otherwise specified by the government as unique to an individual, is restricted except for certain exemptions.[68]

Other ASEAN members take an even weaker form due to the lack of legal framework on data protection. Thailand, for instance, protects privacy by the Civil and Commercial Code and certain sector-specific laws. In practice, therefore, moving data abroad relies on the consent of the data subject to avoid potential civil liability.[69] In Cambodia, Brunei, Laos and Myanmar, the existing data protections are minimal to nonexistent.[70]

18.3.2 Moving Toward Enhanced Connectivity in ASEAN

Despite the seemingly fragmented paradigm illustrated above, there are developments that may help connect the dots in the region. We discuss below.

18.3.2.1 ASEAN's Digital Wall and Its Discontents

On the way toward ASEAN's "enhanced connectivity," any effort solely focusing on the physical dimension would be less fruitful without coordination in institutional settings. This is particularly so in cyberspace. Almost two decades ago, ASEAN leaders pointed out that the network infrastructure is one of but many steps to creating an ASEAN e-space. Much on the agenda of the e-ASEAN Framework Agreement – from the Common Marketplace for ICT Goods and Services, e-Society, e-Commerce Friendly Environment, to e-Government – turns on data flows.[71] As the building blocks of cyberspace, data matters to almost every online activity. Yet, data is multifaceted and means different things to different people. This can be manifested by diversified regulatory

[67] An Act Protecting Individual Personal Information in Information and Communications Systems in the Government and the Private Sector, Creating for this Purpose a National Privacy Commission, and for Other Purpose § 21 (Rep. Act. No. 10723) (Philippines) (Data Privacy Act 2012).

[68] *Id.*, § 3.

[69] *See Data Protection Laws of the World: Thailand – Transfer*, DLA Piper, www.dlapiperdataprotection.com/index.html?t=law&c=TH&c2=TH (last visited Dec. 30, 2017).

[70] Greenleaf, *supra* note 56, at 389–400.

[71] ASEAN, e-ASEAN Framework Agreement (Nov. 24, 2000).

approaches to privacy and data protection. Some treat it as a matter of human rights; others see it as a vehicle to promote electronic commerce. More problematic is the fact that still others tend to link this issue back to national security. All these complexities hamper the development of a universally agreed-upon framework on data protection. This is a daunting task for ASEAN too. The full realization of ASEAN connectivity rests upon more coordinated efforts to curb barriers to data flows by considering cultural, economic, social and political diversities across the region, which, in turn, depend upon ASEAN leaders' political will. Nevertheless, some observations at this juncture are noteworthy and may contribute to follow-up policy debates.

First, ASEAN members that have governed data flows in Type I form, i.e., local data storage, are urged to reflect upon the costs and benefits of such policies. This is particularly true for those that use privacy or data protection as a pretext to serve industrial policies. It is hardly a secret, for instance, that domestic economic development is yet another major driver behind Indonesia's Regulation 82 and the MOCI Regulation.[72] These measures were considered as leverage to force foreign OTT firms to maintain onshore offices and infrastructure. Indeed, this is understandable: Indonesia would love to have "the likes of Google and Microsoft open up data centres" within its border "rather than in neighboring Thailand or Malaysia."[73] Yet, the costs and risks would outweigh these potential benefits. First, creating and operating data server farms is expensive and requires enormous energy.[74] Even building a comparatively small one, as a study shows, would entail upfront investment costs, which can easily reach upward of $50 million.[75] Thus, "mega-investment of this kind" is not a problem for the ICT giants who operate globally, but would not make sense for the limited scale of local businesses.[76]

Second, counterintuitively, despite the huge investment, data centers create only limited jobs locally; reports show that while typical company

[72] Jennie M. Xue, *Indonesia among the Worst Mercantilists?*, The Jakarta Post, Jan. 19, 2017, www.thejakartapost.com/academia/2017/01/19/indonesia-among-the-worst-mercantilists.html (last visited Dec. 31, 2017).

[73] Mishra, *Data Localization*, *supra* note 40, at 148.

[74] Chander & Lê, *supra* note 9, at 723–4.

[75] The Asia Pacific Carrier's Coalition (APPC) & The Asia Cloud Computing Association (ACCA), Cloud Data Regulations: A Contribution on How to Reduce the Compliancy Costs of Cross-Border Data Transfers: A Joint Report 11 (Jun. 2014) (APPC-ACCA Joint Report).

[76] *Id.*

headquarters can have between 200 and 1,000 on-site jobs, the number of jobs at an average data center is generally capped somewhere between five and thirty.[77] Next, local data storage limits local companies' choices for more reliable and cost-effective solutions available in the global market. This would cause harm to SMEs, which are vital to the ASEAN economy, as stated in the AEC Blueprint 2025. Worse, Indonesia's weak ICT infrastructure implies that "sites hosted locally experience delayed loading time" and could be vulnerable to hacking.[78] Indonesia's onshore data storage policy would, on net, result in a decrease of foreign investment by 2.3 percent and a loss of GDP of 0.7 percent.[79] Similarly, this could also backfire in Vietnam,[80] though its data localization is tied to a more compelling rationale, i.e., national security. The above analysis may, arguably, apply to Singapore and Malaysia, depending on how they interpret and apply the laws in practice. As for law enforcement – another policy ground invoked by Indonesia and Vietnam for onshore data storage – is not plausible as a rationale, either, at least in the context of intra-ASEAN data transfer insofar as ASEAN members can improve the Treaty on Mutual Legal Assistance in Criminal Matters concluded some a decade ago.[81]

Third, equally challenging are those ASEAN members with minimal to zero data protection schemes. While the Type I data localization rules can operate to the contrary of "enhanced connectivity," the immature or even nonexistent data protection framework in much of ASEAN can be equally harmful, for their inadequacy means they can hardly be recognized by others that adopt an adequate protection approach, like the European Union, Malaysia and Singapore, for the purpose of data flows. The underdeveloped data protection laws can impede intra- and extra-ASEAN data transfer.

18.3.2.2 ASEAN Framework on Personal Data Protection: (Some) Light in the Tunnel?

Naturally, the above observations highlight the need to formulate a more harmonious approach to data protection in ASEAN. In fact, data

[77] John Lenio, *The Mystery Impact of Data Centers on Local Economies Revealed*, www.areadevelopment.com/data-centers/Data-Centers-Q1-2015/impact-of-data-center-development-locally-2262766.shtml (last visited Dec. 31, 2017).

[78] Chander & Lê, *supra* note 9, at 725.

[79] Bauer et al., *supra* note 41, at 2.

[80] The estimated losses in GDP are 1.7 percent. *See id.*

[81] ASEAN, Treaty on Mutual Legal Assistance in Criminal Matters (Nov. 29, 2004).

protection has long been on ASEAN leaders' agenda; for instance, since 2000 the e-ASEAN Framework Agreement has encouraged members to "take measures to promote personal data protection and consumer privacy."[82] While this element was somewhat missing from the AIM 2015, it was restored in the AIM 2025 and the AEC Blueprint 2025. These efforts eventually materialized into the ASEAN Framework on Personal Data Protection, adopted in November 2016 by the telecommunications and IT ministers of ASEAN states.[83]

This framework delivers several advantages to ASEAN connectivity. First, by referring to the APEC Privacy Framework,[84] which was largely based on the 1980 Guidelines Governing the Protection of Privacy and Transborder Data Flows of Personal Data issued by the OECD,[85] it offers a set of principles.[86] Of particular importance here are data flows and accountability. On cross-border data transfer, the framework states that "before transferring personal data to another country or territory, the organization should either obtain the consent of the individual for the overseas transfer or take reasonable steps to ensure that the receiving organization will protect the personal data consistently with these principles."[87] This provision, read in conjunction with the accountability principle, which stipulates that "an organization should be accountable for complying with measures which give effect to the principles,"[88] seems to adopt a lax approach that is weaker than the model adopted by the OECD and APEC. This framework has no local data storage requirement, nor does it subject cross-border data flows to various mechanisms. Rather, the default rule seems to generally allow data transfer by way of consent and the accountability principle. In this light, it seems relatively closer to the Philippine model with some variants.

[82] E-ASEAN Framework Agreement, *supra* note 72, art. 5(e).

[83] ASEAN Framework on Data Protection (Nov. 25, 2016).

[84] Asia-Pacific Economic Cooperation, APEC Privacy Framework (2005), www.apec.org/Groups/Committee-on-Trade-and-Investment/~/media/Files/Groups/ECSG/05_ecsg_privacyframewk.ashx (last visited Dec. 31, 2017).

[85] OECD Guidelines on the Protection of Privacy and Transborder Flows of Personal Data (Sept. 23, 1980), www.oecd.org/sti/ieconomy/2013-oecd-privacy-guidelines.pdf (last visited Dec. 31, 2017). There are, however, differences between the APEC Privacy Framework and the OECD Guidelines.

[86] These principles relate to (1) consent, notification and purpose; (2) accuracy of personal data; (3) security safeguards; (4) access and correction; (5) transfers to another country or territory; (6) retention; and (7) accountability. ASEAN Framework on Data Protection, *supra* note 83, para. 6.

[87] *Id.*, para. 6(f).

[88] *Id.*, para. 6(h).

But the ASEAN Framework on Personal Data Protection has its drawbacks too. First and foremost, ASEAN states made it clear at the outset that this document is nonbinding and "serves only as a record of the participants' intentions" and "is not intended to constitute or create obligations under domestic or international law."[89] Moreover, the framework offers only high-level guiding principles, as such a nonprescriptive approach and a wide range of exemptions would leave participants much discretion to implement domestically, which, in turn, may be delayed by a given ASEAN country "until such time that it is ready to implement it."[90]

The ASEAN Framework on Personal Data Protection, though not perfect, marks the first step toward a region-wide, more harmonious approach to data protection.

While it remains to be seen whether this and other ASEAN-led initiatives can remove the barriers to data flows, recent developments in megaregionalism in relation to ASEAN deserve attention, as considered in Section 18.3.2.3.

18.3.2.3 Lessons from the Recent Megaregional Negotiation: the TPP and beyond

Led by the United States, the TPP was the first of its kind to prohibit interference with transborder data transfer by electronic means. Recognizing the enabling role of electronic commerce in terms of "economic growth and opportunities" and the "importance of frameworks that promote consumer confidence in electronic commerce and of avoiding unnecessary barriers to its use and development," Chapter 14 of the TPP sets out principles on electronic commerce, fixing some of the loopholes in the WTO framework, including data flows.[91] Article 14.8 begins by highlighting the "economic and social benefits of protection of the personal information of users of electronic commerce and the contribution that this makes to enhancing consumer confidence in electronic commerce."[92] Toward this end, it requires that "each party shall adopt or maintain a legal framework that provides for the protection of the personal information of the users of

[89] *Id.*, para. 2.

[90] *Id.*, para. 7.

[91] *See e.g.*, Neha Mishra, *The Role of the Trans-Pacific Partnership Agreement in the Internet Ecosystem: Uneasy Liaison or Synergistic Alliance?*, 20 J. Int'l Econ. L. 31–60 (2016).

[92] Trans-Pacific Partnership Agreement, art. 14.8.1, Feb. 4, 2016, www.mfat.govt.nz/en/about-us/who-we-are/treaties/trans-pacific-partnership-agreement-tpp/text-of-the-trans-pacific-partnership (last visited Dec. 31, 2017).

electronic commerce."[93] In creating a relevant legal framework, the TPP encourages each party to "take into account principles and guidelines of relevant international bodies."[94] Such legal framework can be in the form of a comprehensive privacy or personal data protection law, sector-specific law covering privacy or laws that provide for the enforcement of voluntary undertakings by enterprises relating to privacy.[95] On this basis, the TPP then proceeds to balance data protection and free information flows by way of Articles 14.11 and 14.13. The former reads:

> Each party shall allow the cross-border transfer of information by electronic means, including personal information, when this activity is for the conduct of the business of a covered person.

This clause is qualified by an exception that allows the TPP party to adopt measures to "achieve legitimate public objective," so long as such a measure is "not applied in a manner which would constitute a means of arbitrary or unjustifiable discrimination or disguise restriction on trade" and meet the necessity test.[96] The TPP then moves on to address explicitly forced local data storage via Article 14.13, which prohibits a party from "requir[ing] a covered person to use or locate computing facilities in that Party's territory as a condition for conducting business in that territory." This provision is also subject to a qualification similar to those under Article 14.11, however.

There are lessons that ASEAN, and more broadly, the trade community as a whole can draw from the above clauses. First, despite its emphasis on data protection or privacy, the TPP seeks to reverse the trend of data localization by setting free data transfer as a default rule. Such a default setting, as provided for under Articles 14.11 and 14.13, applies to data localization manifested in Types I, II and III. This would burden those governments with data localization measures as they have to invoke the exceptions and distinguish between data protection and protectionism. An immediate implication for ASEAN is that Malaysia and Vietnam, as parties to the TPP, would have to carefully review their relevant policies, though the TPP has granted a two-year transition period.[97] Even with Trump's withdrawal from the TPP, similar rules would be channeled into other, more likely bilateral, trade negotiations

93 *Id.*, art. 14.8.2
94 *Id.*
95 *Id.*
96 *Id.*, art. 14.11.3.
97 *Id.*, art. 14.18.

to which the United States is a party.[98] On the other hand, while the TPP reconfigured the default rule of data flows, it did urge countries to take into account "principles and guidelines of relevant international bodies" when enacting data protection laws or the like. The term "principles and guidelines of relevant international bodies," though left undefined, could arguably refer to those high-level guiding principles issued by the OECD, APEC or otherwise.[99] Therefore, the fact that the ASEAN Framework on Personal Data Protection incorporates to some extent the elements of the APEC Privacy Framework seems in line with the TPP.

Nevertheless, it may be too early to consider unfettered data flows as becoming a new template for digital trade. Other challenges include the uncertainty of how the RCEP and the TIS would address this issue. On the RCEP, while countries like Japan are more liberal toward cross-border data flows,[100] and industry stakeholders have urged trade negotiators to craft rules that enable "information flows and prohibit data localization, allow the cross-border provision of services" for the benefit of the SMEs and Internet users,[101] several hurdles remain. For one, while ASEAN plays a central role in the RCEP, and logically, the recent Framework on Personal Data Protection seems a vantage point from which to embark on negotiations vis-à-vis their counterparts, the way in which many ASEAN states shape and implement their data protection laws casts doubt on whether this nonbinding document represents the baseline for that purpose. To further complicate the matter is another powerful player, China. As illustrated, China maintains a rigorous regime on cross-border data flows. Certain regulations – like the Cybersecurity Law – were passed or went into effect while the RCEP negotiations were already underway. The complexities are compounded by the fact that other RCEP participants, e.g., South Korea, Australia and India, have also maintained or considered data localization measures.[102] It can be equally,

[98] Alex Capri, *What's Next for Asia After Trump's America Leaves TPP?*, Forbes, Jan. 26, 2017, www.forbes.com/sites/alexcapri/2017/01/26/whats-next-for-asia-after-trumps-america-leaves-tpp/#52c2cf61e479 (last visited Dec. 31, 2017).

[99] Typically, literature would also include, say, the Council of Europe Convention 108 and Additional Protocol, and Madrid Resolution, as part of international instruments. *See* Kuner, Transborder Data Flows, *supra* note 6, at 36–9, 58.

[100] Greenleaf, *supra* note 56, at 249.

[101] E-*Commerce and Digital Trade Proposals for RCEP* (Asian Trade Centre Working Paper, Auckland Round Jun. 2016), https://deborah-elms.squarespace.com/s/RCEP-E-commerce-Jun.-2016.pdf (last visited Dec. 31, 2017).

[102] Chander & Lê, *supra* note 9, at 717–18. A somewhat related point, though not in megaregionalism, is that the ASEAN-Australia-New Zealand Free Trade Agreement

if not more, problematic to achieve a consensus on data flows in the context of the TIS, as EU negotiators also voiced their concerns about arrangements that would jeopardize personal data, which is central to fundamental human rights and is not tradable.[103]

18.4 Concluding Remarks

The future of ASEAN rests, in large part, on digital technologies, i.e., the building blocks of a connected and innovative region by 2025 and the driver for realizing the full potential of new economic activities and its young demographic. At the center of this ASEAN digital journey resides the connectivity that forges physical, institutional and interpersonal communication channels. Yet, the way toward connectivity remains bumpy. Among other hurdles are the barriers to cross-border data flows. In the aftermath of the NSA revelations, the movement for data localization has gained a new momentum and swept through much of the world, including ASEAN. Indonesia and Vietnam followed China and Russia by imposing an in-country data storage requirement; Malaysia and Singapore modeled the EU approach by subjecting data transfer to certain requirements. The cited benefits of such restrictions, however, seem to be undercut by the risks and costs to trade and investment within and outside ASEAN.

While data localization has attracted much attention, one should not overlook the underdeveloped data protection framework in the rest of ASEAN, as it may also impede free data flows insofar as their existing data protection laws (if any) can hardly be recognized by others. All these point to the need for a more harmonious approach to data protection, which requires ASEAN leaders' sustained coordinated efforts and political will. The ASEAN Framework on Personal Data Protection presents a good point of departure for continued dialogue of a regional-wide strategy. Such a strategy would not be formulated in isolation; rather, it would evolve in a two-way interactive process with the megaregional initiative playing a role.

does prohibit barriers to data transfer if it is necessary for "the conduct of the ordinary business of a financial service supplier."

103 *See e.g.*, Ralf Bendrath, *Trading Away Privacy: TTIP, TiSA and European Data Protection*, Eurozine, Dec. 19, 2014, www.eurozine.com/trading-away-privacy/ (last visited Dec. 31, 2017).

19

Consumer Contracts and Product Safety Law in Southeast Asia: Partly Trading Up?

LUKE NOTTAGE AND JEANNIE PATERSON*

19.1 Introduction: Consumer Protection for the ASEAN Economic Community

This chapter explores the efforts by the ten Member States of ASEAN to implement harmonized standards of consumer protection. This project seeks to avoid a "regulatory race to the bottom"[1] alongside trade and investment liberalization, especially pursuant to the establishment of the AEC by the end of 2015.[2] The original AEC Blueprint 2015 identified consumer protection as a significant issue for creating a "competitive economic region,"[3] consistently with the prognosis that by 2020 the middle class in ASEAN economies is expected to reach 120 million people.[4] Pursuant to the agenda, the ASEAN Committee for Consumer Protection (ACCP) was created to encourage higher and more harmonized standards of consumer law across Southeast Asia.[5] The ACCP has engaged with outside agencies to

* We thank Kirsten Gan for fine research and editorial assistance as well as Gary Low for helpful information and feedback on earlier drafts. All responsibility lies with the authors.

1 *See generally* Luke Nottage, *Legal Harmonization*, *in* International Encyclopedia of Law and the Social Sciences: American and Global Perspectives 686, 686–92 (David Clark ed., 2006).

2 Luke Nottage & Sakda Thanitcul, ASEAN Product Liability and Consumer Product Safety Law (2016). *See also generally*, Tham Siew Yean & Sanchita Basu Das, *Introduction: Economic Interests and the ASEAN Economic Community*, *in* Moving the AEC Beyond 2015: Managing Domestic Consensus for Community-Building 1, 1–23 (Tham Siew Yean & Sanchita Basu Das eds., 2016).

3 Association of Southeast Asian Nations Economic Community Blueprint (2007), para 19–20.

4 *See* Austrade & DFAT, *Why ASEAN and Why Now* (2015), https://dfat.gov.au/about-us/publications/Documents/why-asean-and-why-now.pdf (last visited Jan. 28, 2018).

5 *See* ASEAN Committee on Consumer Protection, aseanconsumer.org/accp/ (last visited Jan. 28, 2018).

further this goal, including teams of consultants funded by the Australian Government.[6]

The AEC Blueprint 2025, published in November 2015, reiterates that "consumer protection [is] an integral part of a modern, efficient, effective and fair market place." Accordingly, it aims to[7]

> establish a common ASEAN consumer protection framework through higher levels of consumer protection legislation, improve enforcement and monitoring of consumer protection legislation, and make available redress mechanisms, including alternative dispute resolution (ADR);

as well as to

> build higher consumer confidence and cross-border commercial transactions by strengthening product safety enforcement, stronger participation of consumer representatives, and promotion of sustainable consumption.

Nonetheless, law and policy development has proceeded in this field predominantly on the basis of voluntary and unilateral reforms by each Member State. This is consistent with the traditional (consensus-based and noninterventionist) ASEAN Way, despite that approach itself being challenged by the ASEAN Charter (in force from 2008)[8] and treaty-based commitments culminating in the AEC project. The realistic aim therefore is not uniform law, which is unlikely to be achieved without a significant degree of concerted effort and even some coercion, but substantively

[6] In particular, both present authors contributed toward a suite of twenty-four policy digests as well as four longer case studies addressing key consumer law and policy challenges facing ASEAN Member States: *see* Consumer Protection Digests and Case Studies: A Policy Guide vol. II (2015). (These and related consumer law issues were discussed in the first-ever ASEAN Consumer Protection Conferences, *see* ASEAN Economic Community Press Release, *2nd ASEAN Consumer Protection Conference focuses on Consumer Safety and Laws*, Dec. 20, 2015.) In addition, in 2015, Nottage contributed a regulators' training module on "Product Safety and Labelling" for a project coordinated by the United Nations Conference on Trade and Development.

[7] *See* ASEAN Economic Community Blueprint 2025 (2015). This Blueprint goes on (at 14) to highlight several services sectors (finance, air transport and telecommunications), but also areas implicating products (e-commerce and energy), for future consumer protection measures.

[8] *See* Charter of the Association of Southeast Asian Nations (2007). *See generally* Walter Woon, The ASEAN Charter: A Commentary (2015) and Jacques Pelkmans, The ASEAN Economic Community: A Conceptual Approach (2016).

harmonized law that raises the overall level of consumer protection throughout the region.

By 2018, all ten Member States had reported enactment of general consumer protection laws, except Cambodia.[9] This trend began with several Member States influenced by developments in the United Nations resulting in the 1985 Guidelines on Consumer Protection,[10] but the last decade has seen new rounds of general consumer law enactments,[11] inspired also by reference to other Member States' laws as well as consumer law regimes outside Southeast Asia. Interestingly, law reform in this field seems to appeal even to military governments (e.g., in Myanmar, Thailand).

Yet public commentary stating that the ten ASEAN states have already harmonized more than 90 percent of their consumer protection laws is very misleading.[12] Some states still lack consolidated consumer legislation (e.g., Singapore,[13] Brunei) and/or have significant gaps (e.g., Brunei: generic consumer product safety regulation[14]), while others have large gaps despite enacting new general laws (e.g., Myanmar: unfair consumer contract terms, as discussed further in Section 19.3 below). Access to justice for redress and enforcement of consumer law add further challenges to legal harmonization, especially in less developed Member States (e.g., in Vietnam, as mentioned further in Section 19.2. below), while consumer NGOs play limited roles (except in Thailand,[15] and Malaysia to a lesser extent[16]).

[9] *C.f.* Chea Vannak, *Consumer Protection Draft Law Almost Ready*, Khmer Times, Aug. 17, 2016.

[10] Namely Thailand (with the Consumer Protection Law enacted already in 1979), Indonesia and Malaysia (both in 1999). On the general influence of the Guidelines, *see* David Harland, *The United Nations Guidelines for Consumer Protection*, 10 J. Consumer Policy 245 (1987). For a comparison with the recent revisions to those Guidelines, *see* Luke Nottage, *Policy Digest 21: Best Practices for Developing Consumer Protection Policy, in* Consumer Protection Digests and Case Studies: A Policy Guide, *supra* note 6.

[11] Namely in Vietnam and Laos (both enacted in 2010), and Myanmar (2014), as discussed further below.

[12] Bernie Magkilat, *ASEAN Harmonizes Consumer Protection*, Manila Bulletin, Apr. 24, 2014.

[13] Lawrence Teh & Ng Hui Min, *Singapore, in* ASEAN Product Liability and Consumer Product Safety Law (2016), *supra* note 2, 253–71.

[14] Colin Ong, *Brunei Darusaalam, in* ASEAN Product Liability and Consumer Product Safety Law (2016), *supra* note 2, 67–87.

[15] *See generally* Frank Munger, *Revolution Imagined: Cause Advocacy, Consumer Rights, and the Evolving Role of NGOs in Thailand*, 9 As. J. Comp. L. 29 (2014); and Sakda Thanitcul, *Thailand, in* ASEAN Product Liability and Consumer Product Safety Law (2016), *supra* note 2, 273–302.

[16] Matthew Hilton, *The Consumer Movement and Civil Society in Malaysia*, 52 Int'l Rev. Soc. Hist. 373 (2007).

This chapter examines such impediments to "trading up"[17] to higher harmonized standards for consumer protection across Southeast Asia, focusing on two main fields: product safety (focusing on general consumer goods rather than safety regulations for high-risk products such as pharmaceuticals or automobiles) and regulation aimed at ensuring minimum quality standards in consumer contracts for the supply of goods and services (consumer guarantees). The two areas are related given that the primary focus of both forms of regulation is in meeting basic consumer expectations of safe and functional products. Moreover, rules setting minimum quality standards for goods and services, and importantly, limitations on the ability to suppliers to contract out of these baseline obligations, can act as a direct incentive to suppliers to proactively monitor the overall quality of the products they supply.

First, Section 19.2.1 shows how consumer product safety regulation by public authorities remains characterized by limited jurisdiction and/or resources for general consumer regulators compared to "line ministries," especially for premarket interventions (e.g., setting minimum safety standards for specify types of products). In addition, only Malaysia has a general safety provision (GSP) (inspired by legislation introduced from 1992 in the European Union)[18] requiring all consumer goods to be safe, although Singapore has recently required that all comply with ISO, EU or other specified standards. Another gap arises because only Vietnam has a partial analogue to a duty on suppliers to report serious product-related accidents to regulators, as introduced in the United States, the European Union and then several major developed economies in recent years.

As for private law mechanisms enhancing consumer protection with respect to unsafe products, Section 19.2.2 outlines how five out of ten ASEAN countries have enacted EU-inspired statutes providing compensation for consumers (and sometimes indeed others) based on strict liability for product safety defects. Yet, despite going beyond the EU model[19] in various pro-consumer ways, this more pro-plaintiff substantive law has generated very few court case filings, except in Thailand, and almost no reported judgments. Anyway, Indonesia retains a negligence-based liability

[17] *See generally* David Vogel, Trading Up: Consumer and Environmental Regulation in a Global Economy (1995).

[18] Directive 2001/95/EC of the European Parliament and of the Council of Dec. 3, 2001 on General Product Safety (2001) O.J. L11/4. (Elsewhere in Asia, Macau and Hong Kong – as former colonies of Portugal and the United Kingdom, respectively – provide for a GSP.)

[19] Geraint Howells, *Product Liability along the Belt and Road, in* ASEAN Product Liability and Consumer Product Safety Law (2016), *supra* note 2, 55–65.

regime – albeit reversing the burden of proof so manufacturers must provide that they took due care in supplying goods that ended up causing harm to consumers. Singapore and Brunei require proof of negligence. They arguably impose strict liability only for consumers harmed by unsafe products containing "warning" or information defects, due to enactments providing redress for misleading conduct,[20] but this possibility appears to be virtually unknown and certainly has never been invoked in reported judgments.

Turning to consumer contract law, Section 19.3 shows that all ASEAN states have consumer protection regimes that aim to address the baseline objectives of ensuring that consumers are free from misinformation, undue pressure and coercion in contracting. Regulation of substantive concerns, relating to the content of consumer contracts, is more haphazard and uneven. Only some ASEAN states provide statutory guarantees of quality, acceptable quality and fitness for purpose in the supply of goods to consumers and of due care in the provision of services. Significantly fewer have rules that prohibit traders from contracting out of those guarantees. Yet these types of statutory guarantees and restrictions on contracting out of their protection are a fundamental protection promoting consider confidence, as well as an effective means of promoting the delivery of safe and effective products.

One suspects, and this is certainly the case in Singapore, that the rhetoric associated with neoliberal values of consumer autonomy (and concomitant "self-responsibility"),[21] along with regional and cultural factors, has impeded the appetite for this type of regulation. Certainly, the more recent literature, primarily from the United States, on behavioral economics and the limits of rational consumer decision-making does not appear to have influenced the regulatory agenda in new and developing economies in the ASEAN region in the way it appears to be doing in Europe, Australia and New Zealand.

As summarized in the conclusions in Section 19.4, much work therefore remains to be done to address gaps and implementation problems in enhancing ASEAN consumer protection law in both fields outlined in this chapter. Arguably, consumer contract law requires the most attention. The safety of tangible goods – beginning with higher-risk and/or everyday products such as foods – meets a fundamental physical need,

[20] Luke Nottage & Sakda Thanitcul, *Introduction, in* ASEAN Product Liability and Consumer Product Safety Law (2016), *supra* note 2, 1–14.

[21] *See also* Eugene Dili Liow, *The Neoliberal-Developmental State: Singapore as Case Study*, 38 Crit. Sociol. 241 (2011).

rather than an economic interest. Introducing and enhancing consumer product safety law has therefore long appealed to governments of all stripes. In addition, there may be more widespread business opposition to trading up to higher standards regarding consumer contracts than for the safety of tangible products.

Given the prevalence of standard form contracts in many areas of consumer contracting, including in the supply of what would now be considered essential services such as telecommunications and energy, and recent growth in the proportionate share of services sectors within Southeast Asian economies,[22] greater and more coordinated efforts may be required to address the unfair shifting of risk to consumers *en masse* through these contracts. The relatively recent enactment of the "lemon law" in Singapore, and the publicity surrounding the enactment of the protections in this law, show the potential for further efforts at substantive harmonization fueled by consumer demand and the recognition even in a robust economy such as Singapore of the social capital that can be found in consumer contract protections.

19.2 Consumer Product Safety Law

Historically, worldwide and within ASEAN, direct product safety regulation has tended to be implemented first, especially for high-risk products such as foodstuffs or cosmetics.[23] This tends to be followed by regulation of general consumer products (outlined in Section 19.2.1 below), which has been introduced in three phases across Southeast Asia since the 1970s. This has been followed by two phases of product liability law reforms since the 1990s (with some highlights set out in Section 19.2.2).[24] However, enforcement remains very problematic in this field as well.[25]

[22] In 2014, the services sector made up 74.5% of total GDP in Singapore, 54.0% in Malaysia, 42.3% in Indonesia and 53% in Thailand: *see* World Bank, *Services, etc., Value Added (% of GDP) 1995–2014*, data.worldbank.org/indicator/NV.SRV.TETC.ZS (last visited Jan. 28, 2018).

[23] Indeed, with full effect from 2012, ASEAN has adopted an EU-style regime for pharmaceutical regulation. *See* Zalina Zakaria, *Regulation of Cosmetics: What Has Malaysia Learnt from the European System?*, 38 J. Consumer Policy 39 (2015).

[24] For more details, including the historical progression in both fields, *see* Caron Beaton-Wells, Justin Malbon, Luke Nottage & Jeannie Paterson, *Product Safety Law: Fragmentation in Regulation and Emergent Product Liability Regimes*, ASEAN Consumer Law Harmonisation and Cooperation (forthcoming).

[25] *Id.* Compare also the challenges to enforcing substantive protections for consumers regarding financial products, prompting recent calls for ASEAN Secretariat assisted coordination to improve dispute resolution options: Vivien Chen, Andrew Godwin &

19.2.1 Product Safety Regulation: Direct Protection for Consumers

Public regulation to secure product safety for consumers is particularly important especially if a country lacks strict product liability legislation, and/or effective representative action procedures for large-scale disputes, or small claims court or tribunal procedures offering redress for more isolated product accidents.[26] Regulatory controls exercised by public authorities remain significant even in an era of trade liberalization, underpinned by treaties prohibiting disguised nontariff barriers as disguised protectionism favoring local firms.[27] Despite ongoing attempts at harmonization, there remains considerable disparity among ASEAN Member States in terms of when general consumer product laws were enacted, as well as their scope with respect to key components of consumer product safety regulation. There are also widespread difficulties regarding enforcement.

Beginning with postmarket interventions, for example, only one mandatory recall has been ordered by consumer regulators in Malaysia under the Consumer Protection Act 1999.[28] In addition, from a broader comparative perspective, no Member State requires suppliers to notify national regulators if conducting a voluntary recall, let alone a broader notification requirement in the event of any serious product-related accident or health risk.[29] The closest provision is Article 22 of Vietnam's Consumer Protection Law of 2010, which requires manufacturers and importers to

Ian Ramsay, *An ASEAN Framework for Cross-border Cooperation in Financial Consumer Dispute Resolution*, 12 As. J. Comp. L. 167 (2017).

26 *See generally* Luke Nottage, *Product Safety Regulation*, *in* Handbook of Research on International Consumer Law (Geraint Howells et al. eds., 2nd ed, 2018).

27 *See* Luke Nottage, *ASEAN Product Liability and Consumer Product Safety Regulation: Comparing National Laws and Free Trade Agreements*, 15/07 Sydney Law School Research Paper (2015). The Appendix to this paper summarizes the key legislative features and provisions in ASEAN Member States' general consumer product safety regulations and product liability statutes.

28 *See also* the reform proposals in *Consumers Association of Penang, An Effective Product Recall Mechanism Badly Needed*, consumer.org.my/index.php/safety/household/514-an-effective-product-recall-mechanism-badly-needed (last visited Jan. 28, 2018).

29 However, there may exist a notification for some types of higher-risk goods, such as health products under Singaporean law: *see* Health Sciences Authority, *Product Defect Reporting and Recall Procedures*, www.hsa.gov.sg/content/hsa/en/Health_Products_Regulation/Safety_Information_and_Product_Recalls/product-defect-reportingandrecallprocedures.html (last visited Jan. 28, 2018). *See e.g., High Mercury Levels Found in Two Glow Glowing Creams, Sellers to Stop Selling Immediately: HSA*, AsiaOne, Jul. 18, 2017.

announce and conduct a public recall of goods they find to be "defective," and to notify local authorities about the results of the recall. The central regulator can then monitor this information and has begun uploading such recall information on its website.[30]

Thailand was one of the first Member States to enact a general consumer law that included provisions regulating product safety. Under the Consumer Protection Act 1979, creating the Office of the Consumer Protection Board (OCPB) as the general consumer affairs regulator, section 10(3) allows the OCPB to publicize information about suppliers of products that may harm consumers – a power to issue warnings. Further, under section 36, the OCPB can order a supplier to test goods if suspected of being harmful to consumers and then can order their modification, ban from future sale or destruction (similar to a mandatory recall power) – all at the expense of the supplier. Noncompliance attracts criminal sanctions under section 56. However, the OCPB interpreted section 36 as only allowing it to issue "cease supply" instructions to the relevant supplier until the results of its tests (or otherwise the OCPB's own tests) have been completed. Only after that period, which may be quite lengthy, will the OCPB publicly announce a ban.

By contrast, for example, Singaporean regulators have greater access to their own testing facilities. Accordingly, they can quickly conduct tests if concerned about safety, and then promptly take public measures including product bans. However, even this developed country seems to have trouble enforcing the law. In 2008, for example, melamine-laced milk in China prompted bans on imported products, yet the mainstream media still noted that some shops were still stocking banned items, with one reportedly declaring that they were just for display but not for sale.[31] In late 2016, Samsung seems to have given less priority to Singapore when embarking on a world-wide recall of its faulty Galaxy Note 7 mobile phone.[32] Making matters worse, pre-market powers and enforcement capacity are even more problematic across ASEAN Member States. For

[30] *See* Vietnam Competition Authority, Consumer Protection Portal – Defective Goods Recall, www.vca.gov.vn/tinbvntd.aspx?Cate_ID=475 (last visited Jan. 28, 2018).

[31] Quoted in Luke Nottage, *Consequences of Melamine-Laced Milk for China, NZ, Japan and Beyond*, Japanese Law and the Asia-Pacific Blog (2008), blogs.usyd.edu.au/japaneselaw/2008/10/consequences_of_melaminelaced.html.

[32] Compare *Samsung Galaxy Note 7: Key Developments in the Recall Crisis*, ABC News, Oct. 12, 2016, with *Samsung's Woes Continue as Customers Complain about Note 7 Exchange and Refund Process in Singapore*, The Straits Times, Nov. 6, 2016.

example, in Thailand, the OCPB's powers to set minimum safety standards before goods are allowed into market circulation are limited.

Until recently, Malaysia was the only ASEAN country to expressly set out a GSP, found also under EU law. Under section 21 of its Consumer Protection Act 1999, no goods may be supplied that are "not reasonably safe." In addition, section 19(4) provides that a supplier "shall adopt and observe a reasonable standard of safety to be expected by a reasonable consumer, due regard being had to the nature of the goods or services concerned." This duty applies even if the general safety regulator has not set any minimum safety standard for specific (classes of) goods or services, as provided separately under section 19(1). Under section 19(3), the general consumer regulator can, but is not required to, adopt standards set by a separate "competent agency" (section 19(5)). However, this part of the Act on standard setting does not apply to "healthcare products" or foods (ss 19(6)–(7)), whereas the GSP under section 21 extends to all consumer goods.

With effect from April 1, 2011, Singapore has achieved a compromise position, going part of the way toward introducing a GSP. The Consumer Protection (Consumer Goods Safety Requirements) Regulations 2011 was introduced pursuant to section 11 of the Consumer Protection (Trade Descriptions and Safety Requirements) Act (originally enacted in 1975), which allows the Minister to declare safety standards for specified classes of goods. Essentially, these regulations now require all goods supplied to comply with (i) standards set by four specified international bodies (e.g., ISO, EU and US bodies together with any further standards set by the general regulator, SPRING), or otherwise (ii) standards "formulated or adopted and published by any regional or national standards body." But safety-related standards may not exist for all products, it is costly for suppliers to access those of international bodies, suppliers may select those setting less demanding requirements and the Regulation sets no direct sanction for noncompliance.

By contrast, in Vietnam, Article 5(1) of the 2008 Law on Quality of Products and Goods only envisages safety standards set separately by other regulators, because it refers simply to "announced applicable standards and relevant technical regulations." This means the general consumer affairs regulator cannot set even information/labelling standards (as the OCPB can arguably do in Thailand, at least for products other than foods that are exclusively regulated by other government departments) or other types of minimum safety standards (as under section 19 of Malaysia's 1999 Act, except for foods and healthcare products).

Vietnam's legislation limits powers to banning unsafe goods, for example, under Article 8(1).

Vietnam's Consumer Protection Law 2010 does not add any further powers in respect of setting mandatory minimum safety standards, although other specific legislation and/or informal interagency collaboration may allow involvement of the Vietnam Competition Authority. Leaving standard-setting activity exclusively or predominantly to other government bodies in this manner is particularly problematic if consumer NGOs involved in safety-setting (such as Vinastas, the Vietnam Standards and Consumers Association) lack resources and capacity. However, as mentioned briefly above, Article 22 does require manufacturers and importers to recall any "defective product" (defined in Article 3(3)) that threatens harm to health or property, by specified public media announcements, and after completing a report to relevant local consumer regulators.[33] Under Decree 80 of 2013, goods subject to such recall include goods that are unsafe for consumers (generally), as well as those whose quality does not conform with certified standards or applicable technical regulations.[34]

A similar gap regarding minimum safety standard-setting arises in Myanmar under the Consumer Protection Act 2014. It does not presently allow for Myanmar's general consumer affairs regulatory bodies to set minimum standards (as in Malaysia, except for foods or healthcare products) or ban entire categories of unsafe consumer goods that cause harm to consumers (as in Malaysia or Thailand).

19.2.2 Product Liability Law: Indirect Protection for Consumers

As in several other Asia-Pacific economies,[35] the European Union's 1985 Product Liability Directive has provided a model for legislation now

[33] There still appear to be some difficulties with enforcement. For example, Canon initially conducted a recall of its Powershot SX50 HS camera (with a viewfinder that could cause allergic reactions) instead only via its own website, until the regulator queried this, and Canon announced a recall via the public media specified in the 2010 Law. Once recalls are notified in this way or after completion, the regulator generally announces them also via its own website.

[34] Other goods subject to such recalls are those violating labelling laws and certain barcodes. *See* Decree 80/2013/ND-CP of the Government dated Jul. 19, 2013 on Administrative Sanctions against Violations in Standards, Measurements, and Quality of Products and Goods, arts. 18.5, 19.7, 25.3, 26.7 and 27.4.

[35] David Harland & Luke Nottage, *Conclusions, in* Product Liability in the Asia-Pacific 559 (Jocelyn Kellam ed., 2009).

enacted in five out of ten ASEAN Member States. Indeed, compared to the European Union law, these statutes mostly expand the liability of manufacturers in various potentially significant ways.[36]

For example, in the statutes enacted in Thailand and the Philippines (as also in China and Taiwan), the consumer does not have the full burden of proving that the goods were unsafe because they had a defect. The supplier, which typically has much better access to relevant information, must instead prove the goods were safe to avoid liability. In Vietnam, at least one commentator argues that the 2010 Consumer Protection Law should be interpreted so that traders have the burden of proving their products are not defective, once consumers prove product-related damages.[37]

In Thailand (similarly to Taiwan and China),[38] additional ("punitive") damages may be awarded to plaintiffs in specified situations. In addition, as under Article 751 of the new Cambodian Civil Code (drafted under the influence of Japanese legal technical assistance from 1999),[39] plaintiffs in Thai courts can claim for personal injury and all forms of consequential property loss. Malaysia instead follows the European Union (and e.g., Australia since 1992) in its version of the 1985 European Directive: under ss 68–9, plaintiffs can only be awarded damages for personal injury and losses to property (other than the defective product itself) that is ordinarily and actually intended for personal or household use. In addition, however, section 51 of Malaysia's Consumer Protection Act 1999 (derived from New Zealand's Consumer Guarantees Act 1993) allows anyone to claim against the manufacturer for all types of consequential damages caused by a lack of "acceptable quality" (including safety: section 32) in a consumer good. The latter is defined in section 3 to mean a product ordinarily for personal use, and not for resupply or using up in a manufacturing process; but (in contrast to the EU Directive) there is no similar limitation placed on the

[36] Nottage & Thanitcul, *supra* note 20.

[37] Pham Thi Phuong Anh, *Vietnamese Law on Consumer Protection: Some Points for Traders*, Vietnam Law & Legal Forum, 16–20 (2013).

[38] *C.f.* e.g., Jing Jin, *National Report – China* (Jan. 13–14, 2016) (paper presented at the Conference on Consumer Protection in Asia, City University of Hong Kong) (explaining how this has led to "entrepreneurial" litigation by individuals and organizations "on behalf of" consumer victims).

[39] *See* Yuta Kaneko, *Catalistic Role of Legal Assistance between Formal Law and Social Norms: Hints from Japanese Assistance*, 15 J. Int'l Coop. 54 (2008) (focusing on tensions regarding the land law provisions); and *see generally* Veronica Taylor, *The Law Reform Olympics: Measuring the Effects of Law Reform in Transition Economies*, *in* Law Reform in Developing and Transitional States (Tim Lindsey ed., 2007).

scope of goods that may be consequentially affected and therefore subject to claims for damages.

In other words, other firms can sue in all three of these ASEAN countries for certain business losses caused by defective goods. Such heightened liability, compared to the EU regime limited to losses incurred by consumers, increases the potential incentive effect on manufacturers to supply safe goods.[40] Yet this effect has not been unleashed, because it seems that this extra scope to bring suit so far has been almost unknown among businesses in any of these three countries.

In addition, Thailand and the Philippines omit the "development risks" defense, found in almost all EU Member States (and e.g., Australia and Japan). This exempts manufacturers and importers from liability where the state of scientific or technical knowledge did not permit the defect to be discovered when the goods were put into circulation.[41] Article 99 of the Consumer Act in the Philippines also extends strict liability for certain consumer services.[42]

In Vietnam, the 2008 Law on the Quality of Products and Goods, also dealing with defects in goods, remains in effect. It has a "development risks" defense that is more demanding (assessing scientific knowledge as at the time damage arises) than the 2010 Consumer Protection Law (assessing knowledge when the goods were put into circulation, as under the EU directive).[43]

By contrast, more general laws in Brunei Darussalam, Laos,[44] Myanmar and Singapore retain a negligence-based liability regime for compensating

[40] This expanded liability regime may disadvantage consumers by cross-subsidizing businesses, but only if manufacturers then raise their product costs more than plaintiff firms lower their own costs for consumers.

[41] *See generally* Luke Nottage, Product Safety and Liability Law in Japan (2004). The omission of the development risks defense in the Philippines, for example, could facilitate any product liability lawsuits that may be filed regarding recent deaths associated with dengue fever vaccine. For background, *see Controversial Dengue Vaccine in Spotlight After Death of Filipino Children*, Sydney Morning Herald, Jan. 6, 2017, www.smh.com.au/world/controversial-dengue-vaccine-in-spotlight-after-death-of-filipino-children-20180106-h0edmv.html (last visited Jan. 28, 2018).

[42] Patricia-Ann T. Prodigalidad & Dyan Danika Lim, *Philippines*, *in* ASEAN Product Liability and Consumer Product Safety Law (2016), *supra* note 2, 221–2.

[43] *Vietnamese Law on Consumer Protection: Some Points for Traders*, *supra* note 37, at 20. This commentator also remarks that under the 2008 Law, manufacturers and importers are not responsible for damage caused by defective goods when public notice of a recall has been issued before the products cause harm (Art 62.1(c)). However, this would constitute an unusual extra defense compared to the EU model, and the interpretation has been doubted.

[44] Sornpheth Douangdy, *Lao PDR*, *in* ASEAN Product Liability and Consumer Product Safety Law (2016), *supra* note 2, 135–51.

consumers (and others) for injury and consequential property loss from defective goods. Proving lack of fault by manufacturers with respect to safety, let alone intermediaries in the supply chain, is more difficult for consumers compared to claiming under strict liability statutes.

In 2015, the Consumers Association of Singapore (CASE, the main NGO but in close cooperation with the government) apparently floated the idea of extending liability for some mandatory consumer warranties from retailers to manufacturers[45] – including perhaps importers. However, in rather typical Singaporean fashion, no formal proposal seems to have been made public and there is certainly no media discussion of this potential enactment of a form of strict product liability. It is possible that manufacturers (and their peak associations or advisors) expressed opposition when consulted informally by CASE and/or the government, which was enough to torpedo this initiative, even though in Singapore a significant proportion of manufacturers are foreign owned or major exporters (e.g., for pharmaceuticals), and therefore potentially already familiar with higher product liability standards in other jurisdictions worldwide. (One commentary suggests that opposition to the proposed reform may have come especially instead from retailers purchasing from "manufacturers of cheaper goods who might find it cost-ineffective to continue doing business in Singapore,"[46] even though retailers are already subject to liability for selling unsafe products directly to consumers.) Another factor may have been the neoliberal and "light-touch" regulatory style persistently favored in Singapore, despite the global financial crisis in 2008.[47]

Nonetheless, Singapore (since 2003) and Brunei (since 2011) have enacted consumer protection laws establishing liability for various types of misleading statements and conduct, including pertinently for misleading omissions.[48] It is possible that such legislation might be invoked by consumers to claim a form of strict liability at least for "warning" or "instruction" defects (not one-off "manufacturing defects" or generic "design defects"). Yet, ongoing research reveals no example of court judgments on this point. Indonesia's Consumer Protection Act of 1999 adopts a compromise approach. Article 19(1)

[45] *Singapore, supra* note 13, 266–8.

[46] *Id*, at 268.

[47] *C.f. generally* Liow, *supra* note 21.

[48] *See* ss 2, 4(a) and 7(4) of Singapore's Consumer Protection (Fair Trading Act) 2003, largely replicated in Brunei's Consumer Protection (Fair Trading) Order 2011.

is subject to Article 28, so the regime is fault-based rather than strict liability, but subject to a reversed burden of proof compared to Indonesian Civil Code provisions on negligence.[49]

Challenges under the substantive law providing redress for product liability are compounded when courts are not well-resourced and judgments are not widely publicized (as in Myanmar and Lao PDR).[50] Even in more developed countries that have enacted strict liability statutes, there appear to be very few reported judgments applying them, let alone finding in favor of consumers. The most functional regime is found in Thailand. Many out-of-court settlements have been reached since 2008, thanks primarily to the active roles played by consumer organizations and the OCPB (including one instance where it publicly committed to bring a representative action against an automobile manufacturer).[51] Publicity through social media may also be leading to more settlements. Consequently, even the active consumer protection working group established within the Thai legislature after the 2014 coup has not been prioritizing further reforms to its substantive law on product liability.

In Vietnam, it is difficult to locate even media reports about product liability claim filings in court, and no representative suits have even been threatened. In researching for his PhD thesis focusing on the consumer protection law of 2010, Cuong Nguyen found that in the lead-up to enactment, the Supreme People's Court reported almost no lawsuits brought by consumers. A survey of consumers in 2010 reportedly found that most would not complain even in urban Hanoi – mostly because they did not know where to make claims or thought they would not obtain fair compensation.[52] Nguyen also notes that although Vinastas is a type of NGO, it was established by retired officials and

[49] *See also e.g.*, Ian Dodds-Smith & Michael Spence, International Comparative Legal Guide To: Product Liability 2016 (2016), and Hutabarat, Halim & Rekan Lawyers, *Product Liability Defenses in Indonesia* (Oct. 6, 2004), www.hnrlawyers.com/files/hhr-oct04.pdf (last visited Jan. 28, 2018).

[50] *See generally e.g.*, Nick Cheesman, Opposing the Rule of Law: How Myanmar's Courts Make Law and Order (2015).

[51] Thanitcul, *supra* note 15, 299–302.

[52] Cuong Nguyen, PhD Thesis – *The Drafting of Vietnam's Consumer Protection Law – An Analysis from Legal Transplantation Theories* 137–8 (2011), https://dspace.library.uvic.ca/bitstream/handle/1828/3404/Nguyen_Cuong_PhD_2011.pdf?sequence=1&isAllowed=y (last visited Jan. 28, 2018).

has a limited budget, mostly therefore instead relying on media campaigns.[53]

Recent cases involving motorbikes catching fire (possibly from gasoline formulations) and allegedly defective beverages do not seem to have generated any lawsuits filed by consumers. Indeed, as of December 2011, only one complaint had been lodged with Vinastas,[54] and one consumer who claimed compensation from a major beverages manufacturer in 2015 was arrested for extortion.[55] In late 2016, the government sharply rebuked Vinastas for publicizing misleading results from tests of fish sauce, allegedly not distinguishing between organic and non-organic arsenic content and thereby "causing fear among the public."[56] In Myanmar, the 2014 Consumer Protection Law does not even provide for the possibility of representative suits, either by regulators or certified NGOs.

Experiences in Thailand, and indeed in countries like Japan that have strict liability regimes, suggest that there is unlikely to be a major increase in product liability litigation, although Japan has built up some significant case law since 1995 and settlements in favor of consumers appeared to have increased somewhat in both countries.[57] To make strict product liability statutes work better in practice, arguably an opt-out class action would be useful, as in Australia (and some parts of Canada) based on the US approach. Under such an approach, all harmed consumers in a class benefit from any judgment or settlement approved by the court, unless they opt out after notification of the class action.

[53] *Id.*, at 144. Vinastas cannot raise funds by way of membership fees (as in other main consumer organizations in ASEAN Member States and beyond) as this arguably would conflict with its mandate to represent the interests of all consumers in Vietnam.

[54] *See Tighter Checks Needed on Motorbike Safety*, Vietnam News, Dec. 26, 2011, http://vietnamnews.vn/opinion/219052/tighter-checks-needed-on-motorbike-safety.html (last visited Jan. 28, 2018).

[55] *See Probe Investigates Soft Drink Producer*, Vietnam Breaking News, Feb. 13, 2015, http://vietnamnews.vn/society/266517/probe-investigates-soft-drink-producer.html (last visited Jan. 28, 2018). *See also Tan Hiep Phat Inspective Results Released*, Vietnam Economic Times, Jun. 6, 2015. In addition, a lawsuit was mentioned as having been filed in a provincial court by a local consumer group regarding around one hundred victims of contaminated cakes.

[56] *Fish Sauce Scandal Suspension?*, Vietnam News, Oct. 28, 2016, www.vir.com.vn/fish-sauce-scandal-suspension.html (last visited Jan. 28, 2018).

[57] Nottage, Product Safety and Liability Law, *supra* note 41, especially ch. 4.

It will therefore be interesting to follow the impact from enacting such a regime in early 2015 in Thailand, after more than a decade of law reform discussion.[58] Appropriate implementing legislation has impeded the development of product liability class actions in Indonesia.[59]

Even when an opt-out class action system is fully implemented, the Australian experience shows that the impact remains far less extensive than in the United States, which has a comparatively unique civil justice and socioeconomic system. Accordingly, a functional product liability system for ASEAN Member States also needs to bolster other dispute resolution mechanisms.[60] These include small claims courts or tribunals, or fast-track procedures supporting consumer lawsuits generally (as in Thailand under the Consumer Case Procedure Act of 2008, including a waiver of court fees and access to a government lawyer[61]). Such procedures are especially useful for more isolated product-related accidents. In fact, it appears that almost all Product Liability Act claims filed in Thai courts have either settled (or else withdrawn) at an early stage, even before being assigned to the regime provided by the Consumer Case Procedure Act.

19.3 Consumer Contract Law: Legal Guarantees and Limits on Contracting Out

As with the consumer protection regimes in other regions, most ASEAN nations have laws that prohibit misleading conduct by traders,[62] as well

[58] Compare Chukiert Ratanachaichan, *A Primer on the Thai Draft Law on Class Actions* (2006) (paper presented at the Ninth General Assembly of the ASEAN Law Association, with Chinnawat Thongpakdee et al., *New Class Action Law in Thailand*, Lexology, May 19, 2015), www.lexology.com/library/detail.aspx?g=e104b041-025a-4a5f-a150-a656bb1472cb (last visited Jan. 28, 2018).

[59] *C.f.* e.g., Elisabeth Sundari, *The Cost Barrier of Consumers Class Action in Indonesia*, 9 E. S. J. 97 (2013).

[60] *See generally* Allan Asher et al., *Development of Complaint and Consumer Redress Models in ASEAN: Output 8 – ASEAN Complaint and Redress Mechanism Models*, (Dec. 6, 2013), especially at 20, http://aseanconsumer.org/misc/Output%208%20i.Complaint%20and%20Redress%20Models%20-%209Jan14.pdf.

[61] Thanitcul, *supra* note 15, 293–5.

[62] Consumer Protection (Fair Trading) Order 2011 (No S 64 of 2011) (Brunei), s 4(a) (CPFTO); Law on the Management of Quality and Safety of Products and Services 2000 (No NS/RKM/0600/001) (Cambodia), art. 21 (LMQSPS); Law on Consumers' Protection 1999 (No 8 of 1999) (Indonesia), arts. 7, 9–11 (LCP); Consumer Protection Act 1999 (No 599 of 1999) (Malaysia), ss 9–10 (CP); Consumer Protection Law 2014 (Myanmar), s 13; Consumer Act of the Philippines 1992 (No. 7394 of 1992) (Philippines), arts. 50–1, Title III Cap VI) (CAP); Consumer Protection (Fair Trading) Act 2003 (Cap

as predatory conduct directed at disadvantaged consumers.[63] There is noticeably greater variation in regulatory attention given to issues concerning the content of consumer contracts. For example, the consumer law in the developing economies of Cambodia,[64] Myanmar[65] and Laos[66] have no provisions dealing expressly with the substance of consumer contracts. By contrast, other states, most notably Malaysia, have legislation specifically directed to regulating the terms of consumer contracts.[67] Significantly, and importantly in the context of product safety, the treatment of mandatory guarantees of quality in supply of goods and services is highly uneven.

Statutory guarantees imposing minimum quality standards in the supply of goods and services (e.g., "acceptable quality" for goods and "reasonable care" for services) protect consumers against sub-standard or shoddy goods and carelessly provided services, and provide rights of redress when these do not meet their reasonable expectations. Statutory guarantees of quality also provide an important complement to product liability regimes of manufacturers. By imposing minimum standards of quality in the supply of goods and services to consumers and by restricting exclusion or limitation clauses (e.g., for negligence causing personal injury), retailers can be incentivized to source and on-supply only safe products. In some jurisdictions, moreover, it is regarded as never acceptable for traders to avoid liability for negligence resulting in death or serious injury to consumers. This strongly expressed intolerance for contracting out of liability provides a significant buttress to any existing product liability regime.

As with product liability, in this context of statutory quality guarantees we can observe an uneven approach across the ASEAN region and relatively less reform as part of the AEC project. The AEC Blueprint 2025 identifies the strong consumer demand for "products and services

52A, 2009 Rev Ed) (Singapore), s 4(a) (CPFTA); Consumer Protection Act 1979 (BE 2522) (Thailand), ss 4(1), 22 (CPA); Law on Protection of Consumers' Rights 2010 (No 59/2010/QH12) (Vietnam), arts. 8, 10 (LPCR).

63 CPFTO (Brunei), s 4(c); CPA (Malaysia), s 24C; CAP (Philippines), art. 52; CPFTA (Singapore), s 4(c); LPCR (Vietnam), art. 10(3). On these types of protections directed at the sanctity of the contracting *see* Jeannie Marie Paterson, *Consumer Protection in Singapore: Statute and the Ongoing Influence of the General Law*, 28 S.Ac. L. J. 1079 (2016).

64 LMQSPS (Cambodia).

65 Consumer Protection Law 2014 (Myanmar), s 13.

66 Law on Consumer Protection 2010 (Lao PDR) – *see* the general commitment to quality of goods and services in arts. 12 and 13.

67 *See further* Beaton-Wells et al, *supra* note 21, ch. 5 (*Consumer Contracts: Regional Responses to Changing Contract Practices and Complex Standardised Terms*).

that meet standard and safety requirements."[68] However, many Member States have given little real attention to the role of statutory guarantees in promoting consumer confidence, and thus in benefiting the economy. Yet unease over a lack of effective response to sub-standard goods and services, particularly from the growing number of middle-class and more affluent consumers,[69] may lead to a push for reform in this area. As we shall see, of central importance to the success of any future reform will be control over exclusion and limitations clauses, restricting the ability of traders to contract out of these important protections.

19.3.1 Legal Guarantees

A number of ASEAN countries have legislation that provides consumers with a statutory guarantee that the goods, and in some states, services, will meet basic quality standards. Indonesia does this through general principles: the Law Number 8 Year 1999 on Consumer Protection (Article 7) obliges entrepreneurs to "guarantee the goods and/or services produced and/or traded based on the prevailing quality standard provisions of the goods and/or services."[70] Brunei,[71] Malaysia,[72] Singapore[73] and the Philippines[74] have legislation that provides specific guarantees of quality applying to the supply of goods to consumers similar in form to those found in the consumer protection regimes in the European Union,[75] the United Kingdom[76] and in Australia.[77] As such, these

[68] AEC Blueprint 2025, *supra* note 7, para. 28.

[69] *See e.g.*, Hang Sukenthea, *Study Shines Light on Growing Cambodian Consumer Class*, The Cambodia Daily, Apr. 6, 2017, www.cambodiadaily.com/business/study-shines-light-on-growing-cambodian-consumer-class-127614/ (last visited Jan. 28, 2018).

[70] *See also* CPA (Thailand) s 4 listing the rights of protection for consumer as below:
"(1) the right to receive correct and sufficient information and description as to the quality of goods or services . . .
(4) the right to have the injury considered and compensated in accordance with the laws on such matters or with the provision of this Act."

[71] Sale of Goods Act 1999 (Brunei), ss 14–18 (SGA).

[72] CPA (Malaysia), pts. V – IX.

[73] Sale of Goods Act 1979 (SGA); CPA (Singapore), as amended by the Consumer Protection (Fair Trading) Amendment Act 2012 (CPFTA), ss 12A–12E.

[74] CAP (Philippines), Ch. III.

[75] Directive 99/44/EC of the European Parliament and of the Council of 25 May 1999 on Certain Aspects of the Sale of Consumer Goods and Associated Guarantees, and Directive 2011/83/EC of the European Parliament and of the Council on Consumer Rights.

[76] Consumer Rights Act 2015 (UK), Chs. 2-4 (CRA).

[77] Competition and Consumer Act 2010 (Cth), Sch. 2, The Australian Consumer Law, pt 3-2 (ACL).

guarantees include requirements of acceptable/satisfactory quality[78] and fitness for purpose,[79] along with guarantees relating to title[80] and correspondence with description.[81]

The guarantees most commonly relied upon by consumers are of acceptable, or satisfactory, quality and fitness for a disclosed purpose. Importantly, the guarantee of acceptable quality gives courts scope to consider a wide range of matters including information provided about the goods and their general safety, thereby providing an express link with product safety requirements.

Singapore has gone further in ensuring protection for consumers from the harm caused by defective or sub-standard goods through the technique of statutory presumptions in favor of the consumer as complainant, a model also utilized in the United Kingdom, based on EU law.[82] Under Singapore's so-called lemon law,[83] introduced with considerable fanfare in 2012, where defects are detected within six months, there is a presumption that goods were defective at the time of sale or delivery,[84] unless such a presumption is incompatible with the nature of the goods or the seller can prove otherwise.[85] The Philippines introduced a bright-line lemon law in 2013 applying to new motor vehicles.[86] This law provides rights of repair or replacement within the first twelve months from delivery in the case of established nonconformity amounting to a defect or fault, which the supplier or manufacturer has not been able to repair after four attempts.[87]

78 SGA (Brunei), s 16(2); CPA (Malaysia), s 32; SGA (Singapore), s 14.

79 SGA (Brunei), s 16(3); CPA (Malaysia), s 33; SGA (Singapore), s 15.

80 SGA (Brunei), s 14; CPA (Malaysia), s 31; SGA (Singapore), s 12.

81 SGA (Brunei), s 15; CPA (Malaysia), s 34; SGA (Singapore), s 13.

82 CRA (UK), s 20. *See also* European Commission, *Sales and Guarantees*, ec.europa.eu /consumers/consumer_rights/rights-contracts/sales-guarantee/index_en.htm.

83 *See further* Alexander Loke, *The Lemon Law and the Integrated Enhancement of Consumer Rights in Singapore*, Sing. J.L.S. 285 (2014).

84 CPA (Singapore), as amended by the CPFTA, s 12B(3).

85 CPA (Singapore), as amended by the CPFTA, s 12B(4).

86 *See e.g.*, New York State Dispute Resolution Association Inc, *Lemon Law Arbitration*, www.nysdra.org/?page=LemonLaw (last visited Jan. 28, 2018); California Department of Consumer Affairs, *Arbitration Certification Program* (2016), www.dca.ca.gov/acp/ (last visited Jan. 28, 2018); California Department of Consumer Affairs, *Lemon-Aid: For Consumers* (2016), www.dca.ca.gov/acp/pdf_files/englemn.pdf (last visited Jan. 28, 2018).

87 An Act Strengthening Consumer Protection in the Purchase of Brand New Motor Vehicles 2013 (Philippines). Given evidence of extensive faults reported in new vehicles sold in Australia in recent years, there have also been calls for further legislative intervention there: Stephen Corones, *Why Australia Needs a Motor Vehicle "Lemon" Law*, 39 U. N. S. W. L. J. 625 (2016).

19.3.2 Services

Services have assumed increasing importance in the consumer landscape as a way of delivering a range of products. Many of these repackaged consumer products include services that are essential to participation in civil society, such as those relating to energy, transport and telecommunications.[88] Yet only a few ASEAN nations, primarily Malaysia and the Philippines, provide direct legal guarantees of quality, of due care and skill[89] and fitness for purpose[90] in the provision of services to consumers.[91] The standard imposed by the guarantee of due care and skill requires the trader to take care in delivering the services, but does not require the trader to ensure that the consumer will obtain the desired result.[92] Unlike the guarantee that goods must be of acceptable quality, this guarantee requires the consumer to prove fault and imposes a similar liability to the tort of negligence. It nonetheless provides an effective safeguard for consumers as an incentive for traders to take care in the provision of services and a relatively clear avenue for remedies when this does not occur.

19.3.3 Attempts to Exclude or Limit Liability

The force of any regime of statutory guarantee of minimum standards of quality in the supply of goods and services to consumers can be measured through its response to contracting out. If suppliers can exclude or limit their liability under statute they are likely to do so, and consumers will again be left with little recourse for sub-standard goods or services. Legislation providing statutory guarantees should therefore ensure that the guarantees are mandatory, meaning that traders cannot exclude the guarantees by contract.

[88] *See also* T. Wilhelmsson, *Services of General Interest and European Private Law, in* International Perspectives on Consumers' Access to Justice 153 (Charles E. F. Rickett & Thomas G. W. Telfer eds., 2003).

[89] CPA (Malaysia), s 53; CAP (Philippines), Ch. III art. 69(a).

[90] CPA (Malaysia), s 54; CAP (Philippines), Ch. III art. 69(b).

[91] *See also* (Thailand) Consumer Protection Act 1979, s 4, giving consumers: (1) the right to receive correct and sufficient information and description as to the quality of goods or services; (2) the right to enjoy freedom in the choice of goods or service.

[92] Jeannie Marie Paterson & Kate Tokeley, *Consumer Guarantees, in* Consumer Law and Policy in Australia and New Zealand 97–128 (Justin Malbon & Luke Nottage eds., 2013).

Brunei,[93] Indonesia,[94] Malaysia[95] and Singapore[96] restrict the ability of traders to exclude their liability for breach of the statutory guarantees of quality, such as acceptable quality and fitness for purpose.[97] In other ASEAN states, the mandatory nature of the legal guarantees is not secure and must rely – if at all – for their efficacy on protection against contracting out and other forms of overreaching exclusion for clauses offered by other provisions. Here a variety of models are found across the region. Vietnam invalidates terms that purport to exclude legal rights,[98] although notably with minimal consumer guarantee rights.[99] Singapore[100] and Brunei[101] have legislation based on the United Kingdom's Unfair Contract Terms Act 1977,[102] which prohibits the exclusion of liability for negligence resulting in death or personal injury and subjects other types of exclusion clauses to a test or reasonableness.[103] Thailand equally subjects terms restricting liability for breach of contract to a test of reasonableness.[104]

19.3.4 Disclosure

For consumers to exercise their rights to goods and services that meet the statutory guarantees of quality, they must be aware of these rights. This calls for education by regulators and advocates about consumers' rights. Thus, for example, an extensive consumer education program by CASE accompanied the introduction of Singapore's lemon law.[105] In addition, to effectively resolve disputes about product quality and performance,

93 *See e.g.*, Unfair Contract Terms Act 1999 (Brunei), s 8 (UCTA).

94 LCP (Indonesia), art. 18.

95 CPA (Malaysia), s 6.

96 CPA (Singapore), s 13 and Unfair Contract Terms Act 1996 (Singapore), s 6 (UCTA).

97 *See also* ACL, s 64; Control of Exemption Clauses Ordinance 1990 (Hong Kong), Ch. 71 s 11 (CECO).

98 LPCR (Vietnam), art. 16. *See also* controls on exclusion clauses in LCP (Indonesia), art. 18.

99 *Id.*, art. 8.

100 UCTA (Singapore).

101 UCTA (Brunei), Ch. 171.

102 *See now* also the CRA (UK).

103 However, there has been very little reported litigation: Sandra Booysen, *Twenty Years (and more) of Controlling Unfair Contract Terms in Singapore*, Sing. J. L. S. 219 (2016). This may be due to the difficulties associated with proving unreasonableness, in addition to the usual problems of access to justice for consumers. *See also* the CECO (Hong Kong), Ch. 71.

104 Unfair Contract Terms Act 1997 (BE 2540) (Thailand), s 4 (UCTA).

105 *See also* Speedo Motoring Pte Ltd *v.* Ong Gek Sing (2014) 2 SLR 1398.

consumers must also have sufficient information about the relevant product, their contractual rights and the trader itself.[106] To this end, the EU Consumer Rights Directive[107] usefully requires traders to provide information to consumers setting out matters such as the characteristics of the goods, the cost of the goods, delivery arrangements, the contact details of the supplier and the supplier's complaint handling policy.[108] There is no equivalent in ASEAN states, and it may be that increasing information and transparency obligations is the key to a more practically effective regime for both product liability and quality regimes.

19.4 Conclusion

This survey of product safety/liability and consumer contract regimes has identified gaps in the substantive law as well as persistent enforcement problems in these two main aspects of consumer protection across ASEAN countries, even in developed countries such as Singapore and Brunei. In addition, the renewed recognition in the AEC Blueprint 2025 of the important role of consumer protection in promoting competition and improving markets along with the drive for harmonization reflects an uneven commitment.

On the one hand, consumer product safety is a highly prominent issue and thus tends to be more politically palatable for reforms, although much remains to be done throughout Southeast Asia. There still seems to be more prospects for successful reforms in this realm than for substantive guarantees of quality other than in the product safety realm. As cross-border trade and investment liberalization have accelerated more recently, coalitions can form that that are more likely to press for trading up[109] to higher levels of consumer protection in the case of end-product standards, such as requirements that goods achieve minimum environmental or safety features.

On the other hand, mandatory legislative guarantees of quality with limits on contracting out currently attract much less attention in the region. To implement and then enforce these types of protection requires a greater willingness to openly acknowledge the limits of neoliberal emphasis on the self-responsibility of consumers regarding their

[106] *See e.g.*, Manjit Kaur, *Online Purchasing Gone Bad*, The Star (Malaysia), Nov. 3, 2016.

[107] Directive 2011/83/EC of the European Parliament and of the Council on Consumer Rights.

[108] *Id.*, arts. 5 and 6.

[109] *See generally* Vogel, *supra* note 17.

purchases. Moreover, pressures for trading up may have been fewer exports of services to consumers, associated with detailed contract terms, compared to exports of tangible goods where safety features may also be more obvious. Anyway, pressures for trading up are less likely to be evident for process standards that focus on how goods or services are generated, such as regulations on factory emissions, rather than standards for the end products themselves.[110] Rules governing unfairness in consumer contracts may be more like such process standards, especially rules regulating procedural unfairness, but also arguably some rules regulating the substantive content of consumer contracts, such as ensuring mandatory guarantees of quality in the supply of goods and services to consumers.[111]

Accordingly, one major possible source of pressure for reform toward greater harmonization across all fields of consumer law, and therefore overall higher levels of consumer protection within ASEAN, may come from the expansion of cross-border business-to-consumer trade in services, as well as goods, and growth in foreign direct investment that also requires the home country firms to consider whether and how they adapt their contract terms and practices despite initially lower levels of protection in the destination markets. A second major impetus for reform should come from the increasingly affluent consumer base across many ASEAN countries. To the extent this politically influential cohort expresses dissatisfaction with a lack of effective redress for unsafe as well as more broadly sub-standard goods and services, this may catalyze political commitment to effective coordinated reform across the ASEAN region.

[110] David Vogel & Robert Kagan, *Introduction: National Regulations in a Global Economy*, *in* The Dynamics of Regulatory Change: How Globalization Affects National Regulatory Policies 1 (David Vogel & Robert Kagan eds., 2004), especially at 10.

[111] *See further* Beaton-Wells et al., *supra* note 24, ch. 1.3.2.

20

Conclusion: Realizing the AEC Blueprint 2025

PASHA L. HSIEH AND BRYAN MERCURIO

In this collection, we have surveyed regulatory and business aspects of ASEAN law in the NREO. We undertook this survey in order to gain greater insight and understanding of the concept of ASEAN law in relation to the development of the AEC and proliferating Asia-Pacific FTAs. Notably, the global trends and shifting paradigms in trade law and politics that we assessed in the book form the basis of a legal roadmap for realizing the AEC Blueprint 2025 and offer valuable implications for a new generation of South-South trade cooperation.

Our detailed investigation of the impact of the ASEAN regional framework on domestic business and commercial laws further enriches the conventional theories of economic integration and crystalizes the normative framework of the NREO. In this final chapter, we will reflect on the key observations of the legal experts who contributed to this book and their assessment of potential legal issues for the AEC Blueprint 2025. More importantly, we will offer concise but concrete legal and policy advice that benefits the Global South, as well as academic and professional communities.

20.1 New Regionalism and a Global ASEAN

From a global perspective, the evolution of ASEAN law in the context of NREO illustrates critical developments in the current Third Regionalism, a period in which South-South FTAs have undergone substantial transformation. While the European Union serves as useful reference, ASEAN's horizontal integration model makes it inherently different from the EU. ASEAN's experience in forging the AEC and connecting with Asia-Pacific economic powers thus provide an alternative model for developing nations. To a different extent, the case studies in the book collectively demonstrate that national governments have attempted to harmonize domestic frameworks in line with AEC requirements. The divergence at the implementation level does not necessarily correspond with disparate stages of development in ASEAN Member States. Instead, the political will of the government and economic gain that domestic industries could expect have primarily driven ASEAN's integration.[1]

In terms of economic integration, the conventional notion of hard law obligations stresses enforcement by a dispute settlement mechanism, whereas soft law commitments are carried out through "naming and shaming."[2] The ASEAN Way sits in between the two theories.[3] Albeit derived from soft law origins, ASEAN states have placed their obligations in economic agreements of a hard law nature. However, no ASEAN member has resorted to the bloc's dispute settlement mechanism. In practice, ASEAN countries and FTA partners frequently review and resolve disputes during annual dialogues and ongoing negotiations. Undoubtedly this practice has its limits, but it has so far continued to be the functional operation of the AEC.

It is the endeavor of the AEC Blueprint 2025 to retain ASEAN's "centrality in global and regional engagements."[4] ASEAN as a bloc plays a pivotal role in global regionalism. The potential expansion of the CPTPP and the European Union's FTAs with additional Asian economies reinforces ASEAN's strategic position. In particular, all ASEAN Member States are parties to the RCEP, which is built upon existing ASEAN+1 FTAs.[5] Insight into ASEAN's trade liberalization is therefore critical to the RCEP and other trade agreements.

Minh Hue Nguyen, Deborah Elms and Lavanya N (Chapter 2) observed the efforts of ASEAN and its trade partners to minimize the "noodle bowl" syndrome caused by different rules of origin under overlapping FTAs. With the introduction of the ASEAN-China Upgrading

[1] Regional initiatives for legal integration include cooperation programs developed by the ASEAN Law Association and the establishment of the Singapore-based ASEAN Law Academy program that commenced in Jul. 2018. ASEAN Political-Security Community Blueprint 2025 (2017), sec. A.2.4(i); *ASEAN Leaders' Vision for a Resilient and Innovative ASEAN* (2018), para. 34.

[2] For more detailed discussions, see Kenneth W. Abbott & Duncan Snidal, *Hard and Soft Law in International Governance*, 54 Int'l Organ. 421, 424–44 (2000); Gregory C. Shaffer & Mark A. Pollack, *Hard vs. Soft Law: Alternatives, Complements, and Antagonists in International Governance*, 94 Minn. L. Rev. 706, 712–27 (2010).

[3] See Charter of the Association of Southeast Asian Nations (2007), preamble & art. 20; Walter Woon, The ASEAN Charter: A Commentary 157–60 (2016).

[4] ASEAN Economic Community Blueprint 2025 (2015), para. 79.

[5] For a detailed analysis of the Regional Comprehensive Economic Partnership, see Pasha L. Hsieh, *The RCEP, New Asian Regionalism and the Global South*, IILJ Working Paper (MegaReg Series) 2017/4 (2017), at 11–23.

Protocol, the rules of origin under the ASEAN Trade in Goods Agreement are now in line with those of ASEAN's FTAs with China, Japan and Korea. The ASEAN-India FTA remains the sole exception. Moreover, going beyond tariff cuts, ASEAN should tackle rising nontariff measures and further harmonize Member States' tariff codes.

Heng Wang (Chapter 3) pointed out different issues based on the evolution of the ASEAN-China FTA. The flexible approach of this FTA can be a foundation for the RCEP's special and differential treatment accorded to ASEAN's least developed nations. Nevertheless, RCEP negotiators should assess the reasons for the low utilization of the ASEAN-China FTA and its limited regulatory obligations. Also, Henry Gao suggested (Chapter 4) that the RCEP is an opportunity to consolidate dispute settlement mechanisms under ASEAN's FTAs. The established World Trade Organization (WTO) system can be a reference for prospective reforms, such as establishing an indicative list of panelists and easing the cost burden on developing countries' participation in proceedings. The following sections on trade in services, investment and intellectual property similarly enhances ASEAN's integration into global supply chains.

20.2 Reforms for Integrating the Services Market

Arguably more important than trade in goods in the new era, services trade-oriented development is critical to the competitiveness of the AEC. The AEC Blueprint 2025 aims to maximize the potential of the service sector for industrial development and economic growth.[6] Certain reforms are required to achieve the intended goals. While ASEAN Member States are negotiating the integrated ASEAN Trade in Services Agreement, Bryan Mercurio (Chapter 5) recommended the inclusion of the MFN clause and transparency obligations. Other essential changes include a further clarification of the current 15 percent flexibility rule and the switch to the positive list approach for scheduling services commitments.

More specific to Mode 4 of service trade, Yoshifumi Fukunaga (Chapter 6) discovered the main loopholes of ASEAN MRAs, which regional professionals have rarely used. As ASEAN Member States have provided alternative legal regimes for foreign professionals, ASEAN nationals are in essence accorded limited or no benefits. Hence,

[6] AEC Blueprint 2025, para. 11.

ASEAN is advised to use such alternative regimes as the reference point for the regulatory design of MRAs. Based on the NAFTA visa model, ASEAN should also synergize MRAs with immigration rules. As for integrating ASEAN's financial services, Federico Lupo-Pasini (Chapter 7) and Michelle Dy (Chapter 8) analyzed banking and capital markets, respectively. Both studies show that distinct from the EU model, ASEAN countries prefer to have a regional framework that allows for liberalization on a bilateral basis. This approach facilitates incremental harmonization of domestic rules without undermining host states' regulatory sovereignty.

To support commercial operations in the financial market, the provision of transnational legal services is pivotal. In assessing ASEAN states' legal services commitments, Pasha L. Hsieh (Chapter 9) reinforced the findings of Fukunaga (Chapter 6). Pursuant to selected members' obligations under bilateral FTAs and self-initiated FTA-plus measures, domestic legal regimes that attract foreign law firms and lawyers are often operated on an MFN basis. He specifically noted the failure of joint ventures as a step for legal services liberalization and recommended recent bilateral FTAs and the CPTPP as the benchmarks for regulatory changes. Jae Woon Lee (Chapter 10) presented different issues that arise from the implementation of air services commitments. Under multilayered air services agreements, ASEAN's aviation integration has gradually progressed. Yet, ASEAN should tackle remaining challenges, which lie in selected ASEAN countries' insufficient infrastructure and lack of commitments in agreements with external partners.

20.3 New Directions for the Investment Environment and Disputes

The AEC Blueprint 2025 prioritizes strengthening ASEAN's status as a global investment destination.[7] Sufian Jusoh (Chapter 11) and Julien Chaisse (Chapter 12) investigated areas of investment liberalization and protection under the ACIA, respectively. Both authors pointed out the much-improved design of the agreement in line with modern FTAs and bilateral investment treaties. Serving as the guide for legal reforms, the impact of the ACIA on investment regimes of least developed countries is noteworthy. Under domestic investment laws, what is critical is the

[7] *Id.*, para. 14.

harmonization of the definition of the negative list and the textual incorporation of MFN and national treatment principles.

Central to investment protection and a rule-based ASEAN, ISDS has engendered much controversy. Comparing the ACIA with ASEAN's investment treaties, Trinh Hai Yen (Chapter 13) identified the ACIA's pro-state features in ISDS provisions. Bearing in mind the investment court system provisions under EU FTAs, she warned ASEAN governments of potential issues, including the limited scope of party autonomy in appointing panelists, the rise in financial costs and the broad mandate of the appeal tribunal.

Yip Man (Chapter 14) observed the prodevelopment effect of alternative dispute resolution mechanisms. Akin to Jusoh's suggestions for the ACIA (Chapter 11), she advised ASEAN to further harmonize domestic interpretations of legal concepts such as public policy as a ground to refuse to enforce foreign arbitral awards. Furthermore, promoting online dispute resolution and regional judicial cooperation will contribute to the commercial usefulness of ASEAN law. Nimnual Piewthongngam (Chapter 15) also linked foreign investment with ASEAN's initiative to narrow the development gap that the AEC Blueprint 2025 emphasizes. Other than legal reforms to ease investment restrictions, she echoed the view of Hsieh (Chapter 9) that modernized legal education and profession are indispensable impetuses for multilateral investment.

20.4 Enhancing Regional Innovation and Technological Connectivity

The AEC Blueprint 2025 underscores the significance of transforming ASEAN into a knowledge-based economy that can energize a competitive and innovative market. Tellingly, seamless cooperation of IP rights is indispensable for the bloc "to move higher up in the technology ladder."[8] Based on the analysis of Irene Calboli (Chapter 16), the free movement of goods is not simply affected by tariffs and nontariff measures that Nguyen et al. (Chapter 2) detailed. The doctrine of IP exhaustion can be an important factor. At present, the laws of ASEAN Member States differ in trademark, patent and copyright exhaustion. An option for the bloc is to follow the European Union's concept of regional exhaustion under which national laws permit intra-ASEAN free

[8] *Id.*, para. 30.

movement of goods but prohibit parallel imports from outside ASEAN. Alternatively, Calboli proposed the NAFTA model where members follow a principle of international exhaustion for domestic IP rights.

From different perspectives, Eliza Mik (Chapter 17) and Han-Wei Liu (Chapter 18) shed light on e-commerce, which the AEC Blueprint 2025 emphasizes for buttressing cross-border transactions and market access by micro, small and medium enterprises. Mik recommended that ASEAN establish a legal and technical infrastructure for mutual recognition of digital signatures. Such recognition requires regional technical standards and regulatory frameworks that rely on the cooperation of certification authorities in Member States. Moreover, the promotion of e-commerce should be accompanied by the creation of effective consumer protection regimes and instruments safeguarding privacy rights.

Liu found that data flows in cyberspace are necessary to enhance economic connectivity within the AEC. Neither employment growth nor national security concerns can justify present data localization requirements, which presumably result in data protectionism. Hence, ASEAN Member States should refer to Trans-Pacific Partnership provisions on e-commerce to avoid undue interference with cross-border data transfer. A closely intertwined topic is consumer protection. Luke Nottage and Jeannie Paterson (Chapter 19) reviewed contract laws and product safety and liability legislation in ASEAN. Regulators are advised to focus on reforms on consumer production safety and statutory guarantees of quality that restrict contracting out liability. In tandem with the AEC goals, the expansion of intra-ASEAN trade in goods and services, investment and the regional consumer base should prompt greater harmonization of consumer protection rules.

ASEAN has undergone multiple stages of development since the 1960s. Amid the Doha Round impasse and rising populist isolationism, the creation of the AEC signifies the bloc's collective commitments to advancing trade liberalization. This collection provides a holistic and focused analysis of evolving ASEAN law vis-à-vis feasible pathways to accomplish the AEC Blueprint 2025. We hope that the case studies and recommendations in the book both enrich theoretical debates on economic integration and practically benefit trade-oriented development of the Global South.

INDEX